AF378792

PARIS POST WAR

ART AND EXISTENTIALISM 1945–55

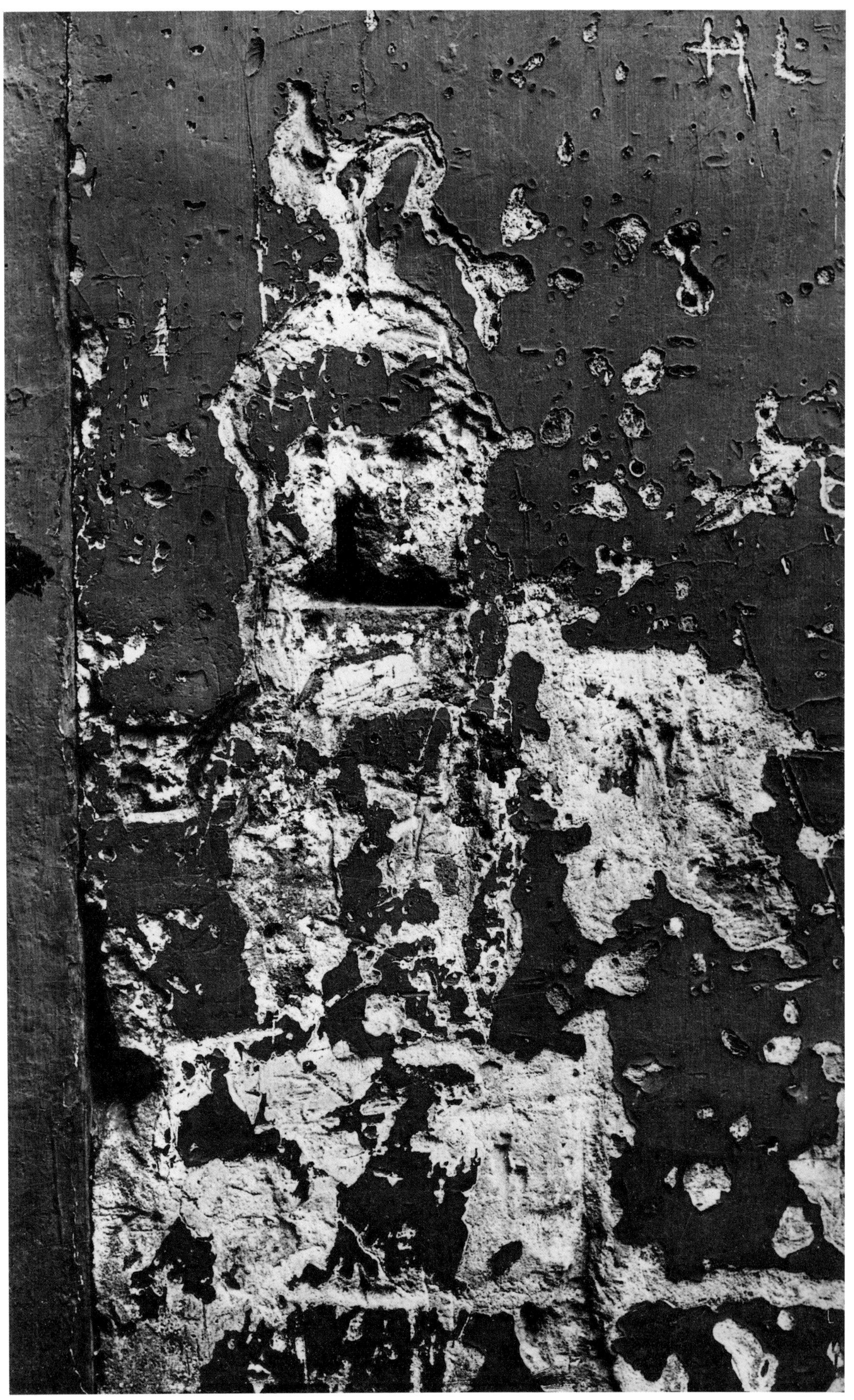

FRANCES MORRIS

PARIS POST WAR

ART AND EXISTENTIALISM 1945–55

TATE GALLERY

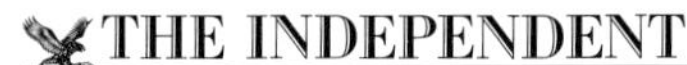 THE INDEPENDENT 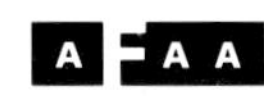 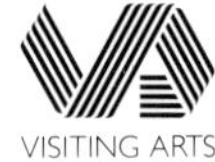 VISITING ARTS

Sponsored by *The Independent*
Supported by AFAA, Association Française d'Action Artistique,
Ministère des Affaires Etrangères, The Cultural Service of the French
Embassy, London
With assistance from Visiting Arts

Cover:
Germaine Richier **Diabolo** 1950 (no.99)

Frontispiece:
Brassaï **Graffiti** 1950
Musée National d'Art Moderne,
Centre Georges Pompidou, Paris.
Donation Daniel Cordier 1989
© *Gilberte Brassaï*

ISBN 1 85437 124 X

Published by order of the Trustees 1993
for the exhibition at the Tate Gallery 9 June – 5 September 1993
Published by Tate Gallery Publications, Millbank, London SW1P 4RG
Designed by Caroline Johnston

Typeset by August Filmsetting, St Helens
Printed in Great Britain by Balding + Mansell plc, Wisbech, Cambridgeshire

CONTENTS

FOREWORD

Paris Post War explores the rich and provocative fields of interaction between art, literature and philosophy in Paris during the decade following the Second World War. It is a field not now familiar in Britain, although several of the artists are well known. The exhibition follows earlier exhibitions at the Tate Gallery, such as *Abstraction: Towards a New Art* or *On Classic Ground* which have examined the achievements of major artists of the twentieth century within the broader context of their period.

In recent years exhibitions like *Westkunst* in Cologne and *Paris–Paris* in Paris, both in 1981, followed by *Aftermath* in London in 1982, which was a substantially reduced version of *Paris–Paris*, prompted a re-evaluation of much of the art of the immediate post-war period. The original and very selective view of the decade celebrated in *Paris Post War* could not have been possible without these earlier surveys.

The exhibition has been conceived and selected by Frances Morris, Assistant Keeper in the Modern Collection. She has also written the introductory texts for the catalogue to which Sarah Wilson and David Mellor have also contributed. Sarah Wilson's scholarly essay is the result of extensive research and introduces many new and original ideas. David Mellor's essay extends the scope of the exhibition by exploring related aspects of British art during the post-war decade. Vincent Gille has advised us on the selection for the documentary section. We should like to thank him for his help in securing loans and for compiling biographical and chronological material on writers and contemporary events.

No exhibition can be mounted without the support of owners, whether public institutions or private collectors. We were delighted to receive such a generous response to our requests and to all lenders we extend our most grateful thanks.

I should especially like to thank the many relatives, descendants and friends of the artists included, as well as the Musée national d'art moderne, Paris, the Fondation Maeght, Saint-Paul, and the Menil Foundation in Houston, all of whose generosity has been quite exceptional.

We are most grateful to *The Independent* which responded so positively to the project and which has undertaken to support the exhibition in various ways.

Finally, I should like to thank the Association Française d'Action Artistique (AFAA) for their great enthusiasm which has led not only to their support for *Paris Post War*, but also to their collaboration on the organisation and support of a related programme of events in London during the period of the exhibition.

Nicholas Serota
Director

ACKNOWLEDGMENTS

Many people have been involved in the preparation of this exhibition and catalogue and I much appreciate all their advice and help.

The project was given immense support at an early stage by Mme Françoise Guiter, Germaine Richier's niece and biographer and I am indebted to her and to all the family of Germaine Richier. Others who were close to these artists during their lives have also been helpful and generous. I am particularly indebted to Mme Jacqueline Hélion, Mme Annette Giacometti, Dr Micheline Phankim-Koupernik, Mme Catherine Beraud-Putman, Mme Georges Gruber, Mme Catherine Bernad-Gruber and Mme Armande de Trentinian-Ponge.

Much of the art of this period is poorly documented and the whereabouts of important paintings and sculptures not widely known. In tracing key works and, in certain cases helping secure loans, I therefore thank Lisa Palmer, Agnès de la Beaumelle, Claire Stoullig, Jacqueline Jahan, Cary Lochtenberg, Pierre Brullé, Keith Hartley, Howard Karshan, Patrice Trigano, Baudoin Lebon and Wolfgang Günther.

Putting together a documentary display can be as complex as selecting an exhibition. I am very grateful to Vincent Gille, Chargé de mission au Pavillon des arts, Musée de la ville de Paris, for researching this supplementary display and for providing the catalogue with its detailed chronology and literary biographies. In this he was ably assisted during the final stages by Emmanuelle Lepic. The Bibliothèque nationale and, in particular, Andrée Pouderoux, Catherine Schmitt and the Documentation du Musée national d'art moderne, Claire Fons, and the Library of the French Institute in London, were especially helpful with advice and generous with loans to the documentary display. Thanks are also due to Barbara Wright for her exacting and precise translations.

At the Tate Gallery I would particularly like to thank Ruth Rattenbury, Helen Sainsbury, Clarissa Little, Sionaigh Durrant, Judith Severne and Tim Holton along with many other colleagues in the Exhibitions, Registrars and Publications Departments for coping with the complexities of such an exhibition, as well as colleagues in the Modern Collection for allowing me extended leave from departmental duties.

Richard Morphet's enthusiasm for the project has been a source of continual encouragement. I am also grateful to him for reading the catalogue essays and making so many helpful suggestions. I have consulted Martin Caiger-Smith at all stages during the selection of the exhibition and writing of the catalogue. His comments and editorial skills have been invaluable and I therefore owe him especial thanks.

Frances Morris

SPONSORS' PREFACES

The Independent

The Independent's support for *Paris Post War: Art and Existentialism 1945–55* follows our successful collaboration with the Tate Gallery on the *Otto Dix* exhibition in 1992. We are pleased to be able to continue our tradition of commitment to the visual arts.

Like the *Otto Dix* exhibition, *Paris Post War* concerns art produced in the aftermath of brutal European war. That is why, I believe, such painting and sculpture speaks to us today, as we find the end of the Cold War marked by atrocities not seen in Europe since 1945.

Some of the artists here are scarcely known in this country. But we feel familiar with the period, the Paris of Jean-Paul Sartre, Simone de Beauvoir, Albert Camus, Juliette Gréco, Existentialism, the Left Bank, the Fourth Republic and unstable governments. Vibrant cultural developments and weak governments – it begins to sound like the early 1990s.

Andreas Whittam Smith
Editor, *The Independent*

L'Association Française d'Action Artistique (AFAA)

Peut-être écrira-t-on un jour l'histoire des échanges artistiques entre la France et le Royaume-Uni. Dans tous les domaines de l'art et de la culture, la matière en est riche, ancienne, et remarquable. Les échanges entre nos deux pays suscitent une curiosité toujours très vive de nos publics respectifs.

L'Association Française d'Action Artistique (AFAA); Ministère des Affaires Etrangères, peut se féliciter d'y avoir, à sa manière contribué au xxe siècle. En 1931 déjà, Londres avait découvert à la Royal Academy of Arts une *Rétrospective d'art français* puis, quelques années plus tard, en 1945, une exposition des œuvres d'Henri Matisse et de Pablo Picasso au Victoria and Albert Museum. Suivirent en 1947 une présentation des *Peintres cubistes* à la London Gallery et une *Rétrospective Max Ernst* en 1950.

Souvent montré en France grâce au British Council, l'art contemporain britannique est également bien représenté dans nos collections publiques et privées. C'est aussi avec cette institution que L'AFAA et la Réunion des Musées Nationaux ont organisé à Paris l'une des plus belles rétrospectives consacrées à Turner.

Depuis cette époque, si le public parisien a eu à son tour l'occasion de mieux connaître les grands aspects du patrimoine pictural anglais, une manifestation consacrée à l'art français d'une telle ampleur n'avait pas eu lieu. L'exposition présentée aujourd'hui à la Tate Gallery à Londres est donc exceptionnelle à plus d'un titre.

Paris après guerre, art et existentialisme 1945–55 – cette période est peut-être l'une des moins connues du grand public anglais. Pourtant, le bouillonnement d'idées et l'effervescence créatrice qui se manifestèrent en France – et particulièrement à Paris – au cours de cette décade, furent essentiels dans l'histoire des arts et de la pensée en France, au point d'en devenir très vite mythiques.

Cette exposition va bien au-delà de la seule présentation d'œuvres plastiques. Elle montre comment les arts visuels, la littérature, le cinéma, la musique, la philosophie, la photographie se nourrirent et s'enrichirent les uns les autres par un jeu extraordinaire d'influences réciproques.

Enfin, elle est pour l'Association Française d'Action Artistique une occasion exceptionnelle de travailler en étroite collaboration avec l'un des musées les plus prestigieux au monde, la Tate Gallery. La qualité de cette institution, sa notoriété l'excellence des partenaires, l'intérêt pour l'art français et la pertinence des choix effectués sont des gages certains du succès de cette manifestation.

Jean Digne
Directeur de l'AFAA

The history of the artistic exchanges between France and the United Kingdom may perhaps be written one day. Every aspect of art and culture provides a rich, ancient and remarkable vein of material. Exchanges between our two countries continue to give rise to a lively curiosity on the part of our respective publics.

L'Association Française d'Action Artistique (AFAA), Ministry of Foreign Affairs, should be congratulated for having, in its own way, made a contribution to the twentieth century. In 1931 London enjoyed a retrospective of French art at the Royal Academy of Art. Then, some years later, in 1945, an exhibition of Henri Matisse and Pablo Picasso was shown at the Victoria and Albert Museum. This was followed in 1947 by a display of Cubist painters at the London Gallery, and a Max Ernst retrospective at the Institute of Contemporary Art in 1952.

Contemporary British art is often shown in France, thanks to the British Council. It is also well represented in our public and private collections. Moreover, it was with the backing of the British Council that AFAA and the Réunion des Musées Nationaux organised one of the finest Turner retrospectives in Paris, in 1983–4.

While the people of Paris have been given many opportunities to become familiar with key aspects of the English pictorial heritage, there have not been many events devoted to French art in London. This exhibition at the Tate Gallery is therefore exceptional in more than one respect.

Paris Post War: Art and Existentialism 1945–55 concentrates on a period which is probably one of the least well known to the English public. However, the outburst of ideas and the creative energy in France, particularly in Paris, during this decade, were so crucial to the history of French art and thought that they almost immediately became legendary.

This exhibition is more than simply a presentation of the visual arts. It shows how art, literature, the cinema, music, philosophy and photography sustained and enriched one another in an extraordinary interplay of mutual influences.

Finally, for the Association Française d'Action Artistique this is an exceptional opportunity to work closely with the Tate Gallery, one of the major museums of the world. The standing of this institution, its reputation, its interest in French art and the appropriateness of its choices are sure guarantees of success for this exhibition.

Jean Digne
Director, AFAA

PRESENTATION

Les dix années qui suivirent la deuxième guerre mondiale furent une période de bouleversements tant pour les individus que pour les nations. L'euphorie des parisiens libérés au terme de quatre ans d'occupation allemande fut de courte durée. Tous ceux qui s'attendaient à une renaissance furent déçus par l'âpre réalité de la vie d'après guerre, par l'austérité, l'instabilité politique, le climat d'incertitude et de représailles.

Paris Post War est, en Grande Bretagne, la première exposition majeure à se consacrer aux peintres et aux sculpteurs dont le travail fut profondément marqué et souvent définitivement transformé par les nouvelles idées qu'engendra cette période tourmentée.

L'exposition présente des oeuvres qui témoignent des épreuves morales d'une ville successivement vaincue, occupée et enfin libérée. Elle expose notamment les natures mortes obsédantes de Pablo Picasso, les visions de personnages émaciés et solitaires de Francis Gruber et les scènes de Jean Hélion, vibrantes et souvent érotiques, tirées de la vie quotidienne de la rue et de l'atelier. Tous ces artistes ont su rendre l'atmosphère d'une époque où le malaise spirituel et les privations matérielles cotoyaient l'espoir et le défi. Cette ambiance fut propice à l'émergence d'une nouvelle philosophie de la liberté qui en vint à pénétrer chaque aspect de la vie parisienne, de la politique à la culture en passant par la mode.

Cette philosophie ce fut l'existentialisme. Son leader-symbole, son maître à penser charismatique en fut Jean-Paul Sartre: philosophe, dramaturge, romancier, journaliste et activiste. Les préoccupations majeures de cette philosophie étaient l'angoisse, l'aliénation, l'absurdité, la liberté, l'engagement et la révolte. Ces idées se répandirent par l'intermédiaire des romans et des pièces de théâtre de Sartre, de Simone de Beauvoir, d'Albert Camus et de Jean Genet. Les thèmes de l'existentialisme eurent, sur le Paris d'après guerre, un impact considérable et immédiat. Son aspect le plus connu, qu'immortalisent pour nous bars et caves de Saint-Germain-des-Prés et les photographies de Robert Doisneau et Brassaï, est aujourd'hui source de nostalgie.

Le rôle des artistes gravitant dans la mouvance existentialiste par les liens d'amitié, de collaboration et d'influence réciproque est, lui, bien moins connu. *Paris Post War* se consacre à ces artistes.

Sartre voyait en Alberto Giacometti et Alfred Otto Wolfgang Schulze, plus connu sous le nom de Wols, les artistes existentialistes par excellence. Giacometti travaillait en solitaire dans son atelier légendaire mi-laboratoire, mi-cave primitive. Il s'était engagé dans une quête obsessionnelle ayant pour objet de perfectionner la 'ressemblance' dans son art. Par là il entendait la création d'images se rapprochant le plus possible de sa propre vision de la réalité. En 1951 Wols mourut prématurément après avoir vécu dans une extrême pauvreté pendant des années. De sa minuscule chambre d'hôtel à Saint-Germain il réalisa des peintures abstraites d'une intensité troublante que Sartre qualifia de vision inhumaine et dont la chaotique et bouillonnante liberté d'exécution gestuelle sembla entièrement nouvelle à ses contemporains.

Un grand nombre des oeuvres les plus intéressantes de cette période furent conçues par des artistes travaillant dans un isolement de la société et de ses normes et éprouvant souvent une tension psychologique extrême. Dans un tel contexte, les artistes réagirent en développant des formes nouvelles et en expérimentant des procédés et des matériaux nouveaux. En 1946 le poète et dramaturge Antonin Artaud sortit de plusieurs années de traitement psychiatrique. Les portraits et auto-portraits aux expressions angoissés qu'il dessina durant les deux dernières années de sa vie portent la marque de sa nature tourmentée. Ses gestes se prolongent dans des attaques violentes et physiques du papier. De même, les visages troublants des aquarelles de Henri Michaux découlent d'un état d'instabilité psychologique aigu. Et la série extraordinaire des 'Otages' de Jean Fautrier témoigne de la déchirante expérience qu'il subît pendant la guerre où, de sa cachette, il entendait le bruit des atrocités nazies. Ses images de visages mutilés et désagrégés surgissent d'une pâte dense de couches superposées de peinture à l'huile, une technique radicalement différente des procédés traditionnels dont Fautrier fut le précurseur. Jean Dubuffet était fasciné par la technique et la vision à l'état brut et par la liberté créatrice révélées dans le travail d'artistes 'naïfs', vierges de toute éducation, dans l'art des fous, dans l'art non-européen et dans l'art 'primitif' des cultures pré-industrielles. Il adopta lui-même dans son oeuvre les procédés du graffiti et le style schématique de cet art 'marginal' ou art 'brut'.

En rejetant les conventions, ces artistes se trouvèrent confrontés à des défis nouveaux et inconnus. La peur de l'échec était constamment présente. Les corps hybrides de la sculpture de Germaine Richier semblent avoir été conçus lors d'une lutte avec les éléments où l'être humain finalement triomphe. Elle avoua que nous ne pouvons dissimuler l'expression humaine dans le drame de notre temps. Le labyrinthe complexe des formes abstraites de Bram van Velde amena son ami intime, Samuel Beckett, à parler d'impossibilité d'expression. En fait ces peintures sont intensément métaphoriques, hantées par un sentiment d'enfermement et d'incarcération qui rappelle la littérature existentialiste contemporaine.

Les artistes de *Paris Post War* travaillaient pour la plupart hors du cercle des galeries établies et des musées. Ils repoussaient les actions collectives mais s'attachaient tous à développer des méthodes de création artistique radicalement nouvelles: des méthodes qui engageaient le corps de l'artiste dans un rapport dynamique et expressif avec l'oeuvre, qui repensaient et modifiaient les matériaux de base de l'art et qui posaient un regard nouveau et intense sur le corps humain. Ces concepts étaient très étroitement liés à la volonté existentialiste de transformer notre conception du monde et la place que nous y occupons.

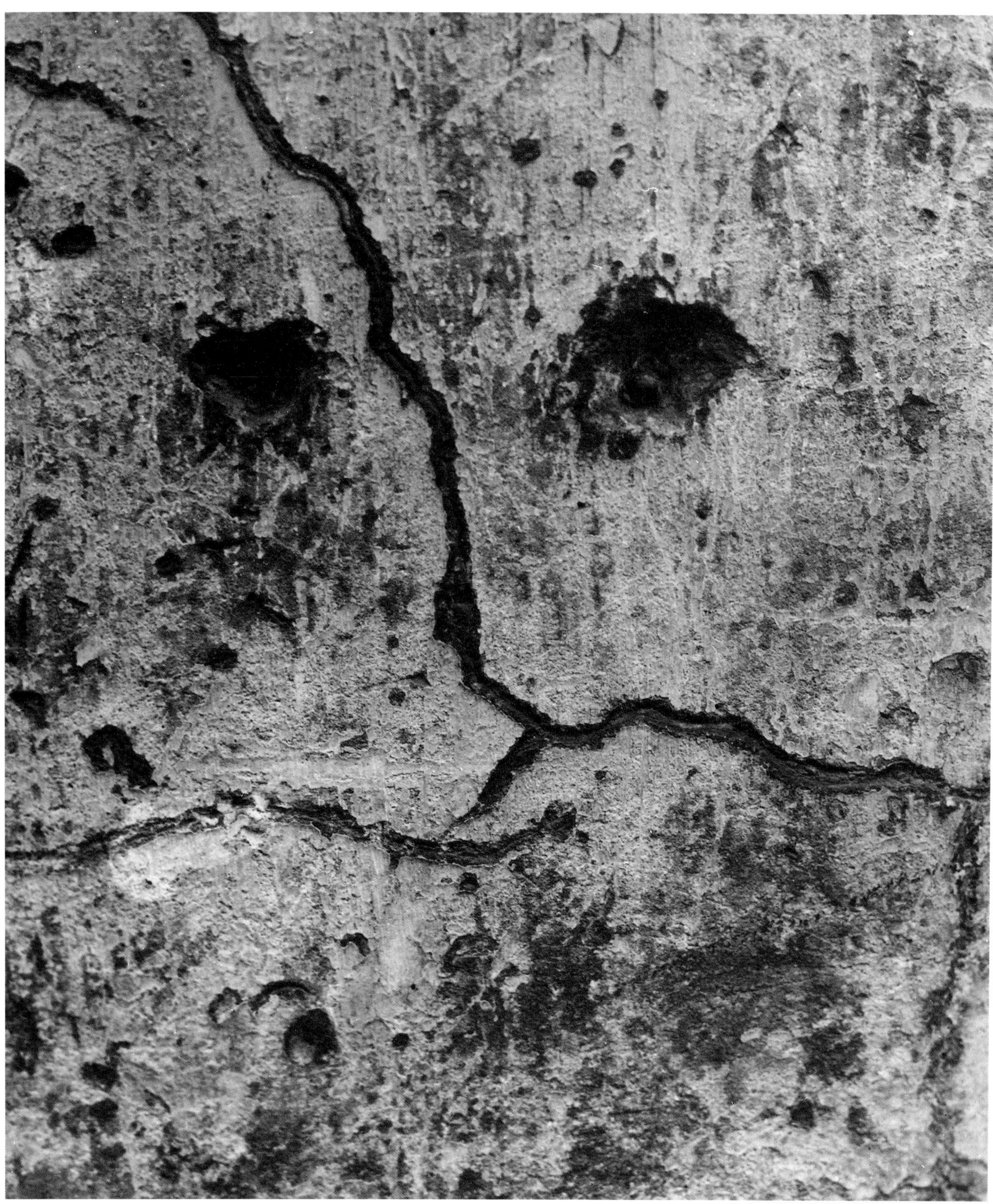

Brassaï **Graffiti 'Birth of the Face, Belleville'**
Photograph *Musée National d'Art Moderne, Centre Georges Pompidou, Paris. Donation Daniel Cordier* 1989 © *Gilberte Brassaï*

INTRODUCTION

Frances Morris

'There was nothing else to do but work seriously and devotedly, struggle for food, see friends quietly, and look forward to freedom' said Picasso.[1] Freedom, for Picasso and for Paris, came with the liberation of the city in August 1944, after four years of German occupation, but the peace was not easy. As the occupying forces retreated, in their wake came revelations of Nazi atrocities and of the full horror of the concentration camps – first in the press following the Russian troops' arrival at Auschwitz in January 1945, and then on the return of deportees in May. And with the unravelling of clandestine networks of Resistance came accusations of collaboration, and retribution, both official and unofficial. Then in August 1945 the atomic explosions at Hiroshima and Nagasaki, which brought to an end the global war, introduced a devastating new dimension both for the individual and for world politics. As Simone de Beauvoir commented: 'the war was over; it remained on our hands like a great, unwanted corpse, and there was no place on earth to bury it.'[2]

The first post-war Salon d'Automne opened in Paris in October 1944, only weeks after the Germans had been expelled from the city. It was titled, appropriately, the *Salon of the Liberation*. One image that caused a stir among the many visitors was the painting 'Job', by Francis Gruber (no.68). The figure of an old man, caught between faith and disillusion, evoked the hardships of the war years and the spirit of survival amongst the oppressed citizens of occupied Paris. As the euphoric mood of the first days of Liberation was dispelled before the sobering realities of post-war life, the painting's blend of hope and despair remained apposite. On his return to Paris in 1946 from his wartime exile in New York, Jean Hélion pictured the slow readjustment of its citizens to peace-time conditions. A sense of deprivation haunts his grandiose compositions in the years following. They concentrate on the bare essentials of life. His crusty baguettes (no.75) have a special poignancy at a time when, three years after the war's end, the bread ration had dropped to two-thirds of its 1942 level. His juxtapositions of the clothes-store mannequin and the *clochard* (no.74) seem to dramatise that odious by-product of economic reconstruction, a widening gap between profits and salaries, between the rich and the poor. So too, perhaps, the persistent pressure of political events – with fifteen cabinets in office from January 1947 to June 1954 – unfolds in the countless newspapers that recur in his paintings (no.73).

Picasso, unlike Hélion, had remained in Paris throughout the war. During the first years of peace, spent mostly in Antibes in the South of France, he celebrated his freedom first in hedonistic classical and Mediterranean themes and then, in a quieter and more domestic spirit, in images focusing on his young family. He could not, however, remain aloof from the ideological debates of the period – indeed his declared commitment to the Communist Party in 1944 had itself stimulated considerable debate within the political art world. When world peace was again threatened, in Korea in 1950, the restless obsession with mortality that had pervaded his still-life paintings of the war years once again surfaced in the potent symbolism of death and human frailty. Although couched in the language of tradition, a modernist Cubist tradition and the seventeenth-century tradition of *vanitas* painting, Picasso's still lifes speak powerfully of an unease that was endemic in those post-war years. For Picasso, as for de Beauvoir, 'no serenity was possible'.[3]

The image presented by the *fonctionnaires* of the artistic community in post-war
Paris, by contrast, was one of cultural continuity and of the resurgence of pre-war
masters. Museums and critics lionised Picasso, Braque, Léger and Matisse, originators
of the French traditions of Cubism and Fauvism (as opposed to the more international
phenomena of Expressionism, Surrealism and Abstraction). Their status was confirmed by prizes awarded at successive Venice Biennales from 1948, to Braque,
Matisse and Dufy. Such apotheoses encouraged a proliferation of Cubist and Fauvist
styles among the next generation. One such, the young painter André Marchand,
now barely remembered, was widely considered the worthy successor to Picasso and
Braque.

The terms of the most enduring critical arguments had been largely established
before the war. Now, in its aftermath, the renewed debates between abstraction and
figuration were especially vocal, fanned in 1947 by the promulgation of an official
Soviet policy advocating a Socialist Realism. Surrealism as a movement was, by the
late 1940s, largely a spent force and was further compromised, in the eyes of many,
by its lack of Resistance credentials and the defections of its important members to the
Communist Party. Its experimental techniques, however, and the innovations it had
generated in the interwar period, continued to provide inspiration for many artists.

For the wider public in Paris, art was most accessible through the annual Salons.
Three new Salons opened during this period. The Salon de Mai was devoted to
avant-garde art, and especially figurative and Surrealist styles, but younger artists
without the influence of a major gallery found themselves largely excluded. The
Salon des Réalités Nouvelles first took place in 1946 and was swiftly dominated by
hard-edged and 'constructivist' abstraction, a tendency which was also the focus of
the review *Art d'Aujourd'hui* and which was supported by the gallery-owner Denise
René and the influential critics Léon Degand and Michel Seuphor. In terms of sheer
visibility, geometric abstraction provided a dominating presence in the post-war art
scene.

Finally, distancing itself from both communist realism and abstraction was a
group of young and earnest figurative painters who formed, in 1951, their own
Salon des Peintres Témoins de leur Temps, concentrating each year on a different
theme. Prominent in this group was Bernard Buffet, an artist whose paintings of
emaciated youths popularised *misérabiliste* despair in easily digested images. Amid the
resurrection of previous debates there were, however, voices for change – voices
which considered the polarised positions around realism and abstraction as inade-
quate or irrelevant to the task of addressing modern concerns. The argument for a
reorientation of artistic values was frequently expressed as a desire to begin anew. No
one was more eloquent in pleading for such a rebirth than the poet Antonin Artaud,
who had been released, finally, from psychiatric care in 1946. In the months left to
him he devoted his brittle energies to attacking cultural conventions and to originating radically alternative ways of expression. Shortly before his death in 1948 he
described his own position as one of beginning, not ending, with everything essential
still to be defined. His words evoked a contemporary world as if at the beginning of
time: 'We are not yet born, we are not yet in the world, there is not yet a world,
things have not yet been made, the reason for being has not yet been found.'[4]

Paris Post War shows how a number of artists were starting again from zero,
outside the museums, salons and more established galleries and consciously isolated
from the protective structures of movements or shared aesthetics. Their wartime
experiences had been of suffering. Wols, for example, was interned as an enemy alien,
Hélion as a prisoner of war, Germaine Richier and Alberto Giacometti were
marooned in neutral Switzerland, Jean Fautrier in hiding in the suburbs of Paris and

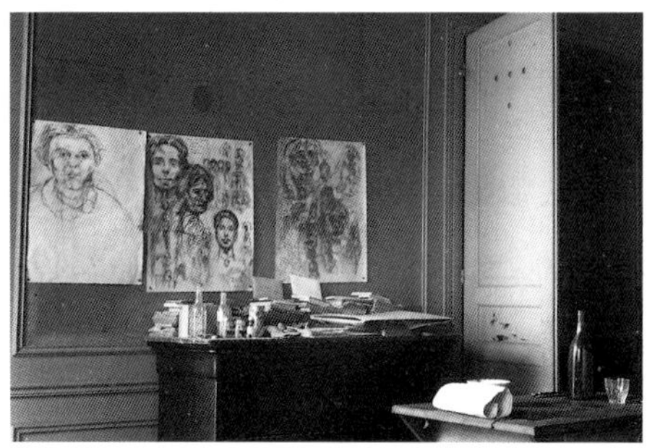

Antonin Artaud's bedroom at the clinic of Ivry-
sur-Seine 1947 Photograph by Denise Colomb
© Ministère de la Culture, France

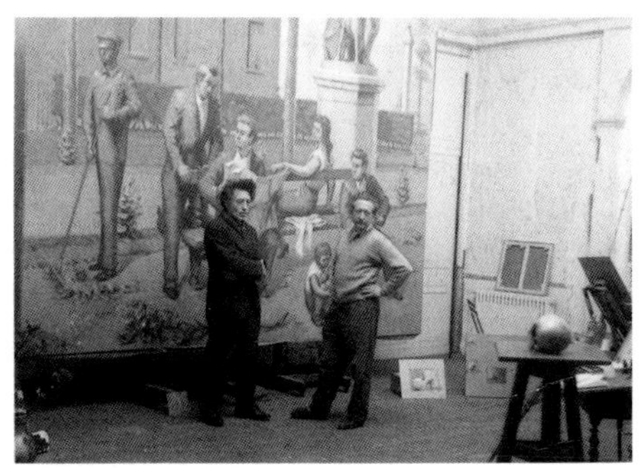

Jean Hélion and Alberto Giacometti in front of Hélion's **Luxembourg** 1955 Photograph by P. Bruguière

Gruber and Bram van Velde remained in Paris where privations – of poverty and solitude – were severe. For all of them the Liberation was cathartic, and the decade 1945–55 a crucial period of achievement in which they developed new styles and approaches for a new era, approaches that were profoundly removed from those of André Marchand and the fashionable painters of the day.

Their friends, supporters and collectors were, in the main, drawn from a small circle of writers – philosophers, poets, novelists, playwrights and critics – associated with the post-war phenomenon of existentialism. *Paris Post War* is a group show of isolated parts. That each artist worked in relative isolation and produced a highly distinctive oeuvre was an 'existential' condition of authenticity. Much of their work went largely unremarked at the time, and only rarely did one exhibit work alongside another. They never exhibited as a group and no critic, at the time, drew them all together for purposes of comparison. However, their individual trajectories did meet. They were linked by complex lines of acquaintance, friendship, admiration and influence, which can be unravelled through the memoirs and records of the period: Brassaï's memories of Picasso,[5] Simone de Beauvoir's diaries,[6] Hélion's studio note-books,[7] Jean Paulhan's correspondence,[8] Boris Vian's guide to the community of Saint-Germain-des-Prés[9]... Their revelations are sometimes surprising. Hélion, who having turned his back on abstract art felt cold-shouldered by his former friends and supporters, found allies within the community represented here. His notebooks describe his growing friendship with the 'phenomenological' poet Francis Ponge, the understanding and appreciation shown by Henri Michaux, the warmth of Claude Lévi-Strauss, the encouragement of Giacometti.

Although none of them could be said to have inspired a 'school', they were not without influence, even at the time; certain emphatic features of their styles provided others of their generation with a way forward. Giacometti and Richier, for example, demonstrated how formal disintegration, through both the paring down of form and its metamorphosis, could heighten the expressive presence of the human figure; and pioneering experiments by Wols, Henri Michaux, Jean Dubuffet and Fautrier, with materials and with bodily gesture underpinned the proliferating tendencies variously defined as *Matière* painting, *Tachisme* and the *Informel*.

Above all there is in this art and in the statements of its makers a telescoping of time – an insistent atavism which supported all that seemed most forward looking. Dubuffet's much-vaunted primitivism, itself a reflection of current thought in the worlds of ethnography, archaeology and the medical sciences, was taken up through the Cobra group and widely beyond Paris.

And in such influence, perhaps, lay the seeds of its own dissolution. The art of *Paris Post War* was born in antagonism to an established school of Paris and independent of a burgeoning American avant-garde. By the middle of the 1950s the art which this art had spawned was beginning to look increasingly like a new establishment, shading into an international style of expressionist abstraction and a 'humanist' figuration. The social, economic, political and philosophical structures that nurtured its progenitors were no longer in place.

The single most important contribution to a definition of the climate for the art of *Paris Post War* came from the philosopher, novelist and playwright Jean-Paul Sartre. Sartre's vast and often intractable philosophical treatise, *Being and Nothingness*, was published in occupied Paris in 1943 in a softback edition of two thousand. No one reviewed it. No one knows who read it. Yet only two years later when Sartre was called on to defend his thesis in a public lecture, 'Is Existentialism a Humanism?', delivered at the Club Maintenant, the packed audience was so overwrought that several spectators fainted – an unusual happening at a philosophy lecture, even in

Alberto Giacometti **Portrait of Jean-Paul Sartre** 1946 Pencil on paper *Private Collection, Paris*

1945. During the heated debate that followed the talk, Sartre observed that philosophy was indeed spreading its roots fast and furiously:

> Until recently philosophers were attacked only by other philosophers. The public understood nothing of it and cared less. Now, however, they have made philosophy come right down into the market-place.[10]

Existentialism as a philosophy was marketed to a large public through books, plays and journalism. What de Beauvoir called the 'existentialist offensive'[11] was launched during 1945. De Beauvoir's 'existentialist' novel *Blood of Others* appeared in September to widespread critical acclaim. The same month saw the publication of Sartre's two novels about freedom, individualism and commitment, *The Age of Reason* and *The Reprieve*. In the very week of Sartre's lecture de Beauvoir's drama *Useless Mouths* opened at the Théâtre du Carrefour. All these events were given significant publicity by sympathetic publications like *Combat*, the mass circulation newspaper founded and published secretly during the Occupation by Pascal Pia and Albert Camus, who remained editor until 1946.

De Beauvoir herself acutely defined existentialism's insistent appeal. Sartre's supporters had, she wrote,

> lost their faith in perpetual peace, in eternal progress, in unchanging essences; they had discovered History in its most terrible form. They needed an ideology which would include such revelations without forcing them to jettison their old excuses. Existentialism, struggling to reconcile history and morality, authorised them to accept their transitory condition without renouncing a certain absolute, to face horror and absurdity while still retaining their human dignity, to preserve their individuality.[12]

Existentialism's 'popular' base spread rapidly, its apprentices ingesting a diet of Kafka, Sartre, Genet and Camus. It was not so much the serious moral tone of Sartre's work that set the pace but the heady notion that pre-existing moral codes had nothing to do with authentic existence. Camus, in his evocation of the absurdity of the world and of the freedom of alienated man, *The Outsider* (1942) offered, in the figure of his central character Patrice Meursault, a powerful role model. For young Parisians maturing through the Occupation years the message was enticing. For a brief period every style-conscious youth on the Left Bank could profess him or herself existentialist. The jazz musician and novelist Boris Vian was their Pied Piper and the young singer Juliette Gréco their voice. In its wider manifestations, existentialism was a shortlived explosion – a lifestyle philosophy acted out day and night in the new bars and caves, the cellar nightclubs of Saint-Germain-des-Prés.

Long before Sartre turned to the art of his contemporaries he had included thinking about art within his philosophical and literary enterprise. Creative endeavour was, naturally, of crucial significance to a philosophy which called upon man to seek his own essence, defining himself through his actions. Sartre drew on the artist as a paradigm for authentic existence: 'In life, a man commits himself, draws his own portrait and there is nothing but that portrait.' To this moral imperative Sartre adds another, insisting on a *tabula rasa*: 'As everyone knows there are no aesthetic values *a priori* . . . no one can tell what the painting of tomorrow will be like.'[13]

To talk of a style of existentialist art was thus a contradiction in terms. Sartre offered an implicit call to artists to make art without preconceptions. He found two artists rising to the challenge: Giacometti and Alfred Otto Wolfgang Schulze, commonly known as Wols.

Giacometti and Sartre met in 1941. Sartre was writing *Being and Nothingness* at

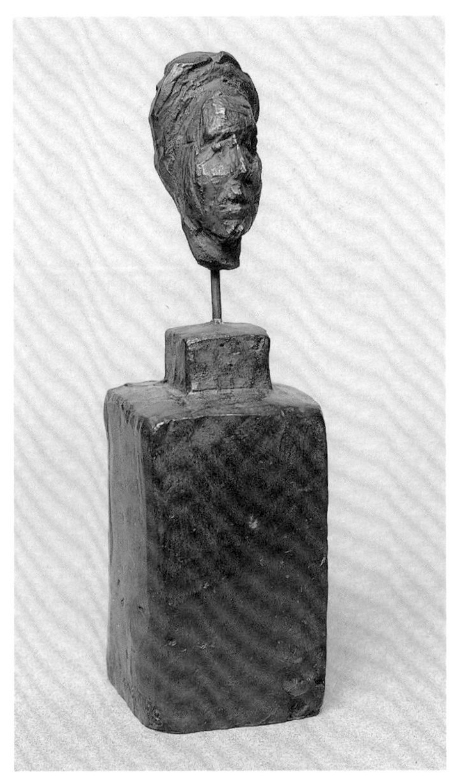

Alberto Giacometti **Head of Simone de Beauvoir** 1946 Bronze *Private Collection, Paris*

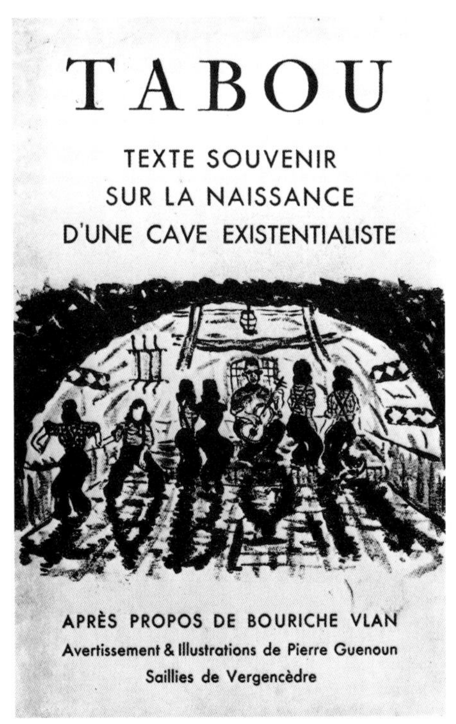

Boris Vian, *Tabou*, Paris

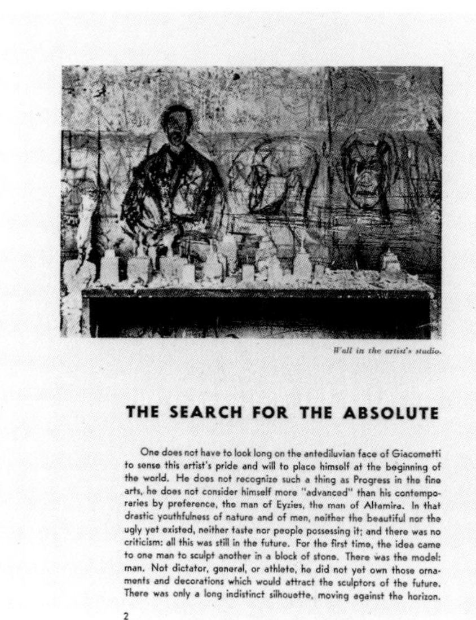

Jean-Paul Sartre, 'The Search for the Absolute', in *Alberto Giacometti: Exhibition of Sculptures, Paintings, Drawings*, exh. cat., Pierre Matisse Gallery, New York 1948

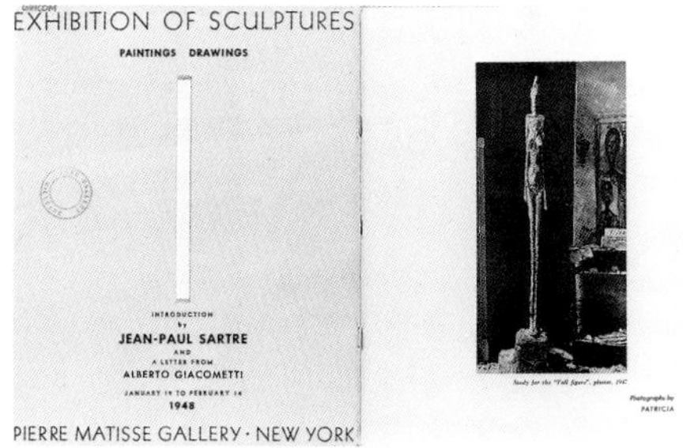

Alberto Giacometti: Exhibition of Sculptures, Paintings, Drawings, exh. cat., Pierre Matisse Gallery, New York 1948

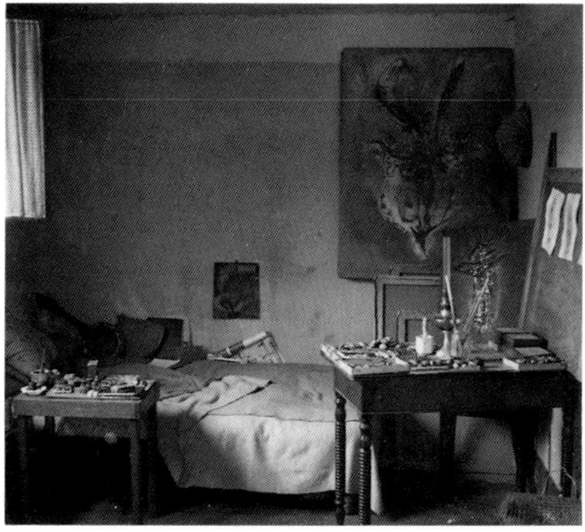

Wols's bedroom, Champigny 1951 Photograph
Private Collection

the time and Giacometti was searching for direction, having rejected the premises of Surrealism in the mid-1930s. According to de Beauvoir the two were drawn to each other because 'both had bet everything on one card, the one on literature, the other on art; impossible to say which was more possessed. Success, fame, money – Giacometti was indifferent to them all. He wanted only to reach his goal.'[14]

Giacometti many times described his goal as that of 'likeness' in art. The manner in which he proceeded evokes the phenomenological methodology of Sartre, while the language with which he disclosed his struggles evokes, at different times, Sartre, Camus, Samuel Beckett and Maurice Merleau-Ponty – his confidants and guides. Sartre first wrote about Giacometti's sculpture in a text, 'The Search for the Absolute', prefacing the catalogue to his first post-war show at the Pierre Matisse Gallery in New York in 1948.[15] Sartre portrays the sculptor's 'contemporaries by preference' as the prehistoric artists of the Altamira caves, drawing attention not only to Giacometti's struggle to reformulate the purpose of art – his rejection of *a priori* rules – but also to his hermetic lifestyle which made him, in Sartre's eyes, an ideal exemplar for his contemporaries. Although Giacometti did not show his work in Paris after the war until 1951, he was a familiar figure in the bars and cafés of Saint-Germain and was often visited in his Montparnasse studio where his obsessional deliberations extended on to the walls themselves. Brassaï, the photographer of urban graffiti, was one of the first to record the ravaged plaster surfaces of Giacometti's modern-day 'cave'.

Wols, who was to die prematurely in 1951, spent much of the war interned as an enemy alien. Sartre met him in 1945 and was fascinated by his tragic and dissolute lifestyle as much as by his obsessive art. In Sartre's first novel, *Nausea*, of 1938, his hero, Roquentin, undergoes a perceptual confrontation with nature through which he realises the fundamental difference between consciousness and the brute existence of things in the world (the difference between 'no-thingness' and 'being'). The experience of metaphysical disgust conveyed in Sartre's account is frightening and cathartic. Sartre described Wols as seeing with the eyes of an alien, unencumbered by conceptual knowledge. In Wols's images Sartre saw the painter's experience, like Roquentin before him, of the 'universal horror of being-in-the-world'.[16]

The first exhibition of Wols's watercolours took place at the Galerie René Drouin in December 1945. On minute sheets, most no larger than a postcard, they were displayed in deep box-like frames, painted black and individually illuminated to enhance their hallucinatory intensity. A tiny catalogue contained quotations and aphorisms selected by the artist, including a passage from Sartre's *Nausea*.

In engaging with the work of Giacometti and Wols, Sartre followed his own preferences for images, materials and styles that best described his vision of human existence. In general he preferred light and ephemeral materials, hesitant and incomplete images, qualities that evoked notions of becoming rather than the fixity of 'being'.

Much of what Sartre wrote on art had been anticipated and was echoed by others of his generation, like Merleau-Ponty, whose existentialist portrayal of Cézanne, 'Cézanne's Doubt',[17] predates Sartre's first text on Giacometti by three years. Sartre's philosophical stance drew on the phenomenological writings of the German Edmund Husserl, which date from the early years of the century, and the philosophy of Martin Heidegger in the 1920s. He was indebted to the French philosopher Henri Bergson who died in 1941, and his writing was richly infused with ideas generated by Marxism and Surrealism. Furthermore, current trends in the philosophy of science, through Gaston Bachelard's writings, in psychoanalysis and in the relatively new science of social anthropology (Lévi-Strauss was beginning to express himself), were as exciting and influential among Sartre's close contemporaries as they were to him.

Sartre's journal *Les Temps Modernes* (named after the Chaplin film *Modern Times*) was first published in 1945. Sartre intended it to be a mouthpiece for himself and a forum of debate for like-minded thinkers. It took over, in part, the role of the former *La Nouvelle Revue Française* which had been published by Gallimard. Jean Paulhan, novelist, critic, collector and former editor of the *NRF*, was on Sartre's imposing editorial board, alongside Merleau-Ponty and Michel Leiris, one-time Surrealist, writer and anthropologist. This cross-cultural editorial policy was mirrored also by Jean Paulhan's own journal *Les Cahiers de la Pléiade*, published from 1946 with a cover designed by Fautrier.

This community, located in Saint-Germain, functioned amid the wider colony of artists who lived, worked and had exhibitions in the mediaeval quarter between Saint Michel and Montparnasse. Hardly surprisingly, these writers perceived the visual arts as integral to moral and political issues, the worthy object of serious intellectual consideration. Partnerships between established writers and obscure artists were not unusual. Sartre's intellectual patronage of Wols and Giacometti was echoed in Paulhan's support for Artaud, the poet Francis Ponge's writings on Richier and Hélion, and Samuel Beckett's on van Velde. But it was to the work of Fautrier and Dubuffet that writers were most commonly attracted.

In the work of Fautrier, as in that of Wols, Artaud and van Velde, a fundamental link can be drawn between the artist's creativity and his isolation, his alienation from society. In one of his very rare recorded statements Fautrier spoke of the 'total expansion of being in solitude'[18]; and it was his 'Otage' (Hostage) paintings (nos. 26–36), made after witnessing Nazi atrocities in circumstances of absolute solitude, that marked the beginning of his post-war career. The works' total freedom from traditional procedures assured Fautrier an important place as a precursor of the *Informel*. What was perceived as especially radical was the thick substance which he had developed as an alternative to oil paint and which supported and embodied the imagery of physical annihilation. Described by André Malraux as an 'incarnation' of horror,[19] the impasto appeared as a metaphor of wounded flesh. Others, like Ponge, found one key to their meaning in the close and intense relationship of the artist to his materials, in the working of the material itself – he once described Fautrier as a cat 'relieving himself in the embers'.[20]

The exhibition of the 'Otages' at the Galerie René Drouin in 1945 was as carefully stage-managed as had been the Wols exhibition. The small panels were hung in monotonous rows, unmistakably evoking both the 'factory' style of Nazi extermination techniques and the 'anonymity' of their victims.

The affinity between Fautrier's work and that of Dubuffet lies in the use of informal methods of composition and in the way that matter itself communicates. Dubuffet was a self-proclaimed iconoclast, consciously looking for ways of breaking the mould. He acknowledged the influence of Fautrier[21] and indeed was one of the few to penetrate the latter's isolation (he painted and drew him several times and used his press to run prints through[22]). Dubuffet's exhibition *Mirobolus, Macadam et Cie* took place at the Galerie René Drouin in 1946. Crude, schematic images of people were scratched into the dense, sticky surfaces of the works. Dubuffet's critics were quick to perceive his originality and to link it to a new sensibility in literature. Such interpretations were not misplaced. Although he had only taken up painting as a profession in 1942, by the end of 1946 his work had been written about by the poets Francis Ponge, Paul Eluard and Eugène Guillevic and by Jean Paulhan, Georges Limbour and Michel Tapié. Sartre was said to be an early admirer[23]; Dubuffet, in his turn, was a self-confessed convert to existentialism. The network of mutual interest and influence was a close and intense one: it was what the painter Georges Mathieu

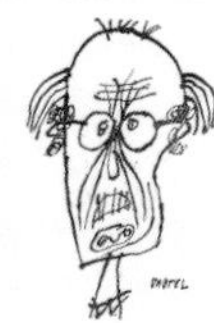

Jean Dubuffet, *Portraits*, exh. cat., Galerie René Drouin, Paris 1947

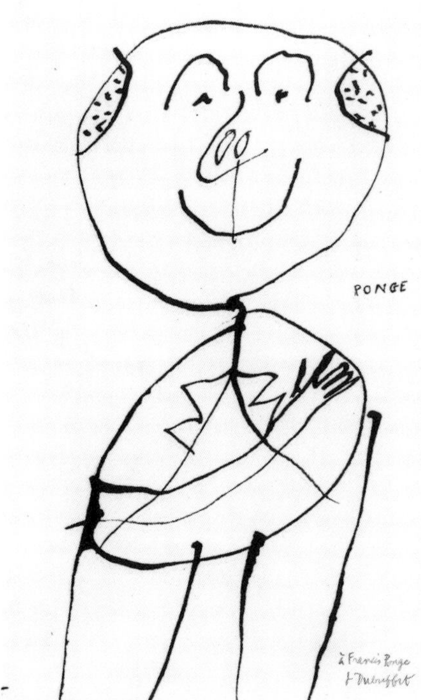

Jean Dubuffet **Portrait of Francis Ponge** 1947
Ink on writing paper *Armande Ponge, Paris*

unkindly described as the 'cocktail-littéraire-Gallimard' set[24] that Dubuffet portrayed in the second series of portraits exhibited at Drouin's the following year (nos.16–17).

The role of the dealer René Drouin in promoting Dubuffet, Fautrier and Wols was surely a significant one. Drouin had been an architect and designer before opening his gallery in the Place Vendôme, in collaboration with Leo Castelli, on the eve of the Second World War. The gallery's early exhibitions were devoted to displaying modern art alongside modern furniture and this may account for its financial survival through the war. Castelli left for America in 1941 and Drouin carried on alone. His post-war programme embraced pioneer abstract painters like Wassily Kandinsky, Surrealists such as Jean Arp and Max Ernst, and painters of the school of Paris currently in vogue including Roger Bissière, Alfred (Mac) Manessier and Gustav Singier. Drouin was also prepared to take risks and listen to the passions of close friends like Paulhan, and the author H.P. Roché who first introduced him to the work of Wols. He published a number of important catalogues in small editions and the actual staging of his exhibitions, as for Wols and Fautrier, contributed significantly to the interpretation of the work. When in 1948 he showed the drawings which the poet Henri Michaux had executed in an intense period of creativity after the death of his wife (nos.80–7), he hung the works so densely that the walls appeared as if 'splattered when some uncontrollable wave had broken'.[25] The venue for much of the newest and most difficult art in Paris, the Galerie René Drouin also harboured Dubuffet's growing collection of psychotic and naïve outsider art or *art brut*, to which Drouin gave over his basement, and which went on temporary public exhibition in the main galleries in October 1949. In such close proximity the relationships between the new and the old could not have been more cogently revealed.

The first attempts to articulate a shared sensibility among the artists of post-war Paris were made by the jazz musician, sculptor and avant-garde entrepreneur Michel Tapié. It was Tapié who began to use the term *Informel*, applied first to the 'formless' art of Wols. By 1951 he was using the term in relation to Dubuffet, Michaux, Fautrier and others. *Les Signifiants de l'Informel*, an exhibition Tapié organised at the Galerie Nina Dausset in Saint-Germain in March of that year, brought together Dubuffet, Fautrier, Georges Mathieu, Michaux, Jean-Paul Riopelle and Iaroslav Serpan.

In 1952 Tapié published his manifesto calling for *Un art autre*,[26] an 'other' or different art, freed from formal aesthetic conventions. The first few reproductions were given over to Fautrier, Dubuffet, Michaux and Wols, thus acknowledging their status, in Tapié's eyes, as precursors. The introduction of Americans Mark Tobey, Sam Francis, Jackson Pollock and Hans Hofmann illustrates Tapié's quite precocious appreciation of new American art. The spirit of internationalism extended to Italy, through the inclusion of Mario Sironi and Marino Marini, to the United Kingdom with Graham Sutherland, Reg Butler and Eduardo Paolozzi, and to the short-lived but important Cobra group, in the work of the Dutch artist Karel Appel. French representatives included Richier and several artists who played significant roles in extending the vocabulary of gestural abstraction like Hans Hartung and Pierre Soulages. Mathieu, whose theatrical performances of gestural painting brought him a perhaps inflated reputation in these years, was given prominence, as was Camille Bryen. Both had been profoundly influenced by Wols and both helped promote his legacy by helping stage a number of small but interesting group shows during the late 1940s.

Tapié's hyperbolic manifesto drew on the language of existentialism for its vocabulary and philosophical justification: individualism, authenticity, aggression, violence and transgression were celebrated.[27] From out of his dense and florid prose, matter and gesture repeatedly emerge as defining elements of a new aesthetic.

This notion that the gesture of the artist might be of significance had its roots in the aesthetic experiments of earlier Surrealists and Expressionists, notably Paul Klee and Kandinsky. For Tapié, however, automatist techniques were no longer merely a means of liberating the imagination of the artist. Sartre, likewise, had rejected Surrealism's preoccupation with the unconscious and with dreams because it ignored the totality of man, allowing only for the liberation of 'pure imagination'. Existential- ism, for *art autre*, as for the work of the artists in *Paris Post War*, provided a context and a language which took the artist's action as a register of authenticity and his marks as an affirmation of essence. Art was to be an activity performed by the whole man. As important as the rhetoric of Sartre was the thinking of his close friend Maurice Merleau-Ponty, whose work in existential phenomenology developed from the same roots as that of Sartre's but soon diverged. Merleau-Ponty's philosophical texts and his writings on art and artists focus on the problem of perception. His second philosophical treatise, *Phenomenology of Perception* (1945), countered Sartre's vision of man's consciousness with an alternative model in which mind and body are unified both in perception and in the creative act. It was Merleau-Ponty's writing more than anything else that so radically redefined the role of the body and bodily action for contemporary art practice. The body was, stressed Merleau-Ponty, man's anchor in the world, the interface between consciousness and the world of objects and materials.

Parallel to the focus given to the expressive gesture was the upsetting of the hierarchical relationship between image and materials that the art of Fautrier and Dubuffet appeared to effect. Although the romance of lowly materials is inescapably present in much of the art on display – appropriately enough in an age of scarcity – these artists did not just reiterate the already well-worn idea that non-art materials could be expressive. They affirmed that art should arise from an encounter with mat- erials, that materials are what unites and differentiates man and the world of objects. Paulhan, whose views were elaborated in lengthy correspondence with Fautrier, Dubuffet and others, believed that it was only through wrestling with materials, grappling with the hazardous effects of chance and challenging the independent will of resistant matter, that artists could find a new way forward. He pointed to Georges Braque, Georges Rouault and Chaim Soutine as precursors. Each, he argued, had found a means of renewal through engaging physically with materials.

The artists whom Tapié gathered together were an eclectic group and loosely bound. Many others could well have found a place in his exhibitions or writings. Giacometti, who would undoubtedly have rejected Tapié's advances, might have featured. Giacometti's struggles involved the kind of trial that Tapié advocated as the basis for self-expression and the extraordinary appearance of his work could be said to demonstrate aspects of an *autre* aesthetic. The characteristics of Giacometti's style have become by now so thoroughly assimilated that we have to rely on accounts of contemporary encounters in order to appreciate them fully in an *autre* context. When the American painter Barnett Newman saw the sculpture in the 1948 exhibition at the Pierre Matisse Gallery in New York, he described them as if they were 'made out of spit – new things with no form, no texture, but somehow filled'.[28] Here is the notion both of the *Informel* and of material as metaphor for the body of the artist. Another oeuvre which might interestingly be seen in an *autre* context is that of Antonin Artaud. Although his mental health, his early death and his predominant involvement with drama and poetry reinforce his 'marginal' status as an artist, he advocated an art-theatre 'of compulsive gesture and physical crisis . . . a dangerous theatre'[29] which he later embodied, literally, in his own crazed portrait drawings. Interestingly, Michel Tapié was one of only two people to commission portrait drawings from Artaud.

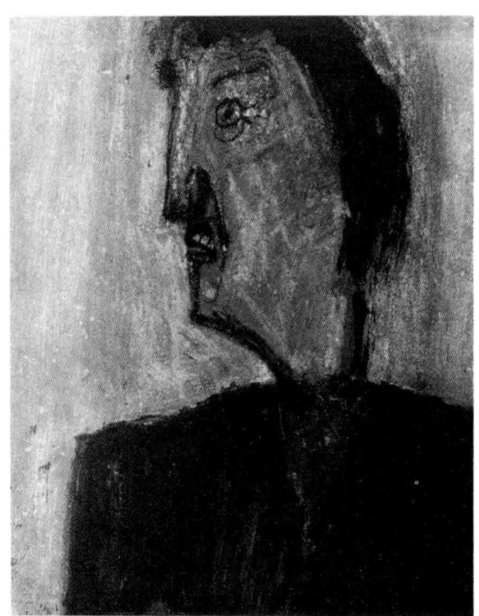

Jean Dubuffet **Portrait of Jean Paulhan** 1945
Gouache and ink on paper *Private Collection*

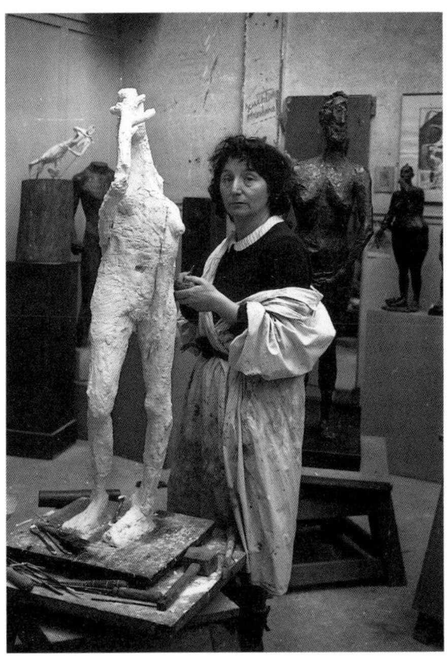

Germaine Richier in her studio with **Forest Man**
1948 Photograph by Brassaï *F. Guiter Collection*

Germaine Richier and Bram van Velde were also, in effect, outsiders, Richier by virtue of her sex, van Velde, who remained outside Tapié's purview, through his reclusive life and almost total lack of admirers. Beyond the extraordinary Kafkaesque imagery that Richier evolved during the post-war decade it is the physical materiality of her work that impresses: her lifesize figures appear to have resulted from some Dionysian struggle with Nature itself. In the context of the aftermath of war it is almost impossible to avoid seeing her hybrid creatures as metaphors for the survival of humanity under threat. 'We cannot', she confessed, 'conceal human expression in the drama of our time.'[30] For van Velde it was the impossibility of expression that Samuel Beckett chose to explore when writing about his art, echoing a leitmotif of the dramatist's own work. Van Velde's paintings have dry, 'ugly' surfaces, far removed from School of Paris sophistication. Residual figurative references refuse to surface; they are lost in van Velde's confusing labyrinthine structures. Beckett's texts on the artist were really about language and its limitations. However the apparent failure – in Beckett's eyes – of van Velde's paintings to communicate was widely (mis)interpreted by others as their meaning and their justification.

Silence has a particular resonance in the art of *Paris Post War*. The emphatic reduction of dialogue in the plays of Beckett offers a parallel to Sartre's notion of man's alienation from man: the impossibility of authentic communication between individuals. Art, too, could be beyond language. So Beckett thought in relation to van Velde, so Sartre asserted when he found Wols's art 'full of nameless things',[31] and so Dubuffet argued when he suggested that to 'name' something was to destroy it.[32] Ironically, the redundancy of language itself could be eloquent, and the notion that in the face of overwhelming historical despair – the War, the Holocaust, the Bomb – artists turned away from a literal description of the world was frequently expressed. With or without language, the works themselves share a rich range of visual metaphors: of engulfing space, of the abyss, of viscosity; of human frailty, isolation, fear; of freedom, action and bodily engagement. That these are at the same time metaphors made familiar in the literature of existentialism and the absurd is the inescapable legacy of a free interchange of ideas and of the networks of friendship and interaction that bound the artists and writers of post-war Paris.

NOTES

1   Picasso, quoted by Harriet and Sidney Janis, *Picasso: The Recent Years, 1939–1946*, New York 1946, p.4.

2   Simone de Beauvoir, *Force of Circumstance*, Paris 1965, London 1968, p.39.

3   Ibid., p.43.

4   Antonin Artaud, *84* (Paris), nos.8/9, p.282, trans. Stephen Barber in Stephen Barber, *Antonin Artaud: Blows and Bombs*, 1993, p.149.

5   Brassaï, *Picasso & Co.*, 1966.

6   De Beauvoir, 1968.

7   Jean Hélion, *Journal d'un peintre: carnets 1929–1984*, Paris 1992.

8   Selected letters to and from Jean Paulhan are published in *Jean Paulhan à travers ses peintres*, exh. cat., Grand Palais, Paris 1974.

9   Boris Vian, *Manuel de Saint-Germain-des-Prés*, Paris 1974.

10   Jean-Paul Sartre, *Existentialism and Humanism*, Paris 1946, London 1989, p.58.

11   De Beauvoir 1968, p.46.

12   Ibid., p.47.

13   Sartre 1989, p.49.

14   Simone de Beauvoir, *The Prime of Life*, Paris 1960, London 1963, p.487.

15   Jean-Paul Sartre, 'La Recherche de l'absolu', *Les Temps Modernes*, vol.III, no.28, 1948, pp.1153–63; trans. as 'The Search for the Absolute', in *Alberto Giacometti: Exhibition of Sculpture, Paintings, Drawings*, exh. cat., Pierre Matisse Gallery, New York 1948, pp.2–22.

16   Jean-Paul Sartre, 'Doigts et non-doigts' in Jean-Paul Sartre, Henri-Pierre Roché, Werner Haftmann, *Wols en personne*, Paris 1963, p.18.

17   Maurice Merleau-Ponty, 'La Doute de Cézanne', *Fontaine*, no.47, Dec. 45, pp.80–100.

18   Jean Fautrier, quoted by Sarah Wilson, 'Jean Fautrier: Orthodoxy and the Outsider', *Art International* vol.4, Autumn 1988, pp.33–40, p.33.

19   André Malraux, 'Les Otages' in *Les Otages, peintures et sculptures de Fautrier*, exh. cat., Galerie René Drouin, Paris 1945, reprinted in *Jean Fautrier 1898–1964*, exh. cat., Musée d'art moderne de la ville de Paris 1989, p.222.

20   Francis Ponge, *Note sur Les Otages peintures de Fautrier*, Paris 1946, unpag.

21   Jean Dubuffet, letter to Jean Paulhan, in *Jean Fautrier 1898–1964*, p.222.

22   Jean Dubuffet, letter to Jean Paulhan (undated), cat.116 in *Jean Paulhan à travers ses peintres* 1974, p.98.

23   According to *Ici Paris*, 21 May 1946, quoted in 'Extraits de presse', Max Loreau, *Catalogue des travaux de Jean Dubuffet*, fascicule II, Paris 1966, p.124.

24   Georges Mathieu, *Au-delà du Tachisme*, Paris 1963, p.43 note.

25   René Bertelé, trans. by Michael Fineberg and quoted by Alfred Pacquement in *Henri Michaux*, exh. cat., The Solomon R. Guggenheim Museum, New York 1978, p.55.

26   Michel Tapié, *Un art autre, où il s'agit de nouveaux dévidages du réel*, Paris 1952.

27   The subject is explored by Yule F. Heibel, 'New Unravellings of the Real? Autre Art's threadbare subject meets the new universalism', *Rutgers Art Review*, vol.VII, 1986, pp.75–103.

28   Barnett Newman in Thomas B. Hess, *Barnett Newman*, New York 1969, p.39.

29   Barber 1993, p.43.

PARIS POST WAR: IN SEARCH OF THE ABSOLUTE

Sarah Wilson

I Introduction to Existentialisms

> Auschwitz – schwitz – schwitz
> Auschwitz – schwitz – schwitz
> Buchenwald!
> Bouhn*wald!*
> ADONOOOI ADONOI!
>
> Isidore Isou, 1947[1]

The Europe of bombed ghost towns is no more ravaged than the idea Europe has made for itself of man.

> André Malraux, 1947[2]

Paris post war was a city which embraced existentialism as a philosophy and as a way of life. But 'existentialism' was a portmanteau-word which teemed with ambiguities. A word which became a sign for nihilism and the extreme, it was dialectically related to the retrieval of tradition, the spirit of reconstruction and indeed the pursuit of happiness, in a city whose nerve-centre became Saint-Germain-des-Prés.

In April 1945, eight months after the Liberation euphoria in Paris, the first newsreels and photographs of the concentration camps reached France, proof of a policy of industrialised genocide. Emaciated deportees arriving at the Gare Saint-Lazare soon offered their eye-witness accounts. In August 1945, atomic bombs were dropped on Hiroshima and Nagasaki ending the global war. They were the ultimate demonstration of the 'revenge of technology' as predicted by Walter Benjamin; and the ultimate refutation of the claims of Western humanism to a tradition of enlightenment and progress.[3] Existentialism, a many-branched philosophy which emphasised crises of being, personal action and commitment – in its most intellectualised or most popular forms – offered coordinates for decision which could be brought to bear upon individual choices at a moment whose unbearable intensity seemed to announce the end of history itself.

Yet new philosophies for reconstruction in 1945 were challenged by the atrocities committed in the name of the *épuration*: the purging of institutions or individuals deemed to have collaborated with the Nazis. The crux of political debate focused upon the notion of legitimacy, which in turn governed policies of continuity versus those of caesura, of the radical break. The psychology of the post-war period, deeply bound up in the simultaneous desire for both caesura, continuity and catharsis, was reflected in contemporary art and thought. Debates around existentialism extended into all domains, in particular religion and politics. The key word 'humanism' became an indicator. Sartre, whose *Being and Nothingness* had appeared in 1943, posited humanism within existentialism, two years later, as being 'present through absence', a contention central to the whole existentialist/humanist controversy.

The debate on humanism in post-war France was complex. It mirrored the political tripartism of the coalition governments of the Fourth Republic with a 'philosophical tripartism': existentialism, Marxism and Catholic personalism, each of which claimed humanism as their own. All three movements held dissident positions in the 1930s, which had matured in clandestinity during the Occupation.[4] Sartre gave his lecture 'Is Existentialism a Humanism?' in October 1945, as a riposte to attacks on all sides: the Communists had attacked the emphasis on the sordid, the quietism of 'despair', and the lack of solidarity with the rest of mankind implied by the existentialist position; the Catholics attacked Sartre's 'freedom' for its nihilism and irresponsibility, its denial of the reality and seriousness of human affairs. Sartre himself, at the beginning of his lecture acknowledged the two strands of the movement: the Christian strand (originating in Kierkegaard's attack on Hegel) via Jaspers and Gabriel Marcel, and that of existential atheism via Heidegger.[5]

As far as Catholicism was concerned, France was of course historically split, to some extent along class lines, into a nation of believers and unbelievers; the lay education of the working classes coincided with the proclaimed atheism of the Communist Party, but tradition and church ritual lingered. The Catholic church, which had been passive if not downright collaborative during the Occupation, actively sought new recruits; Catholic personalism attempted to engage in dialogue both with Sartre and the Marxists; the Communist 'extended hand' policy likewise sought to poach the Catholic vote. Catholic 'personalist' arguments were exemplified by the writings of Emmanuel Mounier and his review *Esprit*. While taking on the Marxists, Mounier constantly challenged Sartre and the position of *Les Temps Modernes*, while his *Introduction to Existentialisms* (1946), claimed priority for the Christian existentialist position.[6]

The conservatism of the Catholic church was matched by that of the Communist Party, which enjoined a similarly ascetic discipline and sexual conformism. Sartre's particular brand of existentialism had the philosophical and intellectual credentials to compete with these two systems; his emphasis on 'engagement' implied a commitment as demanding as his rivals. But Sartre flouted the precepts of the Catholic and Communist establishments in two ways: he exemplified uncompromising atheism and a certain sexual freedom – at least a working redefinition of the couple – in a way which was exhilarating for a younger, post-war generation. Moreover, the 'existential' predicaments dramatised by Sartre in a series of successful novels and plays involved real choices in the real world – with all the absurdity of contingent life. Thus he was perceived as a threat to an older generation who saw what Sartre's 'freedom' might imply in terms of irrevocable social and structural changes in society. Nowhere was this more transparent than in *Existentialism*, a serious but popular guide of 1946, which aimed at explaining the different historical strands of the movement – and its overriding moral consensus – from which Sartre most conspicuously diverged. The author's anxieties focus upon the 'immorality, perversion, pornography' of existentialist novels, and Sartre in particular.[7]

Sartre's philosophy in its popularised form thus offered new freedoms to the young 'existentialists' of Saint-Germain-des-Prés, freedoms by definition ascetic in austerity conditions, but modern freedoms expressed through jazz music, American literature and fashion, new forms of song and dance, sexual experimentation and innovation in the arts. The satirists were quick to attack: 'The existentialists who don't go to bed any more meet from ten to midnight at the Bar Vert, rue Jacob, where they carve existentialist graffiti in the water closets and telephone booths ... no obscenities, no hearts and arrows, but grave thoughts which ponder about the void, the tomb, suicide and Bikini atoll. Here is a random sample of these sombre aphorisms: "Day and night I dream about the animals on Bikini atoll." "Man – that animal that sings the Marseillaise" ... "If you don't feel too good, get yourself felt by an Other." '[8]

These youthful 'existentialists' of Saint-Germain-des-Prés were direct descendants of the 'zazou' teenage movement of the Occupation, who themselves espoused flicked-back hair, platform shoes, and jazz music, 'le swing'. The 'zazous' had rebelled in a politically intolerable situation.[9] The jazz refrain to Isou's poem 'Swing':

> Jingilingi, tingi lingi
> ... Bamagoula bamba goula
> Sale juif ... Vichy ... heil Hitler

recalls the racial hatred, the round-ups, the deportations to French transit camps which were 'normal' at the time – which indeed, fifty years later, have only just been officially acknowledged by the French government.[10]

Isou's poem marks a collision between history, experience and avant-gardism. With his deliberate echo of the score structure of Cabaret Voltaire poems of 1916, he was promoting a Dada revivalism along with artists and critics such as Michel Tapié, whose strategies will be discussed subsequently. Isou's new movement, *Lettrisme*, claimed to return poetry and literature to origins in the letter itself – the sign's priority over even the phoneme – that was just one of an explosion of attempts to define a new beginning for art as a return to origins, literally a starting from scratch.[11] Dubuffet's graffiti art, Michaux's ink blotches, Artaud's screams, Giacometti's minute, thread-like sculptures all share this concern. Despite the fact that these artists had reached maturity in the 1930s, they now aimed to retrieve an authenticity, a sense of beginning at the beginning which was the only way to begin from nothing, the imperative contained in Samuel Beckett's existentialist pun: 'Comment c'est/[Commencez]' (How it is/[Begin]).[12] While the proliferating arenas of artistic debate in post-war Paris never specified a category of 'existentialist art' as such, the ethos of 'beginning from nothing' corresponds to Sartre's theory, expounded in the existentialism and humanism essay, that existence precedes essence: 'We mean that man first of all exists, encounters himself, surges up in the world and defines himself afterwards.'[13] Primal chaos, new beginnings: echoes of Sartrean 'authenticity' informed these discussions of the new painting and sculpture.

II Humanism and Terror

> We were never so free as under the German Occupation ... each thought was a conquest; as an all powerful police sought to silence us, each word became as precious as a declaration of principle; as we were pursued, each gesture had the weight of an engagement.
>
> Jean-Paul Sartre, 1944[1]

How is it possible that the period of *épuration* could in itself contain a nostalgia for the period of Occupation? Paris under Occupation became the privileged site of the double code – not only for the age-old 'civil war' amongst the French – but as a *lieu de mémoire*, a place of memory, in which questions of authenticity and moral value became retrospectively unproblematic absolutes. Sartre recalled the hollowness of the appearance of normality in occupied Paris, the ghost town with curfews and no traffic, with its fake culture of theatrical gaiety, and the window displays in food and wine shops, belied by the notice *étalage factice* (artificial display).[2] This was very much the scene pilloried in Dubuffet's first Occupation series of paintings including the canvas called with bitter humour 'View of Paris, Life of Pleasure' (fig.1). A child-like excitement was conveyed by Dubuffet's friend Jean Paulhan in his evocation of the 'cops and robbers' atmosphere of clandestinity[3]: but his light, anarchic tone belied a deep moral disgust.[4]

Not for Paulhan was Sartre's retrospectively dignified vision of moral clarity. Paris, the 'place of enunciation', the seat of the Académie Française and the institutions and publishing houses that constituted the intellectual life of the nation, had been sullied. The purge campaign conducted by the National Writers' Committee focused on writers for their symbolic function as scapegoats – and for the simple reason that incriminating files of published articles were easy to collate. The publishers, the speculators, the industrialists who financed publishing ventures during the Occupation escaped unscathed. Moral probity, choice, compromise – or writing at the behest of the official regime – these were the dilemmas 'judged' by *épuration* committees. They precipitated the suicide of Drieu la Rochelle, who had run Paulhan's *Nouvelle Revue Fran-*

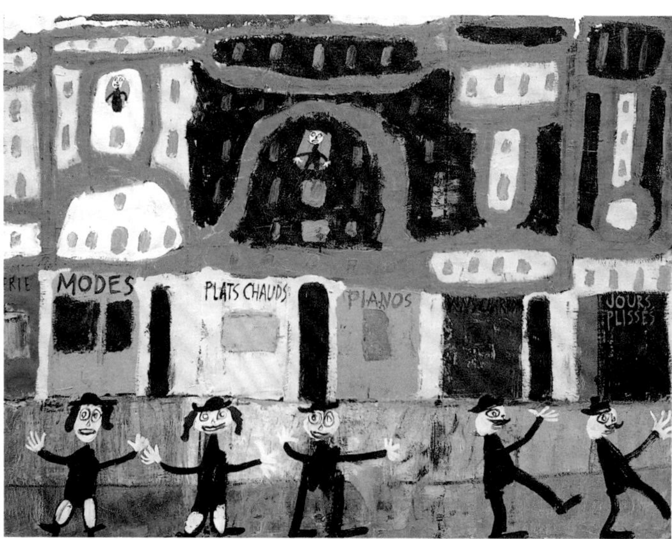

fig.1 Jean Dubuffet **View of Paris, Life of Pleasure** February 1944
Oil on canvas *Private Collection*

çaise during the Occupation. The first death penalty was announced for a thirty-one year old journalist; opponents of the purge waged an unsuccessful campaign to save the brilliant young writer Robert Brasillach.[5] He spent his final days in the Fresnes prison whose walls bore the last messages of deportees, despatched to their deaths in Germany or Poland. Their pathetic graffiti are the key to suppressed tragic resonances in Dubuffet's art.[6]

Well before the Liberation of Paris, a purge campaign had been planned for the arts as part of the general programme laid down by the Front National Resistance organisation in March 1944. A questionnaire for a post-war arts policy widely circulated in August 1944 by the old administration merely provided a useful list of collaborators for the new appointees. The Communist gallery director of the late 1930s, Joseph Billiet, became Directeur Général des Beaux-Arts during the battle for Paris on 24 August. Arrest warrants for certain curators were issued the next day. An *épuration* session was held to discuss the Salon d'Automne, and manifestos and press releases denounced the French artists who had toured Germany in November 1941. The first president of the Front National des Arts, Maurice Denis, had died in 1943, and was replaced by Picasso who became the recipient of letters begging for mercy. Picasso timed the momentous announcement that he had joined the Communist Party to coincide with the 'purged' Salon d'Automne, where his retrospective of recent works, many filled with the imagery of death, caused an uproar involving the laceration of many canvases. Defended in the name of the National Writer's Committee, who were responsible for the *épuration* of writers, it was unthinkable that Picasso could renounce his links with the policies of the purge. Despite Billiet's fall from grace, the *épuration* policy in the fine arts continued and the necessary bureaucracy and machinery for punishment was set up, involving the confiscation of works, withdrawal of exhibiting rights, public trial and fines.

The *épuration*, however, was far more bloody than this specific situation in the art world would suggest. It was a period of denunciation, revenge killings, the settling of old scores and jealousies, and above all of public trials with hastily assembled judicial apparatus, which led to the deaths of thousands of Frenchmen. Thus Fautrier's *Otages* exhibition, the hostage paintings and sculptures shown at the Galerie René Drouin in 1945, had not merely a retrospective resonance. While 'Oradour-sur-Glane' (no.35), one of his most recent paintings, commemorated the ultimate, apparently inexplicable German atrocity, the massacre of 642 men, women and children, in a small southern village as late as June 1944, the serial presentation of the 'Otages' emphasised the anonymity of the tortured victims and implied the continuity of arrests, shootings, and deaths that were the day-to-day stuff of the popular press.[8] 'The shot victim replaces the crucified One, the anonymous man replaces the painted Christs', said Francis Ponge in his remarkable *Note sur Les Otages* of 1946, but his references to 'anti-German unanimity', 'the desire to kill the torturer' and a 'revengeful wrath' employ the familiar vocabulary of the *épuration*.[9] The working of Fautrier's pictorial matter itself embodied the process of scarring and bloodying, the tenderness and sadism, that were exemplified by the relationship between the torturer and his victim. 'Sarah' and 'The Jewess', of 1942–3 (nos.26–7) brought disturbing elements of eroticism, rape and racial identity into the equation. Indeed the equivalence of the erotic relationship and that of the victim and torturer or executioner was explicitly made by Georges Bataille, with

whom Fautrier collaborated on a clandestine edition of *Madame Edwarda* at the very end of the Occupation. Bataille later chose an epigraph for this text by Georg Hegel: 'Death is what is most terrible, and to sustain the work of death demands the greatest power.' Eroticism itself, Bataille says, is visited upon the conscience like a *déchirure* – a rent or tear of the flesh – and this image is repeated as the narrator kisses Edwarda's sex, 'an open wound'. 'Death itself was at the fête, inasmuch as the nudity of the bordello calls for the butcher's knife.'[11] Metaphors of open wounds, indistinguishable from scars, or from the female sex; these evocations from Bataille coincide with Fautrier's residual figuration and his private, terrifying memories as a 'voyeur of death', witnessing massacres in the Parc de Sceaux. Beauty, horror, intensity – and repetition: Fautrier would create another hostage series in 1956, to commemorate the Soviet invasion of Budapest.

The lugubrious light of the still-vigorous *épuration* campaign illuminates Dubuffet's portrait series of 1947 (nos.16–17), ironically subtitled 'More Beautiful than They Think, Beautiful in Spite of Themselves'. Besides the key figure of Jean Paulhan, others he depicted also contested the justice of the purge. The writer Paul Léautaud, for example, had been a chief signatory of the letter campaigning for the writer Brasillach's release, calling the *épuration* 'a repetition of 1793 in the name of a pretended justice'.[12] 'Paul Léautaud with Caned Chair' (fig.2), 'Léautaud, Red Indian Wizard', 'Léautaud Flabbergasted', 'Léautaud, General of the Empire' featured in Dubuffet's show, as did 'Marcel Jouhandeau: Official Portrait', 'Jouhandeau, Little Secret Portrait', 'Jouhandeau with Big Ears'. Jouhandeau was a writer who had certainly fraternised with the German official litterati, Ernst Junger and Gottfried Heller, during the Occupation.[13] *Cahiers de la Pléiade*, the journal with its cover designed by Fautrier, which published Dubuffet, Michaux, Artaud and the poet Francis Ponge, also published the exiled antisemitic writer Louis-Ferdinand Céline as early as 1948.[14] It was the forum for the anti-*épuration* articles of Jean Paulhan. Paulhan had

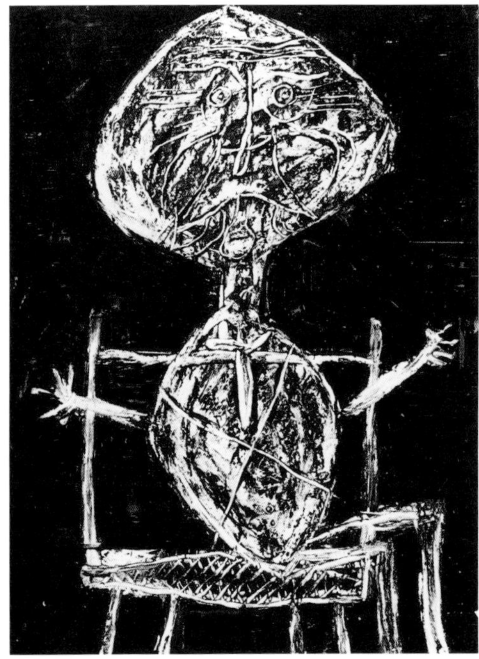

fig.2 Jean Dubuffet **Paul Léautaud with Caned Chair** November 1946
Oil on canvas *Private Collection*

functioned behind the scenes in the Gallimard publishing house during the Occupation, and indeed owed his life to Drieu la Rochelle who officially took over his place. A personal friend to so many writers who published during the Occupation, Paulhan employed metaphor and philological conceits to talk about the political concept of 'Terror' in literature; his position at odds with the punitive writers' committee was clear.[15]

Not only at the moment of Liberation but throughout the 1940s, arguments for the justification of the *épuration* were based on the legitimacy or otherwise of Pétain's government during the Occupation. Chapter and verse of constitutional law were cited by ex-Vichy officials, attacking the legitimacy of the *épuration* – here Louis-Dominique Girard's book *Franco-French Warfare* (1950) is a key document.[16] Yet 'enlightened' and powerful intellectuals such as Paulhan used the same argument: his *Letter to the Directors of the Resistance* (1951), presenting official statistics – around 60,000 Frenchmen tortured, shot or burned alive at the Liberation – appeared at the height of the debate over the mythologising of the Resistance, creating a tremendous furore.[17]

The urge for reparation, for redress, above all for 'normalisation' fought against the horror, just as 'normalisation' had been a policy pursued by the Nazis during the Occupation of Paris. It must be remembered that 1945 and 1946 were years of a kind of mirror-image reversal of artistic events of the war years: the Grand Palais devoted to a multi-faceted show of *European France* during the Occupation held one devoted to *Hitler's Crimes* in 1945. The works of art stolen from French museums through the Occupation – if not destroyed at the Jeu de Paume itself, lost or damaged – were exhibited as 'rediscovered masterpieces' at the Orangerie des Tuileries in 1946.[18] The notion of 'cultural property' was at a premium, and, as with the First World War, in the shadow of the recently bombed cathedrals such as Rouen, 'moral cathedrals' fuelled debates on cultural superiority, art, race, barbarism and reparation, as the School of Paris was re-established.

Before officially reopening in 1947, the Musée national d'art moderne held the exhibition *Art and Resistance* in February 1946, the first to build up images of the French Resistance in painting and sculpture. A talking point was Picasso's 'The Charnel House' (fig.3) with its twisted and intermingled bodies sprawled in death under a bare table, a postscript to 'Guernica'. Seeds of conflict were present, however, in the juxtaposition of work by Picasso and Boris Taslitzky in the show. Taslitzky, born in France, and a young militant for engaged realism in the 1930s, had risked his life making drawings in Buchenwald. These were published with haste by the Communist press, and in the wake of *Art and Resistance*, various Communist ministers attended the opening of his exhibition *Témoignage* (Things Seen) in June 1946, where 'The Small Camp, Buchenwald' (fig.4), a history painting of the scale and aspiration of a Géricault, was purchased for the nation. Immediately it became the centrepiece of the newly opened Resistance Room in the Musée national d'art moderne. Comparisons between Taslitzky's 'authenticity' and Picasso's style generated the bitter debate of autumn 1946 about realism and modernism in the Communist Party rank and file, preceding any call for a 'Socialist Realism' in 1947 (indeed the party had its own promoters of abstract art at the time).[19] Taslitzky's proximity to both Gruber and Giacometti, dating from Popular Front days was evident – and it has been argued that for Giacometti, the Popular Front period and his friendship with Gruber were crucial for his own rejection of Surrealism and return to figuration.[20]

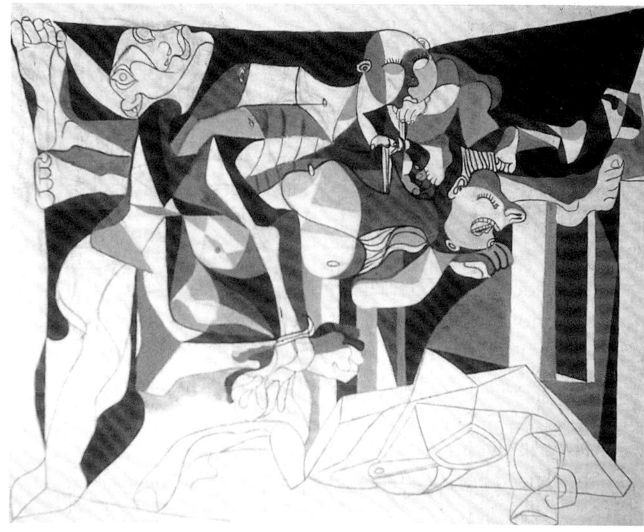

fig.3 Pablo Picasso **The Charnel House** 1945 Oil and charcoal on canvas *Museum of Modern Art, New York*

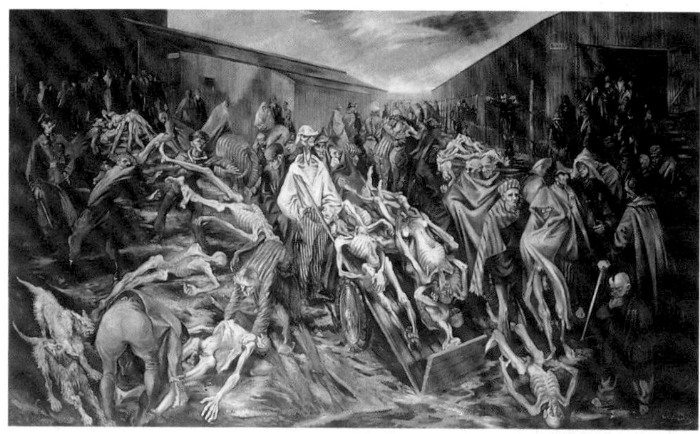

fig.4 Boris Taslitzky **The Small Camp, Buchenwald** 1945 Oil on canvas *Musée National d'Art Moderne, Centre Georges Pompidou, Paris. Courtesy of the Artist*

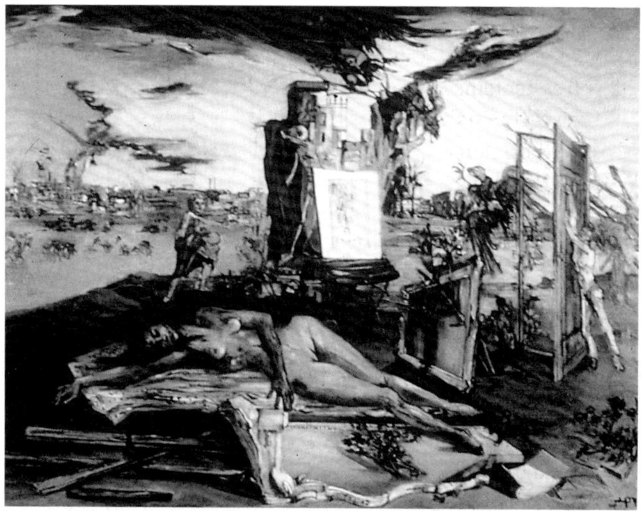

fig.5 Francis Gruber **Homage to Jacques Callot** 1942 Oil on canvas *Jacques Bazaine, Paris*

Gruber's paintings of the early 1940s are strange amalgams; the mutilated remains of history paintings surround conventional depictions of the model in a studio. The naked and violated body in a landscape, 'Homage to Jacques Callot' exhibited in 1942 (fig.5), with its implicit Resistance message, hailed Gruber's precursor from Alsace-Lorraine. Callot's 'Horrors of War' engravings were a source for Gruber's spiky and fantastical facture; Giacometti also saluted Callot in 1945.[21] Gruber's undernourished models in bare interiors recalled all the deprivation of the Occupation period. In 'Job' (no.68) the inside/outside space creates metaphysical ambiguities as regards the notion of threshold. These correspond with Job's lament to Jehovah in a moment of existential choice: the leap of faith or its abandonment. The images of nakedness and dereliction, of fears, agoraphobic and claustrophobic, could, one might specu-late, be related to the inner feelings of doubling and mutilation Gruber experienced because of his father's German/Alsatian back-ground.

Having joined the Communist Party in 1944, Gruber was a founder member, with André Marchand and Emmanuel Auricoste, of the new Salon de Mai, where the writings of Camus, Sartre and the Communist poet Eugène Guillevic were exhibited in the literary section. In *Art and Resistance*, Gruber showed paintings of naked male corpses on an indeterminate ground: the boundaries between the notions of political and religious martyrdom became blurred – as they became between Catholic and Marxist versions of huma-nism. The pro-modernist religious periodical *Cahiers de l'Art Sacré* discussed the 'tragic' in contemporary painting involving not only Catholic figurative painters such as Georges Rouault and Georges Desvallières, but André Marchand's 'Crucifixion' and the work of Gruber.[22]

Certainly Gruber's work seemed to embody the existential pre-dicament in its amplitude, and its ambiguities, its *néant*, one could argue, being pregnant with the absent father in every sense, relig-ious, sexual, political. And in a way, with his death in 1948, Gruber himself became that absent father for a new generation of painters who had emerged from the Salon des Moins de Trente Ans (Salon of the Under-Thirties) started during the Occupation. The future members of the Homme-Témoin (Man as Witness) group, including Bernard Buffet, first exhibited in this forum. Their realism, under the aegis of Gruber, would attempt to distinguish itself from Communist Socialist Realism after 1948. Despite the establishment-orientated later career of Buffet, a direct line may be drawn from the 'Under-Thirties' groupings, via Gruber and Buffet, to the salon of the Peintres Témoins de Leurs Temps (Painters Witness to their Times) of the early 1950s, and the metamorphosis of the 'Under-Thirties' into the Salon de la Jeune Peinture, founded in 1953, which would become the hotbed of the politically engaged, post-Stalinist 'New Figuration' movement in the 1960s.[23]

The dominance of Gruber's heritage and the power of the myth of the 'existentialist' artist as the new *peintre maudit* (damned painter) can be illustrated by a typical article of 1951, Claude Roger-Marx's 'An Art of the Absurd or the Absence of Hope in Con-temporary Painting'.[24] It juxtaposed illustrations of Gruber's hom-age to Rimbaud, 'The Poet' 1942 (fig.6), and Buffet's 'Solitude' 1948 (fig.7), a glum young man seated behind a table with empty bowl, glass and bottle. In both, the adolescent boy and, by implica-tion, dreams of a future thwarted by the 'real', are the focus for a painting whose 'realism' is an ambiguous sign for an imaginary departure from the present. Nineteenth-century artists 'whose exist-

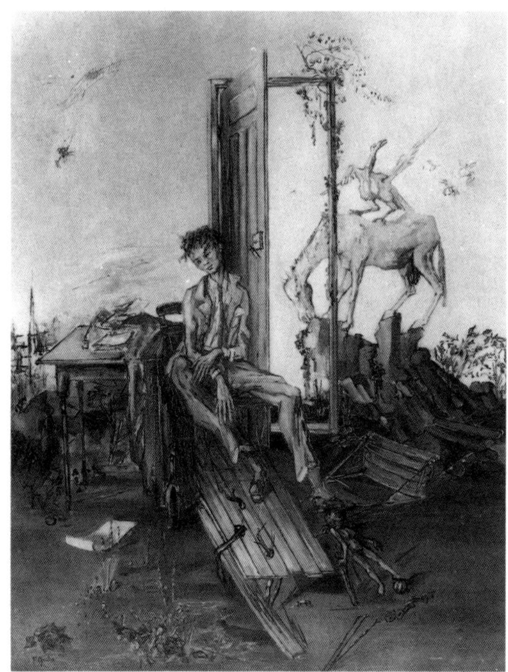

fig.6 Francis Gruber **The Poet** 1942 Oil on canvas
Private Collection

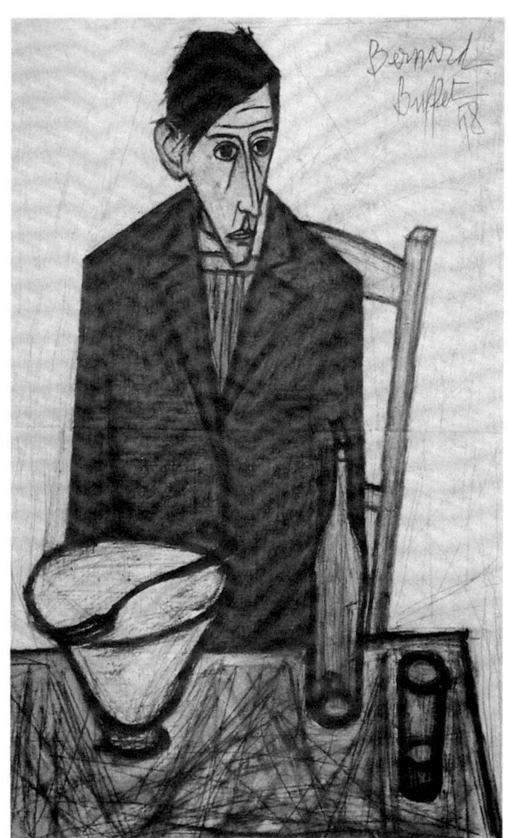

fig.7 Bernard Buffet **Solitude (The Seated Drinker)** 1948
Oil on canvas *Musée d'Art Moderne de la Ville de Paris*

ence was a daily calvary, who were ravaged by misery, madness and suicide … a generation born in suffering' are linked to Buffet and Minaux, whose work evokes 'the cellar air they breathed as children, the terror, the restrictions'. Gruber is the precursor: 'with less austerity Gruber created sinister reds, and spread the odour of crime in a satanic space.' Gruber's Titianesque, almost episcopal luxuriance, the insistence on glazes in his 'The Red Divan' 1944 (no.67) would be abolished in favour of the scraped and scored greys and beiges of Buffet's 'austerity' palette while Buffet appropriated Gruber's motifs. In 1951, Roger-Marx's article was already the sign of a covert nostalgia for the purity of enterprise, authentic poverty and determination (Gruber) which Buffet's meteorically successful career contradicted. Buffet's canvases, easily legible as representations of 'Kafka, Sartre, the concentration camps, food rationing, the housing crisis' spawned a fashion in the 1950s, in direct conjunction with the consumer boom. 'Existentialism' as represented in the *misérabiliste* mode of Buffet and his imitators, became a fashion devoted to the cult of its most glamourous exponents – the very exemplars, ironically, of Sartrean 'bad faith'.[25]

Just as the eschatological dimensions of Gruber's 'Job' (no.68), or of Buffet's 'Crucifixion' series mediated between agnostic and Catholic existentialist positions, so the eschatological dimensions of Communist doctrine, first discussed in the 1930s, were correspondingly emphasised in Socialist Realist painting. After 1947, ousted from government, the French Communist Party opposed the Marshall Plan and espoused Komintern positions in the arts. Conventional religious tropes structured hard-line Socialist Realist paintings, just as hagiographical traditions were employed by writers and propagandists.[26] In 1951, with *misérabilisme* at its height, André Fougeron's 'Le Pays des Mines' series presented a mining accident victim laid out like Holbein's dead Christ; Boris Taslitzky's 'Death of Danielle Casanova' 1950 (fig.8) depicted the Communist heroine's death at Auschwitz in conventional hagiographical terms based on Zurbaran and Géricault. Socialist Realism as a phenomenon is at last acknowledged as a major – albeit not dominant – phenomenon of the period.[27] However, my emphasis here must regard the Communist position in the 'humanism and terror', debate which divided post-war intellectuals.

At the height of the prestige of the Communist Party, the party of '75,000 fusillés' (victims shot dead), Arthur Koestler published *Darkness at Noon*, a ghastly parable of life under Communist rule, implicitly referring to the notorious show trials and purges of the late 1930s. In 1947, Maurice Merleau-Ponty, joint editor of *Les Temps Modernes* with Jean-Paul Sartre, published *Humanism and Terror: Essay on the Communist Problem* in response to Koestler's attack. Merleau-Ponty's explicit resuscitation of the problem of the Soviet show trials of the 1930s and attempts to justify them in terms of the 'greater good' of the revolution presented moral and political conundrums in the context of a purge that had inescapable parallels with the *épuration* climate.[28]

Following Merleau-Ponty's publication, the Kravchenko scandal in 1949 gave the debate over Soviet labour camps new impetus;[29] the threat of atomic destruction and a third world war seemed ever nearer and became a subject for Salon paintings such as Bernard Lorjou's huge 'Anecdotes of the Atomic Age' 1950.[30] As positions polarised, arguments became more strident; the press campaigns in favour of Socialist Realism in *Les Lettres Françaises* for example, are astonishing in their amplitude at the same time as the Communist Party actively promoted the work of the 'late moderns', Picasso,

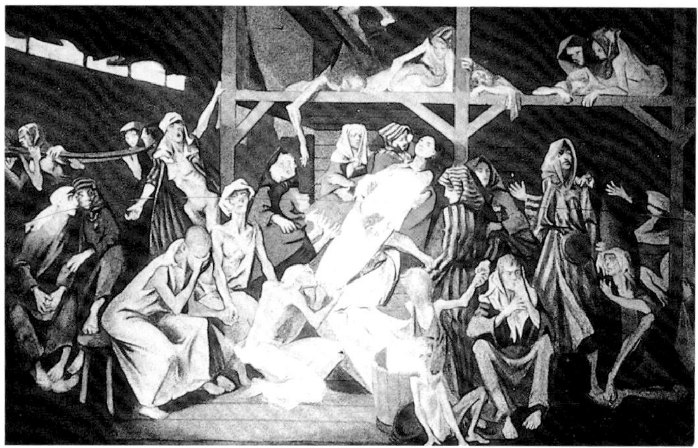

fig.8 Boris Taslitzky **The Death of Danielle Casanova** 1950 *Musée d'Histoire Montreuil. Courtesy of the Artist*

Léger and Matisse. Trotskyist discussions took place in the studios of both the Geometric Abstract artists and the Surrealists. Geneviève Bonnefoi, a participant in the 1950s' art world, now a distinguished critic and curator, has written of the 'mechanism of "two terrors"' at the time: Socialist Realism and Geometric Abstraction. Escape towards the *Informel*, towards 'open' representation in free gesture – the existential alternative – seemed the only possible way out.[31] The political arguments, alas, continued: the Soviet labour camp question continued to split the Left in a vile propaganda war, modified only after 1956 with the revelation of Stalin's crimes. Humanism and terror: the debate would dominate the post-war period.[32]

III Cézanne's Doubt: Painters of Failure

> If, in Cézanne's times, painting an apple was a very advanced intellectual position, to make history painting in the era of 'Guernica' and the extermination camps is also a very progressive intellectual and moral position.
>
> Francis Gruber, 1945[1]

Gruber's position of a realist engagement with history must be directly opposed to painters in post-war Paris who looked to Cézanne. A 'school of Cézanne' was formed in Aix-en-Provence during and after the Second World War that affected the semi-abstract landscape paintings of 'lyrical abstractionists' such as Pierre Tal-Coat.[2] The adoption of Cézanne as both a moral and painterly model by an artist like Giacometti is more significant. Indeed Giacometti's position during the crucial years of friendship with Gruber, 1936–9, hovered between the challenge of political realism as 'engagement' and the lessons of Cézanne: the two 'Apple' paintings and the portrait of his mother, crucial for his work of the 1940s, date from 1937.

Maurice Merleau-Ponty's extensive essay, 'Cézanne's Doubt' was published in the review *Fontaine* in 1945 and in his collection of 1948, *Sense and Non-Sense*.[3] Although more evidence is required of specific responses to Merleau-Ponty's text, it was surely crucial for artists such as Bram van Velde who saw not only their work itself, but their own 'failure' in a Cézannesque mode exemplifying an existentialist predicament. Cézanne reappeared in sections of Merleau-Ponty's *Phenomenology of Perception* (1945), within a vastly complex elaboration of philosophical and perceptual schemata. His exemplary position was thus re-emphasised, and far from pure *misérabilisme*, for painters of the post-war generation, Cézanne's visual power pointed to the ultimate triumph of his fortitude.[4]

'Painting was his world and his existence' Merleau-Ponty declared of the artist. 'Anxiety was the basis of his character.' Cézanne provided a model of asceticism, his life's work doomed to failure as a saint's is doomed to imperfection. Merleau-Ponty posited a 'morbid constitution … schizophrenia … a flight from the world of human beings, the alienation of his humanity'. Cézanne wished to paint 'a primordial world' with an emphasis on the immediate translation of sensation. Moreover 'He did not want to distinguish the fixed objects which appear before our eyes from the fleeting way in which they appear'. Cézanne was deemed able to suspend habits of thought and perception, alienating the spectator in 'a world without familiarity, where we are not at ease'.[5] Merleau-Ponty refers not only to Balzac's artist Frenhofer in *The Unknown Masterpiece* and his canvas of scribbled lines representing nothing[6] – but surprisingly has a long excursus on Sigmund Freud's writings on Leonardo da Vinci: a blueprint for the psychoanalysis of the artist, anticipating Sartre's existential biography of Jean Genet.

Simply, I would propose that, before Sartre's writings on the art of Wols or Giacometti, Merleau-Ponty produced a paradigm of the 'existentialist' artist full of contemporary resonances.[7] His subsequent abandonment of the problems of the individual, the status of individual creation and individual failure, to concentrate upon broader political dilemmas is telling. By considering 'Cézanne's Doubt' in juxtaposition with *Humanism and Terror*, the relative claims of artist, philosopher and the discourse on art versus political writing and political engagement are firmly contextualised in the years 1945–7, with the latter, finally, prioritised.

Echoing and corroborating Merleau-Ponty's text, Bram van Velde wrote in 1948: 'Only men who are sick can be artists. It's their suffering which pushes them to do things which put sense back into the world. The sensitive man or the artist can only be sick in our civilised life full of lies … Painting is man confronting catastrophe … I paint my misery.' The vocabulary of Sartre is also discernible when Bram van Velde speaks of 'Pictorial styles or the struggle with the void … the desire for the non-real, to escape the mesh' (Sartre's metaphor of entrapment, *l'engrenage*).[8]

Samuel Beckett's preface upon the brothers Geer and Bram van Velde, 'Painters of Failure' echoes Merleau-Ponty and Bram himself: 'the knowledge of the contingent preceeds that of substance … Their painting is an analysis of a state of privation … one in terms of light and emptiness, one in terms of the inside, obscurity, fullness and phosphorescences.'[9]

The drawing of the artists into Beckett's own circles of Hell is expressed more punchily: 'The situation is that of him who is helpless, cannot act, in the event cannot paint, since he is obliged to paint, the act is of him who, helpless, unable to act, acts, in the event paints, since he is obliged to paint.'[10]

This topical, existentialist language linked with the imagery of austerity and absurdity, served to mask pictorial struggles, displacing formal analysis. (Was not Bram's failure a failure to escape Picasso in terms of both forms and palette?) Yet the very real deprivations of the early 1940s continued for many into the next decade. The glamorous lifestyle of Buffet or of Georges Mathieu during the 1950s should be compared with that of the far older artist, Bram van Velde, whose support from the Galerie Maeght ended abruptly after his third disastrous show in 1952. Bare walls, simplicity, a dignity which conceals the effort of confronting the blank canvas; poignant images with a mythologising power were caught by photographers such as Brassaï and Denise Colomb. High seriousness, an intense level of creativity and debate, persistence in spite of worldly failure – this paradigm is the very antithesis of those photographs of the craziness of Saint-Germain youth culture: the symbolic release of the youth of the Atomic Age, in carnival, in excess, in the culture of the Tabou.[11]

IV The Theatre of Cruelty

There is a connection between the schizoid constitution and Cézanne's work because the work reveals a metaphysical sense of his illness. If we see schizophrenia as a state of mind in which the world becomes reduced to the sum of all its physical experiences but as if frozen and as a suspension of expressive values, then the illness, in Cézanne's case, ceases to be an absurdity and a fate, and becomes a general possibility of human existence when it resolutely attacks one of its paradoxes: the phenomenon of expression as such.

Maurice Merleau-Ponty, 1945[1]

Schizophrenia as an element in the debate on art and 'authenticity' extended the questions raised under the aegis of existentialism to areas of the mind–body relationship, its dislocation, physical and mental cruelty. 'Insane' art, called in French *l'art des fous* or *l'art psychopathologique* had constituted a parallel discourse with that of modernism since debates about Van Gogh at the turn of the century.[2]

Ironically it was the Van Gogh exhibition in Paris in 1947, possibly the most successful museum exhibition of the period, that precipitated the most savage indictment of society by the writer Antonin Artaud. Artaud, his body consumed by drug abuse, medication and self-neglect had linked the concept of physical catharsis with a ritualistic, violent anti-realism central to his 'Theatre of Cruelty', baptised in 1936. He now spoke with the authority of one recently released from years of incarceration and electroshock treatment in psychiatric hospitals, and in the wake of the first exhibition in the Sainte-Anne psychiatric hospital of the works of the mentally sick in 1946 – a deliberate riposte to the campaign against 'degenerate' art by the Nazis. A great public success, this show had coincided with Jean Dubuffet's first attempts to promote what he called *art brut*, an art made on the margins of society. A 'psychiatric' article on Van Gogh in the weekly *Arts* quoting Dr Joachim Beer's description of the artist as a 'degenerate of the Magnan type' was the catalyst for Artaud's magnificent response: *Van Gogh, the Man Suicided by Society*.[3] His vision was grimmer even than the world of the purge committees: 'And thus, demented as this assertion may seem, present day life goes on in its old atmosphere of prurience, of anarchy, of disorder, of delirium, of dementia, of chronic lunacy, of bourgeois inertia, of psychic anomaly (for it isn't man but the world that has become abnormal) of deliberate dishonesty and downright hypocrisy, of a mean contempt for anything that shows breeding.'[4] In the preface to the exhibition of his own remarkable crayon portraits at the Galerie Pierre in June 1947, Artaud wrote: 'The human face is an empty force, a field of death ... Only Van Gogh knew how to draw from a human head a portrait which would be the explosive smoke from the beating of a bursting heart.'[5].

Artaud had worked alongside Surrealist artists before and during his incarceration; the genuine schizophrenic Guillaume Pujolle was painting at the hospital Rodez when Artaud began his own drawings. Artaud literally embodied and bodied forth the art and madness debate, involving it intimately with considerations of cruelty and abuse. Extreme violence was perpetrated upon language itself: his mother tongue was attacked by reminiscences of Tarahumara Mexican Indian chants and pure glossolalia – a substitute for the tearing and screaming body, bound and subject to electroshock agony, the subject of so many drawings:

> o penis ta penis
> atura
> o petura a petur peni
> ta ksartam
> ta kharon.[6]

Artaud's three-hour performance at the Vieux-Colombier theatre in January 1947, and his group radio recital, 'To Have Done with the Judgement of God' planned for broadcast in February 1948 (prohibited and subsequently pirated), presented almost intolerable sights and sounds of human anguish.[7] The startling realism of Artaud's portraits exhibited in the same year as Dubuffet's portraits, 1947, demonstrates the realisation of his belief in the possibilities of a strong art without origins: 'I have definitely broken with art, style or talent in the drawings displayed here ... cursed be he who considers them works of art, works of the esthetic stimulation of reality. None is properly speaking a work. They are all sketches or should I say staggering blows given in all the directions of chance, possibility, hazard or destiny.'[8]

Artaud's realism is disturbingly self-reflexive: 'Artaud's own face appears in all these portraits, compacted into the face of the sitter, so that they are all double portraits of Artaud and the subject whose face he was interrogating in the drawing.'[9] Recognition becomes identity: the red crayon 'Portrait of Arthur Adamov' (no.10), for example, a homage to the writer's autobiographical exposé, *The Confession*, commemorates a life which like Artaud's was marked, according to his friend Georges Bataille, with 'sickness, neurosis, vice ... Adamov seems to have risen up out of a black imagination avid for a coloured horror that alone might attenuate the grotesque, somehow grandiloquent aspect that crushes the heart.'[10] It is not without relevance to both Artaud's portraits and Michaux's obsessive preoccupation with the head, that Jacques Lacan's essay on the 'mirror stage', conceived in 1936, was published in 1949.[11] Michaux abhorred mirrors and refused to look at his own image; thus his drawings as processes of both apparition and exorcism are intimately related to problems of identity and representation: 'If I paint mad-looking heads, its not to say that I'm mad in those moments ... the madness then of watching the paper soak up the ink too quickly, or the blot making me deviate from my original design, this madness calls up in me almost at once the echo of thousands of madnesses stemming from my none-too-happy past.'[12]

The focus on schizophrenia continued when the *International Exhibition of Psychopathological Art* (planned as early as November

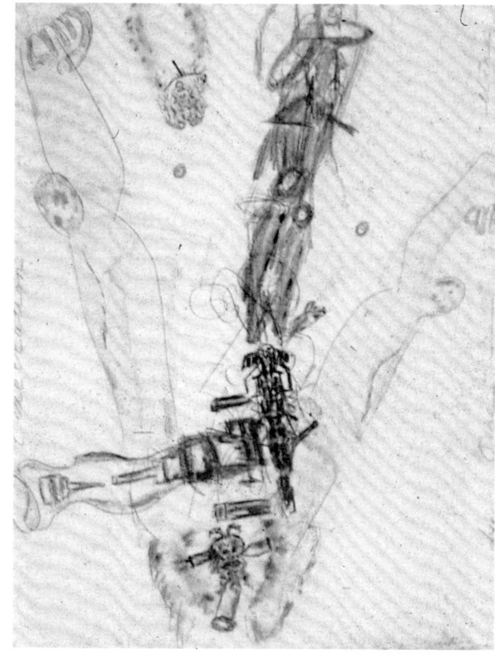

fig.9 Antonin Artaud **Detestation of the Father–Mother** April 1946 Pencil, Pastel and watercolour on paper *Musée National d'Art Moderne, Centre Georges Pompidou, Paris*

1948) was held at the Sainte-Anne psychiatric hospital in 1950, in conjunction with the first World Congress of Psychiatry. Jean Dubuffet, who damned the show, was not asked to lend.[13] Though this exhibition momentarily eclipsed his own *art brut* collection, his promotion of *Art Brut Preferred to Cultural Arts*, as exhibited at the Galerie René Drouin in 1949, a mixture of schizophrenic and naive art, would continue through the decade. While Dubuffet's interest in this kind of art capitalised on discoveries and publications already familiar to the Surrealists, and André Breton's active commitment to the *Foyer de l'art brut* was considerable from 1947–51, the Surrealist leader broke with Dubuffet. Breton's own medical involvement with psychiatry, his awareness of the pain and isolation of dementia, differed vastly from Dubuffet's sense of fête, his celebration of the myth of the 'common man'. In Dubuffet's public presentation of an *art brut* – so ostensibly close at times to aspects of his own work – the artist supressed the tragedy of schizophrenia or of lifelong institutionalisation, only once admitting: 'They are people for whom, indeed, everything is lost. No enterprise can offer them any hope. They have to confront the human condition reduced to a minimum, at its extreme point.'[14] In 1960, a major Dubuffet retrospective at the Musée des arts décoratifs heralded the consecration of the *art brut* collection in the same museum seven years later. The final visibility of schizophrenic art coincided with a stream of posthumously published texts by Artaud. Both Michel Foucault and Jacques Derrida put sanity, identity, and 'voice' at the heart of their writings in the 1960s.

Such issues confronted Sartre's philosophical position from the outset. First, Merleau-Ponty had resited philosophical consciousness within the perceiving, spatialised and sexualised body in *Psychology of Perception* (1945). In addition, he brought both behavioural sciences and Saussurian linguistics onto the agenda of the Collège de France before 1952.[15] Concurrently, the discourses of schizophrenia and with it psychosexual and psychosomatic disturbances involving the rebellious body and its languages, challenged the premises of autodetermination and 'freedom' at the heart of Sartre's critical and philosophical enterprise.

V Matter and Memory: A New Primitivism

The essential gesture of the painter is to cover a surface ... to plunge his hands into full buckets or bowls, and with his palms and fingers to putty over the wall surface with his clay, his pastes, to knead it body to body, to leave as imprints the most immediate traces of his thought, the rhythms and impulses that beat in his arteries and run along his nerves.

Jean Dubuffet, 1945[1]

What Sartre called Henri Bergson's 'philosophical revolution' in *The Imagination* (1936), became crucial for his later writings, as was Gaston Bachelard's focus on imagination, reverie (daydreaming) and primal matter.[2] Bachelard, an extraordinarily imaginative autodidact, took up the chair in the history and philosophy of science at the Sorbonne in 1940. Both Bergson and Bachelard were important and explicitly acknowledged sources for post-war artists before Sartre himself entered the arena of contemporary art criticism. Bergson was saluted in Dubuffet's 'Matière et mémoire' series and Bachelardian ideas of matter permeate his meditations on walls, 'Les Murs' which were exhibited at the Galerie André in April, 1945 (see no.155–6). The poet Francis Ponge's text for Dubuffet, *Matière et mémoire* adopted Bergson's title of 1896, making an explicit homage to the aged philosopher whose refusal to renounce his Jewish roots or seek preferential treatment had led to an ignominious death during the Occupation.[3]

Dubuffet's ferocious lithographs in the 'Matière et mémoire' series of the 'Telephone Torture Victim' (fig.10) or the 'Shorthand Typist' were promoted together with folk art and sign-painting against the 'Greekeries' of the Western humanist tradition in an important lecture of January 1945 that could be seen as the manifesto of his idea of the art of the 'common man'.[4] Reflections upon the 'memory' of the lithographic stone in Ponge's *Matière et mémoire* preface indicated the work itself as the latest 'brutality' in a series of palimpsests going back to 'an ancient Daumier'. Daumier recalls the long tradition of French political caricature which resurfaced in Dubuffet's work, sullying the innocence of his child art sources. And in contrast to Daumier's position at the heart of social life, Ponge's reference to Brassaï's studies of graffiti evoked a disturbing marginality.

The walls in the 'Murs' series of paintings and lithographs represent the area of Paris known as the 'zone', frequented by society's rejects of all descriptions; it was where roads turned into mud tracks, where territory was staked out as allotments, where murder victims were surreptitiously buried, where executions were carried out before and after August 1944. This was the area frequented by Dubuffet's 'common man', whose *argot* (the coded slang of the subculture) was parodied in Dubuffet's own writings which may be compared with those of Louis-Ferdinand Céline. Both men revelled in anarchy, an almost criminal menace and an elevation of the scatological into a metaphysical system.

In the paintings of walls and the images made with ink on lithographic stone a sense of identity between material and representa-

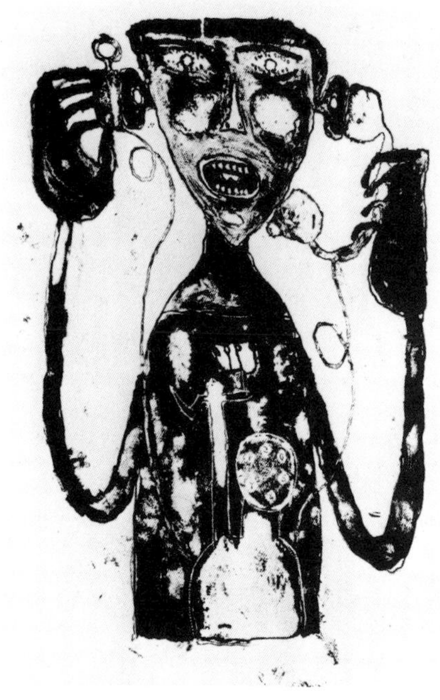

fig.10 Jean Dubuffet **Telephone Torture Victim**
Lithograph from *Matière et mémoire*, pl.30 (n.d.) (1944)

tion was created with stone-coloured, gravelly or tar-macadam surfaces.[5] *Matière* itself became consubstantial with representation as *mémoire*: a fusion of remembered, imaginary and actual images was achieved. Dubuffet's next adventure was to move from gravel and macadam to the *hautes pâtes* or 'raised pastes' which involved a more complex philosophy. 'Buffoon, charlatan, paints with shit, plays the baby, a pimple-scratching aesthetic': the critics were provoked and disturbed.[6] Dubuffet started work on his *hautes pâtes* in April or May 1945. Fautrier's 'Otages', created with thick impastos during the Occupation, were shown in October 1945, before Dubuffet's showed his *hautes pâtes* in the *Mirobolus, Macadam et Cie* exhibition of June 1946, also at the Galerie René Drouin. Beyond any debate on Fautrier's technical precedence, I would propose that Dubuffet and perhaps Fautrier, too, were aware of Gaston Bachelard's lectures at the Collège de France during the Occupation. It was here that the first theorisings upon the *pâte* as primal matter were voiced to a distinguished audience of poets, writers, artists and tramps sheltering from the cold.[7] Bachelard's *Water and Dreams*, published in 1942, posits a 'mesomorphic imagination' in between the formal and the 'material' imagination: 'Mesomorphic dream-objects assume form with difficulty and then lose it, gradually subsiding like dough [*une pâte*]. The viscous, soft, lazy object ... corresponds to the strongest ontological density in dream-life'. The primitive Homo faber is evoked, for whom kneading (clay or dough) is a 'continuous dream, work done with the eyes shut ... intimate reverie'. His work is linked to the dominating character of *la durée* (the flux of time): rhythm. (Bergson as precursor is obvious here.) 'This reverie born from the work of kneading is necessarily linked with a particular will to power, the male joy of penetrating into substance, of feeling the inside of substances ... the hand becomes conscious of the progressive success of the union of earth and water'. The *durée* is inscribed in the matter itself, a *durée* without particular aims, a 'becoming' of substance itself.[8] Compare Dubuffet's *hautes pâtes* with this text, in particular his aggressively naked male figure, 'Will to Power' (fig.11). It combines a rich, thickly worked matter, an outrageous phallicism and a deliberately Nietzschean title. Bachelard's link between his elemental and primordial theorisings of the *pâte* and those of the infant's first material grasp of the world tally with contemporary interest in child mentalities that would reappear in Merleau-Ponty's Sorbonne lectures later in the 1940s.[9] Bachelard declared: 'It is in the flesh, in the organs that the first material images are born. These first material images are dynamic, active, they are linked to desires [*volonté*] that are simple, astonishingly crude'.[10] He refers to Jung, and to the concept of infant libido in psychoanalysis. His discourse may be seen to infuse Fautrier's disturbing 'Baby' series within the 'Otages' (a 'primal' reading of the Massacre of the Innocents?) and to surface again in Dubuffet's 'Corps de Dames' (Ladies' Bodies) (see 'Olympia' fig.12, 'Gymnosophie,' no.20), where the maternal body spreads out, almost coterminous with the canvas boundaries.

Bachelard moves from a consideration of the *pâte* to the *greffe* or graft, and opposes his concept of the 'dynamic hand' to Bergson's concept of the 'geometric hand' of Homo faber – the first man to make tools and designs. Again, compare Dubuffet, whose brilliant reflections upon the *hautes pâtes* are instinct with Bachelardian vocabulary and ideas: 'Nourish yourself with inscriptions, instinctive traces, respect the impulses, the ancestral spontaneities of the human hand when it traces signs. One should feel man and his weaknesses (*maladresses*) in all the details of the picture. Likewise the chance events pertaining to the materials used, the hazards of the hand.'[11]

Bachelard's later writings may continue to be read in tandem with Dubuffet's elaborate productions. Interestingly, in *Earth and the Dreams of Will* (1947) which has another whole chapter on *La Pâte*, Bachelard returns to an extensive analysis of Sartre's *Nausea*, where Roquentin's 'nausea in his hands' stimulates Bachelard's reflections on a 'manual imagination'.[12] Evidently the philosophy of *la pâte*, the key to a reading of the new post-war *Informel* painting was a product of what would now be classified as a highly 'intertextual' situation: a series of interpenetrating readings and quotations from texts that were translated into *matière*, into painting practice (one must emphasise that both Sartre's and Bachelard's books were highly popular).

Yet other sources interfered with these readings from the start. The *Mirobolus, Macadam et Cie, hautes pâtes de Jean Dubuffet* exhibition catalogue was prefaced by the writer, neo-Dadaist and jazz player Michel Tapié. While acknowledging an array of powerful artistic precursors, as had Dubuffet himself, it was Tapié's emphasis upon indigenous and anonymous sources, prehistoric, Gallic and Romanesque, that signalled the definition of a new primitivism for the 1940s. This primitivism was divorced from the spoils and the 'anthropology' of the Trocadero, the exotic fascinations of the returning Surrealists: 'Dubuffet must certainly descend from the god LAUGHTER of our ancestors the gauls'.[13] Yet, with his epigraph by Nietzsche: 'one must have chaos within', Tapié called Dubuffet's works 'less paintings than benevolently endothermic supports' and proclaimed that Dubuffet's man is 'entirely open, aware of himself in the present and his potential future and in certain signs as old as the world.' Tapié's writing on the *Informel*, pulling away from the Bergsonian and Bachelardian nexus of matter and memory towards neo-Dada and the new, multidisciplinary inputs of what he called an *art autre* (an other art) is discussed on pp.45–6.

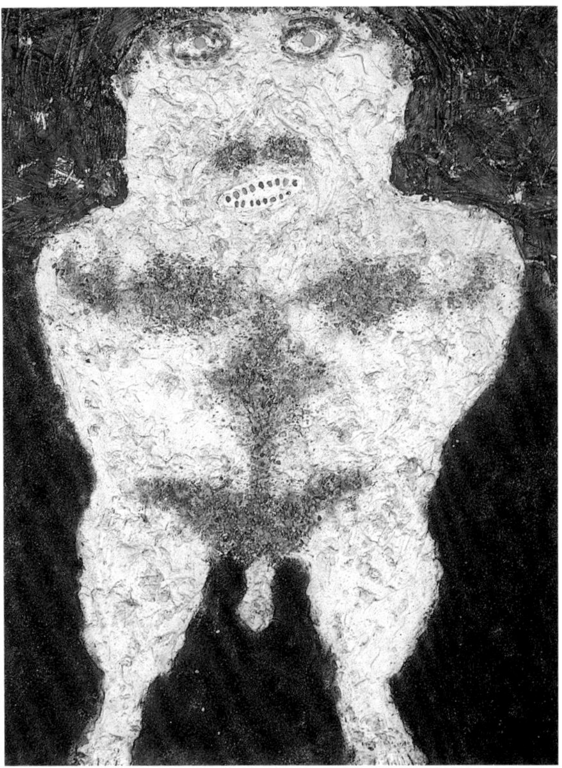

fig.11 Jean Dubuffet **Will to Power** 1947 Oil with gravel, string, pebbles and broken glass on canvas *Private Collection*

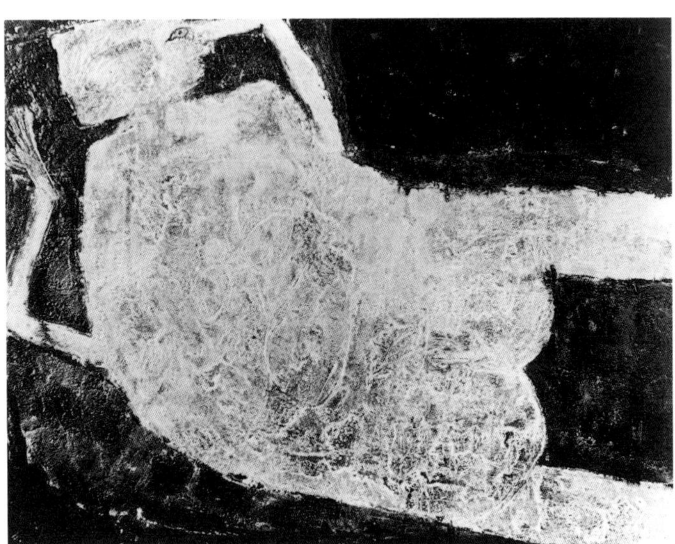

fig.12 Jean Dubuffet **Olympia** April 1950 Oil on canvas *Private Collection*

VI Under the Sign of Sartre

Read Heidegger and the phenomenologers: you will find all the detail of the appearance 'with angst' of the object.

Jean Paulhan to Fautrier, *c.*1942–4[1]

I haven't quite got round to any precise conception of what existentialism actually is . . . Nonetheless I feel and declare myself to be warmly existentialist.

Jean Dubuffet, 1946[2]

The writings of Bachelard, of Merleau-Ponty, of Paulhan, of Ponge, of Dubuffet himself were articulating important ideas about postwar art long before Sartre's first exhibition preface of 1946. Paulhan's advice to Fautrier proves that artists and writers were going back for 'phenomenological' inspiration to the same sources as Sartre himself, without the philosopher's mediation. Can one, indeed, define an 'existentialist art'? As a term it did not exist. The collision between the cult of Saint-Germain-des-Prés and Sartre's philosophy created fields of interference and interaction which only the memoirs of figures like Simone de Beauvoir, the singer Juliette Gréco and the writer and jazz musician Boris Vian can chronicle with justice. However, under discussion here is Sartre's specific relationships with artists and his impact upon certain cultural discourses.

Sartre's *The Imagination* and *The Psychology of the Imagination* of 1936 and 1940 posed the problem of the imagined versus the perceived image. His writings on art published in the luxury art magazine *Verve* before the war, like his novel *Nausea*, are concerned with contingent organic life, consciousness and its meaning versus 'Official Portraits' which petrify a politically controlled image in paint or bronze.[3] In *The Psychology of the Imagination*, Sartre posited presence through absence: 'The imagining consciousness poses its object as an absence' (*un néant*). Pierre is in Berlin but is imagined in Paris, a concept adduced, as I have shown, in the existentialism versus humanism controversy. More importantly in terms of post-

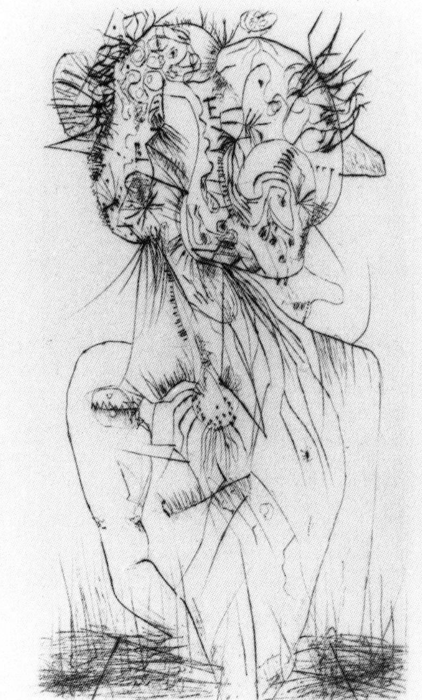

fig.13 Wols, frontispiece for Jean-Paul Sartre, *Visages*, 1948 Drypoint

war developments in *Informel* painting – but without mentioning any artists – Sartre discussed the irrational, 'magic' status of the image, 'Faces in flames, stains on walls, rocks in human form', hypnagogic and crystal ball images and the shift from the pictorial matter of a portrait to mental images. A final section, written as a postscript, specifically addresses the 'existential type of the work of art' where the portrait image versus its material analogue is again the crux of the chapter although music and the concept of beauty are also addressed.[4]

Sartre's later notion of man as 'not definable . . . because to begin with he is nothing' subscribed to an 'autochthonic' myth, an 'unborn' being of 'pure consciousness', consonant with both the Descartes's *cogito* and the traditional authorial position in philosophical writings. This consciousness was essentially divorced from the material world: 'We are left alone, without excuse. Man is condemned to be free . . . There is no reality except in action.'[5]

The whole thrust of the writings of Sartre's rival, Merleau-Ponty, whose *Phenomenology of Perception* came out in 1945, was to root the tradition of transcendental philosophy from Descartes to Kant and beyond, back in the living, perceiving, sexualised body. The argument – of freedom versus embodiment – 'pure' consciousness versus a consciousness at every moment steeped in awareness of itself and its mental and bodily memories can be seen to echo the arguments for new beginnings, an *art autre* (Tapié), versus memory-laden readings of the *Informel*.

Indeed, Sartre's promotion of a free and self-determining consciousness stands in contrast to the loss of perceptual control under the influence of drugs and hallucinations that informed his first drafts of *The Psychology of the Imagination* – some time after his encounter with German phenomenology in Berlin and his first drafts of 'Melancholia', later renamed *Nausea*.[6] These experiences paradoxically allied his writing to the Surrealist precedent. The melancholy and the viscosity at the heart of the vision of a Dalí became transformed in *Nausea*, which was eventually published in 1938.[7] A passage was quoted by Wols in the preface to his first watercolour exhibition, at the Galerie René Drouin in 1945: 'Objects shouldn't touch, for they don't live. And yet they touch me: It's unbearable. I'm afraid of coming into contact with them.'[8]

Sartre's pre-war writings, published with often inappropriate illustrations in *Verve* were transformed by their republication in the 1940s with images by Wols. Even with the black and white of fine drypoint, Wols was able to convey the hairs and the follicles, the 'rosy and porous' matter of the human face as described by Sartre. Ingres's 'Napoleon', in Sartre's text of 1939, becomes for Wols the submerged memory of George Grosz's generals, apparent through the microbiological imagery etched as the 'Official Portrait' frontispiece – a rare intimation of the political in Wols's work (fig.13). Whilst things, to quote Sartre, are but the 'absurd thrust of the nearest masses . . . The Gaze, perceiving at a distance can make the Universe appear . . . the meaning of a face is to be visible transcendence. The rest is secondary: the abundance of flesh can paste over that transcendence.'[9]

'Food', an extract from Sartre's 1936 novella *Dépaysement*, (Exile, Estrangement) also published in *Verve*, reappeared with unpublished extracts from *Nausea* and Wols's illustrations in 1948, thanks to the young publisher Jacques Damase. It was a philanthropic gesture by Sartre, but nonetheless created a conjunction of text and image that had very contemporary resonances.[10] When Sartre wrote about Wols in 1963 he recalled Wols quoting to him those same lines from *Nausea*: 'Objects . . . touch me'. 'It hardly matters what these words mean here for me', Sartre said, 'what he means is that objects touch him because he is afraid of letting his touch fall on them. They are him outside himself; to see them is to dream himself . . . he deciphers himself on the knots of tree bark, in the fissures of a wall; roots, rootlets, vacuoles, pullulating viruses under a microscope, the hairy furrows of women and the turgid flaccidness of male fungi compromise him . . . Inversely, with his eyes shut, withdrawn inside his night, he feels the universal horror of being-in-the-world . . . his automatism is only the fascinated attention he has for his own products when they give themselves to him as external objects.'[11] Before Sartre's work on Giacometti, Wols already embodied the perfect 'existentialist' artist: 'I met Wols in '45, bald, with a bottle and a beggars' pouch. In the pouch was the world, his worry, in the bottle his death . . . He had few projects; a man who renewed himself non-stop, eternal in each instant . . . in fact I believe now that he had thrown himself into one short-term project, only one: to kill himself, convinced as he was that there can be no expression without self-destruction.'[12] Sartre later confessed that in his studies of painters and writers 'I've always looked for the drinking or drug-taking aspects . . . which are revealed in their works. I've always been passionately keen to discover not the man constructed via the work, but beyond that, the man who paints or writes without restraint.'[13] Such was Wols, who from his first moments as a prisoner of war drank to achieve the oblivion from which he drew – an experience quite distinct from the 'automatist' experiments of the Surrealists. Wols's organic, 'inner' abstraction, when expressed in oils for the first time in 1947 (he had no prior experience in the medium) was a painting precisely 'without restraint', where paint tricklings and surface scratches appeared to relate directly to the vision behind tortured eyelids of a wounded or bleeding body. Private unconstrained experience appears as emblematic of the state of humanity – microcosm equates with macrocosm.[14]

Sartre's first published post-war preface, however, was linked to sculptural preoccupations of the past, despite the fact that the works in question were Alexander Calder's mobiles at the Galerie Louis Carré in 1946.[15] The show may be seen retrospectively as an anticipation of kinetic art trends in the later 1950s. Sartre's text, in many ways so close to the *Verve* pieces, nonetheless enlarges the parameters of his thoughts on sculpture: 'With vile, inconsistent substances, with tiny slivers of bone or tin or zinc he fashions strange arrangements of stems and branches, of rings and feathers and petals. They are resonators or traps; the object is always midway between the servility of statues and the independence of natural elements. It's a little hot-jazz tune, unique, ephemeral like the sky, like the morning.'[16] Sartre's conjunctions here between musical improvisation, chance and freedom interestingly anticipate Umberto Eco, who used Calder as the first of his artistic examples in *The Open Work*.

Whilst Calder was American and hardly an orthodox Bretonian Surrealist, Sartre's diatribes against Surrealism are a major element of *What is Literature?* of 1947. The *International Exhibition of Surrealism* dominated critical and popular attention at the time. Tintoretto, Lessing, Winckelman, Vermeer, Cézanne, Picasso's harlequins were all deployed by Sartre in a demonstration of art's relationship to dominating power structures; these culminated, he said, in the bourgeois stranglehold on literature in the first half of this century in France. The Surrealists, 'revolting against "leur papa", achieve

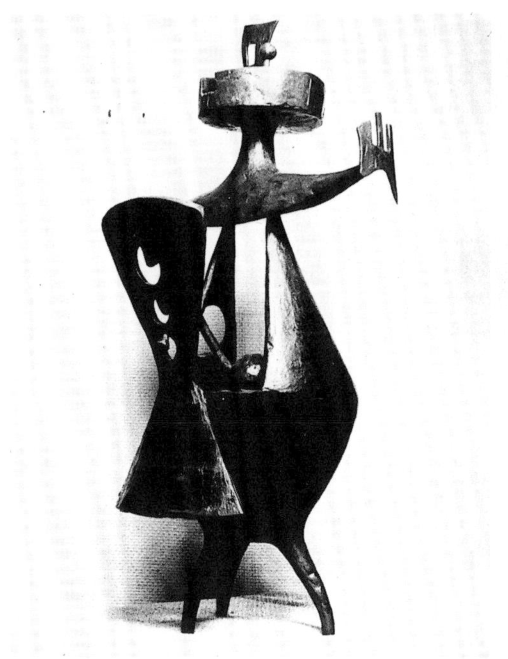

fig.14 David Hare **Man with a Drum** 1947 Bronze *Private Collection*

the void through an over-fullness of being' with a deluge of purposeless objects and the philosophy of the booby-trap. Duchamp's marble sugar cubes were the paradigm of futility, the Surrealist lifestyle a parade of bad faith. Their advocacy of violence was 'illiterate'. Although Sartre wrote: 'we have no wish to "engage" painting, sculpture and music . . . at least not in the same way', he seemed, nonetheless, to see Surrealism as a mystification, just like those he denounced later in the text: Nazism, Gaullism, Catholicism, Communism.

How capricious then, of Sartre, to preface David Hare's exhibition of Surrealist bronze sculpture which was held at the Galerie Maeght in December 1947 – the very premises where the *International Exhibition of Surrealism* had been held in the summer. As usual Sartre contemplated the paradox of living and desiring matter versus sculptural 'petrifaction', but while a sculpture by Praxiteles or Donatello is complicit with our passions, he said, 'the sculpture of Hare – like that of Giacometti – shows us man from the outside; it attempts to dehumanise our gaze, like Kafka who sees (*fait voir*) transcendence back to front' (fig.14). Not only does Hare introduce movement into his works like Calder, he effects an etymological reversal: his gorilla becomes 'horror which gorillas'. Sartre also evokes the personal ('hodological') space around a being which extends beyond its boundaries, anticipating his writing on Giacometti.[17] Sartre's relationship with André Masson, whose work he published in *Les Temps Modernes* in 1947, was yet another friendship with an erstwhile Surrealist.[18] Giacometti had of course been linked with the Surrealist movement himself, but his refusal to continue with Surrealist sculpture and a period of silence before a return to figuration (he had no public exhibition in Paris between 1935 and 1951) demonstrated a personal integrity which bound him to Sartre from the spring of 1941. Sartre was attracted to those who had experienced extreme situations, in life or in action, that he had not experienced himself, the precarious lives of Baudelaire, Wols or Jean Genet are obvious examples. Although Giacometti was hardly a man of action, his witnessing, by absurd chance, of a

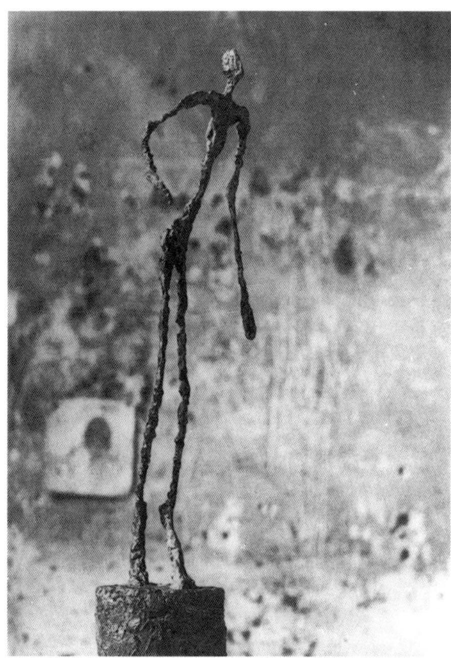

fig.15 Alberto Giacometti **Falling Man** 1950–1 Bronze *Kunsthaus, Zurich*
Photograph by Ernest Scheidegger from Jean Genet, *L'Atelier d'Alberto
Giacometti*, 1958

human death – a life and a look reverting to an absolutely lifeless
object – had been a crucial and formative experience for the artist
in 1921. The ensuing sense of panic, the extension and elasticity of
space, as recounted by Giacometti in 1946, were close to experiences described by Sartre.[19] The two men shared a proximity of
experience and vocabulary from the moment of their meeting,
when Sartre was writing *Being and Nothingness*. Their earliest conversations are indicated, for example, by Sartre's description in his
second Giacometti preface (1954) of his own feelings of agorapho-
bia on release from prisoner-of-war camp: 'So it is with Giacometti:
distance for him is not voluntary isolation, nor is it recoil.'[20]
Simone de Beauvoir quotes Giacometti in 1941: 'A face, he told us,
was an indivisible whole, a mood, an expression, but the lifeless
material, marble, bronze, or plaster was infinitely divisible. Every
particle stood apart, contradicted the whole and destroyed it, he
said.' So close to the Sartre of 'Official Portraits', Giacometti's words
here anticipate Sartre's later statements on Hare.[21] And the influence was surely mutual: take Sartre in *Being and Notthingness*, and
his discussion of vertigo: 'Vertigo announces itself through fear;
I am on a narrow path – without a guard rail – which goes along
a precipice. The precipice presents itself to me as to be avoided; it
represents a danger of death.'[22] Giacometti's sculpture of 1950–1,
'Falling Man' (fig.15) (in French *L'Homme qui chavire*, which implies
wavering, tottering) – is extraordinary as an idea of a 'sculptural
situation' and yet is precisely the embodiment of Sartre's cliff-edge
experience in which anguish and vertigo, self-consciousness and
the instinct for self-preservation play their part.[23] The solitariness of
Giacometti's figures seems to embody what Sartre in *Being and Nothingness* called the 'nothingness' which human reality carries 'within
itself as the nothing which separates its present from all its past.'[24]

Sartre's discourse on the Other – sometimes simply another
being, sometimes specifically a woman (in the chapter 'Patterns of
Bad Faith') – can be seen to be expressed in Giacometti's sculptures
through the juxtaposition of figures. In 'City Square. Seven Women
and One Head' 1950 (Fondation Maeght, Saint-Paul), the gaze of
the male bust represents desire, feelings of distance and sexual difference: the tall, full-length female figures stand with their backs to
him. Alternatively, separation from the Other can be expressed
through metaphors of distance itself, where perceptual size – the
trapezoid sculptural base for 'Four Figurines on a Base' 1950
(no.41) – can represent the recession of a stage and dancing floor.[25]
Just as Sartre's narrative 'exemplars' in *Being and Nothingness* (see,
for example, the section on 'The Caress' in 'Concrete Relations with
Others') link his philosophy with his novels, they provide philosophical coordinates for situations, which, remarkably, Giacometti
could envisage in sculptural terms.

The meeting of Sartre and Giacometti preceded full knowledge
in Paris of the concentration camps, made painfully visible by the
sight of returning deportees. Yet when Sartre came to write the
preface for Giacometti's first show at the Pierre Matisse Gallery in
1948, 'The Search for the Absolute', two metaphors were insistent
– metaphors of the beginning and the end of history. The man of
Eyzies and the man of Altamira who preceded 'three thousand
years of sculpture of the dead' are contrasted with 'the fleshless
martyrs of Buchenwald … This martyr was only a woman. But a
woman complete, glimpsed, furtively desired.'[26] These images of
beginnings and of *dépouillement* (the stripping away of flesh and of
identity) confront a plethora of cultural references in Sartre's preface of 1948: the paradoxes of Zeno, Dostoevsky, Kafka – in particular Pascal, who offers a gloss on 'for months [Giacometti] came and
went with an abyss at his side'.[27]

Not before 1950 would Sartre have encountered Martin Heidegger's essay of 1936, 'The Origin of the Work of Art' with its famous
disquisition on Van Gogh's pair of peasant shoes.[28] Heidegger's
notion of truth as *aletheia* (unconcealment, disclosure) is developed
in the 1936 essay, and becomes an important subtext in Sartre's
second preface for Giacometti's Galerie Maeght exhibition of 1954,
'Giacometti in Search of Space'.

So many limpid ideas from Heidegger's text clarify Sartre's developing relationship to the work of art. Heidegger declared: 'The artist
is the origin of the work. The work is the origin of the artist. Neither
is without the other … If there occurs in the work a disclosure of a
particular being, disclosing what and how it is, then there is here
an occurring, a happening of truth at work … To be a work means
to set up a world … In setting up a world, the work sets forth the
earth.'[29] Sartre's writing and Giacometti's post-war sculpture, a
major historical conjunction, are illuminated by this earlier text
which confirmed the importance of the work of art as a philosophical point of departure.

The encounter with Jean Genet, whom Sartre had publicly supported since 1947, would complicate the Sartre/Giacometti relationship, indeed would set up a latently homoerotic triangle. While
Genet had indeed lived through the extreme situations that Sartre
could only dramatise, his life was 'appropriated' in the most astound-
ing way into Sartre's writing with *Saint Genet, Actor and Martyr*,
serialised from 1950 in *Les Temps Modernes*.[30] Sartre propelled
Genet into the long encounter with Giacometti: Genet's writing, not
Sartre's, would preface Giacometti's third solo show at the Galerie
Maeght in June 1957. The three portraits in oils that Giacometti
made of Genet from 1954–7 were an act of mutual recognition:
it has been implied that the two men's attitude to horror, the attrac-
tion of death and a sense of tragic solidarity between beings was a

common bond whose intensity excluded Sartre (fig.16). The insistent phallic sexuality in the work of Genet and Giacometti, explicit in Giacometti's sculpture 'The Nose' 1947 (fig.17), and implicit in the mechanisms of the reciprocal gaze between artist and model, was another level at which Sartre was potentially excluded – he had been drawn by Giacometti between 1946 and 1949 bespectacled, his eyes downcast squinting.[31] Moreover the intensity of the triangular relationship involving Giacometti affected both writers' attitude to fiction. Sartre was to find in biography and his writings on art a release from the perils of fictitious political action;[32] reciprocally, Genet, master of the disguised autobiography, found a mode of truth-telling which displaced the fictional in his text *Alberto Giacometti's Studio* (1958). Here he insisted on the paradoxes of intersubjectivity, representation, 'resemblance' and commemoration implicit in the process of portraiture. Genet, the 'captive scribe', was depicted by Giacometti in the pose of an Egyptian sculpture in the Louvre – not merely a historical reference, but a play of the here and now with an immemorial humanity (see no.61).[33] Genet himself evokes the Osiris sculpture in the Louvre crypt as he thinks of Giacometti's 'Women of Venice' (nos.46–54). The hieratic immobility of the 'Women of Venice' series fills him with terror and estrangement; they are both millenial and familiar, above all 'a victory for bronze' – yet a man on a train, the street life of Paris, conversations and memories of sexual encounters create a new decorum for the text. Beyond Sartre's philosophical and time/space coordinates and his dream of the vanished flesh of a martyred woman, Genet insists upon the contingencies of life within the absurdities of 'real time' and is explicit, for example, about the connection between Giacometti's female sculptures and the artist's prostrate and adoring behaviour in the brothel: 'Between each naked prostitute and him, there was perhaps this distance which ceaselessly established itself between each of his statues and ourselves. Each statue seemed to recede – or come forward – in a night so distant and dense that it mingles with death.'[34] Genet establishes, against the 'disclosure' of Heidegger and Sartre, a different order of truth.

Ernest Scheidegger's photographs accompanied the publication of Genet's full-version text in 1958. Beyond the literary and imaginative encounters of reader, writer and artist, the black and white images of Giacometti working (fig.18), the disarray of sculptures in the bare *atelier*, works photographed in the street, close-ups of paintings and drawings, provided another rhythm and dimension for Genet's writing. In Scheidegger's close-up photographs of specific figure paintings, likeness appears through the proliferation of precise contour marks. Cézanne's influence appears locked in a struggle with Giacometti's rage of lines which seem to seek their own obliteration. Perhaps the most striking images to accompany Genet's text were those of Giacometti's studio walls, flaking, pitted and scratched with graffiti of the human form. 'To be a work means to set up a world' (see nos.57–9). From the first marks of depiction to the apex of representation: history is collapsed in the extended moment of the *atelier*.

Genet's 'takeover' from Sartre in terms of Sartre's art criticism must be situated in terms of political crisis and Sartre's alignment with the French Communist Party in 1952. His own party, the R.D.P. (Rassemblement Démocratique Populaire) had initially proposed mediation between the superpowers, but Sartre's change of position became clear as instalments of *The Communists and Peace* were published in *Les Temps Modernes* from 1952–4. Sartre's about-turn involved disturbing silences as regards both previous editorial

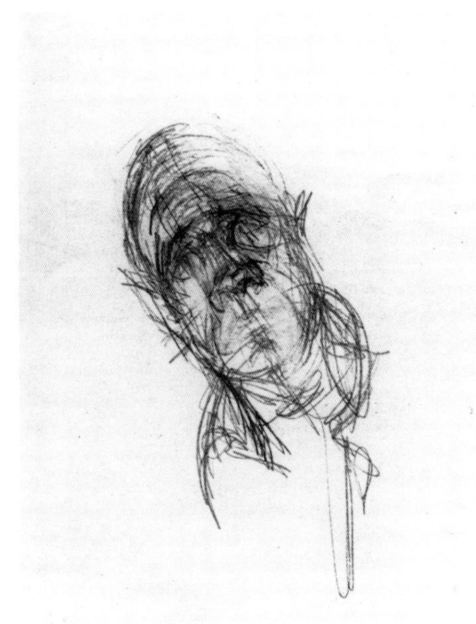

fig.16 Alberto Giacometti **Portrait of Jean Genet** 1954 Crayon Photograph by Ernest Scheidegger from Jean Genet, *L'Atelier d'Alberto Giacometti*, 1958

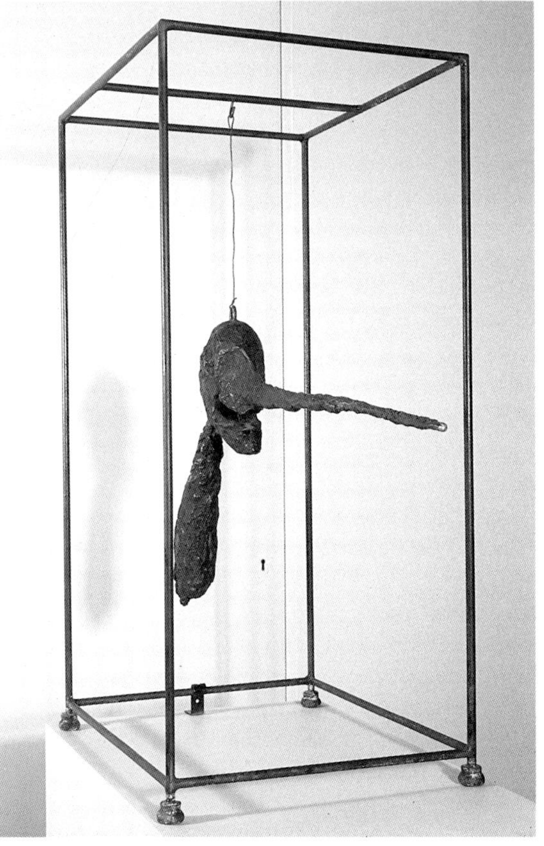

fig.17 Alberto Giacometti **The Nose** 1947 Bronze *Galerie Adrien Maeght, Paris*

exposés of Soviet labour camps, and the Communist Party position on art – the strident Socialist Realism campaign. However, the repressive nature of French colonial policy at the time forced Sartre to conclude that only from within the Communist Party could opposition have any effect.[35] Sartre would continue to write about art, but the 'engagement' of a painter such as Robert Lapoujade who combined a lyrical abstractionist technique and palette with explicit political subject matter on the Algerian War in 1961, vividly demonstrates the aesthetic problems posed by Sartre's politics. This 'other' Sartre, this 'other' engagement in a time of political crisis and colonial war offers an explanation for Sartre's ostensibly inexplicable changes in artistic taste. The radical incompatibility between his existentialist criticism and his subsequent artistic *parti pris* accounts for the demise of his plan for an *Aesthetics*, in which he had originally intended, like Heidegger, to republish his writings on art as part of his overall philosophical project.[36]

VII The Second Sex

One is not born, but rather becomes, a woman.

Simone de Beauvoir, 1949[1]

. . . in a world where so many men are women, she was a man! Her work in its quantity, importance and grandeur manifests a male virtue.

Dor de la Souchère on Germaine Richier, 1966[2]

The move from Sartre and Giacometti to the 'problem of woman' as addressed in the post-war era involves a major change of register. Despite the enduring affinities between Sartre and Simone de Beauvoir, the space and thoughts he shared with Giacometti and with Genet would be distinctly separated from her domain and that of the female characters in his successful plays.

    To recall the war and its immediate aftermath: the indomitable femininity symbolised by the extravagant wood-shaving and newspaper hats of the Occupation and the miniature couture mannequins of the recently rediscovered 'Theatre of Fashion' hid the more voracious passions of a period of deprivation. These were symbolised by Picasso's play of 1941, *Desire Caught by the Tail*, performed at a reading on 19 March 1944 with Sartre, de Beauvoir and Camus among the participants.[3] De Gaulle granted Frenchwomen the vote in October 1945, in recognition of their indispensable role as workers and often as Resistance-fighters during the war. The recognition at this late date of women's dignity and equality within the rubric of the French *droits de l'homme* (rights of man) must be contrasted with the savage treatment of female 'collaborators' during the *épuration* period. Paraded, shaved and tarred, they were denounced by women as viciously as by men. This ritualised vengeance was doubtless the most naked expression of France's profound humiliation during the war. Appalling photographs reached America and were published in the Surrealist periodical *View* of 1946 (fig.19). Prinner's poem of February 1945, 'The Shaved Woman' echoed the litany of insults: 'Whore! – Tart! – Carcass! – Piece of shit! – Disgusting! – Look at her!' The shaved woman replies: 'Remember, Humanity, that I am your work, that you have made me in your image.' The poem's form, a tribunal recalling the trial of Joan of Arc, expresses a sado-masochistic rage

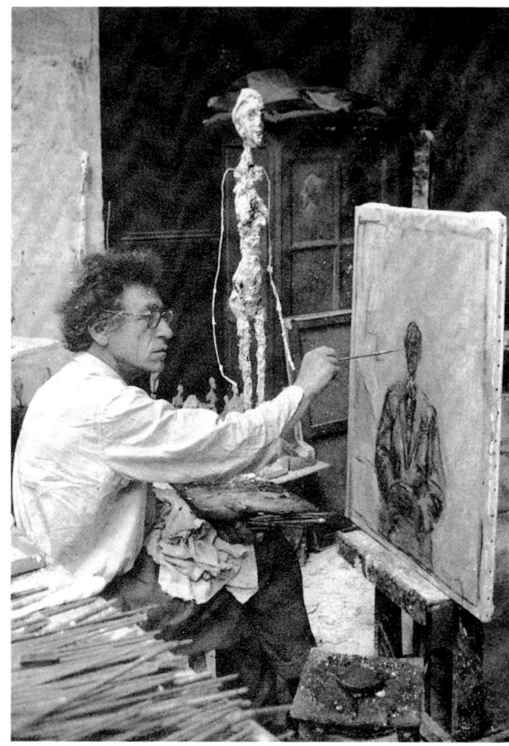

fig.18 Giacometti at work Photograph by Ernest Scheidegger, from Jean Genet, *L'Atelier d'Alberto Giacometti*, 1958

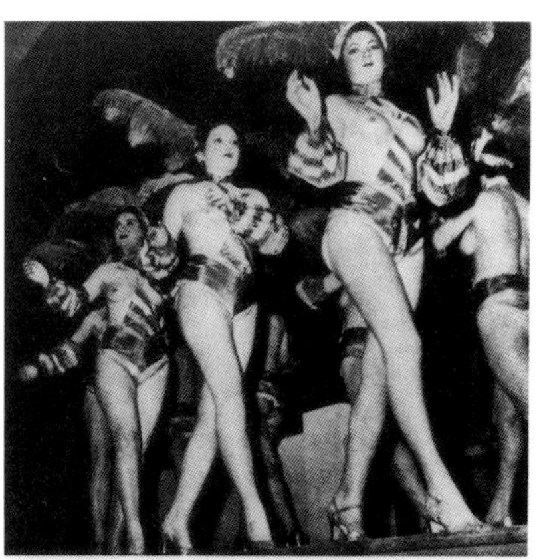

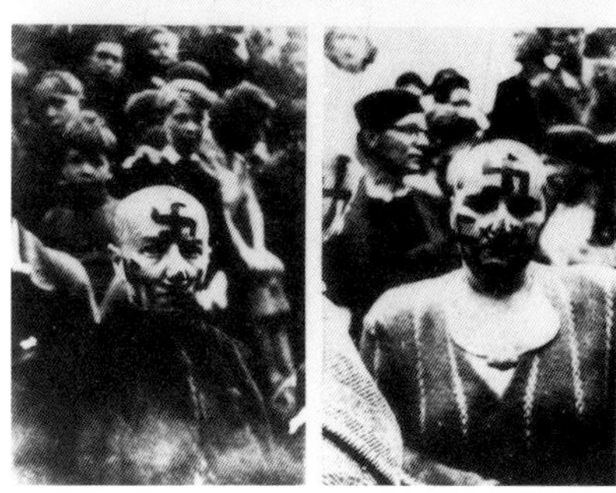

fig.19 Detail from *View*, no.6, 1946, p.9, from Jean Eparvier, *A Paris sous la botte nazie* (n.d.) Photographs by Raymond Schall. Photographs of shaved and tattooed women by Francis Lee

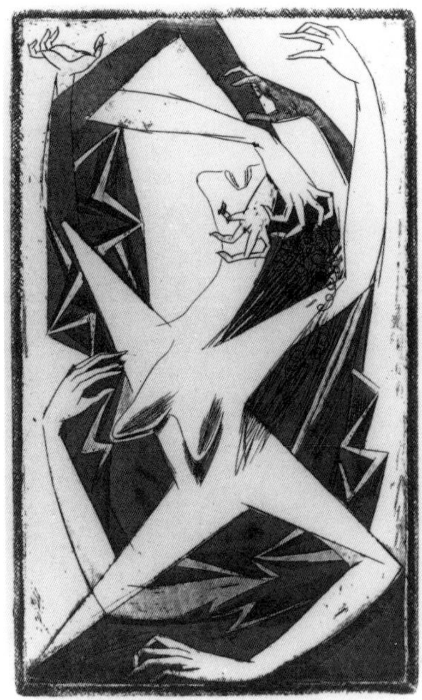

fig.20 Hans Anton Prinner **The Shaved Woman**
1946 Drypoint *Courtesy of Mme Anne Ferdière*

echoed by the artist's stylised engravings (fig.20).[4] The theme of the shaved woman would inspire the Marguerite Duras/Alain Resnais collaboration on the film *Hiroshima mon amour* (1960), in which the collective memories of such atrocities, and the desire to obliterate them is seen to characterise the later 1950s.[6]

De Beauvoir's *The Second Sex*, serialised in *Les Temps Modernes* from May 1948, and published in 1949, discussed in its contemporary sections the tension between women's 'image', her economic dependence on husband, lover, or pimp, and the struggles of the (barely) independent woman – whether seamstress, factory worker or intellectual. Despite the abolition of licensed brothels in 1946, French society still functioned upon a sexual economy of bourgeois marriage together with the 'seduction' of mistresses and prostitutes. Women had been enfranchised for only three years in the France of 1948, and despite their role in the Resistance were excluded from playing any part in national reconstruction.[6] Momentarily, with this massive work of scholarship which touched upon history, anthropology, psychoanalysis and Marxist theory as well as literary criticism, de Beauvoir – insulted by Camus, Merleau-Ponty, François Mauriac, the Communists *en bloc* – stole thunder from Sartre. The book was as thick a tome as *Being and Nothingness*; 22,000 copies were sold in its first week of publication. De Beauvoir was specific in her redefinition of Sartre's fluctuatingly-sexed 'Other': 'He is the Subject, he is the Absolute: she is the Other.'[7]

De Beauvoir's impact coincided with that of the Kinsey reports on male and female sexuality in France (too clinical to have a major success) and the stirrings of a new sexual freedom expressed first through popular song and stars like Juliette Gréco and Catharine Savage, later through the younger role models, Françoise Sagan in literature, Brigitte Bardot in film.[8] De Beauvoir herself was wise to the power of stereotypes: she intervened, perhaps disappointingly, in the very topical controversies about the Marquis de Sade – much loved by contemporary writers such as Bataille, Paulhan, Pierre

Klossoswki, the Surrealists – and published *Brigitte Bardot or the Lolita Syndrome* in 1955. When such stereotypes were confronted by the scandal of the rape and torture of women by French soldiers during the Algerian War, she was again an important voice of protest.[9]

While Giacometti may be seen to desiccate, to desexualise his bodies, paring his work down to its minimal essence and its gaze, for most post-war artists the genre of the nude was still central. The age-old relationship between the female body and painting – the notions of beauty and 'art' – were specific targets, of course, for Dubuffet, from his 'Desnuda' of 1945 (private collection), a reference to Goya, to 'Olympia' (fig.12) in the 'Corps des Dames' series (see 'Gymnosophie', no.20). This shockingly caricatured Manet's 'Olympia', who had achieved her status as modernism's primary icon when the Impressionist collections from the Louvre were installed in the Musée du Jeu de Paume in May 1947. *Dames* were not ladies, but prostitutes, so-called with the chivalry of those who accepted the inevitability of the situation (600,000 *dames* were working in Paris in 1948, two years after the official closure of the brothels).[10] Dubuffet's 'Olympia' took her place next to other ladies in his series such as 'Piece of Butchery' (Sidney Janis Gallery, New York). These are violent works, despite their mock-insouciance. Dubuffet, while keeping his work in completely traditional formats and genres (landscape, portraits – here the nude) was attempting another 'anticultural' transformation. The spreading and wrinkled, rosy images extend squarely, almost to the edges of the canvas. They correspond in their interiority and dissolution not only to Merleau-Ponty's embodied *cogito*, but to an archetypal enunciation by Sartre in 1936, in his chapter on the work of art in *The Psychology of the Imagination*: 'The real is never beautiful.' To desire a woman 'we must forget that she is beautiful, because desire is a plunge into the heart of existence, into what is contingent and most absurd.'[11] Desire – or an infantile, aggressive rage – spreads out contiguously with painterly matter, attempting to obliterate the subject-ground relationship by engulfing it. The ugliness of these 'Dames' invokes with both humour and terror the Devouring Mother: Dubuffet's 'Dames' would be the mothers of Niki de Saint-Phalle's 'Nanas' of the 1960s.

The *Informel* nudes of Dubuffet and Fautrier were presented as absolutes on blank grounds. While 'situational' rather than narrative, Jean Hélion's paintings of fleshy, naked women – in groups, in between men, upside down (viewed at the moment of departure . . .) covertly emphasised the transactional nature of the prostitute's role. The rhythmical linkages of curves and crescents recall Hélion's abstract painting of the past, while depersonalising the nudes as individual models: they are not people but 'tokens of exchange' between men: an indication of Hélion's reading of the contemporary writings of Lévi-Strauss.[12] Hélion's delight in painting itself, the rule-breaking of his figuration in the generally abstract and *Informel* 1950s, his humour and irony in detail and handling, create complex works whose psychological and painterly symmetries both invite and resist our decodings.

Thus immemorial practice, balanced with contingency and desire were fronted by a patriarchal political and intellectual establishment. Sartre as both man and Logos was the most immediate manifestation of this order for de Beauvoir. He penetrated her writing, it has been argued, with his own horror of 'viscous', feminine, biological nature.[13] However, 'equality of achievement' was the yardstick for the talented women in the early 1940s, for Simone

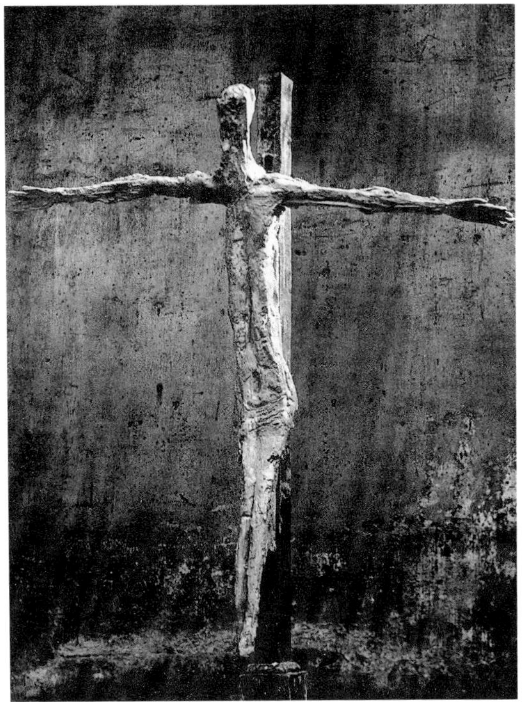

fig.21 Germaine Richier **Crucifix** 1950 Bronze
Church of Assy, Haute Savoie

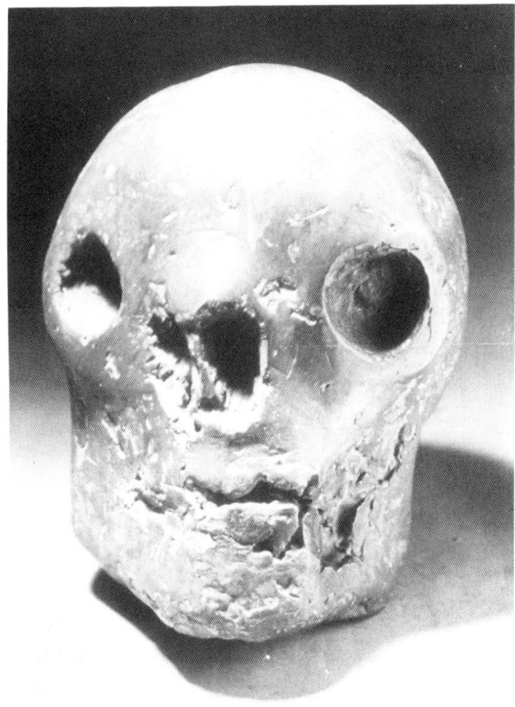

fig.22 Pablo Picasso **Skull** 1943 Bronze
Musée Picasso, Paris

Weil as farmhand, Resistance-worker and religious mystic,[14] de Beauvoir in her novels, travelogues, scholarship, for Germaine Richier in sculpture. Richier frequented the cafés of Montparnasse in the company of figures such as Colette, Nathalie Sarraute and other figures around the prestigious *Nouvelle Revue Française* group, such as Dominique Aury. While Aury, in her picaresque, neo-Sadian novel *Story of O* buried her identity and paradoxically her sex with the pseudonym Pauline Réage (linked instantly to her companion, Paulhan), complicitly adopting Sadean stereotypes, Richier's sexuality in conjunction with her work challenged and disturbed conventional notions. The poet, René de Solier, wrote in the special number of 1948 *Derrière le Miroir* which accompanied Richier's show at the Galerie Maeght: 'I dare not pronounce the word "virility" as regards her work, although that's the most appropriate term.' 'Le sculpteur', 'l'artiste' (masculine nouns) – and Richier's 'unfeminine' working ski-outfit – are balanced against 'this universe, where woman is sovereign, which returns to origins' a clear case of confusion surrounding the classical dichotomy: male creativity versus female nature.[15] André Pierre de Mandiargues, the Provence-based, Surrealist-affiliated writer and follower of the Marquis de Sade, used sadism as a metaphor for Richier the sculptor, who kneads, twists, breaks, pokes and scratches prior to the 'orgasm' of consummation between artist and sculpture as the work is deemed finished. He invoked Otto Weiniger's theories of the sadist who ornaments and then strips sculptures to humiliate them – but then hastened to make a compensatory statement: 'I've never known a woman so good, so discreet, full of spiritual bounty, a force of nature'.[16]

Richier's lack of the reputation she deserves beyond France (although complicated by litigation after her death) is not unconnected with the ambiguous reactions her oeuvre provoked in critics. In contrast to Giacometti, whose works were not shown to a French public until 1951, Richier had become, by 1950, the focus of national controversy with her scarred, eroded crucifix for the church of Assy (fig.21). A comparison of the exhibiting history of the two artists from 1935–55 would establish Richier's greater contemporary reputation without doubt. Her work never became a commodity, a matter for financial speculation. To what extent was the contrary true of Giacometti, precisely because of the myth-making process which would link him so inextricably with the existentialist writings of Sartre? The fact that, unlike Giacometti, Richier's work had an immediate posterity in the School of London sculptors, and in the work of César in France, bears a more eloquent witness to her fecundity than any uncomfortable contemporary praise.

Giacometti's art originating in Surrealism, was poised in the 1940s between the tragedy of the existential predicament and a sophisticated, urban absurd. Richier's came from a pure lineage of monumental sculpture directly affiliated to Auguste Rodin and Emile Bourdelle, in her case modified through her anti-Parisian, Provençal, background. The most powerful and fleshy of Richier's male figures, 'Storm Man' 1948 (no.96), used the very model, now an old man, Nardone, who had posed in his youth for Rodin's nude 'Balzac' (1896–8) – the very paradigm of male potency and creativity. Just as Richier would work with Rodin's models, she worked with his foundries, Rodier, Valsuani and Susse, and embraced both the hard physical labour and the Vulcanic imagery of worker with metal and fire. While the imagery of death in Giacometti's emaciated figures was perhaps starker than Richier's,

Richier's, her relationship to the male and female body and issues of
sexuality and death is equally fascinating.[17] Picasso's bronze 'Skull'
1943 (fig.22) and his 'Man with a Lamb' 1944 (Musée Picasso,
Paris) are key sculptures of the early post-war period, as are Fautrier's scratched and scored 'Otage' pieces in bronze (see nos.22–5),
but is it not perhaps to Richier, rather than Giacometti, that the tradition of post-war sculpture owes its characteristically 'brutalised'
surfaces, along with the configurations that would be baptised in
Britain the 'Geometry of Fear'? Her scarified surfaces and the death-
like ugliness of some of her female creations countered notions of
sculptural beauty with intimations of deformity and mutilation. Yet
a unifying totality, in tension with a totalising sense of desire in her
work, conformed perfectly to Sartre's later definition of the Beautiful.[18] She created explicit metaphors of nature's physical invasion
of sculpture: in 'Forest Man' 1946 (no.95), a disturbing metamorphosis occurs: Richier cast found twigs and branches as arms and
limbs; leaves were pressed into the wet clay to leave their silhou-
ettes prior to casting. Nature invaded the monument – and the
monument would find its home in nature, leaving Giacometti's city
square. 'The Preying Mantis' 1946, represents, upright and death-
like, the insect celebrated by the Surrealists as a token of female
sexual power: she devours the male after copulation. Figures such
as 'The Ant' 1953 (Staatsgalerie Moderner Kunst, Munich), evoke
both creativity and entrapment with their web-like imagery –
ambivalently always, as the spinner, one of the three Fates is a primeval image of female power. In the aftermath of the death camps
and Hiroshima, the idea of a reversal of evolution, the degenerating
of the human through mammal and bat to bird and insect forms
was a powerful metaphor in Richier's work, not only of nature, but
of regression to a more bestial universe.

It was this element of regression and decay which caused fear
and repulsion in Richier's crucifix for the church of Assy in 1950.
On a poetic and etymological level, the fusion of body and bark in
Richier's crucifix evoked the metamorphosis of event to symbol.
A spectrum of modern artists were involved with the Assy project.
Yet Fernand Léger's magnificent mosaic portals were dubbed a bla-
sphemy; Richier's crucifix caused a riot. The so-called Angers tract,
entitled 'God Shall not thus be Mocked' was issued by the right-
wing Integrists. It juxtaposed Richier's work with a typical head
of Christ, with the caption 'The Face of Christ? No! A Scandal for
Christian Piety.' The work was finally removed by the Bishop of
Annecy. The Vatican attacked in 1951.[19] After the Assy scandal,
Richier continued to work and exhibit during the 1950s. In contrast with the spikiness of the insect women certain works achieved
a solemn and monumental dignity. They remained deeply rooted in
Richier's native Provence, using objects found on the land and the
sea-shore: 'The Shepherd of Landes' 1951 (no.100) has his face
made from a brick pierced and rubbed smooth by the sea. Richier's
collaborations, in particular with Maria Helena Vieira da Silva, the
most important woman painter in the School of Paris, gave her
work a new dimension, in which the notion of sculptural patina
and base extended to embrace a painted enamel background.

The awkward, scratched surfaces of Richier's 'Diabolo' (no.99),
the *Informel* nudes – Fautrier's scarred and iridescent 'Sarah'(no.26)
or Dubuffet's 'Olympia' (fig.12 on p.34) – must read 'against' the
frou-frou of the New Look, the 'Miss Tabou' beauty contest in Saint-
Germain-des-Prés, the historical costume dramas in the theatres
and the cinema, the taste for a 'fantastic forties', all of which played
their role in characterising the reborn *femme française*. A certain

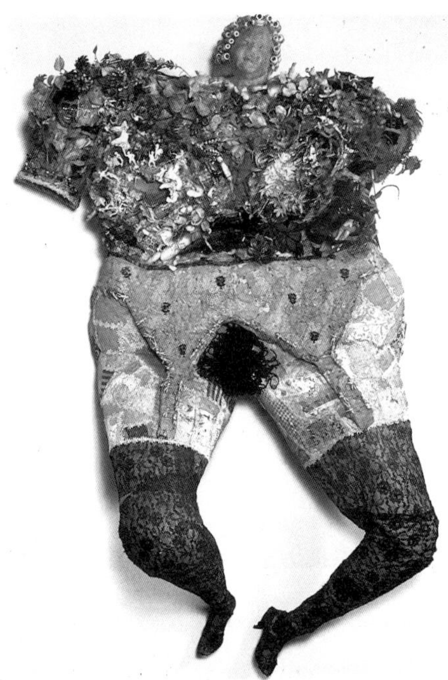

fig.23 Niki de Saint Phalle **Crucifixion** 1963 Mixed media assemblage
Musée National d'Art Moderne, Centre Georges Pompidou, Paris

excess of femininity expressed anxieties that the Surrealists were
soon to sense: long after Duchamp's 'Please Touch', rubber breast
on the cover of the catalogue for the *International Surrealist Exhibition* of 1947, Man Ray, in an exasperated exposé, contrasted the
dark existentialist waif (Juliette Gréco) with the blonde Marilyn in
1958, quoting Christian Dior's lipstick adverts and Jean Paulhan's
preface to the *Story of O*: 'all is sex in them [women] even the spirit.
They must be continually fed, washed, painted with make-up and
beaten.'[20] The next *International Surrealist Exhibition*, *EROS* of 1959,
would signal both an apotheosis of these attitudes and a more
aware exploration of social and anthropological issues.

Was de Beauvoir's battle completely lost? The challenge of popular culture had to be confronted before her message could be reacti-
vated more positively in the early 1960s. Significantly, it was not
Germaine Richier's aspiration, her affiliations with past masters,
her rigorous training or her travail with bronze that could point a
way forward to other women artists. Marginal sources, *bricolage*
techniques, the impact of Dubuffet and an encounter between
Duchamp's ready-mades and her children's toys would generate
Niki de Saint Phalle's monumental sculptures of the 1960s. Yet de
Saint Phalle's 'Crucifixion' 1963 (fig.23), her altarpieces and the
political 'surface' of her works situate her surprisingly, but convinc-
ingly as Richier's successor.[21] Her status throughout the 1960s
was just as unusual as Richier's during the previous decade.

For sociological reasons – and purely financial ones – womens'
real power in the post-war Paris art world was as gallery owners,
caring for and promoting their artists: Jeanne Castel, Fautrier's
patron in the 1930s continued after the war; Jeanne Bucher died
tragically in 1946, but her gallery has faithfully promoted Dubuffet;
Colette Allendy would pioneer Dada, neo-Dada and *Informel* exhibitions from her house in the 16th arondissement; Nina Dausset promoted the Surrealists, Iris Clert the Nouveaux Réalistes. Denise
René whose first exhibition was held in 1944 continues, magnifi-

cently, to promote her changing stable of geometric abstract and kinetic artists. Betty Friedan's *The Feminine Mystique* (1963) took up the torch from de Beauvoir in *Les Temps Modernes* in summer 1964; *The Second Sex* was subjected to a sharp feminist analysis in 1969.[22] Yet the grip of the status quo – particularly in conservative, essentially Catholic countries like France – is the reason why de Beauvoir's account of the 'Second Sex' has hardly dated. Marguerite Duras became the first woman member of the Académie Française in 1980 – six years before de Beauvoir's death.

VIII The Imaginary Museum

The role of museums in our relationship with art works is so great that we can scarcely imagine that there are none, none will ever exist where modern European civilisation rests unknown ... They are but a two-centuries old invention. The nineteenth century lived from them. We live from them still.

Andre Malraux, 1947[1]

The new and very 'masculine' art produced in the immediate postwar period was fighting against two paradigms: that of 'art' in the sense of the art of the museums as represented by the Louvre and that of the 'tradition of modernism', as established prior to 1939 and exhibited at the Musée national d'art moderne and other venues during the period.[2] André Malraux's influential concept of the *Musée imaginaire* (imaginary museum) and its relationship to the art of the Louvre should be seen as complicating the impasse of late modernism. *Informel* painting and the *brut* art of an Artaud owed their 'originality', their evocation of origins, precisely to their by-passing of these two discourses, each of which was entrammelled in specific appurtenances of power. As Malraux himself commented: 'European art is not a heritage but a system of will and Europe will not remain a heritage but a system of will or death.'[3]

The *Musée imaginaire* contemplates the status of the art work and the museum in the age of photographic reproduction and cinema. It exults in the 'extreme intellectualisation' newly offered to art history as a comparative discipline (thanks to photography) while dematerialising the art work and its 'real' presence. Walter Benjamin was not the only – and most obvious – source for this huge cultural enterprise. The comparative technique used in the *Blaue Reiter Almanach* as early as 1912 was brought home to Malraux by an encounter with the Cologne-based art historian André Salmony in the early 1920s. Equally important were Malraux's thoughts on contemporary German and Soviet film, which intensified after meeting Sergei Eisenstein in the Soviet Union in 1934, when a complete shooting script for his anti-imperialist novel, *Man's Fate* was made – and lost. The theme of personal versus historical destiny, the relationship between epic historical and cultural themes and cinema's penetration of the masses, the implications of close-up, montage, travelling, were there before Malraux read Benjamin's now celebrated essay, 'The Work of Art in the Age of Mechanical Reproduction' published in Paris in 1936.[4] The concept of the *Musée imaginaire* was formed in the late 1930s in tandem with Malraux's own experience as a film director, and the happy coincidence of the publication by the Louvre of the *Photographic Encyclopedia of Art*.[5] Four articles by Malraux in *Verve* from 1937–40 would herald the seminal publications of 1946–50: *Sketch for a Psy-*

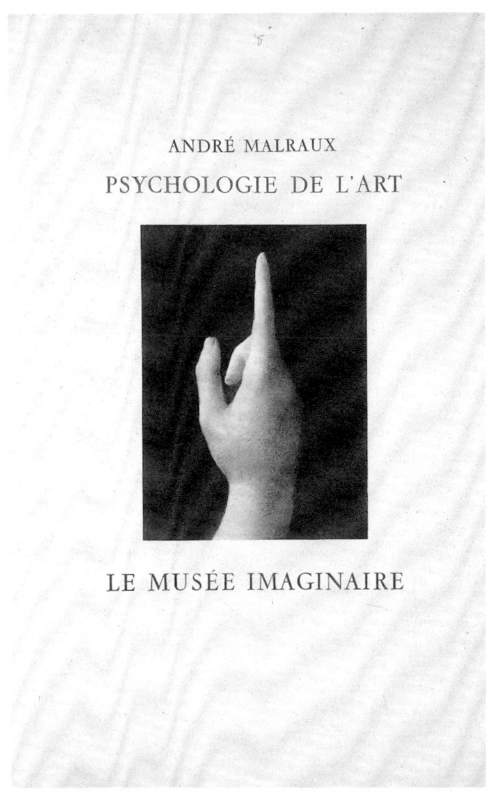

fig.24 André Malraux, *Le Musée imaginaire* 1947, cover

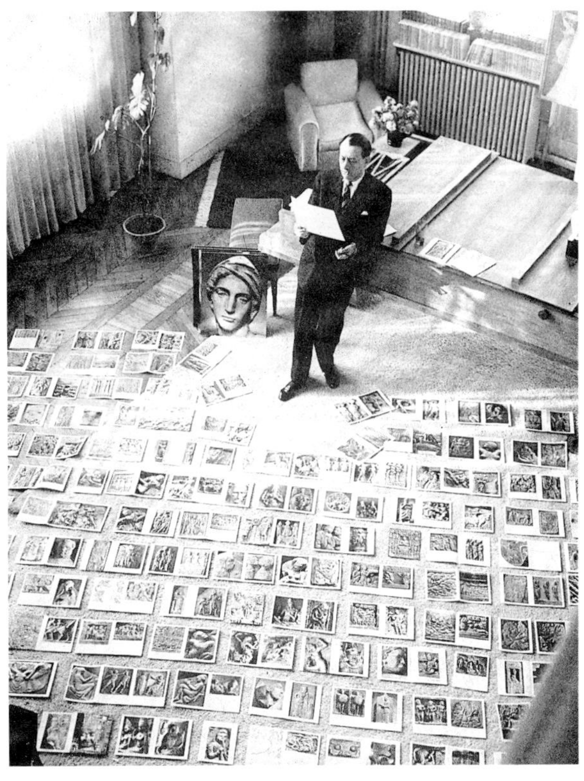

fig.25 André Malraux choosing photographs for the *Voices of Silence* c.1950 Photograph by Maurice Jarnoux for *Paris-Match*

chology of Cinema (1946), and the three volumes that constituted his *Psychology of Art. Le Musée imaginaire* was the first of these, appearing in 1947.[6] The twin estrangements effected upon the art work, first its removal from its context to the museum, a space for the 'confrontation of metamorphoses', secondly its dematerialisation through photography, losing colour, scale, texture and presence correspond not merely to Benjamin's lamentation for the 'loss of aura' but engender an exultation at the possession of 'the first universal artistic culture, which doubtless will transform modern art ... one of the supreme conquests of the West.'[7] In the *Musée imaginaire*, humanism is confronted with a painful awareness of a cyclical history, in which the passage of a smile from a Khmer Buddha to the angel of Reims cathedral transcends millions of deaths. The origins of Malraux's museum lie in booty and pillage; knowledge, too, is presented in terms of conquest. In the last volume, the analogy between art and a secular religion is made explicit: 'This art is not a god, it is an absolute; but this absolute which has its fanatics and its martyrs is not an abstraction ... Modern Art, which no longer knows what could be an exemplary ideal of man often suggests to us an exemplary ideal of the artist.'[8] While in contemporary terms Malraux reaches Cézanne and Rouault (with a nod at Braque), Picasso becomes the sign of the artist who has appropriated the *Musée imaginaire* in his diversity of style, and whose is consciously creating his own posterity: 'Picasso is painting his complete works.'[9] Malraux's delirium of verbal and pictorial juxtapositions deliberately mimics a range of cinematic devices, orchestrating his theory that the photographic 'museum of reproductions allows a style to come alive just as accelerated film can show a plant blooming.' The art work as photograph becomes an 'instant of art', like a film cell.[10]

Malraux's novels and editorials in the late 1920s and the 1930s were those of a virulent anti-colonialist.[11] His vision had been created by the East; extensive travels in his youth were intimately linked to self-knowledge via the same comparative method he applied to works of art; he saw the artistic roots of Christendom itself in the East's assault on Rome. The powerful idea of the *Musée imaginaire* had initially been democratic, linked with Popular Front ideas of art's widest possible audience at a time when Malraux was close to the Communist left.[12] As Malraux began to play an important but increasingly conservative role in the political life of post-war France, he became increasingly elitist; so, as a corollary, did his belief in the autonomy of the art work and its development. He posited a history of style independent of positivist and determinist accounts or the social considerations offered by Taine, Hegel, Marx or contemporary Communist critics. The *Musée imaginaire* became an ever-enlarging proposition, dotted with the names of great artists and illustrated with world masterpieces, yet ultimately a display of Malraux's own metamorphoses and the mastery of his own style.[13] Its popularising role and the quality of reproductions nonetheless had an inestimable impact, not the least in providing artists with a repertory of primitive French, Eastern and pre-Renaissance forms as well as works from the Louvre.

As Minister of Information in de Gaulle's 1945–6 government Malraux witnessed France's expulsion from Indochina by the Japanese in March 1945, a situation abruptly altered by the atomic bombs dropped on Hiroshima. French administration was re-established, but insurrection in Vietnam led ineluctably to the start of the Indochinese war. In an era marked by France's ignominious end as a colonial power, Malraux's was, ironically, an imperialist,

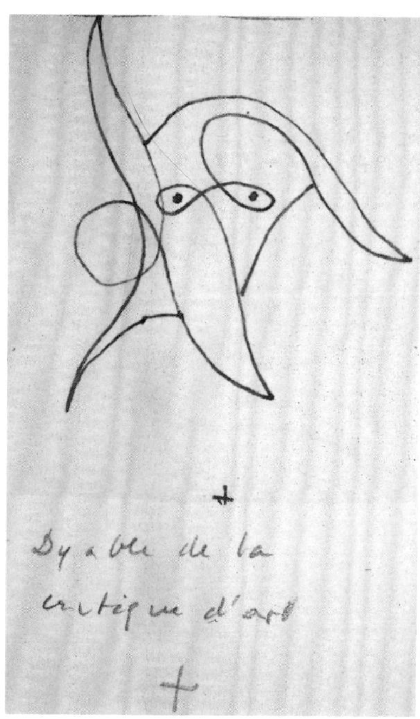

fig.26 André Malraux **Art Critic Devil** (n.d.) *Courtesy Mme Madeleine Malraux, Paris*

not an empirical history of art:'the words conquest, annexation, possession reverberate incessantly in the *Voices of Silence* like so many clarion calls', Georges Duthuit protested in his three-volume riposte, *Le Musée inimaginable* (The Unimaginable Museum) of 1956.[14]

In 1947, Malraux, the despairing humanist of the *Musée imaginaire* asked: 'What nineteenth century state would have dared to employ torture?' Yet in 1958, as Minister of Culture for the Fifth Republic, Malraux was finally forced to take his stand against the government, against torture as practiced by the French State in the context of the Algerian War – no longer the practice of the barbarous Other, but that of France herself.[15] While never wavering in his allegiance to de Gaulle, Malraux's subsequent career as Minister of Culture during this later period which signalled France's loss of political and cultural power, continued to demonstrate a conflict between self and other, elitism and populism that had been rehearsed in the subtextual confrontation between high art and cinema in his *Psychology of Art* series.

Where was the space here for the contemporary artists Malraux collected? In particular Fautrier whose works he had promoted since the 1920s, whose 'Otages' series he had prefaced in 1945, calling the works 'hieroglyphs of pain?'[16] Malraux's penchant for the fragment, the patina, the imperfect was glossed by his adversary Georges Duthuit: 'the whole body is the body which escapes you', while the scar was the 'sign of possession'.[17] Malraux should be linked to Fautrier, his artist, the painter and sculptor of the scar and the wound; both created bodies of work riven with potential loss.[18]

IX The Open Work

Time, like Nature, proceeding only in leaps, means that life is only a succession of presents. Historical speculations about the past and philosophical ones about the future are sterile and artificial. Let us plunge, perpetually into the present.

Michel Tapié, 1948[1]

That the *Informel* is a concept dialectically related to Malraux's imaginary museum is without doubt – a point anticipated by the cultural antitheses set up by Michel Tapié in his *Mirabolus, Macadam et Cie* preface of 1946, but elaborated explicitly, after Malraux's 1947 publication, in Tapié's contribution to the catalogue of *H.W.P.S.M.T.B.* (Hartung, Wols, Picabia, Stahly, Mathieu, Tapié, Bryen) held at the Galerie Colette Allendy in April 1948: 'It's of no interest to me whatsoever to know whether Bernini's Saint Teresa is better than the Dame de Lespugue or not so good as the Callipygian Venus or better than Filippino's Magdalene or not so good as Ruben's ladies or not so better as La Goulue or even better than the Mona Lisa or not so good as Duchamp's Bride.'[2] The collapsed notion of time here, parodying Malraux's page layout and his rampaging style may be contrasted with Tapié's exhortation to plunge into the present – a Bergsonian *durée*.

The notion of the *Informel* as present and timeless coincides with a presentiment of the era as representative of Hegel's 'end of history' – a point that would be made explicitly by Paulhan[3] – yet the very fact that Fautrier's work is rich with references to the many-breasted Dame de Lespuge, France's most revered prehistoric Venus figure, that Paulhan could read Rembrandt, Soutine and Turner in Fautrier's *pâte* contradicts the notions of timelessness in his work – or rather envisages time itself as a simultaneous coexistence of all moments of history.[4]

While the relationship between Fautrier and the writer Georges Bataille was profound in the 1940s, no use of Bataille's term *informe* of the 1920s as a specific concept ever appeared in conjunction with the substantive *Informel*.[5] *Informe* was of course a common adjective. The critic Waldemar George called the *Otages* exhibition 'a triumph of the formless' linking the works to the failed 'masterpiece', a mere scribble of lines, of Balzac's painter Frenhofer.[6] After his 'Otage' paintings and sculptures Fautrier himself was almost silent until his show of 'Object' paintings of 1955 – except as illustrator for Bataille's *Alleluiah* (1947) and André Frenaud's superbly erotic illustrated book *The Woman of my Life* (1948, fig.27).[7] But *informe* appears again in 1945 in Dubuffet's 'Notes for the Well-Read', written to explain his work to writer friends in the spring and summer of 1945: 'Beginning with the formless: the beginnings of the adventure are the surface which will come to life and the first spot of colour or ink thrown on to it.'[8] In 1947, he judged 'the most summary, the most *informe* portrait', superior to 'the most worked-over portrait in the world'.[9]

The *Informel* ground with its trickling signs next came to be seen as a neo-Dadaistic chaos in the works of Wols or of Camille Bryen for example: the Dada precedent was central to Bryen, whose philosophy of *abhumanisme* interpreted the *Informel* as imagery of life at a visual microlevel.[10] In the preface to the *White and Black* exhibition at the Galerie des Deux-Iles in July 1948, where Fautrier joined Arp, Bryen, Germain, Hartung, Mathieu, Picabia, Ubac, Wols, and Tapié himself, Tapié proclaimed: 'the Incoherent and the *Informe*, set free at last are prevailing in all paintings, for they alone possess the

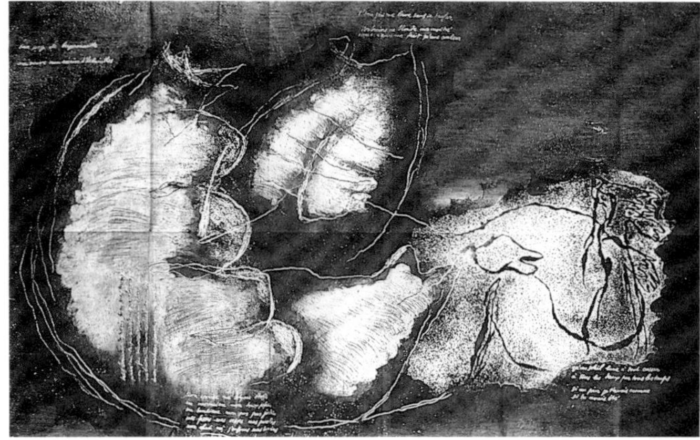

fig.27 Jean Fautrier, illustration for *La Femme de ma vie* 1948 Lithograph

only magico-pyschic force that is actually real: Inertia.' Already he had moved on from references to Far Eastern music and hot-jazz to a consideration of the implications of entropy theory; the influence of the Romanian emigré mathematician, Stéphane Lupasco on the writings of both Tapié and Georges Mathieu would become increasingly insistent.[11] With *Véhémences Confrontées* (Opposing Forces) at the Galerie Nina Dausset in March 1951, where, for the first time the works of American artists confronted the *Informel* school of Paris, Tapié's preamble introduced the metaphors of the conquistador, the epic, the perilous routes and arduous adventures of the 'indefinite domain of the *Informel*'. Saint John of the Cross, Nietzsche and the Dada manifestos were the talismen he claimed, for this period of the 'end of the end of the History of Art'. The figurative/non-figurative debates of the 1940s were grandly dismissed: THE ADVENTURE IS ELSEWHERE AND OTHER.'[12]

Obviously Tapié's own promotional stable linked to the New-York affiliated Studio Fachetti gallery was involved in these broadening definitions, that after *Véhémences Confrontées*, include the eclectic selection seen in the show commemorated in Tapié's publication *Un art autre* of 1952.[13] Tapié's constant emphasis on the 'virility' of the *Informel* may be seen as an overcompensation for the evidently female connotations of primordial matter and the incisive, penetrating, mark-making relationship it posited with the artist. Sexual ambiguitites were strikingly evident in the preface for Jackson Pollock's first one-man show in Paris in February 1952. Tapié used the anarchist image of a bomb for this 'departure from zero'. 'Violence becomes Painting' he declared – but apropos of Pollock's 'She Wolf' 1943 (The Museum of Modern Art, New York) – 'thanks to reproductions, the best-known work in Europe'. With the animal's robustly handled line of full teats it was not only a powerful image of female fecundity but of course a symbol of beginnings of Roman civilisation – neither a bomb nor a 'zero'.[14] This exercise of a 'male' power in turn came to be associated with the 'inhuman'/'antihumanist' characteristics of the *Informel*: as Tapié would later summarise: 'The destruction/creation of Dada strikes a harmonic chord with Nietzsche's *Will to Power*; all humanism liquidated.'

In 1960, Tapié established the International Centre of Aesthetic Research in Turin, promoting his own ideas and publications and international contacts.[15] Umberto Eco's first thoughts upon a painterly *Informel* appeared subsequently in 1961; in *The Open Work in the Visual Arts* (1962), he would expand the definition of the

Informel to the broadest possible rubric, simultaneously opening up the concept to scientific and musical theories and distancing it from its once-promoted connections with past art and art history, still present in the interpretations of Jean Paulhan's *In Praise of the Informel* of 1962.[16]

Concurrently with its growing influence over Europe, and its embrace of American painting, the *Informel* (with Tapié's enthusiastic aid) reached Japan. Just as Tapié with Dubuffet had formulated the premises of a new or 'other' primitivism in the 1940s, so this turning of the *Informel* towards Japan can be seen to signal a new Orientalism. Orientalism had of course been implicit in the very origins of Henri Michaux's *taches* – his experience of the Far East fills *A Barbarian in Asia*, 1933, a disguised autobiography comparable to Malraux's Orientalist *Temptation of the West* (1928): 'Objects are traced, they seem like memories ... The Chinaman possesses the faculty of reducing Being to Being signified.'[17] In Michaux's works, the Western inheritance – Victor Hugo's ink blots, Surrealist automatism and ink decalcomanias, the Rorschach test – a craze in the 1940s Saint-Germain-des-Prés – struggles with the East.[18] Michaux's evocations of 'another place', 'other beings', his signs of 'other beings' in 'other spaces', the metaphors of exorcism, the mysteries of sepia, correspond in his own way to Tapié's *autre*. The motility of the sign and its phenomenology was also important: 'I wanted to draw the consciousness of being and the flux of time' Michaux would say in the 1950s.[19]

The Orient would also be a major point of reference for the 'siting' of the work of Pollock in Paris in 1952: 'America has become the actual geographic crossroads for the confrontation of the great artistic currents of the Orient and the West.'[20] The influence of Japan on the School of Paris itself was felt beyond the field of *art autre*; Hans Hartung and Georges Mathieu forcefully exemplified its impact in terms of gestural abstraction.[21] The Orientalism of some *Informel* painting would entice the second generation of post-

war Surrealists like Iaroslav Serpan and Jean Degottex into its embrace. 'The Second Japanese Mode' merited a whole chapter in *Painting Today* (1959), a popularising overview of art in France by the well-known critic, Michel Ragon. While Malraux's *Musée imaginaire* and Franco-Japanese exchanges dominate the very first page of Ragon's preface, contemporary American competition is dismissed in a phrase.[22] Tapié's trips to Japan, where in 1961, Fautrier won the painting prize at the seventh Tokyo Biennale, the exchanges he set up for Japanese artists in Paris and in Turin, Georges Mathieu's Japanese exhibitions and influence demonstrate the pull of this alternative France/Italy/Japan axis. The intellectual excitement in Europe signified by the interdisciplinary aspects of the writings of Tapié on the *Informel*, taken up by Eco in *The Open Work*, together with these exchanges with the East should counteract over-emphasis on the 1950s as a Franco-American struggle, essentially a question of 'Hot Paint for Cold War'.[23]

X The Return of the Repressed: Revisioning Paris Post War

'Reconstructing modernism' has recently become a tag which takes on the Cold War problem and art/politics issues, but has been both unclear as regards specifics, and unwilling to embrace within its own criteria the ideologies implicit in Michel Tapié's *art autre*, an art defined by its otherness and difference, its existential affiliations and its later geographical perspectives involving Europe as a whole and Japan.[1] This art, which saw itself as marking a specific cultural break with the art of the past (including the 'tradition of modernism') was of course outside the museum – yet paradoxically contemporary with André Malraux's concept of the *Musée imaginaire* and the late modernism promoted by Jean Cassou, director of the Musée national d'art moderne in Paris throughout the post-war period.

Challenging the art of the new museum together with the art of the Louvre, the new *art autre* was sufficiently flexible to rewrite a relationship with a 'different' primitivism, and a 'different' Orientalism in a period in which saw France's collapse as a colonial presence in Indochina and Korea. Of course in the wake of the Marshall Plan for reconstruction, American culture was both celebrated and perceived as a threat. Several of the wealthy G.I.s in Paris would finally end up in Fernand Léger's post-war teaching studio, and the first American paintings were exhibited in 1947. However, cinema, pulp and science fiction, fashion, music, and politics were the arenas where imported American culture or French imitations were most obvious. The impact on form and style in these areas was immense, as was hostility to this 'cultural imperialism' which was countered by nationalists, Communists and the broadly based *Mouvement de la Paix*. For many years, however, America as such was not 'represented' in painting and sculpture, and abstract expressionism was simply subsumed into the *art autre* debates. While Duchamp, Matta and Léger were at home in New York, the first extended trips by Sartre and de Beauvoir provoked a reaction of shock. Both published influential accounts of their experiences.[2]

The painter Jean Hélion is an interesting intermediary figure here: at home in a very 'modernist' America in the late 1930s,[3] his return to realism just before the war was ratified by his humanist

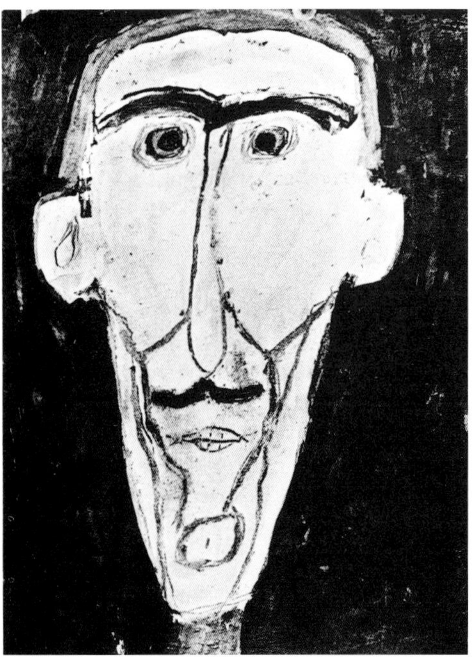

fig.28 Jean Dubuffet **Portrait of Michel Tapié** August 1946 Gouache
Private Collection

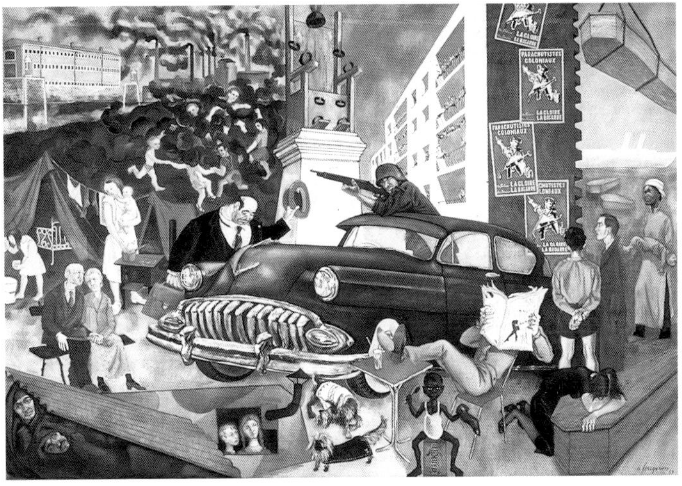

fig.29 André Fougeron **Transatlantic Civilisation** 1953 Oil on canvas
Artist's Collection, Paris

orientation subsequent to imprisonment and escape. He returned to Paris in 1945, but Bowery bums as well as Parisian derelicts inspire his reclining figures and newspaper readers, although the 'Large Mannequin' figures have an undeniable chic (no.74) Samuel Beckett's Pozzo and Lucky, lowlife, farce, the detective novel – all mingle with memories of America in Hélion's ironic populism.[4]

Not until the early 1950s when political antagonisms grew more violent, would the Cold War *per se* become an explicit matter in terms of Realist painting. Just as there was an attempt to 'depict' the Oradour massacre at the *Art and Resistance* exhibition in 1946, so at the Salon d'Automne of 1953, there were Socialist Realist protest paintings of Julius and Ethel Rosenberg, framed by the C.I.A. – it has now been proved – and electrocuted as Soviet spies. Dominating all competition through sheer size was André Fougeron's 'Transatlantic Civilisation' (fig.29), representing the NATO buildings in Paris, a huge Pontiac-Sedan car, replete with armed officer, an American soldier reading a pornographic magazine and various other vignettes, some referring to the Korean War – presided over by an empty electric chair – a reference to the Rosenberg trial. The painting has been discussed extensively elsewhere – and must certainly be given credit as a precursor of the politicised New Figuration movement of the 1960s. What must be emphasised, however, beyond its explicit and visible Cold War content, is the return of the repressed, the appearance of 'low' cultural forms, associated with America and the Cold War debate, within the grandiose 'high' genre of a history painting.[5]

Fougeron's 'Transatlantic Civilisation' was itself, ironically, a response to one of the two American exhibitions at the Musée national d'art moderne in 1953: *Twelve American Painters and Sculptors* was shown from April to June, joined by *Mexican Art from Pre-Columbian Times to Today* from May to July. The latter corroborated Fougeron's creation of a new space for Socialist Realist painting, so reminiscent of the Mexican muralists. Contemporary American drawings were seen in October–November 1954, while *Fifty Years of Art from the United States* was the watershed exhibition of 1955, comprising not only painting, but sculpture, engraving, the decorative arts, typography and advertising. Gestural abstraction, including American varieties, was nothing new by this time: as

early as 1954 Tapié spoke of an 'anarcho-informel sclerosis made of recipes which have nothing more to do with the liberty of the spirit and the imagination'.[6] Responses were ambiguous to the 1955 American show. It anticipated by four years the more celebrated exhibition *The New U.S. Painting* which likewise toured major European capitals, arriving in Paris in January 1959.[7]

A decade separates the 1953 American exhibitions at the Musée national d'art moderne from the symbolic moment of passage so beloved by the adepts of 'Hot Paint for Cold War': 'The whole world recognises that the world art center has moved from Paris to New York.' Alan Solomon's triumphant public statement prior to the awarding of the Venice Biennale painting prize to Robert Rauschenberg was made in 1964.[8] To ignore that decade is to ignore the happy exchanges between Pop artists and the *Nouveaux Réalistes* from the late 1950s, which do not seem to have been contaminated by C.I.A. interests or an obsession with Jackson Pollock. Far more important are the reasons for a genuine epistemological break in the languages of art and society in France in the mid-1950s which explain why the period represented in *Paris Post War* was so soon to acquire a nostalgic and mythical dimension. The decade 1945–55 has become a crucial hinge for debates about 'periodisation'. The year 1953 marked the first balanced retrospective view in France of art of the post-war era.[9] The impending collapse of 'high' and 'low' cultural categories, suggested by Fougeron in 1953 coincided with Stalin's death and subsequent moves for political realignment. Concurrently three events signalled an irrevocable loss of innocence in the cultural field. The first, for artists, was the discovery of Marcel Duchamp: the ready-made offered an unexpected release from the travails of the *métier* of the older generation, the touch of a Bonnard or a Matisse, even the *haute cuisine* of a Dubuffet, and proffered itself for transformation via the anthropological gaze of the *Nouveaux Réalistes*. Secondly, the material nature of life dramatically changed. Giacometti, Richier, Gruber created in an austere Paris where food was as scarce as artists' materials, and wire, plaster, bronze, canvas, oil paint had an integrity and a noble history. The Paris of steak and chips, soap powder and detergents, ornamental cookery and polymorphous plastics – described in Roland Barthes's *Mythologies* of 1957, was materially and coloristically a different universe, a universe of promises and transformations. Finally came the impact of domestic television, long after its domestication in both the United Kingdom and the United States: the boom in television buying in France accelerated with the Coronation of Elizabeth II in July 1953. The relationship between private and public spaces, the role of café and newspaper, the appeal of literature and political journalism – even religion – the conduct of leisure activity as a whole was irrevocably modified by television.[10] As a corollary, the role of the traditional Salons changed; the rejection of Fougeron's 'Transatlantic Civilisation' by Louis Aragon in 1953 was the last moment when the Salon d'Automne, the birthplace of Fauvism in 1905, attracted national headlines.

Caught on the horns of the periodisation dilemma, retrospective accounts of the period have been remarkably inconsistent.[11] The selection of works in *Paris Post War* and my own focus nonetheless redress presentations of the period as one of obsessive Cold War concerns, and counter recent derision of the tradition of writing about art, exemplified by Sartre, which has been so fertile within French culture.[12]

An immense distance separates today's public at the Tate Gallery from the works and the critical positions displayed in *Paris Post War*.

The art of the 1945–55 period, connected loosely to the varying discourses held together under the aegis of the term 'existentialism' moves us with its language of 'authenticity', whether this be realism with roots in the academy and the model (Gruber, Richier, even Giacometti) or the refusal of all but the basics of image-making (Wols, Artaud , Michaux). These artists rejected not merely the notion of style but a late modernist paternity, Picasso in particular, and as such they bracket themselves within a particular sensibility. However the discourse of the Other, the Gaze, the problem of gender: 'One is not born, but rather, becomes a woman', the polysemic utterances of an Artaud, seminal to the writings of a Jacques Derrida or a Julia Kristeva – the 'Imaginary Museum' and the multivalent 'open work', all heralding the 'post-modernist' sensibility – these areas now seen as of vital concern had their genesis in the immediate post-war years.[13] We may now attempt to understand them in a historical context, from today's post-Cold War position, where questions of humanism, questions of Europe have become urgent. *Paris Post War* speaks to us powerfully about these issues.

NOTES

I Introduction to Existentialisms

1 Isidore Isou, 'Cris pour 5,000,000 de juifs égorgés', *Introduction à une nouvelle poésie et une nouvelle musique*, Paris 1947, p.326.
2 André Malraux, *Psychologie de l'art: Le Musée imaginaire*, Geneva 1947, pp.128–9.
3 Walter Benjamin's concept of 'the revolt of technology' appeared in the context of fascism and military build-up in 'The Work of Art in the Age of Mechanical Reproduction', first pub. in French, Paris 1936, trans. Pierre Klossowski.
4 See Michael Kelly, 'Humanism and National Unity: The Ideological Reconstruction of France', in Nicholas Hewitt (ed.), *The Culture of Reconstruction: European Literature, Thought and Film, 1945–1950*, 1989, pp.408–14. For the most recent overview of debates in Paris see Tony Judt, *Past Imperfect: French Intellectuals, 1944–1956*, Berkeley, Los Angeles, Oxford 1992.
5 Jean-Paul Sartre, *Existentialism and Humanism*, 1946, trans. Philip Mairet, 1948. Gabriel Marcel's *Etre et avoir* of 1936, important for both Merleau-Ponty and the personalist Emmanuel Mounier, had challenged the omniscient 'voice' of Kant's philosophy.
6 Mounier's *Introduction aux Existentialismes*, serialised in *Esprit* from Oct. 1946, was published in 1947. See Michael Kelly, *Pioneer of the Catholic Revival: The Ideas and Influence of Emmanuel Mounier*, Oxford 1989, and John Hellman, *Emmanuel Mounier and the New Catholic Left, 1930–1950*, Toronto 1981.
7 Paul Foulquié, *L'Existentialisme, Que sais-je?*, Paris 1946 (3rd ed., 1948), p.6. Existentialism is treated in its theological, conceptual, phenomenological, 'general', atheistic and Christian aspects, prior to a third section devoted entirely to the now-forgotten Louis Lavelle.
8 *Samedi Soir*, 3 May 1947, in Noel Arnaud (ed.), *Boris Vian: Manuel de Saint Germain des Prés*, Paris 1974, p.66.
9 See Jean-Claude l'Oiseau, *Les Zazous*, Paris 1977.
10 Isou 1947, pp.352–4. In Feb. 1993, with 600,000 Jewish votes at stake, seven weeks before a general election, President François Mitterrand (decorated with the *Ordre de la francisque* by Marshall Pétain) finally instigated a national day of mourning commemorating the *Grande Rafle* of 16 July 1942 when 13,000 Jews were rounded up for deportation by the Paris police.
11 See *Le Demi-siècle lettriste*, Paris 1988; Roland Sabatier, *Le Lettrisme, les créations et les créateurs*, Nice 1989. Gabriel Pomerand's *Saint-Ghetto-des-Prêts*, Paris 1947, is particularly relevant to the *Paris Post War* theme.
12 Significantly, Beckett's *Comment c'est*, 1960, followed the impasse in his writing following the odd snippets published in 1955 as *Textes pour rien*.
13 Sartre 1946, p.28.

II Humanism and Terror

1 Jean-Paul Sartre, 'La République du silence', *Les Lettres Françaises*, 1944, republished in Jean Paulhan and Dominique Aury (eds.), *La Patrie se fait tous les jours*, Paris 1947, pp.461–90, quoted from *Situations* III, Paris 1949, p.12.
2 Jean-Paul Sartre, 'Paris sous l'occupation', in *Situations* III 1949, pp.25–7.
3 Jean Paulhan, 'Guide d'un petite voyage en Suisse au mois de juillet 1945', in *Cahiers de la Pléiade*, Aug. 1946, p.200, explaining 'the great wave of depression that swept liberated France in the last months of 1944'.
4 See Michel Ragon, 'Jean Dubuffet, sa rélation aux écrivains libertaires', *Dubuffet, Conférence et Colloque*, Galeries Nationales du Jeu de Paume, Paris 1992, pp.36–42, for Paulhan's relationship in the 1920s with the veteran anarchist Jean Grave and the influence of his circle on Dubuffet's anarchism as well as Dubuffet's relationship with Céline. For Paulhan's anarchist memories see 'Allocution', 1951, in Jean Paulhan, *Oeuvres complètes*, 5, Paris 1970, pp.423–5.
5 See Pierre Assouline, *L'Epuration des intellectuels 1944–1945*, Brussels 1985, pp.42–60. The bitter debate between the intransigent Albert Camus in *Combat* editorials and François Mauriac, who aimed at a more Christian position (described pp.25 and 46–7) is characteristically 'purged' from Albert Camus, *Actuelles, écrits politiques*, Paris 1950 and reprints.
6 See in comparison *Les Graffiti des torturés*, Paris 1971: photographs by Pierre Joly and Véra Cardot of the walls of the Ministry of the Interior, Paris, requisitioned by the Gestapo during the war.
7 See Assouline 1985, Annexe 7, 'Ordonnance no 45-1089 du 30 mai 1945', pp.164–6, relating to the purging of literary authors, composers, painters, graphic artists, sculptors and engravers. For art in wartime France, compare Michèle C. Cone, *Artists under Vichy: A Case of Prejudice and Persecution*, New Jersey 1992 with Laurence Bertand-Dorléac, *L'Art de la défaite 1940–1944*, Paris 1993.
8 Oradour was the subject of several realistic paintings in the *Art and Resistance* exhibition in 1946, as well as poems (Jean Tardieu), and sculptures (Fenosa). Discussion was reanimated with the Bordeaux tribunal on the Oradour atrocities in 1953. For the latest explanations (involving Nazi gold) see Robin Mackiness, *Oradour, Massacre and Aftermath*, 1988.
9 See Francis Ponge, 'Note sur les Otages', Paris 1946 (written 1945), pp.25, 20.
10 Georges Bataille, preface to *Madame Edwarda* in *Oeuvres complètes*, III, Paris 1971, p.9.
11 Pierre Angélique [Georges Bataille], *Madame Edwarda*, with thirty engravings by Jean Perdu [Jean Fautrier], Paris 1945 (deliberately misdated 1942), pp.20, 22.

12 Paul Léautaud, Letter of 6 March 1945. Archives Nationales, f/12 9640, quoted in Assouline 1985, p.94. Léautaud suggested a *Journal des exclus du C.N.E.* (Comité National des Ecrivains) (p.111).
13 Assouline 1985, p.12.
14 See Louis-Fernand Céline, 'Le Casse-pipe', *Les Cahiers de la Pléiade*, Summer 1948, pp.45–87.
15 See Jean Paulhan, *Les Fleurs de Tarbes, ou la terreur dans les lettres*, Paris 1941, discussed by Michael Syrotinski, in Denis Hollier (ed.), *A New History of French Literature*, Harvard 1989, pp.953–7. Paulhan stepped up his campaign with 'De la paille et du grain', pts.I AND II, 'L'Illusion de l'Etymologie', *Les Cahiers de la Pléiade*, April 1947, Autumn 1948/Winter 1949, pp.147–166 and Winter 1950–1, pp.107–31.
16 See Louis Dominique Girard, *La Guerre Franco-française*, Paris 1950, and Jean-Pierre Rioux, 'La Guerre franco-française', in Michael Scriven (ed.), *War and Society in Twentieth-Century France*, New York, Oxford, Munich 1991, pp.237–91.
17 See statistics in Jean Paulhan, *Lettre aux directeurs de la résistance*, Paris 1951, re-edited by Jean Jacques Pauvert, Paris 1968, p.12 and p.23 (quoted). For the context of the 'Resistance' debate see Henry Rousso, *Le Syndrome de Vichy, de 1944 à nos jours*, Paris 1987.
18 *Les Chefs-d'oeuvre des collections privées françaises rétrouvées en Allemagne par la Commission de Récupération artistique et les Services Alliés*, Orangerie des Tuileries, Paris, June 1946.
19 Léon Degand, an advocate of abstract art was art critic for the Communist journal *Les Lettres Françaises* from 1944–7.
20 See Leslie Rubin, 'The Lost Years: Alberto Giacometti's Return to Figuration, 1932–1947', unpublished M.A. thesis, Courtauld Institute of Art, University of London 1990, for which Taslitzky's assistance was crucial.
21 Taslitzky bore Gruber's banner with the portrait of Jacques Callot through the streets in Popular Front processions. See Alberto Giacometti, 'A propos de Jacques Callot', *Labyrinthe* (Geneva/Paris), no.7, April 1945, p.3. Michèle Cone has provided the most elaborate analysis of the 'Hommage to Jacques Callot' allegory, 'to abandon King Philip (Pétain) and follow Charles, Duke of Lorraine (Charles de Gaulle from Lorraine). See Michèle Cone, '"Abstract" Art as a Veil: Tricolor Painting in Vichy France, 1940–44', *Art Bulletin*, June 1992, p.203.
22 See 'Tendances actuelles de l'art chrétien', *Cahiers de l'Art Sacré*, no.7, Aug.–Sept. 1946, pp.12, 35.
23 The fifth Salon de la Jeune Peinture, of Jan. 1954 held an important retrospective of Gruber's work. He was hailed as an influence on young artists for over ten years. Reviewing the sixth Salon of 1955, a critic remarked 'Via tortuous routes – sometimes com-

pletely off-beat above all through Buffet, Gruber has set his seal on many young painters who have found in him, consciously or not, a sort of spiritual fraternity', Guy Dornan, *Libération*, Feb. 1954 and unnamed critic, *Arts*, Jan. 1955, quoted in François Parent and Raymond Perrot, *La Salon de la Jeune Peinture: Une histoire, 1950–1983*, Paris 1983, p.13. See also Guy Vignoht, *La Jeune Peinture, 1941–1961*, Paris 1985.

24 Claude Roger-Marx, 'Une plastique de l'absurde, ou l'absence de l'espoir dans la peinture contemporaine', *Figaro Littéraire*, 1 Sept. 1951, p.9.

25 Ambiguities are rife from the first words of Pierre Descargues's *Bernard Buffet*, Paris 1959. See Michel Ragon, 'Mondanité du "misérabilisme" ', in *La Peinture actuelle*, Paris 1959, pp.56–62 (quotation p.57).

26 See my article 'Catholics, Communists and Art Sacré', in Patrick Marsh (ed.), *The Conscience of the French: Intellectual Life in Post-Liberation France*, New York, Oxford and Munich (forthcoming).

27 See Serge Guilbaut, 'Postwar Painting Games: The Rough and the Slick', in *Reconstructing Modernism: Art in New York, Paris and Montreal, 1945–1964*, Cambridge, Massachusetts and London 1990, pp.30–79; Sarah Wilson, 'Martyrs and Militants', in Scriven 1991, pp.219–46, and *Calls to Realism: Art and Politics in France, 1935–1955*, New Haven and London (forthcoming).

28 See Maurice Merleau-Ponty, *Humanisme et terreur: Essai sur le problème communiste*, Paris 1947, from which 'The Yogi and the Proletarian' is translated in James M. Edie (ed.), *Maurice Merleau-Ponty: The Primacy of Perception and Other Essays on Phenomenological Psychology, the Philosophy of Art History and Politics*, series ed. John Wild, Evanston, Illonois 1964, Chap.7.

29 See Victor A. Kravchenko, *J'ai choisi la Liberté!*, trans. Jean de Kerdeland, Paris 1949. Kravchenko's revelations were denounced as an 'obscene' American imperialist fabrication by the French Communists.

30 Bernard Lorjou shared the *Prix de la Critique* with Buffet in 1948 and was a member of the Homme-Témoin group. See Jean Bouret et al., *L'Age atomique*, Paris 1950. François Fonvielle-Alquier's *La Grande Peur de l'après-guerre*, Paris 1973 describes the general feeling of terror in life and politics.

31 See Geneviève Bonnefoi, *Les Années fertiles, 1940–1960*, Paris 1988, p.23.

32 See David Rousset, *L'Univers concentrationnaire*, Paris 1946 (Buchenwald); *Le Procès concentrationnaire: Pour la verité sur les camps: Extraits des débats: Déclarations de David Rousset*, Paris 1951 (Soviet labour camps).

III Cézanne's Doubt: Painters of Failure

1 Francis Gruber, *Arts de France*, no.5, Paris 1945, p.7.

2 See *Pierre Tal-Coat*, exh. cat., Grand Palais, Paris 1976. Tal-Coat lived in Cézanne's Château Noir during the war and returned to Aix in 1946–7. The combination of Cézannism and *japonisme* of this new 'School of Aix' was enhanced by the presence of André Masson (in his 'orientalist' mode) and Georges Duthuit who had published *Mystique chinoise et peinture moderne*, Paris 1936, three years before Cézanne's centenary celebrations in 1939 (probably the impetus for Merleau-Ponty).

3 Maurice Merleau-Ponty, 'Le Doute de Cézanne', *Fontaine*, no.47, Dec. 1945, pp.80–100, and in *Sens et Non-Sens*, Paris 1948; trans. and with a preface by Hubert L. Dreyfus and Patricia Allen Dreyfus 'Cézanne's Doubt', in *Sense and Non-Sense*, Evanston, Illinois 1964, pp.9–25. Also trans. Sonia Brownell, for *Art and Literature* (Lausanne), Spring 1965, pp.106–24, from which my citations are taken.

4 It is as part of the immense philosophical and phenomenological bibliography of *Le Phénoménologie de la perception*, Paris 1945 that Merleau-Ponty's Cézanne sources appear: Emile Bernard, *La Méthode de Cézanne*, Paris 1920; Joachim Gasquet, *Cézanne*, Paris 1926; and Fritz Novotny, 'Das problem des Menschen Cézanne im Verhaltnis zu seiner Kunst', *Zeitschrift für Aesthetik und allgemeiner Kunstwissenschaft*, no.26, 1932. Cézanne reappears in the section 'La Chose et le monde naturel' in a discussion of

the system of appearances, pre-spatial fileds, the construction of both object and meaning through the painter's marks (1983 ed., p.373).

5 Merleau-Ponty trans. 1965, pp.107–8, 111, 114.

6 Compare Waldemar George on Fautrier's *Otages* exhibition: 'Fautrier's drama is that of the hero of *The Unknown Artist*', in *La Voix de Paris*, 8 Nov. 1945. Cézanne famously recognised himself in Balzac's artist. (The story had been published in several versions in the 1830s.)

7 Dominique Rey's 'La Perception du peintre et le problème de l'être: Essai sur l'esthétique et l'ontologie de Maurice Merleau-Ponty', unpublished doctoral thesis, University of Fribourg, Switzerland 1978, although disappointing, should be mentioned.

8 Bram van Velde in *Derrière le Miroir*, nos.11–12, June 1948, p.13. See also Sartre's play *L'Engrenage*, Paris 1948.

9 Samuel Beckett, 'Peintres de l'empêchement', *Derrière le Miroir*, nos.11–12, June 1948, pp.3–7. See also Germain Viatte, *Geer Van Velde*, Paris 1989.

10 Samuel Beckett, 'Bram van Velde' (first pub. in *Transition 49*, no.5, 1949, pp.97–103), in *Proust and Three Dialogues with Georges Duthuit*, 1965, p.120. The 'School of Aix' provides the link between Duthuit and the other two artists who are the subjects of dialogue, Tal-Coat and André Masson.

11 See Denise Colomb, *Portraits d'artistes des années 50*, no.35, *Bram van Velde*, Paris 1957, and caption, unpag.: 'Bram van Velde gave me a rendezvous in an absolutely empty studio. Of course, I knew his painting but I admit that I never before understood the accord between the man and his work: I hadn't understood the mystic side of his work and the man presented himself to me alone and as peaceful as a monk.'

IV The Theatre of Cruelty

1 Maurice Merleau-Ponty, 'Le Doute de Cézanne', 1945, trans. 1964, p.119.

2 See *Parallel Visions: Modern Artist and Outsider Art*, exh. cat., Los Angeles County Museum of Art 1992, where my essay 'From the Asylum to the Museum: Marginal Art in Paris and New York, 1938–1968' (pp.120–49) contains an extensive discussion of the context for Dubuffet's *art brut* and phenomena such as the Cobra artists from Copenhagen, Brussels and Amsterdam, which are not covered in this *Paris Post War*.

3 First pub. Paris 1947. The article 'Sa Folie?', *Arts*, 31 Jan. 1947, reviewing Dr Beer's publication *Du démon de van Gogh* is reproduced in Artaud, *Oeuvres complètes*, XIII, Paris 1974, pp.302–3.

4 Antonin Artaud, from 'Van Gogh, the Man Suicided by Society', in *Antonin Artaud Anthology*, San Francisco 1970, p.135.

5 Antonin Artaud, preface to *Portraits et dessins*, exh cat., Galerie Pierre, Paris 1947, unpag.

6 See Artaud, 'Cahiers de Rodez', Sept.–Nov. 1945, *Oeuvres complètes*, XVIII, Paris 1974, p.157. Stephen Barber's new biography, *Antonin Artaud: Blows and Bombs*, 1993, sets up an accurate chronology of Artaud's life for the first time and gives a sensitive and comprehensive picture of his creative work in all media.

7 See Artaud, *Oeuvres complètes*, XIII, 1974, pp.67–99; Stephen Barber, 'Artaud: The Final Work, 1946–1948', unpublished Ph.D. thesis, University of London 1990, and Barber 1993, Chap.v 'Ivry – Blows and Bombs', pp.125–63.

8 Antonin Artaud, Preface to *Portraits et dessins*, exh. cat., Galerie Pierre, Paris 1947.

9 Barber 1993, p.143.

10 Georges Bataille, 'Note: Adamov', *Critique*, no.7, 1946, p.654, reproduced in *Oeuvres complètes*, XI, Paris 1988, pp.162–3.

11 Like Raymond Queneau, Bataille and Raymond Aron, Lacan was affected by Alexandre Kojève's Hegel lectures in 1933, his introduction of 'desire' into the master/slave dialectic and his notion of the 'inverted form of the image'. See Alexandre Kojève, *Introduction à la lecture de Hegel* (Raymond Queneau's notes), Paris 1947; Jacques Lacan, 'Le Stade du miroir comme formateur de la fonction du

Je', Paris 1949, in *Ecrits*, Paris 1966, and Elisabeth Roudinesco: 'Jacques Lacan dans le miroir de la philosophie', *Les Enjeux philosophiques des années 50*, Paris 1989, pp.87–98.

12 Henri Michaux, *Peintures et dessins*, Paris 1946. Elisabeth Plessa's unpublished M.A. thesis, 'Henri Michaux, the Supremacy of the Head', Courtauld Institute of Art 1992, alerted me to the problem of Michaux and the mirror.

13 The exhibition dates were 21 Sept. – 14 Oct. 1950. Over 2,000 works from forty-five collections and seventeen countries were exhibited, in geographical sections, attracting over 10,000 visitors in less than a month. See Robert Volmat, *L'Art psychopathologique*, Paris 1956.

14 Jean Dubuffet, 'Honneur aux valeurs sauvages', *Prospectus et tous écrits suivants*, 1, Paris 1967, p.206 (preface to a mixed exhibition Galerie Marcel Evrard, Lille, 1951). See Sarah Wilson, 'Dubuffet, Breton and Art Brut', in 'From the Asylum to the Museum', *Parallel Visions* 1992, pp.128–33.

15 See Merleau-Ponty 1945; *Merleau-Ponty à la Sorbonne. Résumé de cours, 1949–1952*, Dijon 1988; and Vincent Descombes, 'Vers une crise d'identité en philosophie française', *Les Enjeux philosophiques des années 50* 1989, pp.147–67.

V Matter and Memory: A New Primitivism

1 Jean Dubuffet, 'A pleines mains', in 'Notes pour les fins-lettrés', written for interested friends in 1945, published in *Prospectus aux amateurs de tout genre*, Paris 1946, republished in *Prospectus et tous écrits suivants*, 1, Paris 1967, p.71.

2 Jean-Paul Sartre, *L'Imagination*, Nouvelle Encyclopédie Philosophique, Paris 1936, discusses the qualifications and additions to Descartes's mechanistic theory of perception from the mid-nineteenth century onwards, including Bergson's 'philosophical revolution' (p.41).

3 Bergson had secretly converted to Catholicism long before his death. See Henri Bergson, *Exposition centenaire*, *Bibliothèque nationale*, exh. cat., Paris 1959, items 282–6 for Bergson studies during the Occupation, preceding the *Oeuvres complètes*, Geneva 1945–6. The *Etudes Bergsoniennes* published regularly from 1948–56. In 1947, an *Hommage national* was rendered to Bergson, involving the President of the Republic and Minister of Education.

4 Jean Dubuffet, 'Avant-Projet d'une conférence populaire sur la peinture', Jan. 1945, written at Jean Paulhan's request for a projected series on painting for an uninitiated audience and published in *Prospectus aux amateurs de tout genre* 1946. See *Prospectus et tous écrits suivants* 1 1967, pp.31–53.

5 The poet Eugène Guillevic, inspired by the 'Matière and mémoire' series asked Dubuffet to illustrate his poems on the subject of walls. Dubuffet first met Michaux at his Galerie André exhibition.

6 Jean Texcier, *Gavroche*, 30 May 1946.

7 See Jean Lescure, 'Gaston Bachelard' in *L'Express*, 16 Nov. 1961, no.544, pp.34–5. His emphasis as regards the audience for the 1942 lectures is on the poets, alas. He mentions André Frenaud (who wrote the text for Fautrier's *Femme de ma vie*, 1948), Paul Eluard (whose *Dignes de vivre* was illustrated by Fautrier), Raymond Queneau, Eugène Guillevic (whose 'Les Murs' poems were finally published with the 'Les Murs' lithographs in *Les Murs*, Paris 1950), the Surrealist Benjamin Fontaine and the younger Surrealist generation – Jean François Chabrun and Maurice Nadeau, the artist Raoul Ubac: 'for the first time the big names in new literature and new painting were regularly mentioned' in Bachelard's lectures.

8 Gaston Bachelard, *L'Eau et les rêves*, Paris 1942, p.146.

9 Children's drawing exhibitions during the Occupation fuelled a growing interest. An exhibition of children's drawings at the Musée du Luxembourg in 1947 coincided with the publication of the 1920s pioneer Georges-Henri Luquet's *Le Dessin enfantin* (1947). See also Françoise Minkowska, 'De van Gogh et Seurat au dessins d'enfants: A la recherche du monde des formes (RORSCHACH)' in the exh. cat., Musée pedagogique, Paris 1949. *Maurice Merleau-*

Ponty, à la Sorbonne: Resumé de cours, 1949–1952,
Dijon 1988, demonstrates a particular interest in
Piaget, Luquet, the relationship between 'Italian and
modern' painting, 'infantile and adult' painting,
(pp.46, 513–9), besides discussing Lacan's mirror
stage (pp.112–3). His pioneering discussion of Sauss-
urean linguistics at this time (pp.10–90) coincides
with the looser theorisings of a new painting of
'signs'.
10 Bachelard 1942, pp.12–13.
11 Jean Dubuffet, 'La Main parle' in 'Notes pour les fins-
lettrés' in *Prospectus et tous écrits suivants* 1 1967,
p.64, quoted by Michel Tapié in his preface to
*Mirobolus, Macadam et Cie: Hautes pâtes de Jean
Dubuffet*, exh. cat., Galerie René Drouin, Paris 1946,
p.11.
12 See Gaston Bachelard, *La Terre et les rêveries de la
volonté*, Paris 1947, pp.113–4 and, for example,
'Matière et main – inedit' in the co-production with
poets and artists including Eluard, Ponge, Fautrier
and Richier, *A la gloire de la main*, printed under the
auspices of the engraver Albert Flocon and the group
Graphies, in 1949. See also Marcel Schattel, 'Gaston
Bachelard et la lecture de l'oeuvre d'art', unpublished thesis, University of Dijon 1972.
13 Tapié 1946, p.30. A wave of publications on the
French Romanesque before and during the war were
important, as was the exhibition of the Bayeux
tapestry at the Louvre at the end of the war and the
opening of the Musée de la fresque (Romanesque
frescos) in June 1945 at the Palais de Chaillot.

VI Under the Sign of Sartre

1 Unpublished letter from Jean Paulhan to Fautrier,
*c.*1942–4 (undated) quoted in Giorgio Galansini,
'Jean Fautrier: A Catalogue of his Early Works',
unpublished Ph.D. thesis, University of Chicago,
Illinois 1973, p.9, n.1.
2 See 'Trente Quatre lettres de Jean Dubuffet à Jean
Paulhan', item 114, undated, Summer 1946, in *Jean
Paulhan à travers ses peintres*, exh. cat., Grand Palais,
Paris 1974, pp.98–9. About to embark on his second
reading of *Nausea*, Dubuffet muses that baptism precedes catechism.
3 See 'Official Portraits' and 'Faces' in *Verve*, vol.2,
nos.5–6, 1939 (English ed.), pp.12–13 and pp.43–4
respectively.
4 Sartre, *L'Imaginaire*, Paris 1940, pp.23, 53, 74, 78,
104, 362 et seq.
5 Jean-Paul Sartre, *Existentialism and Humanism*,
London 1948, trans. and introduced by Philip
Mairet, pp.28, 34, 41. Ibid., pp.44–5: 'for outside the
Cartesian cogito, all objects are no more than prob-
able . . . Our aim is precisely to establish a pattern of
values in distinction from the material world.'
6 Sartre took mescalin in 1935. He describes the
experiences of seeing an umbrella turn into a vul-
ture, de Beauvoir's slipper into a huge fly, in Alexandre Astruc and Michel Contat, *Sartre, un film*, Paris
1977, pp.52–3. The experiments coincided with the
writing of *L'Imaginaire*. It was the German philosopher in exile, Bernard Groethuysen, who insisted
that Sartre should write a chapter on the art work at
the end of this text (ibid., p.59).
7 See William Plank's extended discussion in *Sartre
and Surrealism*, Ann Arbor, Michigan 1981,
pp.69–78.
8 See Jean-Paul Sartre, *La Nausée*, Paris 1938,
p.22–3, and *Wols*, exh. cat., Galerie René Drouin,
Paris 1945 where Sartre brushes shoulders with
Ecclesiasticus, Poe, Maeterlinck and many Eastern
philosophers.
9 Jean-Paul Sartre, *Visages, précédé de Portraits Offi-
ciels*, Paris 1948 (926 examples, each with four dry-
points by Wols), pp.33, 40–1.
10 See Jean-Paul Sartre, *Nourritures, suivi des extraits de
la Nausée*, Paris 1949 (450 examples).'Nourritures'
– memories of seeing rotting food in Naples – was
first published in *Verve*, no.4, Jan.–March 1939,
p.115. Jacques Damase confirmed to the author (4
Dec. 1984) that the publishing venture was his idea,
'to make Wols work'. Sartre was aware of work in
progress but did not survey the production of the
book and did not come to the publication party. Wols

works were also used to illustrate works by Camille
Bryen, René du Solier, Artaud, Paulhan and Kafka:
see Will Grohmann, 'Das Graphische Werk von
Wols', *Quadrum* (Brussels), no.6, 1959, pp.95–118.
11 Jean-Paul Sartre, 'Doigts et non-doigts', in *Wols en
Personne*, Paris 1963, pp.10–21, trans. Annie Fatet
in Peter Inch (ed.), *Circus Wols: The Life and Work of
Wolfgang Schulze* 1978, unpag.
12 Ibid. The writings on Wols and Giacometti, may be
compared to the literary pieces (Baudelaire, Mall-
armé, Genet, Flaubert, etc.) analysed in Michael
Scriven, *Sartre's Existential Biographies*, 1984.
13 Jean-Paul Sartre and Michel Sicard, 'Penser l'art',
Sartre et les Arts, Obliques, nos.24–5, special number,
1981, p.16.
14 See René Guilly, *Wols*, exh. cat., Galerie René
Drouin, Paris 1947, which reflects existentially upon
the painter's essential solitude: 'As soon as painting
is seen it joins the world of painting lived by others.'
15 Jean-Paul Sartre, 'Les Mobiles de Calder', in *Calder,
mobiles, stabiles, constellations*, exh. cat., Galerie Louis
Carré, Paris 1946. The text appeared with an English
translation in *Style en France*, no.5, April 1947,
pp.7–11, in *Les Temps Modernes*, and then *Situations
III*, Paris 1948. Two English versions appeared in
America within a year, as 'Calder's Mobiles' and as
'Existentialist and Mobilist' for Calder's exhibition at
the Bucholz Gallery, New York. The Paris catalogue
cover was a stroboscopic photograph of a mobile in
motion by Herbert Matter, *c.*1936, the illustrations
inside lithographed and hand-coloured by Mourlot.
Sartre visited Calder's studio in Roxbury thanks to
André Masson. It was Duchamp's idea to send an
exhibition in 'postable' elements to the Galerie Louis
Carré and Duchamp who coined the term 'mobile'.
See *Calder: An Autobiography with Pictures*, 1967,
pp.188–94.
16 From the translation 'The Mobiles of Calder', in Jean-
Paul Sartre, *Essays in Aesthetics*, trans. Wade Baskin,
1963, pp.89–92.
17 Hare had edited the Surrealist periodical *V.V.V.* with
Breton in New York and had purloined his wife, Jacqueline Lamba. For the text see Jean-Paul Sartre,
'Sculpture à 'n' dimensions', in *Exposition David Hare*,
exh. cat., Galerie Maeght, Paris 1947. Extracts published in *Arts*, 12 Dec. 1947. The translation 'N-
Dimensional Sculpture' appeared in *Women: A Collaboration of Artists and Writers*, New York 1948 (not
used here). For the full text see Michel Contat and
Michel Rybalka, *Les Ecrits de Sartre, chronologie,
bibliographie commentée*, Paris 1970, pp.663–9.
Hare's works were inspired by the Surrealist Gia-
cometti of the period of 'Woman with her Throat
Cut' 1935, visible at The Museum of Modern Art,
New York, but not in Paris, an irony lost on Sartre.
18 Masson did the scenery for Sartre's *Morts sans sépul-
ture*, in 1946. See André Masson, 'Balance faussée',
Les Temps Modernes, no.29, Feb. 1948, pp.181–94.
Sartre's text on Masson, 'L'Artiste est un suspect'
written at the same period appeared with Masson's
Vingt-Deux dessins sur le thème de désir, 1961, and as
'Masson' in *Situations IV*, Paris 1964, pp.387–407.
Masson's drawings reappear with Michel Butor's
'Textamorphose ou la réabsorption du commentaire'
with Sartre in *Sartre et les arts*, 1981, pp.205–36.
19 Alberto Giacometti, 'Le Rêve, le sphinx et la mort de
T' in *Labyrinthe* (Geneva), nos.22–3, 15 Dec. 1946,
pp.12–13, reproduced in *Alberto Giacometti*, exh.
cat., Musée d'art moderne de la ville de Paris 1991,
pp.412–14 (unillustrated), discussed at length by Jean
Clair, *Giacometti: Le Nez: Faces de carême, figures de
carnaval*, Paris 1992.
20 Jean-Paul Sartre, 'Les Peintures de Giacometti', *Derrière le Miroir*, no.65, May 1954, preface to Giacometti's second exhibition at the Galerie Maeght,
May 1954, reprinted in *Les Temps Modernes*, June
1954, trans. as 'Giacometti in Search of Space', *Art
News*, vol.54, no.5, Sept. 1955, pp.26–9, 63–5, in
conjunction with Giacometti's exhibition at The
Solomon R. Guggenheim Museum, New York,
retranslation by Wade Baskin 1963, pp.57–70.
21 Simone de Beauvoir, *La Force de l'âge*, Paris 1960,
pp.499–503, trans. Peter Green as *The Prime of Life*,
1963, quoted in Reinhold Hohl, *Giacometti: Sculpture,
Painting, Drawing*, 1972, p.275. Compare Sartre on
Hare: 'marble suddenly reveals its fault, apparently
unchangeable, a secret crumbling eats it away, this
pure hardening of space is made of separable par-
ticles', Contat and Rybalka 1970, p.663.

22 Jean-Paul Sartre, *Being and Nothingness*, trans. Hazel
E. Barnes, 1977, p.30.
23 See *Alberto Giacometti*, exh. cat., Musée d'art
moderne de la ville de Paris 1991, nos.122–3,
pp.218–9, where an analogy is suggested, less con-
vincingly, I think, with Rodin's 'Falling Man' 1882.
24 Sartre, *Being and Nothingness*, p.28.
25 'Four Figures on a Base' 1950, described by Giacometti in a letter to Pierre Matisse, is the point of
departure for Sartre's 'Les Peintures de Giacometti'
1954.
26 Jean-Paul Sartre, 'The Search for the Absolute',
trans. Lionel Abel, in *Albero Giacometti: Exhibition of
Sculpture, Paintings, Drawings*, exh. cat., Pierre Matisse Gallery, New York 1948, pp.2–22, published
with Giacometti's first letter to Pierre Matisse, pp.16,
20. See also 'La Recherche de l'absolu', *Les Temps
Modernes*, no.28, Jan. 1948, pp.1153–63, and
retranslation, Wade Baskin 1963, pp.93–103.
27 Reinhold Hohl nicely juxtaposes Baudelaire's line on
Pascal's solitude: 'Pascale avait son gouffre, avec lui
se mouvant' in *Les Fleurs du mal* (1857), with Sartre's 'Giacometti allait et venait avec un gouffre à son
côté', Hohl 1972, p.207. Sartre's *Baudelaire* was published in 1947.
28 See Steven Ungar, 'Rebellion or Revolution' (15 Oct.
1945) in Denis Hollier (ed.), *A New History of French
Literature*, Cambridge, Massachussetts and London
1989, p.974 for the first reference in this context to
Heidegger's text.
29 Martin Heidegger, 'The Origin of the Work of Art',
1935–6, (first pub. as 'Der Ursprung des Kunst-
werkes', in *Holzwege*, Frankfurt 1950), in David
Farrell Krel (ed.), *Heidegger: Basic Writings*, 1978,
pp.149, 164, 170–1.
30 Sartre's monumental *Saint Genet, Comédien et
Martyr*, Paris 1952, 'rewrote' Genet's life as a tragic
existentialist parable with extraordinary factual dis-
tortions. (Sartre's sub-Freudian desire to explain the
present through the past apparently obfuscated
Genet's happy childhood, enthusiastic military service, etc. Compare Maurice Chevalet's biography in
Genet, 2, Marseille 1989, pp.11–17.) The second
enormity perpetrated by Sartre was literally to
appropriate vol.1 of Genet's *Oeuvres complètes*, Paris
1952, with this text.
31 For the tragedy and absurdity of Giacometti's
obsessively phallocentric universe see Clair 1992.
For a psychoanalytic reading of the Sartrean oeuvre
as a whole, see Andrew N. Leak, *The Perverted Consciousness: Sexuality and Sartre*, 1989.
32 This was discussed at length by Jacques Lecarme,
'Jean-Paul Sartre: Ecrire la guerre' at the first annual
conference of the U.K. Society of Sartrean Studies,
Institute of Romance Studies, 23 Jan. 1993.
33 See Thierry de Duve's comprehensive study, *Giacometti: Portrait de Jean Genet: Le Scribe captif*, Paris
1991.
34 Jean Genet, *L'Atelier d'Alberto Giacometti*, (photographs by Ernest Scheidegger) Paris 1958, unpag.
35 Jean-Paul Sartre, 'Les Communistes et la paix', *Les
Temps Modernes*, no.81, July 1952, nos.84–5,
Oct.–Nov. 1952, and no.101, April 1954, republished in *Situations VI*, Paris 1964.
36 See Sartre and Sicard 1981, p.15. Sartre describes
his intentions for the *Esthétique* as 'Certainly to
contribute to an ensemble of theses on painting: to
attempt to discuss at once what a painter and what
a picture is' . . . 'I thought to do the same one day for
sculpture' he continues (most curiously). A theory of
the Beautiful as 'totalising unification' would have
been central. For the discussion of art in Sartre's
literature and poetry and for artists such as Lapoujade see also George Howard Bauer, *Sartre and the
Artist*, Chicago 1969.

VII The Second Sex

1 Simone de Beauvoir, *The Second Sex*, trans. and ed. by H.M. Parshley, 1953; 1972, opening to pt.II 'Women's Life Today', p.295.
2 Dor de la Souchère, preface to *Germaine Richier 1904–1959*, Galerie Creuzevault, Paris 1966, unpag.
3 See *Le Théâtre de la mode*, Paris 1990. Haute-couture mannequins in theatrical scenery shown at the Pavillon de Marsan, in March 1945, toured to Barcelona, London, Leeds, New York and San Francisco, as a symbol of the renaissance of Parisian woman and the fashion industry. The collection is now on permanent display at the Maryhill Museum of Art, San Francisco.
4 Hans Anton Prinner was a woman, primarily a sculptor (photographed in *View*, no.6, 1946 and profiled in *Horizon*). She was a transvestite whose true sexual identity was unknown to many in the art world. See Prinner, *La Femme tondue*, illustrated with eight engravings, Paris, July, 1946 and Alain Brossat, *Les Tondues: Un carnaval moche*, Paris 1993.
5 Marguerite Duras, *Hiroshima mon amour*. Scenario and dialogue. Film by Alain Resnais, Paris 1960.
6 De Beauvoir quotes the law of 13 April 1946, 'holding that the existence of these houses is incompatible with the essential principles of human dignity and the role awarded to woman in modern society', in *The Second Sex*, p.167.
7 Beauvoir, *The Second Sex*, p.16. See also Chap. 7, 'Le Deuxième sexe' in Paul Webster and Nicholas Powell, *Saint-Germain-des-Prés: French Post-War Culture from Sartre to Bardot*, 1984, p.157. Over one million copies were sold in the United States. The Communist Party's Union des Femmes Françaises and their conservative policy on women at the time is a topic beyond the scope of this essay.
8 Kinsey's report on male sexuality was published in France in 1948; the report on female sexuality (1953) came out in French in October 1954. See Isabelle Moreau, *Mon comportement sexuel: Une française répond au questionnaire Kinsey*, Paris 1953. The impact of film is another dimension: see Gina Lombroso, *L'Ame de la femme*, Paris 1947, or *De la vamp à la femme*, *L'Ecran* no.2, Feb.–March 1958.
9 See Simone de Beauvoir, 'Faut-il bruler Sade?', in *Privilèges*, Paris 1955, pp.9–89; *Brigitte Bardot ou le syndrome Lolita*, Paris 1959, trans. as *Brigitte Bardot and the Lolita Syndrome*, 1960; with Gisèle Halimi et al., *Djamila Boupacha*, Paris 1962.
10 The 600,000 prostitutes indicated an increase of 200,000 since the war (*Combat*, 12 Sept. 1947).
11 Sartre, *L'Imaginaire*, Paris 1940, trans. as *The Psychology of Imagination*, 1950, pp.217–18.
12 See Frances Morris, 'Jean Hélion, from Abstraction to Figuration', unpublished M.A. thesis, Courtauld Institute of Art, University of London 1983, pp.34–6.
13 Sartre's characterisation of the viscous as the sweet and feminine 'revenge of the *en-soi*' in *Being and Nothingness* was challenged by Suzanne Lilar in *A propos de Sartre et l'amour*, Paris 1967, p.77; he was called a 'traditional sexist' by Margery Collins and Christine Pierce, 'Holes and Slime: Sexism in Sartre's Psychoanalysis', in Carol C. Gould and Marx W. Wartofsky (eds.), *Women and Philosophy*, New York 1976, p.125. See Dorothy MacCall, 'Existentialisme ou feminisme', in *Sartre*, special number of *Obliques*, nos.18–19, 1979, pp.311–20.', and Michèle le Doeuff, 'Simone de Beauvoir and Existentialism', *Feminist Studies*, no.6, 1980, pp.277–89.
14 See Simone Weil's posthumous work, *La Pesanteur et la grace*, Paris 1948.
15 René de Solier, 'L'Oeuvre est un rendez-vous', *Derrière le Miroir*, no.13, 1948, pp.4–5.
16 André Pierre de Mandiargues, 'La Main déchaînée', *Le Disque Vert*, no.3, July–Aug. 1953, in *Germaine Richier*, Galerie Creuzevault, Paris 1966.
17 Richier's spiritual forebear and homonym was Ligier Richier, the sixteenth-century French tomb sculptor.
18 See previous section, n.36. Sartre said: 'Beauty is a totalising unification offering through that totalisation the spectre of a never-achieved totality, and it is in the relationship between totalisation and totality that I would find the idea of Beauty.'
19 Celso Constantini's 'Dell'Arte sacra deformatrice', the *Osservatore Romano*'s article of 10 June 1951, was reproduced all over the world. Richier's crucifix

reappeared on the high altar, classified as a historical monument, in 1971. For a full account of the 'Sacred Art quarrel', the theological and political and humanist background, see my article: 'Catholics, Communists and Art Sacré', in Patrick Marsh (ed.), *The Conscience of the French: Intellectual Life in Post-Liberation France*, Oxford, Munich, New York 1993 (forthcoming).
20 Man Ray, 'Des chats et des magnolias', *Le Surréalisme Même*, no.1, 1958, p.7. See also *Exposition, InteRnatiOnale du Surréalisme (EROS)*, exh. cat., Galerie Daniel Cordier, Paris 1959.
21 The seventy-two artist retrospective at the Grand Palais of 1972, *Douze ans d'art contemporain* featured two women: on show were six works by Niki de Saint Phalle and two small textile pieces by the American, Sheila Hicks.
22 See Suzanne Lilar, *Le Malentendu du deuxième sexe*, Paris 1969.

VIII The Imaginary Museum

1 André Malraux, *Le Musée imaginaire: Psychologie de l'art*, Geneva 1947, p.13 (my translation).
2 Exhibitions of Léger, Picasso and Matisse at the Communist-backed Maison de la Pensée Française are but one example.
3 Quoted by Camille Bourniquel in his review of Malraux's *Le Musée imaginaire*, in *Esprit*, March 1948, pp.507–8.
4 Walter Benjamin, 'L'Oeuvre d'art à l'époque de sa reproduction mécanisée', offprint from *Zeitschrift für Sozialforschung*, no.1, Paris 1936, dedicated to Malraux; see *Bibliothèque André Malraux*, Musée national d'art moderne, Centre Georges Pompidou, Paris 1986, item 1764, p.16. Benjamin's text was translated by Pierre Klossowski, the Germanist and brother of Balthus. See Walter Benjamin, *Ecrits français* presented by J.-M. Monnoyer, Paris 1991, pp.114–92 for the various versions and context.
5 See *Encyclopédie photographique de l'art* (3 vols.), Musée du Louvre, Paris 1935–8, in *Bibliothèque André Malraux* 1986, item 966, p.29.
6 See 'La Psychologie de l'art', *Verve*, no.1, Dec. 1937, pp.41–8;'La Psychologie des renaissances', *Verve*, no.2, Spring 1938, pp.21–5; 'De la representation en orient et en occident', *Verve*, no.3, Summer 1938, pp.69–72; 'Esquisse d'une psychologie du cinéma', *Verve*, no.8, June 1940, pp.69–73. Reformulated as *Esquisse d'une psychologie du cinéma*, Paris 1946; *Psychologie de l'art*, I, *Le Musée imaginaire*, Geneva 1947; *Psychologie de l'art*, II, *La Création artistique*, Geneva 1948; *Psychologie de l'art III*, *La Monnaie de l'absolu*, Paris 1949, 1950; the trilogy reissued as *Les Voix du silence*, Paris 1951; trans. Stuart Gilbert as *The Voices of Silence*, New York 1953.
7 Conclusion of *La Monnaie de l'absolu* 1949.
8 *La Monnaie de l'absolu* 1949, pp.128–9.
9 The reference is to Christian Zervos's day-to-day compilation of the Picasso catalogue raisonné, with Picasso's daily dated works: a practice that Dubuffet, characteristically brazen, would be the first to imitate.
10 Reference to the cinema is insistent. Tintoretto's *Ascent to Calvary* (1566) anticipates Eisenstein's *Battleship Potemkin* (1925) and Malraux's own film *Espoir* (1939), for example. See *La Création artistique* 1948, p.200.
11 See Malraux's ironic editorial 'Eloge de la torture' in his protest journal *L'Indochine enchaînée*, no.2, 1925, p.5; *Les Conquérants*, Paris 1928; *La Condition Humaine*, Paris 1933.
12 The ideas of the Maison de la Culture, focus for the broadly based debates of the Association of Revolutionary Artists and Writers in the 1930s, was relaunched, with different politics, through Malraux's own initiatives as Minister of Culture in the 1960s, as part of his decentralisation policy.
13 This is not the place for an assessment of Malraux's career as Minister of Culture for the Fifth Republic, for which see Gérard Monnier, *Des Beaux-Arts aux arts plastiques*, Besançon 1991, pp.259–82.
14 Georges Duthuit, *Le Musée inimaginable*, I, Paris 1956, p.25.
15 See Alec Mellor, *La Torture: Son histoire, son abolition, sa réapparition au XXième siècle*, Paris 1949, esp.

Chap. XI: 'Torture policière: France'. Henri Alleg's *La Question* on torture in Algeria was banned in April 1958, precipitating Malraux's protest to de Gaulle, along with Sartre, Mauriac and Roger Martin du Gard, in the national press, 17 and 18 April.
16 Malraux's exhibitions of Indo-hellenic, 'Gothico-buddhist' and 'Greco-buddhist' sculpture at the Galerie de la Nouvelle Revue Française in 1931 were seminal for Fautrier's early sculptures and his eroded and powdered surfaces. During the same period Fautrier made the lithographic ink proofs for the series of illustrations for Dante's *Inferno* that are the historic precursors of 1940s *Informel* painting, and which Malraux would acquire. Malraux reviewed Fautrier's 1933 exhibition at the Galerie de la Nouvelle Revue Française, renewing his friendship at the time of the *Otages* exhibition at the Galerie René Drouin.
17 Malraux called the metamorphoses of style 'long scars of the passage of fate over the face of the earth'. See also Duthuit I 1956, p.25.
18 For an idea of the breadth of Malraux's output and achievement see *André Malraux*, exh. cat., Saint Paul 1973. Pascal Sabourin's *La Réflexion sur l'art d'André Malraux*, Paris 1972 should also be noted.

IX The Open Work

1 Michel Tapié, Preface, *H.W.P.S.M.T.B.*, exh. cat., Galerie Colette Allendy, Paris 1948, unpag.
2 Michel Tapié, 'Ethique', in *H.W.P.S.M.T.B.* 1948, also reproduced in Francesc Vicens, *Prolégomènes à une esthétique autre de Michel Tapié* Barcelona 1962, p.37.
3 Jean Paulhan, 'L'Art informel', *Eloge*, Paris 1962, p.23.
4 See Fautrier's illustrations to Robert Ganzo's poem, *Lespugue*, 1942 (lithographs by Mourlot, printed by Durand, 1942). References to affinities with Courbet, Redon, Turner, Monet appear in Paulhan's preface to *Fautrier: Oeuvres (1915–1943)*, exh. cat., Galerie René Drouin, Paris 1943, which was the first version of *Fautrier: L'Enragé*, Paris 1949.
5 I thus diverge from Serge Guilbaut's confident opinion that the *Informel* 'derived from what Georges Bataille had named the "formless" in the 1920s' in Serge Guilbaut (ed.), *Reconstructing Modernism: Art in New York, Paris and Montreal, 1945–1964*, Cambridge, Massachusetts and London 1990, pp.50, 59. See my article 'Jean Fautrier and Georges Bataille', to be published in Caroline Gill (ed.), *Georges Bataille: Writing the Sacred*, 1994.
6 Waldemar George in *La Voix de Paris*, 8 Nov. 1945. His analogy preceded Merleau-Ponty's in 'Le Doute de Cézanne' by one month.
7 See my article 'Jean Fautrier, ses écrivains et ses poètes' in *Ecrire la peinture*, ed. and introduced by Philippe Delaveau, Paris 1987, pp.241–51.
8 Jean Dubuffet,'Notes pour les fins-lettrés': 'Partant de l'informe', in *Prospectus et amateurs de tout genre*, Paris 1946 and in *Prospectus et trois écrits suivants*, I, Paris 1967, p.54 and notes, p.464. Compare Gaston Bachelard, 'Une rêverie de la matière', *Rêves d'Encre*, Sept. 1945, unpag. The twenty-five ink decalcomanias introduced by Paul Eluard, René Char, Julien Gracq and Gaston Bachelard evoked the important Surrealist heritage and proximity of the *Informel* to the current Rorschach test craze.
9 Jean Dubuffet, in *Plus beaux qu'ils ne croient, beaux malgré eux*, exh. cat., Galerie René Drouin, Paris 1947, unpag. See also Enrico Crispolti's seven-page discussion of the origins and usage of the term *Informel* in *L'Informale: Storia e poetica*, vol.I, *In Europa, 1940–1951*, Assisi/Rome 1971, pp.47–54; the three numbers of *Preuves*, nos.156–8, Feb.–April 1964 devoted to 'L'Art informel' and Georges Mathieu, 'Mise au point sur l'art informel' in no.159, May 1964 (where he claims his own paternity for the term in 1951). Neither Crispolti nor Mathieu mention Bataille.
10 See Camille Bryen and Jacques Audiberti, *L'Ouvre-boite, colloque abhumaniste*, Paris 1952. Umberto Eco quotes Audiberti on Bryen extensively in 'The Open Work in the Visual Arts', in *The Open Work*, Milan 1962 trans. Anna Cancogni, Harvard 1989, p.92. 'Submedullary staphlococci', 'molecules of the chemical pictorial substances' are evoked: 'And sud-

denly, the painting gives way to a sort of cybernetics … We see the work of art dehumanizing itself, freeing itself from man's signature.'

11 Stéphane Lupasco's publications such as 'Energie et Phénomène Psychique', *Synthèse*, April 1955, culminated for contemporary artists in *Science et art abstrait*, Paris 1963.

12 Michel Tapié, Preface, *Véhémences confrontées*, exh. cat., Galerie Nina Dausset, Paris 1951, reproduced in Vicens 1962, p.41.

13 Tapié had commercial links with the Studio Fachetti gallery which held the show that accompanied the publication of *Un art autre, où il s'agit de nouveaux dévidages du réel*, Paris 1952.

14 Michel Tapié, 'Jackson Pollock avec nous', preface for the one-man show at the Studio Fachetti, Paris, Feb. 1952, reproduced in Vicens 1962, p.44.

15 For Tapié's Centre in Turin see Vicens 1962, pp.258–9.

16 Umberto Eco joined Giulo Carlo Argan (who wrote 'Da Bergson a Fautrier', for *Aut Aut*, Jan. 1960), Renato Barilli and Enrico Crispolti, for the special number of *Il Verri* devoted to the *Informel* in June 1961. Eco's plurivalency was taken up by Crispolti in 1971, when the subtitle for *L'Informale, storia e poetica* was 'Abstract-Expressionism, Abstraction-Lyrique, Action-Painting, Art Autre, Art Brut, Automatismo, Gesto, Informale, New-Dada, Nucléarisme, Spazialismo, Tachisme' (sic).

17 Henri Michaux, *Un barbare en asie*, Paris 1933, pp.156, 160.

18 See Benjamin Peret's articles: 'D'une décalcomanie sans objet préconçu', *Minotaure*, no.8, 1936, pp.18–23, and 'Ruines: Ruines des ruines' with a full-page Victor Hugo ink wash – homage to the great precursor – *Minotaure*, May 1939, p.58. The Rorschach test was published (without plates), Paris 1947. See also Emile Malespine, 'La Peinture intégrale', *Cahiers d'Art*, no.22, 1947, pp.288–92, with decalcomanias, quotes by Leonardo and Rorschach, and Françoise Minkowska.

19 Henri Michaux, 'Vitesse et tempo', *Quadrum*, III, 1956, p.16.

20 Michel Tapié, 'Jackson Pollock avec nous', reproduced in Vicens 1962, p.44.

21 See Pierre Restany, 'L'Art informel et les echanges Paris–Tokyo', 'Anthologie', in *Le Japon des avant-gardes, 1910–1970*, exh. cat., Musée nationale d'art moderne, Centre Georges Pompidou, Paris 1986, pp.262–83.

22 Michel Ragon, *La Peinture actuelle*, Paris 1959, a highly representative text of the period. The 'Avant propos', p.3 mentions an 'anthology' of Japanese art shown in Paris in exchange for a selection of Louvre masterpieces. 'Les Influences étrangères' is certainly not chauvinistic as a section, mentioning the Russian and German avant-gardes, quashed by totalitarianism that sent to Paris a bevy of artists (including those from post-1945 Eastern Europe). Their new talents and ideas 'allow Paris, still today to withstand effortlessly competition with New York, which canvasses for succession as exemplary cultural city', p.27.

23 'Hot Paint for Cold War' was the title of the 1986 symposium at the University of British Columbia, Canada, which gave rise to Serge Guilbaut's publication of 1990.

X The Return of the Repressed: Revisioning Paris Post War

1 See Serge Guilbaut (ed.), *Reconstructing Modernism: Art in New York, Paris and Montreal, 1945–1964*, Cambridge, Massachusetts and London 1990.

2 In Jan. 1945 Sartre, representing the journal *Combat* left to spend several months in the United States. Thirty-two articles on America for *Le Figaro* and *Combat* are listed in Michel Contat and Michel Rybalka, *Les Ecrits de Sartre*, Paris 1970, pp.117–23. See also *Les Temps Modernes*, nos.11–12, Aug.–Sept. 1946, special number on the United States, and Simone de Beauvoir *L'Amérique au jour le jour*, Paris 1948, (originally serialised in *Les Temps Modernes*).

3 Ironically, the expatriate Hélion helped his patron Albert E. Gallatin constitute an important constructivist and abstract collection in New York during the 1930s. See Pierre Arnould, 'Hélion et Gallatin, les échanges entre l'Europe et les Etats-Unis', *XXVIII International Congress of Art Historians* Berlin, July 1992 (Abstracts, pp.30–1).

4 Hélion confirmed to the author that he had seen Roger Blin's *En Attendant Godot* in Jan. 1953. See Sarah Wilson, 'Double Rhythm: Fanfare for Hélion', in *Hélion*, exh. cat., Albermarle Gallery 1987, p.11.

5 See P. Buton and L. Gervereau (eds.), *Le Couteau entre les dents*, Paris 1989, and for the American financing of *Paix et liberté*, François Fonveille-Alquier, *La Grande Peur de l'après-guerre*, Paris 1973, pp.226–8.

6 Tapié, preface to the Mathieu exhibition, Galerie Rive Droite, Paris 1954, in Vicens 1962, p.151.

7 While certainly contributing to the 'Americanisation' of Europe, the charge of C.I.A. funding for these exhibitions, promoted by republications of Eva Cockroft's inaccurate 'Abstract Expressionism, Weapon of the Cold War' (*Artforum*, vol.12, no.10, June 1974, pp.39–41) has been radically challenged by Stacy Tenenbaum, 'A Dialectical Pretzel: The New American Painting, the Museum of Modern Art and American Cultural Diplomacy', unpublished M.A. thesis, Courtauld Institute of Art, London 1992.

8 See Laurie J. Monahan, 'Cultural Cartography: American Designs at the 1964 Venice Biennale', in Guilbaut 1990, pp.369–416.

9 Robert Lebel, *Premier bilan de l'art actuel*, Paris 1953.

10 See J. Queval and J. Thevenot, *Le Télévision*, Paris 1957, and Beno Sternberg and Evelyne Sullerot, *Aspects sociaux de la radio et de la télévision*, *Confluence*, IV, Paris 1966.

11 See Pascal Ory, 'Peut-on parler d'une génération d'après-guerre?', in Patrick Marsh (ed.), *The Conscience of the French*, 1993 (forthcoming) for the periodisation problem. Regarding retrospective readings, Bernard Dorival in *Les Etapes de la nouvelle peinture contemporaine*, Paris 1944, or René Huyghe, *La Peinture française contemporaine*, Paris 1949 saw the (French) School of Paris as dominant; the painter, Georges Mathieu called the period 1944–51 'L'Offensive antigéometrique' in his memoirs, and certainly geometric abstract art was ubiquitous, leading to Charles Estienne's pamphlet: *L'Art abstrait est-il un académicisme?*, Paris 1950. The distinguished historian Pascal Ory constantly declares that Surrealism was the dominant phenomenon of the epoque (Ory, *L'Aventure culturelle française, 1945–1989*, Paris 1989, pp.134 et seq.), whilst Serge Guilbaut claims that Socialist Realism 'monopolised the discourse on art until 1953' in 'Postwar Painting Games: The Rough and the Slick', in Guilbaut 1990, p.44, ignoring the evidence of the *Paris-Paris* exh. cat., Musée national d'art moderne, Centre Georges Pompidou, Paris 1981 (re-edited 1992). This selection in itself excluded the Salon de la Jeune Peinture artists, let alone painting representative of the Parisian Salons or Ecole des Beaux-Arts norms.

12 See Yve-Alain Bois's sarcasms in 'Painting as Model', *Painting as Model*, Cambridge, Massachusetts 1990, p.246. The tradition of the philosopher writing on art continues: see Jacques Derrida's *Mémoires d'aveugle*, Paris 1990.

13 See, for example, as regards Malraux, Rosalind Krauss, 'Le Musée sans murs du postmodernisme', *Cahiers du Musée National d'Art Moderne* (Paris), nos.17–18, 1986, pp.152–8.

EXISTENTIALISM AND POST-WAR BRITISH ART

David Mellor

I Worlds to be Overturned: Authority and Contingency

'It was like a talisman'[1] said David Sylvester about the Giacometti catalogue which he encountered in 1948. That single package between card covers contained 'The Search for the Absolute' – Sartre's essay on Giacometti – the facsimile typewritten 'Letter' from the sculptor, as well as Patricia Echaurren's starkly textured photographs. These were found all together in the Pierre Matisse Gallery catalogue of Giacometti's sculptures of 1948. Passed from hand to hand between a small group of British (in fact mainly Scots) artists living in Paris at the end of the 1940s, were certain texts which reinforced their immediate encounter with an existentialist-based art. For William Turnbull (fig.1), a key member of that group, who had arrived there in the autumn of 1948, a similar talisman took the form of the printed version of Sartre's 1946 lecture, 'Is Existentialism a Humanism?'; it was and remained, he said, 'very important to me'.[2]

For Eduardo Paolozzi, Nigel Henderson and Turnbull (that mix of ex-bomber pilots and radically disenchanted Slade students, supplemented by the presence in Paris of the young critic David Sylvester, all marginal to the English art establishment) Sartre's writing decisively corroded the 'conventionalised hierarchies of merit that

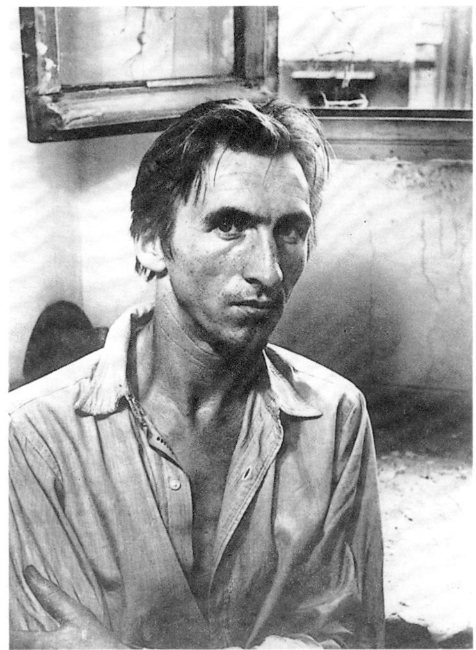

fig.1 William Turnbull, Paris 1949

structured what passed for British art'.[3] As Turnbull read 'Is Existentialism a Humanism?' he found electrifying Sartre's example of a painter freed from *a priori* rules as an allegory of existentialism: 'moral choice is comparable to the construction of a work of art . . . As everyone knows there is no pre-defined picture for him to make . . . the picture that ought to be made is precisely that which he will have made. As everyone knows, there are no aesthetic values *a priori*, but there are values which will appear in due course.'[4] Not only did such a text suggest a weapon for Turnbull in his struggle against 'that habitual English refusal to talk about ideas',[5] but chiefly it indicated the transvaluation of process and contingency in the production of art: Sartre was fundamentally re-orientating for him: 'I began to make a piece of sculpture to find out what a piece of sculpture should be like.'[6]

Such a creation of meaning and value was also profoundly liberating in terms of the seeming impossibility of surpassing Picasso. Across the West the anxiety surrounding Picasso's influence[7] proved a dispiriting blockage and nowhere more so than in London where the Neo-Romantic painter John Minton confided to John Moynihan: 'After Matisse and Picasso, there is nothing more to be done'[8]; here was an overwhelming, stifling paternal authority within modernism which few chose to dissent from. Yet for Turnbull, as he made his first dangling plaster constructions in 1949, the *a priori* claims of Cubist space were to be mistrusted: it was 'a ready made language and a ready made space which might suffocate you. The question was, did you become a second-hand merchant of space?'[9] Others, over the next decade, would also refuse this position of belatedly coming after Picasso and contrarily try to establish a constantly renewed but uncertain personal criteria of authenticity according to existential modes. One was the Royal College of Art action painter and student of Minton's, William Green. Utilising the central existential given of contingency, Green set out in 1955–6 with the chance-driven examples of Georges Mathieu and Jackson Pollock, to disprove that 'Picasso's the limit and that nothing can happen after him'.[10] The citation and deletion of conventionally received authority surfaced, too, in Sylvester's contemporary reading of Francis Bacon's iconography of disaster catching up with the paternal – 'Men seated alone . . . "men of distinction", father figures'.[11] (However, this new sensibility, elaborated first around Paolozzi, Turnbull and Sylvester, then developed by Slade painters such as Victor Willing and Michael Andrews, was unanimous in electing Giacometti as the new, but ambivalent father who could be found, Cézanne-like in Sartre's reading, to be continually disavowing this position through his systematic incertitude).

'To trade continually in the accidental is hazardous; to plan accidents, to make them happen, is a sort of artistic insincerity',[12] wrote Basil Taylor in 1955, taking Willing to task for making paintings 'without a consistent or secure method of forming anything' for his first one-man show at the Hanover Gallery.[13] Willing had violated an unacknowledged criterion then operative in British art, which Bernard Cohen has subsequently called 'the major (pseudo-) issue of stylistic consistency'.[14] Regularity and sincerity offered a predictable factor in the machinery of the rule-bound gentility of certain pedagogic and institutional practices: eliciting the world of the accidental was disruptive. If Willing's spattered runners invited thoughts about contingency, they did so in relation to Bacon's protocols of chance and paint. He was the super opportunist (in Willing's terms) of the accidental: he stood, with Giacometti, as the dominant figure in this climate of existentialist related art that was generated in London by the early 1950s. Bacon gave the contingency of paint and painting a paramount position in his art: 'I feel that anything I've ever liked at all has been the result of an accident on which I have been able to work.'[15]

At this time, in the early 1950s, Paolozzi became close to Bacon and pursued his own experiments to instate chance with a primary role, particularly in his silkscreens of 1950–2 (fig.2). His screen-printer, Anton Ehrenzweig, recalled that they 'could be overprinted on top of each other in almost any position. Paolozzi printed rolls of ceiling paper in ever varying overprints. He left it to the workman who were papering the ceiling[16] to put up the printed rolls according to chance.'[17] These married the still potent residue of Surrealist *hasard* with organic designs that were internally organised by a device Sylvester had identified as an anti-symmetrical, all-over, 'a-focal' compositional procedure inaugurated in the late works of Paul Klee. Sylvester's important essay 'Auguries of Experience',[18] published in the 'Sublime' issue of the New York vanguard magazine *Tiger's Eye* in 1948 (after it had been turned down by various London based magazines[19]) extended – along phenomenological lines – an account of the spectator's vital existential actions in empathising with Klee's paintings. It was significant that Maurice Merleau-Ponty, author of the key study *Phenomenology of Perception* (1945) commissioned Sylvester, who was in Paris for most of the time between 1947 and 1950, to expand his article for *Les Temps Modernes*, where it appeared in January 1951. (What is also striking, in evaluating the dissemination of existentialist related art and theory, is the circuit of vanguard writing that Sylvester's article passed through in New York and Paris, while failing to appear in London: a similar circuit of appreciation and interest attending the Pierre Matisse Gallery's New York catalogue of Giacometti.

II Infra-Human: Pessimism and Violence

Klee's active minimal organisms were re-contextualised by the frame of existentialism: in his acid study *The Writer and the Absolute* (1952), Wyndham Lewis yoked Klee's elemental spaces to 'Heidegger's "despair" and "anguish", [and] . . . Camus' moronic little sleepwalking killers'.[20] The existential universe held at premium neither rank nor privileged humanist meaning – especially not that of the British nature romanticism of the 1940s – but instead appeared as a field of organic endlessness, denuded of transcendence. Within the expatriate circle of ex-Slade students in Paris, this implication seems first to have been realised by Paolozzi. 'He educated me',[21] was Sylvester's later tribute to the sculptor, who produced plaster and wax reliefs of 'insects, leaves and aquatic

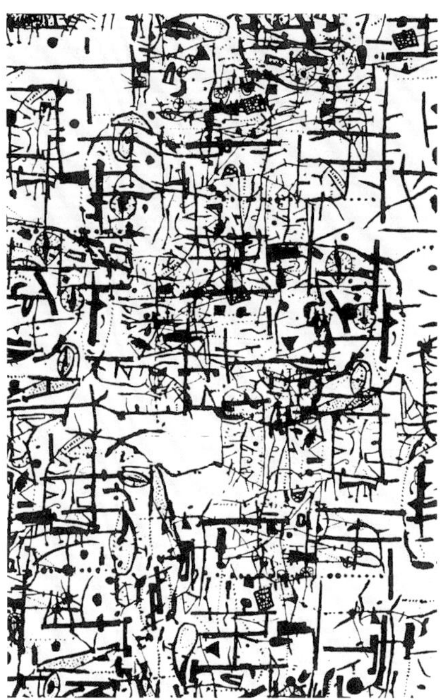

fig.2 Eduardo Paolozzi **Silkscreen Design** 1951

imagery',[22] which he first exhibited at the Mayor Gallery in London in May 1949, and then at Galerie Maeght in Paris in October as part of the group Les Mains Eblouies. The Mayor show of bas-reliefs announced an infra-human, submarine and mutated iconography which would become consensual to avant-garde British sculpture (and became, perhaps, its unique selling point internationally) in the 1950s. There was, claimed J.P. Hodin, presenting contemporary British sculpture to an Indian audience in 1953 'a straight ideological line between the insect forms of Reg Butler's work, certain ideas of Masson, Matta, Klee . . . and Franz Kafka's short story *The Metamorphosis*.[23] Sylvester returned permanently to London in 1950 and emerged as the single most important critic involved in this new sensibility. Closely allied to the Hanover Gallery, Sylvester articulated a discourse of existential pathos which formed a ground for construing the works of Butler, Bacon, Turnbull and Paolozzi. A covert nest of insects mimicking humans (again late, fugitive, Surrealist elements of Matta, Max Ernst and André Masson) was uncovered by Sylvester in his catalogue essay introducing Butler at the Hanover in July 1949: 'Beings which ridicule the human race no more and no less than it deserves . . . Beings affirming the tragic absurdity of existence.'[24] This motif of the affirmation of life in the face of the absurd draws upon that other major influence from existential thought, the writings of Albert Camus. These were, if anything, more significant to British artists – Turnbull again, and the young Bernard Cohen – than those of Sartre.

Perhaps Sylvester's most poetic text from this period is that which introduced both Turnbull and Paolozzi in their exhibition at the Hanover during February and March 1950. Here their sculptures were located phenomenologically, as 'worlds' to be entered by the viewer – Turnbull's 'Aquarium' had previously been placed across the doorway of his Montparnasse apartment so that the unwary visitor would literally come into contact with it. Sylvester populated the sculptors' worlds with those dispersed, existential organisms he had detected in Klee: 'It is as if they are the germs of being, aspiring to grow.'[25] They were to be activated by the spectator, entering 'like a bird among the branches or . . . swim[ming] underwater among the inhabitants, mobile or stationary of the sea'.[26] Existentialist related art redefined the body, casting it into unexpected envelopes of being and action, something Sylvester recognised when he hailed the 'fluid space'[27] of post-Cubism that was generated in Klee's paintings.

Swimming estranged the customs of gravity for Turnbull, but a more traditionally pessimistic version of piscine iconography surfaced in Herbert Read's appropriation of T.S. Eliot's *Love Song of J. Arthur Prufrock* for the British Venice Biennale entry of 1952. Turnbull, Paolozzi, Butler and other sculptors were described as transmitters of collective anxiety, their works scuttling, as in Prufrock's fantasy, like a crab's claws along the ocean bed. Read's 'Geometry of Fear' aesthetic coupled vitalism with Eliot's repertory of guilt and spiritual bleakness; factors which had led Eliot's verse and drama to enjoy unparalleled prestige in the new climate of late 1940s cultural anxiety. (That Gerald Wilde – as early as 1944, in his abstract expressionist illustrations to *Rhapsody on a Windy Night*[28] – together with Bernard Cohen, in his 'The Waste Land' painting of 1952, together with Francis Bacon, all quarried T.S. Eliot's distinctively conservative anxieties of physical disgust and urban horror as paradigms of 'extreme situations' is significant.) A new language of criticism began to circulate in London; one adapting to existential commonplaces but nuanced by previous, more elderly literary structures. Denys Sutton was such a critic; ascribing Hans Hartung with an affective romantic vocabulary which parasitised existential thought. Thus Sartrian 'anguish', with its Heideggerian legacy, reappeared crassly and Byronicly: as Sutton wrote, Hartung's painting 'throbs with fire and a real sense of conquest. On occasion he may tend to mask his real sense of anguish behind too elegant an exterior'.[29]

The 'mortification'[30] that recurred in Herbert Read's construction of native Geometry of Fear sculpture related to a larger cultural perception of a ruinated West laid out in the wake of the Second World War and the onset of the Cold War from 1947–8. As the Second World War had begun, British observers of continental Europe's culture, such as the painter and photographer Peter Rose Pulham, presented Paris on the eve of its fall through a Neo-Romantic prism: 'Romanticism with a discord of sadness, malice and brutality has replaced the desire for a modern classicism.'[31] Given the established structures of British taste, the reception of Germaine Richier at the Hanover Gallery in 1955 was effected through linking her to native Neo-Romanticism, a development not lost on Basil Taylor: 'she should find a following in England more readily perhaps than in any other country . . . She belongs to the kind of "metaphysical" artist which we know here chiefly in the persons of Paul Nash and Graham Sutherland'[32] – otherwise said, there was a congruence in setting her alongside Bacon, Paolozzi and Moore at the Hanover. But Richier was perceived in that double register as simultaneously picturesque and filled with visceral violence. Certainly, by the mid-1950s, the 'taste for violence'[33] had become an issue at the forefront of cultural debate. Robert Melville at first gave a blanket condemnation of action painting as 'a violent, mindless exercise . . . [of] formless demonstrations to besmirch and deface'.[34] An action manner had infiltrated figuration – it was present in Willing, and arguably, Bacon, too. Melville accounted this to be a 'savage and ejaculatory'[35] tactic which turned painting into 'a neurotic branch of athletics'.[36] The iconography of the exerted, destabilised body entering new vectors

of physical suffering and mental stress was at the heart of much existential related art in London.

The lost decorous body was now a prey to violence, in certain paintings by Bacon, Willing and Michael Andrews in the early 1950s. Bernard Cohen, then a student at the Slade, felt that this iconography of catastrophic 'violence in the street' belonged to an English illustrative tradition, 'like Arthur Rackham, except it's not fairies but the moment of violence itself, a camera shutter view of existentialism'.[37] Cohen's preference was equally grounded in Camus's model of the free and absurd predicament of man; but instead of the moment of gratuitous violence (as in the then universal favourite of British artists, *The Outsider*, 1942), Cohen was to seek a moment of pictorial production 'which occurred for the artist as a man alone, without history, without prejudice, with eyes open'.[38]

The endless restartings of his task for Sisyphus in Camus's *Myth of Sisyphus* (1942) were later to provoke some of Cohen's most crucial paintings, those endless repetitions of sprayed trajectories that marked the repetitions of infinite human labour. These paintings belonged to that decentred, anti-symmetric, 'a-focal' category which Sylvester had identified in 1948, embracing a fluid phenomenology of space. Cohen's titles played with Camus's text, as with 'In that Moment' 1965 (Tate Gallery) which echoes the point when Sisyphus, faced with the inevitable, rolling return of the rock to its starting position, considers his absurd fate, 'At that subtle moment . . . One must imagine Sisyphus happy'.[39] If, as Sartre and Camus had argued, man was nothing but the sum of his unfolding actions, then the very act of painting became central and Cohen's meditations on the artist's responsibility for each endless trace are one of the singular monuments of British post-war painting in relation to existentialism. As Cohen began to theorise the 'burden' of the painter (equivalent to Sisyphus's happy but appalling task) it seemed to him a consequence of the 'nuclear truce' of the Cold War: by 1951 the Soviets had acquired atomic weapons, following this, Cohen thought; 'Either there would be a war and we would all be dead or, for the first time in history there wouldn't be one and we would be faced with the burden of thirty to forty years of creative life . . . we artists were now to live the life of Sisyphus.'[40]

The image of catastrophe, the 'chic of contemporary *désespoir*,[41] still lurked, as John Minton apostrophised mid-decade Kitchen Sink painting by Bratby, Middleditch and Smith in 1955: 'Doom being in and Hope being out . . . the atomic theme is unravelled: the existentialist railway station to which there is no more arrival.'[42] Minton's anxiety in the face of the impossible task of making painting after Picasso was matched by his fears of a nihilist action-based art of which he saw the rise in 1956, whose protocols he rounded on in his last RCA Painting School Sketch Club in December that year, just prior to his suicide.[43] In those last few months of his life Minton began to paint an ambitious contemporary history painting of one of the key figures of an emerging pop existentialism, the film actor James Dean. The Italianate scenography of this unfinished painting, 'Composition: The Death of James Dean' (Tate Gallery), together with its neo-baroque style and the Deposition grouping in the manner of Bernard Buffet, rhymed with Wyndham Lewis's perception of Camus as an exponent of 'classical mediterranean pessimism'.[44] Camus himself had, in the moment of his first reception in Britain in the late 1940s, been framed by a nativist desire to represent him as 'blood-boltered' Jacobean, since (another echo of Eliot's influence here) like Webster, 'Camus is much obsessed by death'.[45]

A veritable sub-genre of existentially charged car crash paintings developed amongst painting students at the Royal College of Art during the late 1950s and into the following decade. Tony Messenger won enormous press attention at the *Young Contemporaries* exhibition at the RBA Galleries at the beginning of 1958 with his '22nd September 1955' (fig.3), another portrayal of Dean's violent death, in an oil-on-board collision of Richard Deibenkorn's and John Bratby's painting styles: while Norman Toynton's 'Death of Albert Camus' 1963 (artist's collection) was executed in a Bacon-esque rendition of the writer's fatal road crash in 1960.

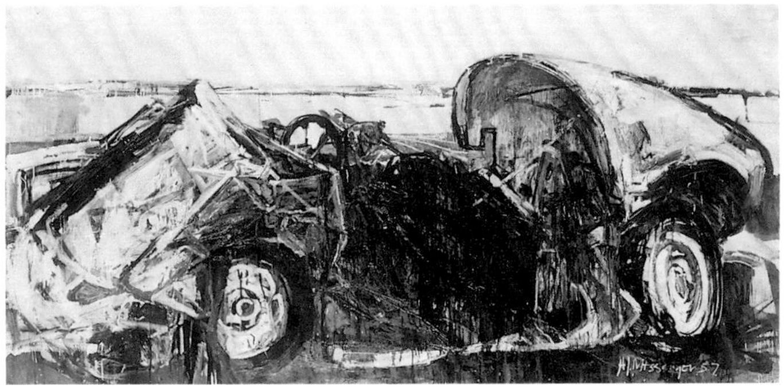

fig.3 Tony Messenger **22nd September 1955** 1958 Oil on board
Private Collection

III A World without Clocks

If a text existed for these memorial paintings it might have been found in Willing's essays, his existential manifesto, 'Travel by Bus' (1954),[46] and his discussion of Jackson Pollock, 'Thoughts after a Car Crash'.[47] The elision of high performance car racing and the act of painting itself is performed by Willing in his edgy and chancy 'Travel by Bus': 'Finally one is always alone, like a driver in a dangerous and delicious race against time with anything around the corner.'[48] The prestige of the car-racer as existentialist hero was immense: just as Willing had represented Pollock as an artist who 'preferred conversation about cars'[49] to that of art, so the action painter William Green was presented, at the time of his 1958 New Vision Centre exhibition, in anti-heroic Beat terms as a motor-infatuated drag-racer who also painted: 'Rather than museum bound he'll be around the breaker's yards. Fingering the surface rust on Buick chrome. Slanging with the grease monkeys ... With an unquelled streak he handles a drag with unhesitant force ... and still has time for long studio workouts.'[50]

Willing imagined the car race as an allegory of the painter's race with time. Disaster was the work of time in endless, Sisyphean repetitions during the 'subtle moments' of Stanley Kubrick's 1955 film *The Killing* – a cult object to the action-painting generation of 1955 at the RCA composed of Green, Dick Smith, Michael Chalk and John Edkins. Its creeping incremental moments of catastrophe seemed to ring in Sylvester's extraordinary commentary on Bacon's painting that was published in 1957; a text couched partially in suspense and thriller mode. This was apt for an Anglo-Saxon existentialist culture that canonised the private detective and the cowboy gunman in its avant-garde magazines *Horizon*,[51] and its successor, *Encounter*.[52] 'There are some', began Sylvester ventri-loquising Peter Lorre as Kierkegaard, 'to whom it is happening now, some who will be taken unawares, some who want to be ravished by disaster ... some who wait and dream about their wreck'.[53] In this view, in the confined Sartrean spaces implied by the title 'In Camera', the body was to be displayed in a seizure of being – in Heidegger's words, 'thrown into the world'. Michael Andrews had already marked Bacon's methods in this respect, particularly in his painting 'A Man who Suddenly Fell Over' 1952 (fig.4) which deals with a middle-aged male figure literally being 'thrown into the world' – losing balance in the street and toppling over, attended by a screaming woman. As such the painting belongs to that major contemporary thematic of illustrating the phenomenology of the body unsettled in space, barely coping with gravity and beset by implacable forces (as with Anthony Caro's

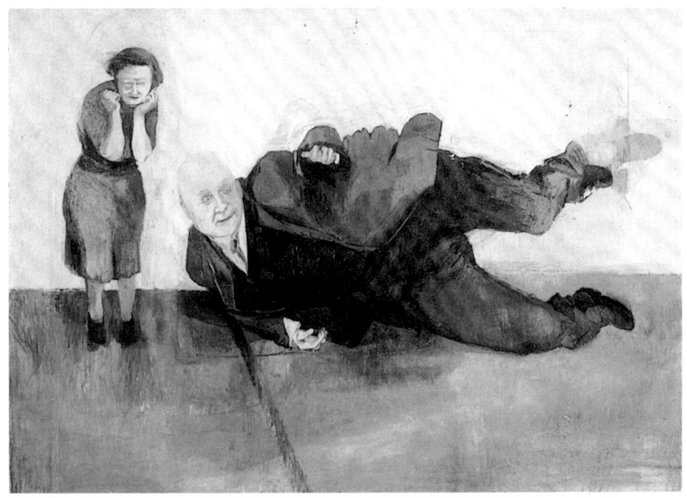

fig.4 Michael Andrews **A Man who Suddenly Fell Over** 1952 Oil on board
Tate Gallery

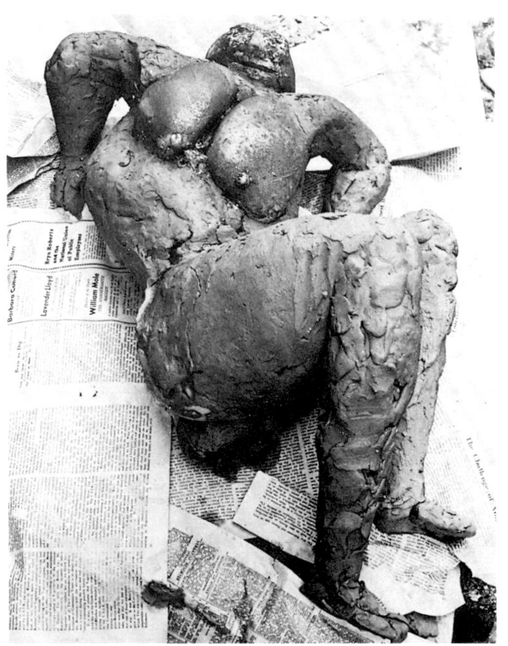

fig.5 Anthony Caro **Woman Waking Up** 1955 Bronze
Arts Council of Great Britain

grounded female figures of 1955, fig.5). 'It's a catastrophe' wrote Michael Andrews, six years after the painting's completion. 'It's about the complete upsetting of someone's . . . equilibrium'.[54]

Apart from the instant notation of embarrassment registered by the man in relation to his disturbed bulk, Andrews suppressed any itemisation of a narrative situation; the falling man and screaming woman are marooned from time, space and milieu. The notion of a basic minimum depiction of human life threaded through existentialist writing and drama: narrative becomes acutely attenuated in Sartre's *In Camera*, which had been first directed by Peter Brook in London in the summer of 1946.[55] This was equally the case in Beckett's *Waiting for Godot* in 1955. Narrative was suspect and Andrews became fond of Beckett's refusal, contained in his phrase 'there's always an excess of circumstance'.[56] Bacon, with his dread of the 'boring' and of any *a priori* meaning that would intrude between the spectator's nervous system and the painting, was a vital influence on Andrews in 1951–2. For Sylvester, Bacon's denial of narrative[57] summoned the memorable description found in his essay 'In Camera' where Bacon's topic is represented as 'somebody seen in a fleeting moment in a world without clocks'.[58] This Schopenhauerian world of beings as objects plucked out of time could even be superimposed upon that heavily sedimented British cultural structure, the urban documentary-drama. An Italian student at the Slade, Lorenza Mazzetti, directed a low-budget film *Together* in the East End of London in the early summer of 1955. Paolozzi and Andrews were cast by her as 'two deaf and dumb labourers in the London Docks'[59] (fig.6), Andrews already having acted for her in a film she had shot at the Slade in 1952 of Kafka's *Metamorphosis*. This stigmatised duo move around in an *art brut* milieu of bleak textures and graffiti, an urban limbo of non-communication. Mazzetti had deliberately set out to make a minimal, stasis-narrative; as she said, 'It was difficult to write as I did not want anything happening in the story'.[60]

Another 'documentary' locus of existentialist influence in London were the street photographs of Nigel Henderson and Roger Mayne. Henderson, a close friend of Turnbull and Paolozzi, had visited Paris for periods in the late 1940s, meeting Giacometti and Henri Cartier-Bresson, another who incarnated the shift from Surrealism to existential discourses of the problematic immediate world and actions within it. In 1951 Cartier-Bresson was commissioned by the London picture magazine, *Illustrated*, to photograph around the East End where Henderson lived (with Paolozzi as temporary lodger on his return from Paris), in Bethnal Green (fig.7). The battered urban spectacle of a post-war London, which Cartier-Bresson represented, was becoming a backdrop for 'extreme-situation'[61] films that united post-war Italian Neo-Realism with excessive, violent versions of traditional crime narratives, such as Jules Dassin's *Night and the City* (1950). Henderson steered Cartier-Bresson away from his most 'picturesque' of *brut* locations (select graffiti, vernacular shop window decorations). It was not so much the tissue of urban textures and organisms (which fascinated the emerging East End Brutalist grouping of Alison and Peter Smithson, Paolozzi and Henderson, and was to culminate in their minimal existence enclosure, the 'Patio and Pavilion' at the *This is Tomorrow* exhibition at the Whitechapel Art Gallery in 1956) – it was also the chance arrangements of street-life which engaged Cartier Bresson. Two years later he drew together many of his photographs in the volume *Images à la sauvette*, published in London and New York as *The Decisive Moment*. An existential rhetoric of poised instants, of

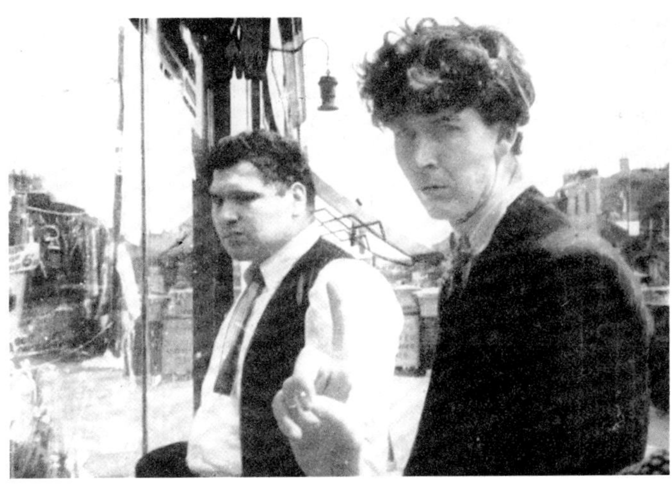

fig.6 Eduardo Paolozzi and Michael Andrews in a scene from *Together* 1955

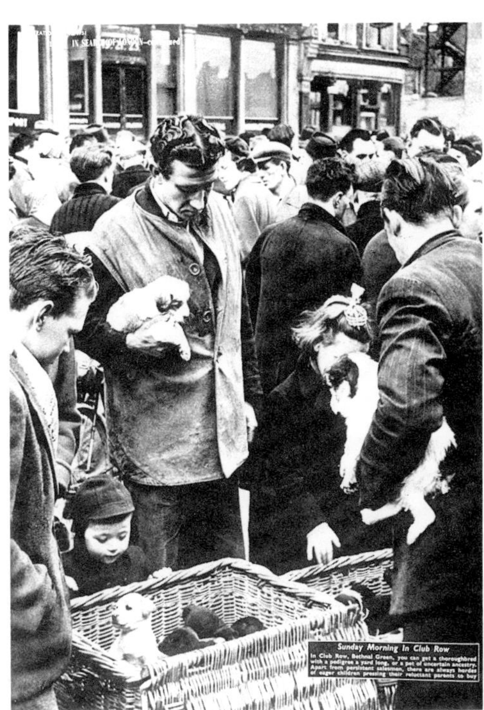

fig.7 Henri Cartier-Bresson, Club Row, Bethnal Green, *Illustrated*, 12 May 1951, p.16

hasards, risks, and of the necessary absolute authenticity of situations coloured the text Cartier-Bresson wrote to accompany his photographs. This rhetoric was entering circulation across a wider horizon of visual representations. Michael Middleton greeted Sylvester's Arts Council Giacometti exhibition in the summer of 1955 with a description of the sculptures: 'They tremble, these extraordinary figures, on the brink of the passing moment.'[62]

IV Exchanging Glances

The motif of existential choosing (when to press the shutter), the instant in time – the brink – of decision when the human act took place, preoccupied photographers such as Roger Mayne and sculptors like Kenneth Armitage. The street was the stage for this concern; the street, that is, and its looks and gestures. When asked to contribute a text for Peter Selz's 1959 exhibition *New Images of Man* at the Museum of Modern Art, New York, celebrating existential humanist figuration, Armitage wrote: 'We are all involved in ceaseless and ruthless scrutiny of others and become adept in making automatic split-second assessments of everybody we meet . . . interpreting every variation of shape.'[63] This was a confrontatory, raw world of rapid ocular shocks and impacts – Baudelaire's experience of the metropolis made over into the epoch of *The Decisive Moment*. In the second half of the 1950s, in the Notting Hill streets Roger Mayne photographed places of voids learned from Cartier-Bresson, dispersed, 'a-focal' spaces populated with playing children and random scatters of young adults from white and black communities (fig.8). His children are poised for a fight, and sometimes in the aftermath of a violent act – a blow, a kick – a gender division arises; of hurt, crying girls, and young boys who stride away from the incident. But Mayne also pictured a kind of grimy out-of-doors domesticity that was more associated with Mediterranean countries – Turnbull, from Dundee, was impressed by the Parisian and South of France spectacle of a 'free life lived out of doors'.[64] Not for nothing did Colin McInnes have his characters in the novel, *Absolute Beginners* (1959), set in Notting Hill, call the district 'Napoli'. Roland Penrose, endorsing Armitage's similarly convivial sculptures of street groups such as 'Children Playing' 1953,[65] wrote: 'Their walks, their games, their dances, their common interests and their loves cement them together so that the group becomes a single multiple figure.'[66] This gave a communalist twist to that omnipresent formal tendency to produce webbed, networked compositions.

This geniality aside, in existential related art the street was the site of stares, where anyone could come under the gaze of others. Raymond Mason, the first of that group of disgruntled art students to arrive in Paris (in 1946), produced his first bas-reliefs in 1952. These concentrated on the topos of the returned urban stare, as the city looks back from a hollow-socketed young male ('Man in the Street' 1952, fig.9, and 'Place St Germain des Prés' 1953) stuck in a Parisian place, an intent semi-spook. Mason re-enacted and perhaps codified Sartre's 1948 'talisman' description of a Giacometti statue: 'In perceiving this statue of a woman of plaster, I encounter athwart her my own glance, chilled.'[67] Certainly the sub-text of the look which (phenomenologically) constitutes the body and presence was apparent to Robert Melville in the first extensive account of Francis Bacon's paintings which *Horizon*

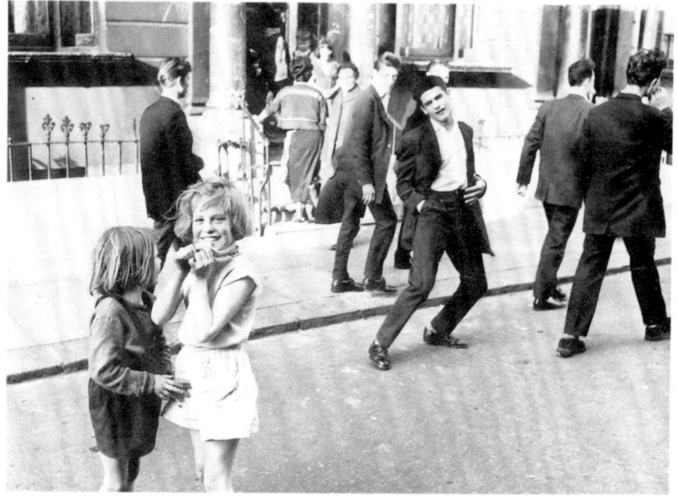

fig.8 Roger Mayne, Southam Street *c.*1957 *Trustees of the Victoria and Albert Museum*

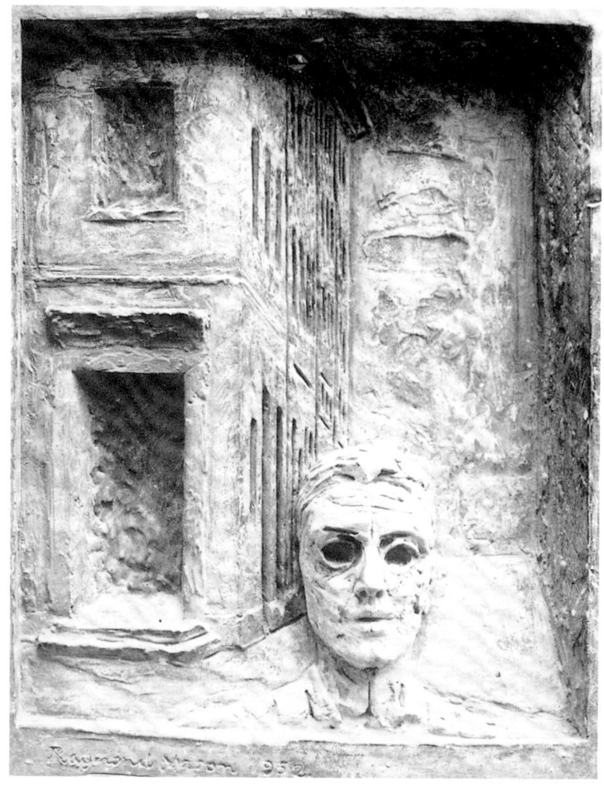

fig.9 Raymond Mason **Man in the Street** 1952 Bronze *Galerie Claude Bernard, Paris*

published in 1949: 'A man turns his head and stares out of the picture through a *pince-nez*; I am more conscious of the stare than of the eyes.'[68] Melville, a veteran of Surrealism, was fascinated in the cross-over point between the Surrealist-uncanny look and this new weighing of the body and sight: he later analysed a Derrick Greaves Beaux Arts Gallery painting according to the significances of the mutual gazes between painter and 'a rather wretched dog'.[69]

The stare of the subject and that of another seer was fundamental to Merleau-Ponty's *Phenomenology of Perception* (1945) and seems to stand over the art of this period. As late as 1964, Jacques Lacan described the intersection, in Merleau-Ponty's text, of the existential presence of the body and the look: 'the regulation of form which is governed not only by the subject's eye, but by his expectations, his movement, his grip, his muscular and visceral emotion – in short, his constitutive presence, directed in what is called his total intentionality ... the essential point – the dependence of the visible on that which places us under the eye of the seer ... this seeing to which I am subjected in an original way.'[70] Elements of this were close to the formulation which Sylvester had independently developed in his original *Tiger's Eye* article on Klee which Merleau-Ponty had so enthusiastically asked him to expand for *Les Temps Moderne*.

From military-industrial coinage and from the ever widening promotional universe, the word 'impact' gave new force to the conjoining of body and eye. The portraits of Bacon's photographer friend John Deakin, made mostly in the early 1950s, were described by Daniel Farson solely in terms of their visceral effect: 'I had never seen such photographs with such an impact. They were portraits to recoil from, brutal portraits.'[71] New thresholds in intimate scrutiny of the body were implied, and while one set of strategies looked to the direct indexical imprint – as in photography – of the body and scene, the other lay along the axis of the most severe surveillance. Giacometti and Bacon were paragons of this latter mode; so was Lucian Freud. When Freud wrote in 1959 – 'The subject must be kept under closest observation: if this is done, day and night, the subject – he, she or it – will eventually reveal the *all*',[72] he revealed metaphors of carcereal and forensic techniques, techniques of an interrogator observing through the prison peephole. The world had grown colder through observation made ominous (a topic of Orwell's *univers concentrationnaire* novel *1984* (1949) – made into a 'horror' television presentation) and presages of brutality. The photomechanical world offered gloomy portents to Minton in his jeremiad interpretation of the Kitchen Sink painters of 1955: 'the over-exposed photograph, the presage of disaster, the dull thud off-stage.'[73] But Bacon was a supreme connoisseur of the violent portents of the photopress and soon after the Algerian War had broken out in 1954, he drew Paolozzi's attention to a dark black and white photo of the aftermath of a terrorist bombing in *Paris Match*, saying, 'It's hard to know what's shadow and what's blood'.[74] The doings of the Notting Hill serial killer, Reginald Christie, who had been arrested in 1953 (fig.10), were a point of fascination and fixation for writers and artists in that particular part of London. A sinister pall lay over the shabby streets of North Kensington. For one of those residents, Colin Wilson, the populariser of existential thought with his study *The Outsider* (1956), Christie was a portent of the amoral. Apparently sociopathic, Christie was unremarkable except as a disposer of bodies: a figure from Camus and Genet, perhaps, but strongly inflected by the mythologies of English murder.

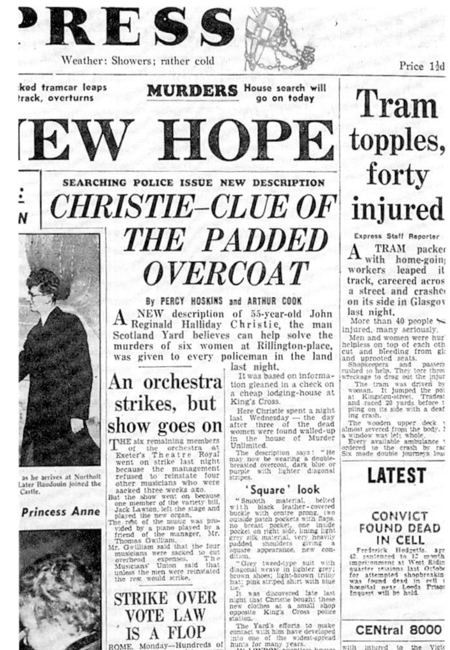

fig.10 Front page article from the *Daily Express*, 31 March 1953

V 'A Kind of Slime': Matter and the Body

Like Freud, Bacon also set out to imprison for observation the absurd human, but his tactic was to take a quasi-photographic trace, manifest as paint, which then balefully shone out of what Wyndham Lewis called his 'lamp-black monochromes'.[75] The Slade was becoming, after its cultural atrophy in the mid-1940s, a centre for the domestication of new currents of existential thought, and Bacon became an occasional visitor in the early 1950s. On 14 November 1950 he lunched with William Coldstream (for whom a separate argument can be made out for alignment with existential interests) and William Townsend. The latter recorded in his diary: 'Francis gave us some wonderful illustrations of the things which interest him, [including] a trap set out and a smear across it, a kind of slime, showing that a human being had passed through.'[76] The base, abject, secreting body is figured by Bacon in transit across a certain frame – perhaps his painted space frames – which, with Giacometti's, would order the imaginary space of British painting and sculpture for nearly two decades. The smear became an indexical sign of the skin, of organic life transferred and deposited within a particular duration in time: it was this implication which by 1954 led John Latham beyond the ranks of Bacon's epigones (Dennis Wirth-Miller, the early RCA Pop painters, David Hockney, Derek Boshier). In that year Latham made his first spray paintings: whilst their iconography began with Matta-like organisms, by 1956 they resembled miniature pre-visions of Yves Klein's corporeally decalcomanic 'Anthropometrie' series – bodies traced in time by paint deposits. For Latham the process of painting with sprays was a gesture of reflexive incorporation – 'producing paintings which would quite literally evince in their configuration, the process of their production.'[77] The sprayed painting was, for Latham, his first, 'small "time-event" ',[78] which the artist existentially chose, acted and performed, and the traces of that event remained.

Such an art was composed, in Melville's arresting phrase, of 'phantasmal tissue',[79] versions of the body metaphorised as paint that was both gross and sensational. Bacon became the demiurge creating a body: his was the distanced brush touch, which for Sylvester demonstrated 'Paint that brings flesh into being and at the same time dissolves it'.[80] For Melville a schoolboy memory of a melodramatic story of luminous paint defiling masculine hands prompted his first full account of Bacon which centred upon the issue of *matière*. Brought to the forefront of Parisian avant-garde practices by Fautrier and especially Dubuffet in 1945–6, the metaphors contained in tar, sand, and plaster were not lost on Turnbull and Paolozzi. In the existential world where metaphysics stood under deletion, a curious romance of abject material began to flourish: 'I was very suspicious about beautiful materials, but there was something about this bag of dust, because the plaster had to be all of you: you making it out of nothing and that defined the thing' said Turnbull,[81] evoking the base power of lowly material. This was certainly the assumption of Sartre in his hymn to Giacometti in 1948: 'He has chosen for himself a material without weight, the most ductile, the most perishable, the most spiritual to hand: plaster.'[82]

Like plaster, skin and bodily organs perished: in the major aesthetic reversal of poles that Dubuffet effected and which was announced in London at the Institute of Contemporary Arts in the spring of 1955 – 'Painting is matter rather than form. It is matter in the same way as the world is matter',[83] and that matter carried a pathos of human evanescence and absurdity. Dubuffet's exhibition came at the point where the young William Green, just out of Wormwood Scrubs gaol for his refusal to serve in the armed forces, was preparing to enter the RCA and begin his own insistence on the primacy of matter with his bitumen paintings. Ken Russell's legendary film of Green, *Painting an Action Painting* (1957) shows a tense,self-absorbed Beat figure in the RCA Painting School yard at South Kensington, a place of grey London urban lacerations, aided in his endeavour to spread tar and plaster dust over a hardboard surface by Tony Messenger. Green's condensation of *matière* and body was present in his large painting 'Napoleon's Chest at Moscow' (destroyed), where in the midst of black whorls an isolated tar mark indicates the broken heart of Napoleon at the point of the reversal of his potency (a painting implicating duration, event, history and the body in a way which cited the activities of Mathieu, the French action artist). Green's debt to Dubuffet was more definitely evident in his caricatural incision, on two 6 × 4 foot boards of bitumen, of the figures of the contemporary BBC TV children's puppets, Pinky and Perky (1959).

Seen in this light, Peter Blake's mid and late 1950s' drift towards a distinctively English form of representing a tattered popular culture of naive vernacular signs (e.g.'Siriol, She Devil of Naked Madness' 1957), is congruent with the diffusion and reception in London of the aims of Dubuffet's Salon de L'Art Brut. These archives were visited by Paolozzi and Henderson at the end of the 1940s and their worn tattooed surfaces run through his photography and emerge at the 'Patio and Pavilion' which he helped construct as a basic (Bethnal Green) shelter, with decorations of signs and organisms for the *This is Tomorrow* exhibition in 1956. His masterpiece, the 'Head of a Man' 1956 (fig.11), looked out of the makeshift garden shed, his skin moulderingly overlaid, like a

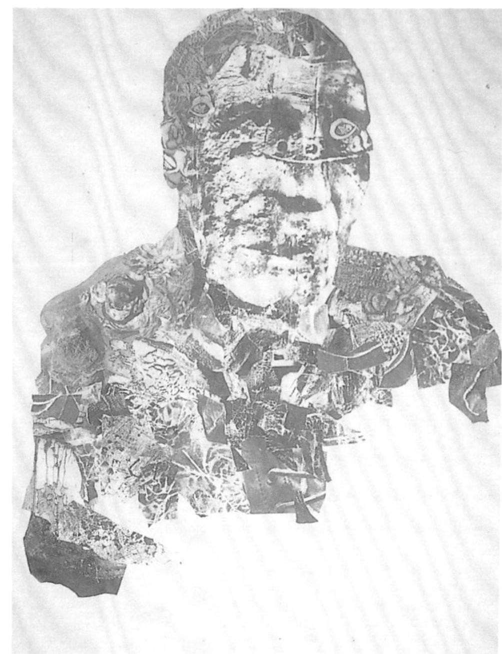

fig.11 Nigel Henderson **Head of a Man** 1956 Photograph on board *Tate Gallery*

humanoid vegetable growth from the new wave of American horror films which had colonised the London Pavilion cinema since 1954. Paolozzi developed his signs of lower organisms (the aquatic ones pressed into clay) of the late 1940s into a more thorough exploration of the epidermis as a site for the impression of a more fragmented and mechanical imagery in the mid and late 1950s. Brutalist breakages in the envelope of the final bronze skin and the disruption of the boundary between the world and the body led to a hollowing out of the internal organs of these mock authority figures which he showed at the Hanover Gallery in 1958. (This iconography of impaired skin – like that of Henderson's 'Head of a Surveyor' – was further refined from Continental artists such as Alberto Burri, and by Michael Fussell, in his Hanover Gallery exhibition in 1962.)

VI Under Pressure of the Ordinary

The 'all too human' paint as skin marred by damage and vulnerability was also embodied in the demonstrative 'ordinariness' of Kitchen Sink painting. The deathly white of the winding sheet was laid out in Jack Smith's interiors, whilst Peter Coker traded in the butcher's block as picture plane. 'On goes the paint, trowel thick in great linear strips that follow the form like livid wheals',[84] wrote Michael Middleton of Bratby's paintings, explicitly raising the conjunction of paint/skin onto the spectacular plane of pain; of damaged, broken skin in 'livid wheals'. But there was also a transcendent banality in the project of the Kitchen Sink artists: their object was the density of the world and, particularly for Bratby, what Iris Murdoch in her study of Sartre in 1953 had called, 'the

crowded superfluity of things'.[85] This was that experience of the
world which, in *The Diary of Antoine Roquentin* (1949),[86] Sartre
dubbed 'nausea' – an overwhelming, contingent, over-abundance
of substances and *matière*. Desperation might follow, at least in the
way John Berger construed the import of Bratby as a specifically
angst-filled artist at the Beaux Arts exhibition in 1954: 'Bratby
paints as though he had only one more day to live. He paints a
packet of cornflakes on a littered kitchen table as though it were
part of the Last Supper; he paints his wife as though she were
staring at him through a grille and he was never to see her
again.'[87] (It was noticeable that Berger mobilised cues that amoun-
ted to clichés from a melodramatic existentialism: the condemned
man; Christ as Buffetesque exemplary universal and timeless suf-
ferer; and the prison).

In one of these table paintings from 1954, Bratby's gaze hits the
anxious stare of Jean Cooke, his wife, across a table of commodities
and utensils, a proto-Pop cornucopia, in which gender roles are
beset by dislocation. Sylvester skilfully recognised the pictured scene
under the sign of nausea in his essay, 'The Kitchen Sink Painters',
that was published in 1954.[88] In his version, Bratby is presented as
a Roquentin-like victim of his uncategorised visual sensations of an
over-full world: 'an act of surrender to the terrible vitality of things.
The objects are piled up in a chaotic profusion.'[89] The 'every-day'
might be a stage set for the appalling absurdity of existence and acts
of violence. Around 1952 the art historian Rudolf Wittkower asked
a group of Slade students – Michael Andrews, Barry Daniels and the
Cohen brothers – whether it was possible to imagine a contemporary scene that would accommodate that paradigm of universal
tragedy, the Crucifixion. Bernard Cohen responded, to the
bafflement of Wittkower: 'By the lamp-posts',[90] that is to say, on the
city street corner, in an everyday place. Bacon had arranged such a
locale for his oil and cotton wool 'Fragment for a Crucifixion' 1950
(Stadliche van Abbe Museum, Einhoven), complete with
Giacometti-esque pedestrians and passing cars (Dubuffet's quotidian urban-scape). Yet as Cohen's work developed by the decade's

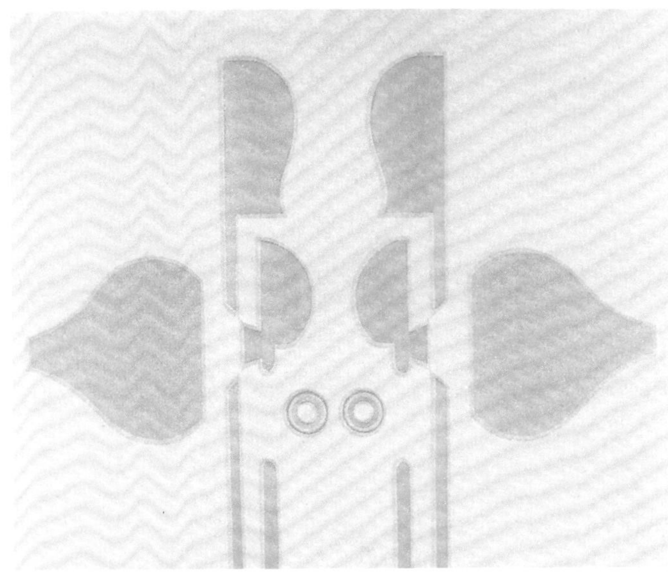

fig.12 Bernard Cohen **Sands** 1951 Oil on canvas

end, such resonant street furniture was transformed into planar
cyphers of domestic furnishings – chests of drawers, fireplaces,
architraved doorways – that all retained the severe symmetries of
crucifixion and an irreducible 'presentness', in his immediately
post-*Situation* paintings of 1961 at the RBA Galleries. After the
turning point of the *Situation* show in the summer of 1960, it
appeared that smear and slime might be relegated from the first division of pictorial languages in British art. But in the longer duration
– even by 1966, with Barry Flanagan – the abject and lowly returned. Perhaps only ordinariness – the room, the street, the flesh of
the subject's body, the dust of 'low' materials – could stand service
to signify fully in the absurd world.

NOTES

1   David Sylvester, conversation with the author, 9 Jan. 1993.
2   William Turnbull, conversation with the author, 21 Dec. 1992.
3   Ibid.
4   Jean-Paul Sartre, 'Existentialism Is a Humanism'. in William Kauffman (ed.), *Existentialism from Doestoevsky to Sartre*, New York 1956, pp.305–6.
5   Turnbull, 21 Dec. 1992.
6   Ibid.
7   Cf. Harold Bloom, *The Anxiety of Influence*, 1972.
8   Daniel Farson, *Soho in the Fifties*, 1987, p.85.
9   Turnbull, 21 Dec. 1992.
10 William Green, conversation with the author, 22 Dec. 1992.
11 David Sylvester, 'In Camera', *Encounter*, April 1957, p.22.
12 Basil Taylor, 'Art', *The Spectator*, 16 Sept. 1955, p.362.
13 Ibid.
14 Bernard Cohen, conversation with the author, 21 Dec. 1992.
15 David Sylvester, *Interviews with Francis Bacon*, 1975, p.53.
16 During the decoration of the offices of R.S. Jenkins, Fitzroy Street, in 1952.
17 Anton Ehrenzwieg, *The Hidden Order of Art*, 1967, p.116.
18 David Sylvester, 'Auguries of Experience', *Tiger's Eye*, no.6, 1948, pp.48–51.
19 Among them *Apollo, Cornhill* and, surprisingly, given its orientation towards current European thought and its role as acting as a conduit for existential literature into Britain, *Horizon*.
20 Percy Wyndham Lewis, *The Writer and the Absolute*, 1952, in R. Rosenthal (ed.), *Wyndham Lewis, A Soldier of Humour and Selected Writings*, New York 1966, p.349.
21 Sylvester, 9 Jan. 1993.
22 Robin Spencer, *Eduardo Paolozzi, Recurring Themes*, 1984, p.58.
23 J.P. Hodin, 'Contemporary British Sculpture', *The Dilemma of Being Modern*, 1956, p.147.
24 David Sylvester, 'Microcosmos of a Sculptor', *Reg Butler: Sculpture and Drawings*, exh. cat., Hanover Gallery 1949.
25 Ibid.
26 Ibid.
27 Sylvester 1948, p.49.
28 *Poetry London*, vol.2, no.10, 1945, p.96.
29 Denys Sutton, *Hans Hartung: Drawings and Paintings*, exh. cat., Hanover Gallery 1949.
30 Herbert Read, *Concise History of Modern Sculpture*, 1964, p.257.
31 Peter Rose Pulham, 'Living in Paris', *Harper's Bazaar*, 26 July 1939, p.52.
32 Basil Taylor, 'Art', *Spectator*, 14 Oct. 1955, pp.499–500.
33 Robert Melville, 'Exhibitions', *Architectural Review*, July 1955, p.53.
34 Ibid.
35 David Sylvester, *Eduardo Paolozzi and William Turnbull*, exh. cat., Hanover Gallery 1950.
36 Ibid.
37 Cohen, 21 Dec. 1992.
38 Ibid.
39 Albert Camus, 'The Myth of Sisyphus'. in Kauffman 1956, p.315.
40 Cohen, 21 Dec. 1992.
41 John Minton, 'Three Young Contemporaries', *Ark*, no.13, Spring 1955, p.14.
42 Ibid.
43 Cf. transcribed extracts from his tirade against action painting in David Mellor, *Sixties Art Scene in London*, 1993, p.28.
44 Wyndham Lewis 1952, p.299.
45 Reyner Heppenstall, 'Albert Camus and the Romantic Revolt', *Penguin New Writing*, no.34, Dec. 1948, p.104.
46 Intended for a projected Slade/RCA student magazine, *Gemini*. This was eventually published in *Victor Willing*, exh. cat., Whitechapel Art Gallery 1986, p.60.

47 *Encounter*, Oct. 1956, pp.66–8.
48 Cf. n.46, above.
49 Cf. n.47, above.
50 Michael Chalk, *William Green*, exh. cat., New Vision Centre Gallery, July 1958.
51 Cf. Albert Votaw, 'The Literature of Extreme Situations', *Horizon*, Sept. 1949, pp.145–59.
52 Cf. Robert Warshaw, 'The Gentleman with a Gun', *Encounter*, March 1954, pp.18–24.
53 Sylvester 1957, p.22.
54 Mary Chamot, Dennis Farr, and Martin Butlin, *Tate Gallery, Modern Paintings, Drawings and Sculpture*, vol.1, 1964, p.9.
55 Stephen Potter, 'Theatre', *New Statesman and Nation*, 27 July 1946, pp.63–4.
56 C. Lampert (ed.), *Michael Andrews*, exh. cat., Arts Council of Great Britain 1981, p.53.
57 'Is Denying Narrativity an Illuminating Gesture?', E.V. Alphen, *Francis Bacon and the Loss of Self*, 1992, p.21.
58 Sylvester 1957, p.22.
59 Lorenza Mazzetti, 'Making a Film', *Ark*, no.17, p.30.
60 Ibid.
61 Votaw 1949, p.145.
62 Michael Middleton, 'Art', *Spectator*, 10 June 1955, p.742.
63 Reprinted as 'Statement', in Norbert Lynton, *Kenneth Armitage*, 1962, unpag.
64 Turnbull, 21 Dec. 1992.
65 For the first suggestion of a linkage between Armitage's vision and that of Roger Mayne. see Lynton 1962.
66 Roland Penrose, *Kenneth Armitage*, Ariswil 1960, p.6.
67 Jean-Paul Sartre, 'The Search for the Absolute', in *Alberto Giacometti: Exhibition of Sculptures, Paintings and Drawings*, exh. cat., Pierre Matisse Gallery, New York 1948, p.14.
68 Robert Melville, 'Francis Bacon', *Horizon*, Dec. 1949 – Jan. 1950, p.422.
69 Robert Melville, 'Exhibitions', *Architectural Review*, Oct. 1955, pp.263–4.
70 Jacques Lacan, *The Four Fundamentals of Pyschoanalysis*, 1975, pp.72–3.
71 Daniel Farson, *Out of Step*, 1974, p.70.
72 Lucian Freud, 'Some Thoughts on Painting', *Encounter*, July 1959, p.24.
73 Minton 1955, p.14.
74 Sir Eduardo Paolozzi in conversation with the author, 20 Sept. 1991.
75 Percy Wyndham Lewis, 'Round the Galleries', *Listener*, 12 May 1949, p.811.
76 *The Townsend Journals*, ed. A. Forge, 1976, p.92. Notice that Townsend's report of Bacon's verbal figuring of the human as abject slime predates Bacon's own statement to this effect in 1955, in *The New Decade: 22 European Painters and Sculptors*, exh. cat., Museum of Modern Art, New York 1955, p.63.
77 Roberta Brooks and John Stezaker, *State of Mind*, exh. cat., Stadtische Kunsthalle, Düsseldorf 1975, p.25.
78 Ibid.
79 Melville, 1949–50, p.419.
80 Sylvester 1957, p.22.
81 William Turnbull, 21 Dec. 1992.
82 Sartre 1948, p.5.
83 Georges Limbour, *Let the Material Speak for Itself, Georges Dubuffet*, exh. cat., Institute of Contemporary Art 1955, unpag.
84 Michael Middleton, 'Art', *The Spectator*, 1 Oct. 1954, p.390.
85 Iris Murdoch, *Sartre*, 1953, p.33.
86 *La Nauseé* was first published under this title in Britain.
87 John Berger, 'John Bratby', *New Statesman and Nation*, 25 Sept. 1954, p.358.
88 David Sylvester, 'The Kitchen Sink Painters', *Encounter*, Dec. 1954, p.63.
89 Ibid.
90 Cohen, 21 Dec. 1992.

THE ARTISTS

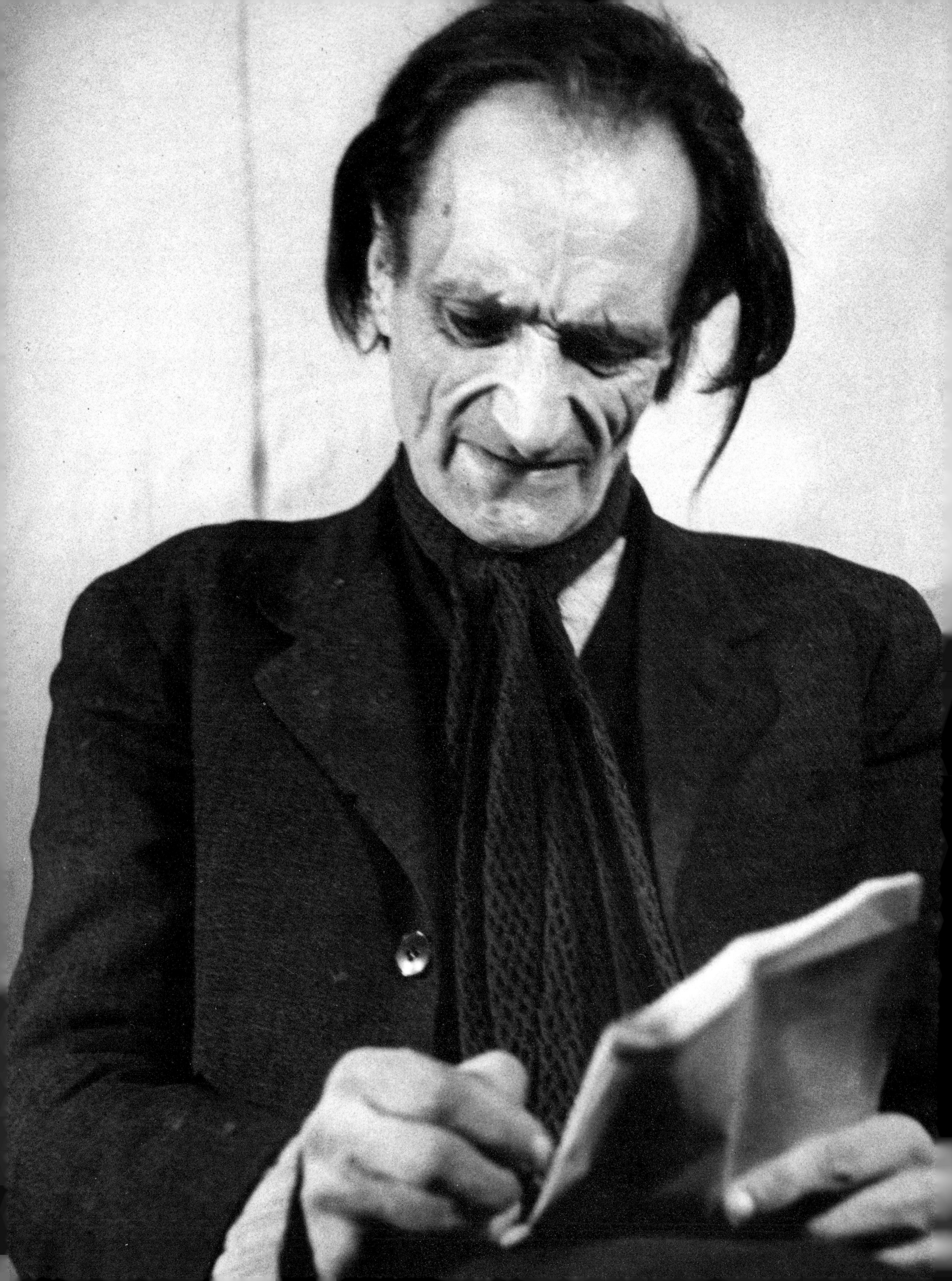

Antonin Artaud (1896–1948)

Actor, director, writer, critic, designer, theatrical innovator, visionary, mystic and madman, Antonin Artaud was also an artist. Towards the end of his life his creative output was dominated increasingly by drawing – as if in answer to an inner need as he emerged from the stranglehold of insanity and asylum after the war. John Dequeker's description of Artaud at work on a self-portrait shortly before his death in 1948, evokes the emotional power of Artaud's relentless and tormented attack on the paper:

> he had drawn the abstract outlines of a face, and in these barely sketched traits, where he had placed black blotches, apparitions of the future, with no mirror for reflection, I saw him create his double, as though in a crucible at the price of nameless torture and cruelty. He worked with rage, broke crayon after crayon, enduring the throes of his own exorcism. Amid cries and the most feverish poems which ever emanated from the spleen of a tortured being, he cursed and cast spells on a nation of obstinate worms; when, suddenly taking on reality, his face appeared.[1]

Artaud had been interested in art for decades. His earliest extant drawings date from 1915 when he was undergoing his first experience of the psychological malaise that was to affect him, with varying degrees of intensity, for the whole of his adult life. Artaud's mental stability was severely impaired by his brief military service during the First World War, which precipitated in him a mystical crisis, a deepening depression and violent mood swings. At the same time he was subjected to unbearable headaches, possibly connected with a childhood episode of meningitis, which led to a lifelong and often debilitating drug dependency. As part of the treatment and therapy offered by Dr Dardel at Neufchâtel in Switzerland, Artaud was encouraged to draw seriously for the first time. He continued to do so after his move to Paris in 1920, until writing and the theatre became his dominant preoccupations. It was not until the 1940s that he began drawing again.

The impulse behind all of Artaud's graphic work was less aesthetic than therapeutic. Drawing was a means of confronting the burden of alienation – expressed often in his writings as a fear of the void – which he experienced at times with an almost unbearable intensity. Artaud's statement in the catalogue of the only one-man show of his drawings held during his life, at the Galerie Pierre in 1947, set out his artistic credo:

> The human face is an empty face, a field of death ... the human face bears in effect a kind of perpetual death on its countenance. It is precisely up to the painter to save this face by restoring its personal features.[2]

The notion of an inner void, expressed as emptiness, fear of the abyss, death and unconsciousness, is the central theme of almost all of Artaud's writings. It was first explored in a series of letters he wrote to Jacques Rivière, then editor of *La Nouvelle Revue Française* (*NRF*), in 1923 and 1924. Artaud had sent Rivière a group of his poems for consideration. The editor rejected the poems – described by Artaud as 'the shreds that I have managed to snatch from complete nothingness'[3] – largely on stylistic grounds. This prompted a correspondence which is extraordinary for the lucid way in which Artaud examines his own mental disorder, and in particular the paralytic seizures of anguish that gripped him periodically and which necessitated an enormous effort of creative will to overcome. With Artaud's full agreement the correspondence was published in the *NRF* in 1924. Artaud's liaison with Rivière and the voice given to him by the *NRF* brought him into contact with avant-garde literary and artistic circles in Paris. Until 1927 he was associated with the Surrealists.

At the same time, in the early 1920s, Artaud was studying to become an actor and also publishing reviews of art exhibitions in journals such as *Demain* and *L'Oeuvre*. His earliest writings on art are interesting primarily for their anticipation of his later belief in the primacy of expressive intensity over any notion of fidelity to reality. When, in 1934, Artaud first met the painter Balthus, it was the eroticism and violence implicit in Balthus's restrained and carefully described images that attracted him. Such ideas were developed by Artaud, not in relation to art (this only came to the fore much later) but to the theatre. In 1926 he co-founded the Alfred Jarry Theatre (with the playwright Roger Vitrac and the essayist Robert Aron). The venture was based on a notion of theatre divested of realism and logic, in which the spectator's involvement would be harnessed, not through the intellect but by touching the nerves and the senses. Artaud later went on to develop his revolutionary concept of a Theatre of Cruelty, inspired by the central place given to facial and bodily gesture by the Balinese artists, whose performances he saw at the Colonial exhibition in Paris in 1931, and in whose work the spoken word was relatively insignificant. This more extreme stance he elaborated in published essays and realised only partially in the 1935 production of his play *The Cenci*.

Artaud's belief in the need for a new form of theatre was based on a view of society that mirrored his own view of himself – that of a society sick and repressed. In Artaud's terms, cruelty 'in the sense of an appetite for life'[4] is a metaphysical concept fulfilling a therapeutic role in fusing man and life and liberating repressed areas of the unconscious. This was to be achieved through violent and irrational means employed theatrically in all dimensions: gesture, decor, sound effects and language. Artaud's new theatre was designed to stun and shock, to rivet and release. The totality and vividness of the spectacle was of fundamental importance in liberating the spectator.

Artaud's ideas and writings about the Theatre of Cruelty have been immensely influential. At the time, however, they were almost universally condemned. The 1935 production of *The Cenci* that Artaud finally managed to promote, with a set designed by Balthus, ran for only seventeen days and was a disaster with the critics.

Following the devastating failure of this venture Artaud left Paris for Mexico, hoping to find amongst the Mexican Indian tribe of the Tarahumaras an example of a primitive society whose ritual beliefs and ceremonies coincided with his own understanding of theatre. On his return to Paris, several painful and abortive attempts to give up his dependency on heroin and a thwarted love affair exacerbated his deepening mental instability and obsessive behaviour. During a visit to Ireland in 1937, from where he was convinced he would witness the end of the world, he became rapidly less able to cope, sending bizarre and often frightening letters to his friends and family in France. He was returned to France by the Irish authorities in a straitjacket and interned at Le Havre. He was thence institutionalised, at various levels of security, for the remaining decade of his life.

The letters Artaud sent from Ireland give the first indication of an interest in the symbolic and psychologically expressive power of visual effects. The writing is agitated and vigorously notated, the papers are stained and often scarred with cigarette burns. Signs, like the symbol for the female sex or the sign of the planet Venus, appear. The letters are angry, incantatory and vindictive. Artaud wrote further letters while in hospital at Ville-Evrard from 1939–43. Conditions at the institution in wartime were dreadful, and many of Artaud's letters were inspired by his overwhelming obsession with release. Finally the poet Robert Desnos arranged for his transfer to the hospital at Rodez where Dr Gaston Ferdière, the psychiatrist and poet, who was interested in Surrealism and collected psychotic art, took over responsibility for his treatment. At Rodez Artaud was subjected to a regime of electro-convulsive therapy, the practice of which was still in its infancy. He was terrified by the threat of memory loss and by the inevitable coma that followed each session. The physical and mental strain of the treatment was immense. On one occasion the shock administered induced a fall from which he sustained a broken vertebra. In a letter to Jacques Latrémolière, one of the psychiatrists at Rodez responsible for administering the shocks, Artaud wrote in desperation:

> Electric shock, Mr. Latrémolière, reduces me to despair, it takes away my memory, it dulls my mind and my heart, it turns me into someone who is absent and who knows he is absent and sees himself for weeks in pursuit of his being, like a dead man alongside a living man who is no longer himself, but who insists on the dead man being present even though he can no longer enter into him. After the last series I remained throughout the months of August and September absolutely incapable of

working, thinking, and *feeling that I was alive.* Each time it brings on those horrible splinterings of the personality which I wrote about in the correspondence with Rivière, but which at that time was a perceptual knowledge and not a living agony as with electric shock.[5]

As well as undergoing this controversial treatment, Artaud was encouraged to write and draw again. He made a very few drawings early in 1944, apparently at the suggestion of Frédéric Delanglade, a minor Surrealist painter whom Dr Ferdière was sheltering from the Nazis. More drawings followed at the beginning of 1945. At the same time Artaud began compiling his notes, now known as the 'Cahiers de Rodez' which include compositions, portraits, lists of his larger drawings often with marginal illustrations, and explanations of certain of his drawings encouraged by Ferdière. Artaud described his drawings of this period as *dessins-écrits* (nos.1, 2, 3, 6), pointing to their status between text and image. Much of their vocabulary of signs, phrases and images drew on his Mexican experiences. Skulls, coffins, guns, human limbs and sexual parts are depicted. Sexuality, dismemberment, brutality, death and destruction are clearly prevalent themes: they show Artaud's lifelong obsessions, as well as reflecting the devastating impact of his electroshock treatment. The drawings reveal Artaud's urge to find an alternative to conventional, linguistic means of expression. In his writings he was beginning to employ his own, invented language, while visitors to Rodez and later to Ivry recall his frequent and sudden self-immersion in glossolalic expression, often combined with weird dancing motions and song.

During 1945 Artaud's condition appeared to his keepers to have stabilised, and with the return of peace his contact with the outside world through visitors increased greatly. At the same time his desire for liberty became acute. Eventually his release was agreed on two conditions: that sufficient funds be found to secure his financial security, and that sheltered accommodation be found for him. The first condition was fulfilled through a fundraising committee headed by Jean Paulhan, which organised a gala performance at the Théâtre Sarah Bernhardt in June 1946 and an auction at Galerie Pierre. For the auction, the young writer Arthur Adamov collected manuscripts and works of art from many sources, including de Beauvoir and Sartre, Picasso, Michaux and Giacometti. The second condition was met when accommodation was found at a home, run by Dr Delmas, at Ivry on the outskirts of Paris. Here Artaud was able to live nourished and nurtured but free to come and go as he pleased. His financial affairs were managed first by Dubuffet (the group of drawings Dubuffet made of Artaud attests their friendship), then by Paulhan and finally by Pierre Loeb.

Briefly, until his death, Artaud became a familiar figure on the streets and in the cafés of Saint-Germain. He spent much time with Adamov (no.10), the director Roger Blin and the young poet Jacques Prevel (nos.4, 7). However he courted isolation, and spurned the renewed advances of André Breton who invited him to participate in the 1947 *International Exhibition of Surrealism* at the Galerie Maeght. He vehemently resisted association with either existentialism (according to his latest biographer[6] Artaud loathed Sartre and ignored Jean Genet) or with the nascent *Lettriste* movement.

On his return to Paris and the relative freedom of Ivry, Artaud almost completely abandoned the practice of *dessins-écrits*, instead turning to portraiture – perhaps, as his close confidante, editor and collaborator from those years Mme Paule Thévenin[7] has suggested, to please friends, perhaps because he saw in portraiture a potential means of earning cash to finance his need for drugs. His first portraits were lively and bold but largely straightforward attempts to render the face as observed. Increasingly they became the vehicle for the sustained exploration of gesture, line and (often) colour in performance which – as recalled by Dequeker (quoted above) and witnessed by Thévenin[8] – engaged the artist's whole body at times, his physical impact making an impression through four or five sheets of paper.

A notion of the image as the result of a sustained physical attack is expressed in Artaud's introduction to the catalogue of his Galerie Pierre exhibition in 1947. Here he speaks of the necessity for a style of 'barbarity and disorder', exploring 'in all the directions of accident, of possibility, of chance or of destiny'. In his seminal text on Van Gogh, also of 1947, the cathartic basis of Artaud's art is made explicit in his claim that 'No one has ever written, painted, sculpted, modelled, built, or invented except literally to get out of hell'.[9] This brilliant and angry text was prompted by Artaud's outrage on reading a review of the Van Gogh exhibition at the Orangerie by the psychiatrist, Dr Joachim Beer. Dr Beer approached Van Gogh's paintings as diagnostic indicators and through them described the artist as 'a degenerate of the type described by [Dr Valentine] Magnan'.[10] At one and the same time eulogising and identifying with Van Gogh, Artaud condemns psychiatry as the defence mechanism of a sick society against admission of its own diseased state. So-called madmen, artists such as Van Gogh, he argues, are in rebellion against society which punishes their 'superior lucidity'. The madman is 'a man who society did not want to hear and whom it prevented from uttering certain intolerable truths'. The reference to Artaud's own incarceration is not difficult to infer.

One of Artaud's last projects, written and organised while he suffered from the anal tumour that would shortly kill him, was a voice and sound performance for radio. Entitled 'To Have Done

With the Judgement of God',[11] it was an attempt to disrupt the structures of language by employing multiple voices, strange accents, rhythm, screams and silences. Like his *dessins-écrits* the text explodes with multiple images – of Christianity, Tarahumara ritual, excrement and the body, sexuality and death, the void. On the eve of the scheduled transmission the radio company cancelled the broadcast: 'just', commented Thévenin, 'as though it were a porno movie.'[12] Artaud's thoughts on Van Gogh were again vindicated.

In his defence, and in affirmation of his life's work, Artaud wrote to René Guilly only four weeks before his death on 4 March 1948:

THE DUTY
of the writer, of the poet
is not to shut himself up like a coward in a text, a
book, a magazine from which he never comes out
but on the contrary to go
into the world
    To jolt
    to attack
    the mind of the public
    otherwise
    what use is he?
And why was he born?[13]

NOTES

1 John Dequeker, 'Birth of the Image', from 'Antonin Artaud ou la santé des Poètes', *La Tour de Feu*, nos.63–4, 1959, excerpt trans. Sarah Wilson in *Aftermath*, exh. cat., Barbican Art Gallery 1982, p.122.
2 Antonin Artaud, 'Le Visage humain', *Portraits et dessins par Antonin Artaud*, exh. cat., Galerie Pierre, Paris 1947.
3 Jack Hirshman (ed.), *Artaud Anthology*, San Francisco 1965, p.8.
4 Antonin Artaud, *The Theatre and its Double*, 1938, trans. Mary C. Richards, New York 1958, p.102.
5 Susan Sontag (ed.), *Antonin Artaud, Selected Writings*, New York 1976, p.11.
6 Stephen Barber, *Antonin Artaud: Blows and Bombs*, 1993, p.11.
7 Paule Thévenin, *Antonin Artaud: Portraits et Dessins*, Paris 1968, pp.35–6.
8 Ibid., pp.36–7.
9 Antonin Artaud, 'Van Gogh, the Man Suicided by Society' (first pub. 1947), in Sontag 1976, pp.483–514.
10 John MacGregor, *The Discovery of the Art of the Insane*, Princeton 1989, p.284.
11 Discussed by Stephen Barber in 'A Foundry of the Figure, Antonin Artaud', *Artforum* (USA), vol.26, pt.1, Sept. 1987, pp.88–95.
12 Paule Thévenin, quoted by Barber 1987, p.92.
13 Letter to René Guilly, 7 Feb. 1948, in Sontag 1976, pp.483–514.

Illustration (p.64) Portrait of Antonin Artaud
1947 Photograph by Denise Colomb
© *Ministère de la Culture, France*

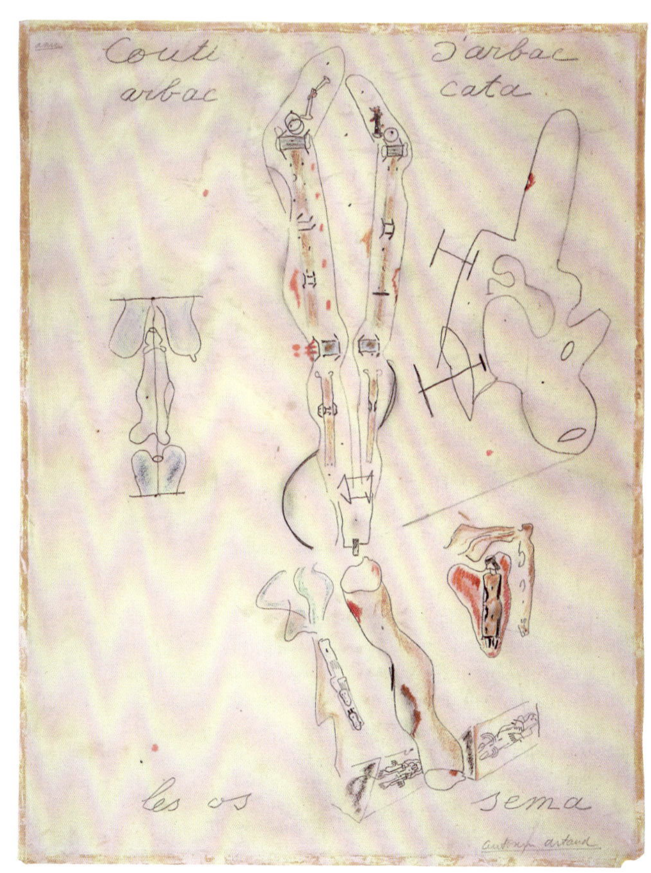

1 **Couti the Anatomy** 1945
65.4 × 50 (25¾ × 19⅝)

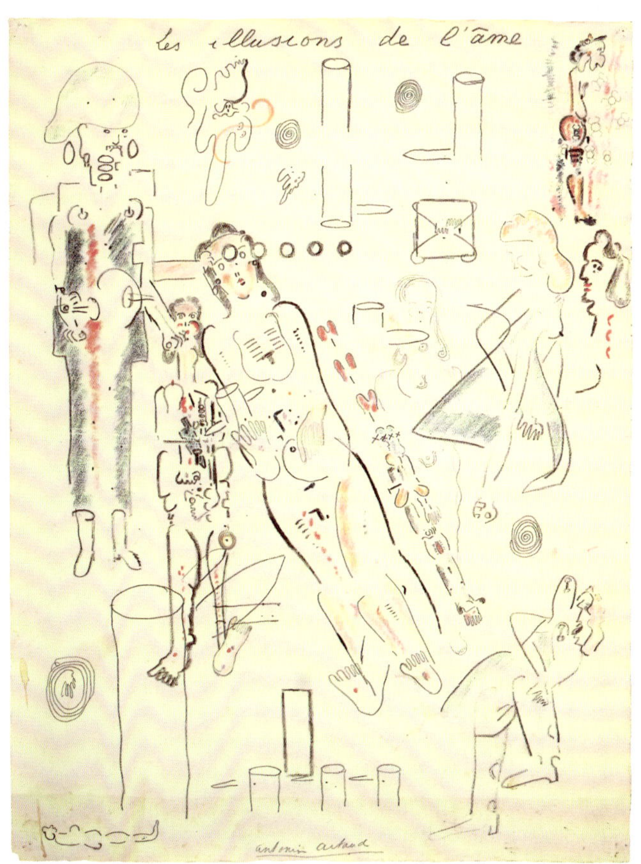

3 **The Illusions of the Soul** 1946
62.5 × 47.8 (24⅝ × 18⅞)

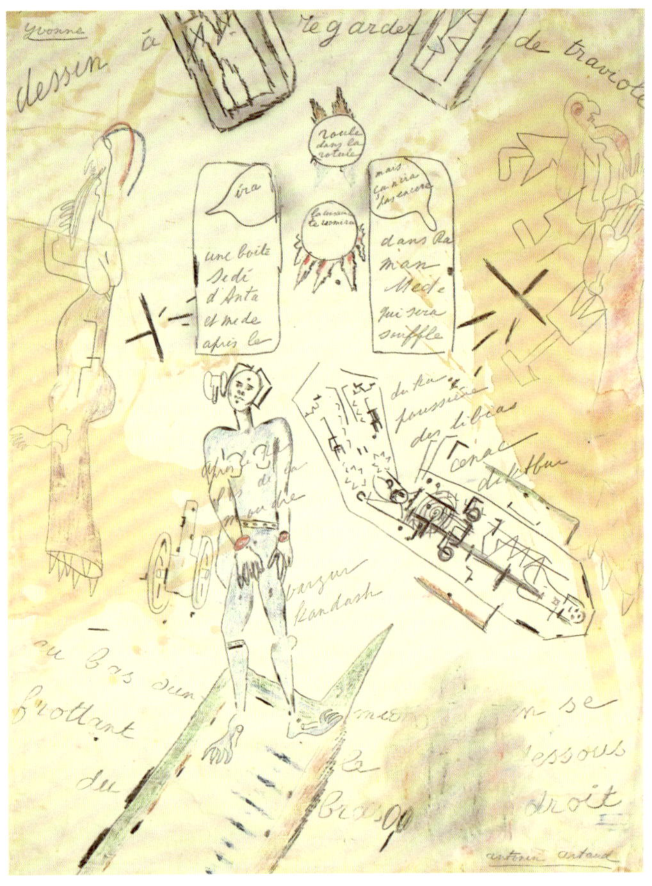

2 The Machine of Being or Drawing
to be Looked at Cockeyed 1946
64.5 × 49.6 (25⅜ × 19½)

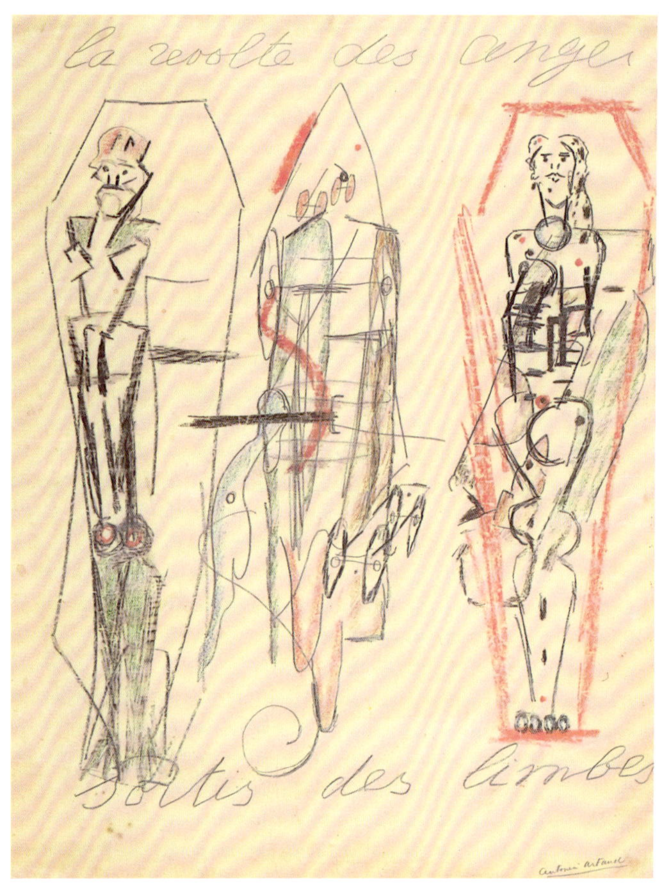

6 The Revolt of the Angels
outside Limbo 1946
65 × 49.5 (25⅝ × 19½)

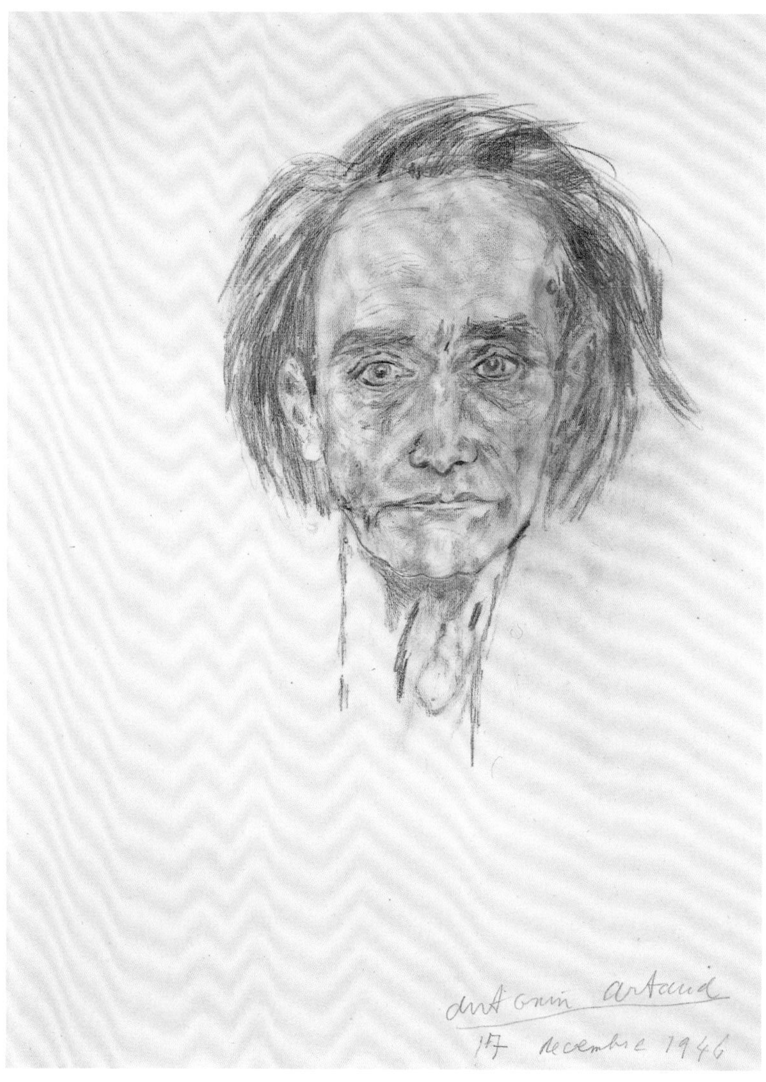

5 Self-Portrait 1946
65 × 50 ($25\frac{5}{8} \times 19\frac{5}{8}$)

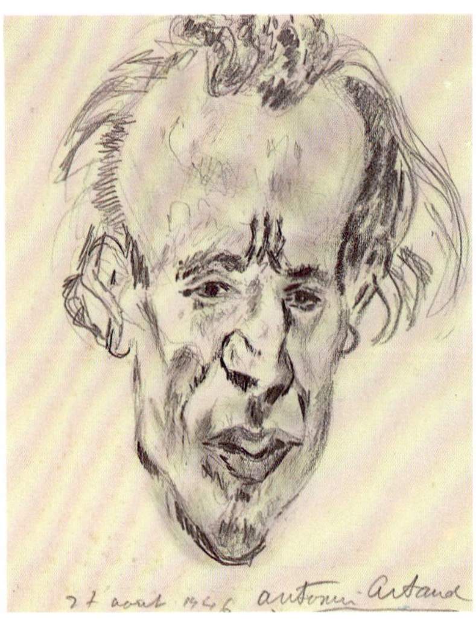

4 Portrait of Jacques Prevel 1946
$28 \times 22.5 \ (11 \times 8\frac{7}{8})$

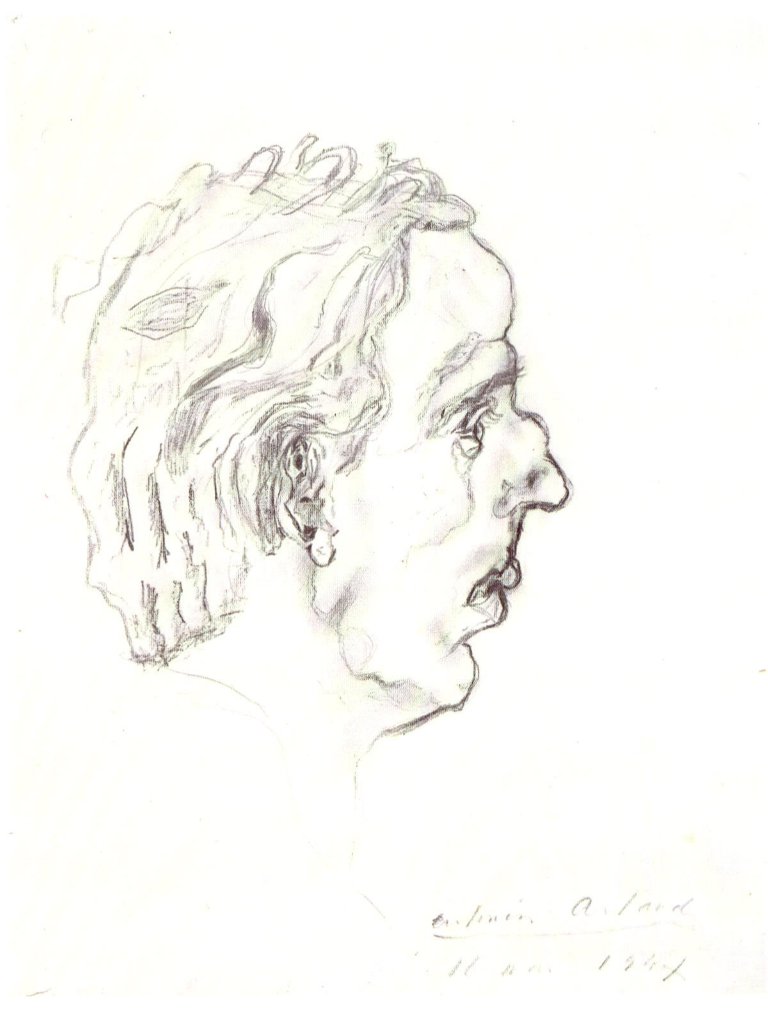

7 Portrait of Jacques Prevel (in Profile) 1947
$56.5 \times 45 \ (22\frac{1}{4} \times 17\frac{3}{4})$

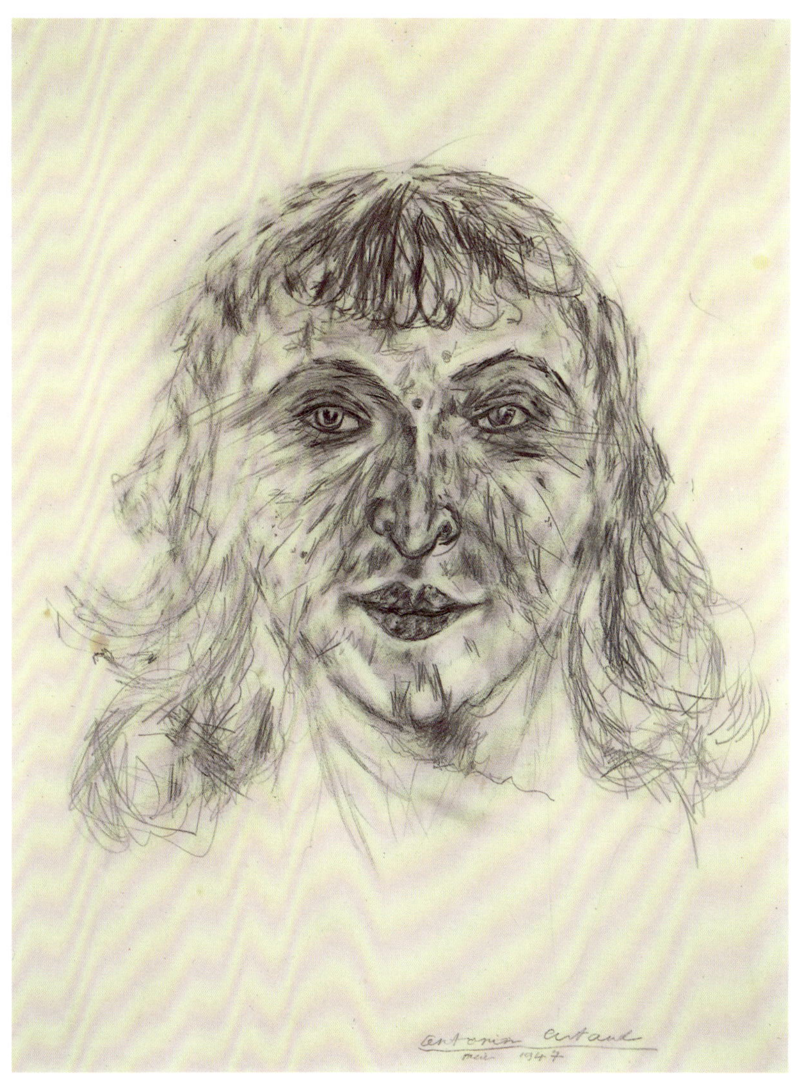

8 Portrait of Mania Oïfer 1947
$64 \times 50 \ (25\frac{1}{4} \times 19\frac{5}{8})$

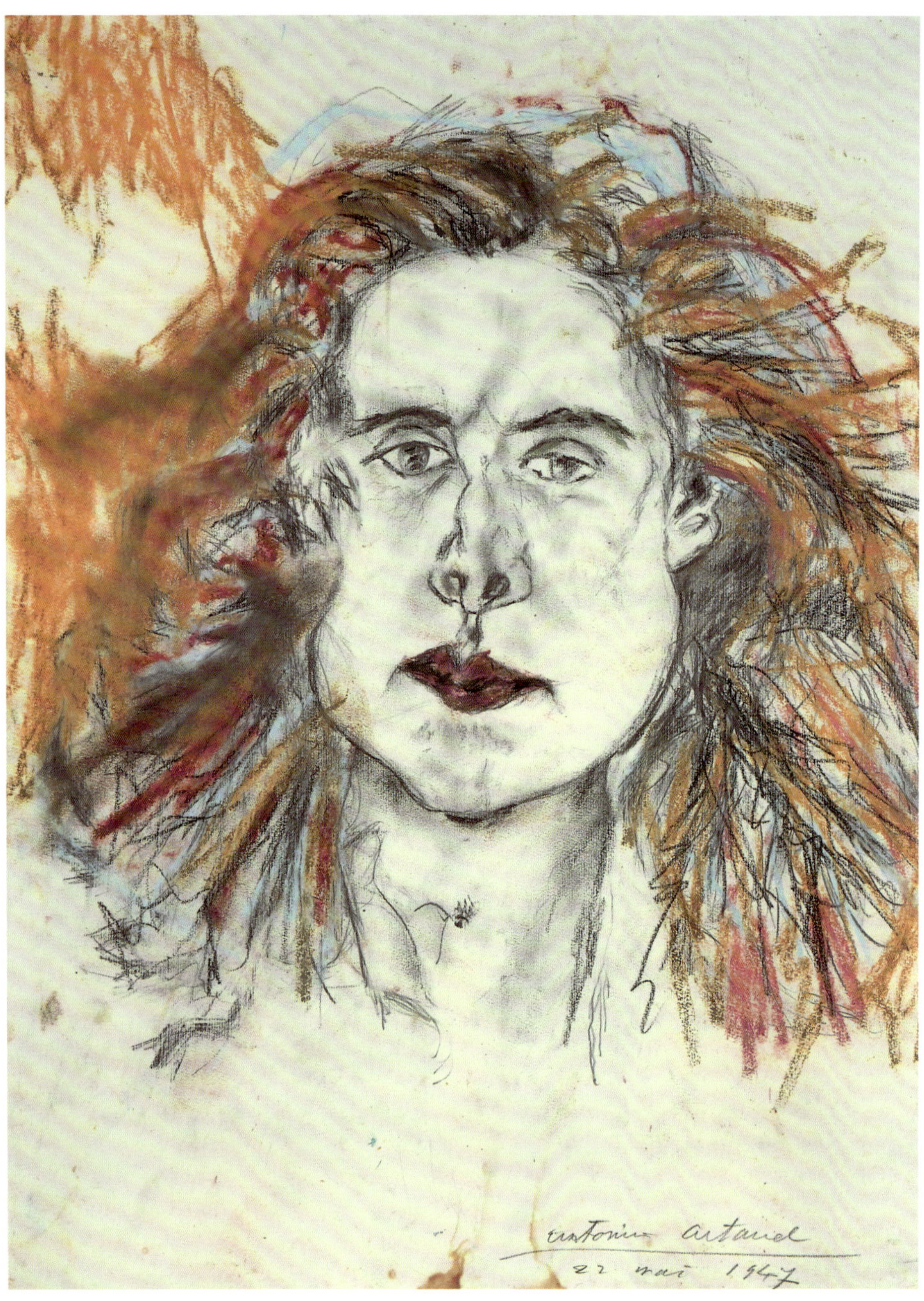

9 Portrait of Minouche Pastier 1947
63.5 × 47.8 (25 × 18⅞)

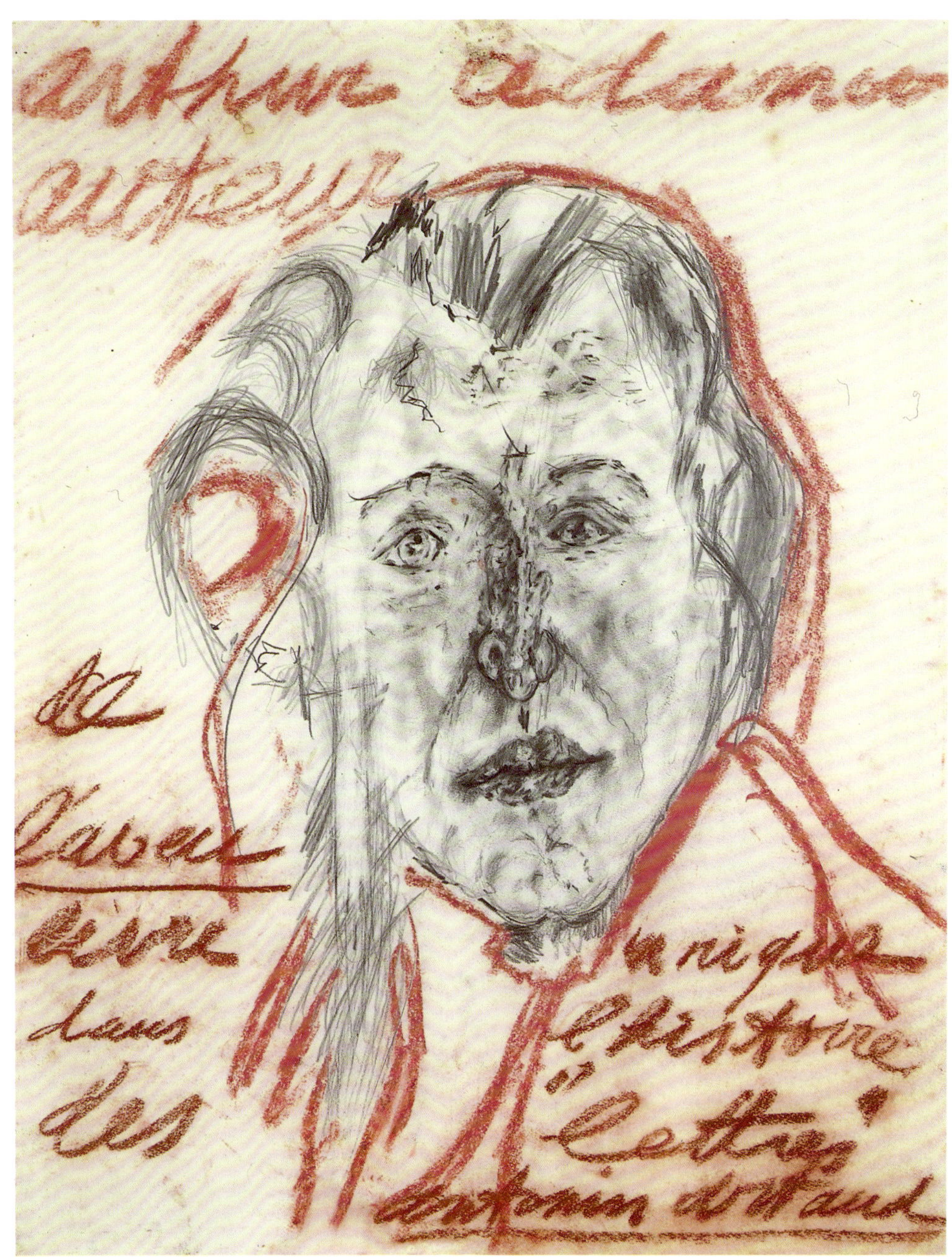

10 **Portrait of Arthur Adamov** 1947
$65 \times 50 \left(25\frac{5}{8} \times 19\frac{5}{8}\right)$

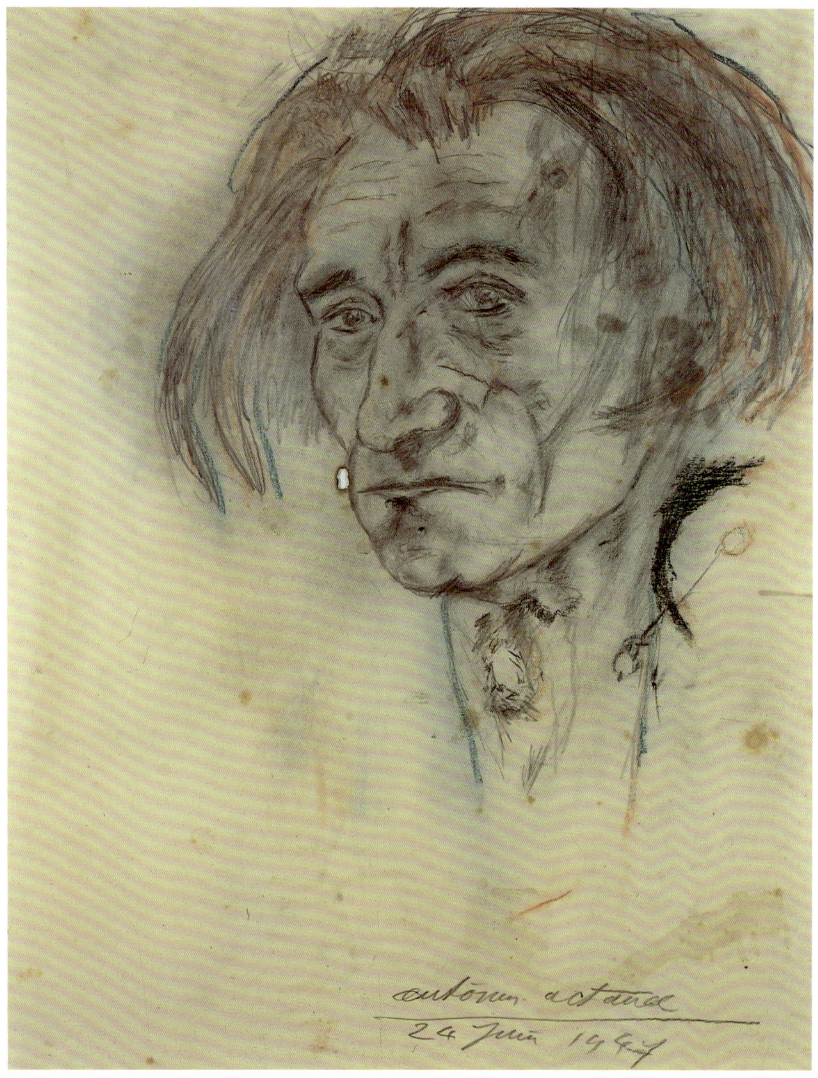

11 **Self-Portrait** 1947
55×45 ($21\frac{5}{8} \times 17\frac{3}{4}$)

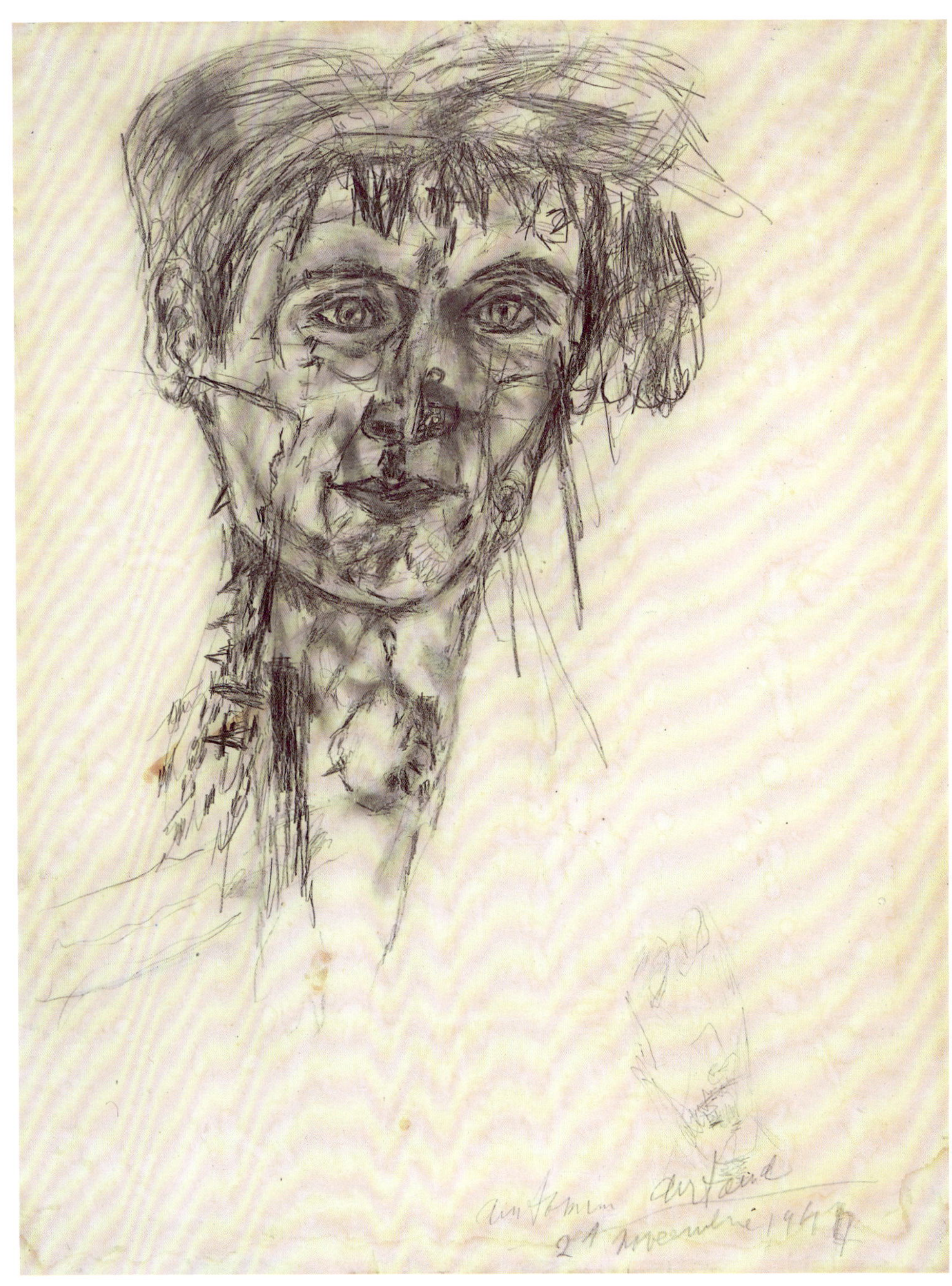

12 Portrait of Henri Pichette or **Gris-Gris** 1947
64.7 × 49.8 (25½ × 19⅝)

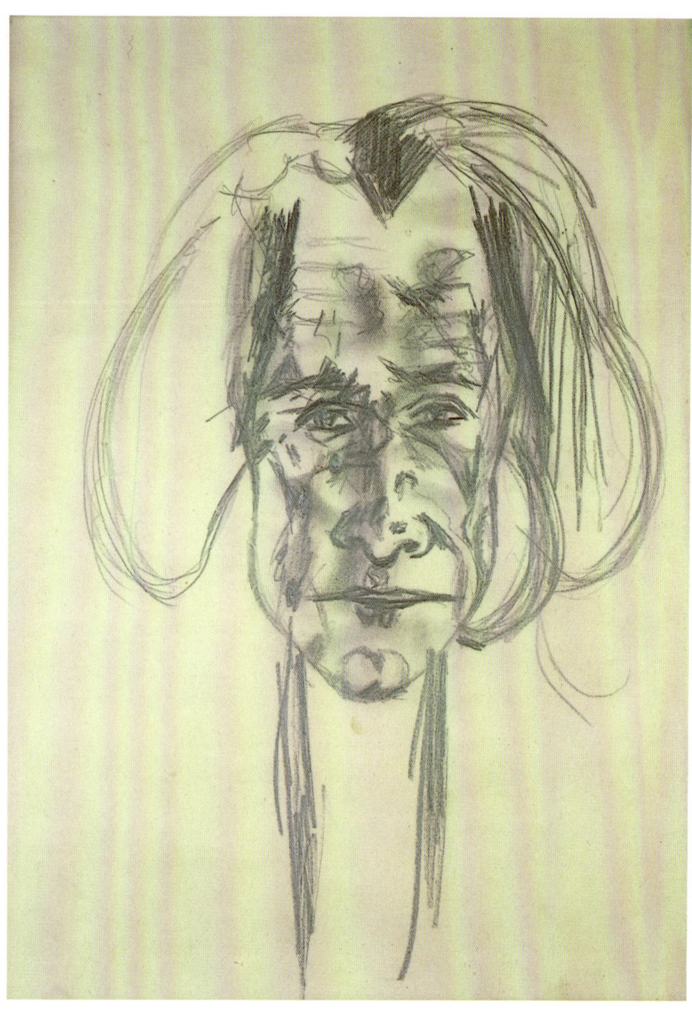

13 Self-Portrait 1947
$37 \times 27 \left(14\frac{1}{2} \times 10\frac{5}{8}\right)$

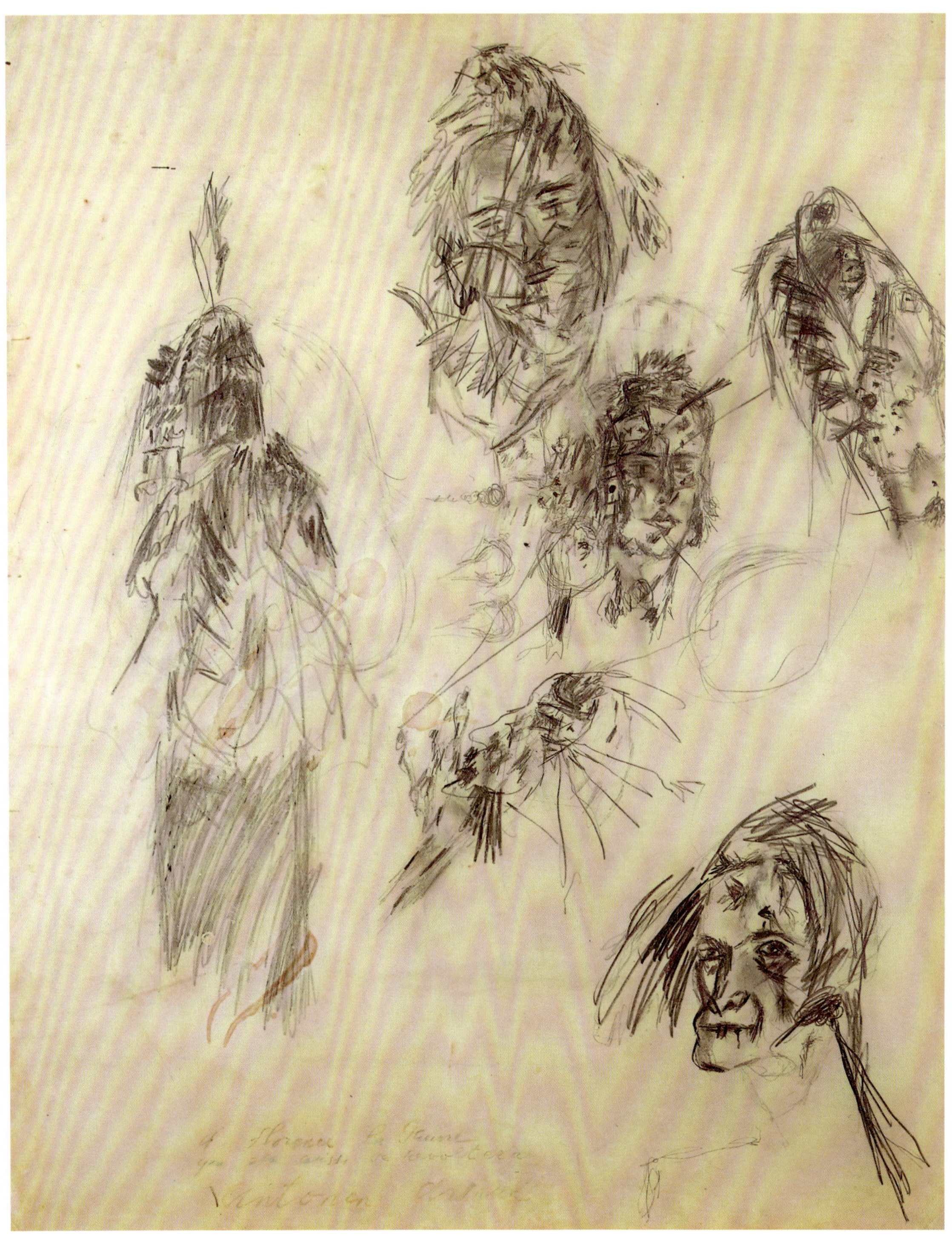

14 Portraits 1947
63 × 50 (24¾ × 19⅝)

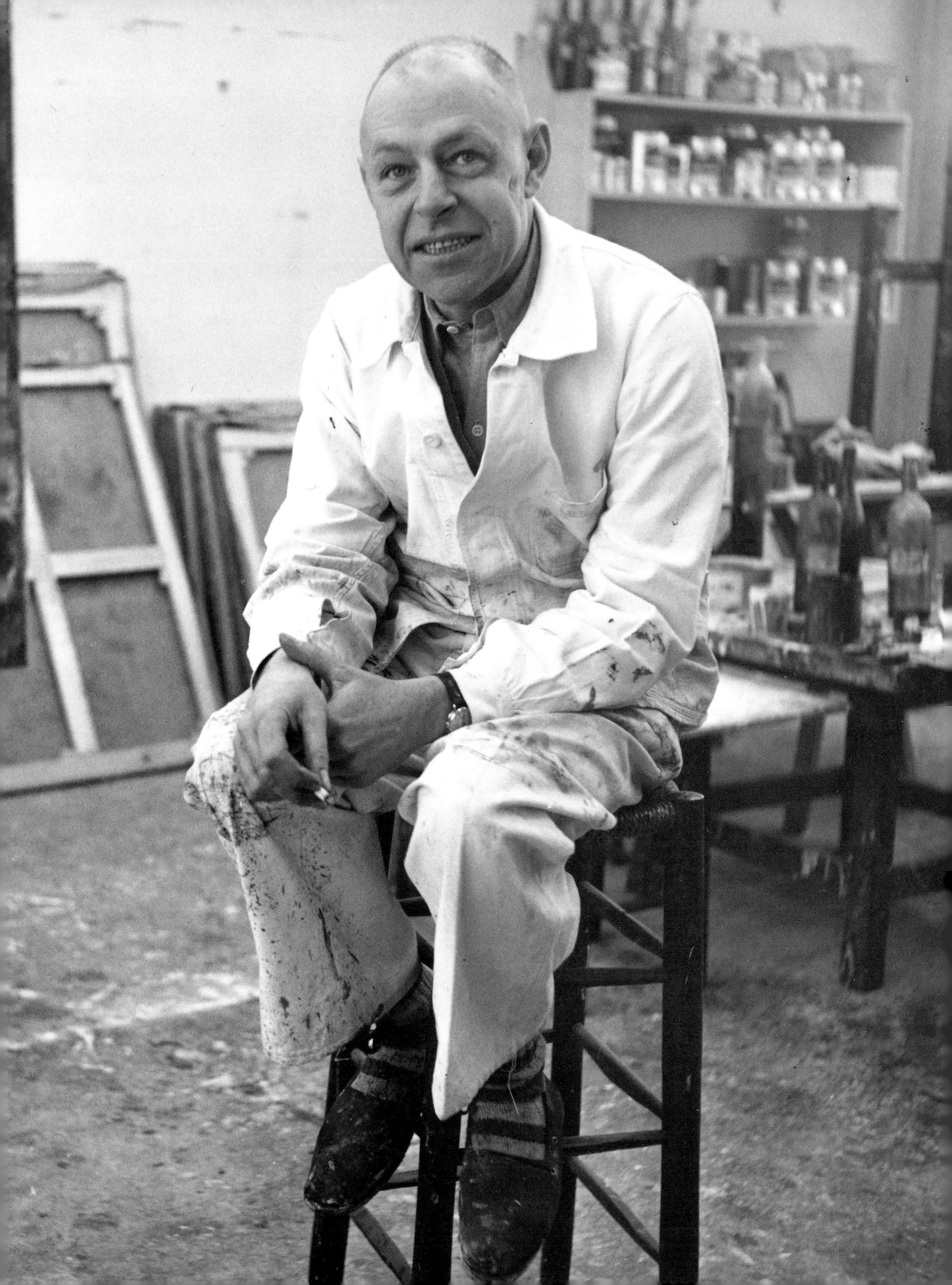

Jean Dubuffet (1901–1985)

Many of those visiting Jean Dubuffet's second exhibition at the Galerie René Drouin in 1946 were horrified by his new series of paintings entitled 'Mirobolus, Macadam et Cie'. They were disturbed not so much by the crudely caricatured depictions of men and women but by the dense, mud-like composite medium, or *haute pâte*, into which these images were incised and collaged. Rarely had they seen such a radical alternative to oil paint.

In his introduction to the exhibition catalogue Michel Tapié described the medium as

> a mixture of céruse and Meudon white . . . ranging from the substance of putty . . . to the coloured liquid that he applies in "streams". Dubuffet pours and blends with this sand, gravel, tar . . . heavy varnish used on boutique fronts . . . plaster mixed with water and oil, drying agents . . . coal dust . . . small stones . . . string, small bits of mirror or coloured glass, Ripolin, Duco: he draws on this using a trowel or soup spoon, a scraper, a knife, a wire brush or his fingers.[1]

Tapié found in Dubuffet's paste a 'sort of living matter working its perpetual magic'. Other critics found 'excrement'[2] and 'filth'[3] appropriate terms with which to disguise their incomprehension.

'Mirobolus, Macadam et Cie' swiftly established Dubuffet's reputation. While becoming the 'bête noire of the bourgeois press, of officialdom, of champions of reason, proportion and decency – of all those who clothe themselves in "common sense"'[4] – he was also, to others, a fascinating and important figure. His first supporters came from the intellectuals gravitating around Jean Paulhan, well known as an author, collector and editor from the Gallimard publishing house. Dubuffet had been introduced to Paulhan by the former Surrealist Georges Limbour, a friend from his student days. In the early 1940s Limbour brought a succession of intellectuals and artists to meet Dubuffet, including the poets Francis Ponge, Paul Eluard and Eugène Guillevic. *Newsweek*, 20 May 1946, described him as 'the darling of the Paris avant-garde' and *Ici Paris* numbered Eluard, Paulhan and Sartre as enthusiasts.[5] Their respect for him was reciprocated. In a letter to Paulhan dated summer 1946 Dubuffet described how he had read *Les Temps Modernes* cover to cover and been deeply impressed. In addition he had just finished reading Sartre's *Nausea* which he had found difficult in parts. He declared himself an enthusiastic convert, 'I feel and declare myself warmly existentialist', making light of his incomprehension and reminding Paulhan that 'in all matters of doctrine baptism precedes catechism'.[6]

Dubuffet was himself an unusually gifted writer on art; this is a major reason for the respect he commanded within literary circles. While finding himself indifferent to Dubuffet's painting, Jean-Jacques Gautier envied his abilities as a writer: was he not 'one of the great writers of today?'[7]

Dubuffet wrote for public consumption and also for a small circle of interested individuals. His 'Notes for the Well-Read'[8] were written in 1945 for private circulation. In them Dubuffet began to explain what he understood as an active and expressive role for materials in art, a role that was crucial in the evolution of his radical theory and practice of *art brut*. He argued that art should be the product of a competitive interaction between the artist, his tools and his medium, and that the finished work should retain the marks of that struggle. He favoured difficult, intractable materials because they heighten the adventure for the artist and introduce the element of chance, 'the whims and aspirations of the bulky material'. Similarly, he felt the artist should tackle his medium directly and boldly, learning how to smear the paint in an expressive way. Dubuffet contrasts an image of a tentative aesthete struggling to recreate the patina of an apple using dabs of paint squeezed from tiny tubes with one of the heroic artist locked in a Dionysiac struggle with brute matter, a struggle that is somehow authentic and primordial.

Dubuffet's development of the *haute pâte* as medium was part of his personal search for practices appropriate to a new era, with which to replace moribund traditions in fine art, traditions conditioned by what he saw as misguided but still prevailing notions of beauty and purpose in art. When Tapié, in his manifesto published in 1952,[9] called for *Un art autre* that was authentic, individualist and violent, matter and gesture were its defining properties, and Wols, Fautrier and Dubuffet its exemplars. In laying stress on the body and matter, Dubuffet and Tapié's *art autre* were doing no more than reflecting current directions of thought within the scientific community and following paths parallel to contemporary existentialist and phenomenological writing. Sartre's *Nausea* (1938), Maurice Merleau-Ponty's *Phenomenology of Perception* (1945) and Gaston Bachelard's *Earth and the Dreams of Will* (1947) explored the ways in which the body and consciousness function within the world of matter.

Although Dubuffet was a pioneering and undoubtedly articulate exponent of *matière* painting he was not the first to explore the expressive potential of the raw material in this way. He had been introduced to Fautrier by Paulhan in 1943 at a crucial moment in Fautrier's career. Fautrier's thickly impastoed 'Otage' paintings (see nos. 26–36) presented a new relationship between the image and the material – one in which the material actively participates in the generation of form. That such a relationship was 'primitive' as well as modern was suggested by parallels found outside the modern, cultured era, for example in non-Western practice (a parallel between Fautrier's 'Otage' imagery and negro masks was described by Francis Ponge[10]).

A year after Fautrier's 'Otage' paintings were first shown[11] and some two years before Sartre compared Giacometti to the cave man of Altamira,[12] Tapié found in Dubuffet's work 'all the magical-incantatory charm of these richly elementary signs that a dumbly resigned scepticism had discreetly buried: graffiti in caves and on dolmens, menhir statues, mother goddesses'.[13]

Like Paulhan, who advocated a return to an artistic 'Stone Age'[14] as a means of rejuvenation, Dubuffet himself gave the 'primitive' a key position within his developing theories. For Dubuffet the 'primitive' was not so much a historical or socio-economic category as a state of consciousness in which freedom and authenticity prevail. Those living outside or on the margins of the prevailing culture were of particular interest to him. Parallels with Sartre's belief in the interdependence of alienation and creativity are of interest. Both men, highly cultured themselves, saw cultural convention as stifling.

In his 1951 lecture, 'Anticultural Positions',[15] Dubuffet claimed that primitive values such as 'instinct, passion, caprice, violence, madness' were very much alive 'on the streets' in the West but were not reflected in contemporary culture, which he saw as an 'ill fitting coat' speaking a dead language. Dubuffet eulogised primitive man's independence from reason and logic as routes to knowledge, his respect for nature and elemental life and his use of visual art as a tool of communication. Dubuffet ridiculed Western notions of beauty and scorned written language as an inferior means of communication. After asserting the importance of delirium in the making of art, Dubuffet explains that, for him, art should go to the roots of mental activity, where 'thought is close to its birth'. The lives and works of his contemporaries Wols, Michaux and Artaud must surely have helped shape this plea for artists to address 'the underground levels of mental spurts'.

Dubuffet's ideas had developed during the two decades that separated his first experience of art, as a student at the Académie Julien in 1918, and his final and successful attempt to work full time as an artist in 1942. In between came military service, success as a wine merchant and an abortive attempt at a career in 'popular' art. Various factors may have contributed to Dubuffet's stance. His dislike of the restraints and prejudices of his art school training fanned a genuine interest in 'popular' arts. This interest prompted his attempt, between 1933 and 1937, to find his way by making marionettes and masks, a project which may also owe something to the example of Fernand Léger (who alongside Dubuffet contributed to the magazine *Aventure* in 1921). Certainly key passages in Dubuffet's 1945 'Notes for the Well-Read' are strongly reminiscent of Léger's celebratory attitude to the common man. Dubuffet's first paintings after his 'return' to art in 1942 demonstrate a vigorous enthusiasm for the everyday life and culture. They are scenes of urban and domestic life depicted in a consciously naive style.

Early on, Dubuffet was drawn to the work of those living on the edge of society. While on military service in 1923 he became fascinated by the work of clairvoyants and mediums through an encounter with the work of a female visionary, Clementine R, who sent her sketches of celestial apparitions to the National Meteorological Office where Dubuffet was stationed. Limbour was very probably responsible for kindling Dubuffet's early interest in art and the insane, and would no doubt have informed him of the Surrealists' interest in such work. Of particular importance to the artist was Hans Prinzhorn's pioneering study of the art of the insane, *Artistry of the Mentally Ill* (*Bildnerei der Geisteskranken*) (1923), which he was given in 1928. The illustrations vividly conveyed an art ignorant of culturally determined aesthetic prejudices yet capable of achieving an unrestrained expressive power. This interest in what he later defined as *art brut* was cemented during a series of visits he made, in the company of Paulhan, to psychiatric hospitals in Switzerland during 1945. The visits gave Dubuffet the opportunity to start buying works of art by schizophrenic artists for a collection which was first displayed in the basement of René Drouin's gallery in 1947. The following year Dubuffet invited interested parties to become part of the Compagnie de l'Art Brut; founding members included André Breton, Jean Paulhan, Henri-Pierre Roché (Wols's champion) and Charles Ratton, who had been one of the first dealers in primitive art in Paris.

Although *art brut* should be seen in the context of a growing public and specialist interest in art and mental illness during the immediate postwar period (with exhibitions at the St-Anne psychiatric hospital in Paris in 1946 and, in 1950, to accompany the first World Congress of Psychiatry in Paris), Dubuffet was vehemently opposed to the notion of 'psychotic' art. He was interested in the art produced by schizophrenic creators only when they were working entirely for their own personal reasons, not on the instruction of doctors to produce images for diagnostic purposes. He rejected received definitions of insanity, seeing it – like Artaud – as a profound act of rebellion against the established order, not as a condition to be cured. For him, only rare individuals among the insane were able to produce *art brut*. In writing of the work of one such individual, Heinrich Anton Müller, Dubuffet claimed that 'the creation of art is [so] worthless when it does not originate in a state of alienation, and when it fails to offer a new conception of the world and new principles for living'.[16]

Another source of 'primitive' art that was perhaps influential and which provided a parallel to Dubuffet's exploration of matter in painting was modern graffiti. The photographer Brassaï, whom Dubuffet met in 1944, had been mapping the imagery of contemporary urban graffiti since the 1930s. Not only did Brassaï's photographs capture evidence of 'our state of civilisation',[17] which was very much the kind of raw and vital on-the-street activity that Dubuffet championed in his 'Anticultural Positions', but they also recorded the physical qualities of the wall as matter battered by warfare and by the activities of anonymous mark-makers. Dubuffet showed more than a passing interest in the subject. It provided him with a range of quotidian imagery that was harsh, urban and appropriately downbeat. The motifs employed in his paintings of urban graffiti and people of the streets (1945) or in the series of etchings made to accompany Guillevic's poems, *Les Murs* (1945), was, as Mildred Glimcher points out, quite new to the world of high art.[18] From a technical point of view the whole process of working with *haute pâte*, of excavating an image from a physically resistant surface, owes much to graffiti. This is emphasised by Dubuffet's rejection of perspective and 'focus', by an overt linearity in composition in which the outline predominates and in which figures are flattened into two dimensions.

If adopting the process and appearance of graffiti was a way of upsetting the conventions of oil painting, in which the medium is the invisible support for colour and composition, another strategy was to destroy received notions of beauty by tackling head-on the favoured subjects of high art. This Dubuffet did to extraordinary effect in his remarkable series of portraits of friends, artists and writers of the avant-garde who gathered for weekly discussions at the home of Mrs Florence Gould. A series of portraits was exhibited in October 1947 (nos.16, 17) and the press release proclaimed: 'People are more handsome than they think. Long live their true faces at the Galerie René Drouin, 17 Place Vendôme. Portraits with a resemblance extracted, with resemblance cooked and conserved in the memory, with a resemblance exploded in the memory of Mr. Jean Dubuffet, painter.' Rejecting the twin aims of traditional portraiture, resemblance and psychological insight, Dubuffet created a series of grotesque masks, bringing wildly caricatured elements of the subject's physiognomy together, often with deliberate crudeness and banality. Peter Selz argues that 'like Beckett, Ionesco and Genet, Dubuffet finds that only a ritual sort of comedy can adequately deal with the human condition'.[19]

More striking in their iconoclasm were the series of 'Corps de Dames', first shown at the Pierre Matisse Gallery in New York in January 1951 (nos.19–20). These were depictions of the female body dehumanised, its form flattened and spread out over the canvas and its sex graphically described. Dubuffet delighted in their expressive complexity and ambiguity:

It amused me (and I believe this propensity to be almost constant in all my paintings) to juxtapose brutally in these female bodies the most general and the most particular, the most subjective and the most objective, the metaphysical and the grotesquely trivial ... This same tendency gives rise to apparently illogical relationships between textures suggesting human flesh ... and other textures which have nothing more to do with anything human but instead suggest earth, or all sorts of things like bark, rocks, botanical or geographical phenomena ... It seems to me that it provokes all sorts of transformations and polarisations which throw objects into an unusual light and can give them new and unknown meanings.[20]

The impression these images gave of the 'body-as-landscape' was intentional. Dubuffet described them as works of 'ardent celebration',[21] products of an art liberated from a moribund culture and demonstrating the 'rehabilitation of scorned values'.[22]

NOTES

1 Michel Tapié, *Mirobolus, Macadam et Cie, Hautes Pâtes de Jean Dubuffet*, Galerie René Drouin, Paris 1946, pp.25–8, trans. in Mildred Glimcher and Jean Dubuffet, *Towards and Alternative Reality*, 1987, p.11.
2 Henri Jeanson, *Le Canard enchaîné*, 15 May 1946, quoted in Max Loreau (ed.), *Catalogue des travaux de Jean Dubuffet*, Paris 1966, fascicule II, p.124.
3 Jean Texcier, *Gavroche*, 30 May 1946, quoted in Loreau ii 1966, p.125.
4 James Fitzsimmons, 'Jean Dubuffet, A Short Introduction to his Work', *Quadrum*, no.4, 1957, p.28.
5 *Ici Paris*, 21 May 1946, quoted in Loreau ii 1966, p.124.
6 Jean Dubuffet, letter to Jean Paulhan, summer 1946, repr. in *Jean Paulhan à travers ses peintres*, exh. cat., Grand Palais, Paris 1974, p.98.
7 Jean-Jacques Gautier, *La Nef*, May 1947, quoted in Loreau II 1966, p.126.
8 Jean Dubuffet, 'Notes pour les fins-lettrés' in Jean Dubuffet, *Prospectus et tous écrits suivants*, I, Paris 1967, pp.54–89: trans. in Glimcher and Dubuffet 1987, pp.67–86.
9 Michel Tapié, *Un art autre, ou il s'agit de nouveau dévidages du réel*, Paris 1952.
10 Francis Ponge, *Note sur Les Otages peintures de Fautrier*, Paris 1946.
11 *Les Otages peintures et sculptures de Fautrier*, Galerie René Drouin, Paris, 16 Oct.–17 Nov. 1945.
12 Jean-Paul Sartre,'La Recherche de l'absolu', *Les Temps Modernes*, vol.III, no.28, 1948, pp.1153–1163, trans. Lionel Abel, 'The Search for the Absolute' in *Alberto Giacometti*, exh. cat., Pierre Matisse Gallery, New York 1948, pp.2–22.
13 Tapié 1946, p.8.
14 André Berne-Joffrey, 'Quand les belles-lettres touchent aux beaux-arts', in *Paris-Paris*, exh.cat., Musée national d'art moderne, Paris 1981, p.38.
15 Jean Dubuffet, 'Anticultural Positions', lecture delivered to the Arts Club of Chicago, Dec. 1951, reprinted in French in Dubuffet I 1967, pp.94–100.
16 Jean Dubuffet, 'Henrich Anton M.' in Dubuffet I 1967, p.269.
17 Brassaï, 'Language of the Wall', quoted in Mildred Glimcher, *De Kooning/Dubuffet: The Women*, exh. cat., Pace Gallery, New York 1991, p.13.
18 Glimcher 1987, p.8.
19 Peter Selz, *Jean Dubuffet: The Early Work*, Museum of Modern Art, New York 1962, p.37.
20 Jean Dubuffet, 'Corps de Dames' in Georges Limbour, *Tableau bon Levain à vous de cuire la pâte*, 1953, p.95, trans. Sarah Wilson in *Aftermath*, exh. cat., Barbican Art Gallery 1982, p.99.
21 Selz 1962, p.64.
22 Ibid.

Illustration (p.78) Portrait of Jean Dubuffet in his studio 1951 Photograph by Robert Doisneau © *Doisneau/Rapho*

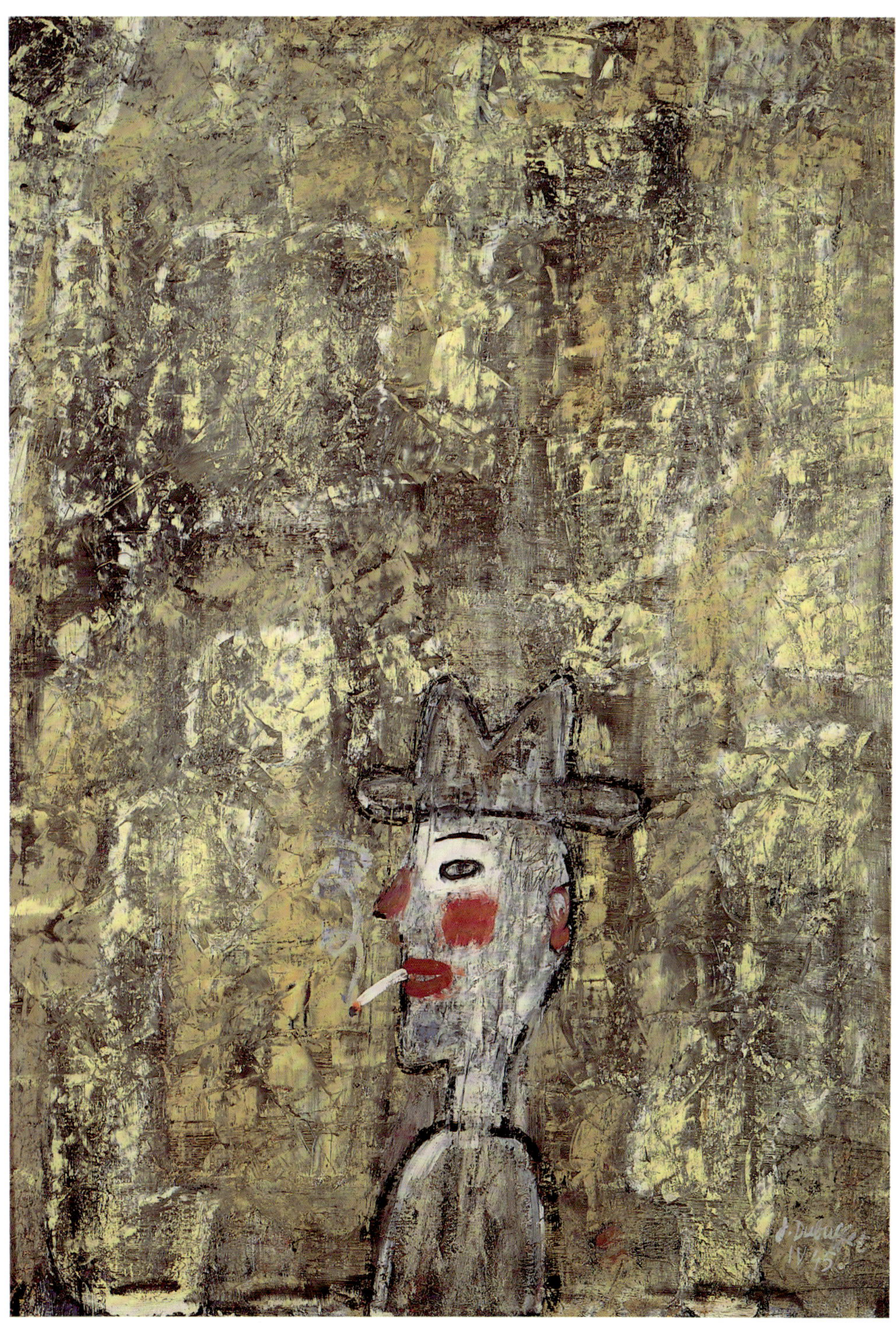

15 Smoker by a Wall 1945
116 × 89 (45⅝ × 35)

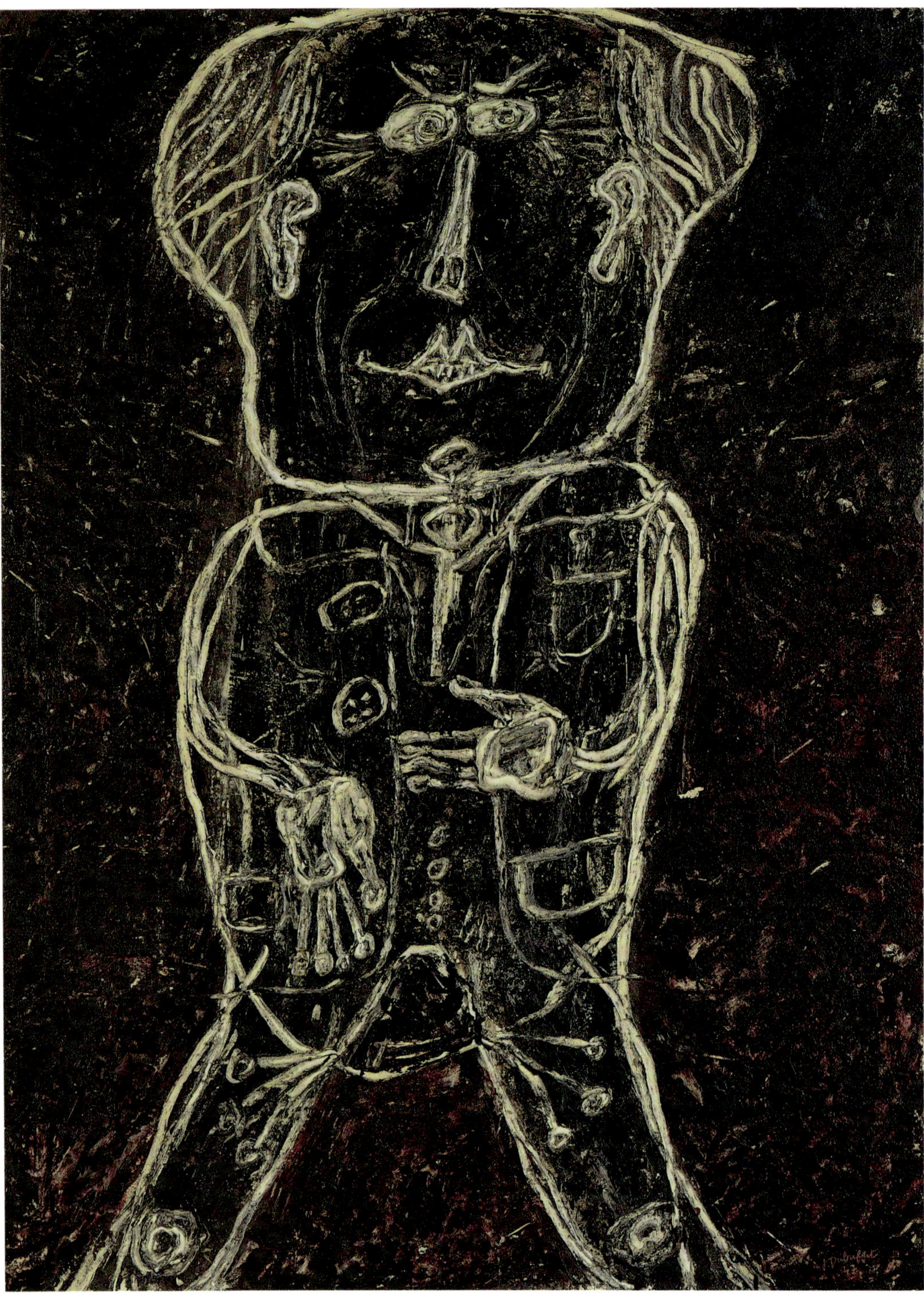

16 Monsieur Plume with Creases in his
Trousers (Portrait of Henri Michaux) 1947
130.2 × 96.5 (51¼ × 38)

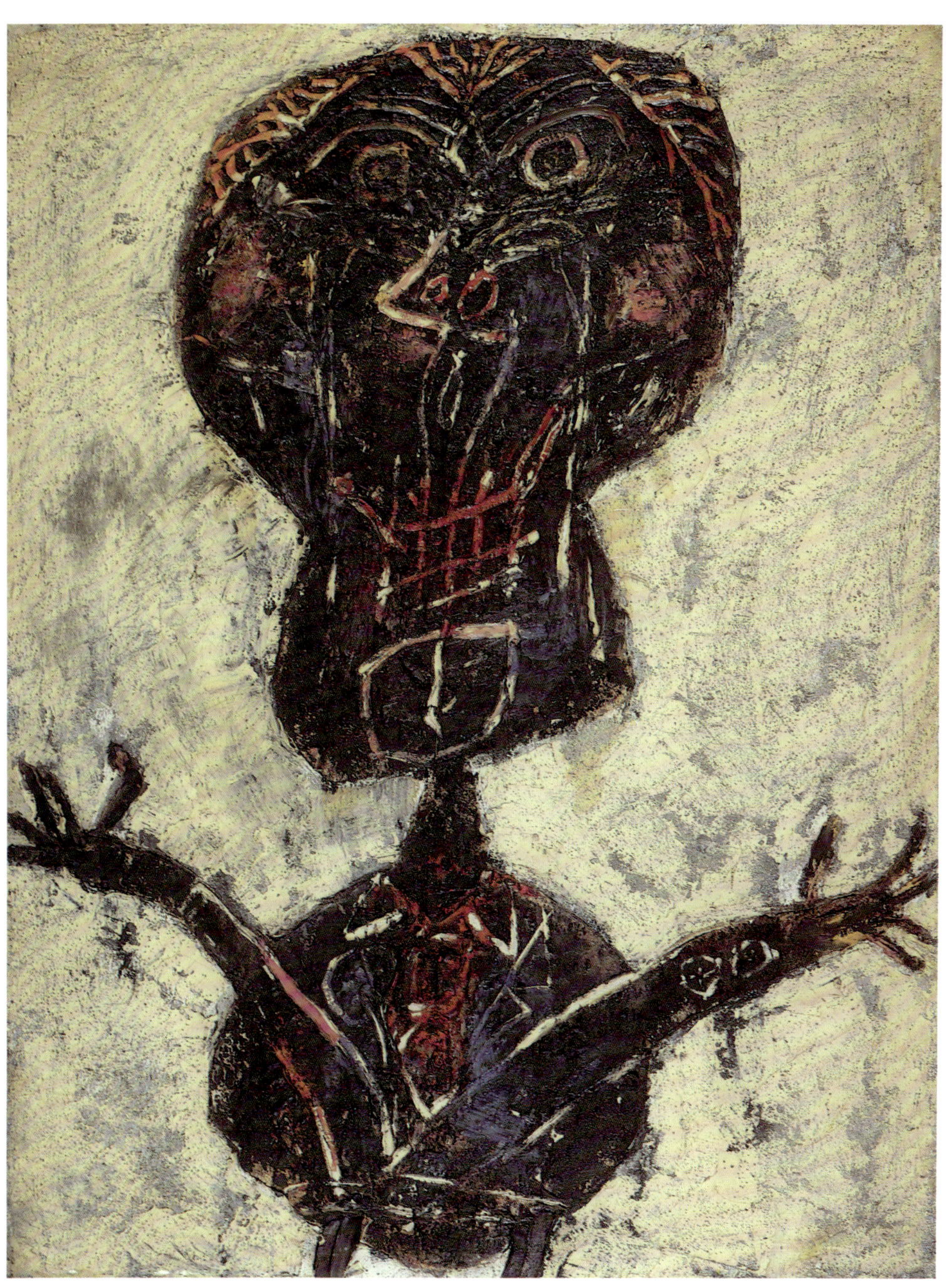

17 Bertelé, Flowered Bouquet,
Parade Portrait 1947
116 × 89 (45$\frac{5}{8}$ × 35)

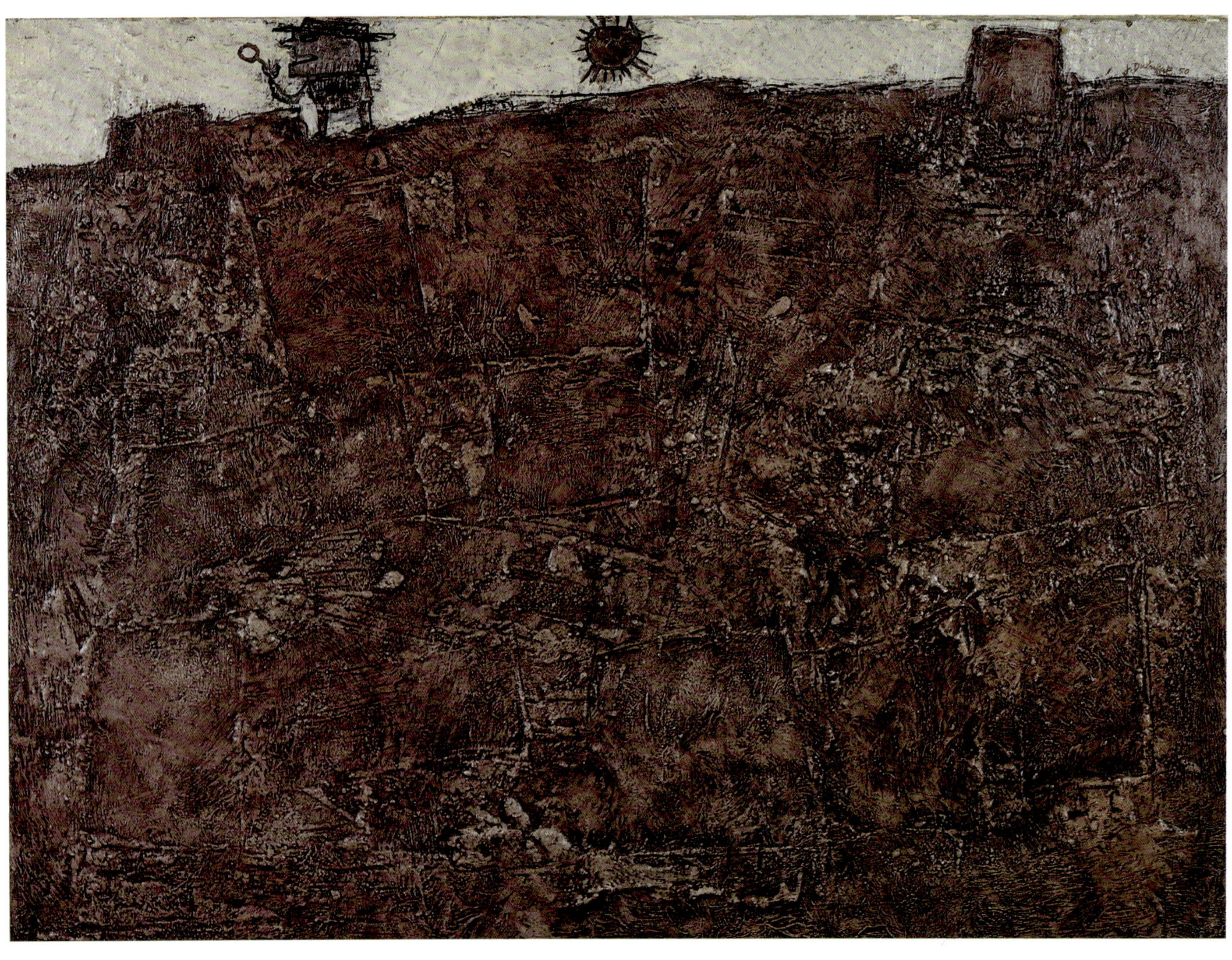

18 **The Geologist** 1950
97 × 130 ($38\frac{1}{4} × 51\frac{1}{8}$)

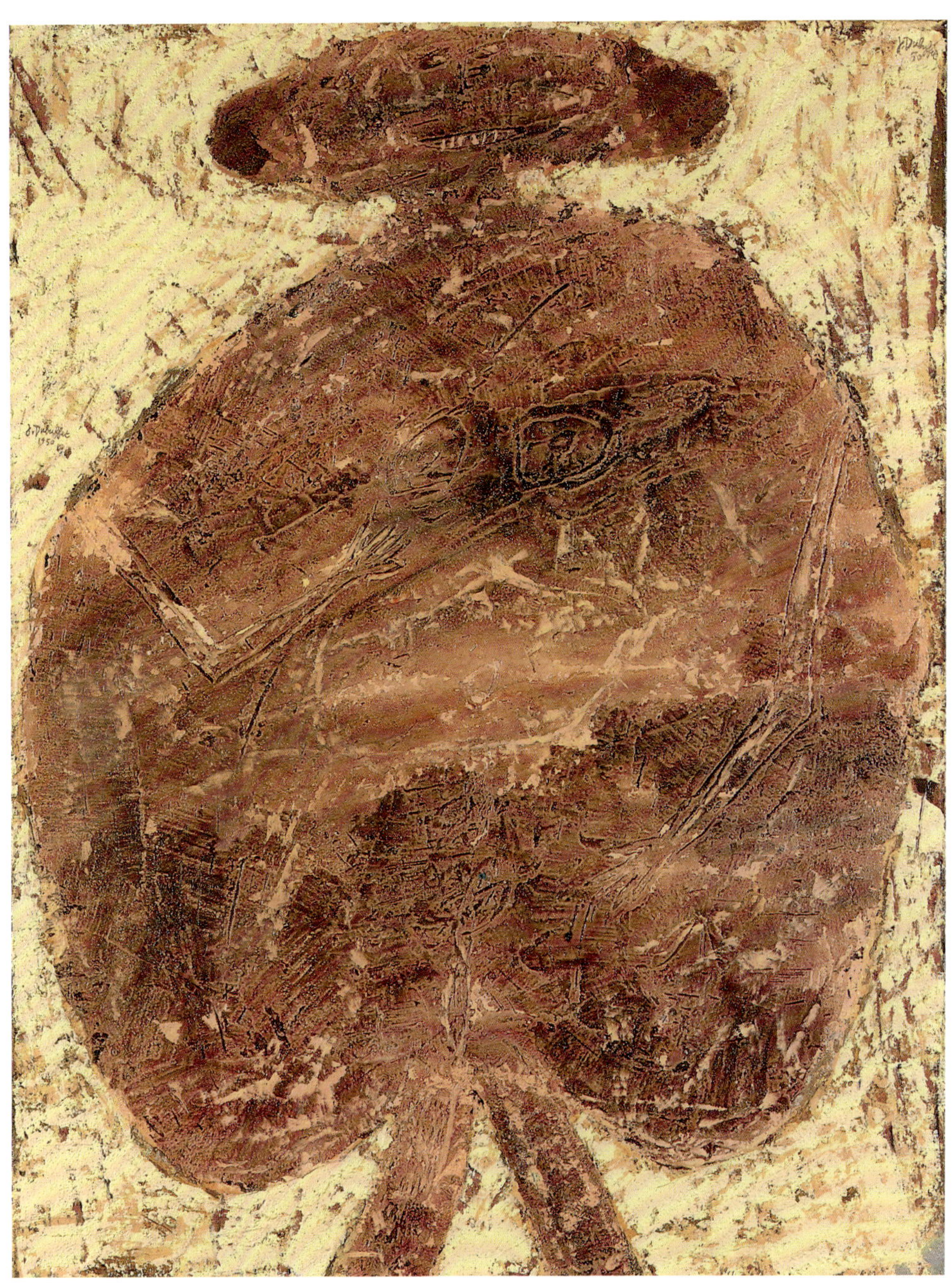

19 **The Uncertain Woman** 1950
116.5×89.5 $(45\frac{7}{8} \times 35\frac{1}{4})$

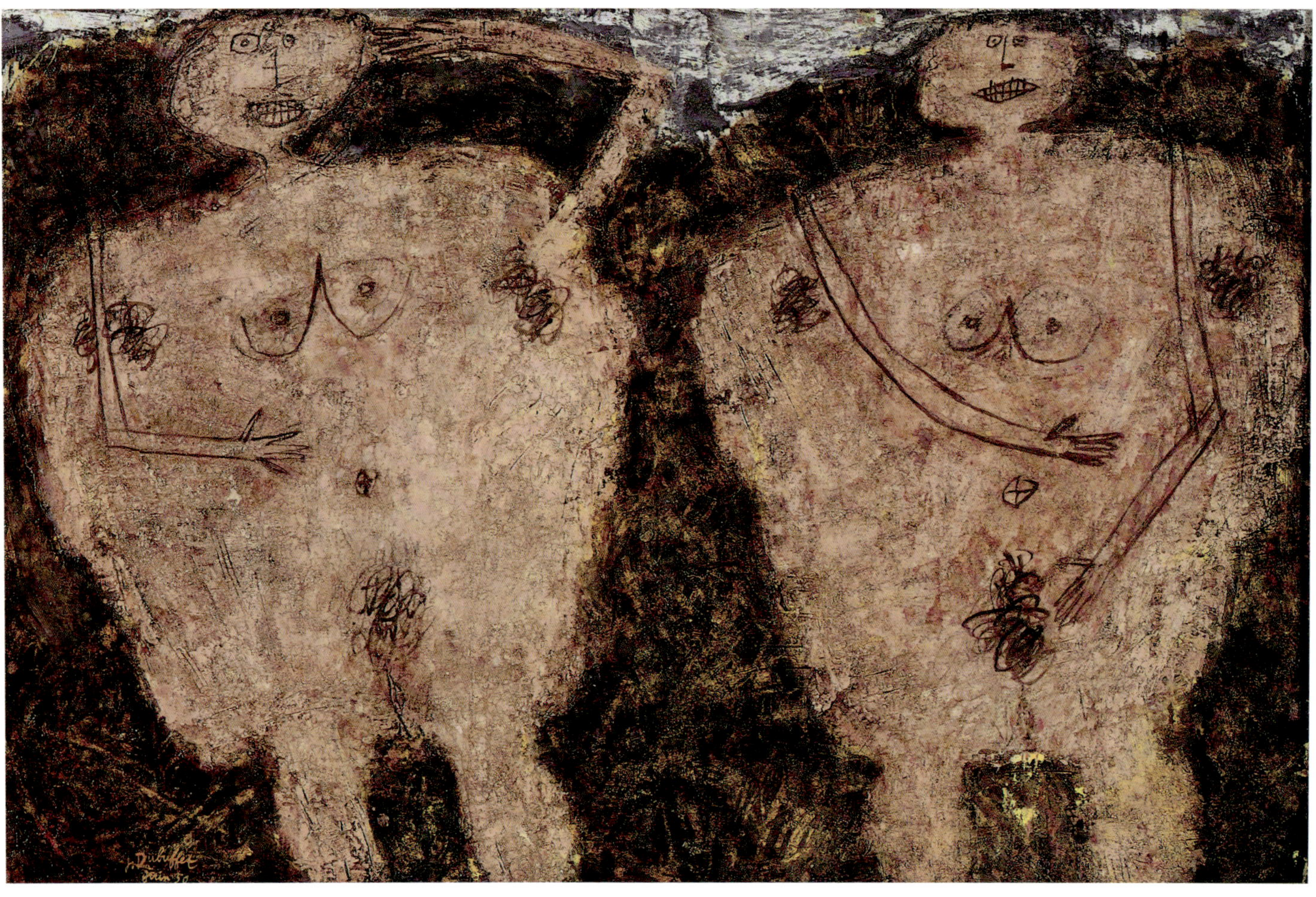

20 Gymnosophie 1950
97 × 146 (38¼ × 57½)

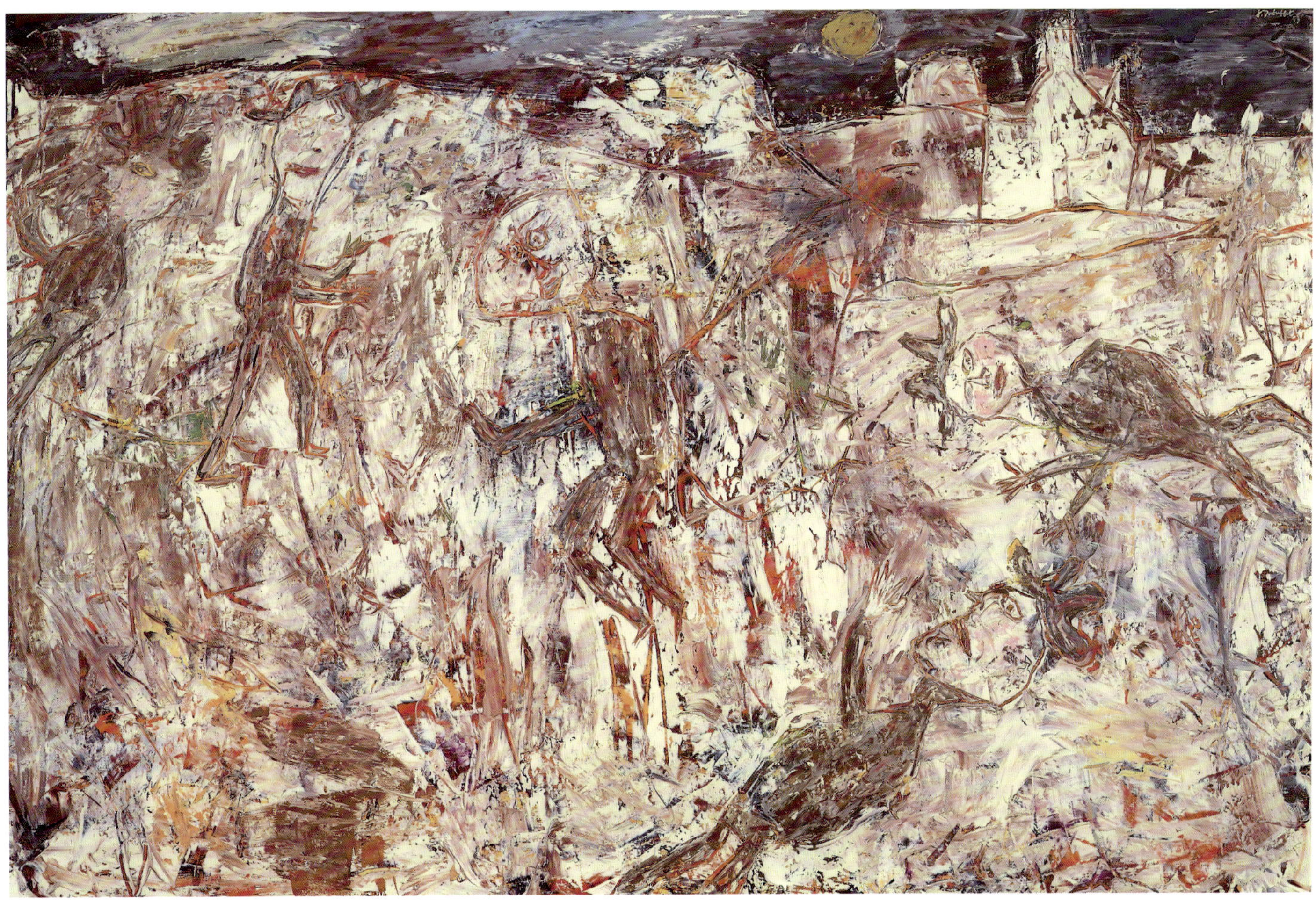

21 **The Busy Life** 1953
130.2 × 195.6 (51¼ × 77)

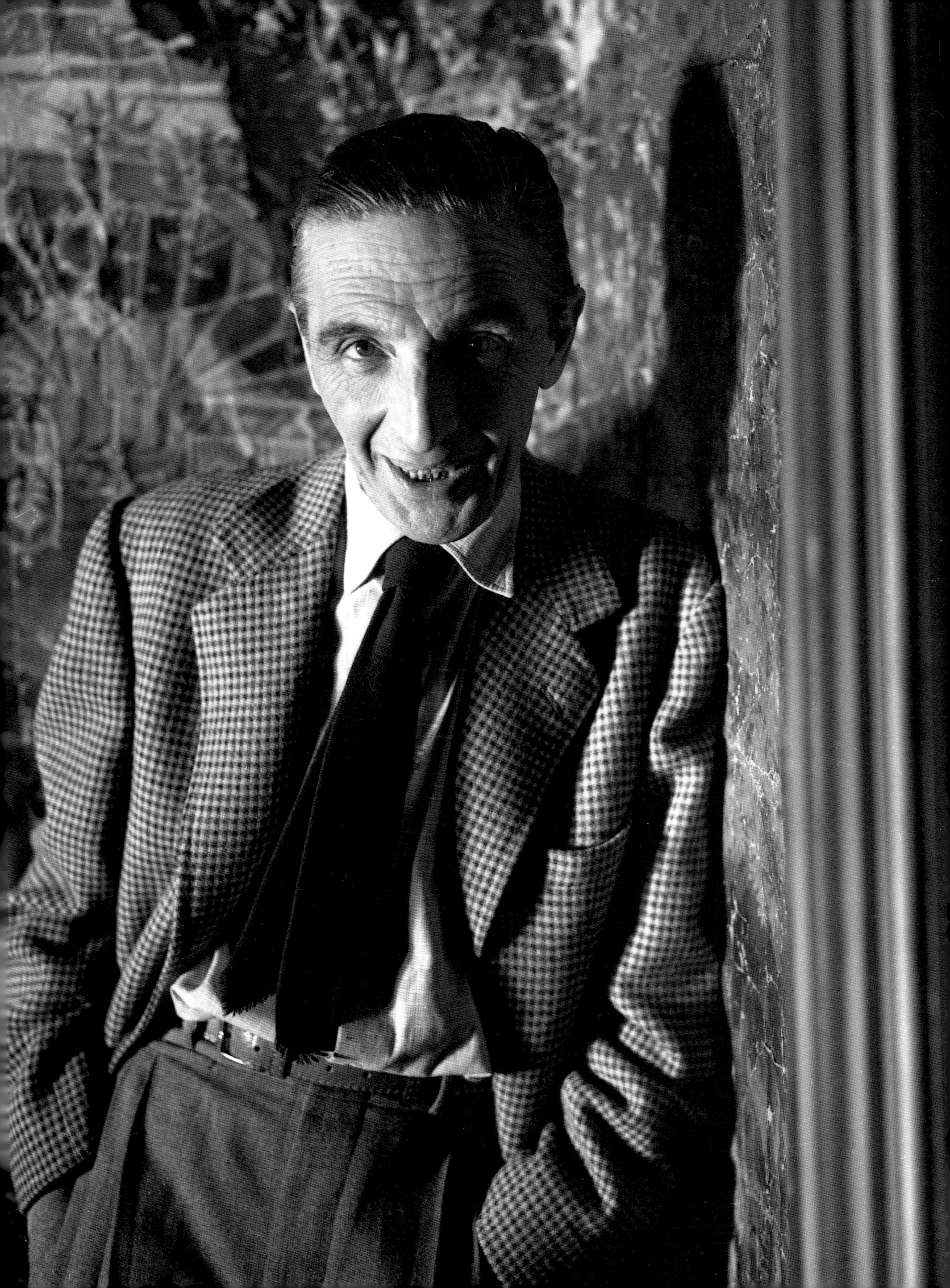

Jean Fautrier (1898–1964)

It was the dealer René Drouin who was largely responsible for revealing Jean Fautrier's work to a wider Parisian public after the Second World War. Unlike Wols and Dubuffet, whose paintings Drouin premiered, Fautrier was not unknown – merely forgotten after an absence of some years. Drouin was re-presenting an artist who had achieved a certain critical stature during the 1920s after being discovered and promoted by the young Jeanne Castel.

Fautrier was brought up in London from the age of ten and received his artistic training at the Royal Academy of Art and the Slade School of Art. His return to France was prompted by the First World War when he was mobilised for active service. Transferred to the auxiliary services as a result of his ill-health, he was finally discharged in 1921. He then turned to painting and during the 1920s developed a singular style, distancing his work from the prevailing styles of Surrealism, late Cubism and hard-edged abstraction. While his themes – landscapes, portrait heads, nudes and still lifes – were not in themselves extraordinary, his techniques and his interpretations often were. They demonstrated an obsession with the macabre and a pervading sense of morbidity. In 1933, André Malraux (who had admired his work since the late 1920s and had prompted Fautrier's ill-fated and eventually abortive project to illustrate Dante's *Inferno*) referred to the 'almost constant tragic resonance'[1] in his work.

During the 1930s Fautrier, the victim of economic recession, withdrew from the art world and Paris, and instead sought a living as ski instructor, night-club patron and hotel proprietor in the French Alps. Whilst he painted very little, he began to explore various sculptural themes at this time. On the outbreak of war he returned to Paris, staying at first with Castel, on whose advice he began painting again. A studio was found for him on boulevard Raspail. In 1941 he submitted two sculptures to the Salon d'Automne and a group of recent works was shown at the Galerie Alfred Poyet in June 1942. The artist was swiftly absorbed into the circle of intellectual resistance around Jean Paulhan, who had been recently deposed as editor of *La Nouvelle Revue Française*. The circle included such avant-garde writers and poets as René Char, Robert Ganzo, Francis Ponge and Paul Eluard. Friendships produced literary-artistic collaborations and Fautrier provided illustrations for Ganzo's *Orénoque* and *Lespugue* in 1942, Eluard's *Dignes de vivre* in 1944 and Paulhan's *Les Causes célèbres* in 1945. It was probably Paulhan who introduced Fautrier to Drouin; Drouin gave him a retrospective exhibition of his sculptures, prints and drawings at his gallery in 1943.

Fautrier had been arrested by the Gestapo in January 1943, suspected of Resistance activity. Although he was swiftly released on the intervention of the German sculptor Arno Breker (persuaded to intercede by Castel), a temporary retreat seemed wise and Paulhan arranged for him to be accommodated in the grounds of a clinic for mental patients run by Dr Le Savoureux at Châtenay-Malabry on the outskirts of Paris. It was here, in a studio space cleared in a former dovecote, that Fautrier produced the extensive series of heavily impastoed and painted panels collectively known as 'Otages' (hostages). They formed the subject of Fautrier's second exhibition at the Galerie René Drouin, in 1945, where they were received with a mixture of rapture and disdain. The subject and meaning of these images are inextricably bound up with Fautrier's experiences at Châtenay-Malabry, where the dense woods surrounding the sanatorium were frequently used by the German occupying forces for torturing prisoners and conducting clandestine, summary executions. Although these atrocities were hidden from view, Fautrier could not but overhear the victims' searing cries.

The 'Otages' (nos.26–36) are small panels, almost in bas-relief, each depicting the half-obliterated remains of a human face. Sometimes it is the eyes that are delineated, sometimes a profile. The physical presence of damaged flesh and bone is conveyed forcefully in the mass of impasto held on each panel. The works are charged with the implication of physical annihilation. In a few of the larger works that punctuate the series, the body is literally dismembered, as in 'Body of a Hostage' 1945 (private collection), for example, or it is truncated, as in the small painting entitled 'Torso' 1943 (no.28). In 'Oradour-sur-Glane' 1945 (no.35) (inspired by the Nazi massacre of the inhabitants of a French village of that name[2]), the schematic heads in profile overlie a spattered ground, like spectral presences released from the brutal anonymity of dead and decaying matter.

André Malraux wrote the preface to the catalogue of the 'Otages' exhibition. The series marked, in his opinion, 'the first attempt to dissect contemporary pain, down to its tragic ideograms, and force it into the world of eternity'.[3] The same theme was taken up by Ponge in his extensive 'Note sur Les Otages'[4] which was published in 1946. Ponge described Fautrier's images as depicting 'tumified faces, crushed profiles, bodies stiffened by execution, dismembered, mutilated, eaten by flies'. For him these paintings addressed the most important issue of their time, epitomising a 'new human resolve' against the horrors of war. The artist's understanding of his subject, Ponge felt was informed by multiple sources from the history of art, from negro masks to saints' faces, from Michelangelo's slaves to Picasso's 'Guernica'. Above all it is the crucifix, suggested by the prominent T-shaped motif that dominates so many of Fautrier's heads, that is evoked – a crucifix in which 'anonymous man replaces Christ'. The anonymity of the victims conjured by Fautrier, the small format of the works and their seemingly repetitive display along the walls of the gallery made, in the eyes of some spectators, for monotony: it created, according to Michel Ragon, a 'disagreeable impression of serial production'.[5] For others it evoked a sense of the massive scale of arbitrary destruction of life in war, suggesting rows of anonymous corpses.

For some visitors this stark confrontation with the horrors of war was ill-timed in those early days after the Liberation when the urge to forget, if not forgive, was widespread. Many were also disturbed by the seemingly misplaced shades of tenderness and eroticism lent to the paintings by the powdery colours laid on their surfaces. Marcel Arland, for example, had serious reservations about the 'prettiness' of the works which he found more 'seductive than horrible'.[6] A former admirer who was outraged by his new paintings saw Fautrier as 'un grand peintre qui commet un suicide'.[7] Even Malraux – looking presumably at works like 'The Jewess' 1943 (no.27), in which the references to the human body are softer and the colours largely pastel shades – allowed a note of doubt to creep into his eulogy, admitting that

> Little by little, Fautrier suppresses the direct suggestion of blood, the complicity of the corpse. Colours free from any rational link with torture are substituted for the initial ones, at the same time as a contour replaces the ravaged profiles, trying to express the drama without representing it.[8]

It was Ponge who explored this ambivalence in real depth, finding in it the prime source for the expressive power of the paintings, locating their ability to communicate and disturb precisely in the coexistence of suffering and horror with beauty and tenderness.

The 'Otages' attracted attention not only for their subject matter and appearance but also for their – at that time – revolutionary technique and consequent status somewhere between painting, sculpture and object. Each work involved lengthy and methodical preparation in order to facilitate a very rapid and intense period of execution. The slow drying time of layers of oil and the incapacity of canvas to provide an absorbent ground had determined Fautrier's move away from traditional easel painting from the early 1930s. The 'Otage' paintings were made from a thick paste, applied in successive layers to an absorbent base of sheets of rag paper laid on canvas. The original and subsequent drawings were obscured by each successive layer of solid matter. Fautrier drew on the final surface and the work was completed with areas coated in coloured (pastel) powder bonded to the surface with a thick finishing coat of varnish. The technique had been largely developed by the time of the first 'Otage' paintings and was remarked upon at the time of the 1943 exhibition when Michel Tapié, discerning the radical nature of Fautrier's stance, 'had the impression for the first time that there was *something else*'.[9]

Nevertheless the period between the two Drouin shows was crucial for Fautrier. He wrote to Paulhan a year after the first show that 'the Drouin exhibition [1943] taught me a vast amount. I had plenty of time to think, and now I realise that the art I see before me is dead forever as far as I am concerned.'[10] The experience of solitude and the practice of sculpture both played a role in the development of the 'Otages'. During 1943 Fautrier, always a singular and solitary figure, was at his most alone in his voluntary asylum at Châtenay-Malabry. For him the experience of solitude was cathartic:

> Alone to the point of longing for the atrocious and total annihilation of everything ... Alone, but ultimately there is a total expansion of being in solitude – it is this state which in every case offers us the purest and the most absolute solutions.[11]

During this period of solitude Fautrier made his final sculpture. Two years later, when the 'Otage' paintings were shown for the first time, Malraux argued for a profound relationship between Fautrier's painting and sculpture:

> The 'Otage' which provides the key to the others is the large 'Otage' sculpture. Rather than coming from Fautrier's paintings these images derive from his sculpture ... which has found, in torture, what it had been searching for so long in vain: a means of incarnation.[12]

Fautrier had made sculpture intermittently throughout his career and this experience may have influenced his growing desire for a more direct contact with the painting process. In the small yet seemingly monumental heads he sculpted from 1940 onwards, the brute substance of the material is marked by the evidence of the sculptor's intervention in a way that is powerfully expressive. In the four latest works made between 1940 and 1943 the human face is systematically ravaged by the artist. In 'Large Tragic Head' 1942 (no.24) it is shockingly disfigured. The artist has clawed away half of the face in a gesture of consummate cruelty. The sculpture which Malraux refers to specifically, 'Hostage' 1943 (no.25), has the appearance of a head brutally torn from its body, battered and burned beyond recognition, so that only its contours and the evocation of flesh and tissue convince us of its human origins.

While Malraux, as a critic, was primarily interested in Fautrier's 'tragic and pitiful side',[13] others were interested in dissecting the expressive content of the material basis of his art – what Ragon refers to as its 'continual allusion to sperm and filth'.[14] Ponge, recognising a parallel between Fautrier's creations and Georges Bataille's concept of the *Inform*, found the substance of the works provocative, primitive and essential:

> Fautrier is a cat relieving himself in the embers. He has his own particular way of being wild. One of the most characteristic ways of wild beasts. Their way of excrement: a pasty, sticky mortar. And over it, by clawing the ashes, with a dash of earth, a dash of ash, (then they sniff), also their way of ritually covering over the excrement.[15]

The perception of reality as formless, incoherent and ambiguous so often found in Ponge's writings lies also at the heart of the vision that Sartre invented for Roquentin in *Nausea*. The notion of the inchoate, implying a freedom from formal categories, from expectations and from traditions, was, too, the single most important element in Tapié's evolving concept of a new, radically 'other' art for the post-war era. He recognised the 'otherness' of Fautrier's painting with matter. When he later came to reflect on the genesis of *art autre*, Tapié claimed that the *Otages* exhibition constituted one of two 'staggering shows [that] marked in 1945 the beginnings of that ''something else'' in which we are now beginning to feel at home'.[16] Tapié's second 'staggering show', was of Dubuffet, who himself acknowledged a fascination and admiration for Fautrier, at the same time as he was experimenting with his own invented impastoes. Due to Tapié's efforts as curator and critic Fautrier was swiftly categorised as a major precursor of the *Informel*. His work was included in two important exhibitions of the new tendency organised by Tapié: *White and Black* at the Galerie des Deux Iles in July 1948, where he showed alongside Jean Arp, Camille Bryen, Hans Hartung, Georges Mathieu, Francis Picabia, Tapié, Raoul Ubac and Wols; and *Les Significants de l'Informel* at the Studio Faccetti in November 1951 where he showed with Dubuffet, Mathieu, Michaux, Jean-Paul Riopelle and Iaroslav Serpan.

It was not only his wartime and post-war work which was seen as a central component of a new expressive stance. His works of the 1920s, and in particular his 'Glaciers' landscapes of 1926 and the images produced in connection with the Dante project, were also seen as revelatory. When wider recognition finally came, within his lifetime – ironically following his return to the more prosaic themes of the nude and still life – his name was continually linked to the new orthodoxy of the *Informel*. His exhibition at the Galerie Rive Droite in 1957 was therefore entitled *Fautrier, 30 années de figuration informelle*. This affinity should not be sought in the most obvious components of the *Informel* vocabulary – non-figuration and gestural improvisation – but rather in Fautrier's manipulation of physical matter as the expressive basis of art, together with his antipathy towards defined form. This antipathy is seen most clearly in the incongruity between the drawn contours of his images and the physical contours of his impastoes.

The artist himself always acknowledged reality as a starting point. In 1957 he told André Verdet that 'in matters of art all that comes from reality, on condition that it serves only as the initial thrust, appears more imaginative, more magic than anything which obstinately turns its back on it'.[17] In 1943 solitude and the experience of sculpture provided Fautrier with the means of developing his work; but it was reality at its most pressing and disturbing that ultimately inspired the 'Otages'.

NOTES

1 André Malraux, 'Notes', *La Nouvelle Revue Française*, no.233, Feb. 1933, reprinted in *Jean Fautrier 1898–1964*, exh. cat., Musée d'art moderne de la ville de Paris 1989, p.216.
2 Dominique de Menil, 'Oradour-sur-Glane', *The Menil Collection*, New York 1987, p.248.
3 André Malraux, 'Les Otages', in *Les Otages, peintures et sculptures de Jean Fautrier*, exh. cat., Galerie René Drouin, Paris 1945, reprinted in Paris 1989, p.222.
4 Francis Ponge, *Note sur Les Otages peintures de Fautrier*, Paris 1946, unpag.
5 Michel Ragon, *Fautrier*, Paris 1957, p.25.
6 Ibid., p.26.
7 Luc Vezin, 'Fautrier, Otage de son siècle' in 'Jean Fautrier', *Beaux Arts*, hors serie/les grandes expositions, 1988, p.8.
8 Malraux 1945.
9 Ragon 1957, p.10.
10 Jean Fautrier, letter to Jean Paulhan 1944, Archives Paulhan.
11 Jean Fautrier, 'Création', in *Jean Fautrier*, exh. cat., Kunstverein, Hamburg 1973, trans. Sarah Wilson in 'Jean Fautrier: Orthodoxy and the Outsider', *Art International*, vol.4, Autumn 1988, p.33.
12 Malraux 1945.
13 Ragon 1957, p.20.
14 Paulhan in Ragan 1957, p.21.
14 Ponge 1946, p.30.
15 Michel Tapié, *Un art autre*, Paris 1952, unpag.
16 Jean Fautrier, quoted in Jean-Yves Mock, 'Jean Fautrier', *Apollo*, vol.68, Sept. 1958, p.83.

Illustration (p.88) Portrait of Jean Fautrier
*c.*1952 Photograph by Paul Facchetti
© *Paul Facchetti*

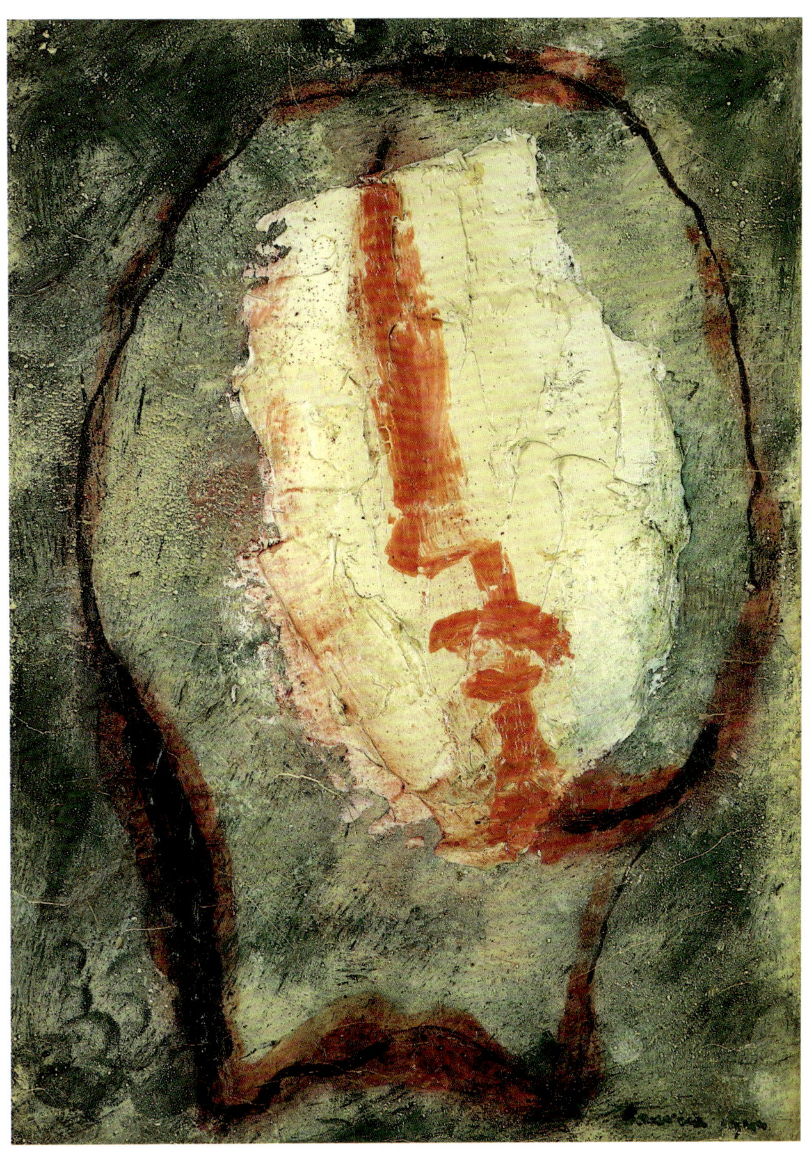

31 **Head of a Hostage No.20** 1944
33×24 ($13 \times 9\frac{1}{2}$)

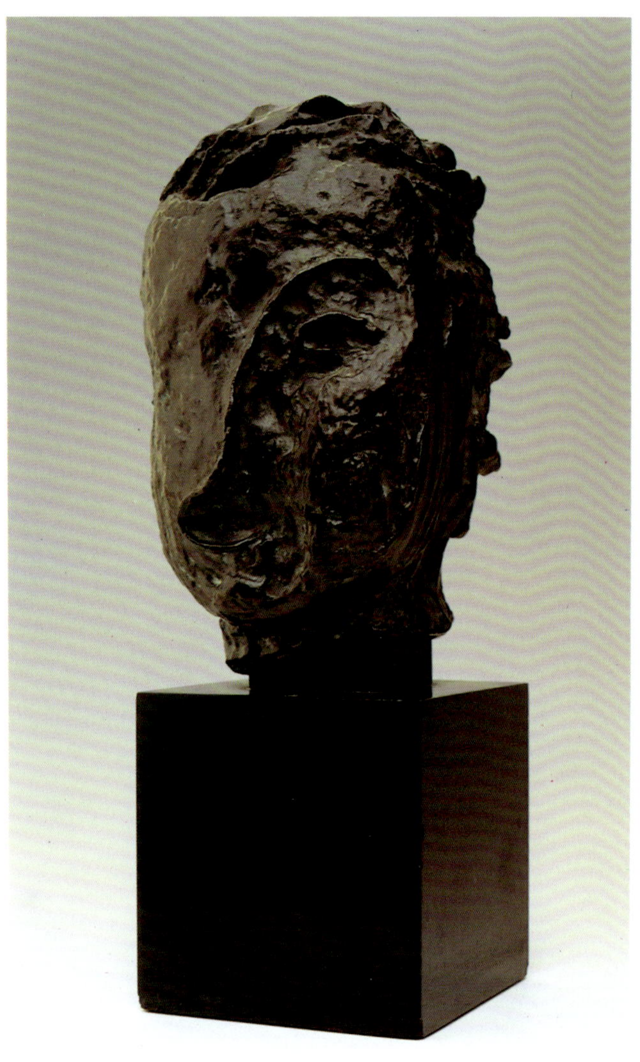

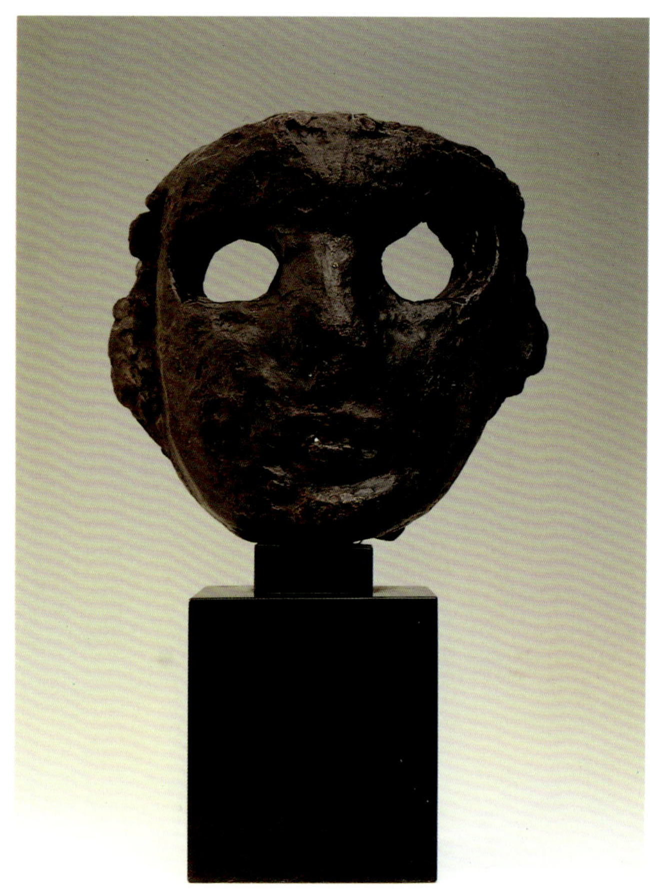

23 The Eyes 1940
14 × 15.5 (5½ × 6⅛)

22 Scored Head 1940
18 × 10 × 15 (7⅛ × 4 × 5⅞)

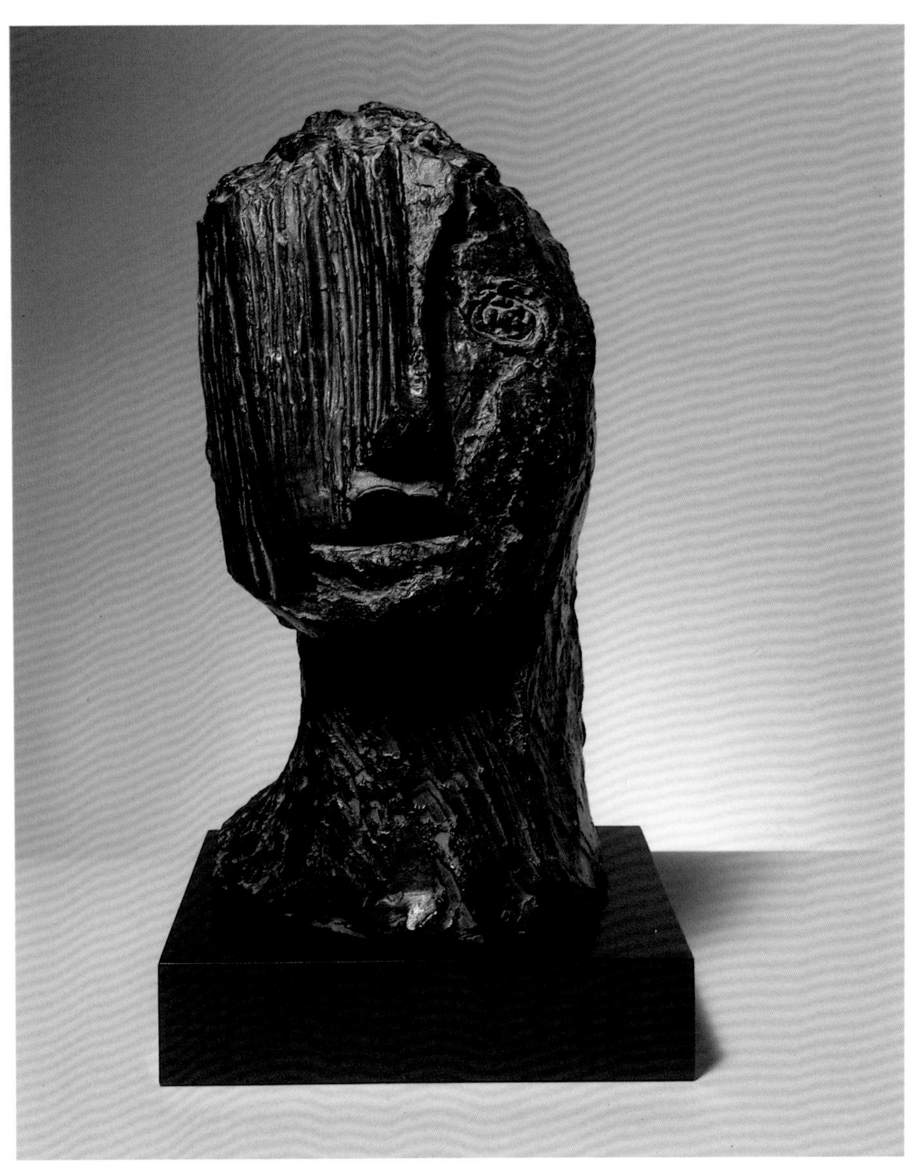

24 Large Tragic Head 1942
38.5 × 21 × 21.5 (15¼ × 8¼ × 8½)

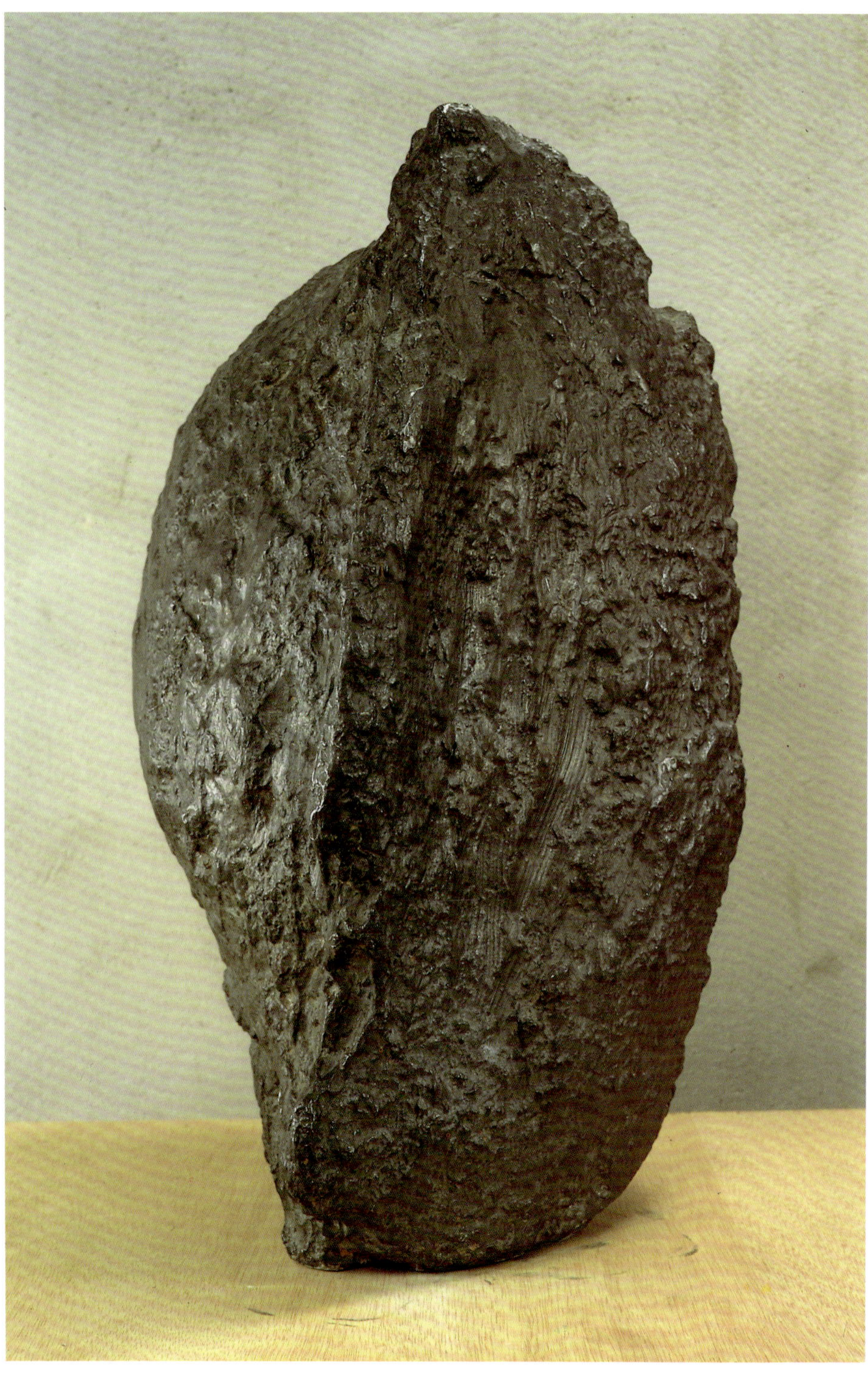

25 Hostage 1943
48 (18⅞) high

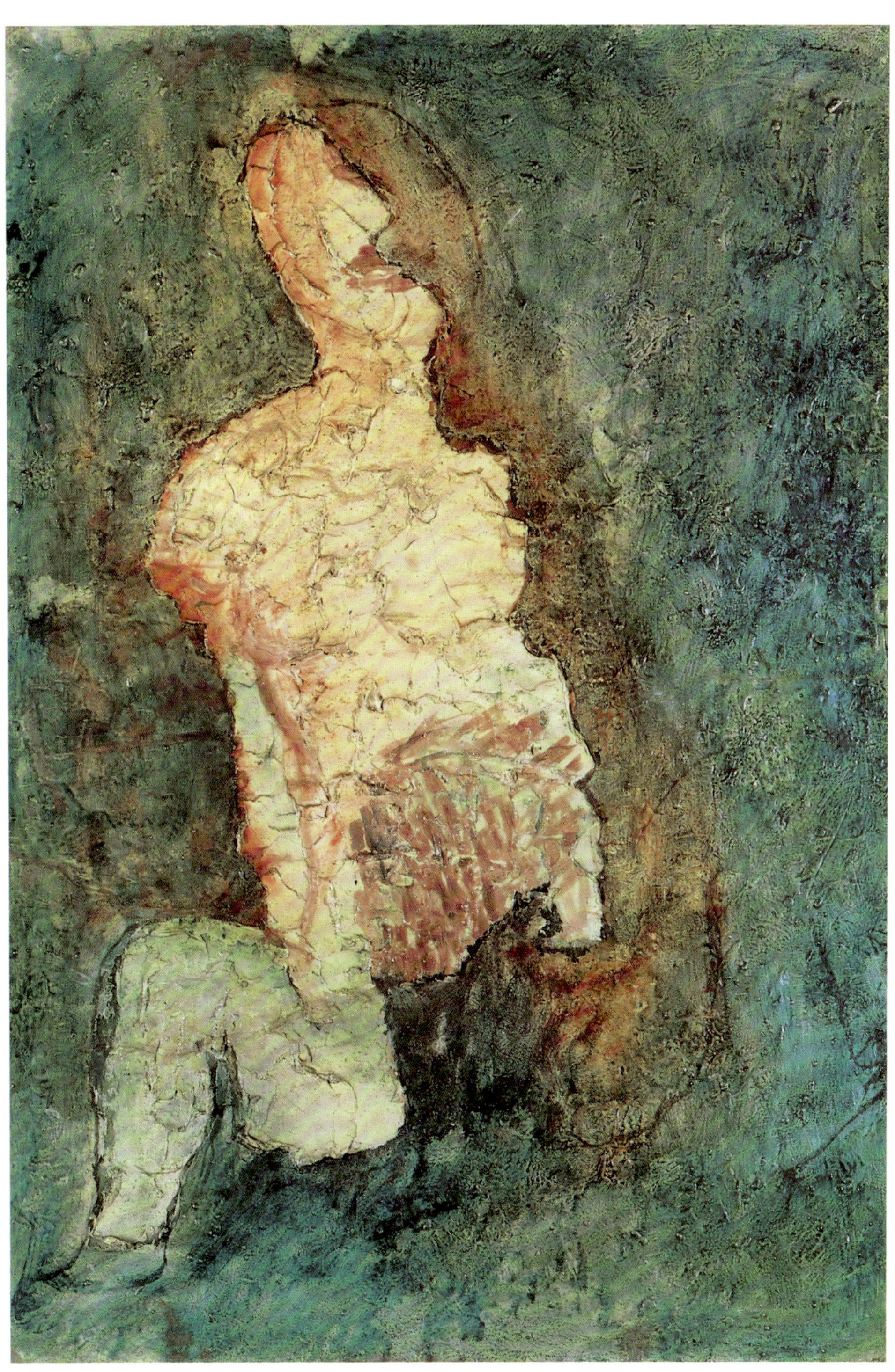

26 Sarah 1942–3
116 × 89 (45⅝ × 35)

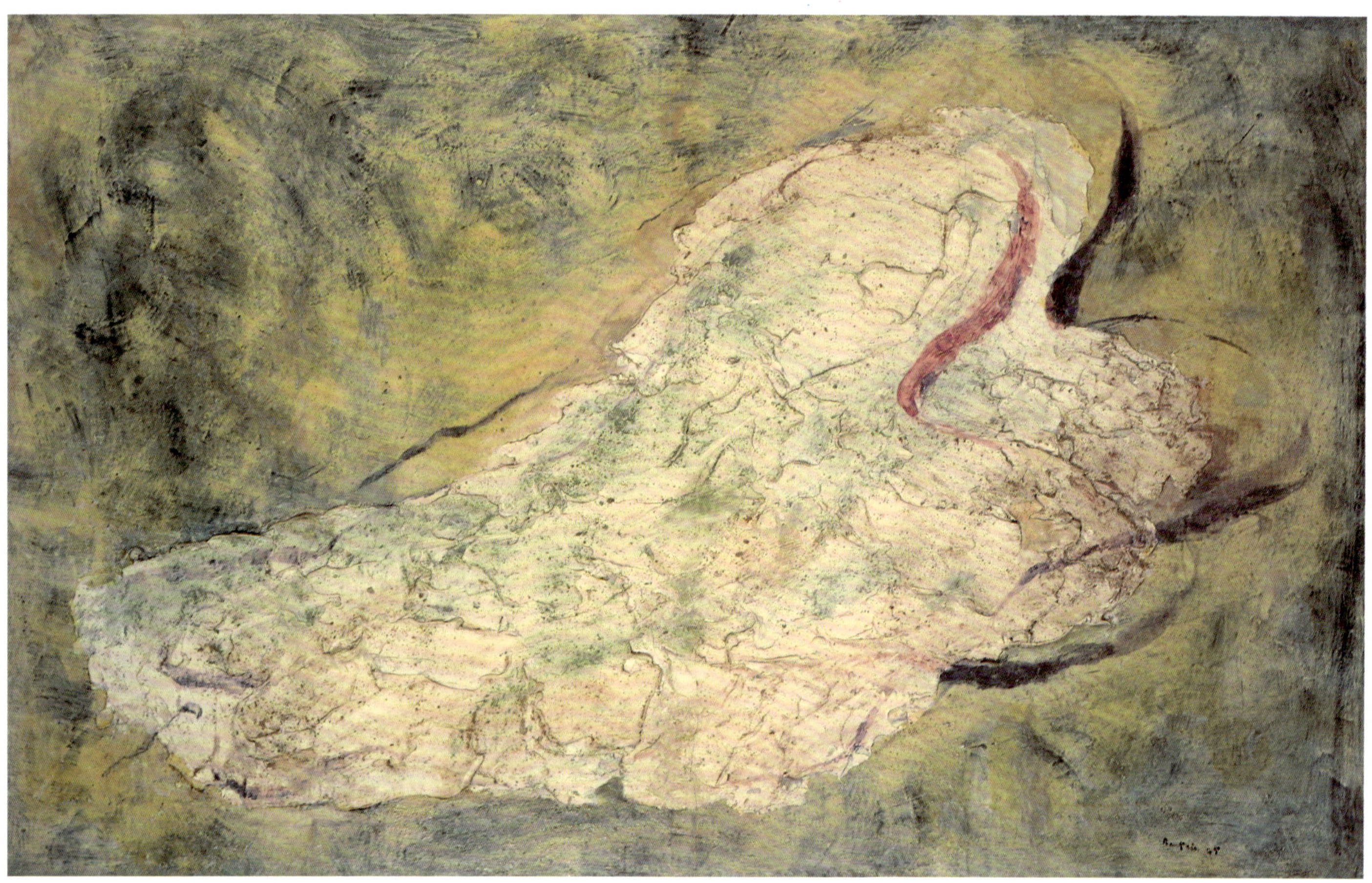

27 The Jewess 1943
73 × 115.5 (28¾ × 45½)

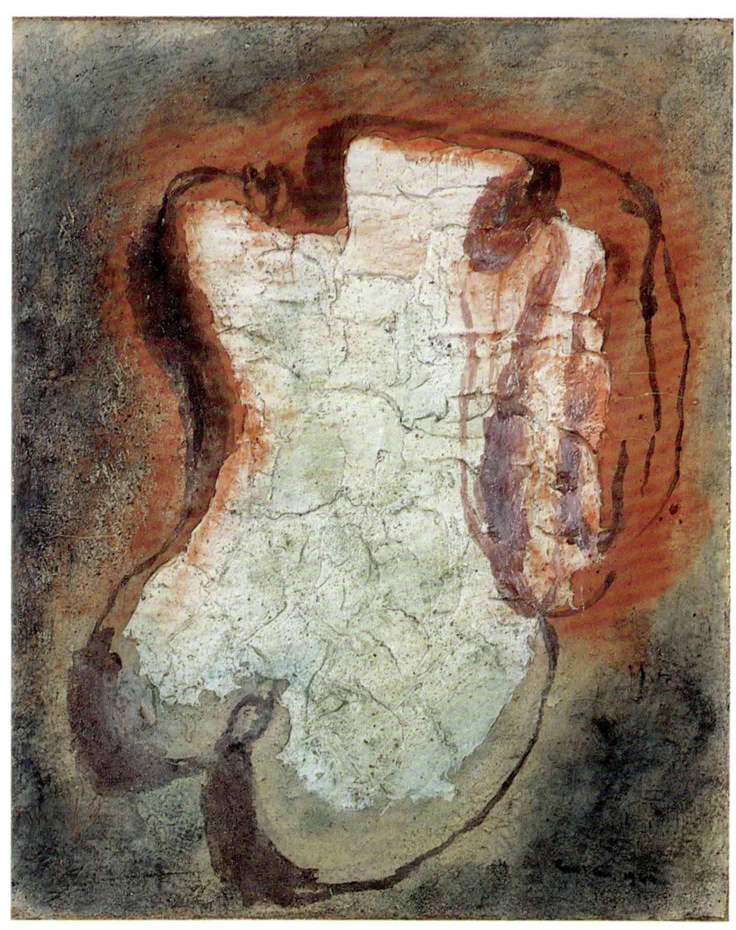

28 Torso 1943
46 × 38 (18⅛ × 15)

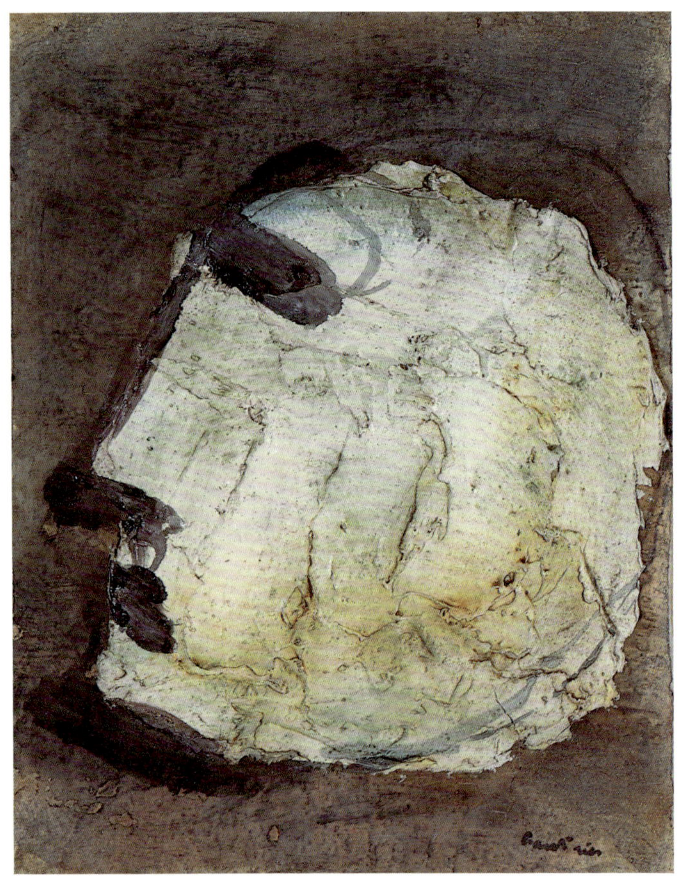

29 Head of a Hostage 1943
$28 \times 22 \ (11 \times 8\frac{5}{8})$

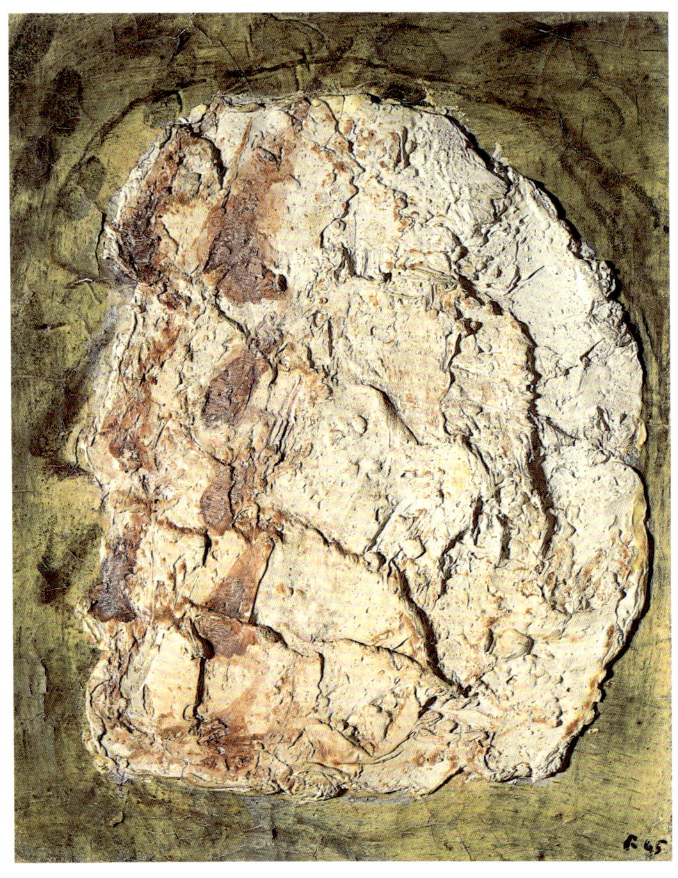

30 Head of a Hostage No.1 1944
$35.6 \times 26.7 \ (14 \times 10\frac{1}{2})$

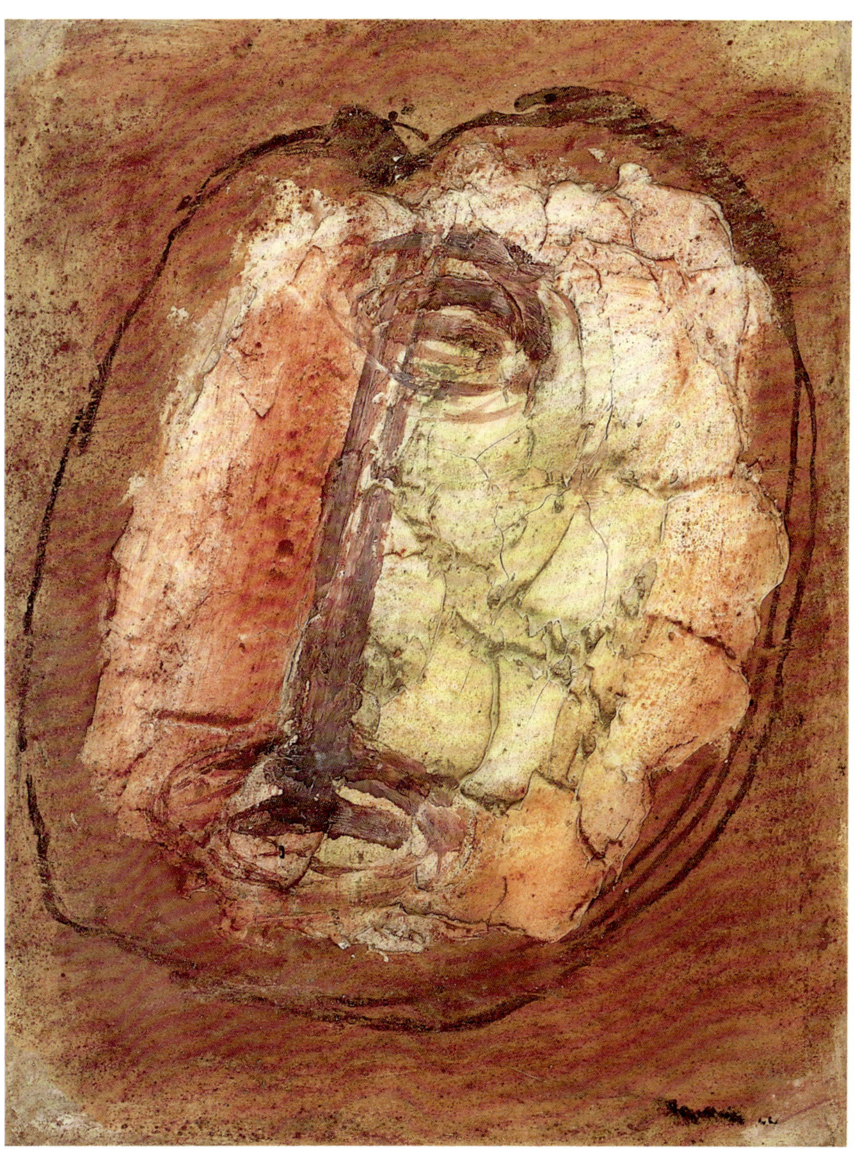

32 Head of a Hostage No.22 1944
$27 \times 22 \, (10\frac{5}{8} \times 8\frac{5}{8})$

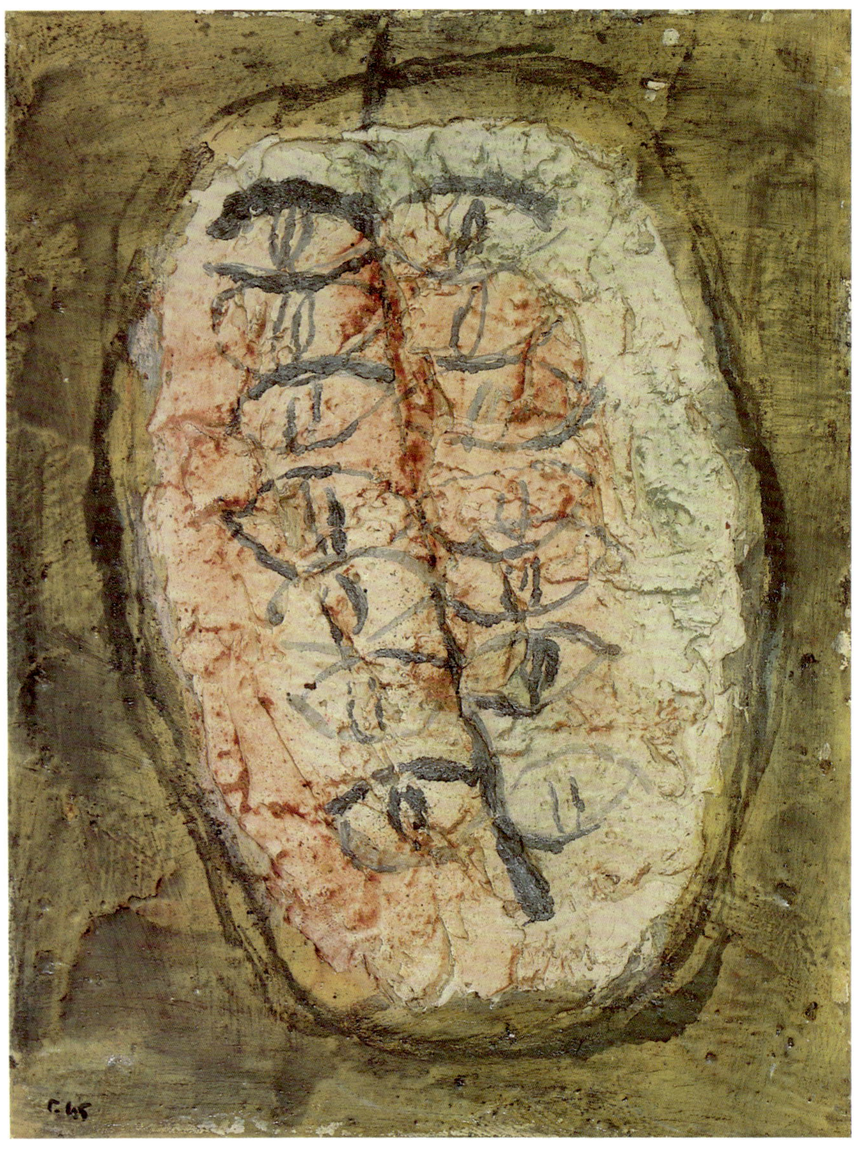

33 Head of a Hostage 1945
$35 \times 27 \ (13\frac{3}{4} \times 10\frac{5}{8})$

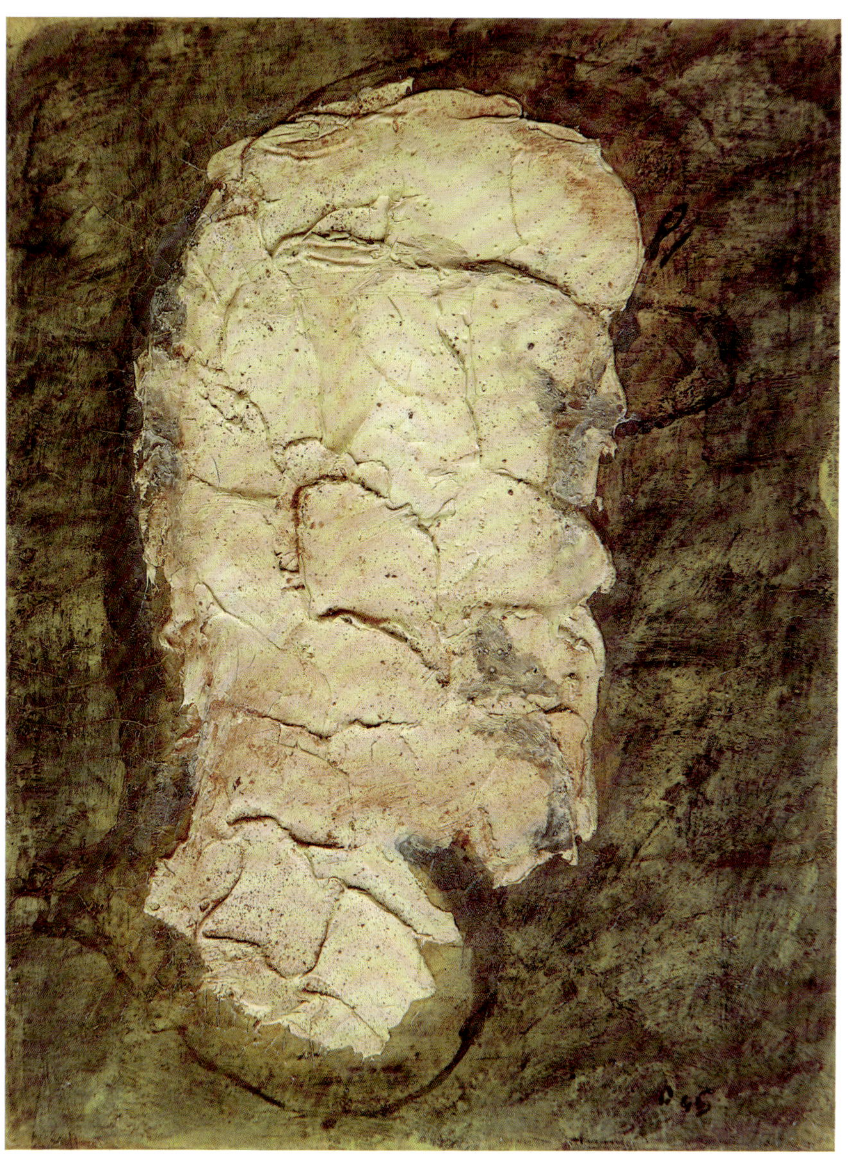

36 Head of a Hostage No.2 1945
35.5 × 26.5 ($14 × 10\frac{3}{8}$)

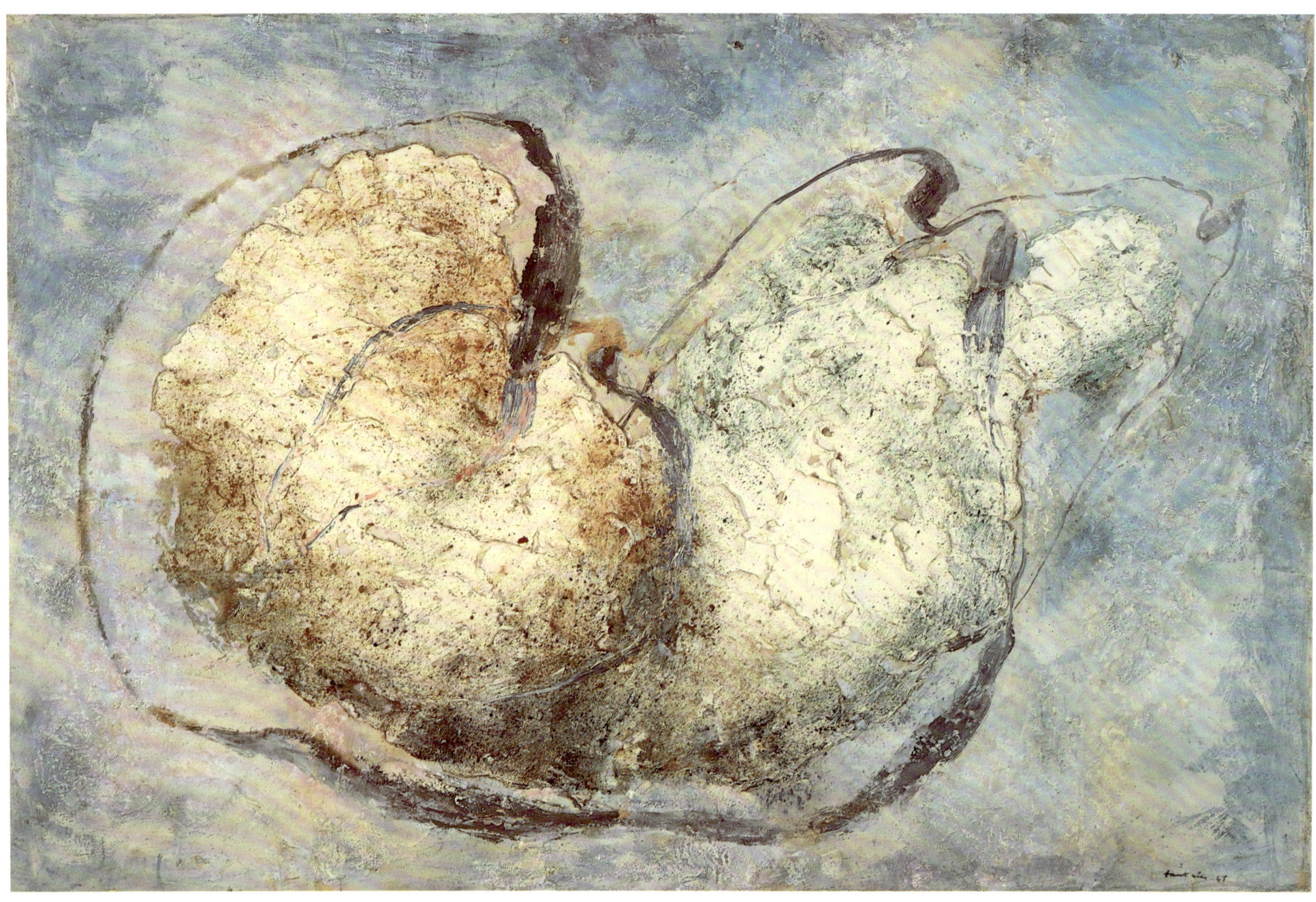

34 Remains 1945
114.3 × 144.8 (45 × 57)

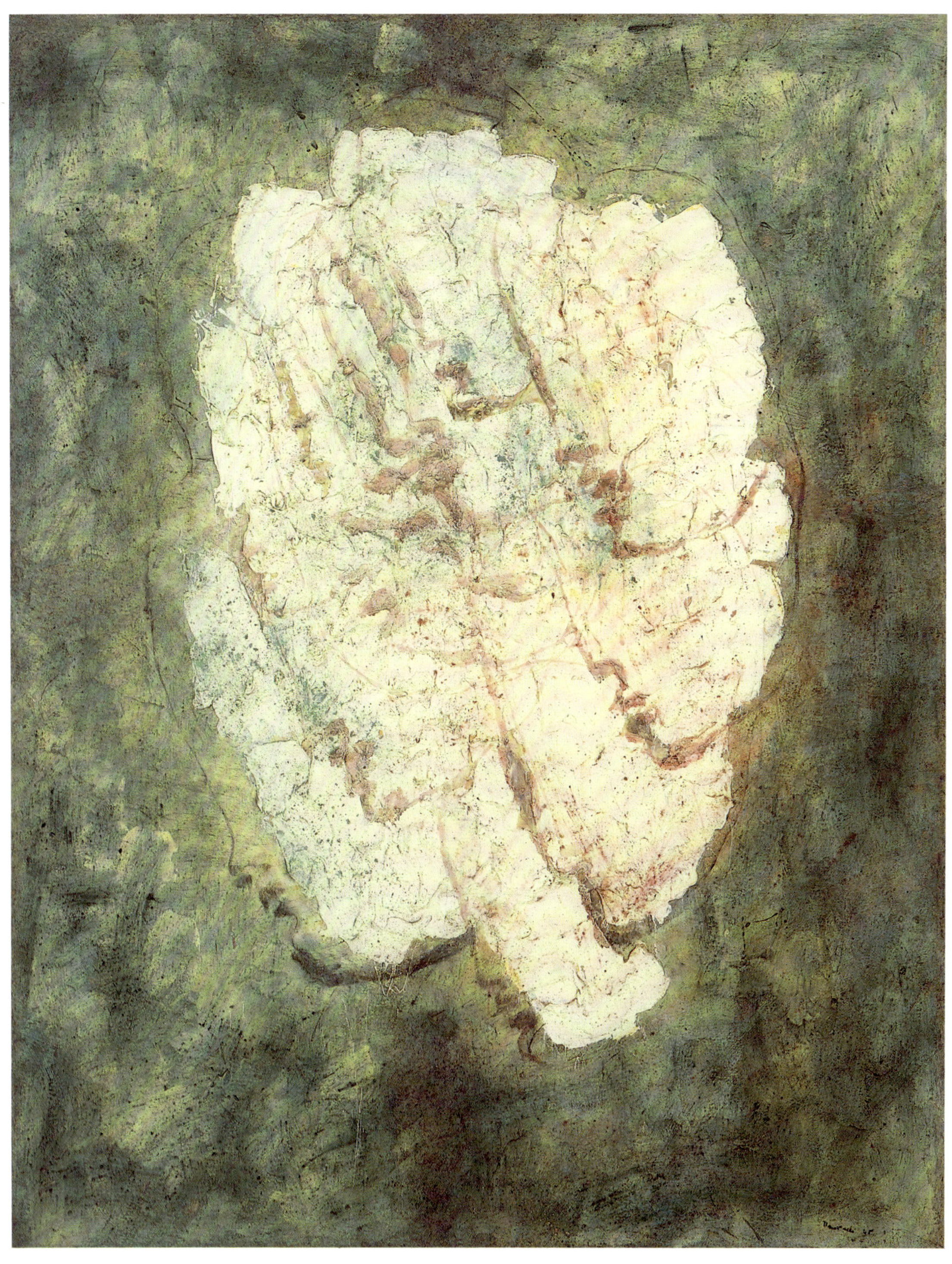

35 Oradour-sur-Glane 1945
145.1 × 113.7 (57⅛ × 44¾)

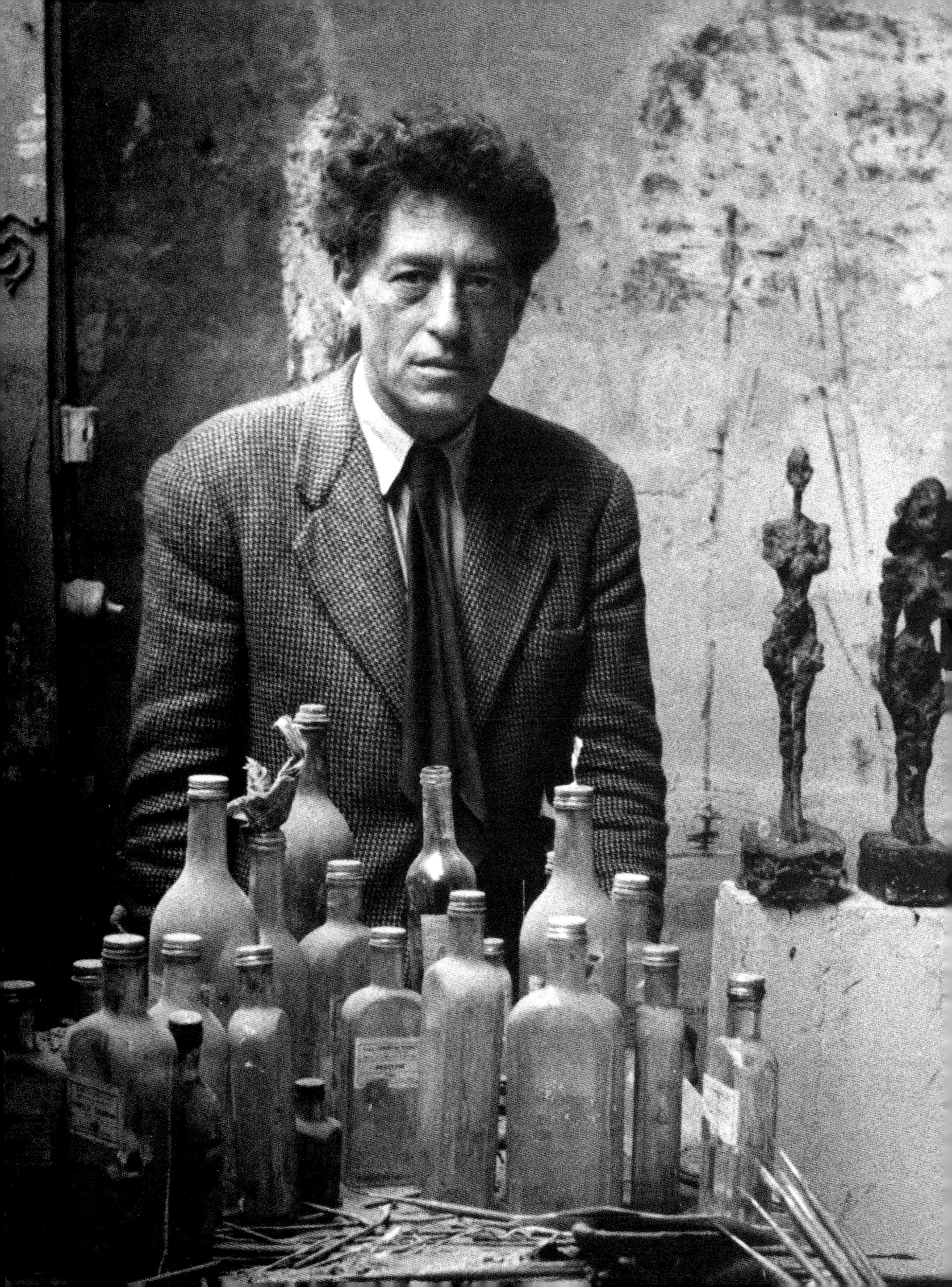

Alberto Giacometti (1901–1966)

A singular figure, relentlessly pursuing a singular goal, Alberto Giacometti remained aloof from the major group manifestations of new, expressionist styles after the war. His 1951 exhibition at the Galerie Maeght was his first Paris show for nineteen years, and even when he became better known in the years after this exhibition, there developed no 'school' of Giacometti. However, in 1948 the American critic Dore Ashton spoke of the 'unmistakable existentialist milieu of his work'[1] and the 1959 *New Images of Man* exhibition in New York assigned him a key role in the creation of an original approach to the figure, focusing on the atmospheric, iconographic and physical attributes of his work, seeing it as part of a widespread investigation of the spiritual essence of humanity. For Giacometti, these evocative stylistic characteristics were intimately bound up with his struggle to find adequate means of representing perceived reality.

Giacometti's struggle to reformulate the role of the artist was first described as heroic and primitive by Jean-Paul Sartre in his 1948 essay on the artist, 'The Search for the Absolute',[2] published in the catalogue of Giacometti's first post-war exhibition, at the Pierre Matisse Gallery, New York. Sartre saw in Giacometti's work a rejection of the traditional 'conceptual' approach to sculpture – in which the sculptor would make a head according to his knowledge – in favour of an approach based on direct visual experience. Comparing Giacometti to 'the man of Eyzies, the man of Altamira', Sartre defined the role of the artist in atavistic terms:

> After three thousand years, the task of Giacometti and of contemporary sculptors is not to enrich the galleries with new works, but to prove that sculpture itself is possible … it is not a question of infinite progression; there is a definite goal to be attained, a single problem to be solved: how to mould a man in stone without petrifying him?[3]

This notion of the artist as caveman was reinforced by Giacometti's austere, almost troglodytic lifestyle, and encouraged by the image the artist projected in conversation and writings. Photographs of him, taken by Patricia Echaurren in his Paris studio on rue Hippolyte-Maindron, just south of Montparnasse, as he hurriedly prepared the magnificent life-size figures for his first Matisse Gallery show, capture the dusty subterranean atmosphere of his gloomy ground-floor rooms. The plaster figures which people the space suggest ancient burial rites. Behind these spectral figures and the detritus of a sculptor's tools, the walls of the studio bear the daubs and scratches of the artist's incessant deliberations, as mysterious and primeval as the recently discovered cave paintings of Lascaux.

In the letter to Pierre Matisse written in 1947 which was also published in the New York exhibition catalogue,[4] Giacometti described the trajectory of his career. Following traditional studies in painting and sculpture in his native Switzerland he studied in Italy and then moved to Paris in 1922 where his work developed through Cubist stylisation to an association with Surrealist modes of composition during the first half of the 1930s. In 1935, growing dissatisfied with Surrealism, he attempted 'one or two studies from nature'.[5] The experience was galvanising. There followed a five-year period in which he concentrated almost exclusively on life drawing. His brother Diego sat for him every morning. Frustrated by his lack of progress Giacometti turned to working from memory, only to find that his sculptures, as they progressed, diminished in size becoming minute. After spending the war years in his native Zurich he was able to return to Paris with his finger-sized sculptures neatly packed in the pockets of his overcoat. He felt himself at an impasse and sought escape once again by a return to the model. Although continuously thwarted by his lack of accomplishment, he had articulated a new goal – that of achieving a 'likeness' or 'resemblance'. These concepts embraced a dual notion of the artist's vision and his encounter with the model, for a head is both an object in space and a living presence.

As the letter to Pierre Matisse demonstrates, Giacometti liked to portray his career as a continuous striving towards a determined goal. In 1962 he acknowledged: 'it's a rather unusual thing for a person to spend more of his time trying to copy a head than in living life'.[6] Commentators from Sartre on have tended to adopt this teleological veneer, effectively isolating Giacometti from his context. Links with other artists are often neglected. For example, the influence of figurative painters like Balthus, Derain and Gruber and the debates of the 1930s over realism have yet to be assessed for their influence on Giacometti's rejection of Surrealism. Parallels can also be found between the austerity of Gruber's solitary figures and Giacometti's concentration on his sitter's studio presence in his first post-war paintings. The relationship between Giacometti's urban figure groups and Balthus's major pre-war painting 'The Street' 1934 (Museum of Modern Art, New York), may be as important as the literary ties so often drawn between Giacometti and Sartre, Camus or Beckett.

However, the rhetoric of struggle and failure, of the artist as a 'driven man', was compelling, and Giacometti was an ideal candidate for Sartre's admiration. Some time before their first encounter in 1939 Sartre had dismissed classical sculpture and portraiture as means of conferring on their subjects a fixed, 'mythical' character at odds with the real nature of man's fragile and ephemeral existence. In Giacometti's figures, by contrast, Sartre found this real nature vividly represented – both iconographically, in the depiction of human solitude, and physically, in the plaster which he modelled and in his light and hesitant touch.

The exchange of ideas between Sartre and Giacometti, and between the artist and the intellectuals who frequented the Montparnasse and Saint-Germain café circuit of which he was a habitué, was mutually stimulating. He is frequently referred to in Simone de Beauvoir's memoirs and Sartre wrote two major texts on his work.[7] He was the subject of an evocative essay by Jean Genet[8] (whom he painted on several occasions between 1953 and 1957) and he became a close friend of Samuel Beckett in the early 1950s. Later on his work was also written about by Maurice Merleau-Ponty. In his seminal essay 'Eye and Mind' (1961) Merleau-Ponty argued that Giacometti's understanding of 'resemblance' was very close to his own phenomenological approach: 'Resemblance is the result of perception, not its mainspring.'[9] Merleau-Ponty distinguished between habitual perception, based on knowledge accumulated over time, and authentic perceptual experience which, like the sight of a newborn child, precedes knowledge.[10] Giacometti too seems to have come to a similar understanding of different qualities of vision. He was especially influenced by several dramatic perceptual experiences. Once, while watching a film in a Montparnasse cinema, he suddenly realised the distinction between the external world and the filmed version of it:

> instead of seeing a person on the screen, I saw vague black taches [blurs] that moved. I looked at the people around me and all of a sudden I saw them as I had never seen them … Everything was different: depth, objects, colours, silence … and completely new … a sort of continual marvelling at everything … That day reality became completely revalued for me; it became the unknown, but a marvellous unknown.[11]

From then on he saw his models anew, as strangers, each time they sat for him. Of Diego he confessed

> [he] has posed ten thousand times for me: the next time he poses I won't recognise him. I should like to work with him some more, to test what I see.[12]

Giacometti found this recurring experience of strangeness frustrating as well as inspiring. His routine was dominated by obsessive reworking of the same themes – standing women, walking men, small groups of figures, busts – and he worked either from memory or with a few key models, intimately known – principally his brother Diego and his wife, Annette. He attempted meticulously to control the circumstances of each sitting, establishing and maintaining the exact distance between artist and model, insisting on the model's immobility and silence. He worked swiftly, making, destroying and remaking. Sculpted figures, modelled in clay on a fragile wire armature, could be revised endlessly before their final casting in bronze and even then the plaster remained to be reworked. Giacometti's 'Venice Women' (nos.46–54), made for the Venice Biennale of 1956, consist of separate states, cast in bronze, of a single female standing figure. There exists no definitive or most accomplished version.[13] Paintings, too, were ruthlessly scraped back and restarted. Seen in a raking light their surfaces show concentrations of paint around the head, vivid proof of their constant revision. The end result was often not so much a finished piece as an abandoned state.

Another moving perceptual experience shaped Giacometti's understanding of the importance of space. In his 1946 text 'The Dream, the Sphinx and the Death of T' he recalls how waking up one morning he had the impression that

> there was no longer any rapport between things, they were separated by endless abysses of space. I looked at my room in terror, and cold sweat ran down my back.[14]

Giacometti recognised the perceptual impossibility of seeing anything outside an enveloping space. This space he describes through a number of different techniques. The exaggeratedly large bases (or feet) of certain pieces can be interpreted as a shorthand for deep perspectival recession and a means of recreating a feeling of the original confrontation of the artist and model. 'Four Figurines on a Base' 1950 (no.41) recaptures the image of four naked women seen at a brothel. According to Giacometti the space in which he saw them was at once physical and psychological:

> The distance which separated us, the polished floor, seemed insurmountable in spite of my desire to cross it, and impressed me as much as the women.[15]

In his paintings, too, Giacometti developed specific techniques for creating the illusion of distance and the substance of space. Early on he began to centre his images within a specially delineated picture area, a frame within a frame, thus enhancing the sense of tunnelling recession often created already by a radical reduction of the size of his sitter's head. Giacometti was not unaware of the expressive potential of distorted and ambiguous spatial effects: 'My figures need a sort of no man's land',[16] he said. Giacometti's contemporaries were fascinated by his treatment of the figure in space: a preoccupation with the void or the abyss pervades contemporary existentialist literature.

Giacometti's treatment of surfaces was also designed to effect an active and expressive relationship between form and space. In painting he used a light, incessantly moving brushstroke to build volume and suggest contour, an effect akin to that given by the roughly pitted surface of the sculptures. Both techniques appear to generate form rather that depict detail. Whilst some have seen in Giacometti's painted strokes visual evidence of the rapidly searching movements of the artist's eye, the marks also seem to bind physical mass to the surrounding space. There is a vital physical quality to his work which is not far from the feeling generated in the sculpture of contemporaries like Richier and Fautrier. All three artists rejected the smooth polished surfaces of earlier modernist styles in favour of roughly pitted textures which project the marks and movements of the artist's hands, evidence of their physical engagement with matter. In Giacometti's bronzes evidence of the restless movements of the artist's hands attests the provisional status of the image.

Despite shifts in emphasis, Giacometti's postwar oeuvre shows a striking stylistic coherence. He saw the elements of his style as his means of translating perceptual experience into art and thus approaching 'resemblance':

> Have you ever noticed that the truer a work is the more stylised it is? That seems strange, because style certainly does not conform to the reality of appearances, and yet the heads that come closest to resembling people I see on the street are those that are least naturalistic – the sculptures of the Egyptians, the Chinese, the archaic Greeks, and the Sumerians.[17]

For his contemporaries, the urge to find metaphors appropriate to the age was overwhelming. At Giacometti's post-war debut in New York, commentators were swift to interpret his excessively attenuated figures as symbols of human despair and hardship. Whilst one critic could find 'in the tall, mysterious, emaciated knotty forms … a sort of desperate struggle for survival',[18] others found the imagery of recent wartime suffering. The reviewer for *Art Digest* saw them as 'fugitives from Dachau'.[19]

Giacometti rejected these interpretations of his work, claiming that the evocative quality of his imagery was largely unintentional. On the rare occasions when he was asked to express his view of humanity and explain the relationship of his work to his era he avoided grandiose sentiments, because, he explained in 1962, 'in art there is no one aspect of life that should be expressed rather than another. There is only the problem of expression'.[20]

NOTES

1 Dore Ashton, in Reinhold Hohl, *Giacometti: Sculpture, Painting, Drawing*, 1972, p.278.

2 Jean-Paul Sartre, 'La Recherche de l'absolu', *Les Temps Modernes* vol.III, no.28, 1948, pp.1153–63; trans. Lionel Abel, 'The Search for the Absolute', in *Alberto Giacometti: Exhibition of Sculptures, Paintings, Drawings*, exh. cat., Pierre Matisse Gallery, New York 1948, pp.2–22.

3 Pierre Matisse Gallery 1948, p.4.

4 'A Letter from Alberto Giacometti', Pierre Matisse Gallery 1948, pp.29–45.

5 Ibid., p.42.

6 Excerpt from André Parinaud, 'Entretien avec Alberto Giacometti: "Pourquoi je suis sculpteur"', *Arts, Lettres, Spectacles*, no.873, 13 June 1962, pp.1, 5, in Hohl 1972, p.274.

7 Sartre 1948, and 'Les Peintures de Giacometti', *Derrière le Miroir*, no.65, 1955, trans. Lionel Abel, 'In Search of Space', *Art News and Review*, Sept. 1955, pp.26–30.

8 Jean Genet, *L'Atelier d'Alberto Giacometti*, Paris 1958, trans. Charles Penwarden in *Alberto Giacometti: The Artist's Studio*, exh. cat., Tate Gallery Liverpool 1991.

9 Maurice Merleau-Ponty, 'L'Oeil et l'esprit', *Art de France*, vol.I, Jan. 1961, trans. Harold Osborne (ed.), in *Aesthetics*, 1972, pp.55–85.

10 This is discussed by Ed Hill, 'The Inherent Phenomenology of Alberto Giacometti's Drawings,' *Drawing*, vol.III, no.5, Jan.–Feb. 1982, p.98.

11 Alberto Giacometti, Interview with Georges Charbonnier, April 1957, in Georges Charbonnier, *Le Monologue du peintre*, Paris 1959, pp.159–70.

12 Pierre Dumayet, 'La Difficulté de faire une tête: Giacometti', *Le Nouveau Candide*, Paris, 6 June 1963, reprinted in Pierre Dumayet, *Vu et entendu*, 1964, pp.37–46, excerpt trans. in Hohl 1972, p.185.

13 David Sylvester, 'The Residue of a Vision', in *Alberto Giacometti*, Arts Council of Great Britain 1965, unpag.

14 Alberto Giacometti, 'Le Rêve, le sphinx et la mort de T', *Labyrinthe*, nos.22/23, 15 Dec. 1946, pp.12–13.

15 Alberto Giacometti, 'Letter to Pierre Matisse 1950', *Alberto Giacometti*, exh. cat., Pierre Matisse Gallery, New York 1950, pp.14–15.

16 Alberto Giacometti, 'Autres propos', 1965, in Pierre Schneider, *Alberto Giacometti dessins*, exh.cat., Galerie Claude Bernard, Paris 1985.

17 Excerpt from André Parinaud, 'Entretien avec Alberto Giacometti: "Pourquoi je suis sculpteur"', *Arts, Lettres, Spectacles*, no.873, 13 June 1962, in Hohl 1972, p.278.

18 Allen Weller, 'Coast to Coast: Chicago', *Art Digest*, no.4, 15 Nov. 1953.

19 Jo Gibbs, 'Attenuated Beauty', *Art Digest*, no.22, 1 Feb. 1948.

20 Quoted in Hohl 1972, p.284.

Illustration (p.104) Alberto Giacometti in his studio 1954 Photograph by Sabine Weiss © *Weiss/Rapho*

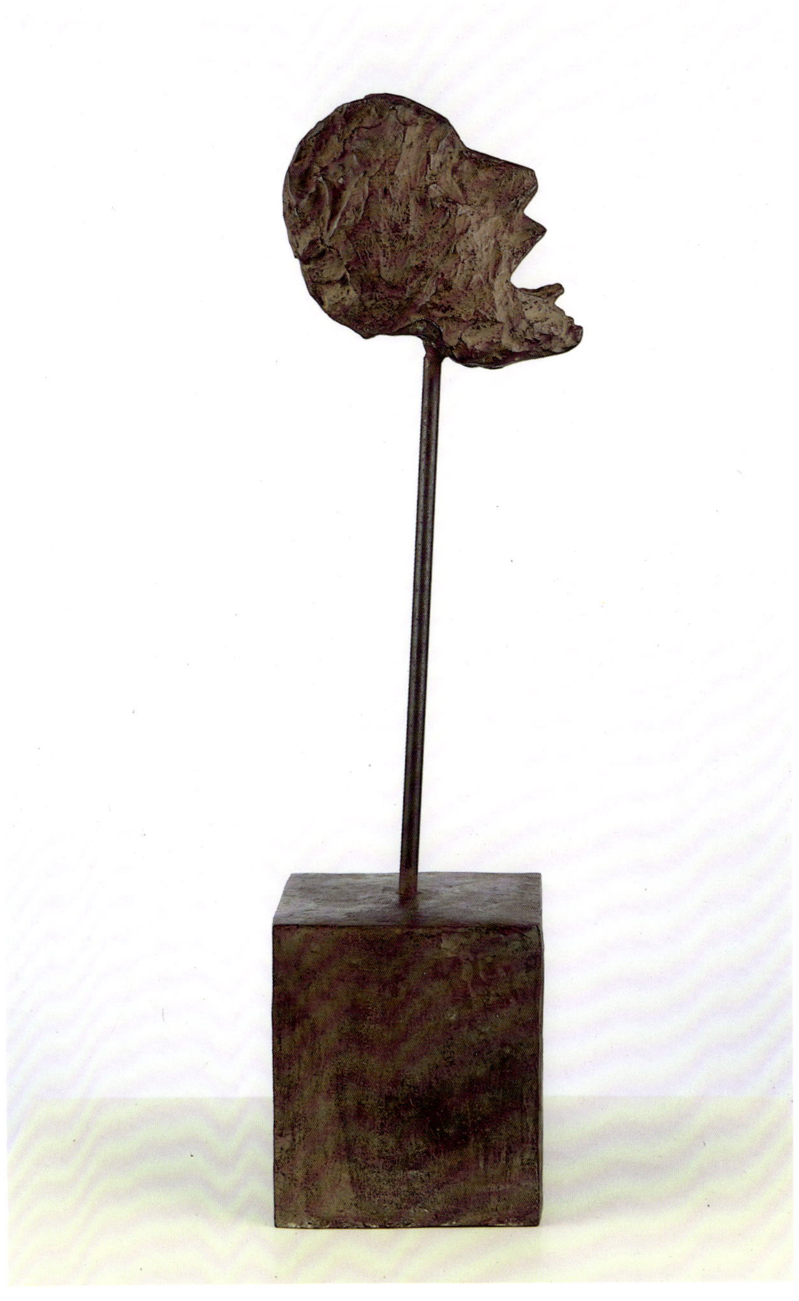

37 Head on a Rod 1947
62.2 × 14.6 × 15.2 (24½ × 5¾ × 6)

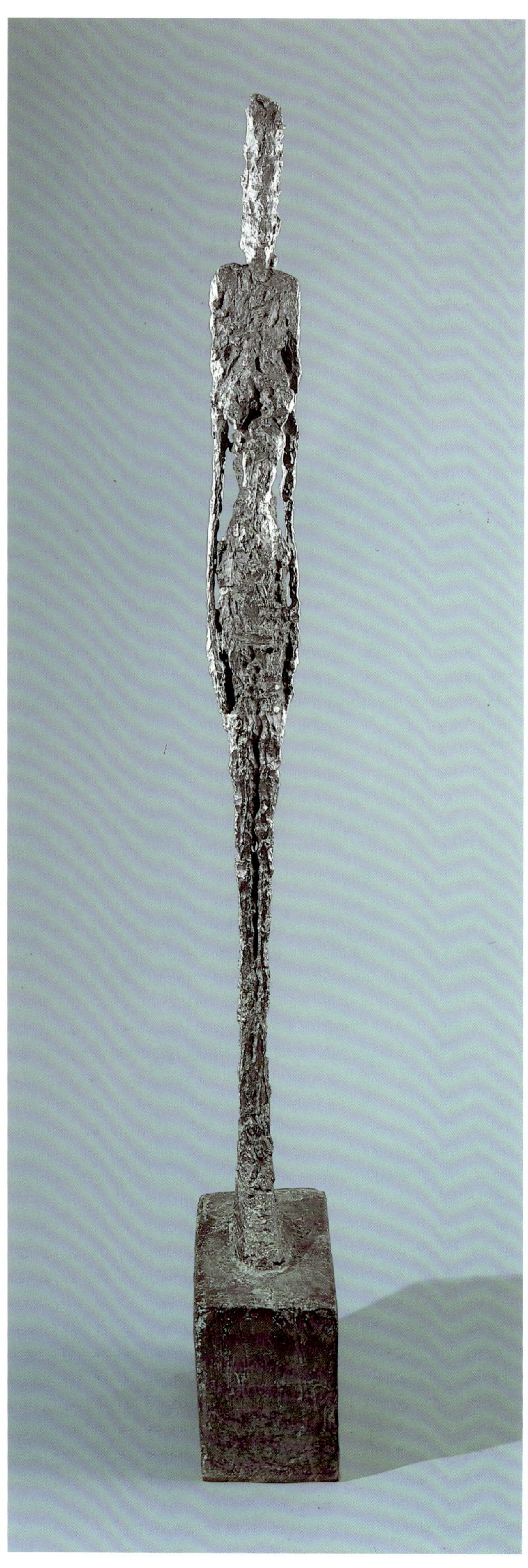

38 Tall Figure 1947
201.3 × 21.3 × 42.2 (79¼ × 8⅜ × 16⅝)

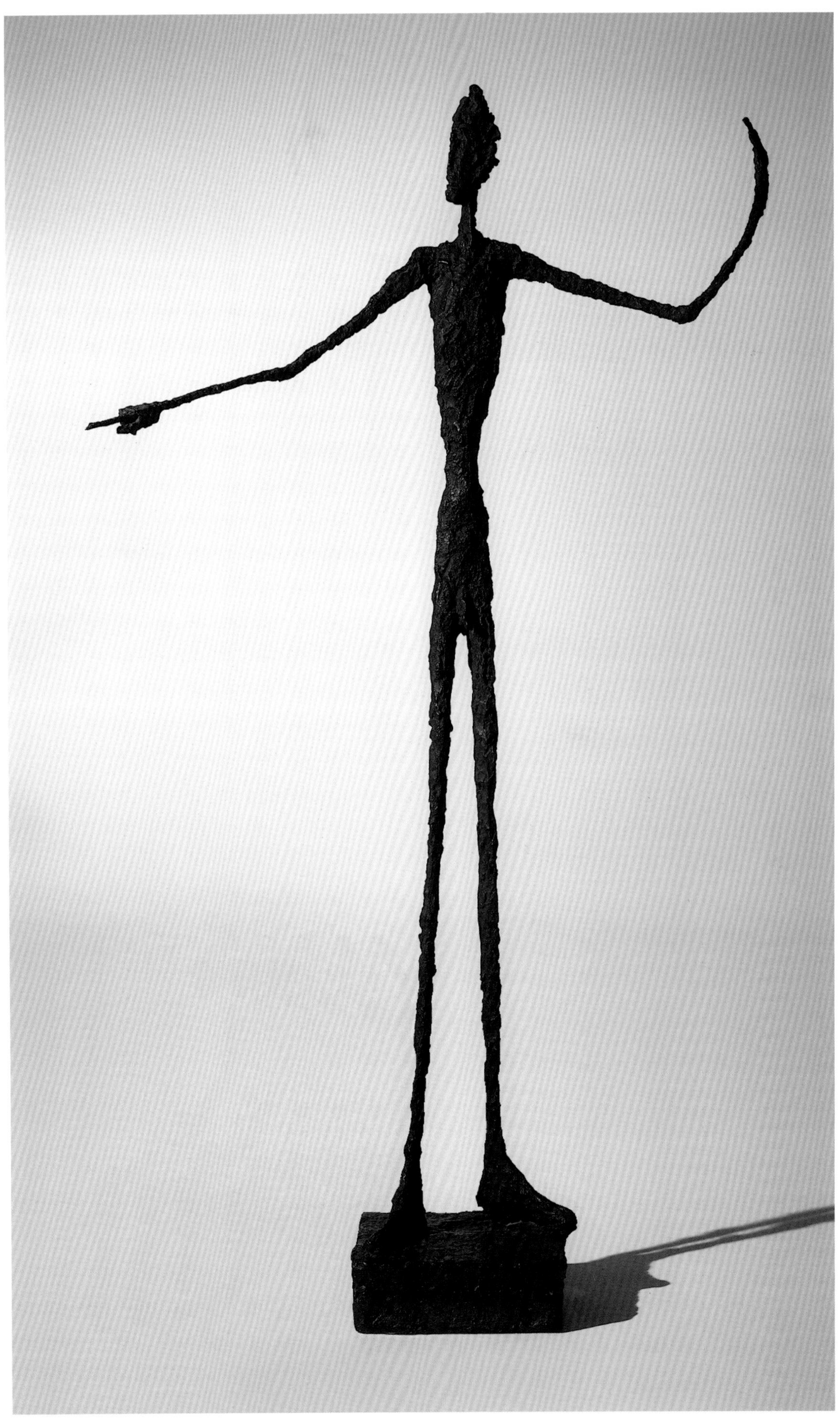

39 Man Pointing 1947
178 × 95 × 52 (70⅛ × 37⅜ × 20½)

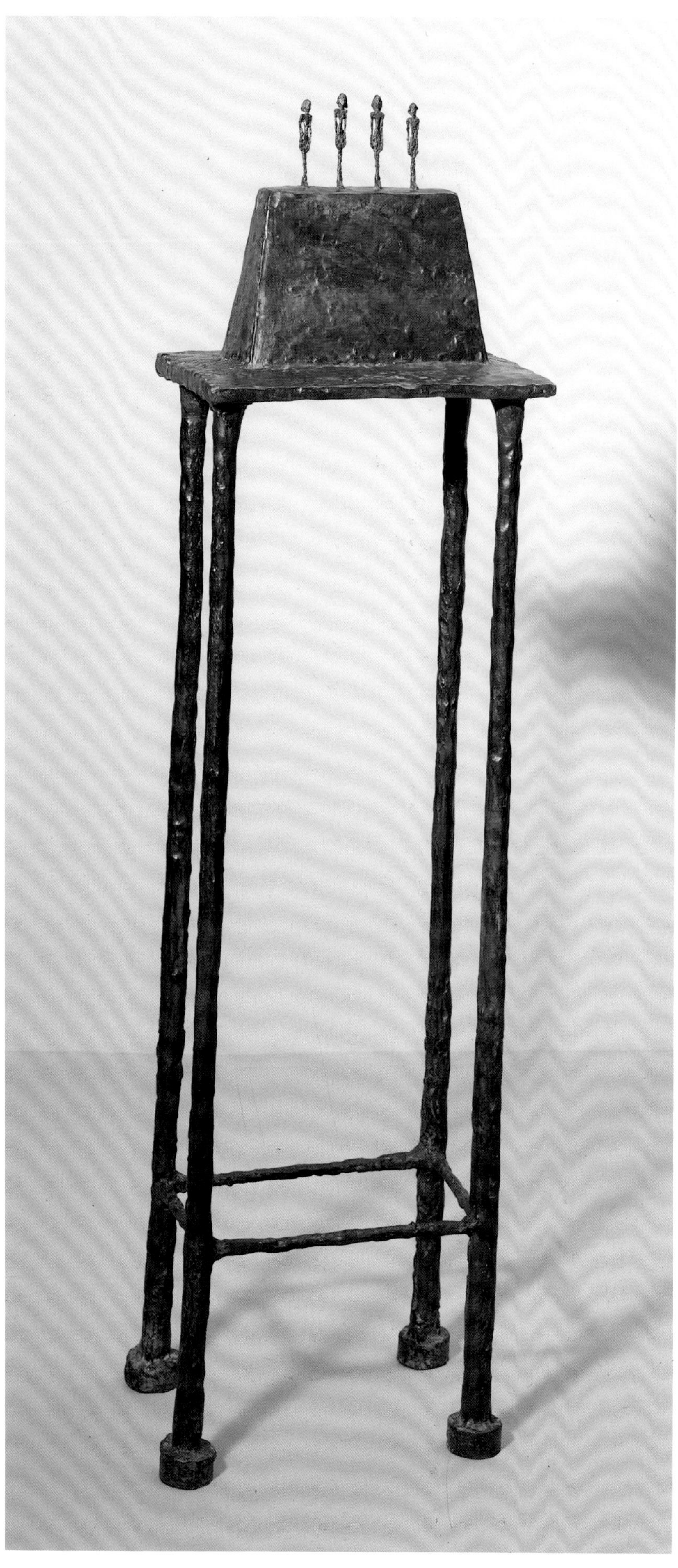

41 Four Figurines on a Base
1950/1965, cast *c*.1965–6
156.2 × 41.9 × 31.4 (61½ × 16½ × 12⅜)

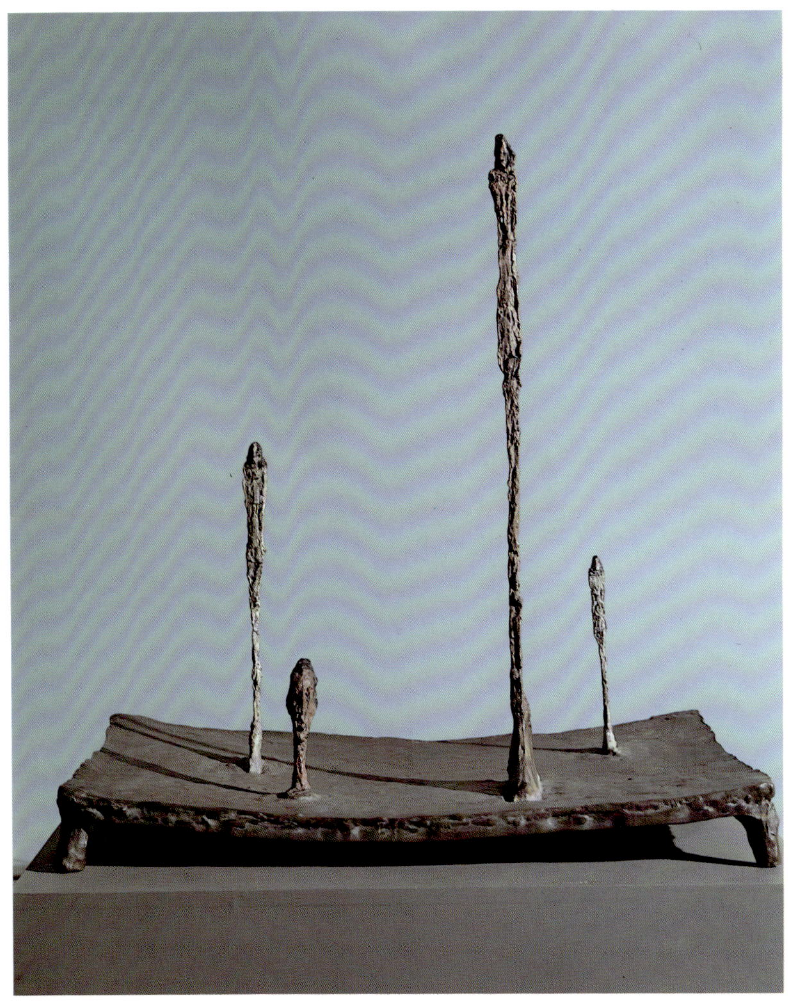

42 Place, Composition with Three
Figures and a Head 1950
$58 \times 57 \times 42$ ($22\frac{7}{8} \times 22\frac{1}{2} \times 16\frac{1}{2}$)

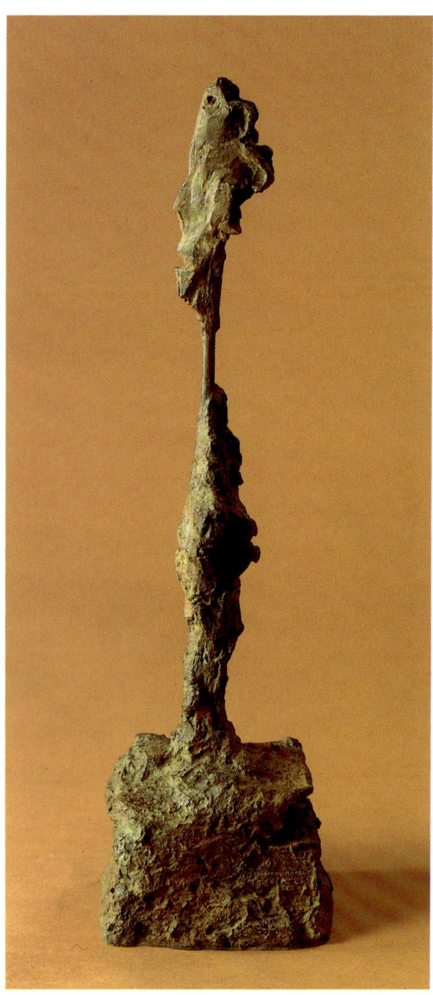

40 Bust of a Man 1950
57 × 15.5 × 16.5 (22½ × 6⅛ × 6½)

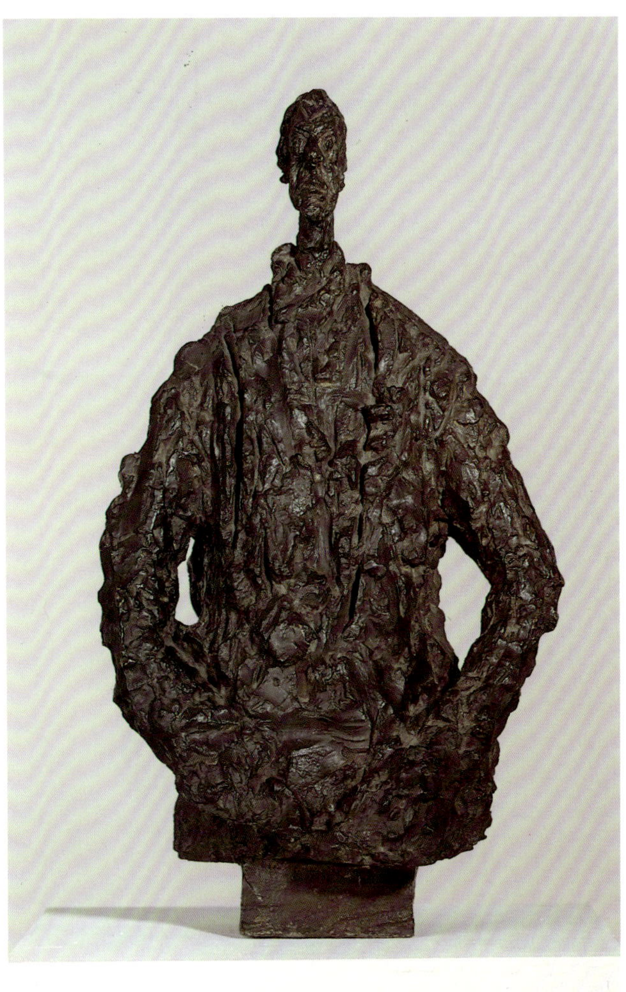

43 Diego in a Sweater 1953
49 × 28 × 22.5 (19⅛ × 11 × 8⅞)

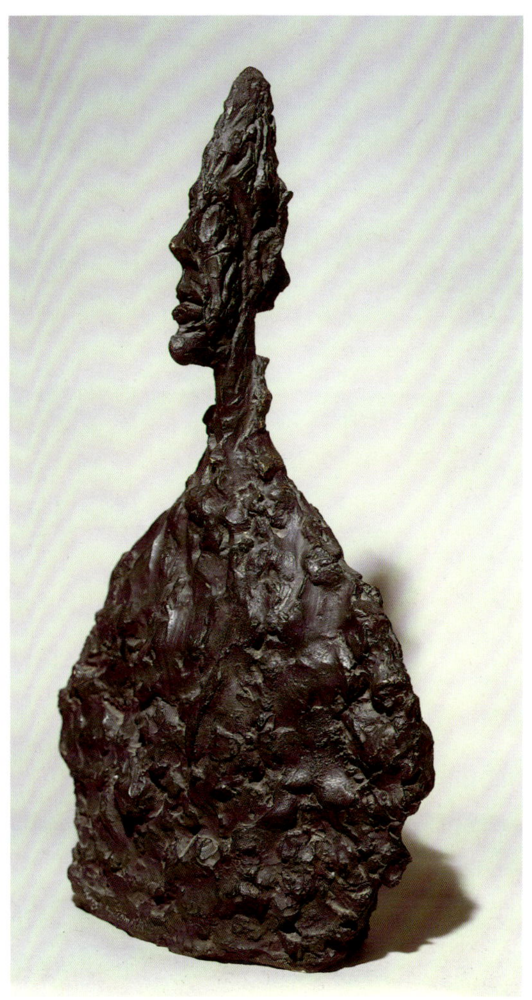

45 Bust of Diego 1955
56.5 × 32 × 14.5 (22¼ × 12⅝ × 5¾)

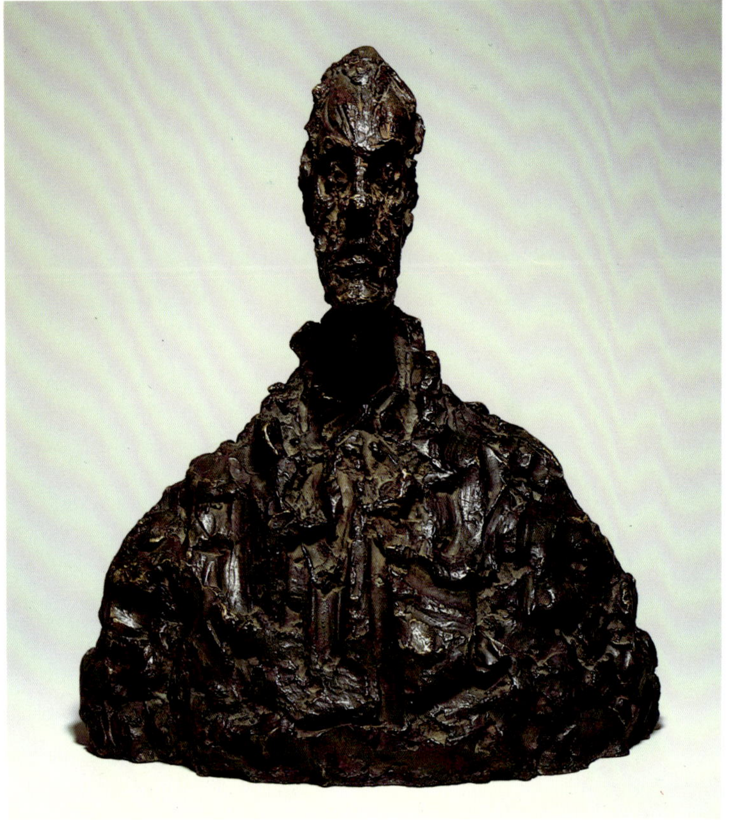

44 Bust of Diego *c.*1954
38.2 × 33.3 × 18.7 (15 × 13⅛ × 7¼)

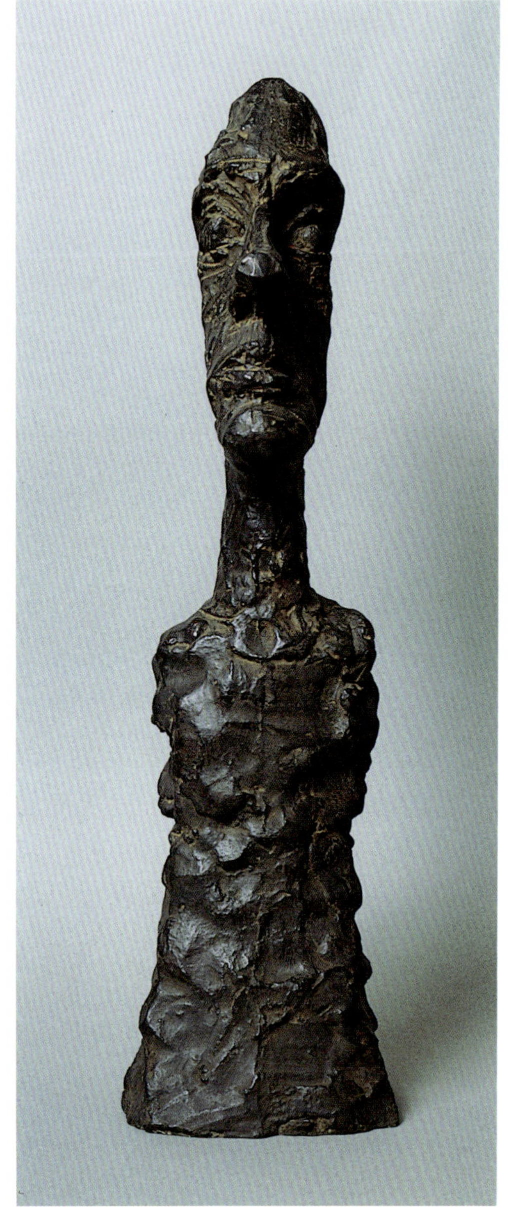

55 Bust with Large Eyes 1957
51.5 × 13.7 × 11 (20¼ × 5⅜ × 4⅛)

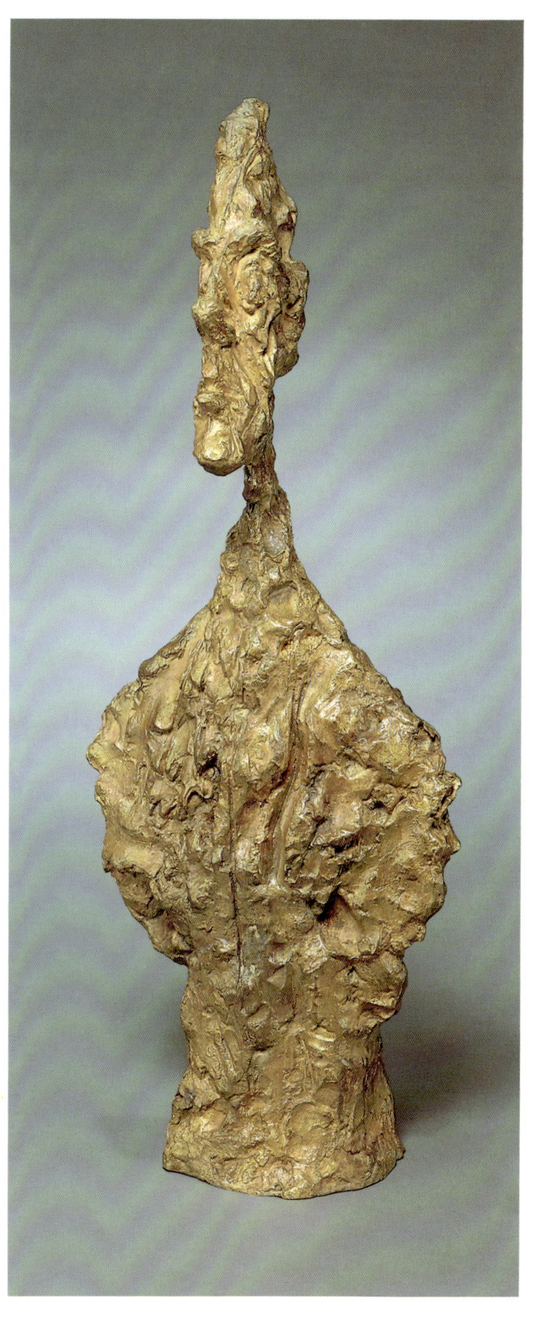

56 Bust of Diego 1957
60.6 × 24.8 × 16.2 ($23\frac{7}{8} × 9\frac{3}{4} × 6\frac{3}{8}$)

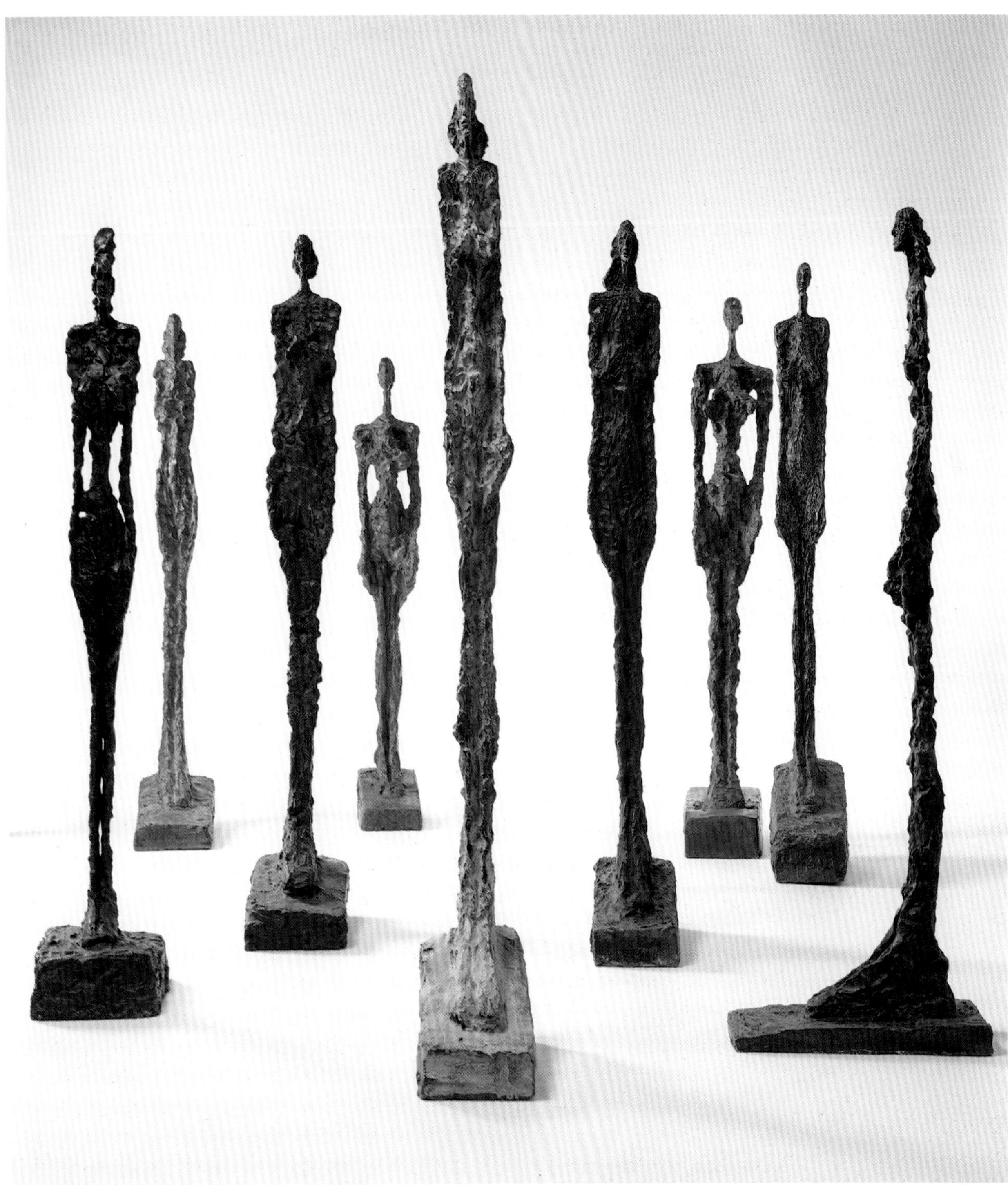

46–54 Venice Woman I–IX 1956
(not illustrated in order)

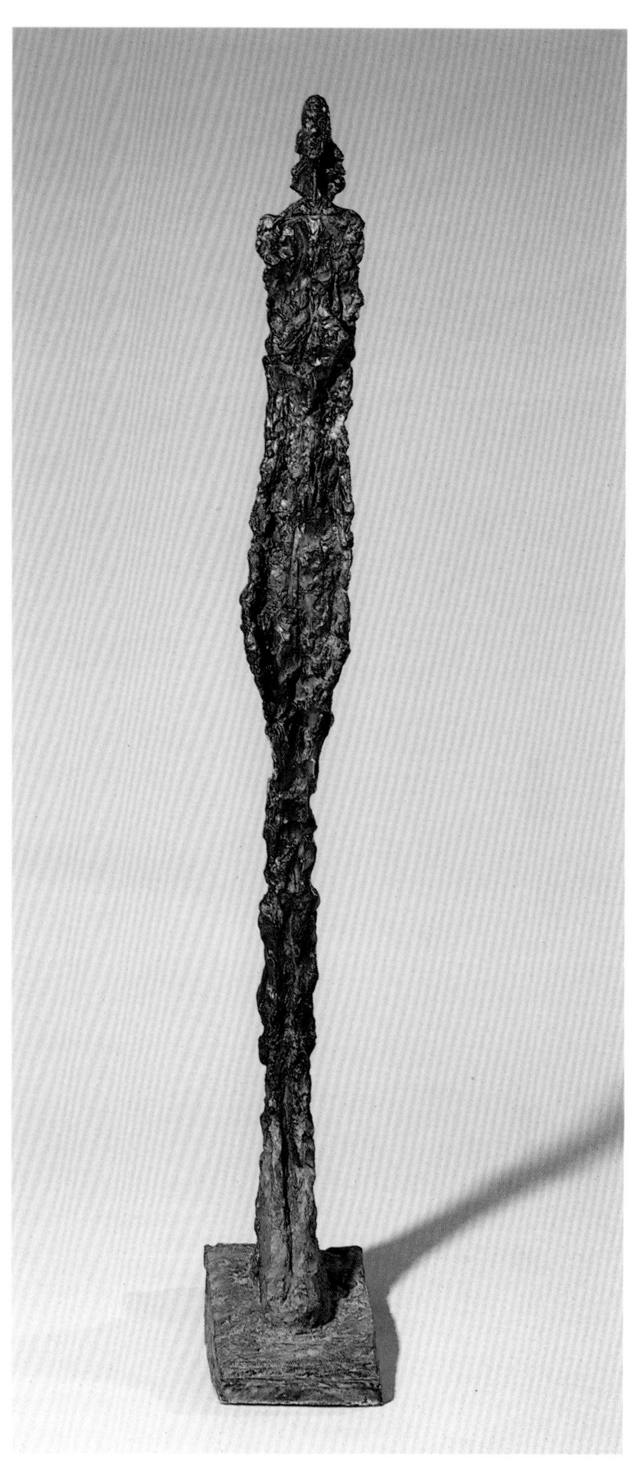

52 Venice Woman VII 1956
117 × 16.5 × 36.5 (46⅛ × 6½ × 14⅜)

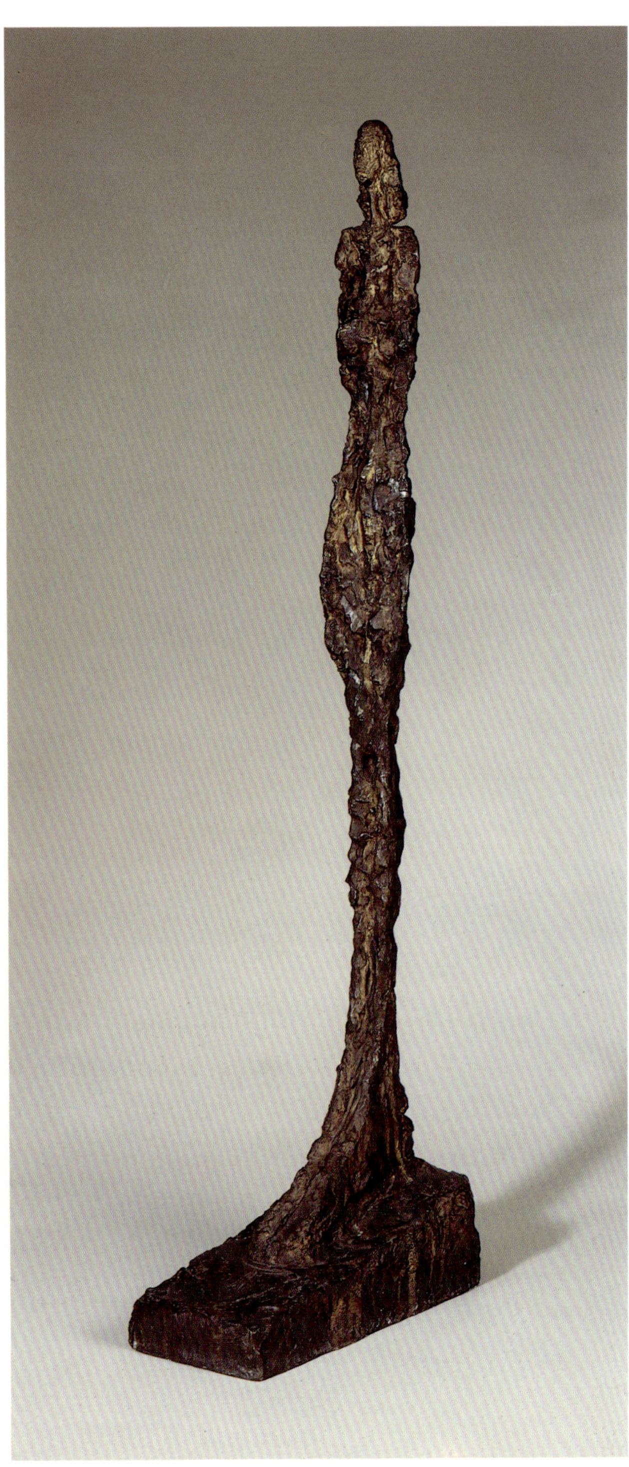

54 Venice Woman IX 1956
113 × 16.5 × 34.6 (44½ × 6½ × 13⅝)

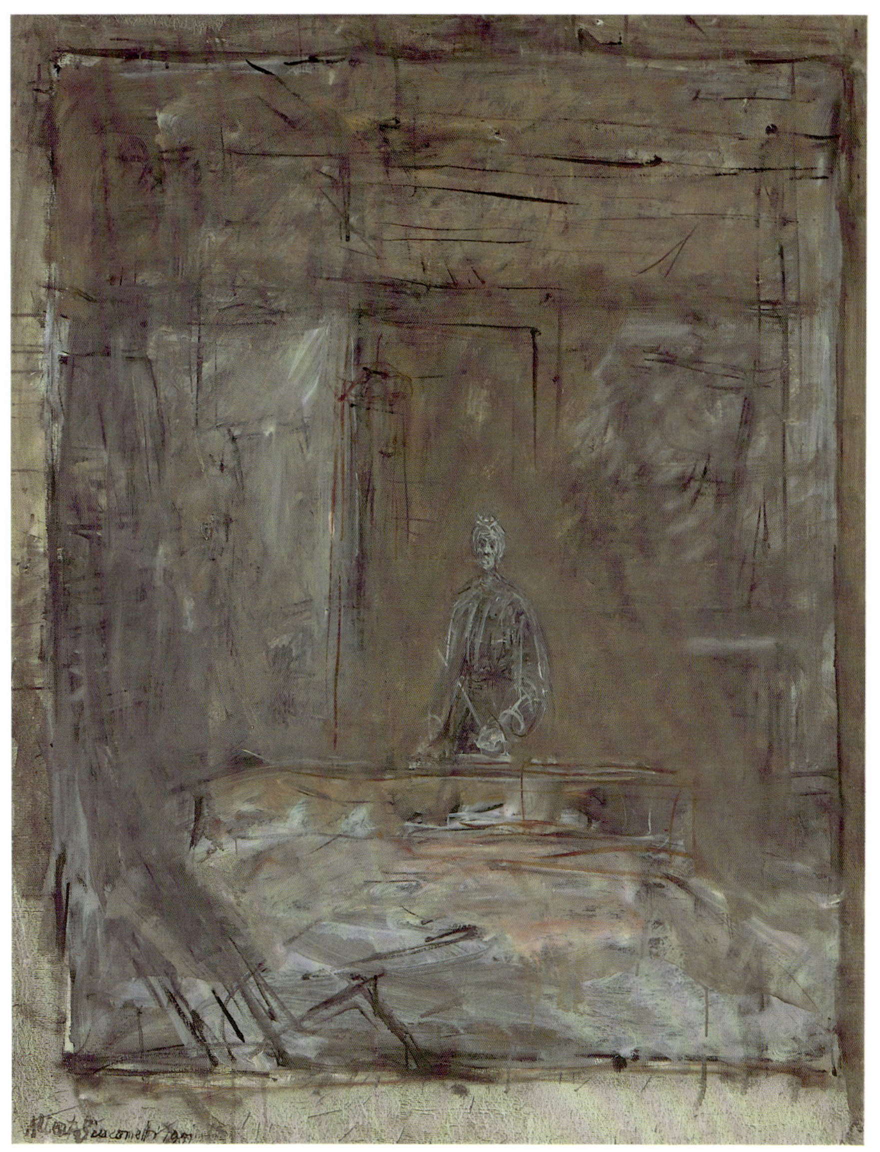

60 The Artist's Mother 1951
91.8 × 72.7 (36⅛ × 28⅝)

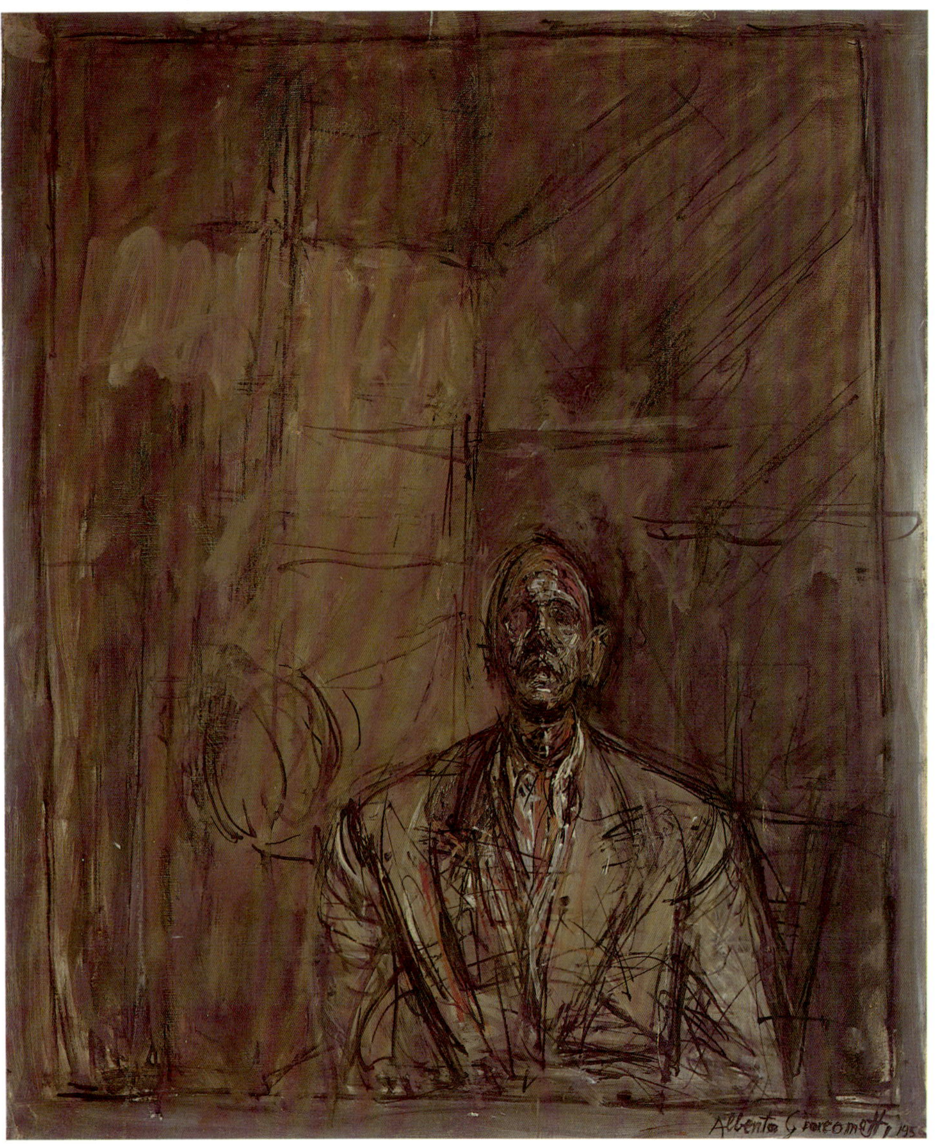

61 Jean Genet 1954–5
65.3 × 54.3 (25¾ × 21⅛)

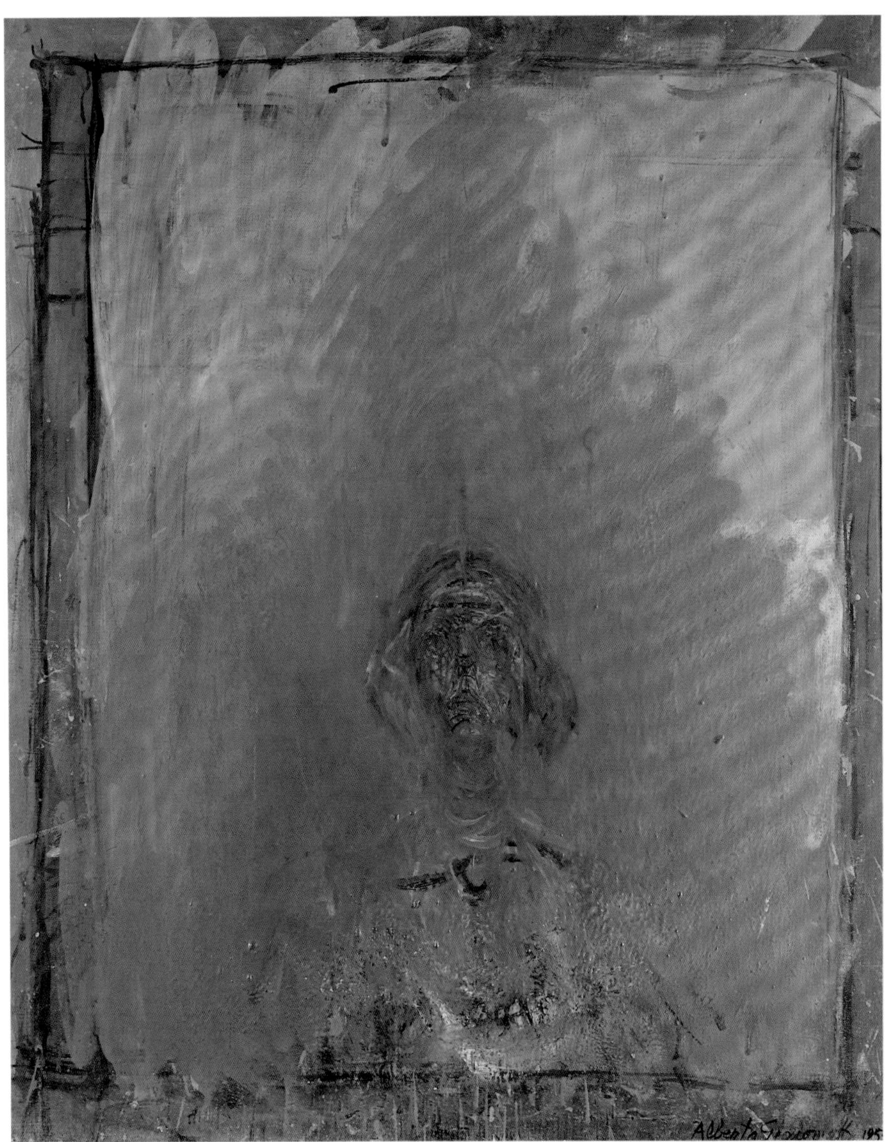

62 Sketch 1957
73 × 60 (28¾ × 23⅜)

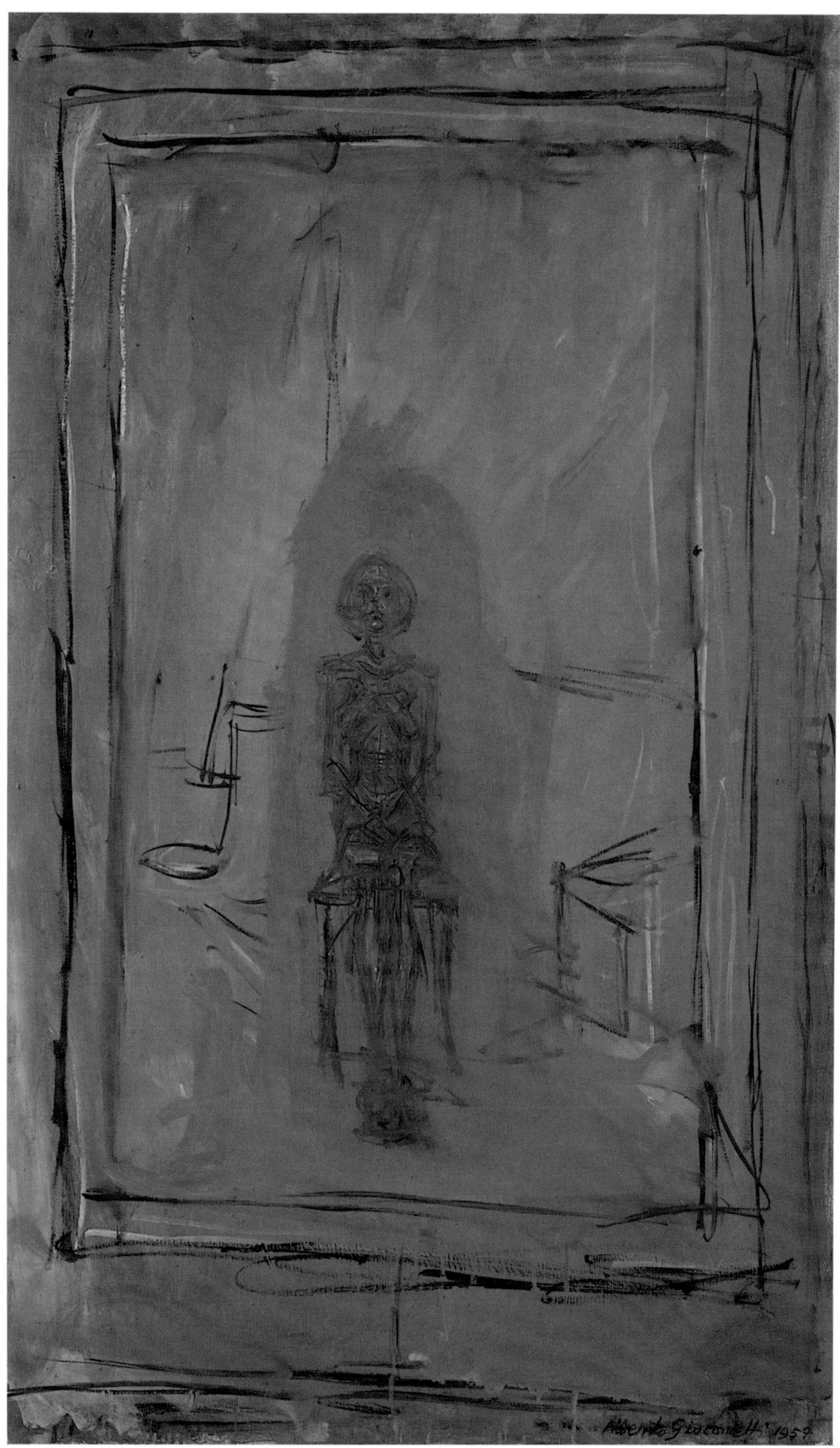

63 Annette Seated 1957
99.5 × 60.5 ($39\frac{1}{8} \times 23\frac{7}{8}$)

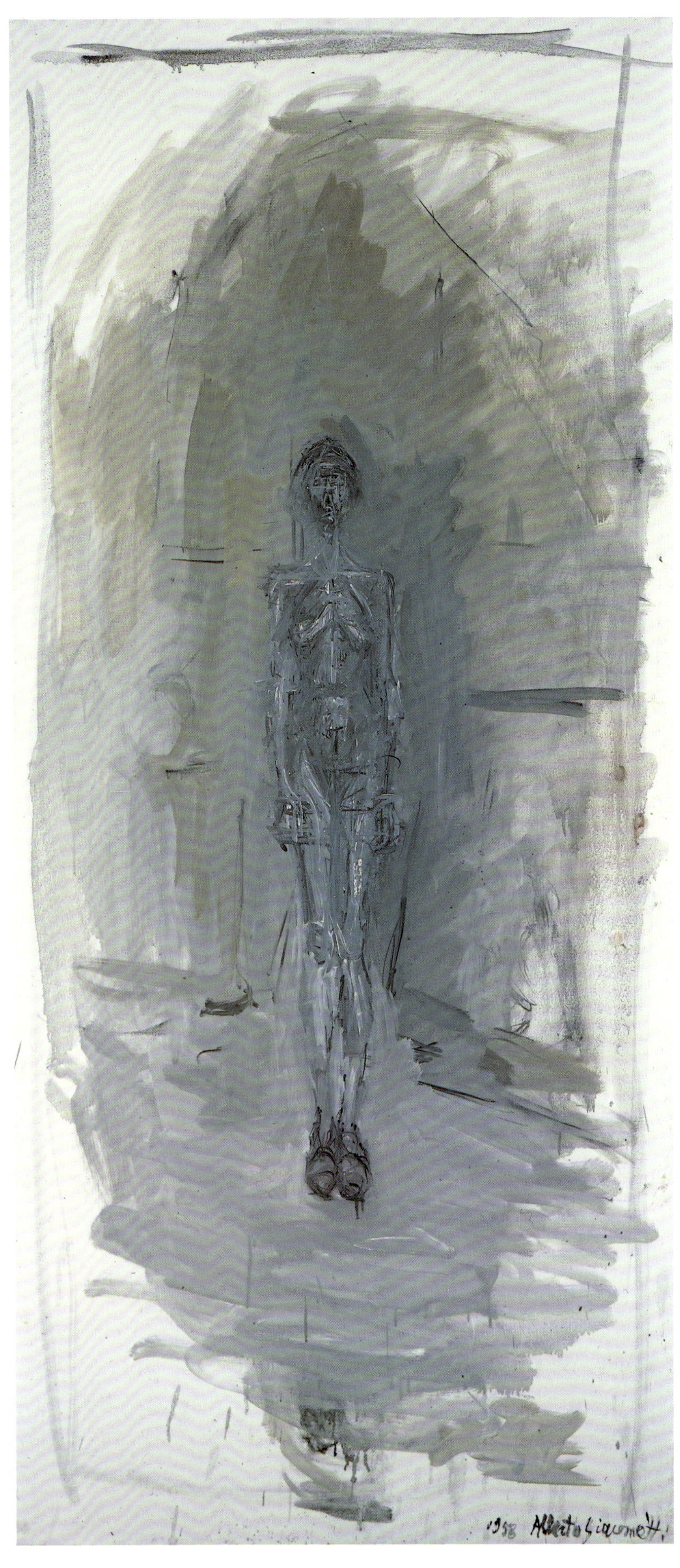

64 Standing Nude 1958
155 × 69.5 (61 × 27⅜)

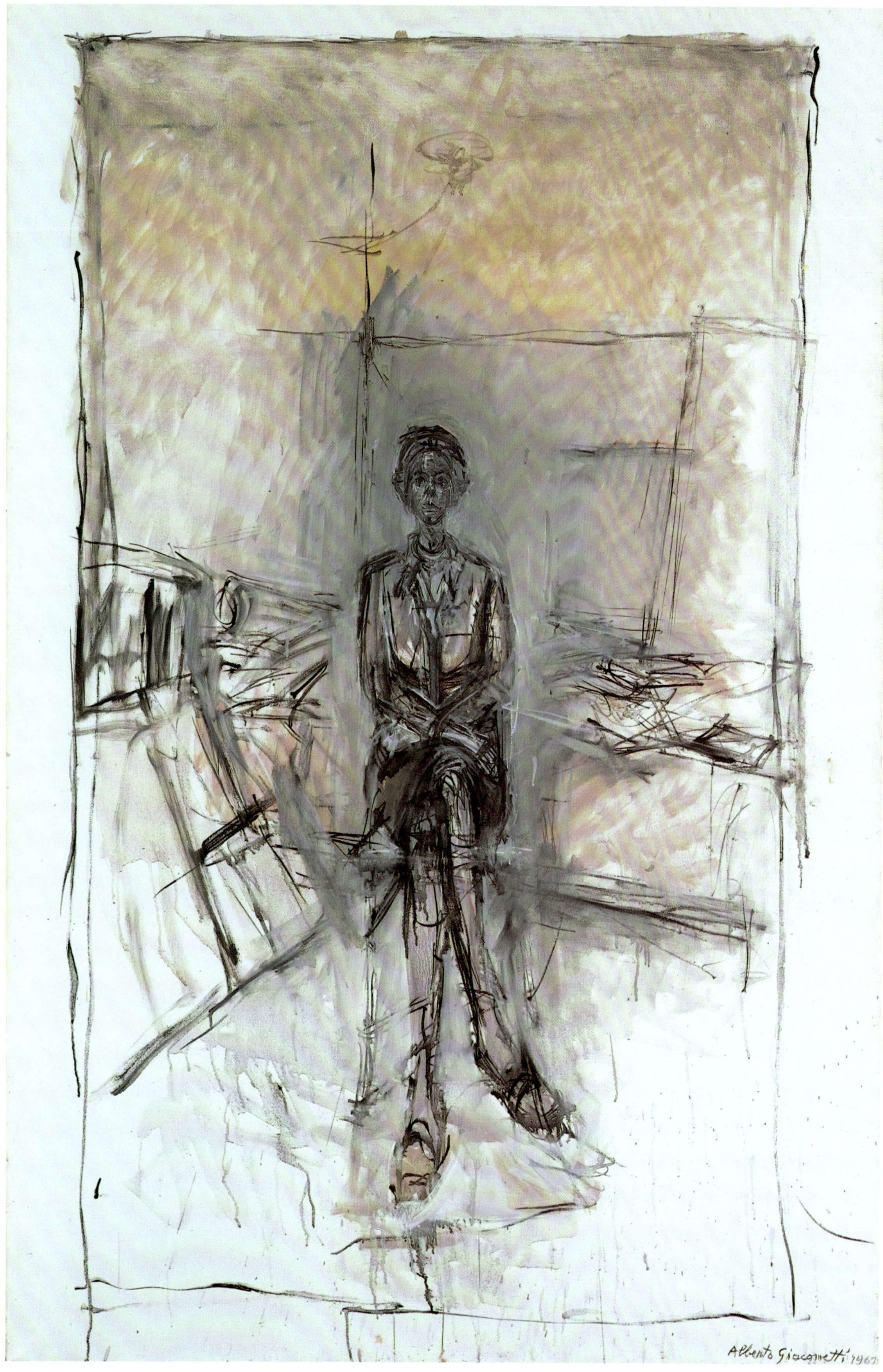

65 Annette in the Studio 1961
146×97 ($57\frac{1}{2} \times 38\frac{1}{4}$)

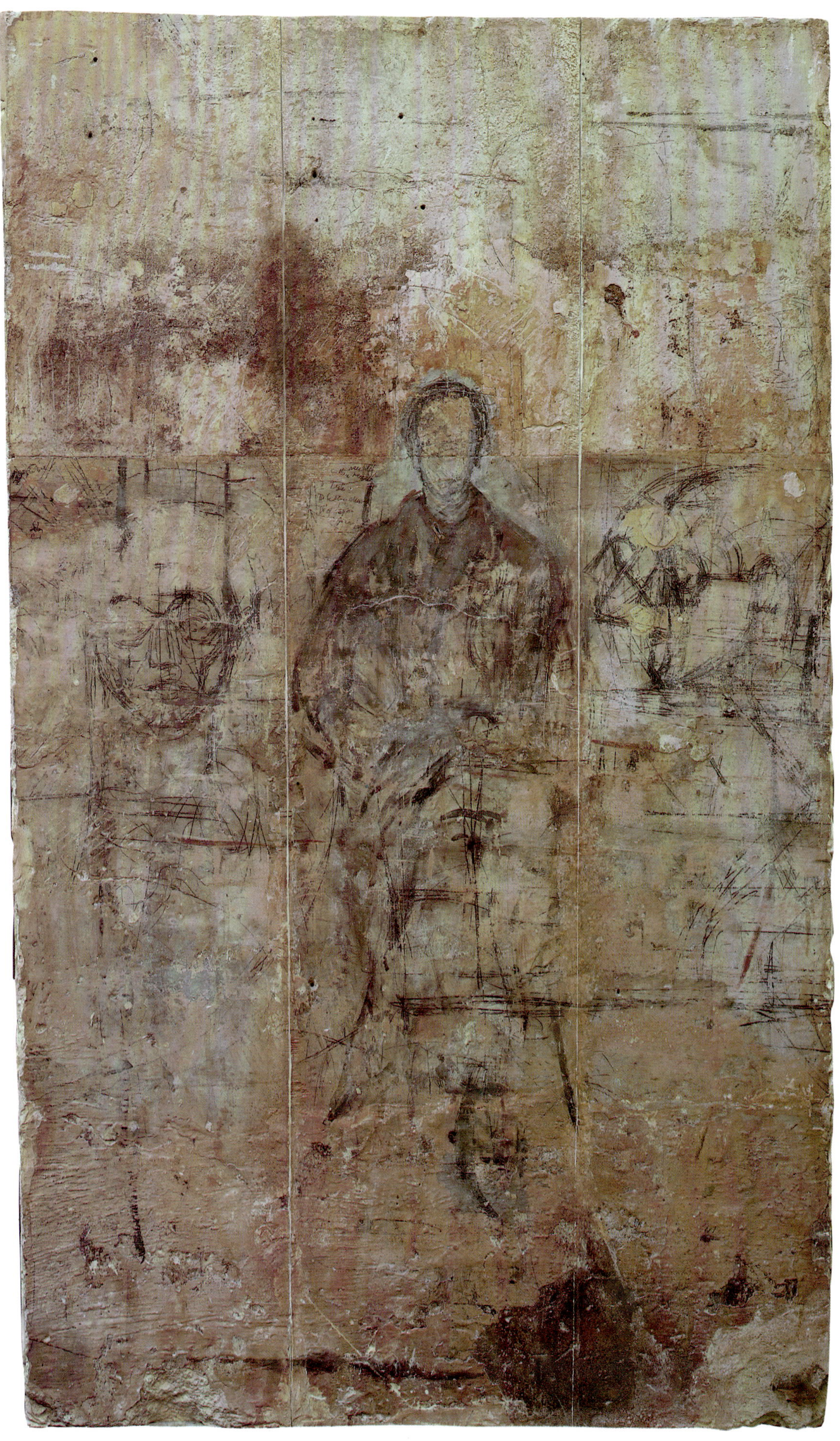

**57 Portrait of Diego Seated,
Head of a Woman, Heads**

160 × 200 (63 × 78¾)

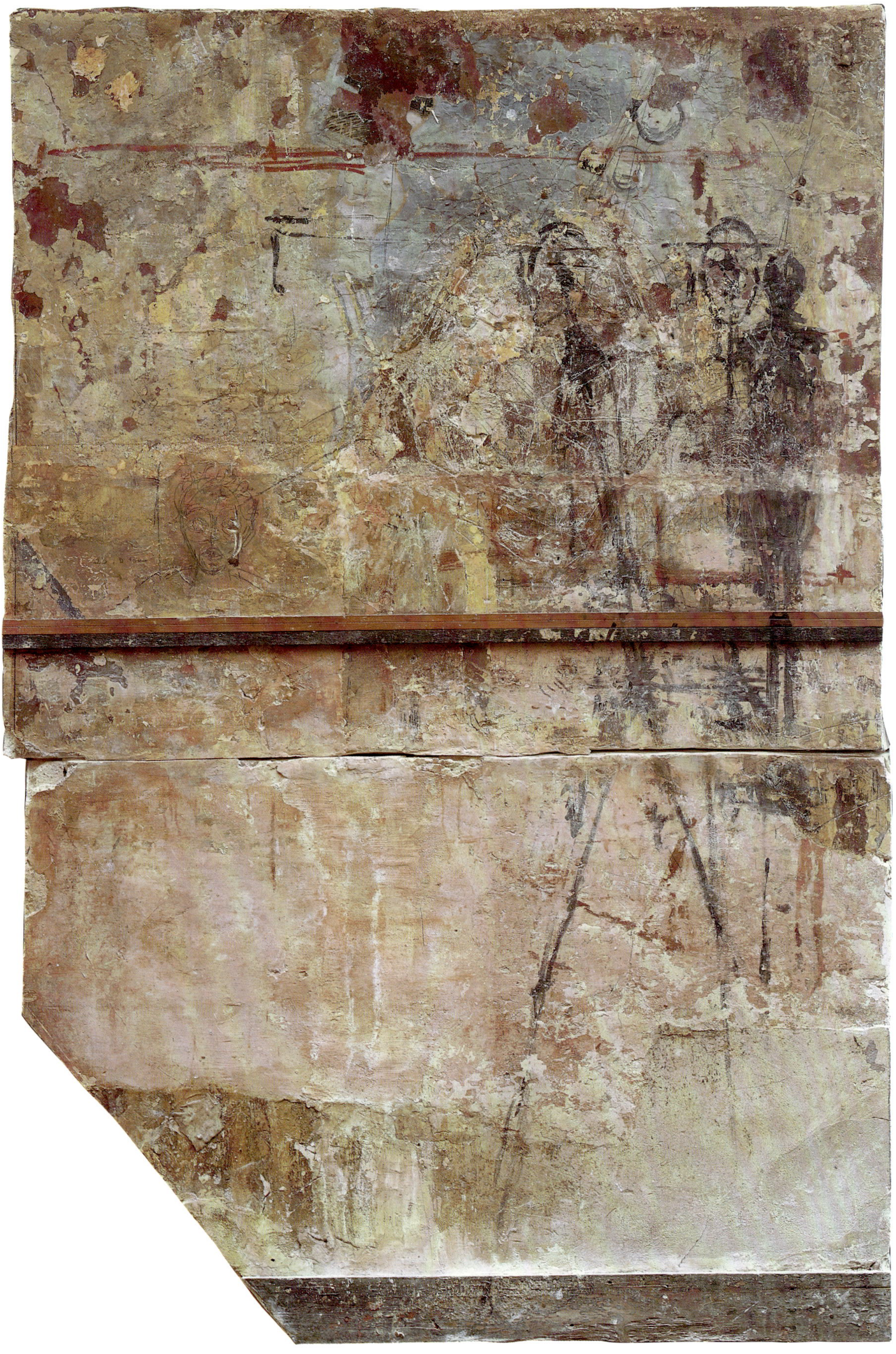

58 Walking Man, Standing Woman,
Head of a Woman
180 × 160 (70⅞ × 63)

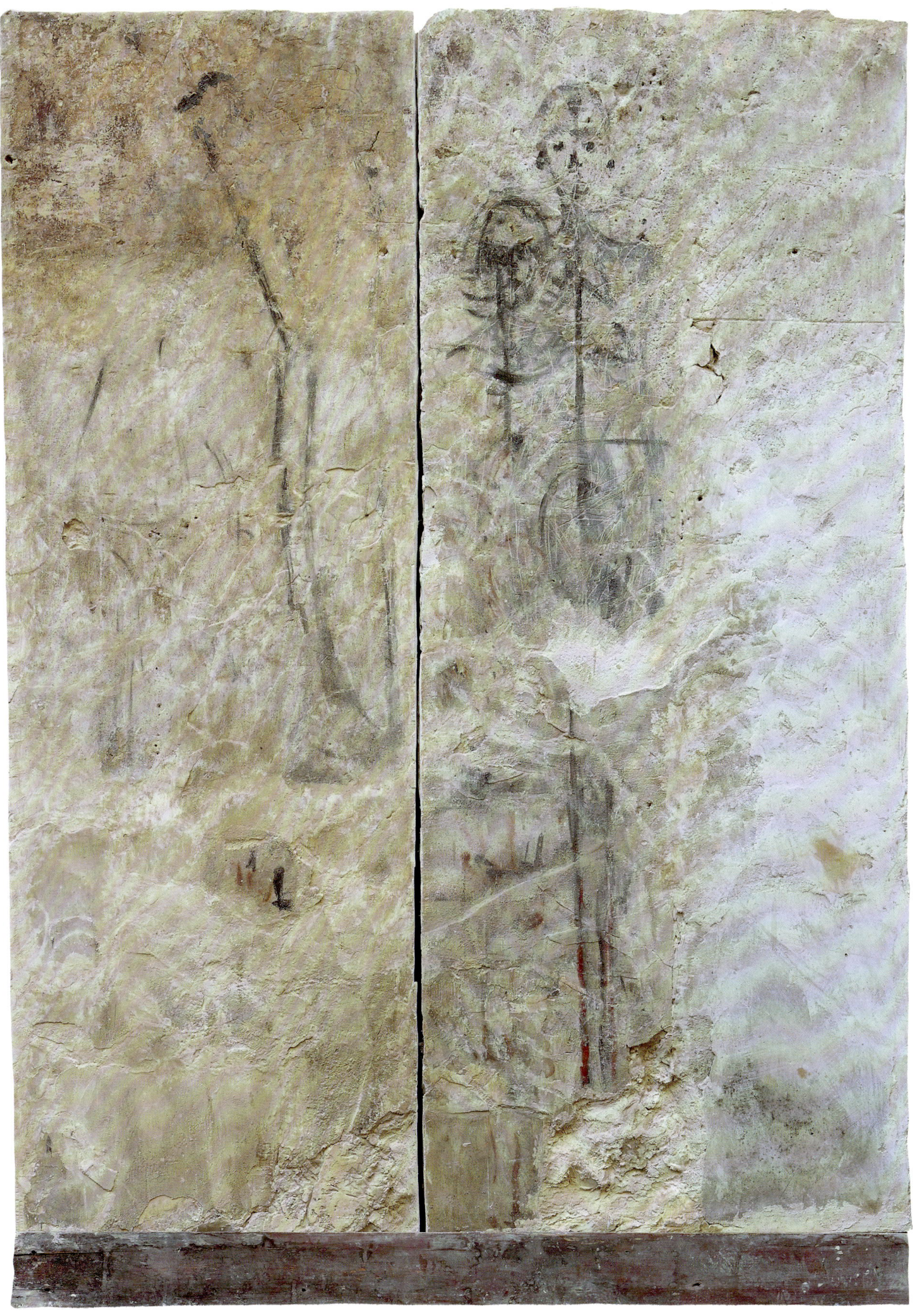

**59 Tall Woman, Annette, The Leg,
Standing Woman**
180 × 150 (70⅞ × 59)

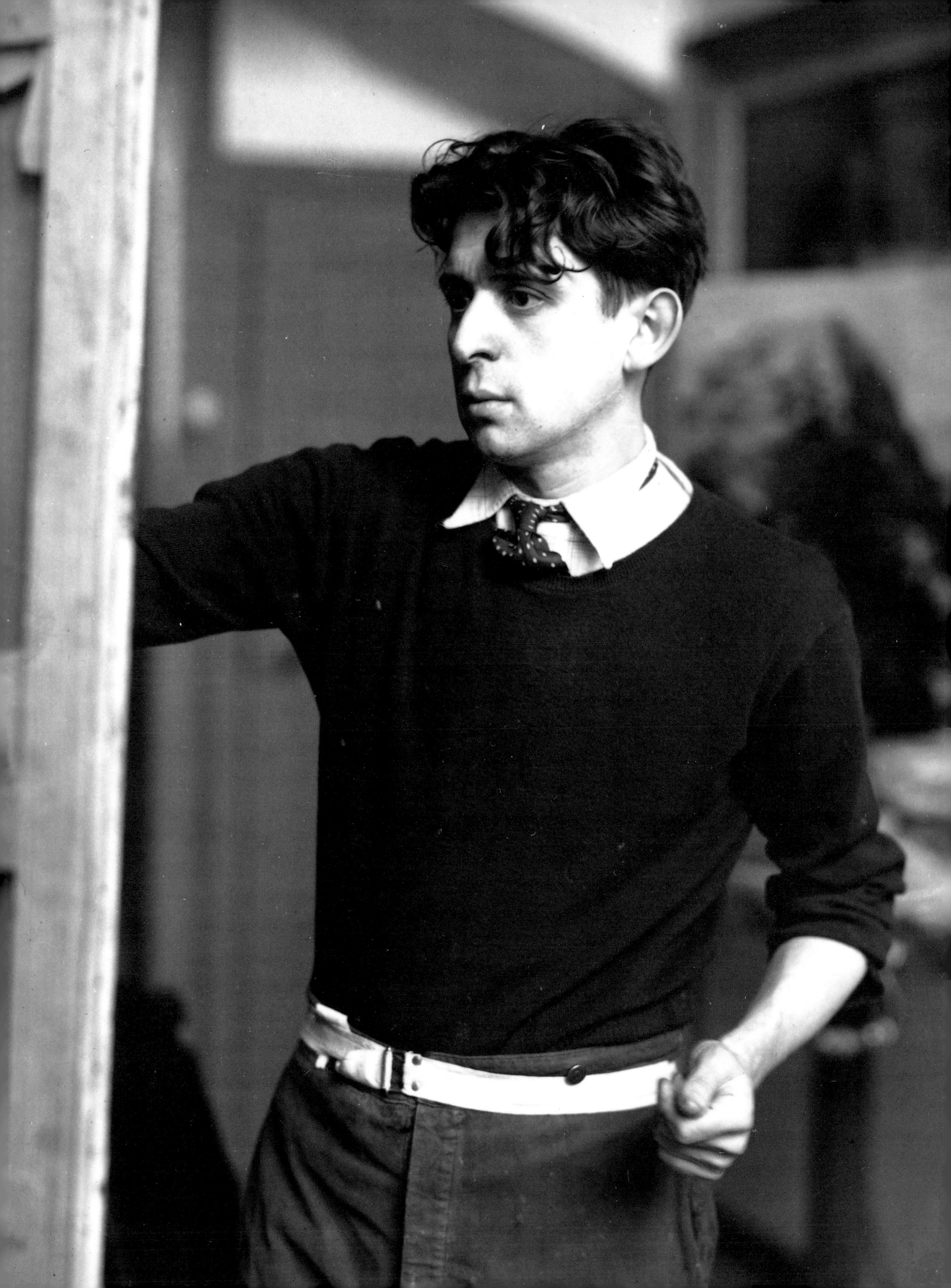

Francis Gruber (1912–1948)

In an interview given to the Communist journal *Arts de France* in April 1945, Francis Gruber declared: 'The painter, conscious above all of man, of the life of man, cannot but be touched profoundly by events. Great painting is history painting.'[1] Most of Gruber's short life was devoted to developing a popular, social art through a modern genre of history painting. Curiously, though, it is not Gruber's ambitious allegorical canvases that best evoke the events of his era but his series of portrait studies made in the Spartan emptiness of his studio during the years of Occupation.

Gruber was born in 1912 and his early life and artistic development can only be seen against a background of war, political instability and economic hardship. As the Popular Front took shape artists and critics began to define their own politico-artistic roles. Gruber's father was a successful stained-glass manufacturer and the family's political orientation was towards left-wing republicanism. Gruber's closest friends, artists who had worked with his father and fellow students at the Académie Scandinave, included a number of politically committed artists, such as Boris Taslitzky, Francis Tailleux and Pierre Tal-Coat. Gruber was involved in various demonstrations in support of the Spanish Republican cause but his contribution was almost entirely artistic. For use in processions he painted a huge banner of Jacques Callot, the seventeenth-century engraver who was something of a personal hero for Gruber and whose famous 'The Horrors of War' was a well-known anti-war statement.

Gruber's career mirrors closely the development of a realism that was consciously 'political' in orientation, one of the cultural features of the Popular Front era. Gruber was involved in the series of debates on social realism in May 1936 known as 'La Querelle du réalisme', and he was in sympathy with the broad aims of the Maison de la Culture (the cultural organisation for professional groups founded by the Communist Party and dominated by Louis Aragon, the former Surrealist poet) which worked towards an art with mass appeal and a redefinition of the role of the artist in society. Following those debates Gruber, Taslitzky, Edouard Pignon, André Marchand and others were included in an exhibition organised in 1936 by the Maison de la Culture entitled *La Réalité et la peinture* at the Galerie Billiet-Vorms. A year later Gruber was among a wide-ranging group of artists protesting against the civil war in Spain in the exhibition *Art cruel*, also at the Galerie Billiet-Vorms and again hosted by the Maison de la Culture. He was a member of the editorial group advising the *Bulletin des Peintres et Sculpteurs de la Maison de la Culture* of which Taslitzky was director. Two new salons, Henry Héraut's Nouvelle Génération, January 1936 at the Galerie Charpentier (at which Gruber exhibited) and the Salon des Jeunes Artistes, distanced themselves from current and preceding isms (Impressionism, Cubism and Surrealism); and the manifesto *Rupture*, published on the

occasion of the second Salon Nouvelle Génération in 1938–9 at the Galerie Billiet-Vorms, expressed the desire to 'break the chains'. While rejecting abstract art as exclusive, the means of renewal were seen as available only via primitive models and through the study of nature. According to his daughter, Gruber claimed Bosch, Grünewald and Dürer as his major influences, and, in acknowledgment of his father's Alsatian birth, liked to call himself the 'last German painter of the Renaissance'.[2]

Gruber's major works of the late 1930s, responding to the call for a populist-realist art, are large allegorical history pieces, referring to France's own renaissance in 'François I Welcoming the Antiques at Fontainebleau' 1935 (Musée d'art moderne de la ville de Paris), and to the contemporary world of the masses in 'Homage to Labour' 1936. More general themes reflect his own involvement with the escalating historical drama. Titles such as 'The Announcement of Winter' 1935 (Musée d'Arras) , 'Melancholia' 1935, and 'The Misfortunes of Love' 1937 punctuate the period leading up to the outbreak of war.

Throughout his career Gruber persisted in giving a primary place to the craft of the painter, especially to the skills of drawing and design. Many drawings survive and many of his paintings were still-life studies. His own brand of history painting took reality as its starting point and observation as the key to invention. Speaking to the newspaper *Combat* in 1948, Gruber argued that the artist should 'seek to rediscover the world through solitude while also possessing the technical abilities necessary for the transcription of those discoveries'.[3] This attitude may derive from the artist's respect for his father's professional skill as a craftsman but it was no doubt reinforced by his friendship, from 1937 (they had first met in 1933), with Giacometti during a key moment in the latter's career when he was becoming more and more intensely preoccupied with the model.

Giacometti left for Switzerland in 1941. Gruber remained in Paris; most of his friends were mobilised and on their return disappeared into the Resistance or into the unoccupied zone. Gruber had suffered severely from asthma since childhood and was unfit for service. He did not leave Paris during the Occupation except for visits to the family house at Thomery in the Forest of Fontainebleau. Solitary and alone (he was diagnosed tubercular in 1942), his daily life and work focused increasingly on his immediate surroundings, the spacious, empty studio which he had occupied since his father's death in 1936.

Throughout the war years the single most revisited motif in Gruber's oeuvre was the female portrait. This was not a new subject in his work: during the 1930s he had produced portraits of great power, including those of his mother and his friend Ulla in 1934. These monumental figures assume languid, if not fatigued, poses which appear melancholic. Their gazes are directed

away from the viewer's into a middle distance dreamland. Their settings are occasionally detailed with symbolically charged still-life groups but are more often reduced to a narrow spatial setting of a domestic character. Gruber returned to the genre in 1940, at first in meeting commissions from Jacques Bazaine, director of the Galerie Friedland with whom Gruber showed his work from 1942–4, and then working from his model Etiennette and from 1942 with his young wife, Georges. The atmosphere of the studio weighs heavily on these delicately portrayed characters. Unlike the penumbrous gloom of Giacometti's settings, Gruber gives his studio a sharp focus. Rarely has emptiness been described with such precision. His models are arranged in simple poses. They are less melodramatically limpid than in his earlier portraits. Like his earlier sitters these models were encouraged to stare out into the distance beyond the viewer, evading eye contact and creating an aura around the model of intense intimacy, solitude and vulnerability. It is these aspects of Gruber's work that appeared so acutely responsive to the desolation of war and the immediate post-war era. His style, in which objects are delineated by a dry and hesitant outline, repels sensuality and warmth.

Gruber also produced more overtly political works. When, in 1942, the Galerie Friedland invited submissions to a theme exhibition intended as a 'Hommage aux anciens', Gruber made his response emphatically political. 'Homage to Jacques Callot' (fig.5 on p.28) was both a private homage to his mentor and also a symbol of artistic resistance. Gruber's painting is of a devastated landscape, dominated in the foreground by the naked body of a female victim of war. Behind the nude an engraving on paper is displayed on a chair. The engraving is of 'The Beggar with a Wooden Leg', an image taken from Callot's famous 'The Horrors of War'. The painting also included a painted tricolour which was removed at the censor's request.

Gruber's major painting of the Liberation caused a sensation when it was shown at the first post-Liberation Salon d'Automne in 1944. This image of a seated male nude, titled 'Job' (no.68), epitomises Gruber's desire to bring observation and social message together in historical allegory. Gruber had found an old Bible in Thomery and was inspired to explore the theme of Job as an allegory for the Occupation of Paris, a symbol of the oppressed inhabitants of the city who experienced great suffering without losing hope and faith. Gruber's Job is portrayed in an attitude of silent contemplation. At his feet lies a sheet of paper bearing an inscription from the Book of Job, 23.2 which reads 'Now, once more my cry is a revolt, and yet my hand suppresses my sobs'.[4]

In the immediate aftermath of war the Communist Party made great efforts to enlist artists and intellectuals and Gruber was among many who joined. In 1946 an exhibition entitled *Art and Resistance* at the Musée nationale d'art moderne brought together a number of artists including Picasso, André Fougeron, Taslitzky and Gruber. Excepting the abstract painter Jean-Michel Atlan, all those who showed worked in figurative styles. The exhibition inevitably revived the issue of the connections between style and politics that had dominated the abstraction versus realism debate of the 1930s. The debate hardened when, in November 1946, Aragon announced the party's doctrine of realism. *Arts de France* and *Les Lettres Française* both swiftly fell into line, while the painters Fougeron and Taslitzky upheld the doctrine through their work.

Although Gruber's early death in 1948 prevented him from making a significant contribution to the debate, he was not without a voice in the Communist press and made his comments felt through published statements in *Arts de France* and *Panorama des Arts*. His influence was also felt in another way, when certain superficial aspects of his style were adopted and adapted by a younger generation of artists – of whom the best

known is Bernard Buffet – aspiring, as he had a decade earlier, to an art rooted in its time.

For this younger generation, which emerged at the Salon des Moins de Trente Ans (Salon of the Under-Thirties) in 1947 and issued a manifesto as the Homme-Témoin (Man as Witness) group, it was not only the pervading atmosphere of existential despair in Gruber's painting that was so compulsive, but his characteristically dry and brittle style. Introducing his work to a British audience for the first time in 1959, René Huyghe put the record straight:

The admirers of Buffet are inclined to forget where he borrowed his draftsmanship from for he has only systematised Gruber's creation. Full of breaks and ruptures, torn and angular, tense and contracted, it may one day enable posterity to read our most intimate preoccupations.'[5]

NOTES

1 Francis Gruber, 'Interviews et Opinions', *Arts de France*, April 1945, pp.27–34.
2 Catherine Bernad-Gruber, with Armelle Vanazzi, *Francis Gruber*, Switzerland 1989, p.27.
3 Quoted by Bernad-Gruber 1989, p.44.
4 Trans. Sarah Wilson in *Aftermath*, exh. cat., Barbican Art Gallery 1982, p.58.
5 René Huyghe, Introduction to *Francis Gruber*, exh. cat., Tate Gallery 1959, p.7.

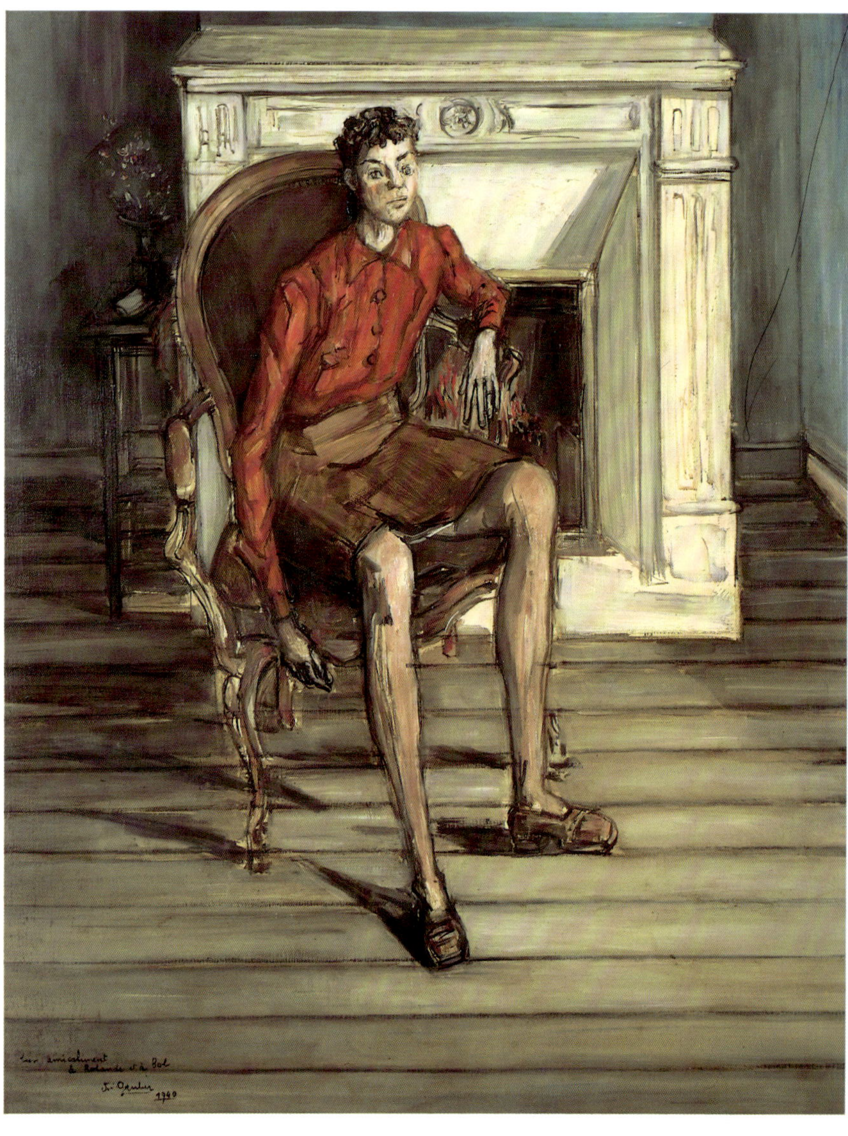

Illustration (p.128) Portrait of Francis Gruber in his studio Photograph by Marc Vaux
Documentation du Musée Nationale d'Art Moderne, Centre Georges Pompidou, Paris

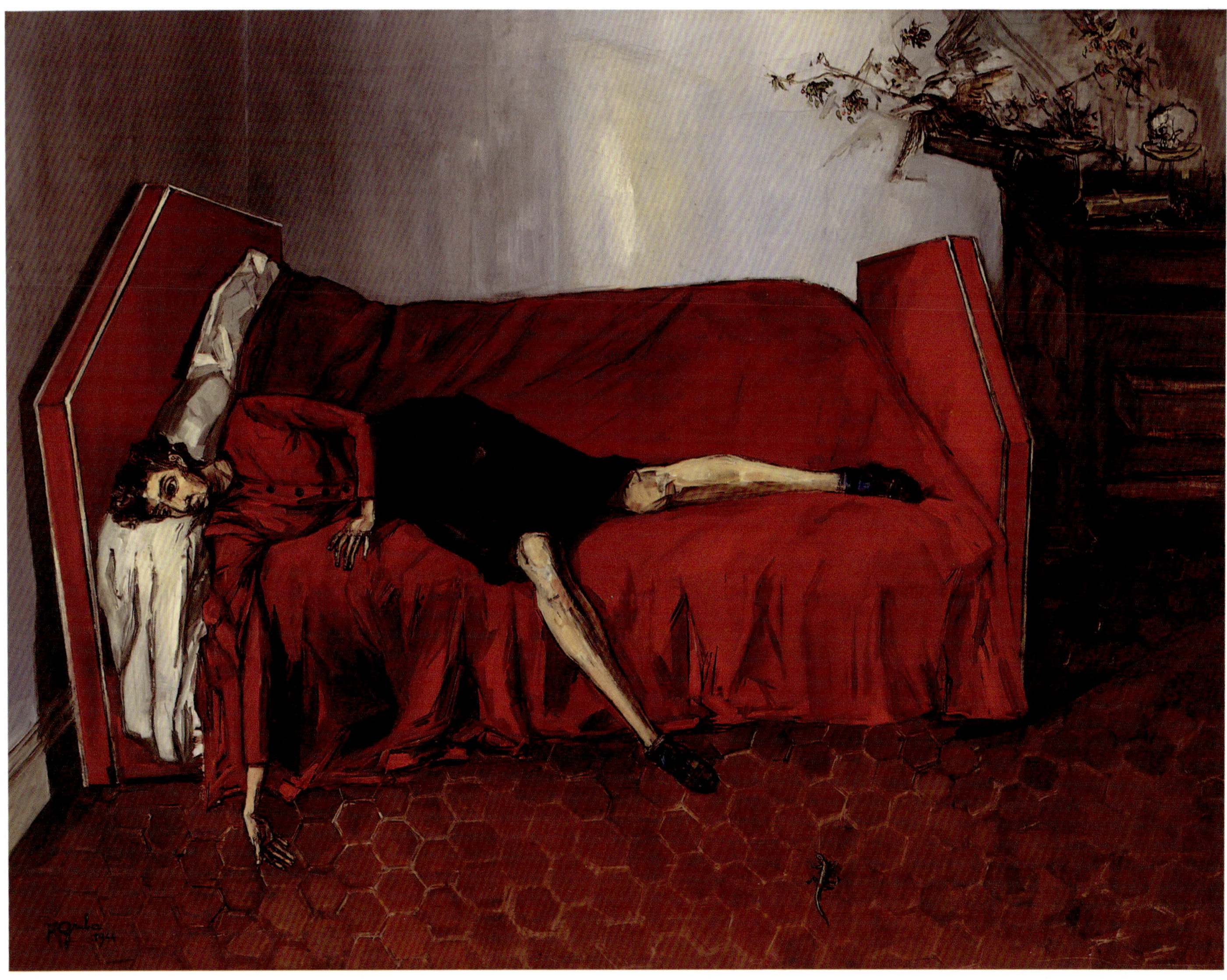

67 The Red Divan 1944
89 × 116 (35 × 45⅝)

opposite
66 Woman Seated in Front of the Fireplace 1940
91 × 72 (35⅞ × 28⅜)

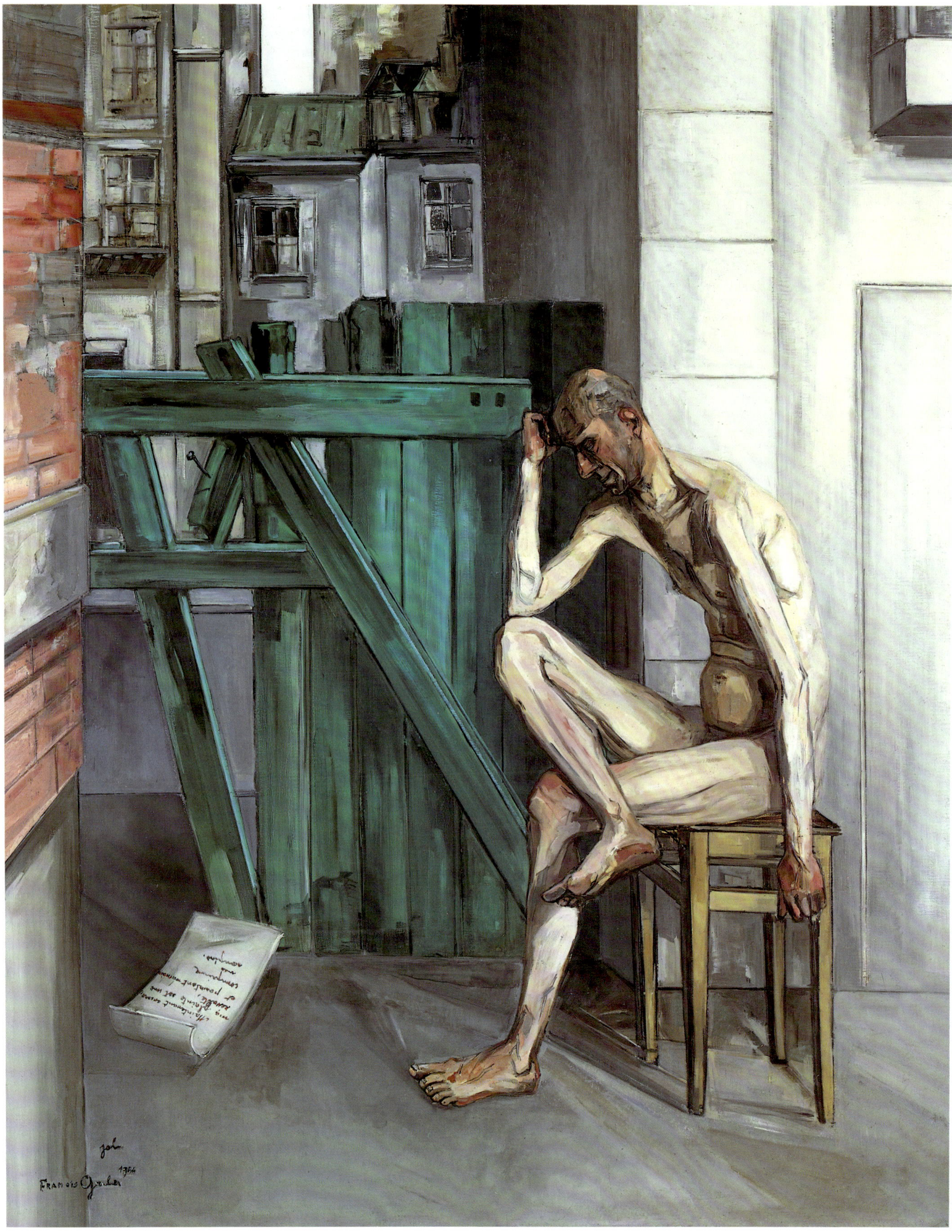

68 Job 1944
161.9 × 129.9 (63¾ × 51⅛)

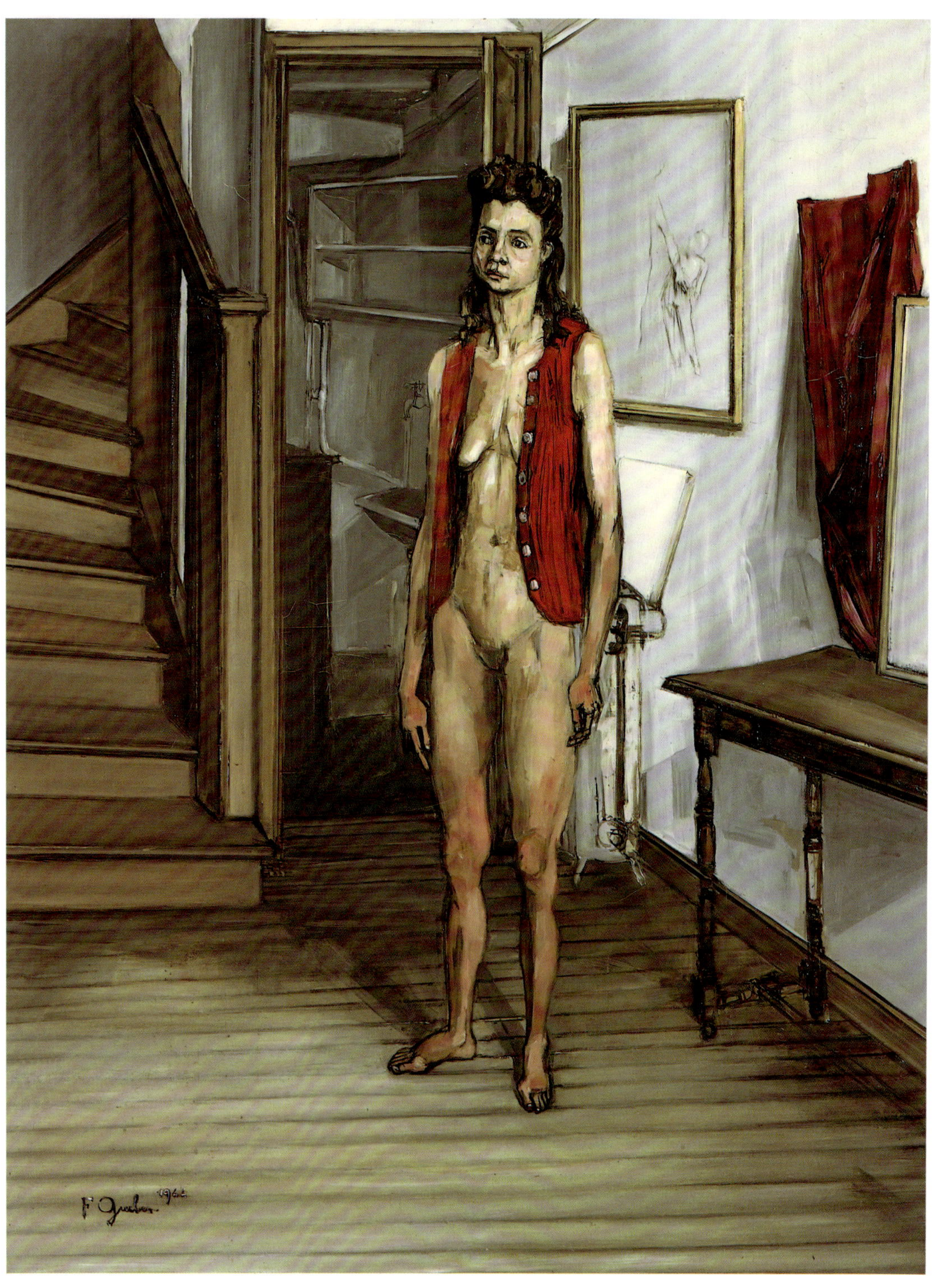

69 Nude in a Red Waistcoat 1944
115×86 ($45\frac{1}{4} \times 33\frac{7}{8}$)

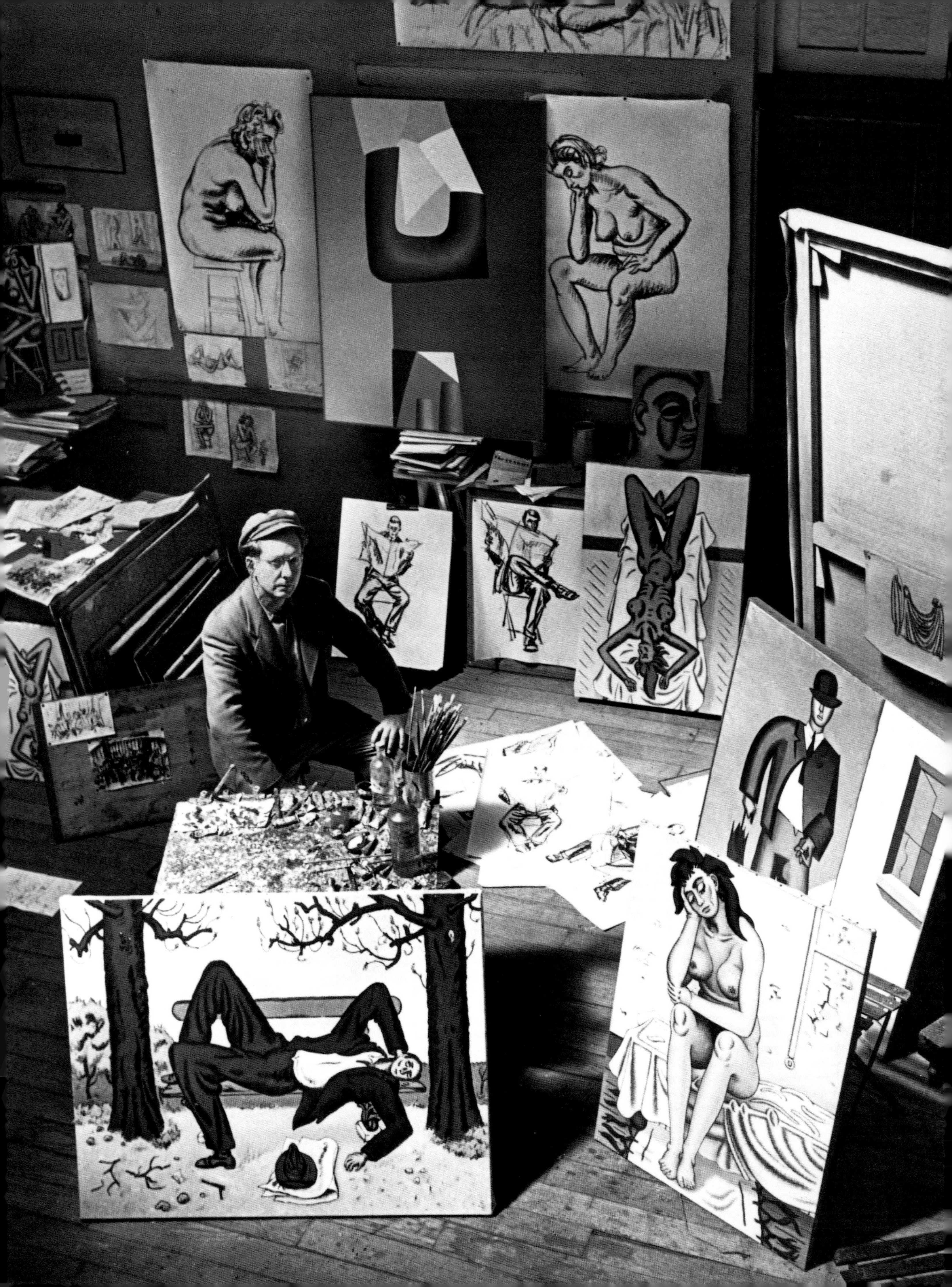

Jean Hélion (1904–1987)

Throughout the 1930s Jean Hélion had been, in his own work and writings, an active and articulate spokesman for hard-edged abstraction. On the brink of war, in 1939, he turned to a figurative idiom. This *volte-face* cost him many friends and plunged his career into critical and financial obscurity. For the rest of his life he pursued an independent line, unaffiliated to any groups.

Although Hélion described his earliest figurative works of 1939 as marking 'merely a more lively abstraction',[1] the motivation behind this development was not only artistic. Recalling the decisive moment from the vantage point of 1950, he wrote of how he had

> suffered until then from an impossible contradiction: painting eight hours a day in one style while living in another ... drinking, eating, loving ... but of all this in my painting no clear relationship?[2]

Hélion's re-examination of the relationship between art and life does not seem to have had an obviously political motivation. Although the artist had been, alongside Auguste Herbin and Otto Freundlich, one of the very few abstract artists involved in the Association des Ecrivains et des Artistes Révolutionnaires, founded in 1932, and though he later found much common ground with Fernand Léger, he never became a member of the Communist Party and he emphatically distanced himself from party or Cold War politics. Added to a growing sense of unease at the gap between his abstract work and the realities of everyday life, Hélion's experience as a prisoner of war hardened his desire for an art capable of communicating 'a violent passion for life, as a whole, as it was denied to me, the streets, the people, the things'.[3]

From 1939 until his move towards a more fastidiously observed genre of realism in 1951–2, he was primarily concerned with urban reality, inspired by a fascination for contemporary rituals and everyday artefacts, and anxious to establish a 'certaine mythologie quotidienne'.[4] In 1949 he wrote:

> the gravest problem is that of the subject ... Time will tell if I have created vain symbols or if, on the contrary, I have identified latent myths.[5]

His project and his means of exploring it undoubtedly drew on a Surrealist heritage and looked ahead to anthropological and structuralist thinking in the post-war years.

Hélion attached special importance to street scenes. In this he has been seen as anticipating the urban realism of the Nouveaux Réalistes in the 1960s.[6] In fact he was not alone in finding inspiration for high art in everyday subjects. Dubuffet's imagery of the metro and the pavement is evidence of a parallel search for meaningful contemporary subject matter. To different ends those artists included within the Homme-Témoin group and certain Socialist Realists were also exploring a vocabulary of urban experience.

While waiting for a passage from Marseilles to the United States following his escape from a Pomeranian prisoner of war camp, Hélion had begun to sketch his observations: women daydreaming, men smoking and greeting one another, war cripples, shabby shop fronts, the cracks in the walls.

During 1945, now settled in New York, Hélion developed some of these subjects into large-scale paintings. His aim as he saw it was to explore those 'gestures and events of daily life, in which I discover or confer an extraordinary quality or appearance (the extraordinary in the banal)'.[7] In the first years of his career, before developing his well-known abstract style, Hélion had been fascinated briefly by Dada and by Dadaist notions of the 'ready-made'. He had filled his studio with found objects, enthralled by their fetishistic potential, building up a 'collection of objects including a collection of reflections ... In a vertical cage suspended against the wall, eight bottles of Bordeaux, each one with a painted reflection – superb!'[8] Two decades later, in an interview given in 1944, Hélion argued that figurative artists should investigate the 'mysterious side of Surrealism'.[9] The war had brought him back into close contact with Surrealist ideas. While married to Pegeen Guggenheim he was, for a while, Max Ernst's step-son-in-law and during the period spent in New York he was closely involved with the group of 'artists in exile' that included Ernst, Marcel Duchamp and André Breton. These contacts were sustained after the war. Breton and André Masson were visitors to his Paris studio and a number of Surrealists, including Breton, were involved, with Hélion and others, in the Internationalist 'Front Humain'.

But although Hélion's exploration of street life and the fetishism of objects does have an important relationship to the 'merveilleux quotidien' discovered by Aragon through a relaxation of the faculties of rational interpretation, Hélion was at pains to distance himself from Surrealist pictorial *dépaysement*.[10] His subjects always remain within the realm of observable reality:

> You see, when Magritte paints bread, he shows baguettes proceeding across the sky like a fleet of Dirigibles. It's supposed to be very surprising. Yet after the initial shock, where's the surprise? When I paint bread, I paint baguettes lying on the table. There's mystery there. Mystery that lasts forever. The mystery of ordinary things.[11]

After Hélion's return to Paris, the shop front became for a period the central theme in his work. There were precedents for this. Louis Aragon had written of the store front as the 'modern spectacle' and Léger's descriptions of window displays combine his affirmation of the 'art' of the common man and his passion for the beauty of ordinary things.[12] Photographers such as Eugène Atget had captured the extraordinary aspects of commercial street life, documenting, for example, window displays of fashion manne-

quins in images much admired by the Surrealists. As part of the *Exposition Internationale du Surréalisme* at the Galerie des Beaux-Arts, Paris 1938, a 'rue surréaliste' featured twenty female mannequins dressed and decorated by the exhibiting artists, who included Arp, Ernst, Dalí, Duchamp, Masson and Miró.

During a period of scarcity and deprivation Hélion's paintings of window displays, bursting with ripe pumpkins or parading immaculately groomed mannequins, symbolised a nation's needs and desires. In 'Large Mannequin Painting' 1951 (no.74), it is the disturbing contrast between the condition of the living man, slumped on the pavement, and the ideal that society makes of his representation which provides the drama of the painting. The image of the *gisant*, a reclining or fallen figure, carries multiple religious, social and political implications. It recurs in Hélion's work, appearing first in the 1939 painting of a 'Fallen Figure' (Musée national d'art moderne, Paris) which signified the collapse of his non-figurative ambitions in a cascade of abstract forms. While in New York during the war, Hélion's childhood fascination with shop window displays was rekindled by the jumbled interiors of the down-at-heel shops along 2nd Avenue. In one such window he glimpsed a man sleeping.[13] Perhaps inspired by this incident, the fallen man then returned to haunt his figurative work, foregrounding compositions of nudes, newspaper readers and store fronts, creating rich and complex iconographic oppositions. Hélion's conception was of the shop window as theatre stage: he saw his invented and often comic drama as essentially Shakespearian.[14] His imagery of urban destitution, epitomised in the *gisant*, crucially anticipates Beckett's tramps, Estragon and Vladimir in *Waiting for Godot*, which was premiered at the Théâtre du Babylon in January 1953.[15] Hélion himself identifies the classic fictional outsider of the era, Charlie Chaplin, or 'Charlot' as the modern hero, a view shared by, among others, Sartre, whose review *Les Temps Modernes* was named after the title of Chaplin's first sound film.[17]

Throughout his abstract years Hélion had written passionately about great art of the past. It was the search for a form of great art appropriate to his age that motivated his quest for subjects with a contemporary meaning. He dreamed 'of a Sistine Chapel in the forms and costumes of our age' but was aware of the problems facing the artist in a non-religious era: 'what will replace the love of God and the fear of Hell?'[18]

Despite his interest in the life of the streets he continued to place traditional genres, such as the female nude and the still life, at the centre of his ambitions. Isolated from the outside world by the studio setting, Hélion's nudes doze or daydream, unaware of each other or of the viewer's gaze. Like Gruber's studio paintings of single female subjects they convey a period melancholy. But Hélion celebrates the nude – 'c'est toujours Vénus'[19] – while simultaneously treating the traditional theme in a pointedly ironic way. These bony figures recall little of the classical nude. Their overtly analytical compositional structures are anti-illusionistic and anti-idealist. Fastidious attention is paid to seemingly incidental elements in the background, to light switches and peeling paint as well as to the placing of bizarre still-life objects. These details are unsettling rather than reassuring. If a psychological dimension seems absent it is perhaps because Hélion is less interested in the inner life of his models than in their anthropological status. It is the exploration of a symbolic social language that most obviously separates Hélion from contemporary realist painters like Giacometti, Gruber or Balthus and from Socialist-Realist painters such as Fougeron. The strangely ritualistic structures and symbolism of these paintings are fascinating. In 'Star-Figure Nude with Smoker and Newspaper Reader' 1949 (no.72) the relationship between the central female nude and the two flanking male figures (both dressed) evokes Claude Lévi-Strauss's thesis that the basis of human exchange and of symbolic thought is the uniquely human phenomenon that a man is able to establish a relationship with another man through the exchange of women. Hélion's description of his formal and symbolic intentions in the slightly later, and seemingly more illusionistic 'Nude with Loaves' 1952 (no.75) is littered with the kind of binary oppositions explored by Lévi-Strauss. Here the nude is seen, as Hélion himself noted:

> from the back, because from the front it would be a person, and the relationship between the flesh and bread would only be seen from a long way off. The male/female relationship is once more expressed in the sombre/white, heavy/light antinomy of the hanging trousers and skirt. Fringed rug, for the nude is offering the fringe of her hair. Bread on the ground; crumbs on the rug; crumbs on the floor . . . Man's shoe, big, heavy and old under the fresh looking petticoat. It's there to provide the composition with a patch of colour – no doubt to balance the trousers, but also to establish the homage to the nude . . . A votive branch for burning. Twigs. On the white tablecloth, two fine loaves, nice and alluring, white . . . the burnt end of bread is also a bud . . . the tip of the breast etc.[20]

In a period of continuing acute deprivation the image concentrates on the bare essentials of life. Hélion's manner of describing things has often been compared to the poetry of Francis Ponge, a close friend of the artist from the late 1940s. But whereas Ponge describes objects dispassionately and in isolation, Hélion is continually interested in an object's symbolic and formal relationship to other objects and the underlying unity of the physical world. This is what underpins the seemingly stylised formal rhythms and echoes that articulate his paintings.

The eloquence with which his work speaks of the post-war period and of the spiritual and social crisis that underpinned existentialism's extraordinary cultural invasion did not go unrecognised at the time. Ponge characterised Hélion's style as a 'Réalisme Absurde', the 'official art of a Republic of the Absurd'.[21] Writing in 1951, the Surrealist writer Pierre Mabille argued that Hélion's paintings were amongst the most eloquent testimonies of the human condition, and saw in his 'Men Reading Newspapers' 1950 (no.73) the imagery of alienation constructed, perversely, from symbols of communication.[22]

NOTES

1 James Johnson Sweeney, 'Eleven Europeans in America: Jean Hélion', *The Museum of Modern Art Bulletin*, New York, vol.12, nos.4–5, 1946, pp.28–31.
2 Jean Hélion in 'Réalisme et réalité, enquête sur la peinture, querelles et fictions du réalisme', *Esprit*, no.168, June 1950, p.941.
3 Jean Hélion, 'Notes de travail' MSS Bibliotèque Nationale, Paris, 29 March 1945.
4 Ibid., 5 Sept. 1949.
5 Ibid., 15 Feb. 1949.
6 Bernard Ceysson, 'Le Cas Hélion', *L'Art en Europe, les années décisives*, Musée d'art moderne de Saint Etienne, 1987–8, p.85.
7 'Notes de travail', 2 Aug. 1945.
8 Jean Hélion interviewed by Daniel Abadie in Daniel Abadie, *Hélion ou la force des choses*, Brussels 1975, p.14.
9 Hélion 1950, pp.941–2.
10 André Breton, *Le Surréalisme et la peinture*, Paris 1928.
11 'Notes de travail', 29 March 1945.
12 Fernand Léger, 'The Machine Aesthetic I' 1925, reprinted in *Functions of Painting*, 1973, p.56.
13 Abadie 1975, p.109.
14 'Notes de travail', 6 May 1947.
15 This point is made by Sarah Wilson, 'Double Rhythm: Fanfare for Hélion', in *Hélion*, exh. cat., Albemarle Gallery 1987, p.11.
16 'Notes de travail', 6 May 1947.
17 According to Simone de Beauvoir in *Force of Circumstance*, 1968, p.22.
18 'Notes de travail', 14 Oct. 1947.
19 Ibid., 15 Feb. 1949.
20 Ibid., 6 March 1952.
21 Francis Ponge, Introduction in *Hélion Paintings*, Hanover Gallery 1951, p.3.
22 Pierre Mabille, 'Jean Hélion et l'homme quotidian', *Elements*, Jan. 1951.

Illustration (p.134) Jean Hélion in his studio 1950 Photograph by Douglas Glass *Mme Jacqueline Hélion*

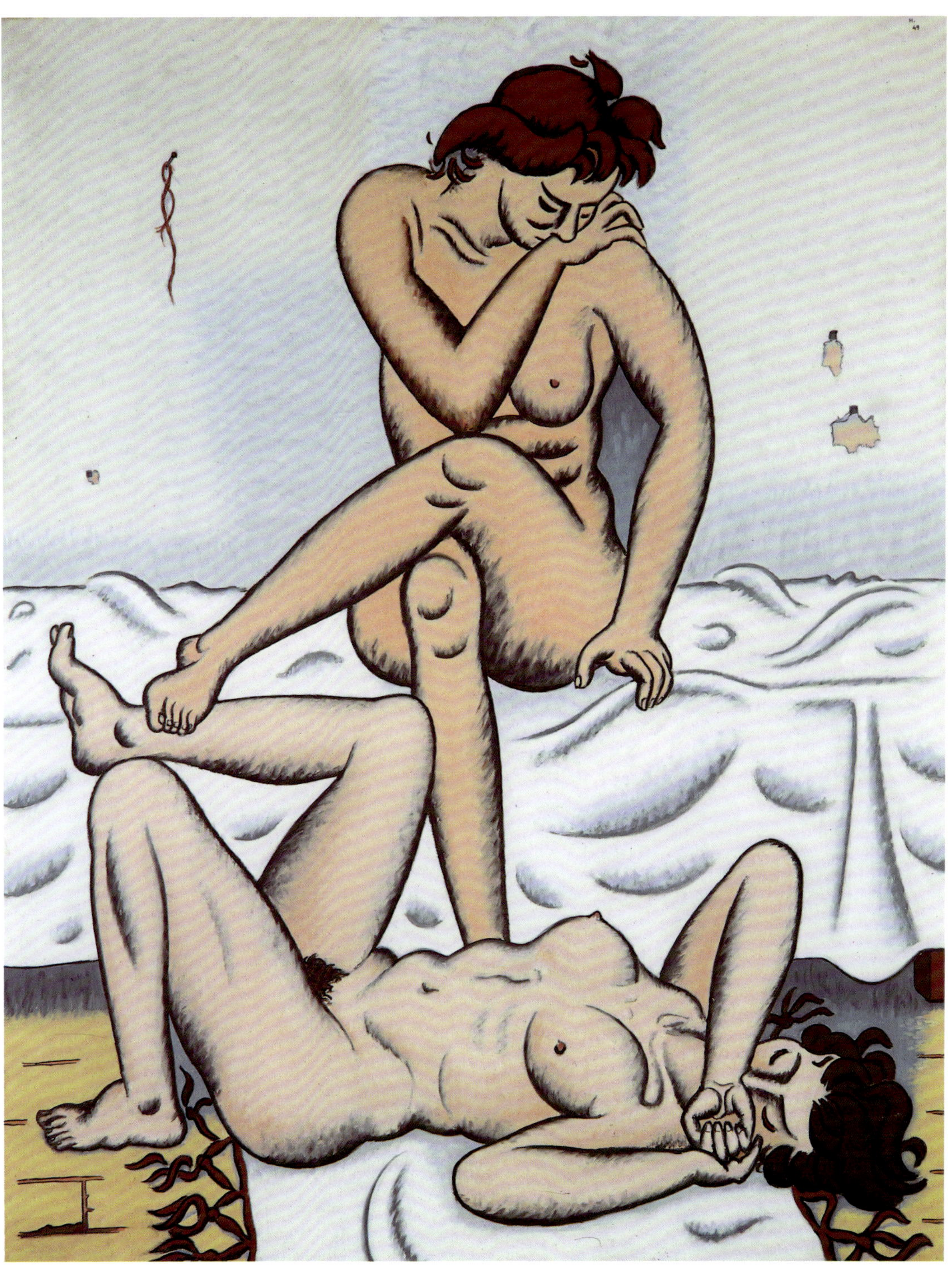

70 Seated Nude, Nude Reclining 1949
146×114 ($57\frac{1}{2} \times 44\frac{7}{8}$)

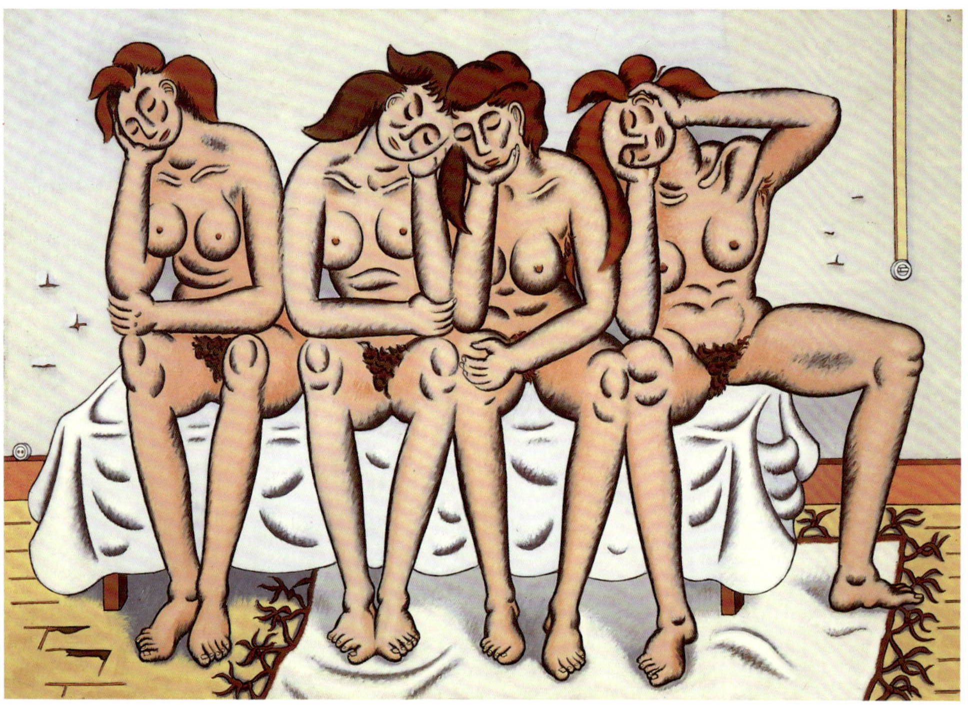

71 Four Seated Nudes 1949
114 × 162 (44⅞ × 63¾)

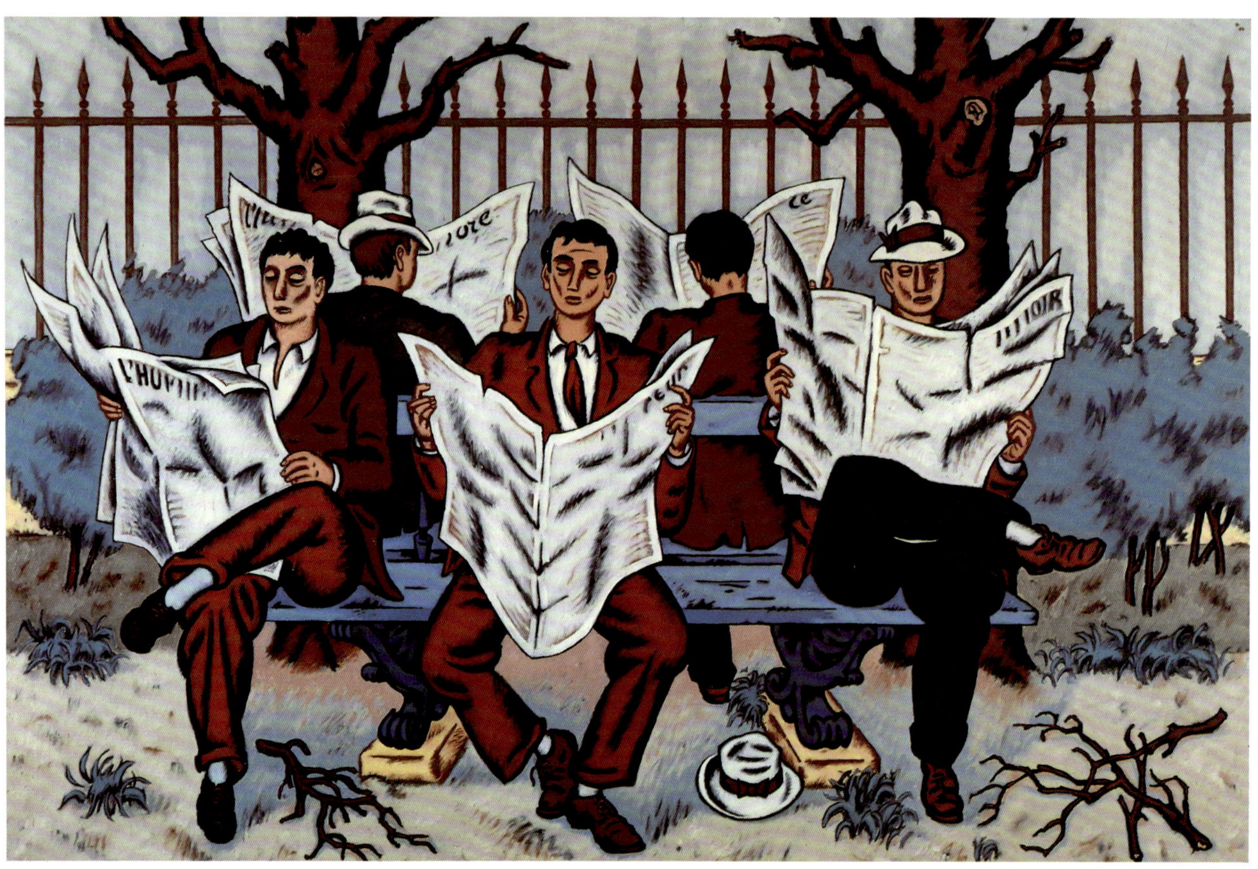

73 Men Reading Newspapers 1950
129.5 × 195 (51 × 76¾)

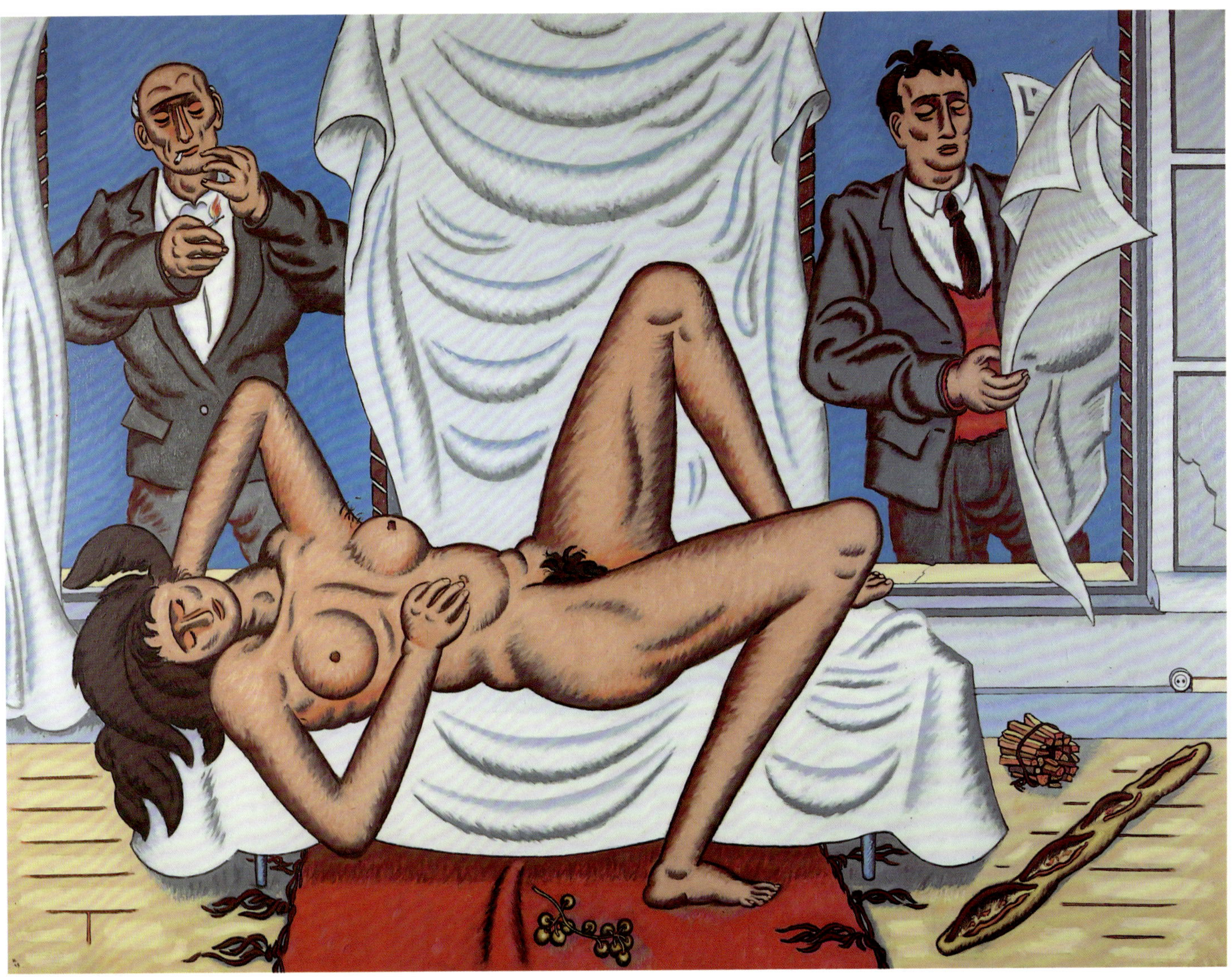

**72 Star-Figure Nude with Smoker
and Newspaper Reader** 1949
150×200 ($59 \times 78\frac{3}{4}$)

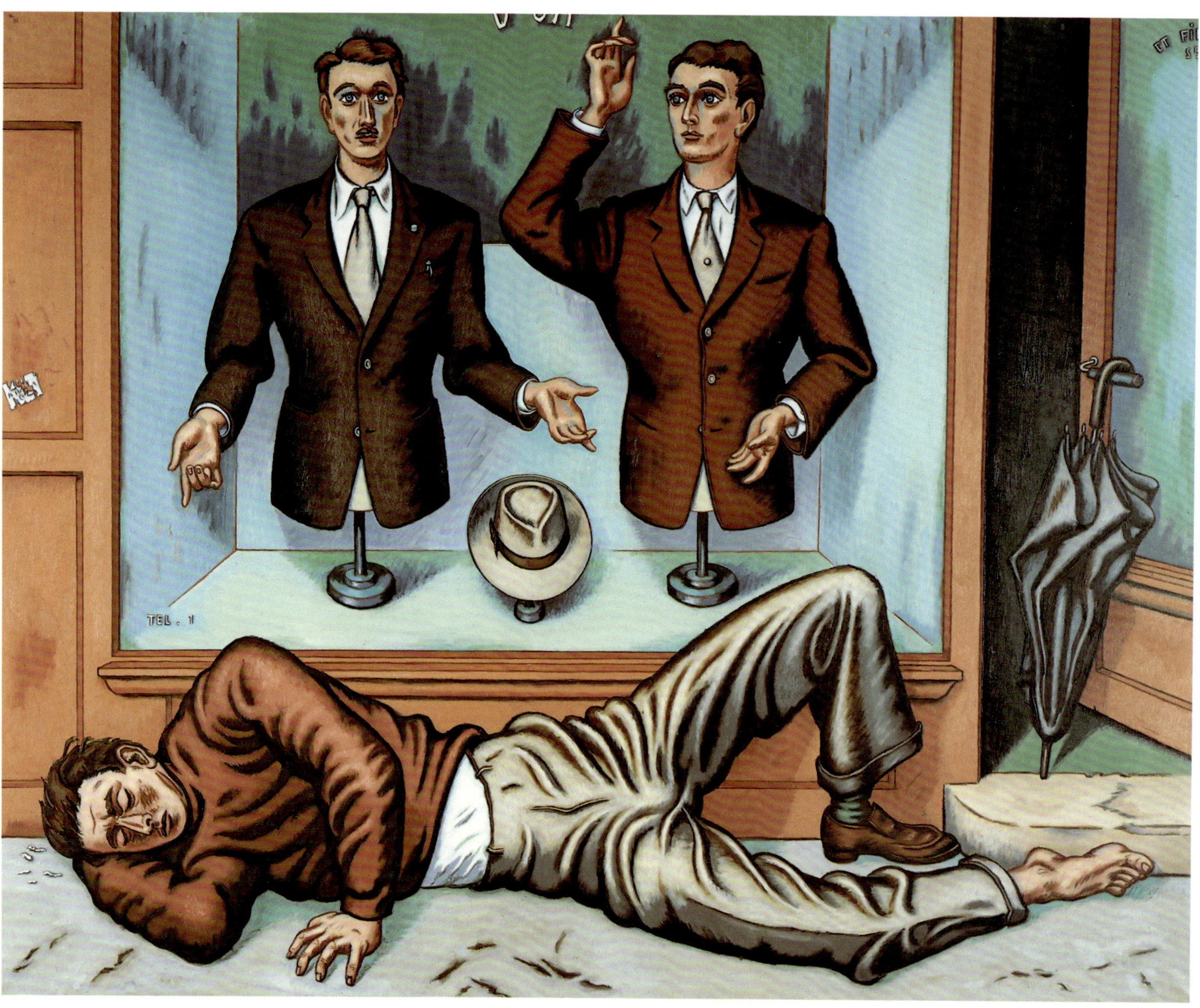

74 Large Mannequin Painting 1951
129.5 × 161.5 (51 × 63⅝)

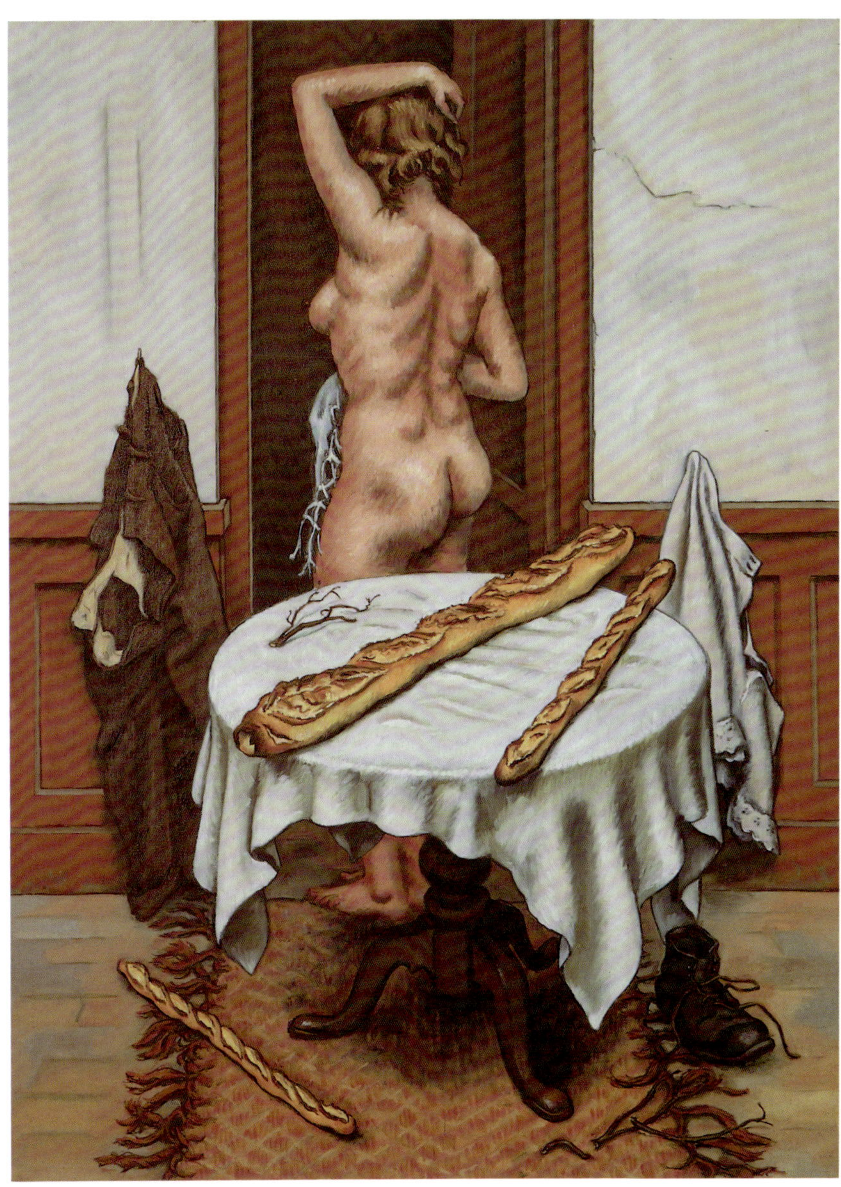

75 Nude with Loaves 1952
130.1 × 97 (51¼ × 38¼)

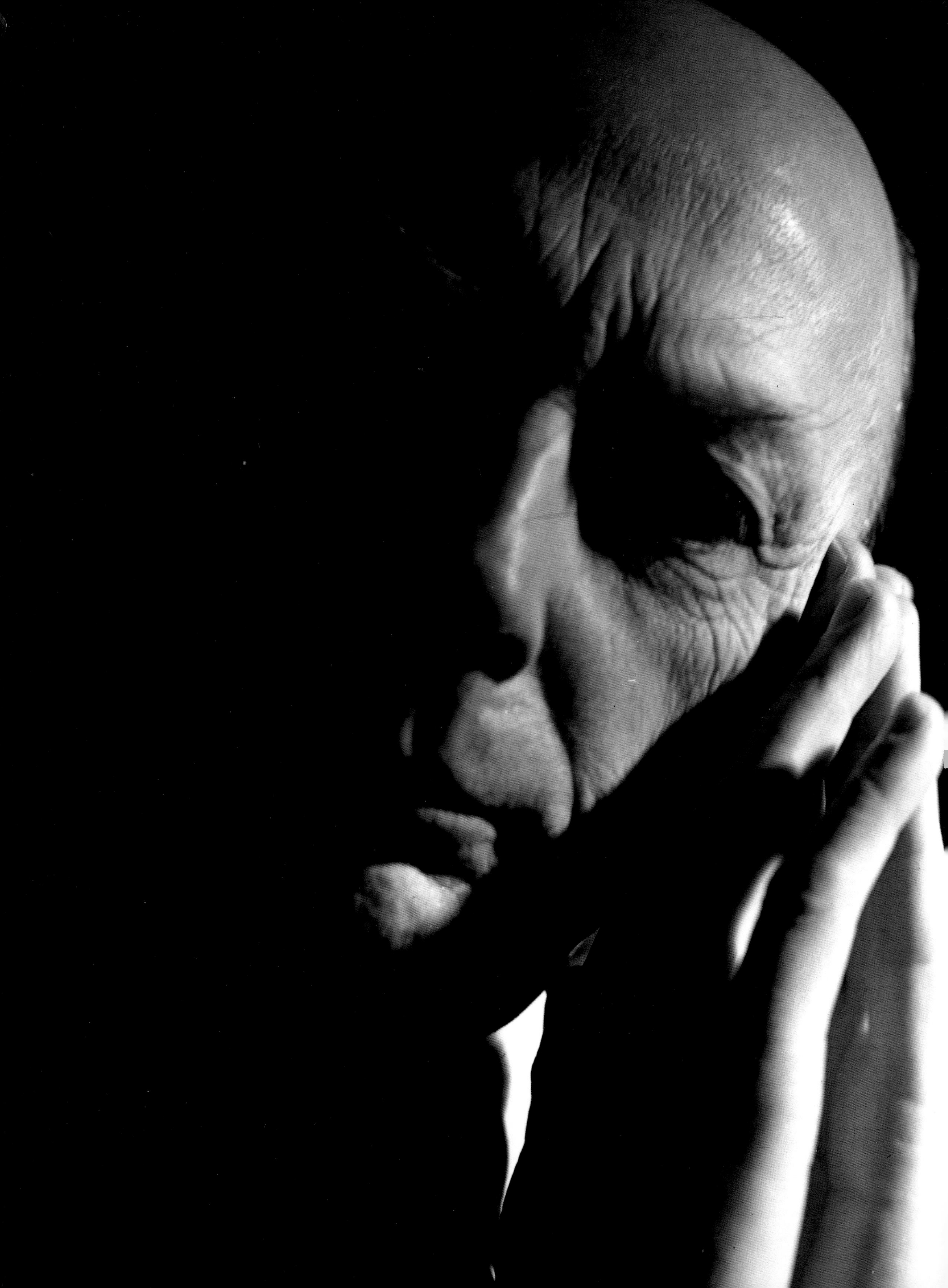

Henri Michaux (1899–1984)

In 1948 the tragic death of his wife, Marie-Louise, precipitated a period of astonishing creativity in which the poet, Henri Michaux, produced hundreds of watercolours in swift and feverish succession. This was not his first exercise in watercolour but hitherto, as he said,

> I had not let myself go completely. I had not flung myself into them. And yet it's only when I've been flung into them that they hold up, that they work. I didn't know that I was holding something back.[1]

When a selection of these paintings was displayed at the Galerie René Drouin in April 1948, the poet and critic René Bertelé remarked that the walls 'looked as though they had been splattered when some uncontrollable wave had broken; they were covered with demented heads or figures about to vanish as suddenly as they had appeared, as though sucked in by violently coloured flames in a dreadful wind'.[2] The exhibition brought real acclaim for Michaux's painting for the first time, with critics like René Guilly claiming in *Combat*: 'Henri Michaux's paintings are as intense and poignant as his writings.'[3]

Most of these paintings comprise coloured grounds onto which the artist drew with black ink before the watercolour had time to dry. A fluid, often blurred, melodious figuration results in which heads and bodies emerge and metamorphose with momentary, hallucinogenic intensity. The paintings clearly reflect the artist's deep personal distress at this time:

> In a hospital fate stands still. No change for better or worse … In a black mood I start … to cover it [the paper] with a few dark colours and sullenly to squirt water onto it at random, not in order to do anything in particular, and certainly not to do a painting. I have nothing to do, I have only to undo. To undo the world of confused, conflicting things in which I am plunged.[4]

His experience of suffering and pain is the key not only to these remarkable and moving images but to Michaux's approach to art and writing. It is through pain, and other extreme, alienating states that the individual can most effectively break through the protective armour of conventional behaviour and thought to intensely personal, primordial mental states. Later, for example, Michaux experimented with the drug mescalin. For him such experiences were both singular, as in the experience of his wife's death, and more general, as in the experience of anguish and alienation at the absurdity of life without a transcendent justification – making of Michaux 'a key witness to the existential crisis of the Twentieth Century'.[5]

Several of Michaux's texts deal with this notion of absurdity, and the idea of anguish as a prelude to self-discovery. In *A Certain Plume* (1930), Michaux's fictional character Plume (who has been compared variously to Camus's Meursault, to Sartre's Roquentin and to Charlie Chaplin) is a frequent – and often comic – victim of absurdity, an outsider who remains indifferent to the blows which life rains upon him. In *My Properties* (1929), Michaux creates an image of gratuitous and purposeless life in which man has to find his own meaning. Michaux's concept of anguish and his probing of the question of personal identity finds echoes in Sartre. Both see man as aspiring to that quality of wholeness which is perceived in objects of the external world. Both also acknowledge anguish as a potentially liberating experience, and the work of art as a means by which man can define himself.

Very early in life Michaux rejected the world of ordinary lived experience as commonplace and insignificant. He spurned family life, refused to eat as a child, dismissed the company of his fellow students at school, and as a young adult chose to travel to faraway, exotic places. When he began writing it was as a therapeutic activity. In his 1942 statement on poetic method he identifies, as the first of three reasons for writing, the impulse 'to liberate myself from an intolerable tension'.[6] Writing became for him a way of investigating inner experience.

Michaux had begun drawing and painting in the late 1920s, only a few years after his first published texts. The practice started as a way of reaching beyond the literary significance and cultural conventions of words to a more direct and pure form of expression: 'born, bred, and educated in a purely verbal milieu and culture, I paint to "de-condition" myself.'[7]

As a young man Michaux had initially dismissed painting in terms that closely echo Sartre's criticism of the classical figurative tradition with its affirmation of bourgeois social and political hierarchies and the status quo. Michaux abandoned this stance when he saw, for the first time, the work of Paul Klee and Max Ernst on his arrival in Paris in the early 1920s:

> Until then I had strongly rejected it [painting]. I hated painters more than anyone else as I considered them to be the voluntary helpers of cumbersome reality and its appearances which form an all too conspicuous screen … At last, thanks to Ernst and Klee I was able to get a glimpse of what goes on beyond the scenes. It was a way, a hope.[8]

Both Klee and Ernst (and, in a different way, Isidore Ducasse, self-styled Comte de Lautréamont, whom Michaux first read at this time) drew Michaux's attention to the possibilities of pictorial automatism as a revelatory tool. In Klee the use of line, a meandering and exploratory trace, may have been of especial significance. For Michaux, the absolutely free and unprejudiced nature of line was its strength; it was free from the kind of associations tied to words, free of form, of focus, of centre, of necessary beginning or end, product alone of tool and body movement.

Michaux's first paintings were made in the mid-1920s, and anticipate his later development in important respects: in the use of media suited to fast and continuous work, of small and intimate formats and of imagery that hovers on the border of abstraction and figuration. Early works include an invented alphabet arranged systematically like Chinese characters, and fluid single-line drawings which demonstrate his early interest in automatism.

From 1927 to 1937, Michaux travelled extensively, to Ecuador, Turkey, South America and Asia. While travelling his most prolific and acclaimed activity was as a writer. Towards the end of this period he began to paint again and in 1938 he had a first exhibition at the Galerie Pierre in Paris. A volume of poems and gouaches, entitled *Paintings*, was published the following year. The illustrations, coloured images on black backgrounds, were described by Louis Cheronnet in his introduction to the volume as 'strange nocturnal celebrations', recalling images glimpsed and imagined on his travels. The book also contained one of Michaux's first statements on his painting in which he describes the experience, new to him, of experimenting with images rather than words:

> He took up painting but lately.
> When one undergoes a shift in creative activity one embarks on one of the strangest voyages within oneself that can be made.
> Strange decongestion, putting part of oneself to sleep, the speaking, writing part … Night. Local death. Gone desire, eloquent appetite. That part of the head which was the most concerned, grows cold. It is a surprising experience.
> It is a strange feeling too when one rediscovers the world through another window. Like a child one must learn how to walk.
> One knows nothing.[9]

Aside from the unmistakable suggestion of landscape, imagined or real, evoked by the black gouaches, the most frequent suggestion is of the human face and head, whether in watercolour or in his experimental frottage drawings from 1945. According to Michaux, although he drew 'with no particular intention, scribble mechanically, nearly always there appear faces on the paper'.[10] As for their identity, they are a

> sort of epiphenomenon of thought … as though one were constantly shaping within oneself a fluid, ideally plastic and malleable face and that it were to form and disintegrate in accordance with ideas and impressions, automatically, in an instantaneous synthesis, all day long and so to speak cinematically.[11]

A characteristic of all Michaux's paintings is the depiction of images in transition, in metamorphosis. His poems too are full of ambiguous images, prompting multiple readings. As in his spontaneous approach to image-making on paper he follows, as a writer, no predetermined creative method and his writings display continual shifts in style and character. In his writings on painting

"

Michaux emphasises the importance of speed and movement as a way of liberating the artist from ordinary consciousness. His seminal 1946 text, entitled 'Thinking about the Phenomenon of Painting', describes how the speed of execution induces a mood in which resonate a 'thousand moments of panic, called up from my not too happy past'.[12] Panic induces a creative struggle in which superficial identities are destroyed. It loosens the mental stranglehold of normal consciousness and allows for a deeper correspondence between image and self:

> It's not in the mirror that one should contemplate oneself.
> Men, look at yourselves in the paper.[13]

Michaux's concept of identity is entirely appropriate to his imagery. He rejects the notion of a single, describable self, in favour of an existence in flux, endlessly redefining itself in relation to the world outside.

The Surrealists early claimed Michaux as one of their number. Michaux was clearly interested in their discoveries, writing in 1925 that he affirmed the principle of automatism and acknowledged the term Surrealist with the reservation that 'the surrealist idea of what is marvellous is monotonous ... but if I have to choose between the marvellous and anything else, long live Surrealism. Even if it is only superficially marvellous, bathing in it does me good.'[14] But despite the acknowledged influence of Klee and Ernst, Michaux was not interested in the systematic exploration of automatic processes. The official Surrealist line held automatism as a process of activating visionary faculties in order to create previously unknown associations of images. André Breton, who always regarded language as supreme, found in Ernst that 'everything is seeking itself [and] is in the process of becoming articulate'.[15] In contrast, Michaux was not interested in seeking relationships between language and images. André Gide spoke tellingly of this pre-verbal quality in Michaux's work in a lecture of 1941, extolling the poet's ability to 'make us feel *intuitively* the strangeness of natural things and the naturalness of strange things'.[16] We find Michaux's imagery, as Sartre found Wols's, full of 'nameless things'.

Michaux was also influenced by the art which he discovered during his travels in China in 1930–1. What he admired about Chinese artists, he explained in *A Barbarian in Asia*, was the tentative quality of their vision, for in Chinese paintings images 'are there and yet they're absent, like delicate phantoms that haven't been summoned by desire. The Chinese especially like distant horizons, what can't be touched.'[17] Later he wrote of the elemental, metamorphic quality of Chinese painting evoking 'the break of day, dusk, and in other places, the rising tide, the ebb tide, the breeze springing up, the great ceremonies of nature'.[18] Chinese painters were poets 'of the incomplete' and approached art in ways that echo Surrealist automatist procedures with 'Lines that dash and flit with the movement of a sudden inspiration and are not drawn prosaically ... that's what said something to me and carried me away'.[19]

The series of Indian ink drawings collectively known as *Movements* that Michaux published in 1951 seems like a visual demonstration of his understanding of a Chinese approach. A few deft strokes, swift and spontaneous, identify a character as part of a group or alphabet disposed, like Chinese characters, neatly across the page. Michaux described them as 'a new language, spurning the verbal ... I see them as liberators'.[20] The emphasis is once again on a realm of expression far from words, the exploration of which is profoundly therapeutic. Michaux prefaced the publication of these drawings with the desire that

> Whoever, having perused my signs, is led by my example to create signs himself according to his being and his needs will, unless I am very much mistaken, discover a source of exhilaration, a release such as he has never known, a disencrustation, a new life open to him, a writing unhoped for, affording relief, in which he will be able at last to express himself far from words, words, the words of others.[21]

When recognition for his art came it was initially from those critics and writers most closely involved in defining and encouraging new informal and gestural styles. Although Michaux ultimately eschewed movements and groups, preferring his own society to that of fellow artists, he was profoundly aware from an early date of a new climate and the necessity for a new art.

Although his own art reached the heights of its expressive potential only in the late 1940s, already in the early years of the war Michaux was advocating a new way forward. Speaking to Brassaï of Picasso's art, Michaux claimed that 'we no longer want the same thing, we're no longer aspiring to the same thing ... his [Picasso's] "monsters" no longer disturb us. We're looking for other monsters down different paths.'[22]

NOTES

1 Henri Michaux, *Emergences-Résurgences*, Switzerland 1972, pp.32–6, trans. Michael Fineberg in *Henri Michaux*, exh. cat., The Solomon R. Guggenheim Museum, New York 1978, p.60.
2 René Bertelé, 'Notes pour un intinéraire de l'oeuvre plastique d'Henri Michaux', *Cahiers de l'Herne*, no.8, 1966, pp.359–60.
3 René Guilly, 'Henri Michaux, peintre de la présence', *Combat*, 21 April 1948.
4 Michaux 1972, pp.32–6 in *Henri Michaux* 1978, p.60.
5 Peter Broome, *Henri Michaux*, London 1977, p.34.
6 Henri Michaux, statement in René Bertelé, *Panorama de la jeune poésie française*, Paris 1942.
7 Michaux 1972, p.9.
8 Quoted in Patrick Waldberg, *Max Ernst*, Paris 1958, p.300.
9 Henri Michaux, 'Qui il est', *Peintures*, Paris 1939, unpag.
10 Henri Michaux, 'En pensent au phénomène de la peinture', *Peintures et dessins*, Paris 1946, pp.1–12.
11 Ibid., pp.2–3.
12 Ibid., p.8.
13 Ibid., p.3.
14 Henri Michaux, *Que je fus* Paris 1927, quoted by Agnès Angliviel de La Beaumelle in *Henri Michaux* 1978, p.49.
15 André Breton, *Le Surréalisme et la peinture*, Paris 1965, p.168.
16 André Gide, *Découvrons Henri Michaux*, Paris 1941.
17 Henri Michaux, *Un Barbare en Asie*, Paris 1933, 1967, p.181.
18 Henri Michaux, quoted by Angliviel de La Beaumelle 1978, p.45.
19 Ibid.
20 Henri Michaux, 'Postface', *Mouvements*, Paris 1951, unpag.
21 Ibid.
22 Quoted by Brassaï, *Picasso & Co*, London 1967, p.57.

Illustration (p.142) Portrait of Henri Michaux
1953 Photograph by Paul Facchetti
© *Paul Facchetti*

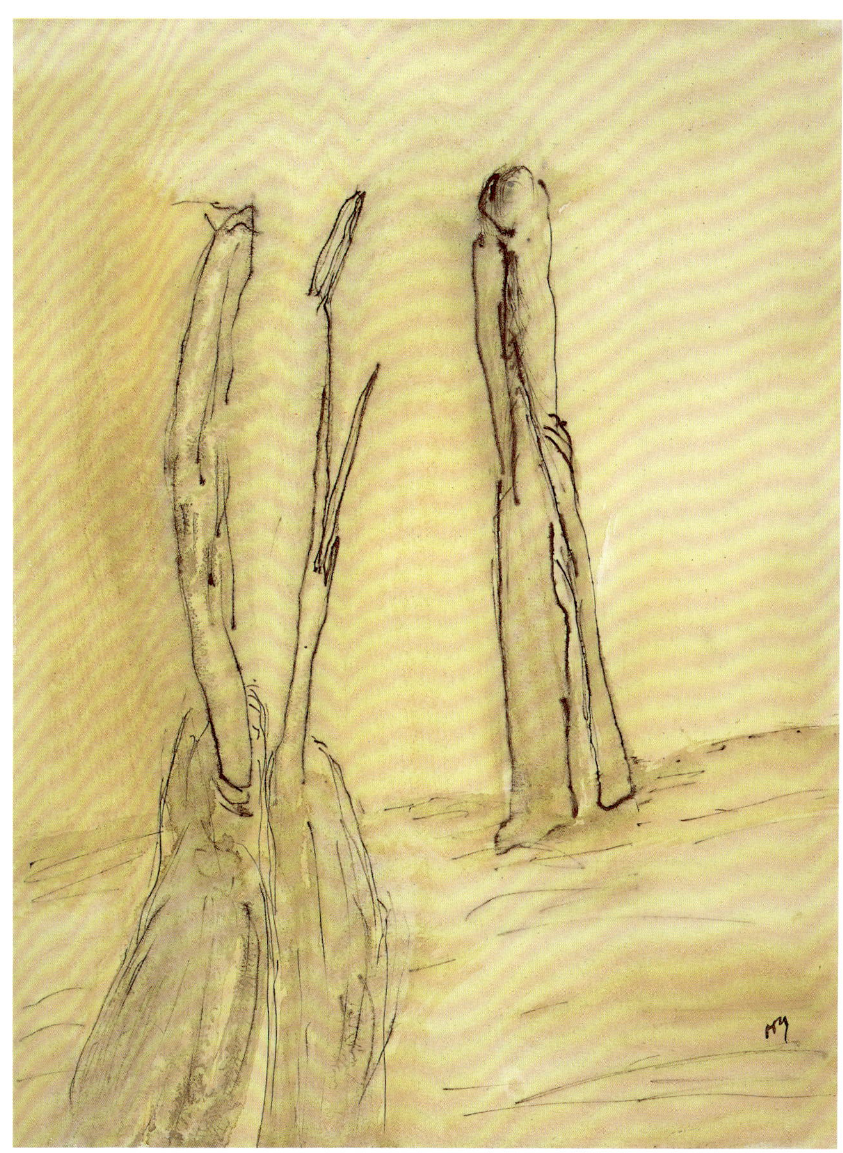

76 Untitled 1946
31.7 × 23.7 ($12\frac{1}{2} \times 9\frac{3}{8}$)

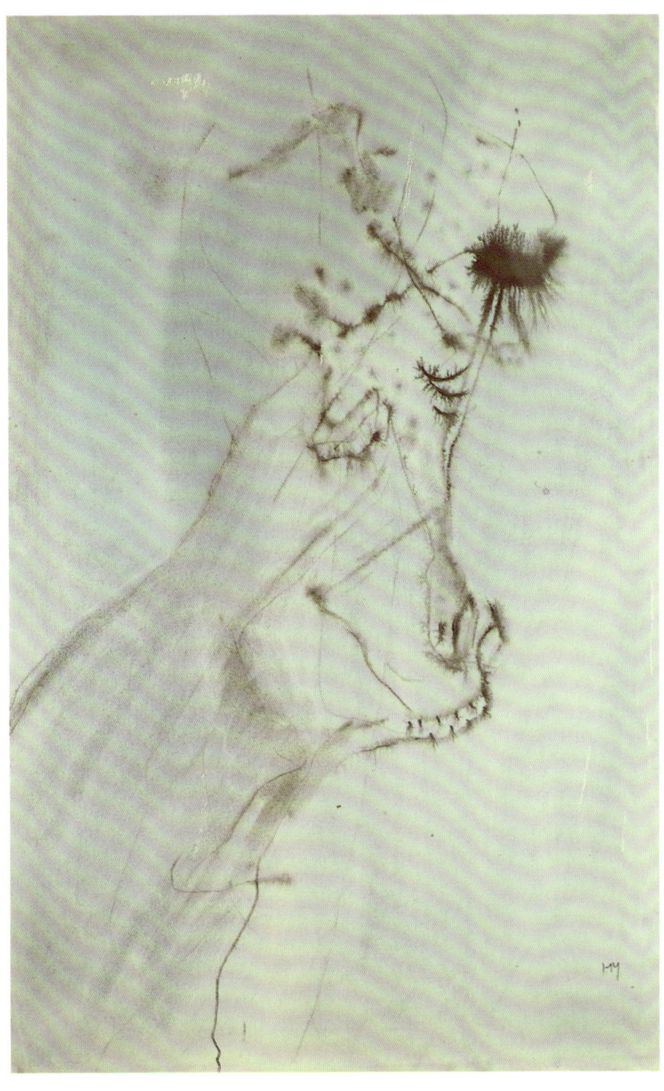

77 **Untitled** *c*.1946
47 × 30 (18½ × 11¾)

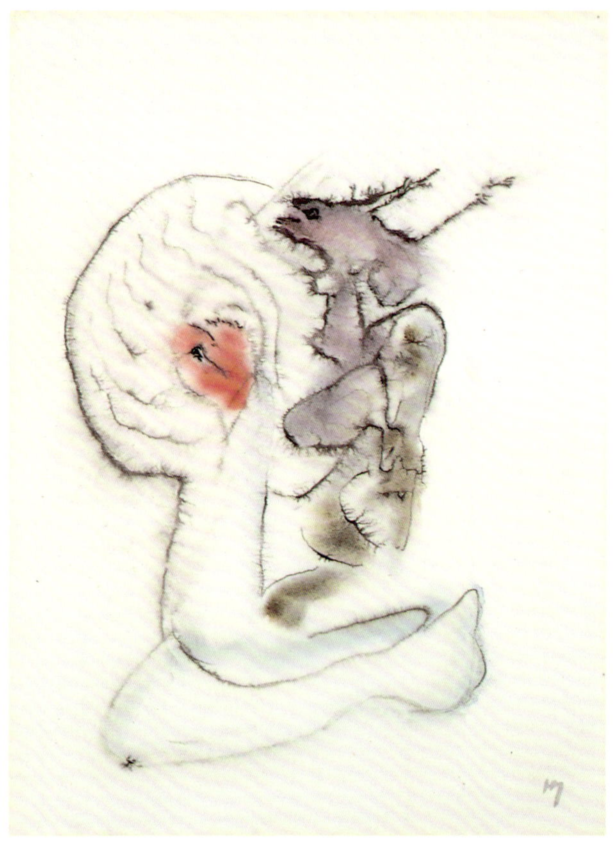

83 **Untitled** 1948
39.1 × 29.2 (15⅝ × 11½)

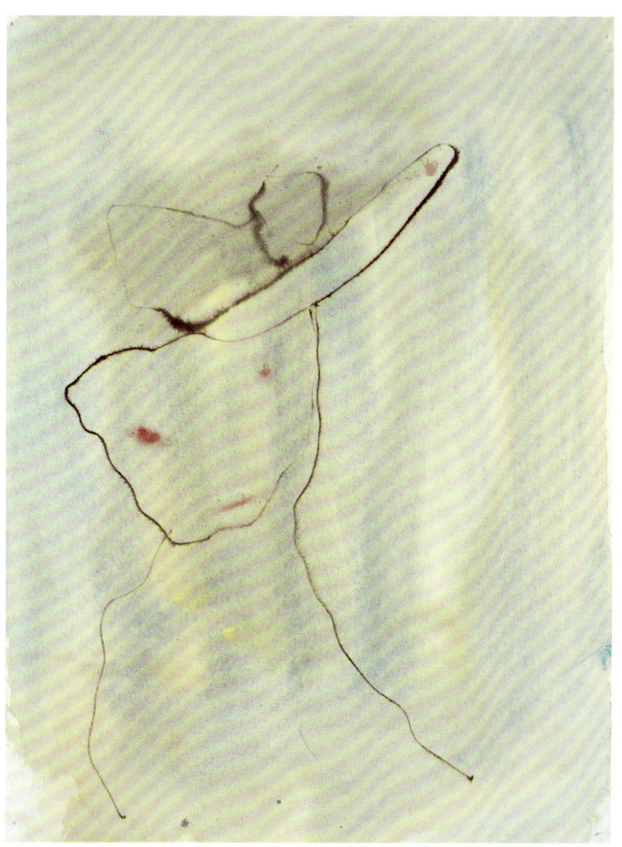

80 Untitled 1947–8
$38 \times 28 \, (15 \times 11)$

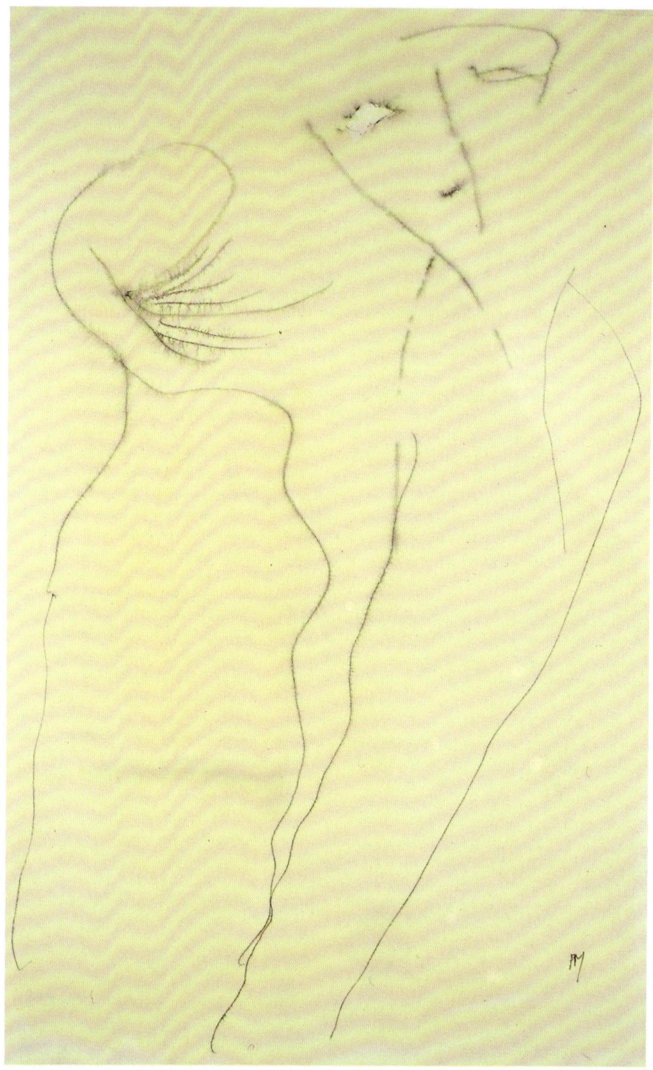

81 Untitled 1947–8
$46 \times 30 \, (18\frac{1}{4} \times 11\frac{3}{4})$

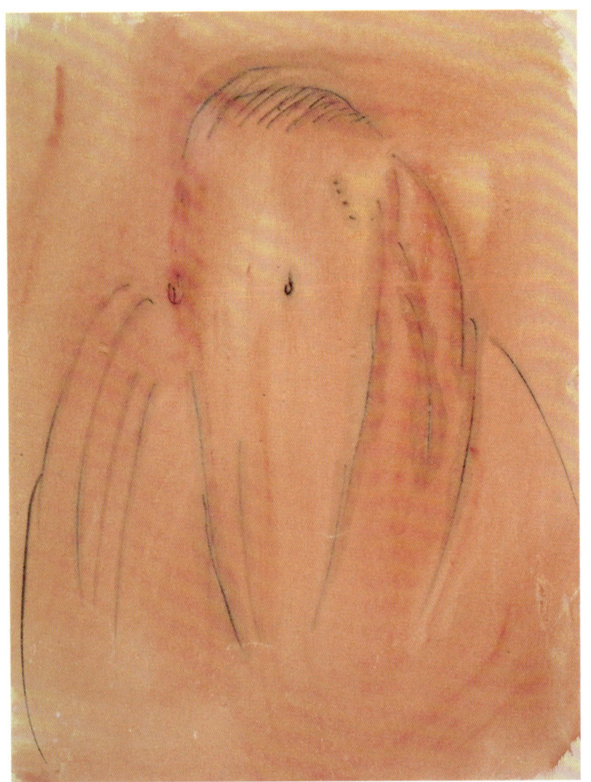

82 Untitled 1948
32×24 ($12\frac{5}{8} \times 9\frac{1}{2}$)

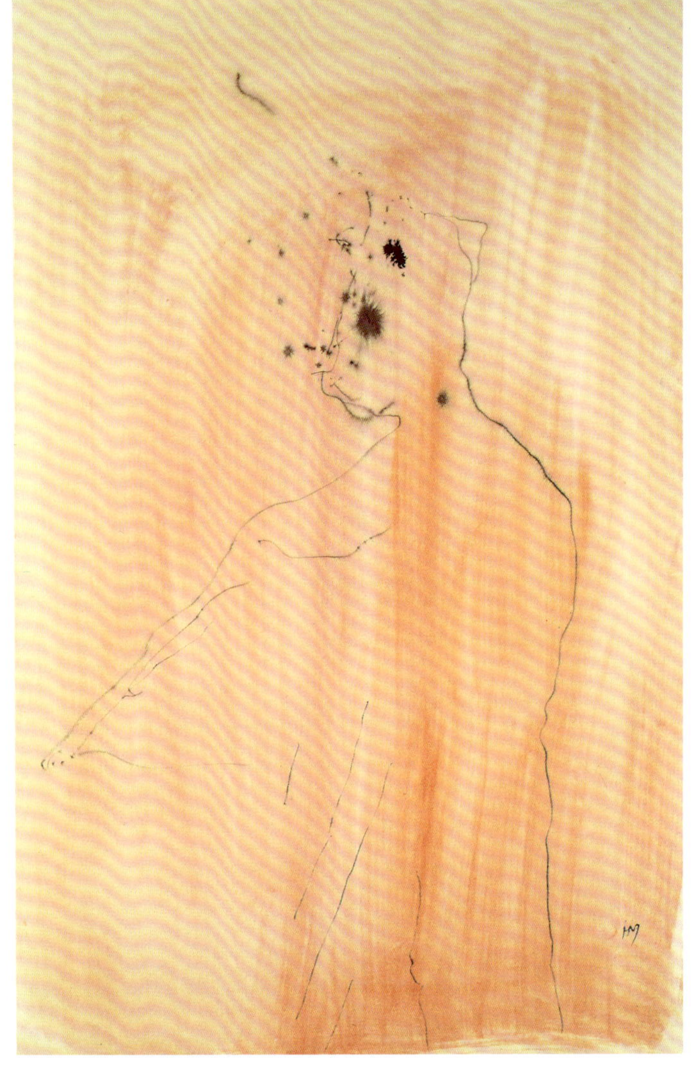

86 Untitled *c.*1948
49.5×32 ($19\frac{1}{2} \times 12\frac{5}{8}$)

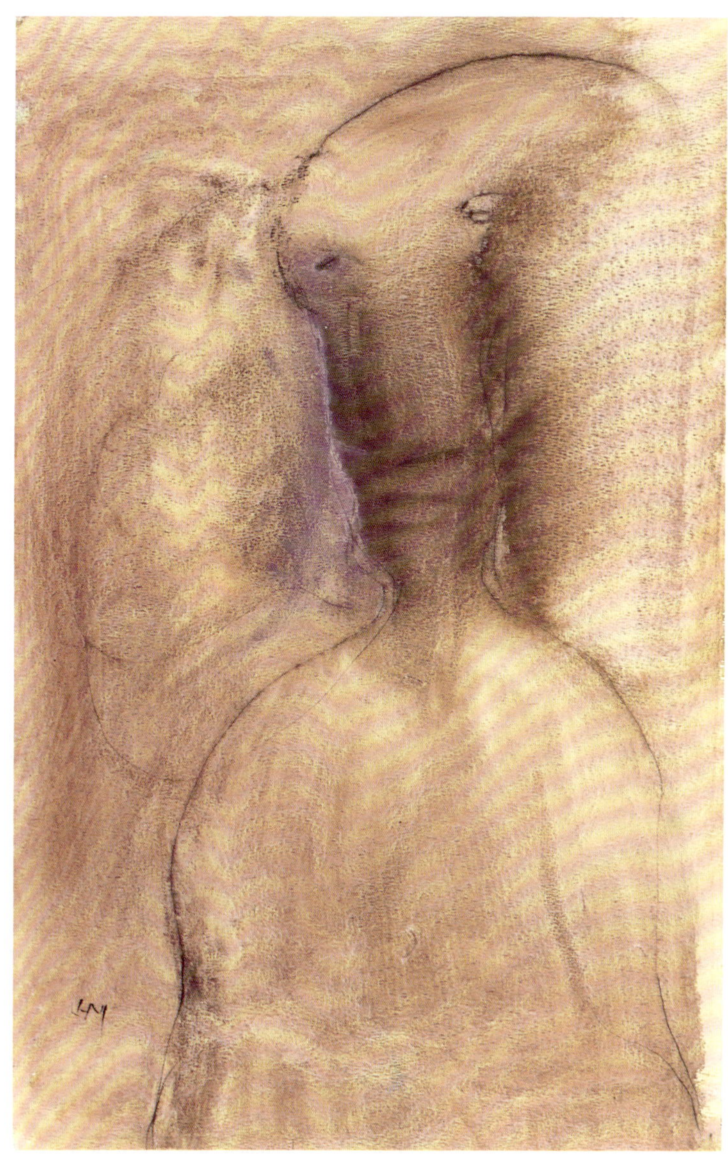

78 Untitled 1946–8
50.8 × 32.7 (20 × 12⅞)

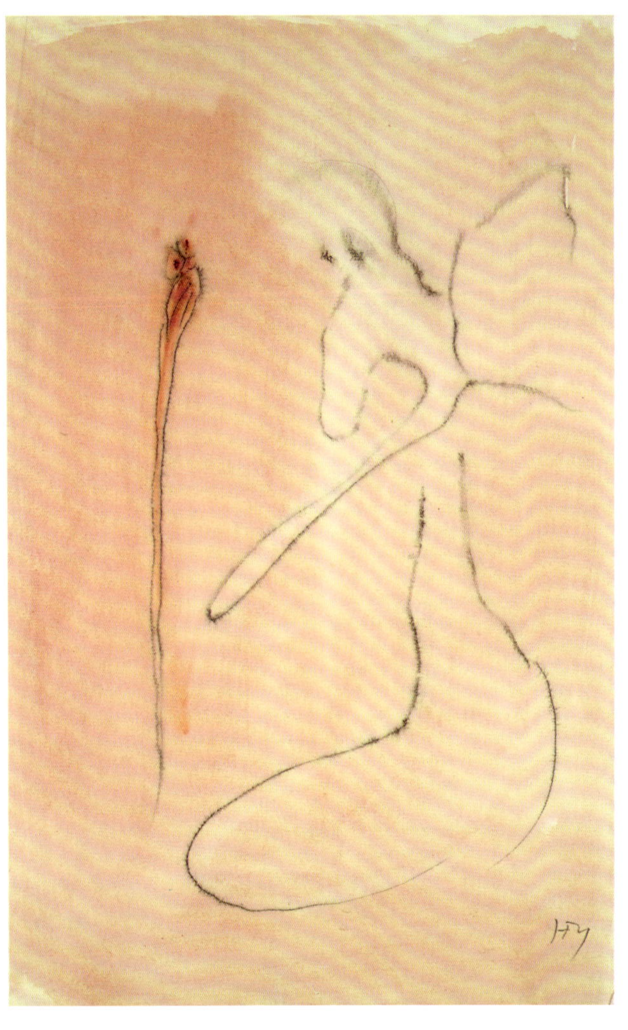

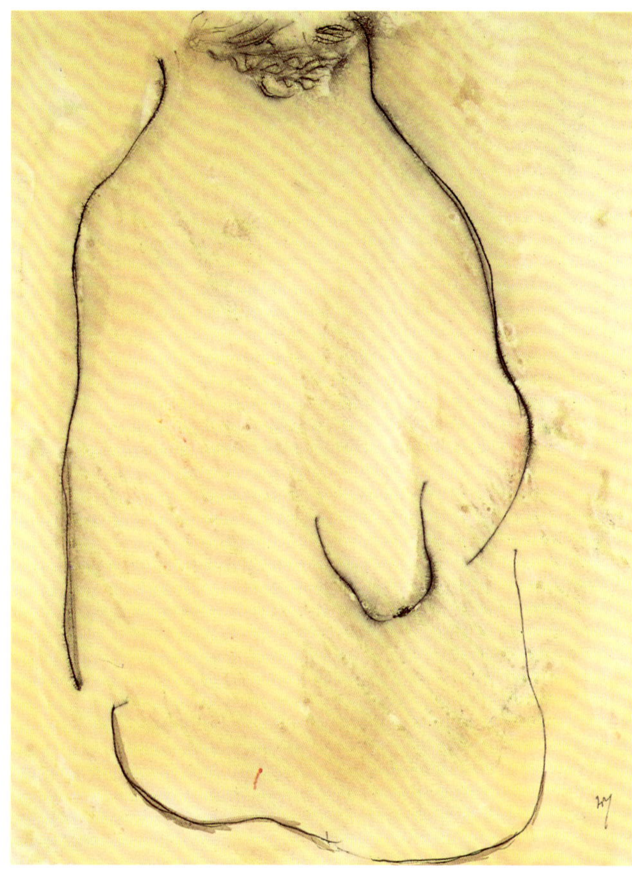

87 Untitled *c.*1948
31.7 × 24.2 ($12\frac{1}{2} \times 9\frac{1}{2}$)

85 Untitled *c.*1948
47.5 × 31 ($18\frac{1}{4} \times 12\frac{1}{4}$)

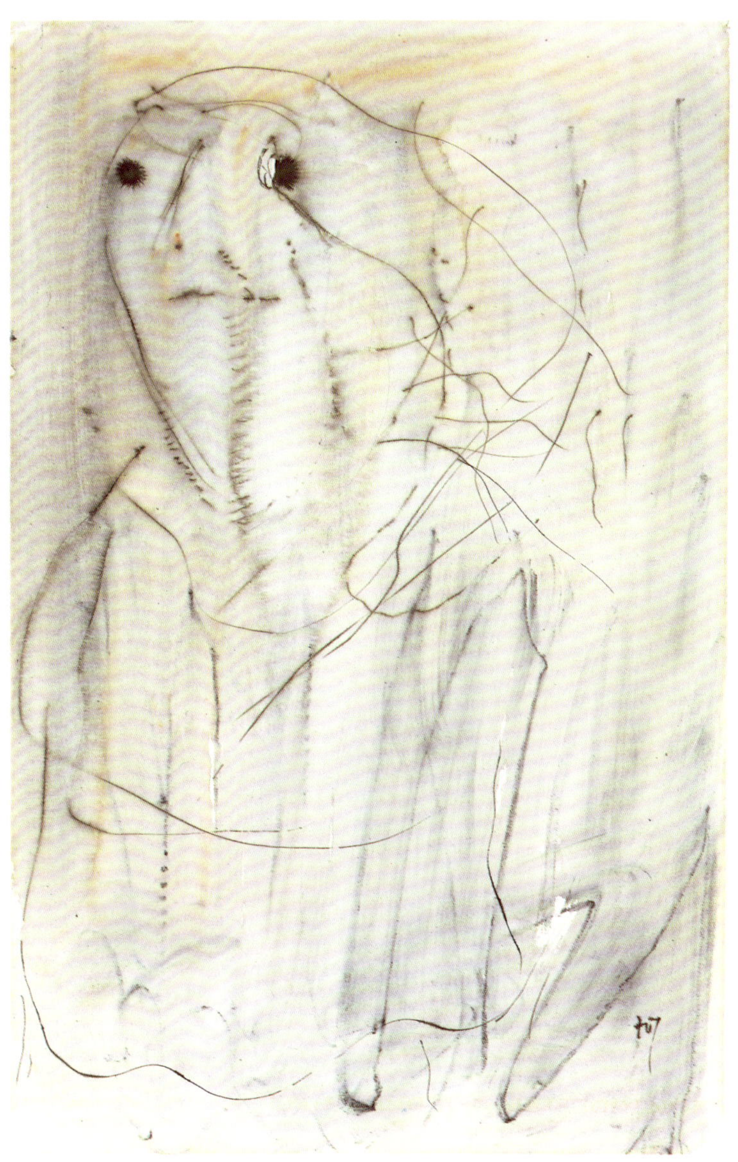

79 Untitled 1946–8
50 × 32 (19⅝ × 12⅝)

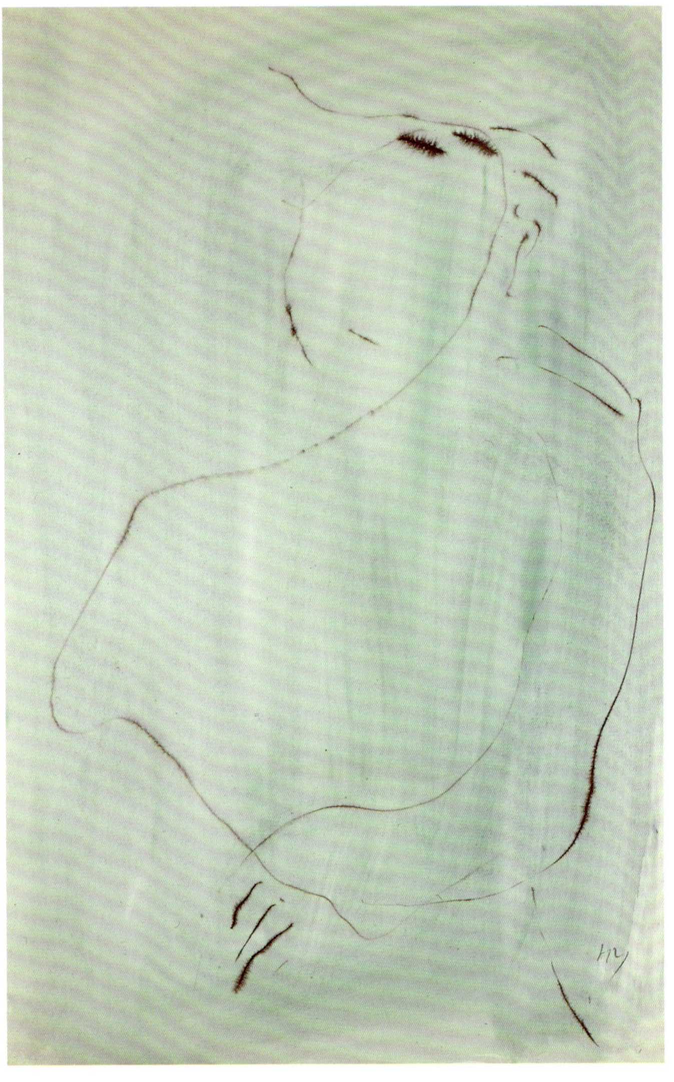

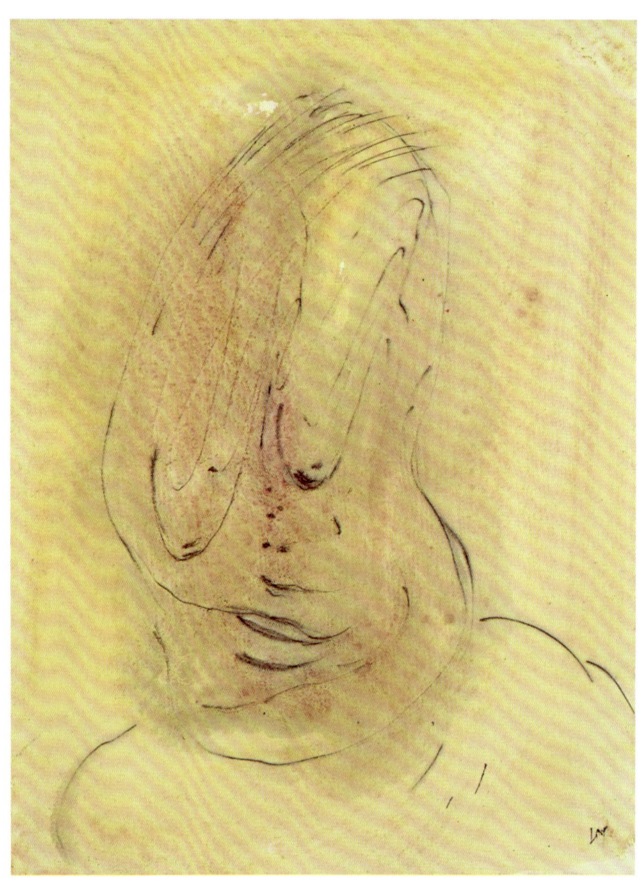

88 Untitled 1948–9
31.5 × 23.5 ($12\frac{3}{8} \times 9\frac{1}{4}$)

84 Untitled *c.*1948
49 × 32 ($19\frac{1}{4} \times 12\frac{5}{8}$)

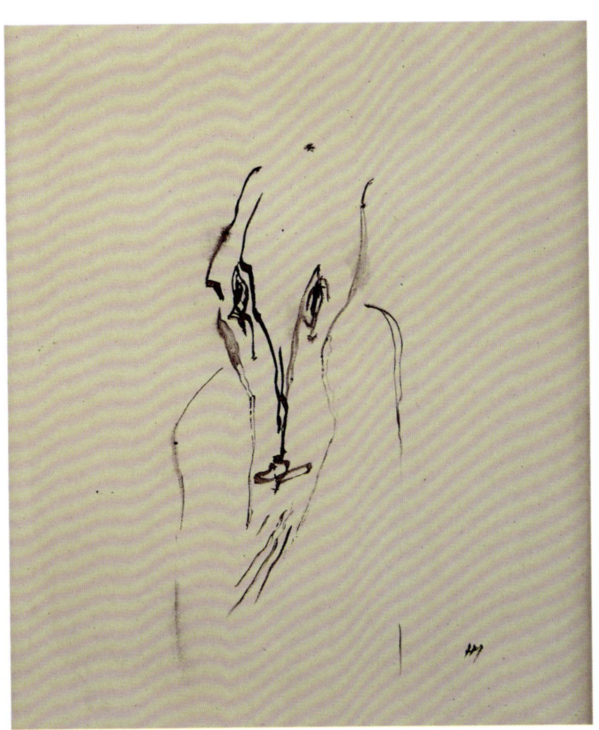

89 Untitled 1950
23.5 × 21 (9¼ × 8¼)

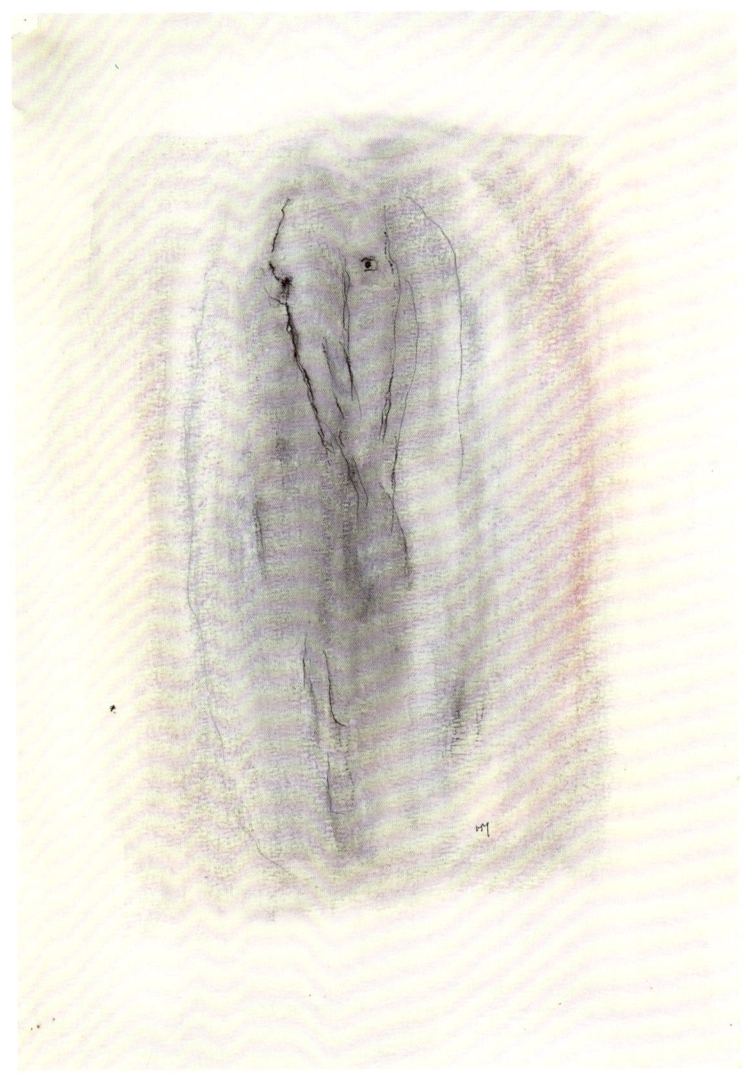

90 Untitled *c.*1950
39 × 27.5 (15⅛ × 10⅞)

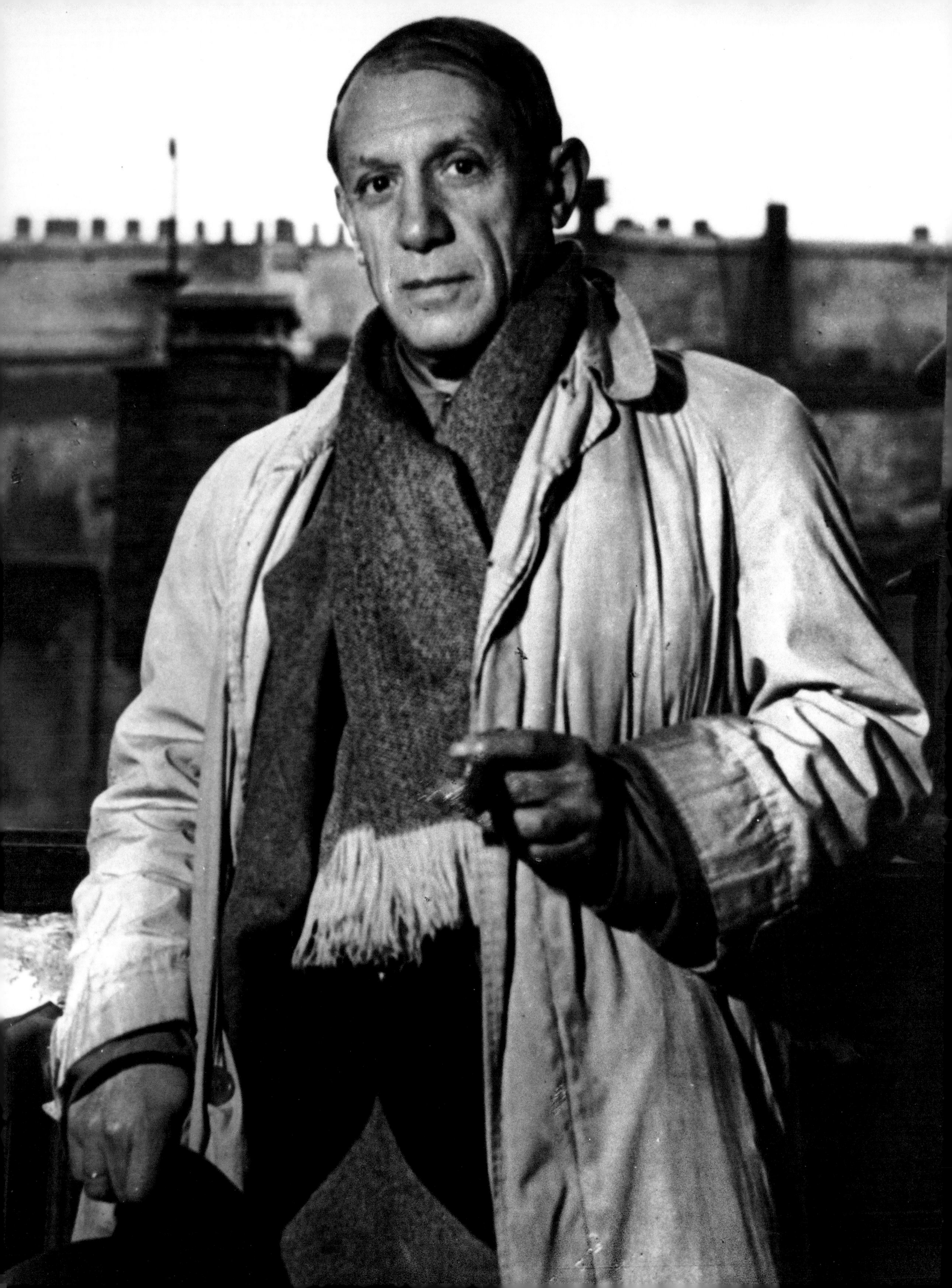

Pablo Picasso (1881–1973)

Picasso remained in Paris throughout the Occupation, working prodigiously in his vast studio on rue des Grands Augustins in Saint-Germain. Although not active in the Resistance, and despite unfounded rumours of easy relations with the occupying forces (he was in fact banned from exhibiting his work by the Nazis), he played a crucial symbolic role as a guardian of creative freedom. Immediately after the Liberation he was inundated with visitors, many of whom were American servicemen, as 'the symbolic courage that had saved him during the enemy occupation proved an irresistible magnet to all with the advent of Liberation'.[1] Six weeks later his adopted country honoured Picasso by making him the subject of the one-man homage – customarily restricted to an artist of French birth – at the Salon d'Automne of 1944, retitled the *Salon de la Libération*.

The Salon included a retrospective survey of Picasso's work of the war and occupation. Many visitors were surprised that no single work appeared to allude directly to the dramas of the period, and that little direct correspondence could be found between Picasso's imagery and specific outside events during the war. During the street fighting in August 1944 Picasso had been preoccupied with exploring a Bacchanale 'after' Poussin and with portraying his daughter Maya. He explained that the 'distance' between his work and the war was more apparent than real:

> I have not painted the war because I am not the kind of painter who goes out like a photographer for something to depict. But I have no doubt that the war is in these paintings that I have done.[2]

Throughout Picasso's life, his own experiences and the people and environment around him appear more important as a source of imagery than any external happenings. His subjects, with several notable exceptions, were drawn from his immediate locality and where there is evidence of outside events these are often filtered through conventional genre. Images like 'Guernica' 1937 (Centro de Arte Reina Sofía, Madrid), and 'The Charnel House' 1945 (Museum of Modern Art, New York) are very rare in his oeuvre. Over the war years he pursued a wide variety of subjects, including female portraits and groups, reclining nudes and children, bullfighting, the 'kissers' series, and landscapes of Paris. But above all it was the still-life genre that Picasso developed into a tool capable of evoking the most complex blend of pathos and defiance, of despair and hope, balancing personal and universal experience in an expression of extraordinary emotional power. The hardships of daily life, the fragility of human existence and the threat of death are themes that haunt Picasso's still-life paintings of the war and Liberation periods.

Using simple objects to serve as allegories of the human condition, Picasso revived the tradition of the *vanitas*. The symbols of life and sustenance, both physical and intellectual (foodstuffs, jugs, candles and lamps and books) are ranged alongside the symbols of mortality to express the evanescence of life in the face of death – eighteen paintings made between 1943 and 1946 are dominated by the human skull (see nos.91–2). The skull was also the subject for one of Picasso's most extraordinary and moving sculptures – the brutal, monolithic 'Death's Head' 1944 (Musée Picasso, Paris), described by Leo Steinberg as 'probably the most powerful single mass sculpture in twentieth century art'.[3]

The motif of the human skull was first developed in the Royan sketchbooks in 1940.[4] Following France's declaration of war on Germany on 3 September 1939 Picasso had moved himself and his various dependants to Royan, an Atlantic coastal town near Bordeaux. In May the German forces crossed the French border. On 14 June they entered Paris and soon after Pétain signed the Armistice with Germany. Picasso's first response to these shattering events can be seen in a sketchbook dating from the period following the fall of Paris, when the image of the weeping woman, based on his mistress Dora Maar, which had grown out of 'Guernica' and was irrevocably associated with the human and domestic tragedy of war, dramatically reappears. Suddenly, in an oil sketch dated 11 June, the head is transformed into a skull, part animal, part human; it retains the posture and distinctive hairstyle of Dora Maar. As the pages of the artist's sketchbook demonstrate, the skull/Maar motif obsessed Picasso between 11 and 24 June. In sketches dated 30 June and 1 July the oblique yet unmistakable references to Dora Maar have been replaced by a more thoroughgoing interest in the human skull as a three-dimensional object.

The image of the human skull had made only a few previous appearances in Picasso's work – in an early sketch for 'Desmoiselles d'Avignon' 1907 (Museum of Modern Art, New York), in the 1907 'Composition with Death's Head' (Hermitage Museum, Saint Petersburg) and related drawings and in the 1913 painting 'Guitar, Skull and Newspaper' (Musée d'art moderne, Villeneuve-d'Ascq). Picasso had, however, made frequent use of animal heads (sheep, bulls and minotaurs) from early on in his career, and skulls of bulls and goats feature in still-life paintings of the war and post-war period. In October 1939 Picasso had made a study of three skulls from recently slaughtered goats and in a painting of the same year an animal skull is juxtaposed with a still bloody section of an animal rib. In 1942, 'Still Life with Steer's Head' (Kunstsammlung Nordrhein-Westfalen, Düsseldorf), a large and moody painting in purples, browns and blues focuses on the head of a steer.

On 23 June 1940 the German forces reached Royan. There was no longer any advantage to be gained from remaining in voluntary exile on the coast. Refusing offers of sanctuary from the United States and Mexico, Picasso returned to the occupied capital on 25 August, moving into his studio on the Left Bank as the daily journey from his apartment on rue La Boétie to the studio was no longer practicable. While eschewing special favours, he quickly established a means of getting on with the occupying forces which appears remarkable given his reputation as the degenerate artist *par excellence*. Picasso's international reputation and his position among French intellectuals may have deterred the German command from upsetting a workable relationship. Although he was one of those fined for dining at his favourite lunchtime venue, Le Catalan, on a day when rationing banned the consumption of meat, the war years were, in general, as hard on Picasso as they were for most Parisians. Food was scarce and the studio was unbearably cold in winter. The photographer Brassaï was a frequent visitor while on an assignment from *Minotaur* to document Picasso's sculptural oeuvre; he often found it too cold to photograph and he recalls periods when the intensity of cold deterred even Picasso from painting.[5] In the short farce Picasso wrote in mid-January 1941, *Desire Caught by the Tail*, the characters are equally obsessed with love, hunger and the cold.

War, the threat to human life and liberty posed by the occupying forces, and frequent news of the death of friends and acquaintances, are condensed in the image of the skull, making it much more than a symbol drawn from the *vanitas* repertoire. Its importance to Picasso, and his recurring fascination with images of mortality throughout this period, may be linked not just to his personal experience of war but to his own increasing age. In 1903 or 1904 his close friend, the poet Max Jacob, had read Picasso's palm and foretold his death at sixty-eight years preceded by ill health and weakness.[6] Picasso was sixty in 1941. Jacob's own death, in the concentration camp at Drancy in 1944, may well have reminded Picasso of the prophecy.

Many of his wartime still-life paintings, often painted at night, have a dark and intense tonality in contrast to the brighter effects of those painted in daylight. The mood is echoed in many of Picasso's single figure studies of women, of Dora Maar and the young Françoise Gilot, mother of Paloma and Claude Picasso, in which sombre colours and formal dignity symbolise restraint and quiet suffering.

Picasso was in daily contact with the intellectual community of Saint-Germain that supported the Resistance and involved itself in clandestine activities. Intellectual freedom and activity were seen as acts of defiance in themselves. When, in the spring of 1944, Michel Leiris organised a reading of *Desire Caught by the Tail*, he had no trouble rounding up a cast of speakers which included Sartre, de Beauvoir, Raymond Queneau, Georges and Germaine Hugnet, Jean and Zanie Aubier and Dora Maar, with Albert Camus as director. According to Roland Penrose

the rendering of the play was so excellent that this single performance in occupied Paris is talked of by those who were there as an event as memorable for its accord between poets and painter as the banquet in honour of the Douanier Rousseau forty years before. In addition it savoured of a clandestine orgy, an insult to the preposterous invaders who had imagined that they could govern Paris.[7]

A few of Picasso's very close friends were deeply involved in the Resistance. Aside from Louis Aragon who had become a Communist in the 1930s, the poet and former Surrealist, Paul Eluard, joined the party in the summer of 1942 and became immediately involved in Resistance work. In September the first issue of *Les Lettres Françaises* was published. Eluard was closely associated with this underground publication which was also supported by young painters and intellectuals, and Picasso quickly came to know its staff and supporters. Despite his known sympathies, the announcement – just before the opening of the great *Salon of the Liberation* – that Picasso had joined the Communist Party came as a surprise to many at both ends of the political spectrum. His motives were widely and hotly debated – as was the likely future relationship between his artistic development and a nascent Socialist Realism. Picasso's reasons for joining the party, given in a statement published in *L'Humanité* and in *New Masses*, appear to have been straightforward: an acknowledgment of the party's role in the Resistance, and respect for its intellectuals and for its desire to 'reconstruct the world'.[8]

Picasso's work, and exhibitions, of the Liberation period were exuberant responses to liberty, dominated by classical and Mediterranean imagery; they were untouched by the increasingly vocal debate on the relationship between style and political affiliation conducted in the press. But politics and continuing human suffering were not entirely absent from his thoughts. Themes of war and hardship return to haunt his work at intervals. Following an attack on his Communist credentials by an American commentator in 1945, Picasso made a declaration on the role of the engaged artist:

> what do you think an artist is? An imbecile who has only his eyes if he is a painter, or his ears if a musician, or a lyre at every level of his heartthrobs if he is a poet, or – even if he is only a boxer – just his muscles? On the contrary, he is at the same time a political being, constantly alert to the heart-rending burning, or happy events in the world, moulding himself in their likeness. How could it be possible to feel no interest in other people and, because of an ivory-tower indifference, detach yourself from the life they bring with such open full hands?[9]

One of Picasso's most inspired 'political' works, entitled 'Massacre in Korea' 1951 (Musée Picasso, Paris), addressed the imperialistic dimension of the Korean War. It paid homage to Goya's painting and etchings commemorating the executions of Third of May 1808 and Manet's paintings of 'The Execution of Maximilian' 1867. In April 1952 the continuation of the war and Picasso's increasing disgust at Western involvement led him to begin a mural scheme on the themes of war and peace to decorate the deconsecrated chapel at Vallauris.

The theme of the skull returned in Picasso's work at this time. In 1951, a painted bronze sculpture of goat's skull and bottle with candle seemed to revive the *vanitas* theme of the Second World War still lifes. At the same time, during late March and early April, Picasso made four very restrained, monochrome still-life paintings each depicting a goat's skull and bottle with candle (nos.93–4). These are telling reminders, that alongside renewal and hope in the post-war era, suffering continued.

NOTES

1 Harriet and Sidney Janis, *Picasso: The Recent Years 1939–1946*, New York 1946, p.3.
2 Peter D. Whitney, 'Picasso Is Safe', *San Francisco Chronicle*, 5 March 1944, quoted by Alfred Barr, *Picasso: Fifty Years of his Art*, exh. cat., Museum of Modern Art, New York 1946, p.223.
3 Leo Steinberg, 'The Skulls of Picasso', in *Other Criteria: Confrontations with Twentieth Century Art*, New York 1972, pp.115–24.
4 Sam Hunter, 'Picasso at War: Royan 1940, Sketchbook no.110, 1940' in Arnold and Marc Glimcher (eds.), *Je suis le cahiers*, 1986, pp.141–77.
5 Brassaï, *Picasso & Co*, Paris 1964, trans. Francis Price, London 1967, p.108.
6 Steinberg 1972, p.121.
7 Roland Penrose, *Picasso: His Life and Work*, 1981, p.338.
8 Janet Flanner, 'The Surprise of the Century', in *Men and Monuments*, New York 1990, p.195.
9 Picasso, letter to *Les Lettres Françaises*, quoted by Flanner 1990, p.198.

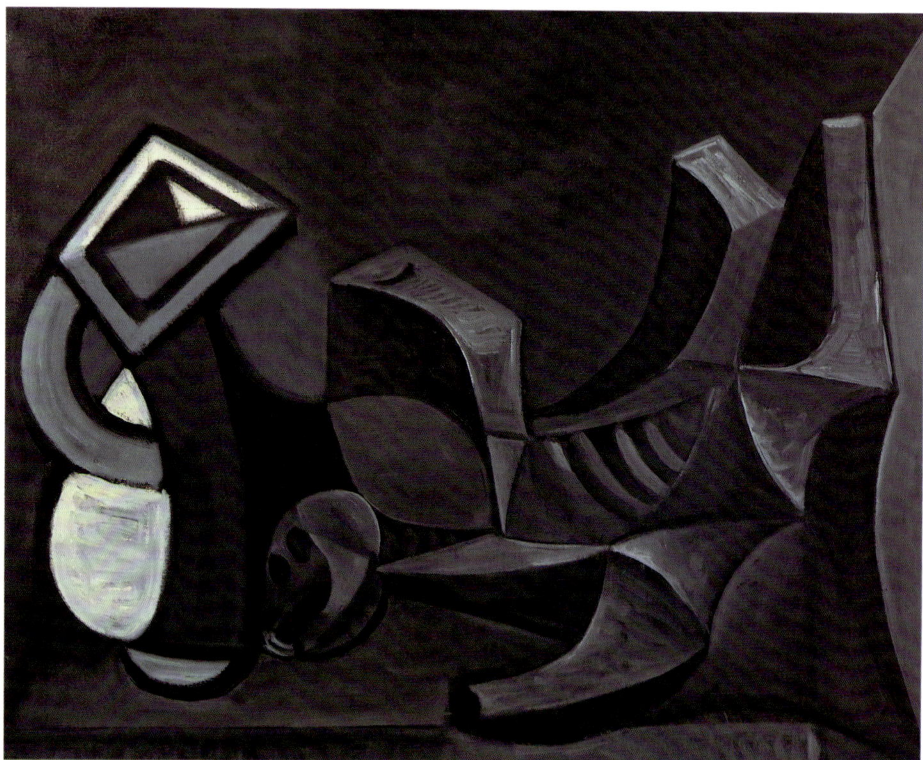

Illustration (p.154) Portrait of Pablo Picasso 1948 Photograph by Brassaï *Bibliothèque Nationale, Départment des Estampes, Paris* © *Gilberte Brassaï*

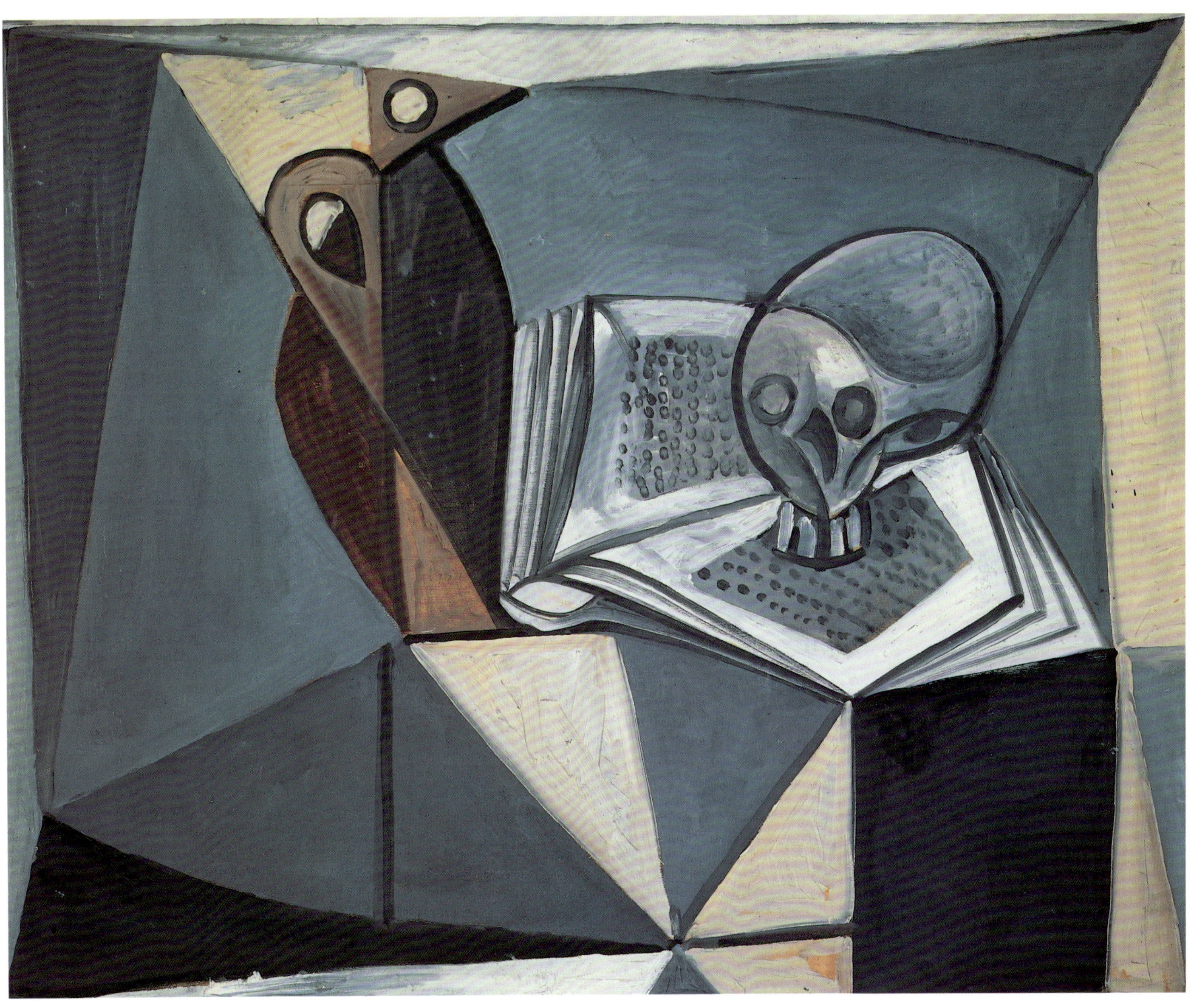

92 Skull and Book 1946
80 × 100 ($31\frac{1}{2} × 39\frac{3}{8}$)

opposite
91 Pitcher and Skeleton 1945
73 × 92.2 ($28\frac{3}{4} × 36\frac{1}{4}$)

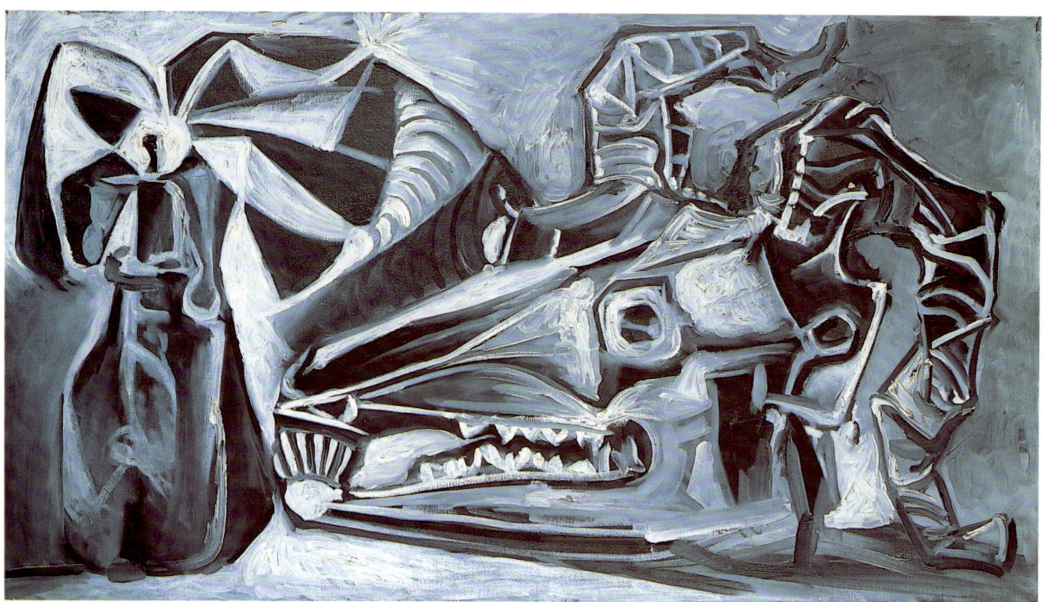

93 Still Life with Goat's Skull,
Bottle and Candle 1952
45×81 ($17\frac{3}{4} \times 31\frac{7}{8}$)

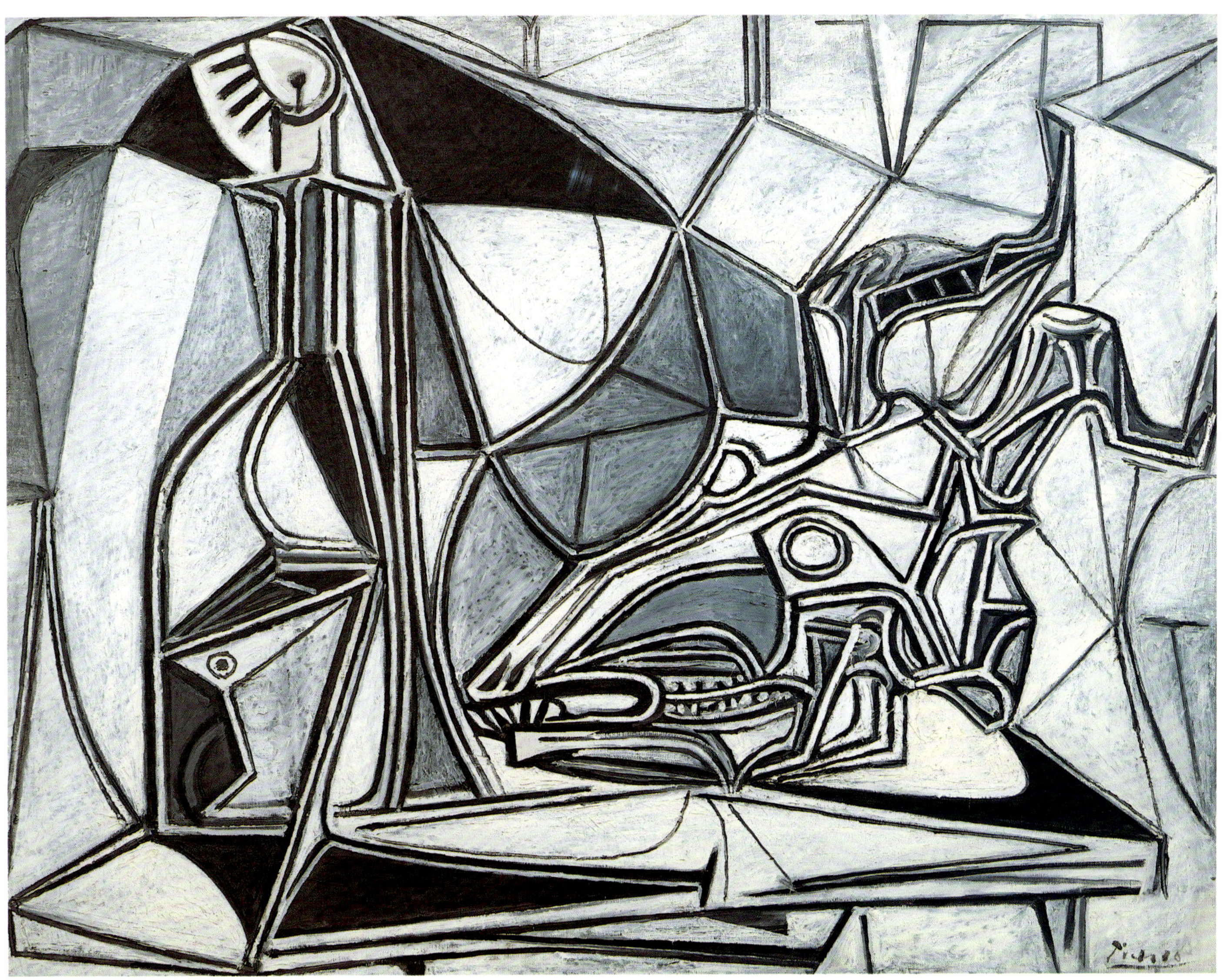

94 Goat's Skull, Bottle and Candle 1952
89.2 × 116.2 (35⅛ × 45¾)

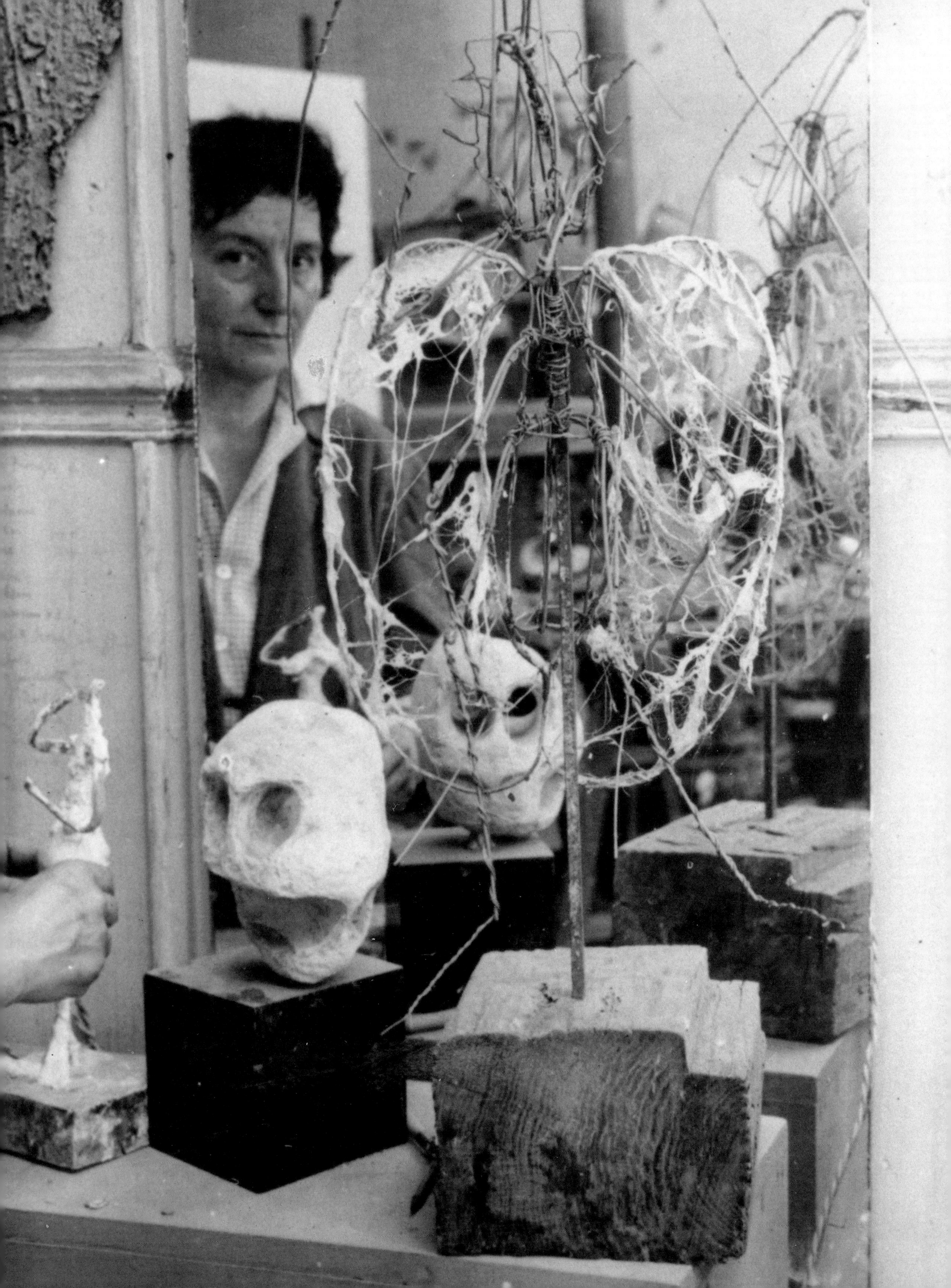

Germaine Richier (1902–1959)

In 1939, on the outbreak of war, Germaine Richier and her first husband, the Swiss-German sculptor Charles Otto Banninger, were holidaying in his native country. They decided to remain in Switzerland until hostilities were over. Alongside Giacometti and Marino Marini, whom they had known in pre-war Paris, they became part of the small circle of artists who congregated in Zurich.

Richier had met Banninger while she was studying in Emile Bourdelle's atelier – he was an assistant to the elderly sculptor. She had come to Paris in 1926 following a training at the Ecole des Beaux-Arts in Montpelier where she had worked under the sculptor Guigues, formerly assistant to Auguste Rodin. These studies had prepared Richier for a mainstream career as sculptor of the female nude and portrait bust. She established her own studio in 1930, taking in pupils from 1933, and was not unsuccessful. Her sculptures were fastidiously observed and crafted, with meticulous attention to the technical analysis of form and proportion.

A radical reorientation in her approach was first hinted at in a small nude piece executed during 1942. Crouching low and with arms extended as if in readiness to pounce, the human figure resembles the 'Toad' of its title. Two years later, in 1944, 'The Grasshopper (Small Version)' revealed a more thoroughgoing fusion of animal and human themes. Shortly after completing the piece she embarked on 'Forest Man' 1945 (no.95), in which plant forms are assimilated into the human figure. These creatures were dubbed by the critics 'hybrid beings' – either Georges Limbour or René de Solier invented the term in 1946.

Richier's early wartime practice in Zurich had been busy and successful. She had had no difficulty finding clients for her work and soon established a lively group of students. Exhibitions followed, in Zurich (1942), Winterthur (1943) and Basel (1944). However, looking back on this period, Richier recalled that dissatisfaction with her work prompted a rethinking of her attitudes: 'I believe I found my way when I grew tired of analysing forms … When something no longer interests you, you want to move on to something else.'[1]

Why the 'something else' arrived at by Richier should have been this strange anthropomorphism achieved through the fusion of animal, plant and human imagery is still a matter for speculation. According to Richier's niece, Françoise Guiter (who was herself a student of the artist's from 1956–59), she turned to memories of her childhood in Provence and in particular to imaginative encounters with the flora and fauna of the region and to the vivid tales of ancient folklore and mythology with which she was familiar from her early years.[2] Such imagery provided Richier with a way of liberating her work from the stranglehold of tradition. One critic, writing in the mid-1950s, realised that

Through these monsters, insects, reptiles, batrachians, humanised birds, leaf-like girls and log-like men, her work induces strange emotions in us, making us experience those primordial feats and passions that a 'civilised' way of life has deadened in us.[3]

This questioning of her sophisticated and cultured practice, an awakening interest in other life forms and in ancient folklore and native tradition, coincided with the interests of a whole generation of artists including Dubuffet and Michaux, who were also seeking in the place of 'culture' more authentic types of experience and finding inspiration in natural and primitive realms. An interest in folklore and national mythologies characterises the work of the Cobra group and is seen in hybrid man-beast imagery in paintings by Asger Jorn and Karel Appel, among others, often combined with an expressive emphasis on physical gesture and on the material substance of the work. In Surrealism, techniques of collage and a concern with unusual juxtaposition and with visual metamorphosis (the legacy of the Comte de Lautréamont) provided obvious sources of inspiration. For Sartre, metamorphosis and ambiguity were key elements in conveying the uncertainties of human existence.

In Richier's hybrid figures the human aspect is almost always to the fore. The maquette for 'Forest Man' comprises a section from a tree branch found by Richier in Le Valais in Switzerland, transformed into the figure's leg and trunk. The distinctive plant-like hand of the creature was derived from a leaf found at the same place. These found objects were not merely a source of inspiration or the basis for reproduction, they were physically incorporated into the work, which was then completed by the more traditional means of modelling in clay. The strength with which the human element asserts itself in the final piece is perhaps due to the remarkable fact that in bringing her found objects to their final figuration Richier relied on a professional model.

On the occasion of her first major showing in Paris after the war, at the Galerie Maeght in 1948, the Maeght house journal *Derrière le Miroir* devoted an issue to the exhibition, with a text by Francis Ponge and an account of his first visit to Richier's studio by Georges Limbour, former Surrealist and close friend of Dubuffet and Jean Paulhan. Limbour was taken to the artist's studio by the writer and critic René de Solier who had met Richier in 1940 and who became her second husband in 1946. This relationship naturally brought Richier closer to the group of writers and artists associated with the pre-war *Nouvelle Revue Française*, and Paulhan became a keen supporter of her work. Limbour's text describes how he was struck by the extraordinary combination, in her work, of the imagination and the model as observed. It was a practice which Richier continued throughout her career, as she later admitted:

All my sculptures, even those that seem to contain the greatest amount of imagination, are based on something true, on an organic truth … The imagination needs a point of departure. It is thence possible to plunge straight into poetry … I invent more easily while contemplating nature – its presence makes me independent.[4]

Richier tended to work with a few chosen models. Nardone, the eighty-year-old who had sat for Rodin's 'Balzac', was a favourite. His combination of great bulk and attenuated limbs lent itself vividly to works such as 'Storm Man' 1947–8 (no.96) and 'Pentacle' 1954 (no.102). In most cases Richier's active reference to the model continued through to the completion of a work. Aside from working to the model she returned, at regular intervals, to modelling portrait busts from life. She enjoyed the discipline of seeking 'resemblance', and described the effort as a 'lesson in humility'.[5]

Photographs of Richier at work reveal an elaborate and precise method. She would use plumb line and compasses to translate proportion and mass from model to invention, squaring up both model and maquette with a web-like structure of lines painted in blue laundry ink. For Richier this was her means of conceptualising forms in space.

Throughout the 1950s, until her death in 1959, Richier's imagination continued to feed on the natural and animal sources that had inspired her first hybrid creatures. In addition to entomological illustrations she filled her studio with other things:

insects, bits of wood, pebbles, grasses, all kinds of things that were being hoarded, biding their time, piled one upon another, gradually crowded the shelves : many of them were from her native Provence and the beaches that surround Les Saintes-Maries-de-la-Mer.[6]

Sometimes items of natural ephemera were used to impress a surface or furnish the detail of a hand or foot. In the case of 'The Shepherd of Landes' 1951 (no.100), the chilling death's-head was cast from a lump of brick and cement, rounded and hollowed through the corroding action of the sea, which the artist had found while scavenging on the beach of Varangeville.

Richier's most complex works are perhaps those in which wires traverse the form, a system which she first explored in a sculpture entitled 'The Spider I' 1946 and later in 'Diabolo' 1950 (no.99) and 'Man with Claws' 1952 (no.101). The idea for adopting an external linear structure may have originated in the image of the spider and its web but it also met more general expressive and structural demands, extending into actual space the vertical, horizontal and oblique lines that she traced on her models. The wires plot this geometry, and suggest Richier's interest in revealing her process, further evidence for which is given in the formal remains of the *pointes fixés* (points at which lines drawn on the figure intersect, marked by the artist with the head of a match) which are clearly visible on works such as 'Diabolo'. These wires are also expressive devices. They have a dramatic role in articulating the predicament of a being in space. The notion of entrapment is difficult to escape, and is enhanced by the original associations of these wires with the spider in its web – both habitat and trap.

If Richier's figures stalk and ensnare space, they are also ensnared by it in turn, for space is invasive in another way, partly as a by-product of the manner in which the artist physically worked her materials, and partly as a function of the cavities and striations that break through the surface and hollow out the interiors of many of her figures. Richier's manipulation of her material finds a parallel in Fautrier's practice. For both artists the same matter provides at once the substance of the work and its skin; it is meaningless to speak of inside and out, surface and form. The surfaces of Richier's sculpture are roughly pitted. External space is therefore not repelled by a smooth, armoured surface but allowed to penetrate and interplay in a way that makes even the largest of her monumental figures appear vulnerable. In certain works the notion of elemental corrosion enhances their expressive power. 'Storm Man' 1947–8 (no.96) and 'Hurricane Woman' 1948–9 (no.97) testify to the ultimate survival of the human form, victim of cataclysmic assault. To Richier the fractured appearance of her works was the key to their meaning:

> What characterises sculpture, in my opinion, is the way in which it renounces the full, solid form. Holes and perforations conduct like flashes of lightning into the material which becomes organic and open, encircled from all sides, lit up in and through the hollows. A form lives to the extent to which it does not withdraw from expression. And we decidedly cannot conceal human expression in the drama of our time.[7]

Many critics have remarked on Richier's aversion to a smooth finish, and have seen in it a key to the works' meaning parallel to the expressive force of her hybrid iconography. In a 1948 review, Limbour found in the surfaces of Richier's work a principal reason for her figures' tormented appearance.[8] Some years later, in a catalogue introduction to her Hanover Gallery exhibition in London in 1955, André Pieyre de Mandiargues was almost overwhelmed by the theme of death:

> She spares the bronze . . . neither privation nor torture nor the ultimate agony. She is not afraid of going as far as the corpse, carrion, even putrefaction . . . the violent wind blowing through Germaine Richier's work carries a sense of death.[9]

Also contributing to the catalogue, the critic and art historian David Sylvester wrote that he found, in her assault on matter, a metaphor for the survival of the human body:

> Richier brings matter to the point of dissolution only to hold it all the more firmly together. In the very process of committing an act of assault and battery, her hands transmit to their victim an energy that will ensure its remaining whole.[10]

Sylvester saw this assault reinforced by her practice of fusing the human figure with animal or plant imagery, because 'for her the assertion of the human figure is achieved through its denial'.[11]

Richier's figures are survivors as well as victims, her ' "subjects" belong to the world of metamorphosis'[12]: and the potential for both life and destruction is thus enshrined in her work. While many critics dwelt on the metaphor of death, others, like Limbour, found in her sculptures 'a world in the process of being born'.[13]

Although firmly individual and undoubtedly distanced from slightly later contemporaries like César, or from the British sculptors Lynn Chadwick, Kenneth Armitage and Reg Butler who have been seen together with Richier as portraying 'Kafkaesque images of tortured, atombombed, pitiful men',[14] Richier's iconography and her approach to materials were deeply rooted in their time. Peter Selz, whose important New York exhibition *New Images of Man* in 1959 set out to demonstrate the emergence of new styles reflecting human anxieties in the modern era, found in Richier's work a powerful reflection of post-war concerns:

> hers is still a world of growth, change and decay. Like that of so many artists of this time, her work is concerned with transmutation, metamorphosis and organic interaction relating to the patterns unraveled by the physical scientists in their discovery of a continuing process in which the absolutes of time, space and matter have been abolished.[15]

NOTES

I am indebted to Mme Françoise Guiter, Germaine Richier's niece and former student, who is currently preparing a catalogue raisonné of the artist's work.

1   Germaine Richier, quoted in the biography compiled by Françoise Guiter, in *Germaine Richier*, Louisiana 1988, p.28 (unpublished trans. by Barbara Shuey).
2   Ibid.
3   André Pieyre de Mandiargues, *Germaine Richier*, Hanover Gallery 1955, unpag.
4   Guiter 1988, p.28.
5   Ibid.
6   Ibid., p.29.
7   Germaine Richier, statement in Peter Selz, *New Images of Man*, exh. cat., Museum of Modern Art, New York 1959, p.130.
8   Georges Limbour, 'Forêts en bronze', *Action* (Paris), no.217, 24–30 Nov. 1948.
9   Pieyre de Mandiargues 1955, unpag.
10 David Sylvester, 'On Germaine Richier' in Pieyre de Mandiargues 1955, unpag.
11 Ibid.
12 Germaine Richier, statement in *The New Decade: 22 European Painters and Sculptors*, exh. cat., Museum of Modern Art, New York 1955, p.35.
13 Limbour 1948, p.10.
14 Margit Rowell, 'La Récuperation de l'objet déchu' in *Qu'est-ce que la sculpture moderne?*, Musée national d'art moderne, Paris 1986, p.188.
15 Selz 1959, p.131.

Illustration (p.160) Germaine Richier in her studio Photograph by Brassaï *Coll. F. Guiter*

[163]

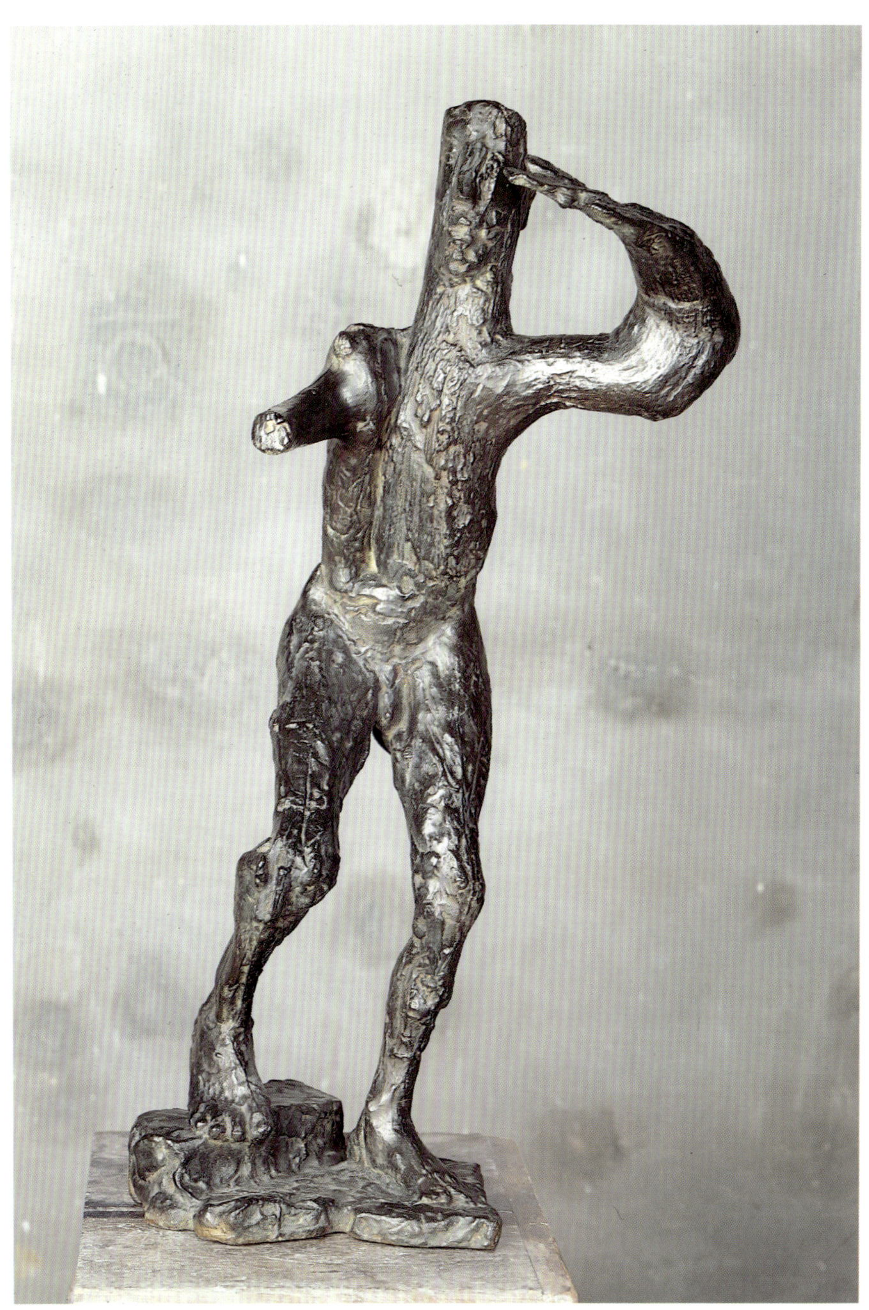

95 Forest Man (Large version) 1945–6
94.3 × 45 × 45 (37⅛ × 17¾ × 17¾)

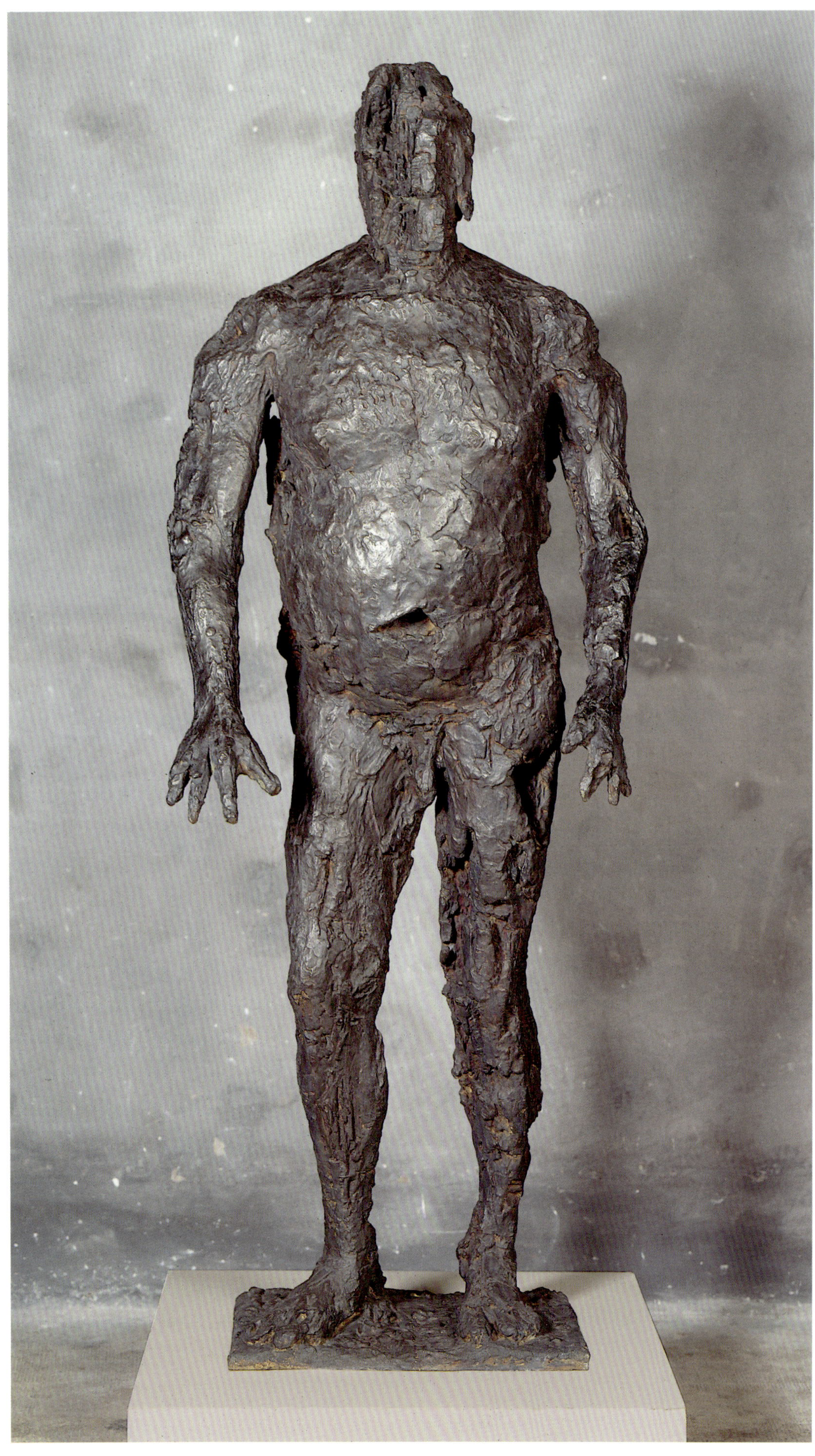

96 Storm Man 1947–8
190.5 × 72 × 57.5 (75 × 28⅜ × 22⅝)

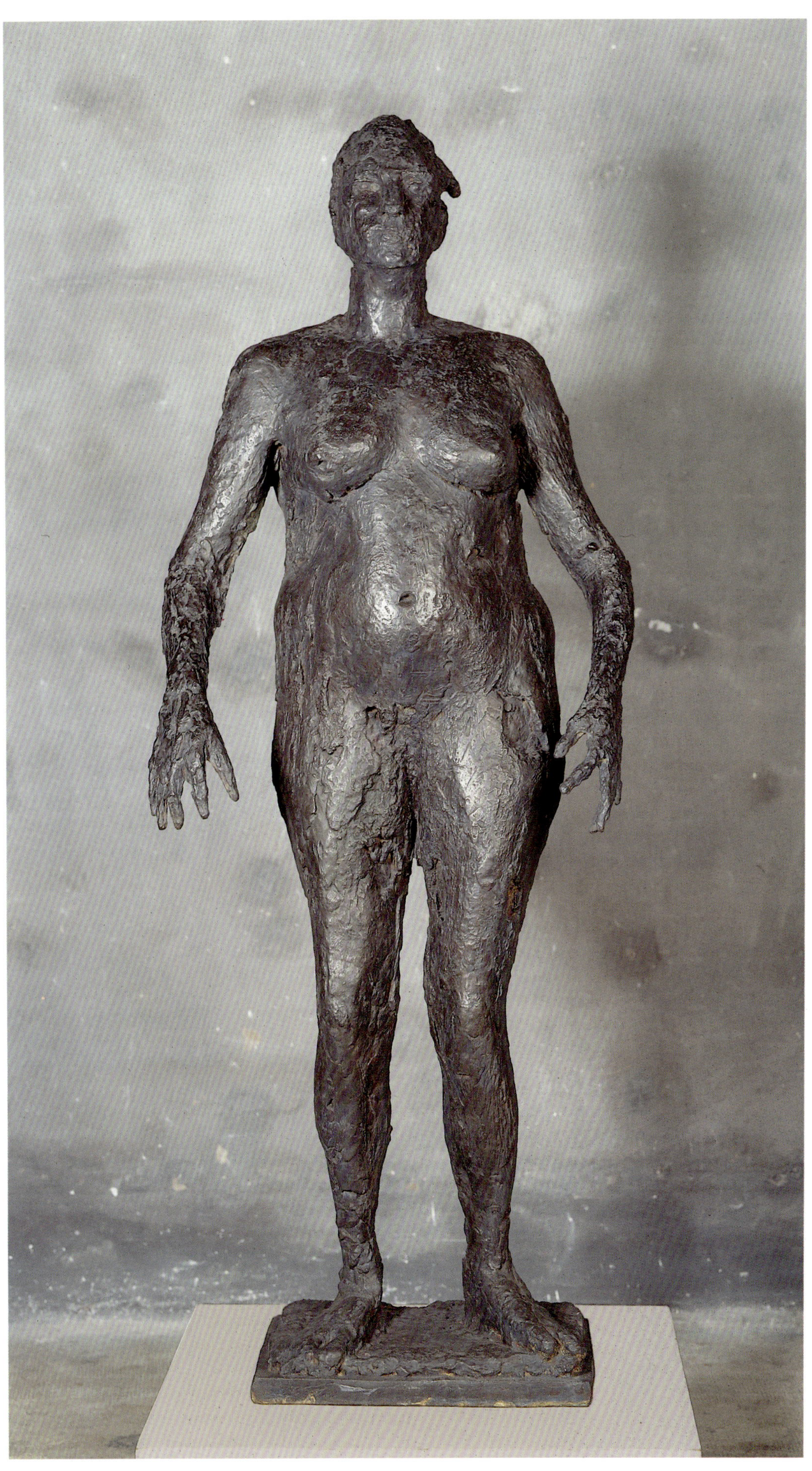

97 Hurricane Woman 1948–9
179.5 × 71 × 47 (70⅝ × 28 × 18½)

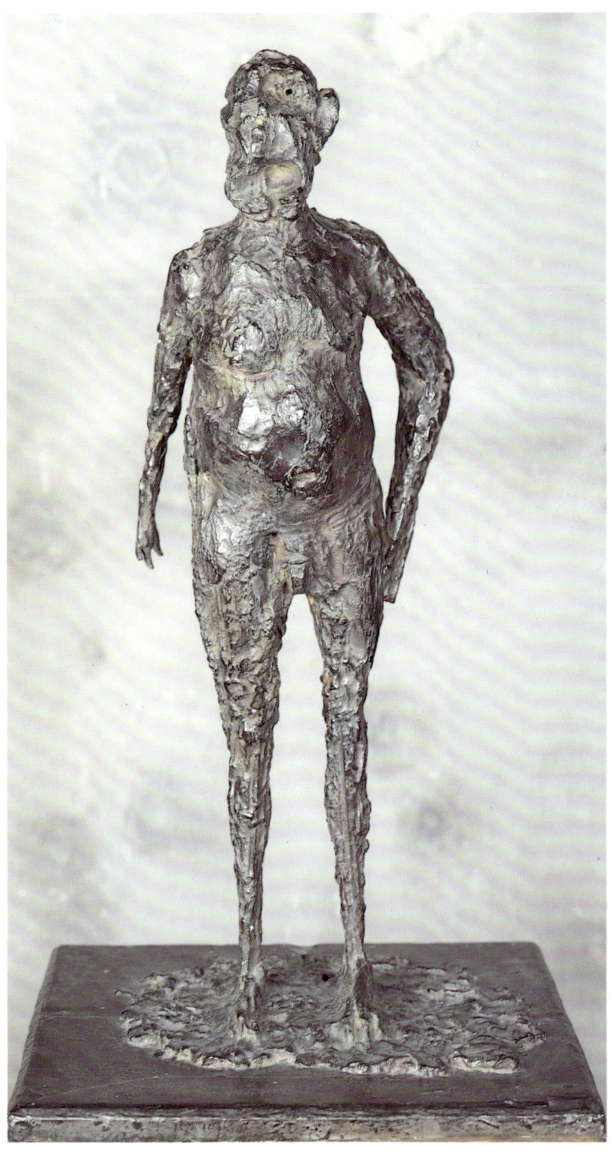

98 Ogre 1949
80.5 × 45 × 41 (31¼ × 17¾ × 16⅛)

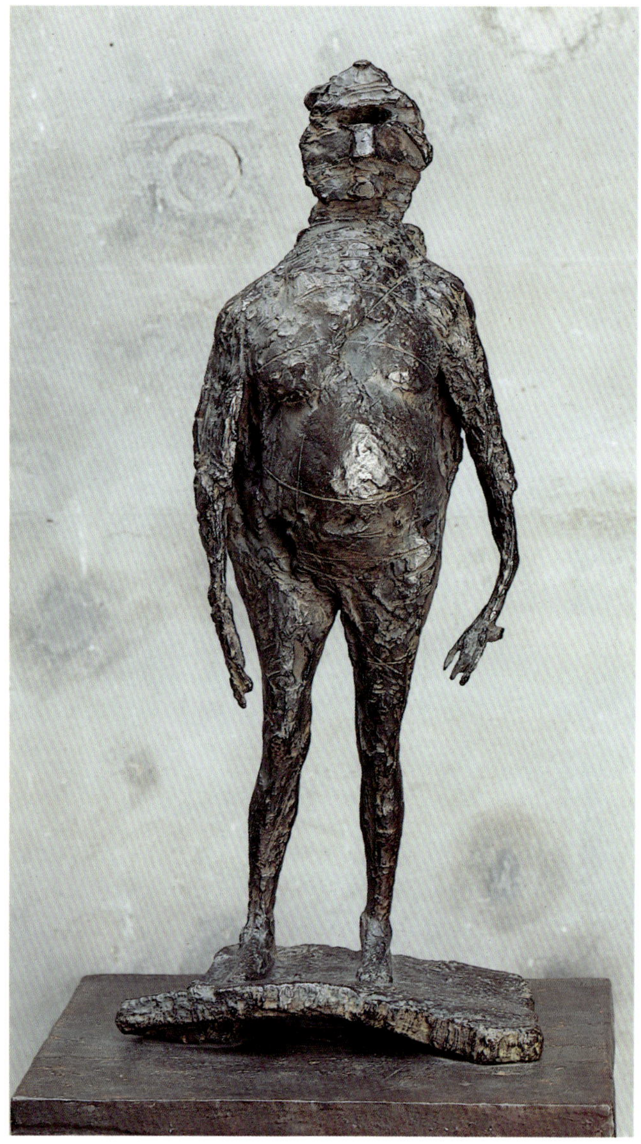

102 Pentacle 1954
82.9 × 36 × 22.5 (32⅝ × 14¼ × 8⅞)

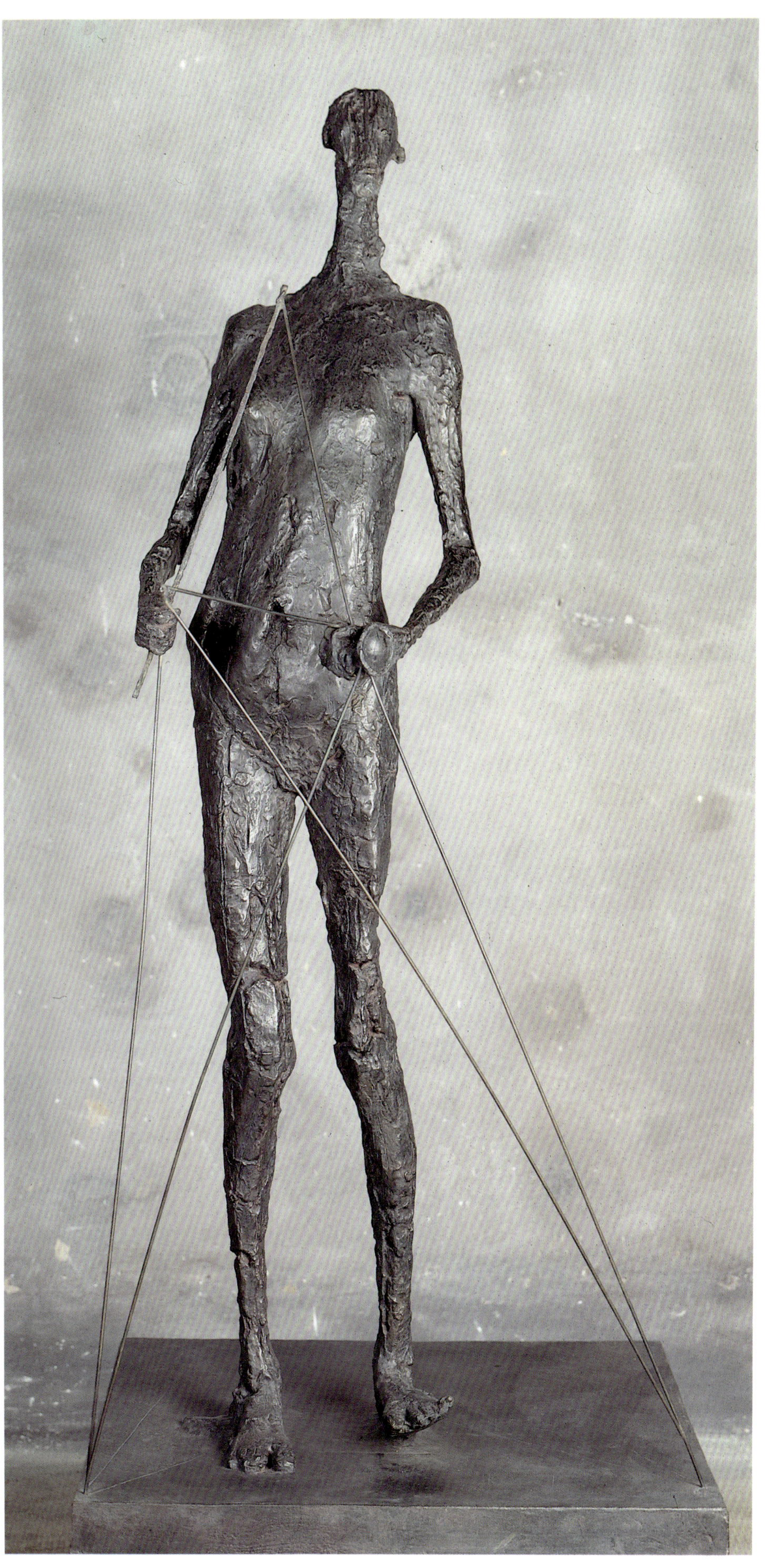

99 Diabolo 1950
167.5 × 74 × 93 (66 × 29⅛ × 36⅝)

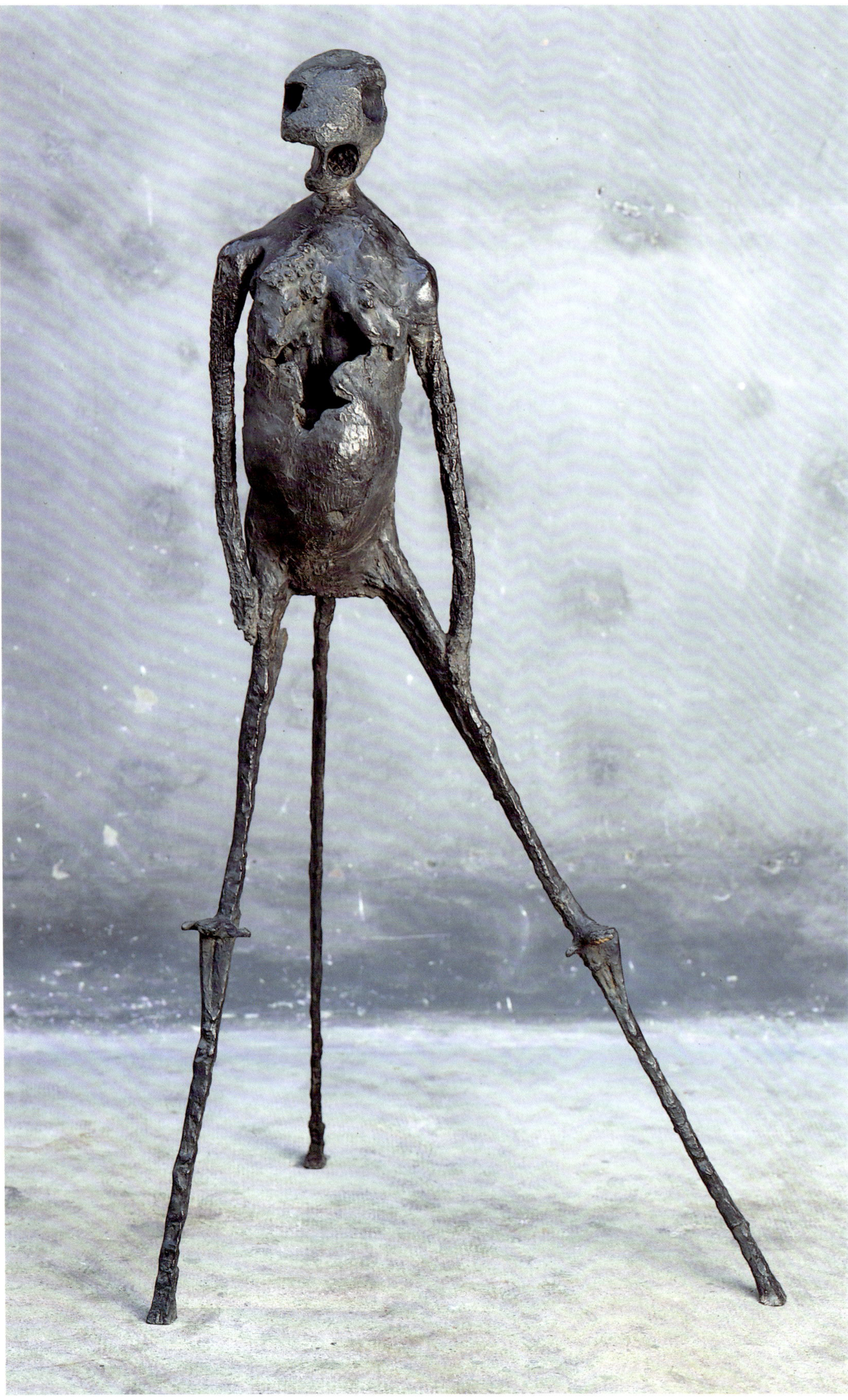

100 **The Shepherd of Landes** 1951
149.9 × 89 × 60 (59 × 35⅛ × 23⅝)

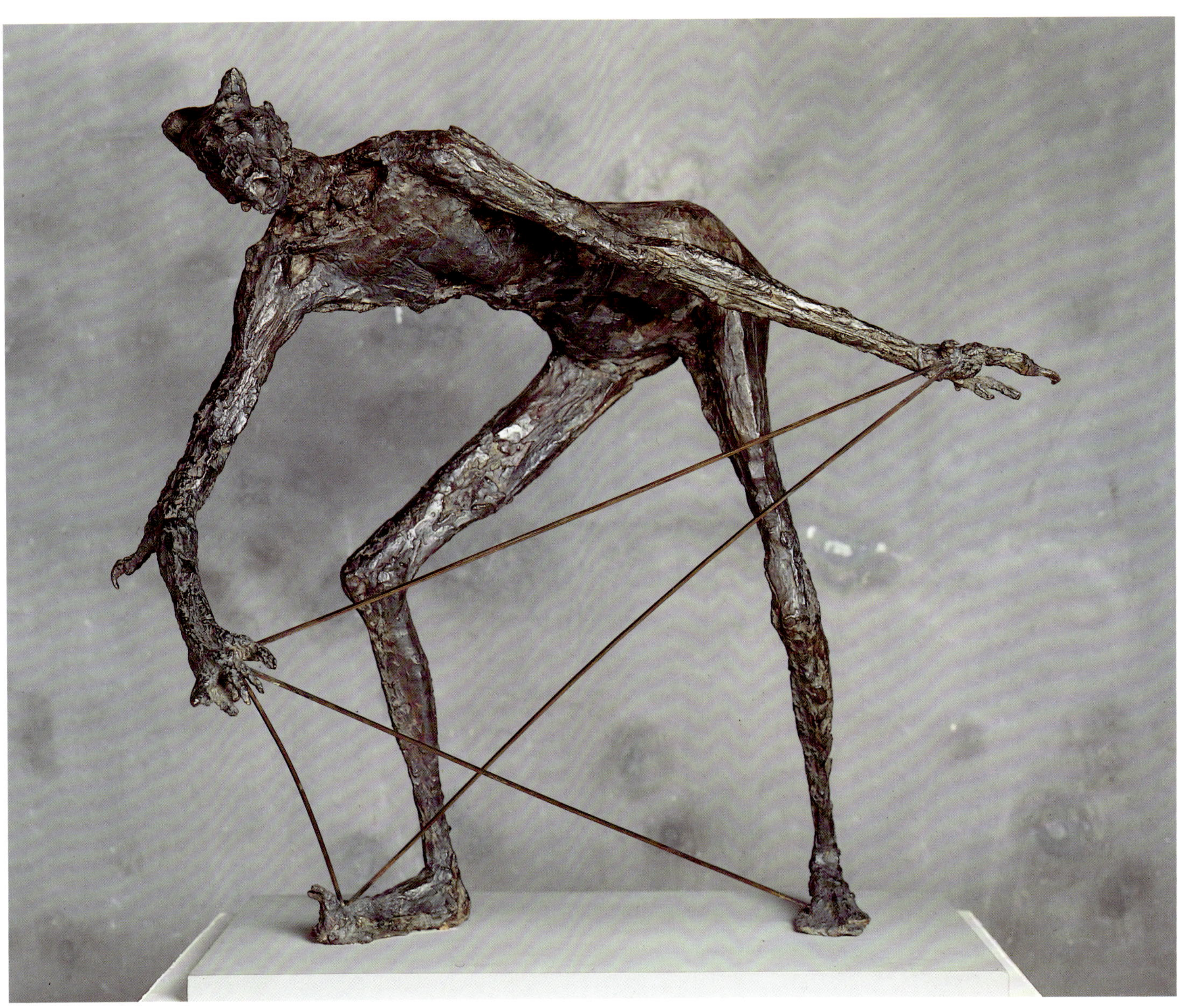

101 **Man with Claws** 1952
$89 \times 98 \times 85 \ (35\frac{1}{8} \times 38\frac{5}{8} \times 33\frac{1}{2})$

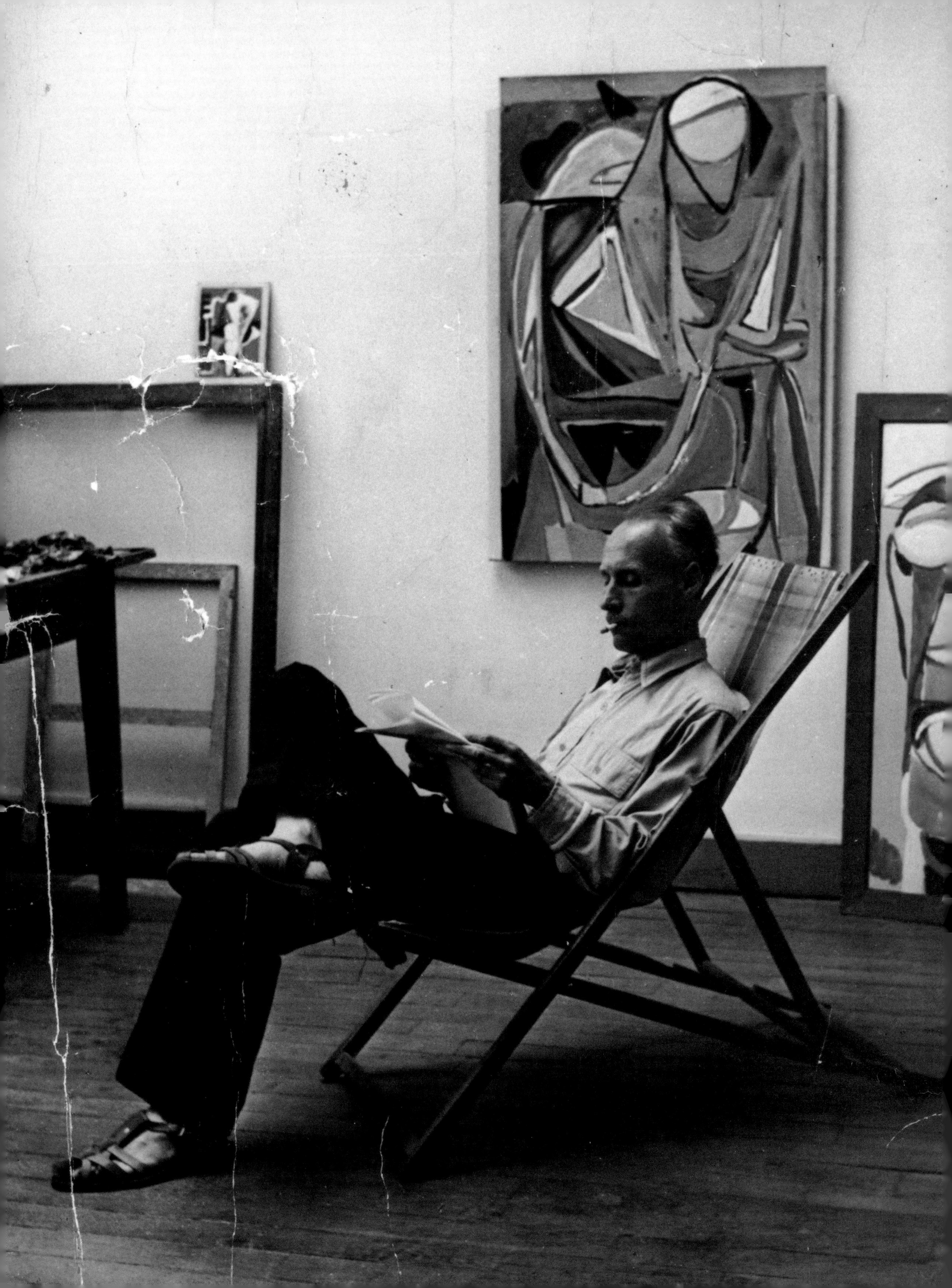

Bram van Velde (1895–1981)

On his first encounter with a group of van Velde paintings in 1952, Patrick Waldberg confessed, he had been 'baffled and disconcerted, torn by conflicting sentiments: a sense of loss, of being lost, of falling'. He concluded that the artist was 'one of the strangest among contemporary painters'.[1] Waldberg was meeting these images some years after van Velde's Paris debut. By this time the heady rhetoric of failure and of expressive intractability had become indissolubly linked to van Velde's work through the critical contributions of Samuel Beckett; Beckett's writings continue to cast a shadow over subsequent interpretations.[2]

In 1946, when Bram van Velde had his first one-man exhibition at the Galerie Mai in Paris, he was already fifty years old. He was born (Abraham van Velde) and brought up in Holland, and a deprived and unsettled childhood was followed by various upheavals induced by artistic and/or financial necessity. Recognising his precocious artistic talent his employer, the collector Eduard H. Kramers, gave him a stipend and then funded a study trip, first to Munich and then to the artist's colony in Worpswede, North Germany, in 1922. From there he moved to Paris in 1924, to Corsica in 1929 and on to Majorca in 1932 in pursuit of a less expensive life. He returned to Paris in 1936, ousted from Spanish territory by the Civil War. His migratory route is mirrored in the development of his work, from the local influence of the Dutch artist Georg-Hendrik Breitner on the naturalistic paintings of his youth to the vigorous Expressionist mode developed following his first encounters with modernist German Expressionism at Worpswede in North Germany, to the development of a linear abstract style derived from Picasso's late Cubist works. He returned to France with a roll of five paintings, the fruits of his four years in Majorca, testimony to a slow and painstaking method. His painting became progressively more abstract in the late 1930s. Figurative details increasingly failed to coalesce into identifiable images while content and structure became more coherently wedded in a dense and linear scaffolding. During the war his output ground to a halt; his creativity was numbed by despair, his life reduced to the bare necessities of existence. Of the twenty-five paintings and gouaches exhibited at the Galerie Mai the most recent was, therefore, dated 1941 and the show literally encompassed his life's work.

The exhibition was the inaugural event of a new gallery, owned by Christian Zervos and directed by Marcel Michaud, formerly a dealer in Lyon. Michaud had been introduced to the artist by the critic Edouard Loeb and had developed a profound respect for his work: so it was with some regret that he handed the management of van Velde's career over to Aimé Maeght the following year. Although not a financial success, this first exhibition excited some favourable comments – *Les Lettres Françaises* described him as 'a painter of remarkable power. His large gouaches and above all his oils are works of rare formal cohesion and a fullness indicative of talent arriving at maturity.'[3] For the invitation card Loeb contributed a short but moving appraisal of the man and his work:

> Amid all the remorse which is the only honourable thing we have left, nothing is more rending than the tense silence which surrounded this exceptional man. However fine they might be, the works of art created during these four years of disgrace, not one of them, to my mind, would be able to dominate Bram Van Velde's silence with its message.[4]

To accompany the exhibition, the magazine *Cahiers d'Art* (edited by Zervos) commissioned Beckett to write an essay on the work of Bram and his brother Geer van Velde,[5] a painter who had already established something of a reputation. When Bram returned to Paris from Majorca in 1936 he initially made a temporary home with his brother. It was through Geer that Bram met Beckett and the former missionary Marthe Arnaud-Kuntz (also a friend of Beckett's) who became a close companion. Although the *Cahiers d'Art* article was the first published account of Beckett's understanding of Bram van Velde's art, it is clear from the correspondence between artist and writer that a deep mutual sympathy already existed in 1940, and it was to Beckett that van Velde appealed for help at the height of his war-time suffering. To Waldberg, van Velde later confessed: 'I awaited each of Beckett's visits with intense eagerness, and I shook with emotion when I showed him my canvases. He spoke of my painting as no one had ever spoken before; his presence was stimulating to me.'[6]

Beckett's essay on the van Velde brothers was entitled 'The World and the Pair of Trousers' after the joke he later employed in *Endgame* about a tailor who unfavourably compares God's achievement of creating the world in six days to the feat of constructing a pair of trousers over six months. Beckett begins by distancing himself from the conventional role of art critic, pouring scorn on contemporary art criticism in general, highlighting the insufficiency of words for understanding and elucidating visual art, and noting the 'curious effect' van Velde's work has in inducing silence on the part of his spectators. While using this as an occasion for furthering his own ideas about his art,[7] Beckett also has several interesting comments to make about Bram van Velde's work. Beckett talks of his paintings as if they are held in suspense, suggesting not just an unfinished quality but an unfinishable situation. Looking at van Velde's mature work there is indeed a very real sense of the incomplete. This is evident not just in the seemingly casual application of paint, which is sometimes dry and papery and sometimes thin and dripping, nor is it just in the assertive presence of unpainted areas. It is also in the lack of resolve his surfaces maintain. Lines go nowhere, have no apparent beginning or end and construct nothing. Depth is suggested, but it is contradictory and impenetrable. Images are hinted at, yet come to nothing.

A second statement by Beckett, 'Painters of Failure' appeared in *Derrière le Miroir* in June 1948 and was published as 'The New Object' in Beckett's English translation for an American audience the same year. In 1947 the French dealer Aimé Maeght and the New York dealer Samuel Kootz had agreed to exchange exhibitions to promote the 'international' status of their artists. The agreement was launched with an exhibition of young Americans in Paris in 1947 and the following year Maeght supplied Kootz with a show of the van Velde brothers' work. The exhibition, in March, was promoted with an illustrated catalogue which carried Beckett's essay. In June a further exhibition was held at Maeght in Paris. Despite some interesting and enthusiastic comments from critics in both cities the exhibitions were financially disastrous. No sales were made. The New York failure has been seen as partly due to the great difficulties avant-garde French art had in penetrating the American consciousness at a time when the influential critic Clement Greenberg was asserting the primacy of the American school and the demise of the French. Although official French efforts to proclaim the post-war hegemony of French styles tended to concentrate on mature strengths rather than on innovation, van Velde's work was shown outside the structures of officialdom, at a gallery of which Greenberg was normally an enthusiastic patron. And yet he either failed to visit the van Velde show or decided to remain silent on the subject. This is especially surprising given the close relationship between Bram's mode of painting and related approaches then being developed by Jackson Pollock and others, something of which a number of critics were not unaware.

In contrast to Greenberg's dismissal of the School of Paris, Beckett's essay claims that the very different painting styles of the brothers van Velde are proof 'that what goes by the name of the Paris School is in its infancy and has a promising future before it'.[8] He situates the two artists within a history of art seen as a history of painting's changing relationship to the object. Beckett sees Bram and Geer as recognising, in their work, the impossibility of representing either the object or its essence for, as the history of art has shown, 'the essence of object is to elude representation'. What remains to be represented, therefore, according to Beckett is 'the conditions of that elusion'. In Bram van Velde's painting the 'analysis of privation' is described by Beckett 'in terms of the within, of dark and full and fulgation', finding its resolution in the

> immovable masses of a being shut away and shut off and turned inward for ever, pathless, airless, cyclopean, lit with flares and torches, coloured with the colours of the spectrum of blackness. An endless unveiling, veil behind veil, plane after plane of imperfect transparencies, light and space themselves veils, an

unveiling towards the unveilable, the nothing, the thing again. And burial in the unique, in a place of impenetrable nearnesses, cell painted on the stone of cell, art of confinement.[9]

Beckett's vision of van Velde's art closely parallels the dislocated world his own invented characters inhabit in much of his later work. His characters are exiles from the physical world of landscapes and objects. Language, no longer located within the framework of identifiable objects, is suspended between speech and silence, meaning and non-meaning.

Beckett comes yet closer to identifying van Velde with his own genre of hero in the third major text he wrote about the artist. This took the form of a 'conversation' with George Duthuit, editor of a bilingual literary and art journal, published as one of three 'Dialogues' (the others being on Pierre Tal Coat and André Masson) in *Transition*. It was here that Beckett most emphatically enunciated the notion of van Velde's failure. He saw van Velde's achievement as that of acknowledging at one and the same time the impossibility of creating and the necessity of continuing to create: 'The situation is that of him who is helpless, cannot act, in the event cannot paint, since he is obliged to paint. The act is of him who, helpless, unable to act, acts, in the event paints, since he is obliged to paint.'[10] Beckett goes on to claim that van Velde is

> The first to admit that to be an artist is to fail, as no other dare fail, that failure is his world and the shrink from it desertion, art and craft, good housekeeping, living ... I know that all that is required now, in order to bring even this horrible matter to an acceptable conclusion, is to make of this submission, this admission, this fidelity to failure, a new occasion, a new term of relation, and of the act which, unable to act, obliged to act, he makes, an expressive act, even if only of itself, of its impossibility, of its obligation.[11]

According to Beckett's biographer Deirdre Bair, some of those most closely associated with *Transition* were extremely critical of Beckett's interpretation and saw the painter as 'an innocent martyr literally created by Beckett's theorising'.[12] They feared that his fragile equilibrium would be unbalanced by such virulent talk of failure and impossibility.

Duthuit's role in the dialogue was rather different. His suggestion that for van Velde 'the occasion of his painting is his predicament', and that the painting is 'expressive of the impossibility to express?'[13] evokes van Velde's own admission that 'Painting is man face to face with his débâcle'[14] and that 'I paint my wretchedness'[15] (referring more to the human condition than to his own impoverished life). In a later piece of criticism Duthuit developed the notion of van Velde's art as an exploration of the unknown, of the abyss,

> a world of blindness and deafness which seems ... impenetrable and yet finally a chink appears and it splits open ... With groping hands and thrusting shoulders we push on past huge trenches of quartz, salt and hard dried mud[16]

developing into a vision of van Velde's art as paralleling structures in the natural world:

> ellipses hardening into spear-heads, right angles on the point of fusion, long shafts of spittle and lava collapsing under their own weight, ovular clots obstructing veinous passages ... hidden, raw, floating masses on the face of which a fat and tangled vegetation forms a network of filtering arteries ... among the scattered fragments of ruined or embryonic cities and in the heavy calm of caverns and phosphorescent wrecks, captive suns levitate and streak about[17]

Van Velde's painting now seems, like that of Wols, forcefully in tune with the disequilibria and dislocations of the period. With its 'abortive geometry',[18] its inconsistencies and awkwardnesses, it is worlds away from the professionalism and sensuousness of much School of Paris abstraction of this period. Van Velde's paintings undermined the formal structures of Cubism, negated the potential for imagery to emerge and took unforgivable liberties with colour and line.

When the artist finally gained a measure of wider recognition at the end of the 1950s this was due less to any radical change in his art than to changed circumstances within the art world itself. As Franz Meyer stated, by the beginning of the 1960s

> the climate of painting had changed. The positive aspect of Bram van Velde's work became apparent: the transfiguration of conventional real space into dramatic experienced space [albeit] achieved at the cost of

painful experiment and agonised self-questioning of slow work and unbearable neglect.[19]

Very few anticipated the artist's later success. His third one-man exhibition, at the Galerie Maeght in 1952, was again a financial and critical disaster. The vernissage was celebrated by five visitors only, all close friends and supporters of the artist: Beckett, Roger Blin, Giacometti, Geer van Velde and Jacques Putman. In its aftermath the gallery withdrew its support.

NOTES

1 Patrick Waldberg, 'Bram van Velde', *Apollo*, no.398, April 1958, pp.130–4.
2 Discussed by Claire Stoullig, 'Bram van Velde: un certain état de la fortune critique', in *Bram van Velde*, exh. cat., Musée national d'art moderne, Paris 1989, pp.13–18.
3 *Les Lettres Françaises*, 19 April 1946, quoted ibid., p.161.
4 Edouard Loeb, invitation to the opening of Galerie Mai, 21 March 1946, reprinted in translation in *Aftermath*, exh. cat., Barbican Art Gallery 1982, p.148.
5 Samuel Beckett, 'La Peinture des van Veldes ou le monde et le pantalon', *Cahiers d'Art*, 1945–6, pp.349–56.
6 Waldberg 1958, p.133.
7 See John P. Harrington, 'Samuel Beckett's Art Criticism and the Literary Use of Critical Circumstance', *Contemporary Literature*, vol.21, no.3, Summer 1980, pp.331–48.
8 Samuel Beckett, 'The New Object', in *Geer and Bram van Velde*, exh. cat., Samuel M. Kootz Gallery, New York 1948, unpag.
9 Ibid.
10 Samuel Beckett and Georges Duthuit, 'Three Dialogues: Tal Coat – Masson – Bram van Velde', *Transition 49*, no.5, 1949, pp.97–103.
11 Ibid., p.103.
12 Deidre Bair, *Samuel Beckett: A Biography*, 1990, p.417.
13 Beckett and Duthuit 1949, p.101.
14 'Some Sayings of Bram van Velde', Beckett and Duthuit 1949, p.104.
15 Ibid.
16 Georges Duthuit, 'Bram van Velde ou aux colonnes d'Hercule', *Derrière le Miroir*, no.43, pp.2–4, 8; excerpts translated in Waldberg 1958.
17 Ibid.
18 Franz Meyer, Introduction in *Bram van Velde, Paintings 1957–1967*, exh. cat., Knoedler Gallery, New York 1968, unpag.

Illustration (p.170) Bram van Velde reading the manuscript of *Waiting for Godot c.*1952
Photograph by Maywald *Catherine Béraud Putman*

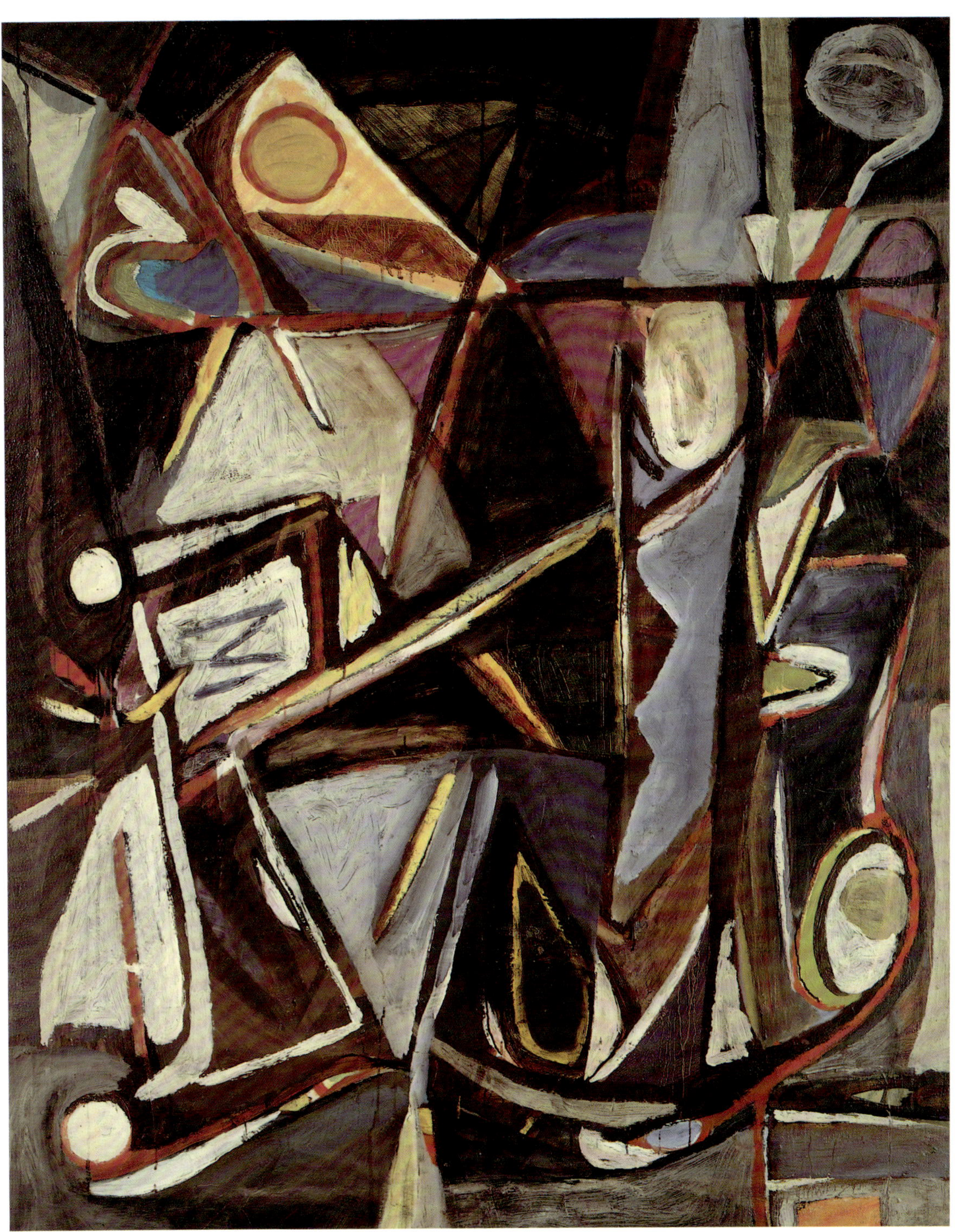

103 Untitled, Montrouge 1951
162 × 130 (63¾ × 51⅛)

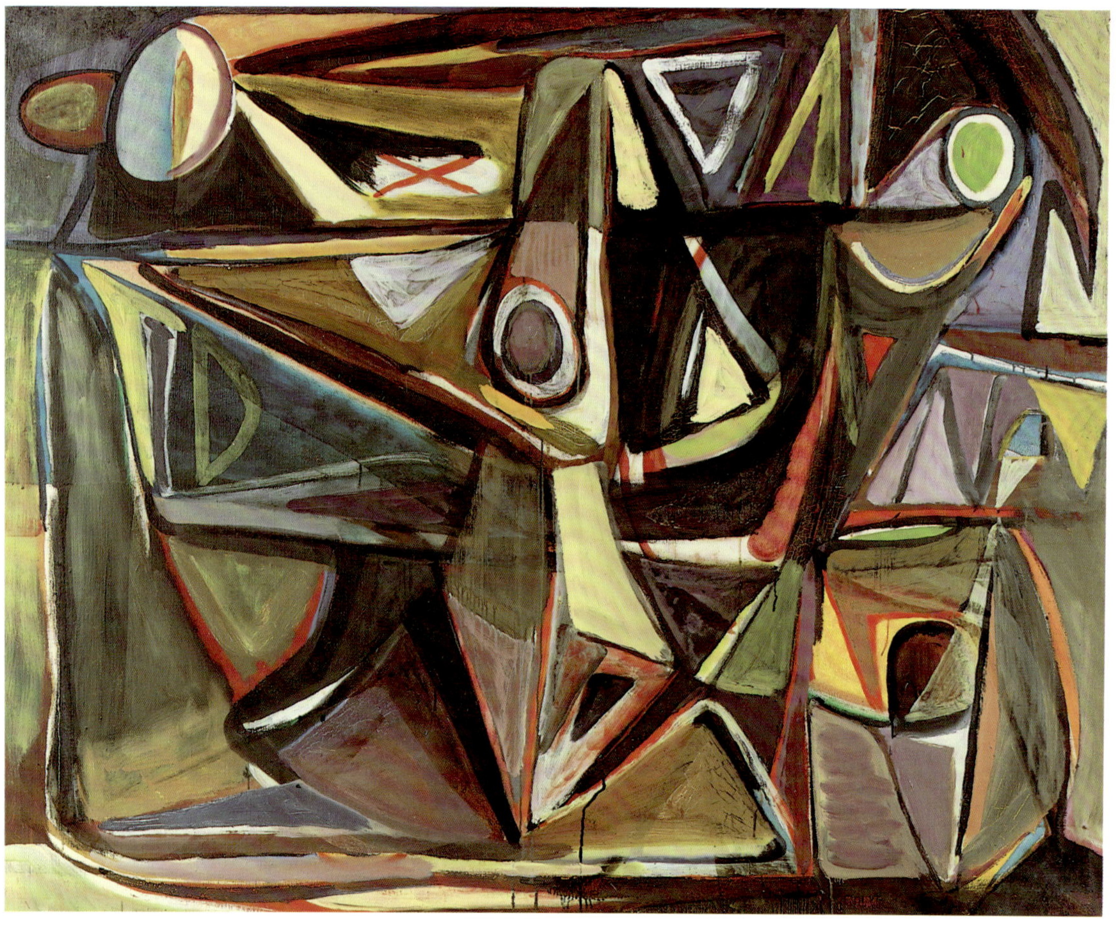

104 **Untitled, Montrouge** 1951–2
130.5 × 162 (51⅛ × 63¾)

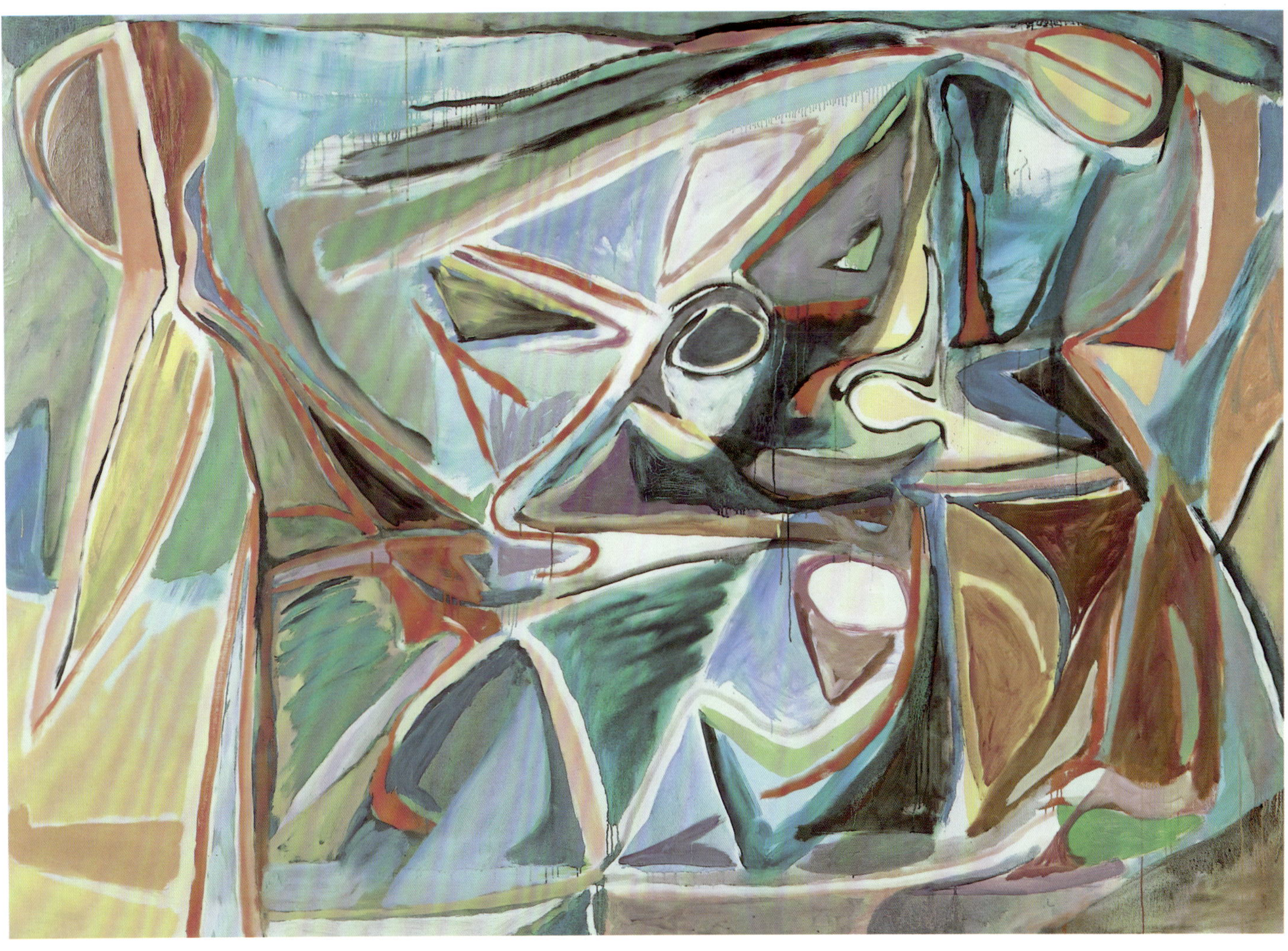

105 Untitled, Paris, Boulevard de la Gare 1956
$170 \times 242.5 \ (66\frac{7}{8} \times 95\frac{1}{2})$

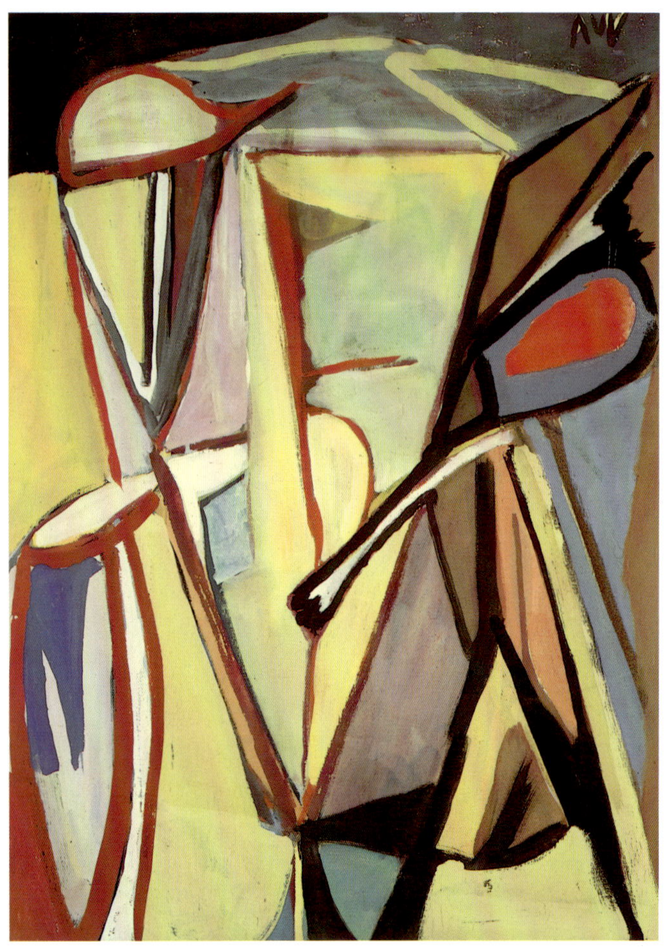

106 Untitled, Montrouge 1945–8
99 × 82 (39 × 32¼)

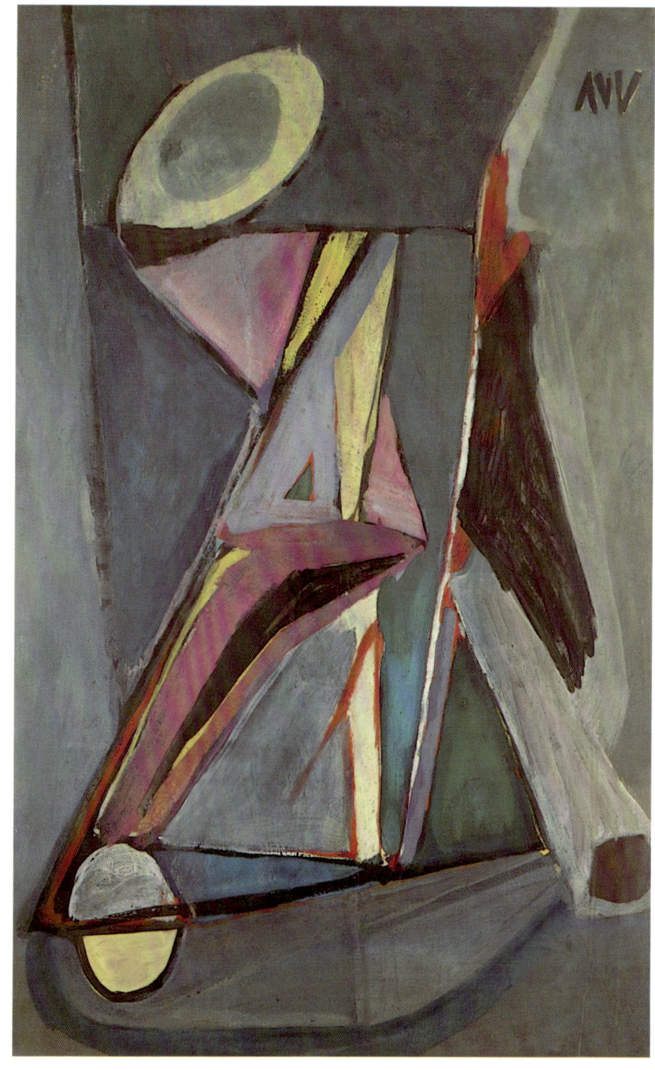

107 Untitled, Montrouge 1946–8
116 × 73 (45⅝ × 28¼)

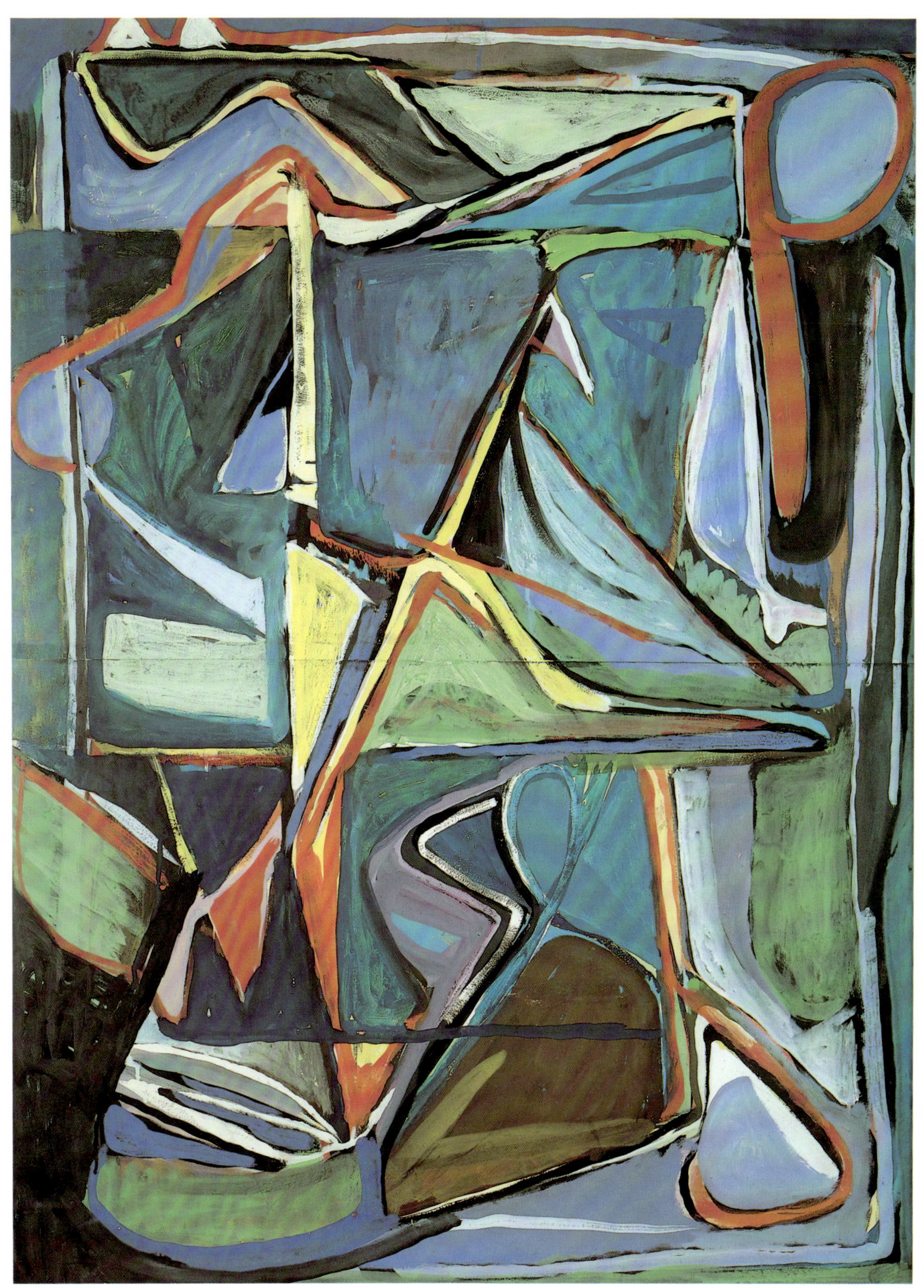

108 Untitled, Montrouge 1953
146 × 108 (57½ × 42½)

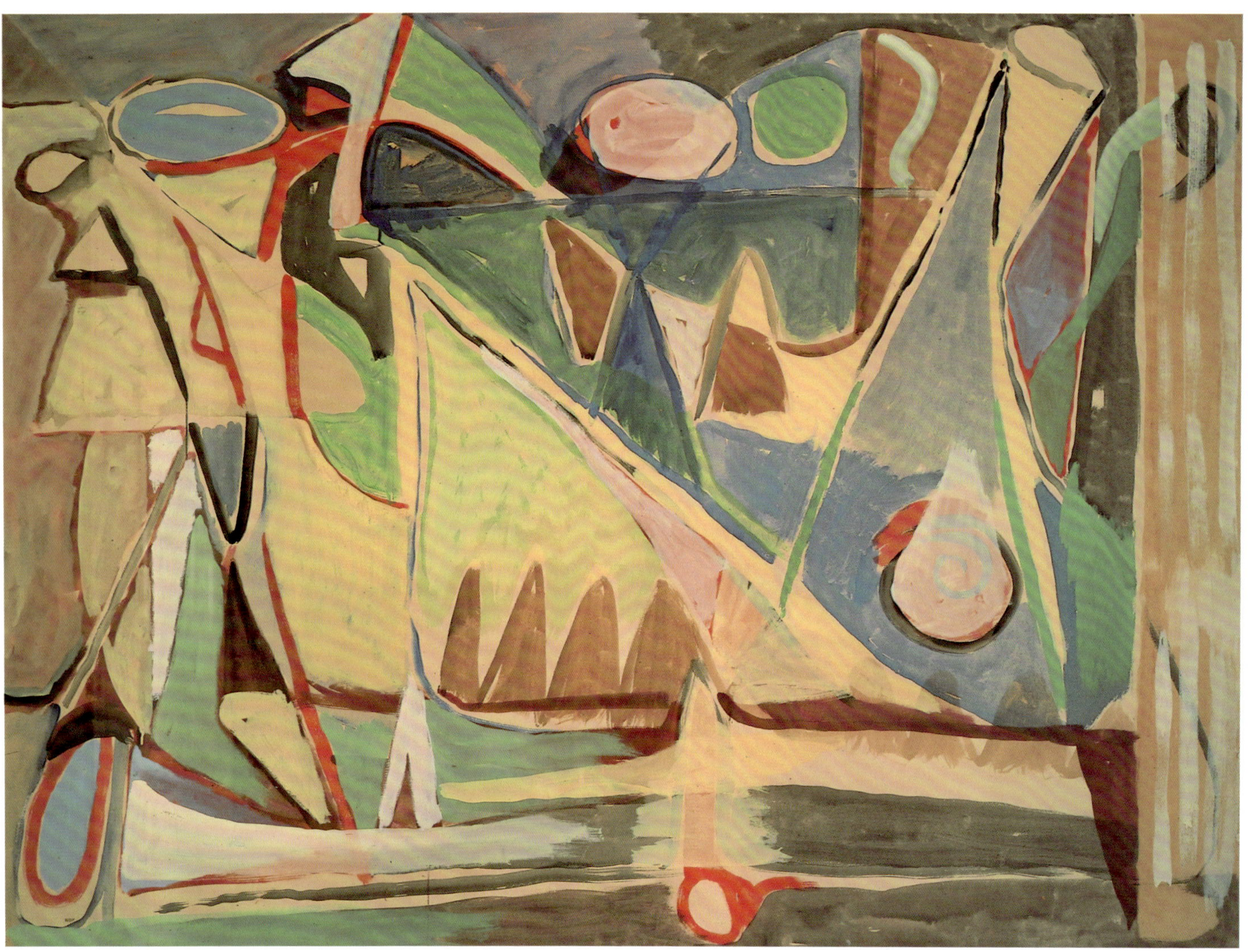

109 Untitled, Bourgogne 1954
150 × 202 (59 × 79½)

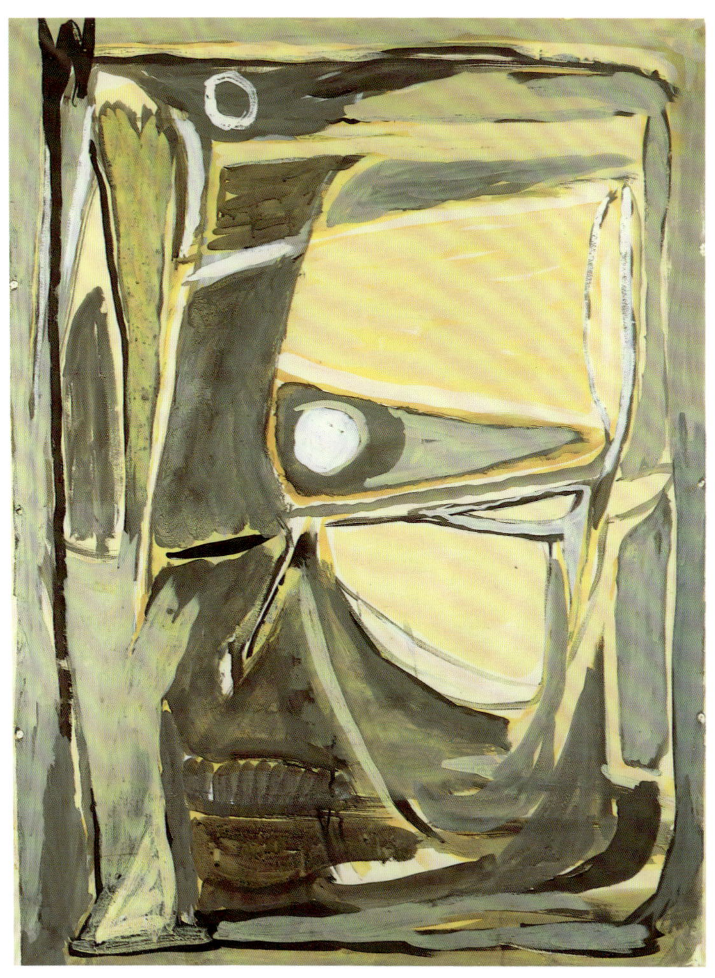

110 Untitled, Fox-Amphoux 1958
124 × 94 (48⅞ × 37)

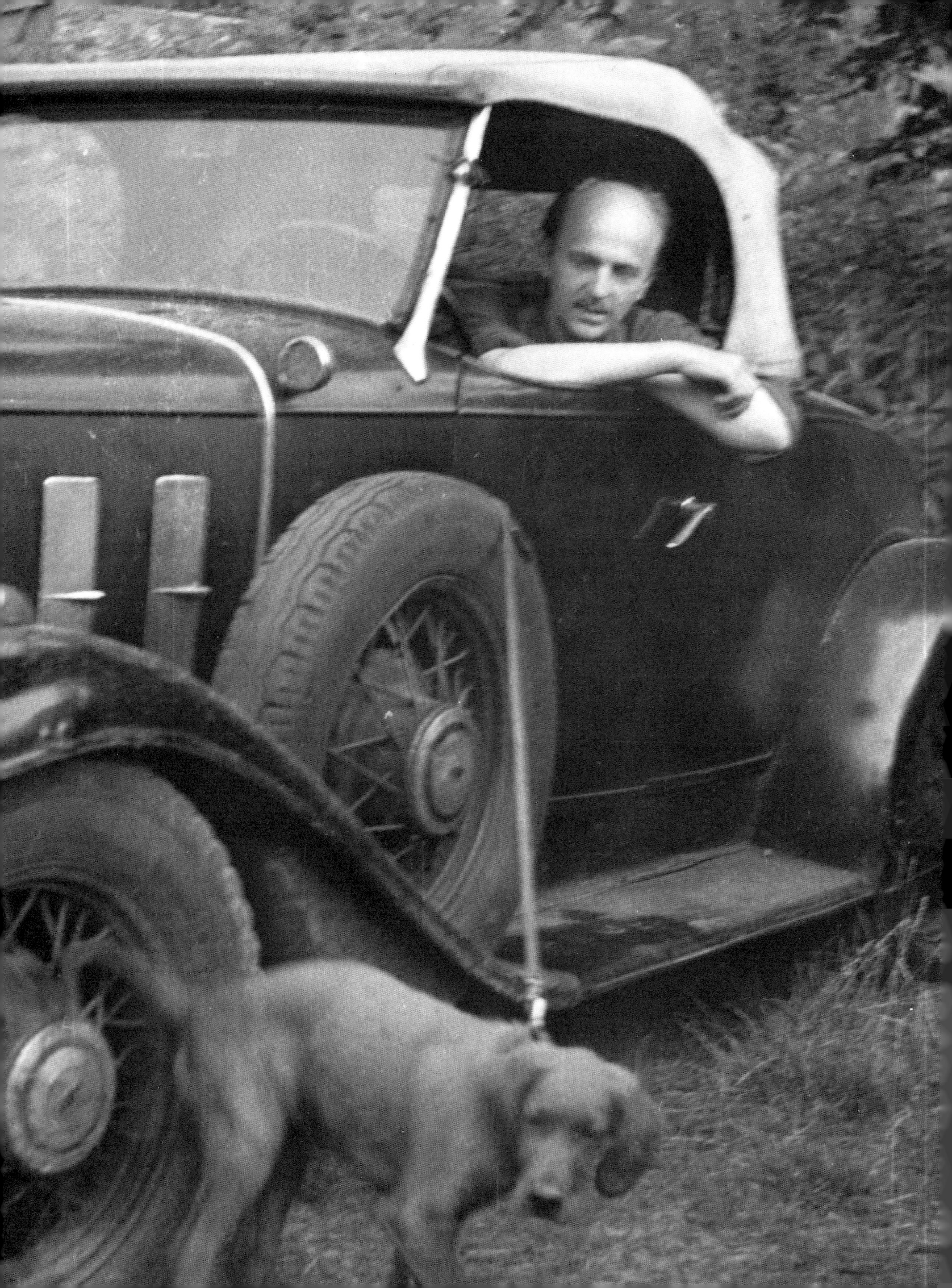

Wols (1913–1951)

In Wols's first exhibition, at the Galerie René Drouin in December 1945, his drawings and watercolours were displayed in illuminated boxes and the show was accompanied by a minute black catalogue. Despite the general indifference of the Parisian art world, the circle of intellectuals (including Jean Paulhan, Francis Ponge, Georges Limbour and André Malraux) that supported Drouin's aesthetic enterprise was fascinated by the mesmerising intensity of these tiny images. They seemed to derive in part from Surrealism but also to make something quite new of automatic processes of visual improvisation.

Wols had been introduced to Drouin by the professor of English and author (of *Jules et Jim*) H.P. Roché, who was a passionate admirer and one of the earliest collectors of the artist's work. Following his first exhibition Drouin provided Wols with canvas and materials, urging him to experiment with oils and on a larger scale. Wols did so: forty paintings were exhibited at Drouin's gallery the following year. They were received by a group of artists and critics as the products of a revolutionary new aesthetic. Michel Tapié, who was shortly to define this new art as *Un art autre*, claimed Wols as the 'catalyst of a lyrical, explosive, anti-geometrical and unformal non-figuration'.[1]

Wols had first made a name for himself as a photographer. It was to facilitate his career within the world of French avant-garde photography that he first adopted the pseudonym Wols – a name taken from a torn fragment of a telegram he had received – in place of his real name, Alfred Otto Wolfgang Schulze. He came to Paris in 1933, aged 19, at the suggestion of Laszlo Moholy-Nagy, whose student he had been at the Berlin Bauhaus. Leaving Germany was also a way of liberating himself from the Nazi threat and from the oppressive hold of his strict bourgeois family. Moholy-Nagy's recommendations brought him into contact with the 'Surrealist' circle around the Prévert brothers, though neither his work nor his retiring personality helped him make an impression. Still, by 1937 he was doing quite well as a photographer. That year he had a one-man exhibition at the Galerie de la Pléiade, one of the key Paris venues for contemporary photography, and his new status was confirmed in the same year when he was contracted to photograph the fashion pavilion at the Paris International Exhibition (*Exposition Internationale des Arts et Techniques dans La Vie Moderne*, 26 May–26 November 1937).

This career was brought to an abrupt end by the war. In 1939 Wols was interned as an enemy alien. Though he was freed a year later, following his marriage to Gréty, a French citizen, such a bourgeois profession was no longer practicable.

Both his photography and the drawings he made in the 1930s show the influence of Surrealism. As a photographer Wols was a master of the close-up, frequently composing his subjects in unexpected focus, destroying constructive coherence and dislocating expectations. His images often alight on seemingly trivial details or show objects in paradoxical relationships, and these aspects of his photography were standard Bauhaus practices. His subjects also demonstrate his obsession with decay and waste. His drawings and watercolours are of imaginary landscapes, often strongly architectural in character, suggesting buildings or cities. The tiny scale and the delicacy of his line, as well as the autonomous ease with which the image appears to emerge, suggest a clear relationship with Paul Klee's work. In other drawings, biomorphic characters are reminiscent of Yves Tanguy, Joan Miró and Max Ernst. Wols's invented personages often combine disparate parts, assertively through juxtaposition and more gently through metamorphosis. Under internment, moved from camp to camp, Wols became more and more absorbed in his art but at the same time began to drink heavily, forming an addiction he never conquered. On his release, he and Gréty made a home at Cassis in the South of France and then at Dieulefit in the Drôme above Montélimar, existing without financial security and constantly mindful of the German occupying forces. However the time at Cassis was crucial in reorientating Wols's approach. His imagery became less and less receptive to precise identification or verbal description, while retaining a strong visceral and metaphoric appeal. Werner Haftmann characterised Wols's new compositions as no longer providing a 'stage or window onto an imagined reality, but as the immaterial ground in which the play of fantasy created a new world appropriate to itself'.[2] Ironically it seems to have been Wols's fascination with the natural world at close hand that stirred this deepening of his abstract vision:

> At Cassis, the pebbles, fish,
> rocks under a magnifying glass
> the salt of the sea and the sky
> made me forget about human pretentions
> invited me to turn my back
> on the chaos of our goings-on
> showed me eternity
> in the little harbour waves,
> which repeat themselves
> without repeating themselves.[3]

In place of imaginary scenarios populated by invented characters, his images begin to describe processes of invention, growth, change and mutation.

Sartre met Wols in 1945, when the artist returned to Paris following the Liberation, came to know him well and on occasion saved him from destitution. The philosopher was intrigued by Wols's work, particularly that of the later years. In a lengthy tribute, written more than a decade after Wols's death, he explained the reasons for this fascination.[4] For Sartre, Wols's early works derived from a meditation on the 'otherness' of phenomena in the world, demonstrating a vision not unlike that obsession with strangeness which grips Sartre's own invented character, Roquentin, in his novel *Nausea* (1938). Roquentin's sensation of nausea, like Wols's experience at Cassis, came from a confrontation with the object, a realisation of man's connection to and separation from the world of objects. In order to explore visually this sense of strangeness, Wols, prior to 1940, depicted recognisable features from the real world but presented them in irrational ways, often using Surrealist formulae. Sartre believed that Wols had found, after 1940, a revolutionary means of expressing this perception of strangeness, by deploying shapes without any relationship to the world: i.e. non-things. The difference between old and new in Wols's work is evoked by Sartre, who repeats an aphorism of the Taoist Chuang-tzu: 'using one's fingers to demonstrate that fingers are not fingers is less effective than using non-fingers to demonstrate that fingers are not fingers.'[5]

From 1942 onwards Wols's drawings suggest microscopic structures of life seen from close to, or alternatively planetary worlds glimpsed from afar. Shapes are predominantly biomorphic and often in metamorphosis. Many of his inventions project a very strong feeling of space and of the concrete physical presence of the depicted object in space. Objects have focal points reminiscent of biological forms, suggesting eggs or cells and cavities evocative of sexual organs.

Although Wols's first paintings on canvas were simply scaled-up versions of his works on paper, he fast became more adventurous with the new scale and medium. His paintings show a total disregard for the niceties of pictorial composition or facture. Increasingly the object is subsumed in a chaos of space. Paint is stencilled, smeared, daubed and flung at the canvas and then incised using fingers or the wrong end of the paint brush. Liquid paint is allowed to flow freely and to coagulate, and the canvas is manipulated to allow rivulets to crisscross the surface. Elsewhere, paint is sprayed or flicked. When using the brush Wols seems to have become more and more confident in expressing a physical relationship with the canvas. Brushstrokes are laid on in curves that rhythmically echo the energetic gestures of the artist's arm. Such arabesques are contrasted with circles of energy where the artist has used his wrist as if to tunnel into the canvas.

This late style of Wols's was described by Haftmann as a form of 'psychic improvisation'[6] and by Sartre as 'automatism', an existential act in which the painter visualises our 'universal horror of being-in-the-world' in painting which unites the self (artist) with the other (object):

> Wols, human and Martian together, applies himself to seeing the earth with inhuman eyes: it is, he thinks, the only way of universalising our experience … it is not our life that they [his paintings] manifest, nor even our materiality, it is our naked being, perceived from outside … foreign, repulsive, but ours; impossible to look at without vertigo, this being which we are, captive in them [his paintings] as the being which they are.[7]

For Sartre, Wols's paintings create a sense of unease in the viewer. They reject the traditional means by which painters have sought to reassure man of his status in the world and instead project, through improvisation, a field of absolute uncertainty and instability where the physical world of objects (animal, vegetable and mineral) is presented in a state of 'transsubstantiation permanente'. Wols's paintings were for Sartre representations of anguish in plastic form, revealing the continuous struggle of the artist to define himself in the world.

It is not difficult to see why Sartre was drawn to Wols. On his return to Paris Wols lived a semi-destitute life, drifting from hotel to hotel on the Left Bank, often drinking, sleeping intermittently and working incessantly, mostly in bed. Ione Robinson, a rare visitor to Wols's room at the Hotel de Seine recalls:

> I will always remember that room. The bent iron bed. The battered wardrobe and chair. The wash basin that made a noise like a trumpet. And Wols lying in bed drawing, with his dog asleep at his feet ... while apologising for the untidiness of his room, he reached for the mandolin hanging on the wall opposite the bed. The room was so narrow, he had no difficulty in reaching for the mandolin and his clothes which were hanging on a nail, or for his box of watercolours on the table under the mandolin.[8]

Such a life took its toll. When Sartre met him in 1945 he was

> bald, with a bottle and a beggar's pouch. In the pouch was the world, his worry; in the bottle, his death. He had been handsome, he wasn't any more: at 33 one would have thought him 50 without the youthful sadness in his eyes. Everyone – to start with him – thought that he would not make old bones ... In the end, his friends had to carry him in the evening to the Rhumerie Martiniquaise, and bring him back in the middle of the night, a little more dead each day, a little more visionary.[9]

Sartre dwells here on the notion of the artist's self-destruction in realising his art, believing 'that he had thrown himself into a short-term adventure, just one: to kill himself convinced that one cannot express anything without destroying oneself'. At the same time he expresses the related notion of the absorption of the artist in his painting: 'Wols ... constructed palaces with his own excretions, as a matter of course. The creature dreamed of his own decomposition with his product.' Expressing a similar idea, Haftmann claims that 'every picture absorbed a part of the painter's psychic vitality; the pictorial texture devoured his living tissue'.[10]

The idea that Wols either worked or drank himself to an early death is factually incorrect. Wols died from food poisoning at a time when he seemed to be successfully fighting off the stranglehold of alcohol. Whilst confessing to Ione Robinson that his drinking was 'a defence [against life]' he also asserted that 'My pictures are not a revolt against anything. In spite of misery, poverty and the fear of becoming blind one day, I love life.'[11] Sartre was not the first to label Wols an existential artist. Pierre Restany had earlier described him as 'une peinture existentielle',[12] and argued that Wols had found in Sartre's philosophy 'a supplementary justification of his refusal of contingency, and a clear analysis of the reign of ''l'En-Soi'' (the Thing in Itself), the existential projection of Being in the Cosmos'. Restany also points to the affinities between Wols's stance and Chinese mystic thought. Many of Wols's poems probably do reflect an interest in Taoist philosophy, especially the idea of an absolute realm embracing microcosm and macrocosm. The poem entitled 'At Cassis', some of which is quoted above, continues:

> Nothing is explicable
> we only know appearances.
> All loves lead to one love.
> Beyond personal loves
> there is the nameless love
> the great mystery
> the absolute
> X
> Tao
> God
> Cosmos
> Holy Ghost
> One
> Infinity
> the abstract that penetrates everything
> is ungraspable;
> in each moment
> in each thing
> eternity is there.

This interest is not at odds with Wols's documented sympathy for Sartrean existentialism. There is in Taoism a concept of K'ai ho, the ability to produce art without effort, in which the intellectual element of consciousness is suppressed and therefore prevented from interfering with the expression of the total person, which parallels Sartre's idea of automatism. Similarly, just as both Wols and Sartre saw in his art unnameable things (Wols never titled his paintings; titles were added later, mostly by his widow and Roché), Tao is ineffable.

For many visitors to Wols's 1947 exhibition, his paintings represented a completely new approach to art, a rejection both of figuration and of cool abstraction, and a projection far beyond the familiar world to a metaphysical plane. For painters like Georges Mathieu the absolute freedom with which he approached the canvas represented a revolutionary break in the history of art: 'After Wols, everything has to be done anew'.[13] Jean Paulhan's description of *art autre* demonstrates how much the philosophy of the new painting styles (variously described as the *Informel*, *Abstraction Lyrique*, and *Tachisme*) owed to Wols:

> one could easily believe that their work betrays the accidents and fundamental ambiguity of another object, a mysterious object they approach from more than one side and which they do not cease viewing, without ever quite being able to embrace it. An unseizable, incorruptible object, compared with which our everyday objects are faults and shatterings.[14]

NOTES

1 Michel Tapié, 'Espaces et Expressions', *Premier bilan de l'art actuel 1937–1953*, p.102.

2 Werner Haftmann, quoted by Roger Cardinal, 'The Later Works of Wols: Abstraction, Transparency, Tao', in Peter Inch (ed.), *Circus Wols*, 1978, unpag.

3 Wols, 'At Cassis', 1944, trans. in Inch 1978, unpag.

4 Jean-Paul Sartre, 'Doigts et non-doigts' in Jean-Paul Sartre, Henri-Pierre Roché, Werner Haftmann, *Wols en personne*, Paris 1963, pp.10–21.

5 Ibid., p.17.

6 Werner Haftmann, *Painting in the Twentieth Century*, I, 1960, p.346.

7 Sartre 1963, p.18.

8 Ione Robinson, 'Talks with Wols' in *Modern Art Yesterday and Tomorrow* [The Selective Eye IV], ed. G.and R. Bernier, Zwemmer 1960, p.111.

9 Sartre 1963, p.10, trans. Annie Fatet in Inch 1978, unpag.

10 Haftmann 1960, p.346.

11 Robinson 1960, p.13.

12 Pierre Restany, 'Peinture existentielle: Wols', *Vingtième Siècle*, no.19, June 1962, pp.53–6.

13 Georges Mathieu, *Au-delà du Tachisme*, Paris 1963, p.35.

14 Jean Paulhan, *L'Art Informel*, Paris 1962, p.4, trans. in Peter Inch, 'The Destruction of Wols', *Art and Artists*, Dec. 1971, p.34.

Illustration (p.180) Wols at Champigny, August 1951 *Private Collection*

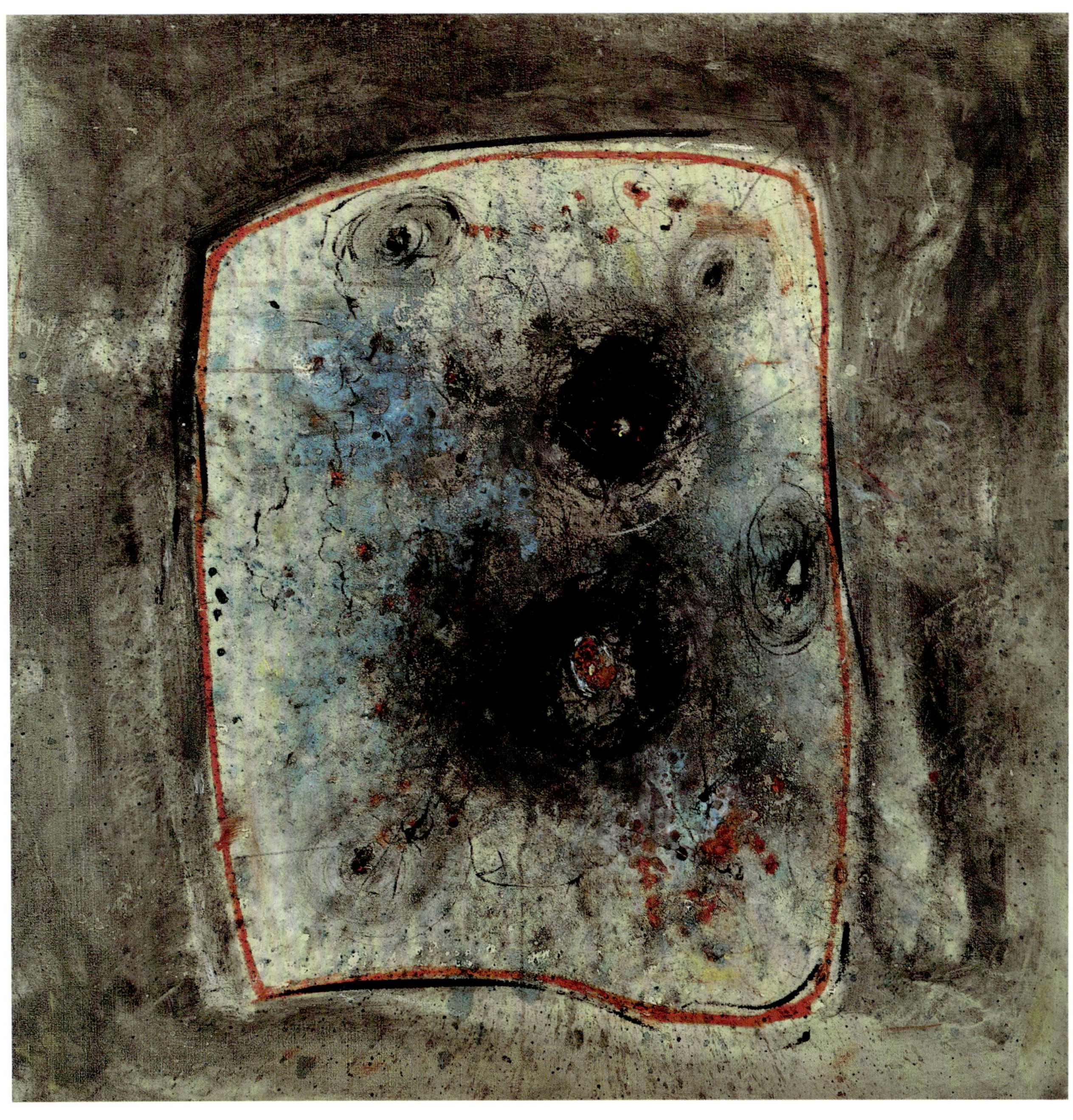

111 **Painting** 1944–5
$81 \times 81.1 \, (31\frac{7}{8} \times 32)$

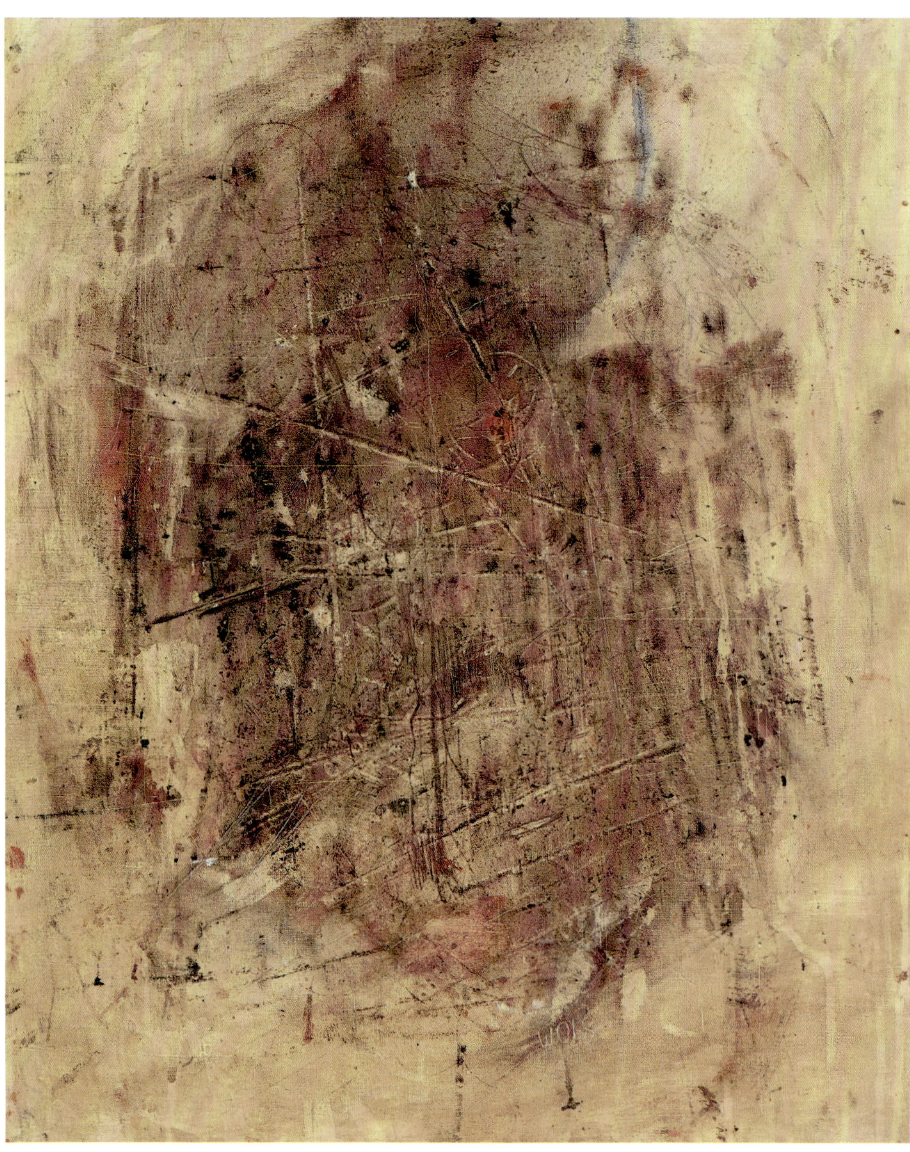

112 **Composition IV** 1946
65×54 $(25\frac{5}{8} \times 21\frac{1}{4})$

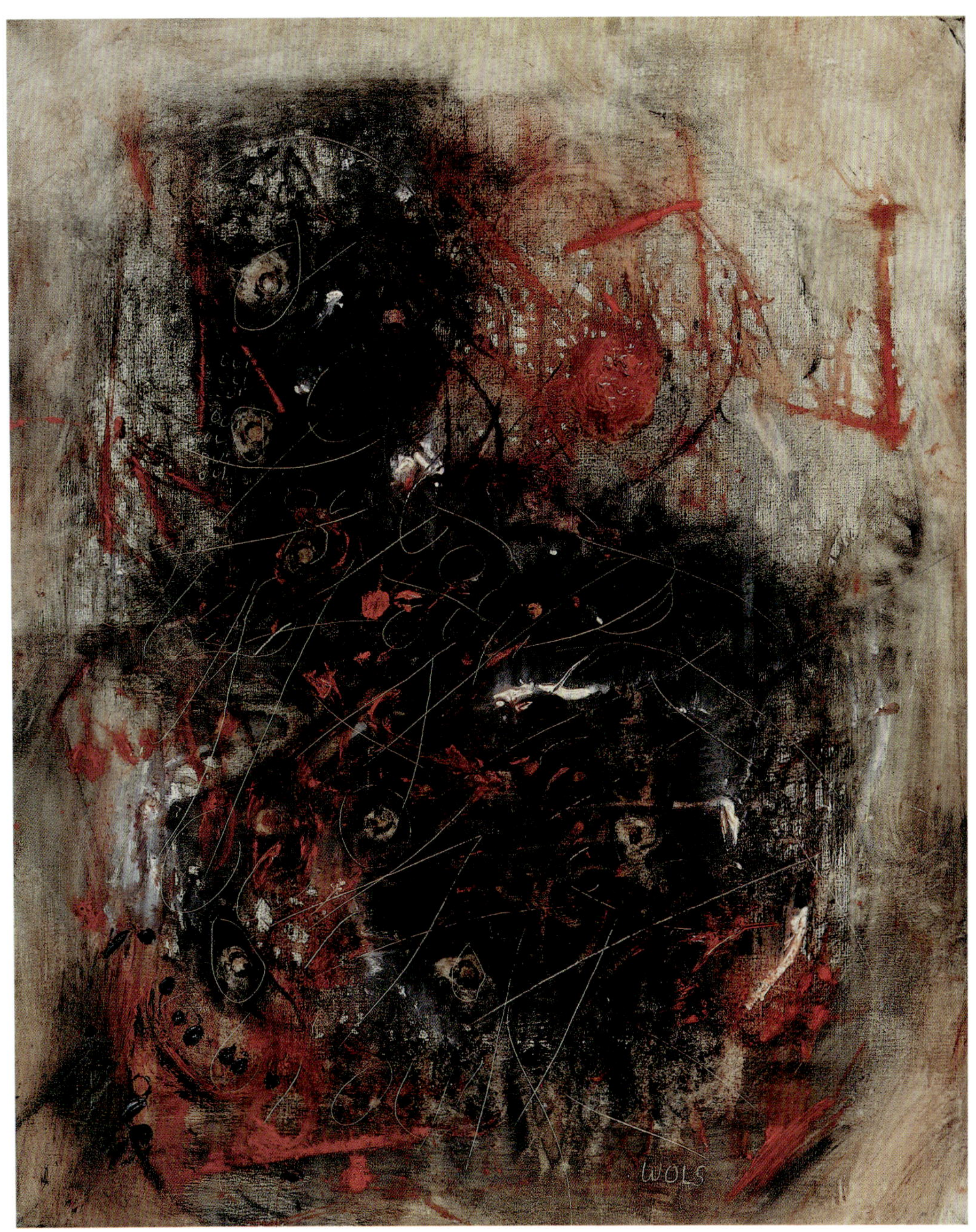

113 Yes, Yes, Yes 1946–7
80.6 × 64.2 (31⅛ × 25⅝)

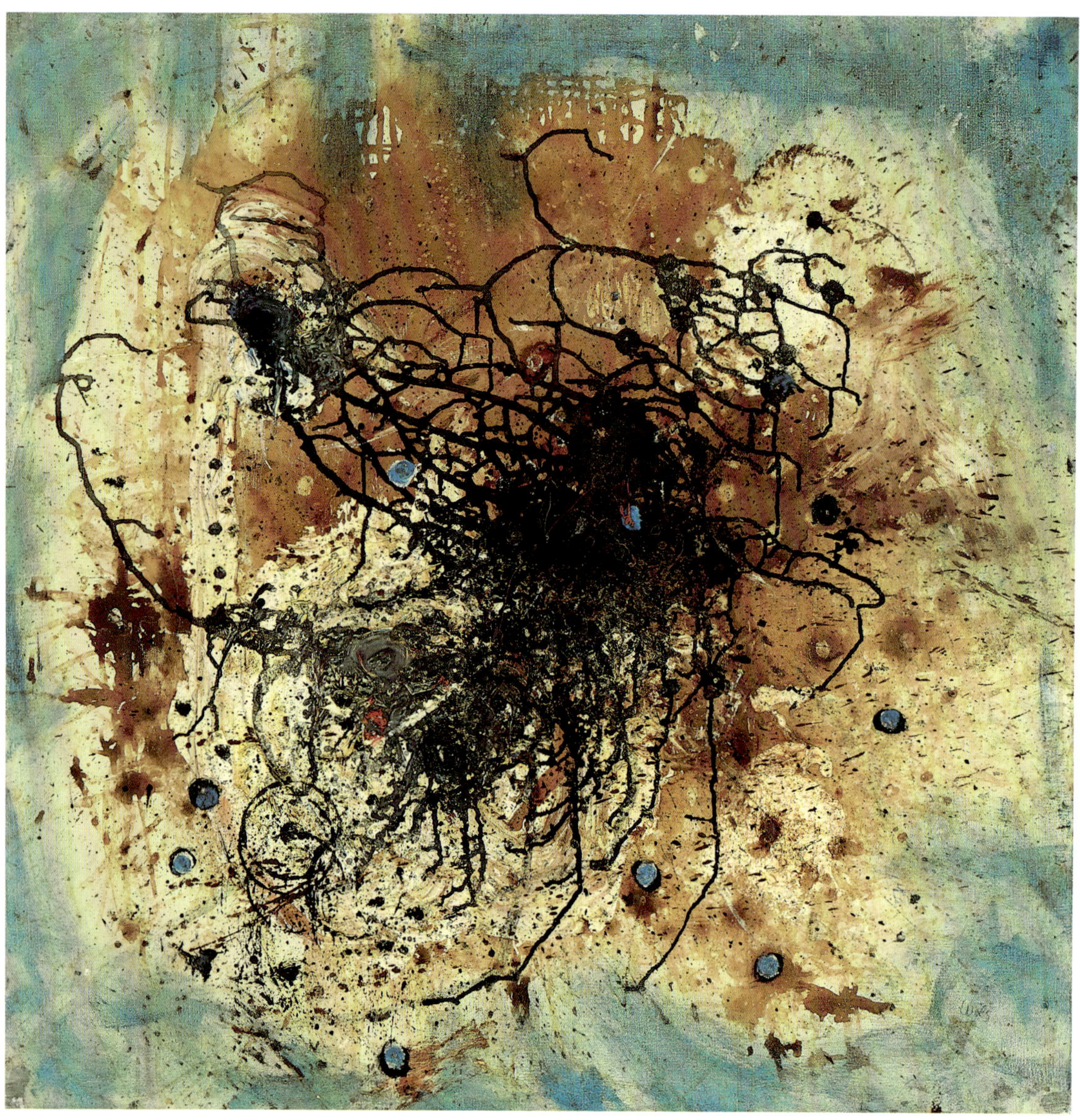

114 Untitled 1946–7
81 × 81 (31⅞ × 31⅞)

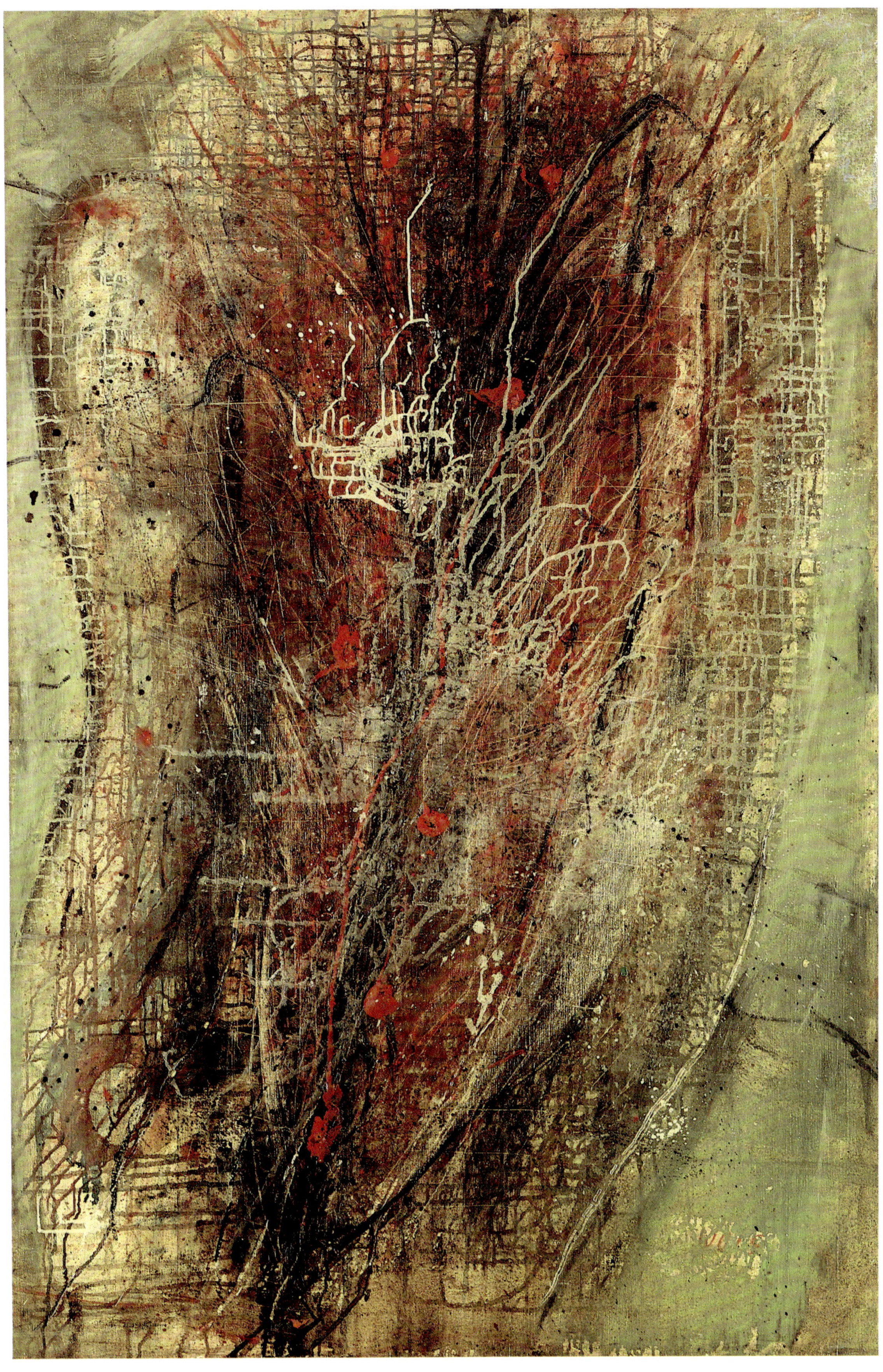

115 Manhattan 1947
146 × 97.5 (57½ × 38⅜)

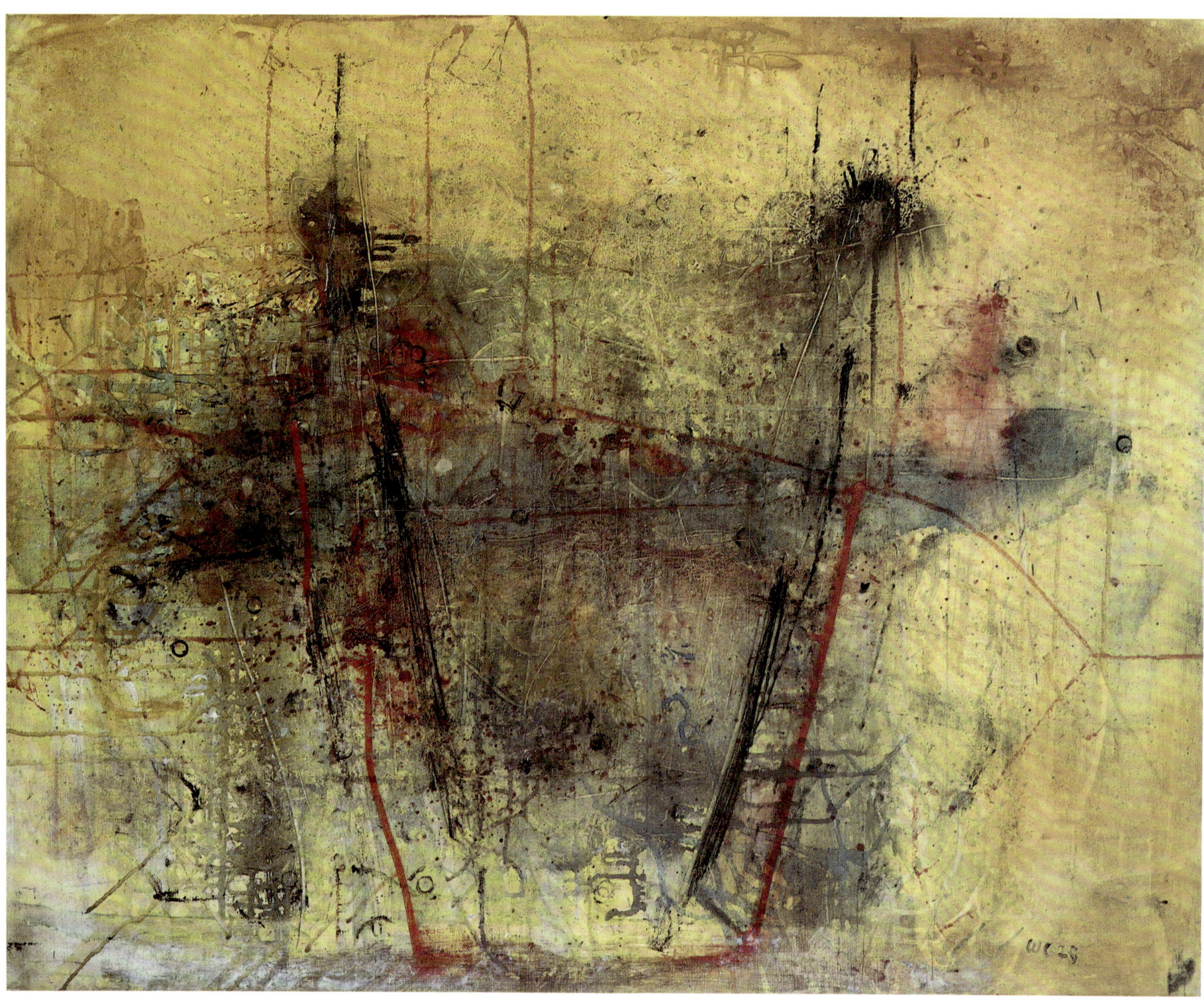

116 Yellow Composition 1947
73 × 92 (28¾ × 36¼)

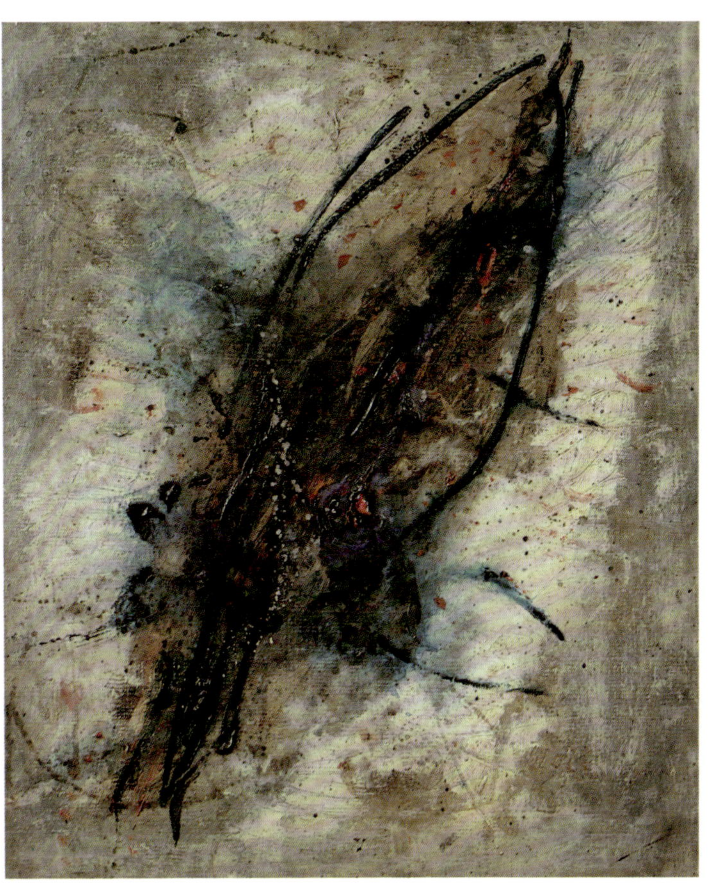

117 Butterfly's Wing 1947
$55 \times 46 \ (21\frac{5}{8} \times 18\frac{1}{8})$

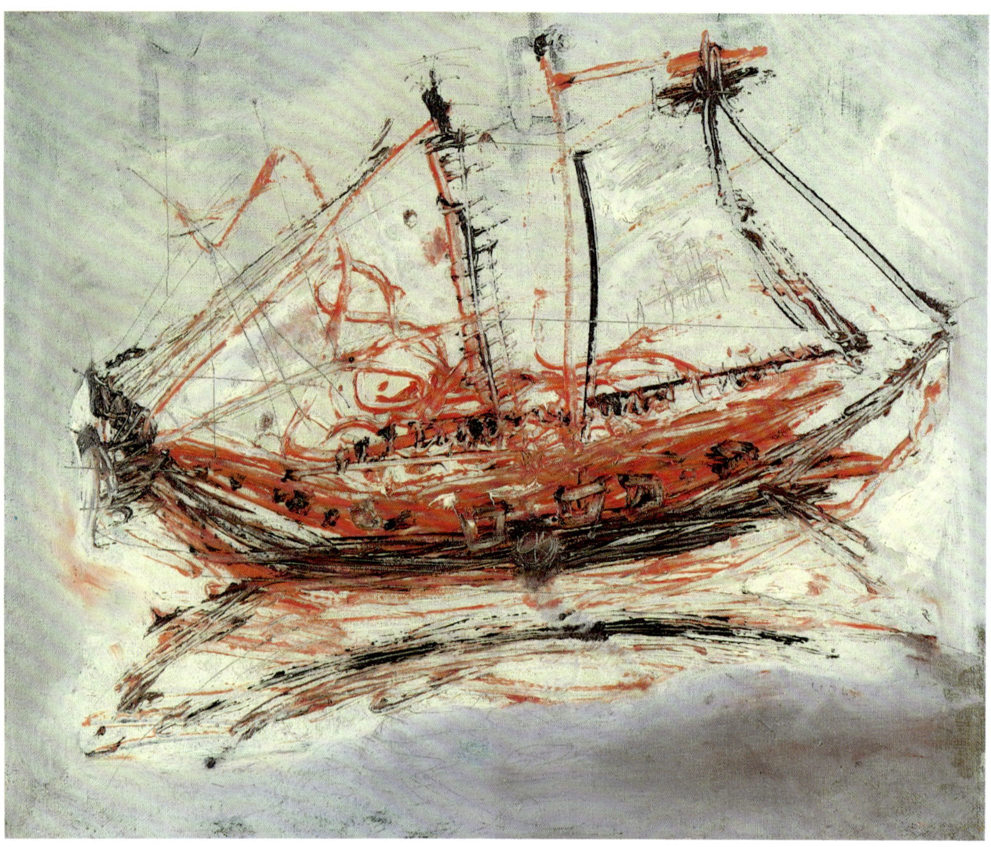

118 The Pink Ship 1949
38 × 46 (15 × 18⅛)

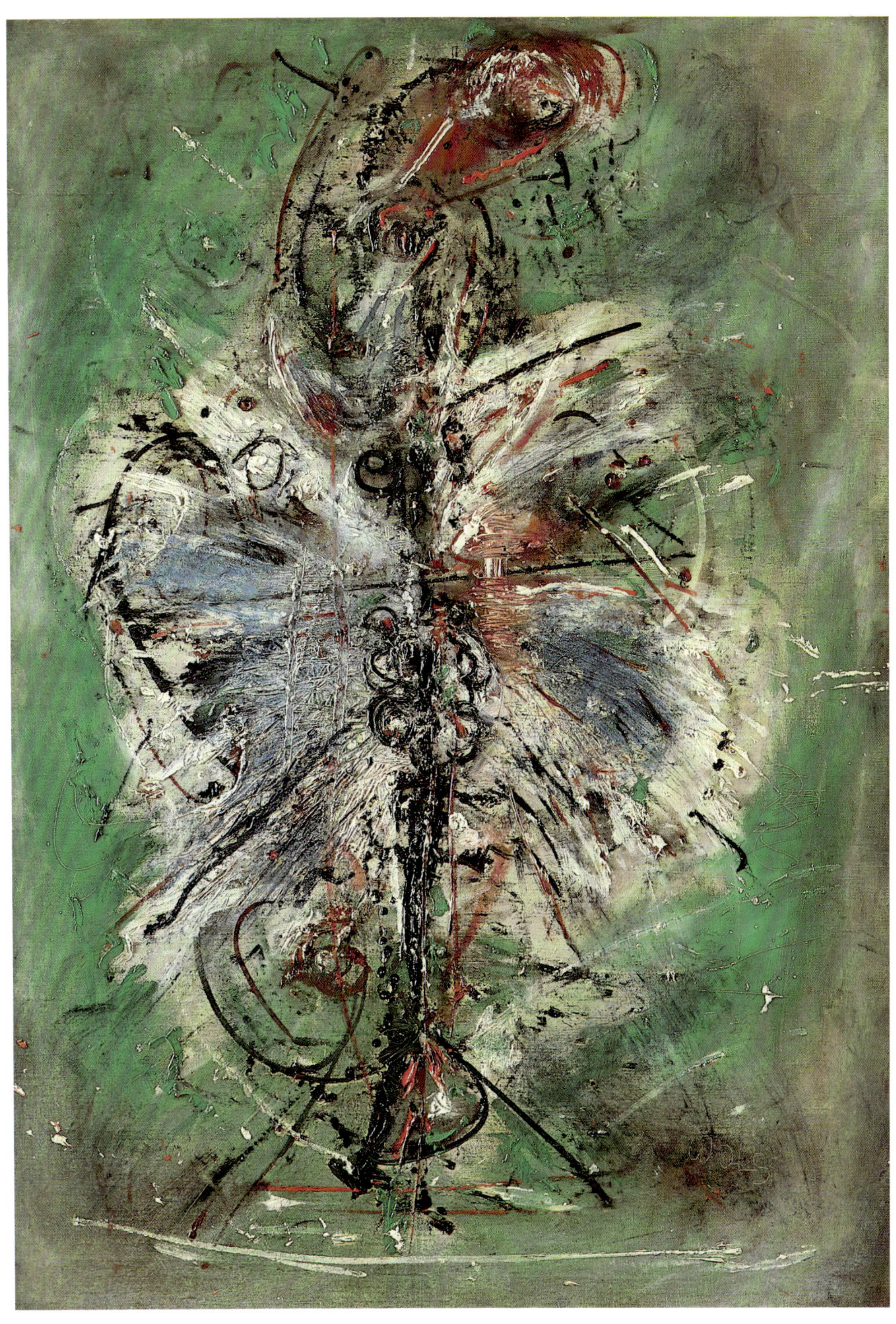

119 **Bird** 1949
92.1 × 65.1 ($36\frac{1}{4} \times 25\frac{3}{4}$)

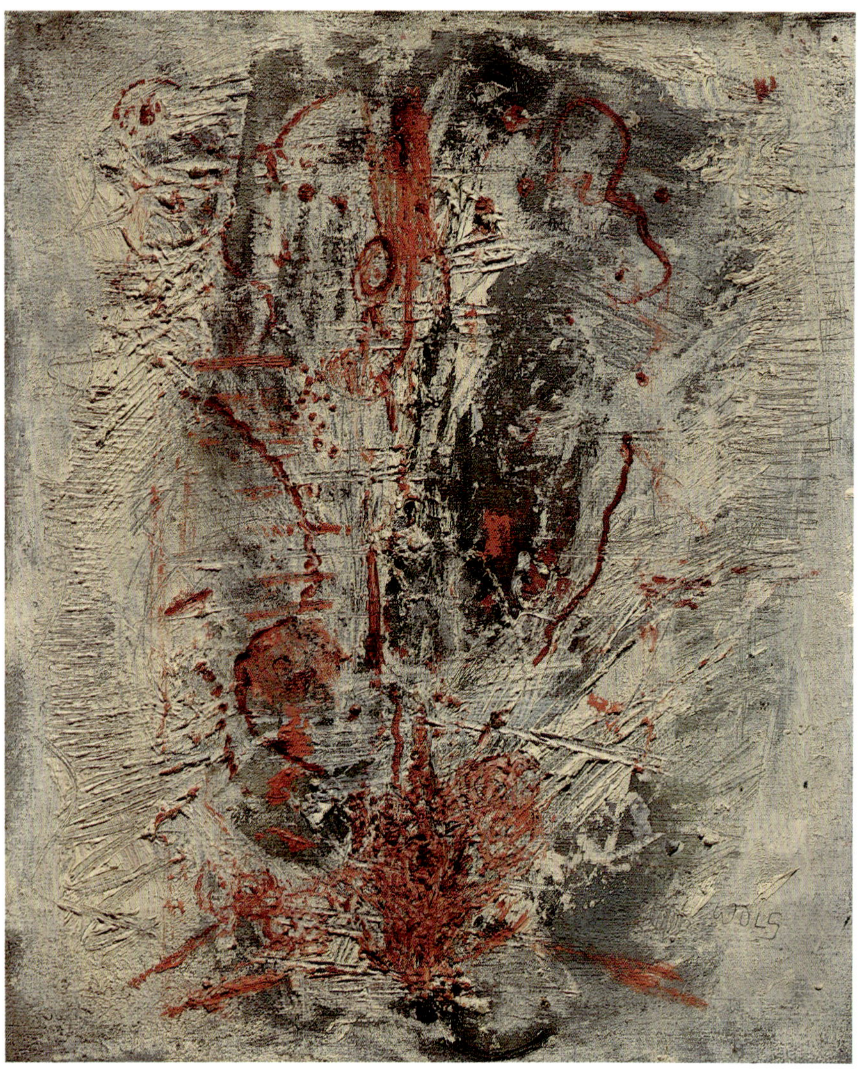

120 Composition on Grey Ground 1949
$46 \times 38\ (18\frac{1}{8} \times 15)$

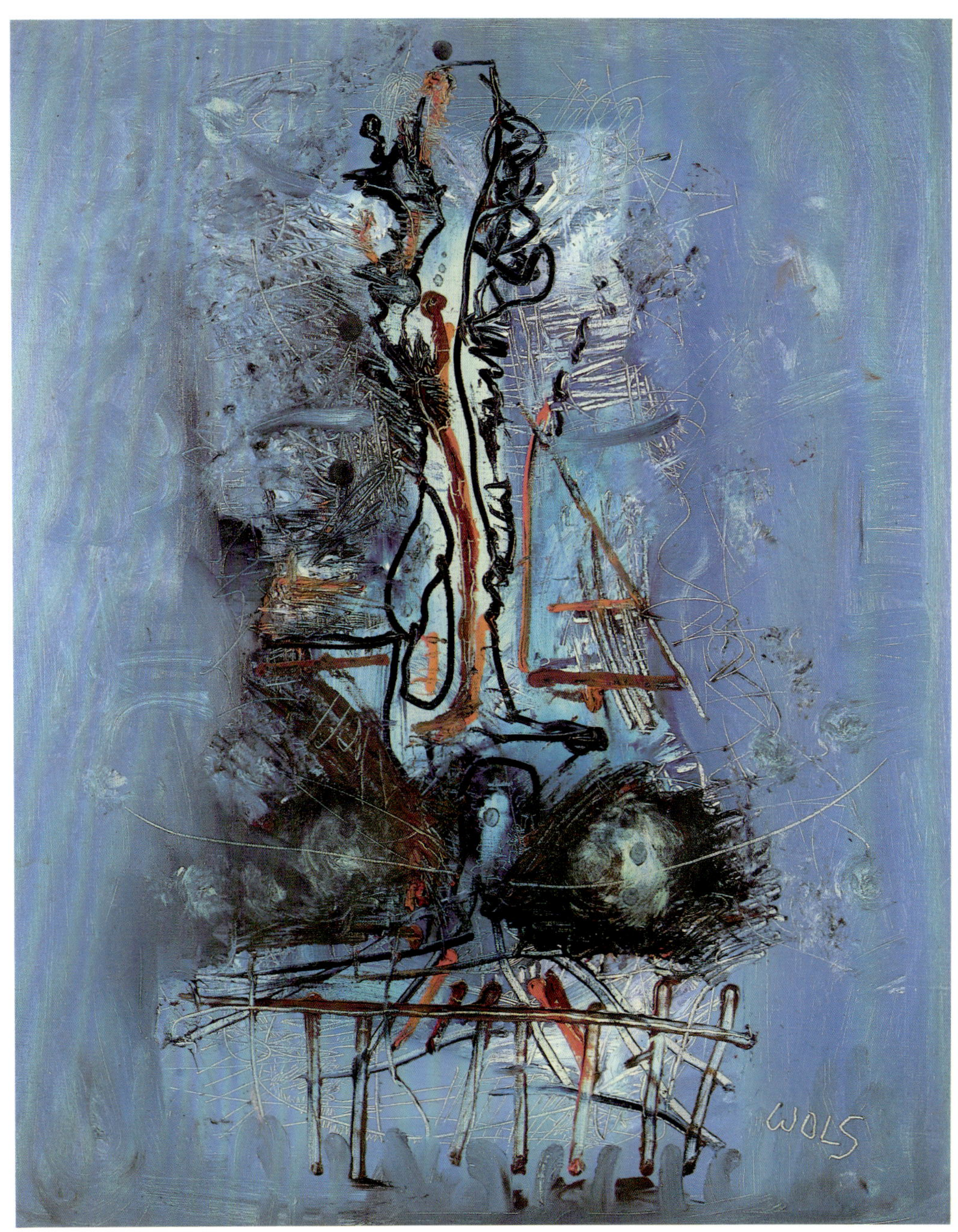

121 Composition Champigny 1951
68 × 57 (26¼ × 22½)

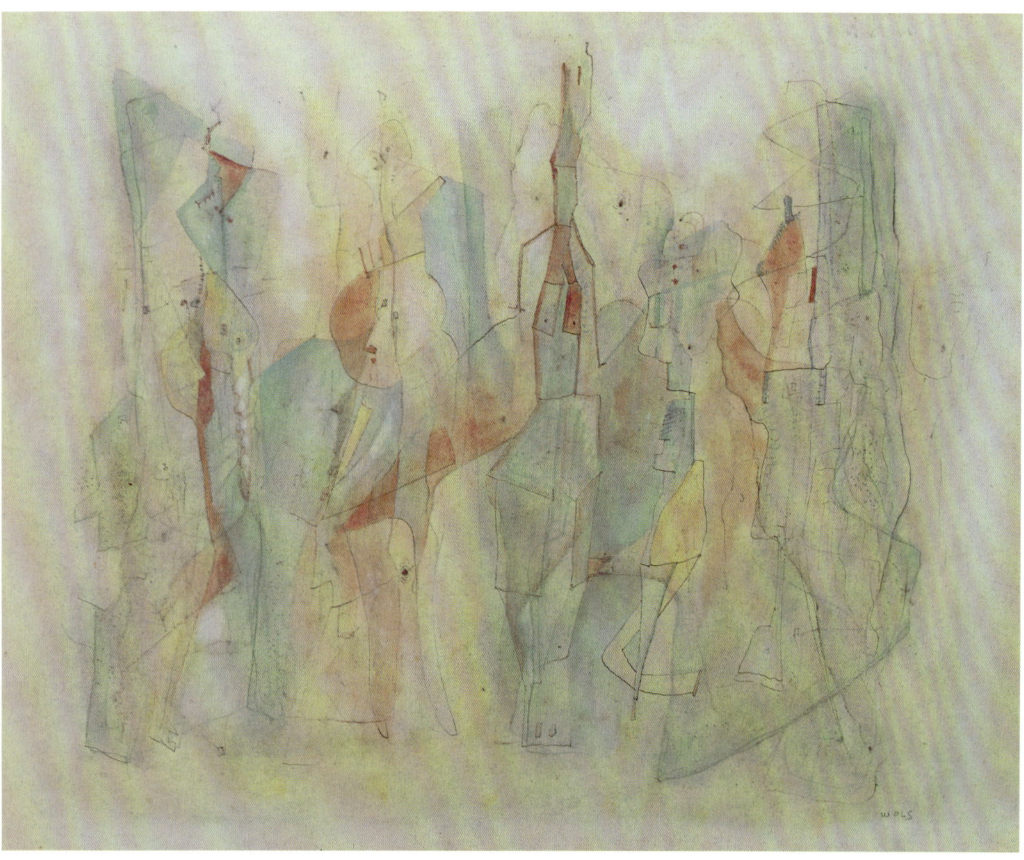

122 Untitled 1940
26.5 × 33 (10⅜ × 13)

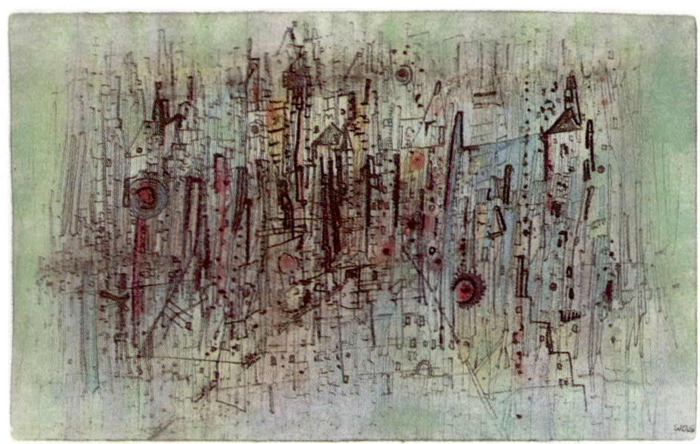

127 The City 1944–5
9.8 × 16.2 (3⅞ × 6⅜)

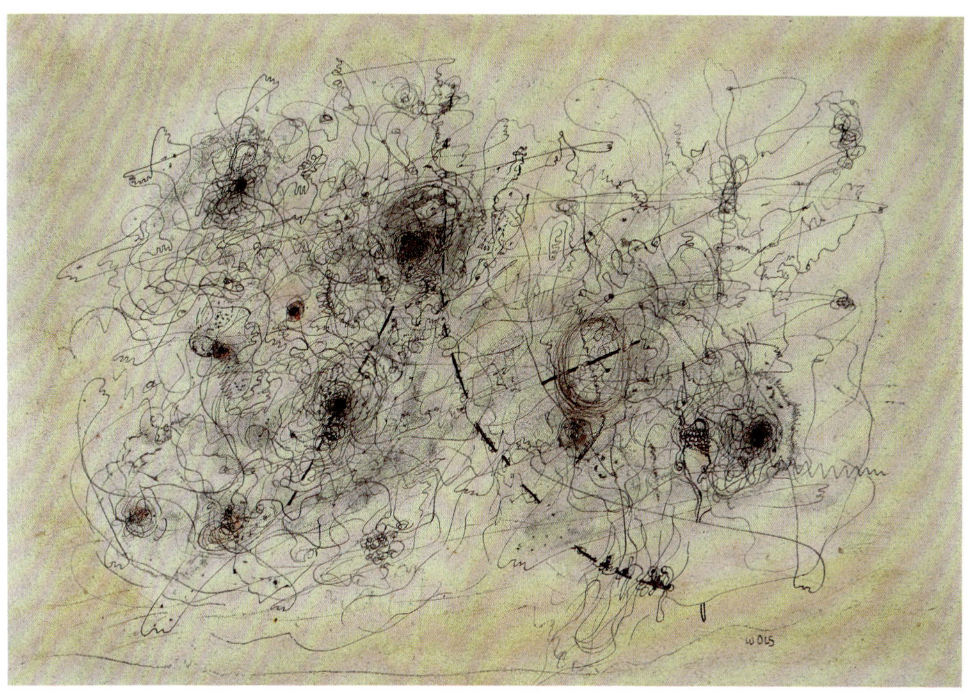

123 Untitled 1942
18 × 26 (7⅛ × 10¼)

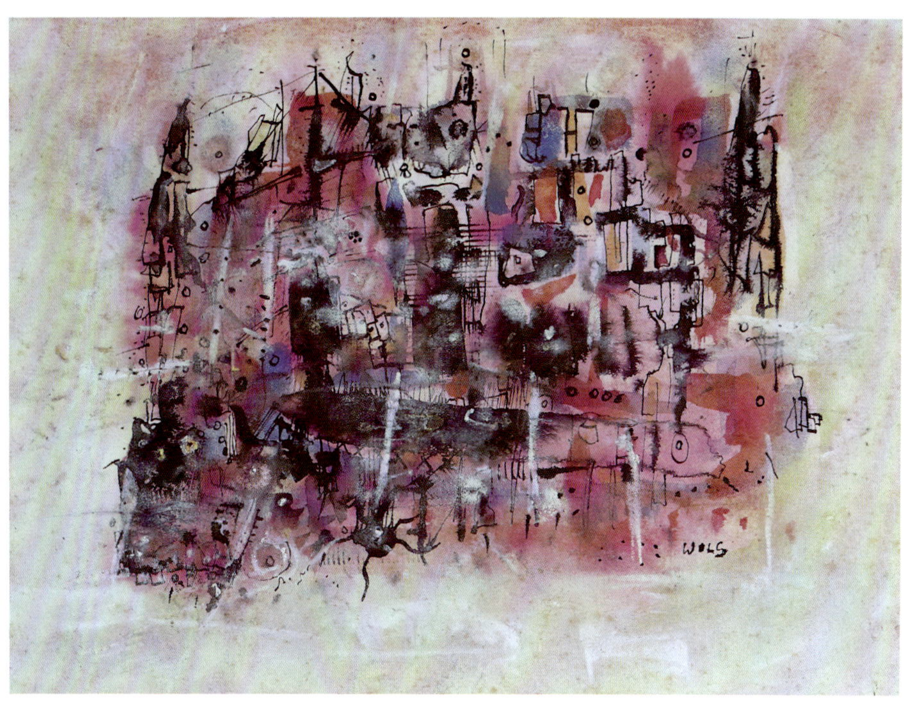

137 The Pink City 1945–6
18.5 × 25 (7¼ × 9⅞)

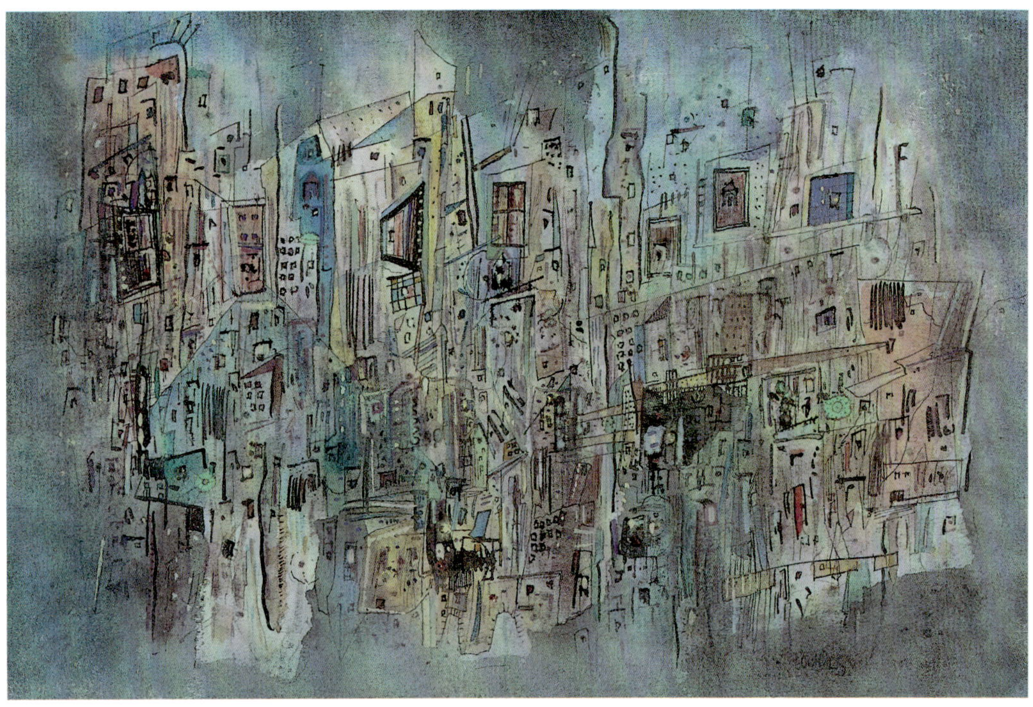

124 Happy City 1942–3
15.7 × 24 (6⅛ × 9½)

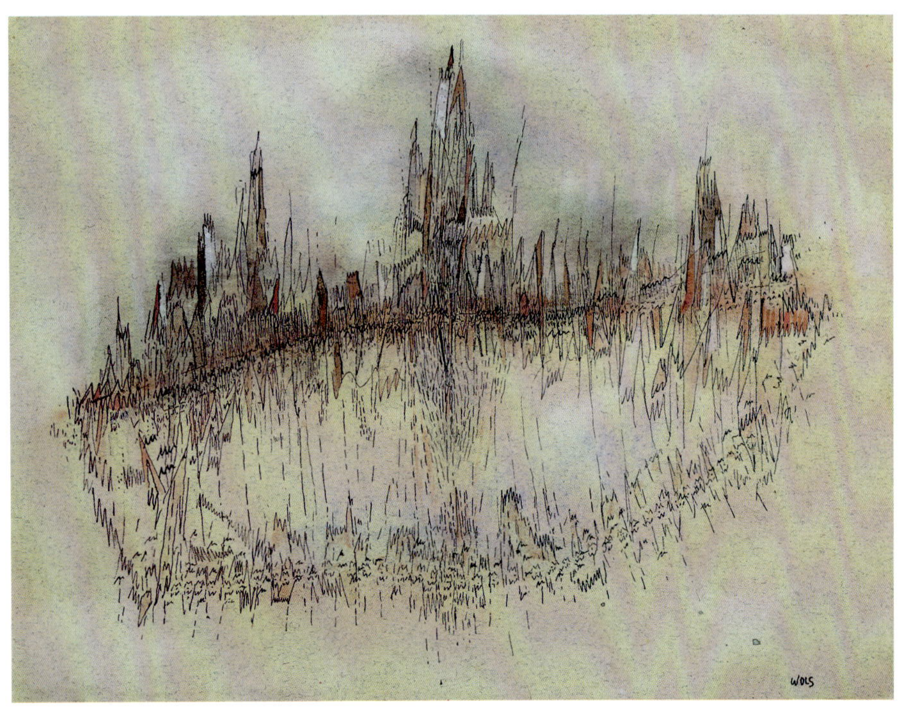

125 Enchantment of a City 1944
15.8 × 21 (6¼ × 8¼)

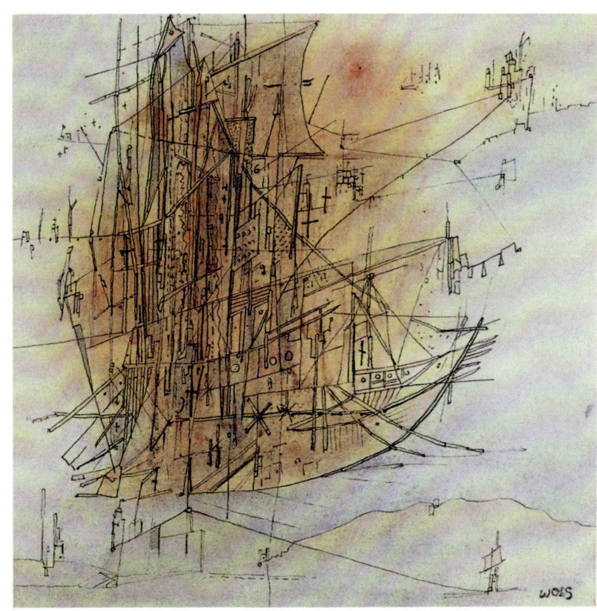

126 Vascello All'ancora 1944–5
13.5 × 13.5 (5¼ × 5¼)

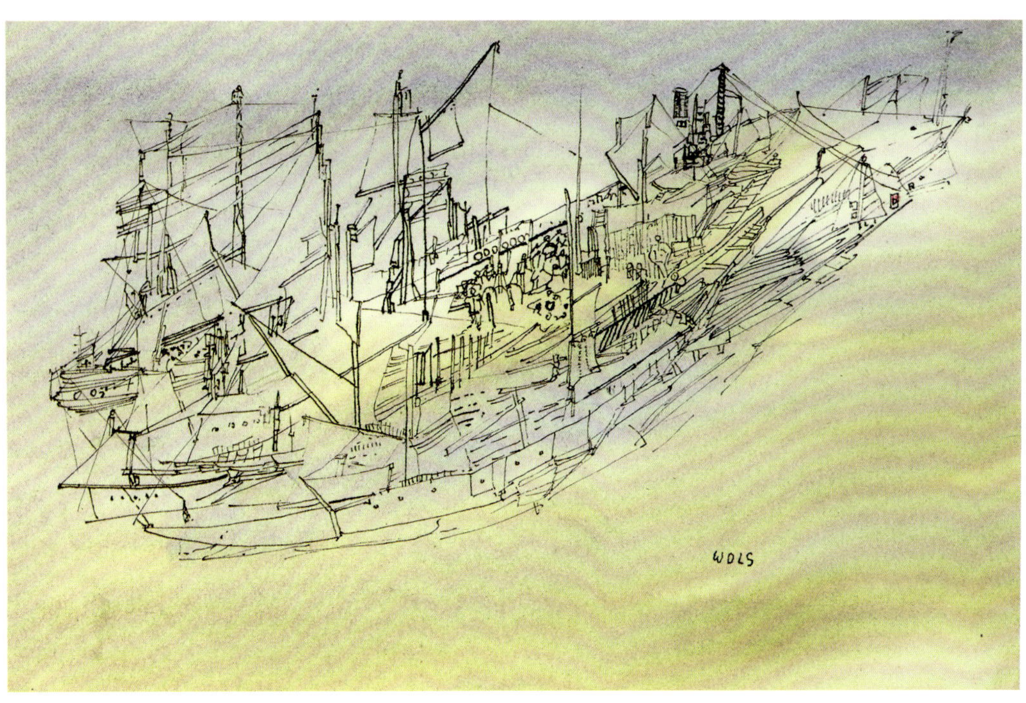

132 Ship on Green and Blue Ground 1945
15.5 × 24 (6⅛ × 9½)

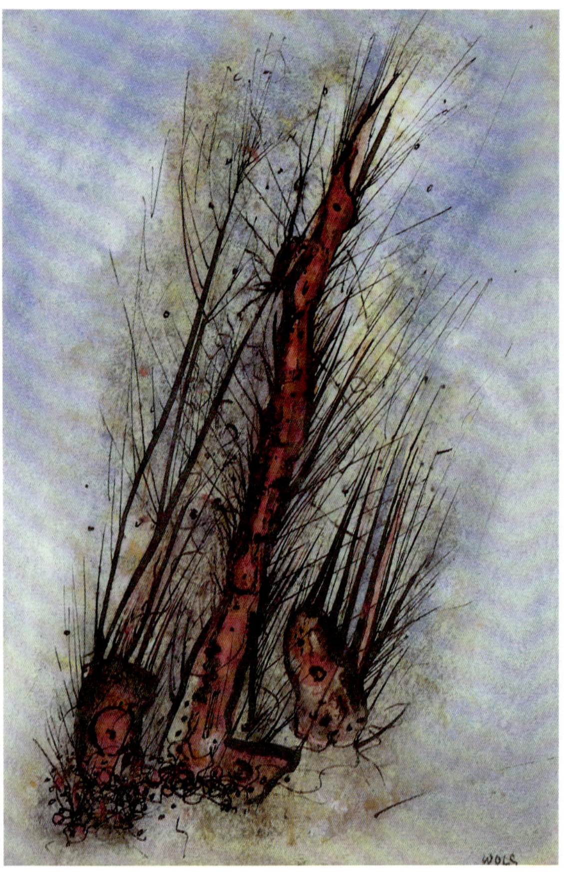

**128 Branching Tree-Stumps
in the Wind** 1944–5
15.7 × 10.5 (6⅛ × 4⅛)

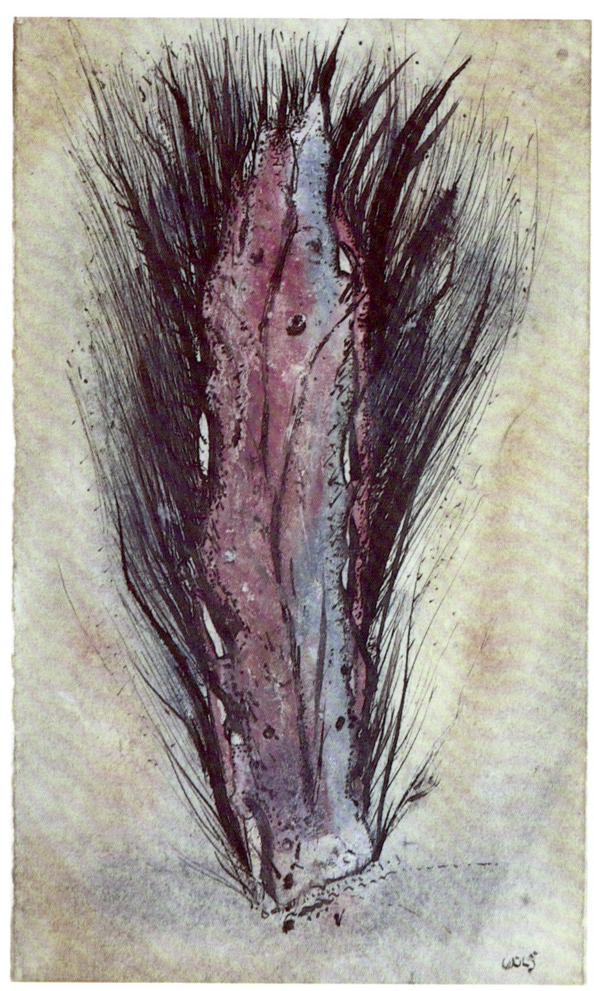

134 The Mad Boar *c.*1945
20.4 × 12.2 (8 × 4¾)

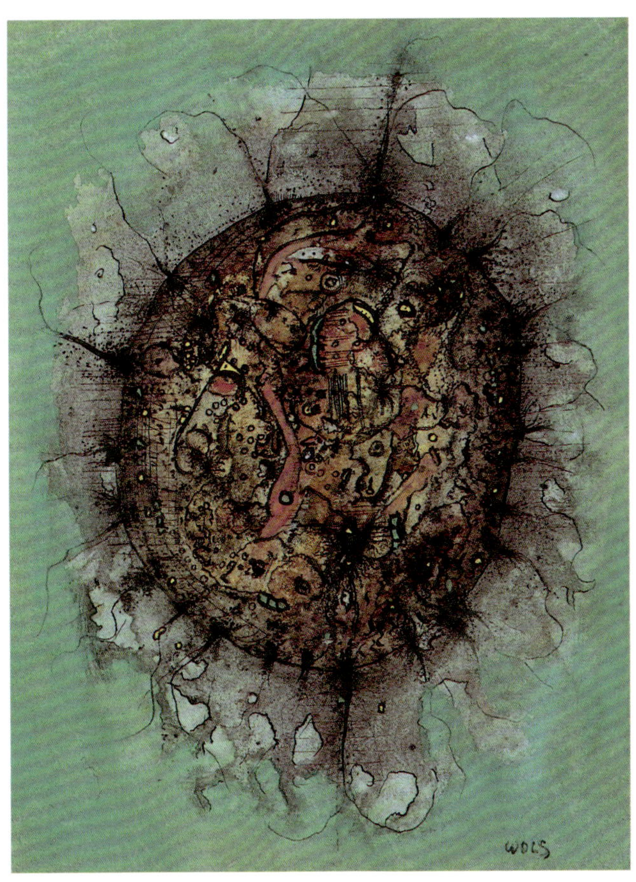

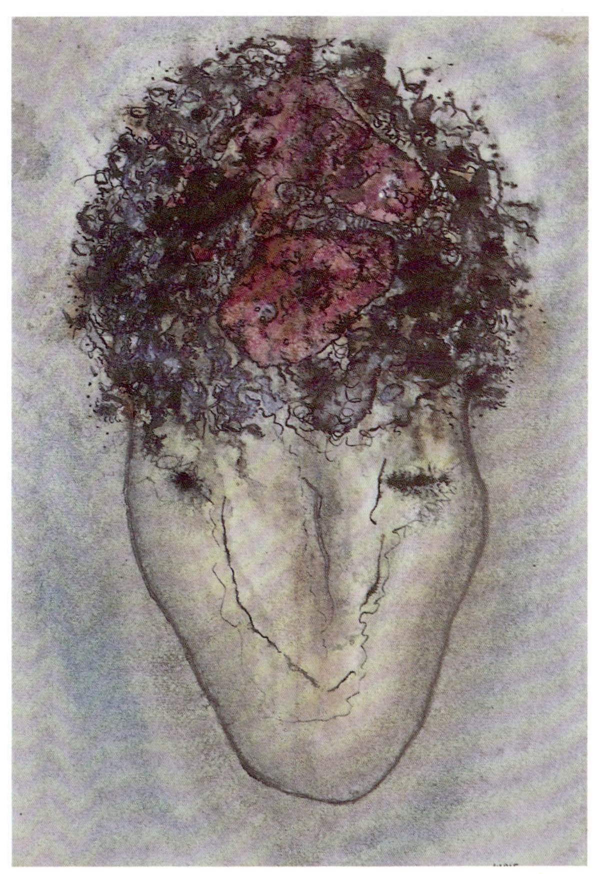

129 Nearby Star (Our Earth) 1944–5
16.7 × 12.3 (6⅝ × 4⅞)

130 Untitled 1944–5
18.7 × 13.3 (7⅜ × 5¼)

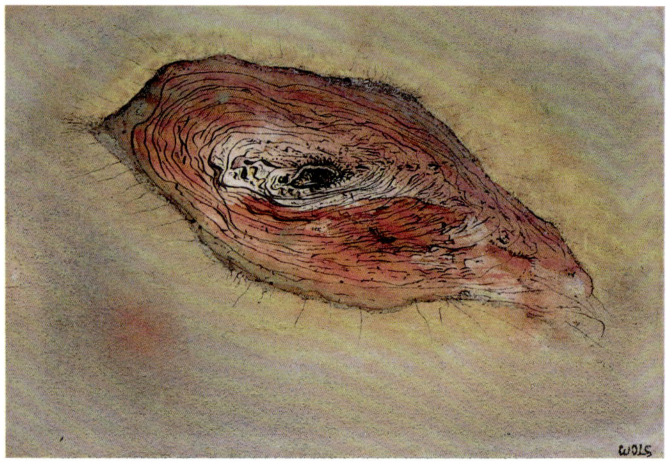

131 Untitled *c.*1944–5
9.2 × 13.5 (3⅝ × 5⅜)

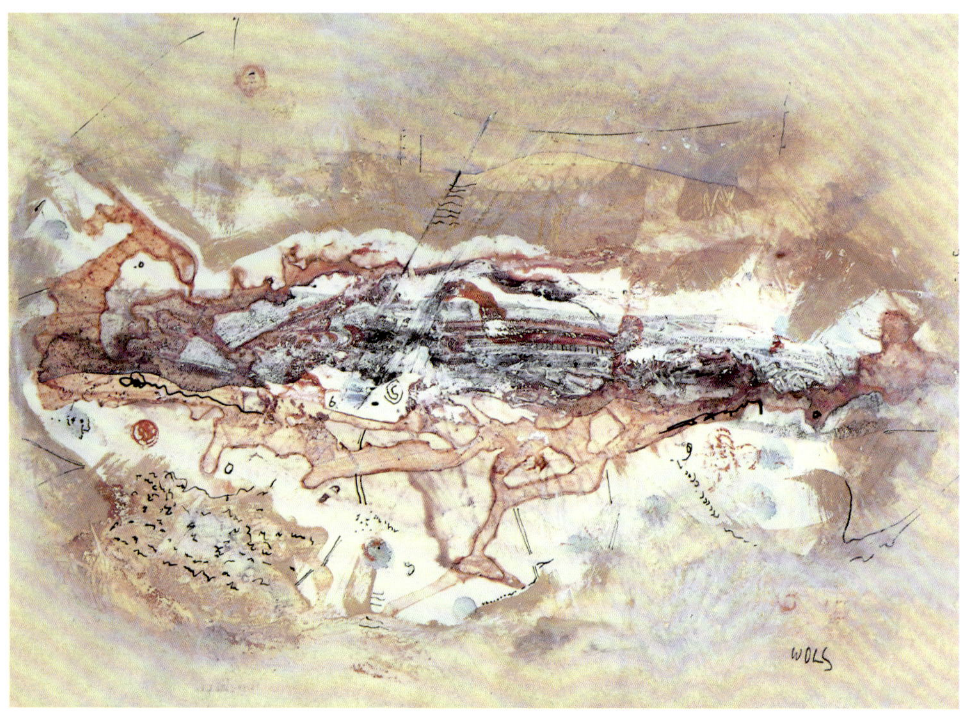

140 Untitled 1946–7
12 × 21.5 (4¾ × 8½)

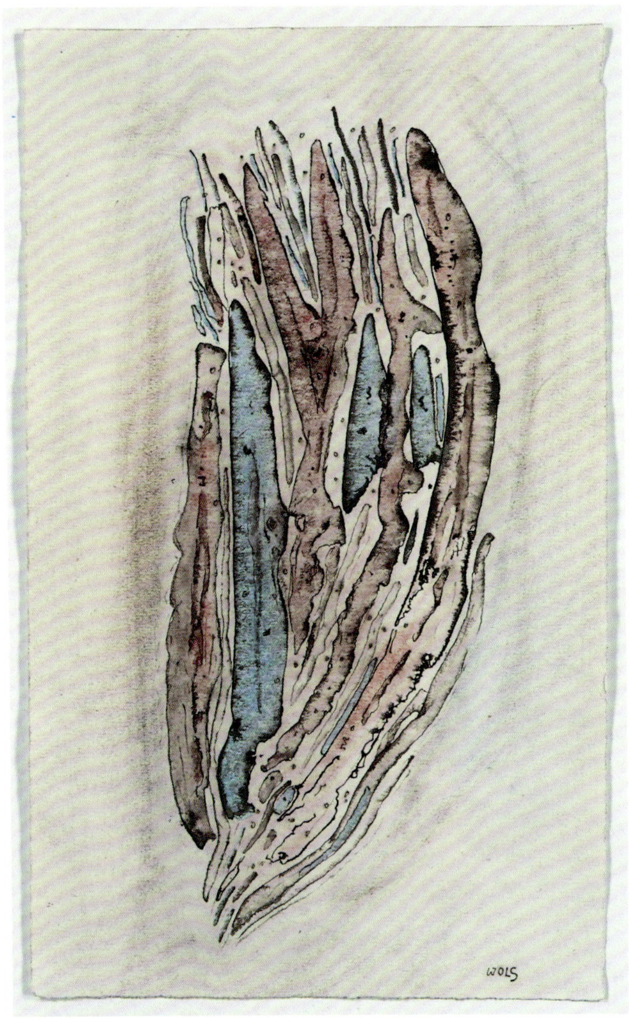

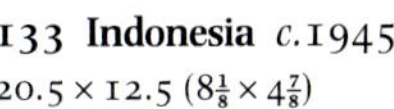

133 Indonesia *c.*1945
20.5 × 12.5 ($8\frac{1}{8} \times 4\frac{7}{8}$)

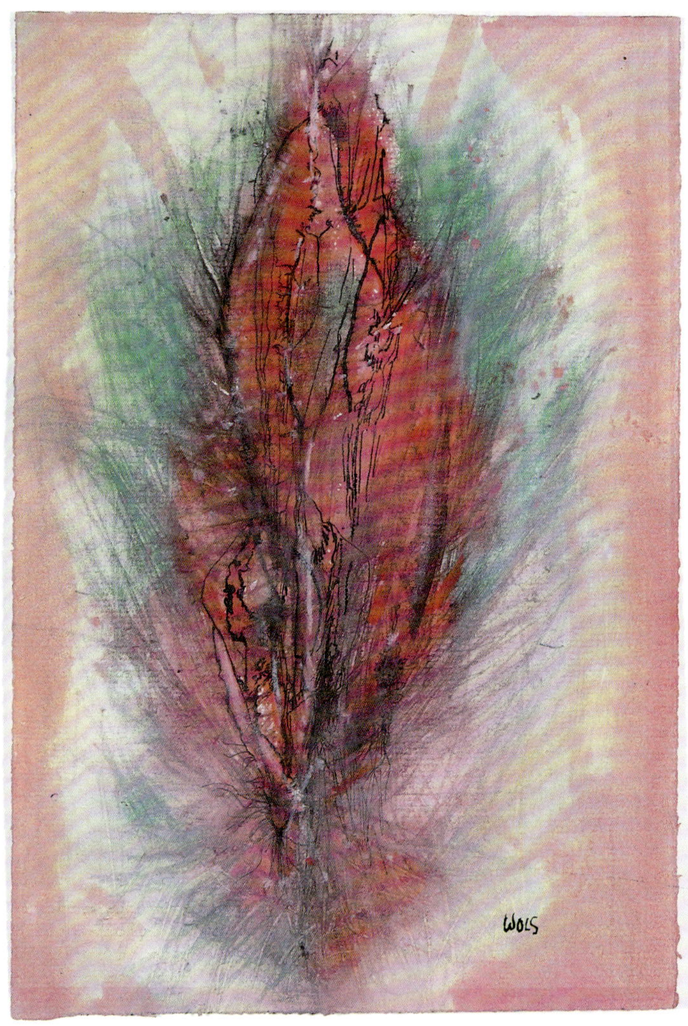

136 The Red Leaf 1945–6
21 × 14.4 ($8\frac{1}{4} \times 5\frac{5}{8}$)

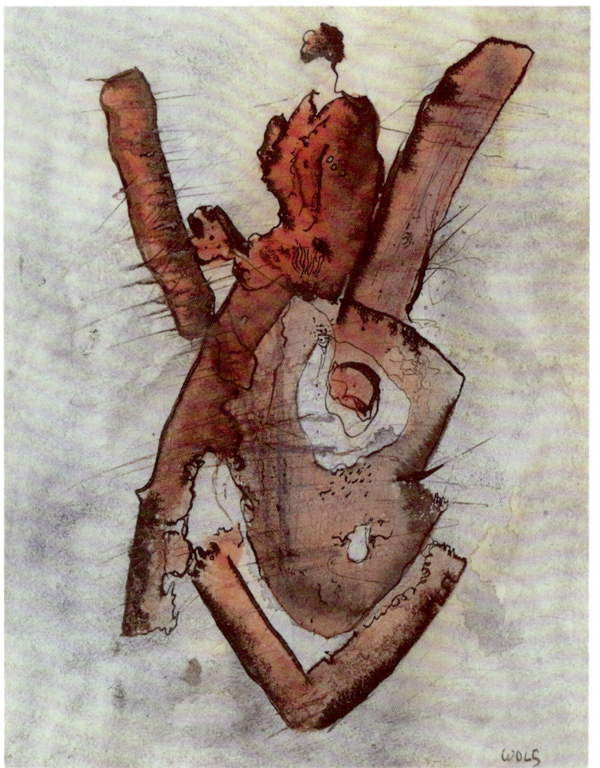

143 Untitled 1950–1
15.5 × 12 ($6\frac{1}{8} \times 4\frac{3}{4}$)

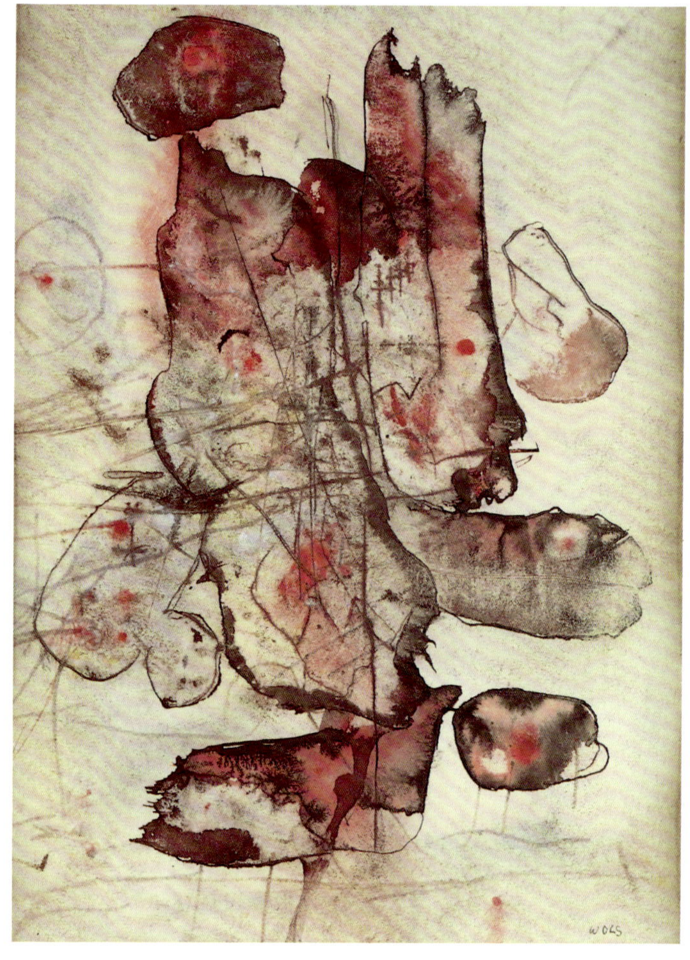

135 Untitled 1945–6
19.5 × 14 ($7\frac{5}{8} \times 5\frac{1}{2}$)

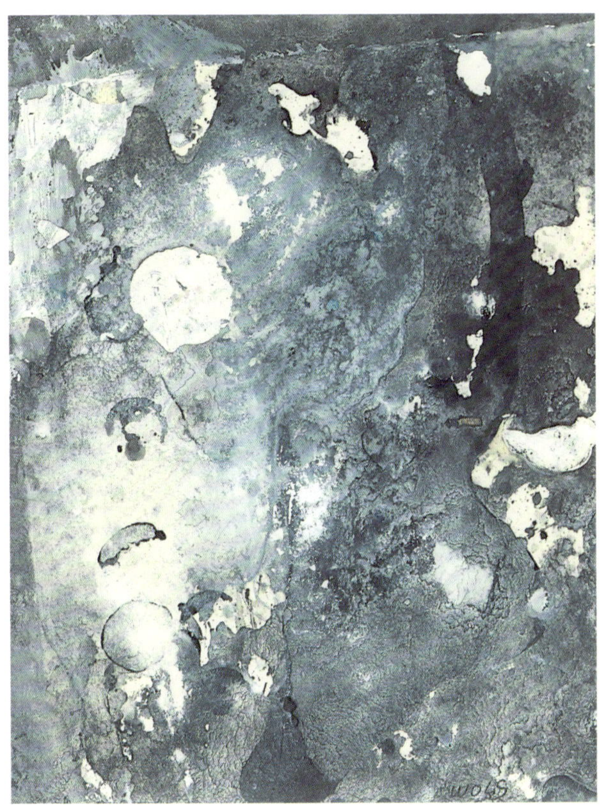

139 Dark Sky 1946–7
16 × 12.2 (6¼ × 4¾)

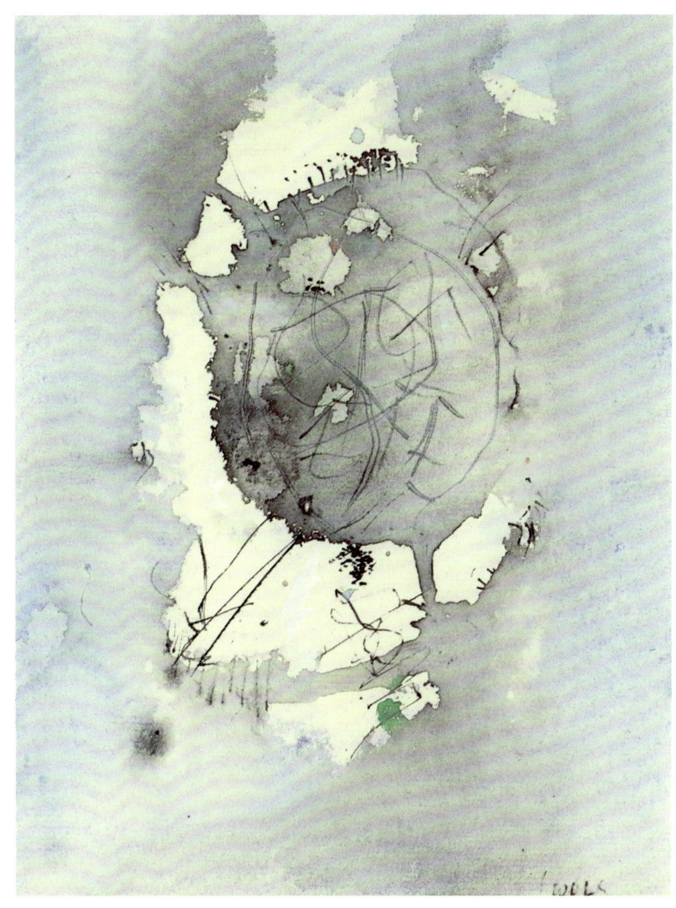

138 Untitled 1945–6
19 × 14.5 (7½ × 5¾)

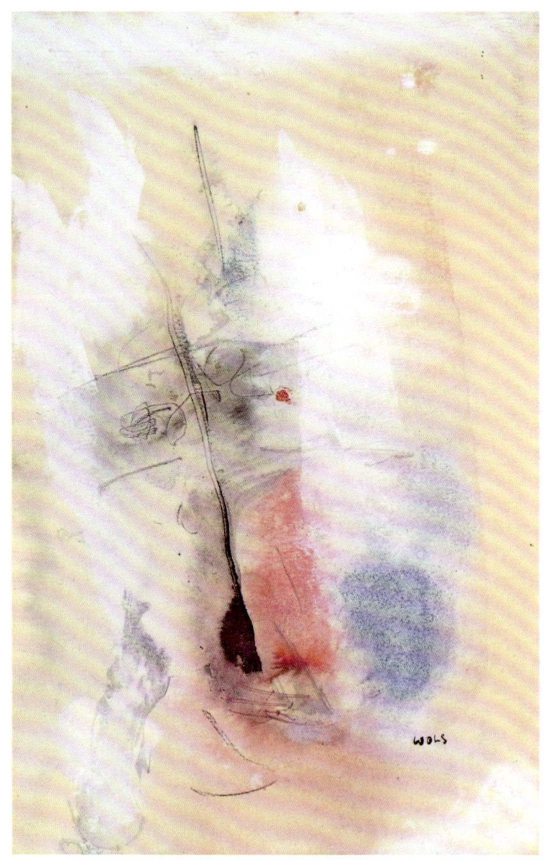

141 Untitled 1949
$25 \times 16.2 \ (9\frac{7}{8} \times 6\frac{3}{8})$

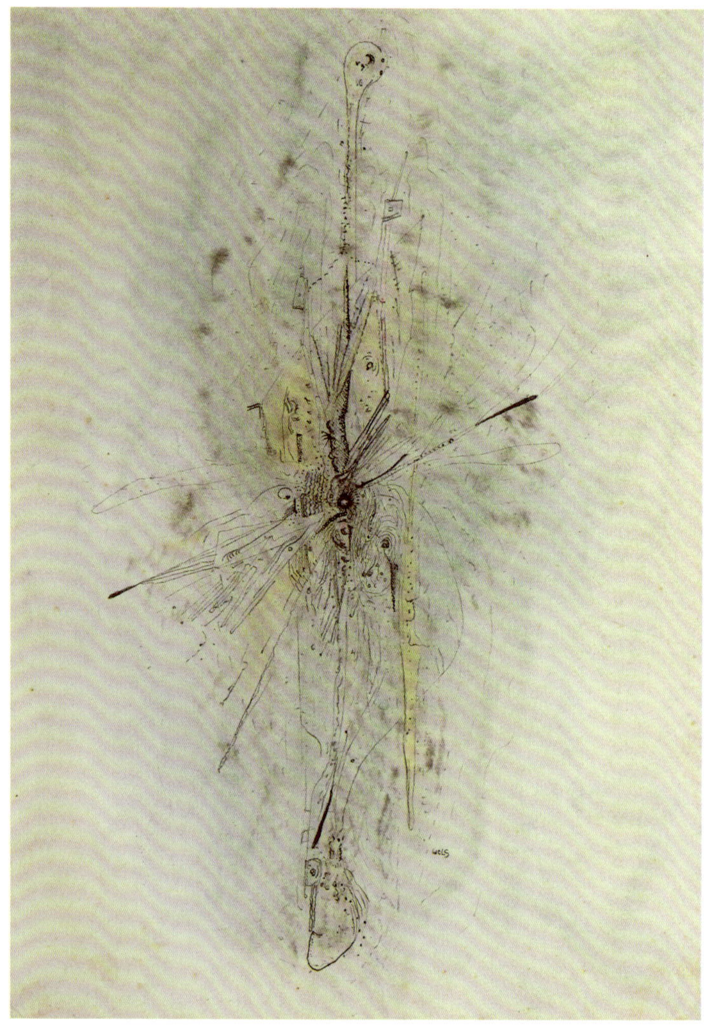

142 Untitled *c.*1949
$30 \times 21.5 \ (11\frac{1}{4} \times 8\frac{1}{2})$

THE WRITERS

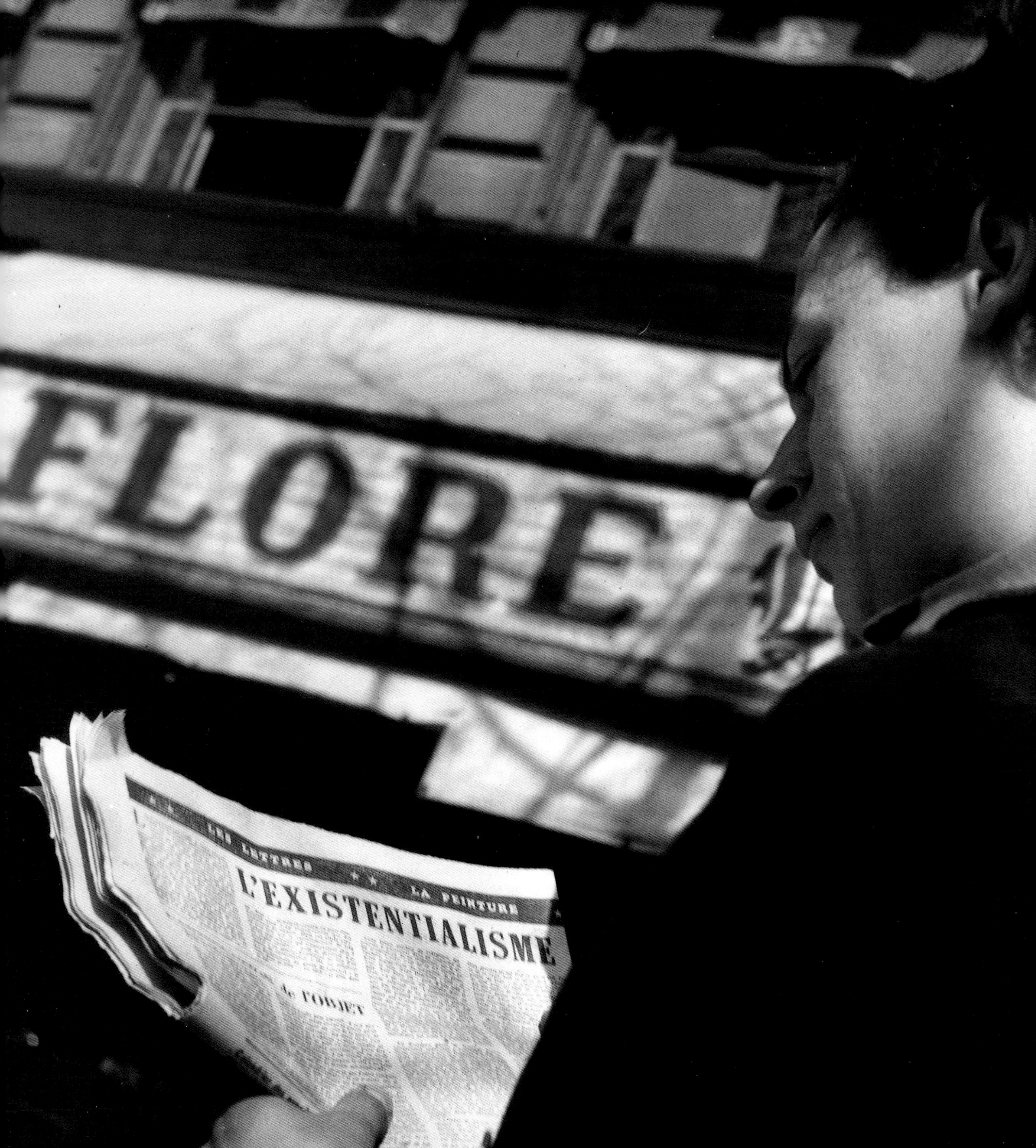
FLORE
LES LETTRES ** LA PEINTURE
L'EXISTENTIALISME

Simone de Beauvoir (1908–1986)

Simone de Beauvoir and Jean-Paul Sartre were famous as a couple during the post-war period: they were lifelong companions and their relationship was both romantic and professional. De Beauvoir was well known in her own right. She trained as a philosopher and went on to create her own distinctive literary and philosophical style despite the difficulties of being the partner of Sartre. 'When they called me "La Grande Sartreuse" or "Notre-Dame de Sartre", it made me laugh, but I was hurt by the way some men looked at me; they were offering a sordid complicity with me in my capacity as an existential – and therefore depraved – woman ... I avoided asking myself any questions about the value of my work, either as it was then or as it would become.'

De Beauvoir was an active figure in the existentialist circle, a vocal left-wing intellectual and a contributor to the review *Les Temps Modernes*. She remains one of the main historiographers of her time: a key eye-witness of the period. *Les Mandarins*, 1954 is a fictional account of the left-wing intellectual community in Paris and the ideological tensions of the early Cold War years. The characters of Sartre, Camus, Raymond Aron and many of their contemporaries are only thinly veiled. The work was a great success and won the *Prix Goncourt* when it was published. The volume of her extensive memoirs entitled *La Force des Choses*, 1963 (*Force of Circumstance*) in which she describes many of the same events is a more direct and detailed but equally vivid account of the post-war period.

Much of de Beauvoir's writing is concerned with issues of existentialist philosophy. *Pyrrhus et Cinéas*, 1944, and *Pour une morale de l'ambiguïté*, 1947 (*The Ethics of Ambiguity*) explores the existentialist notion that man must determine his own relationship to the world since the world is never given to him. Her first novel *L'invitée*, 1943 (*She Came to Stay*), considers the difficulties individuals encounter in their relationships with other individuals. *Le Sang des autres*, 1945 (*The Blood of Others*) is a long meditation on the responsibility involved in action. Set in the 1930s and 1940s, its heroine discovers through love her ability to die for freedom. Having first embraced Nazi ideology she eventually fights for the Resistance. A number of lesser works such as *Tous les hommes sont mortels*, 1946 (*All Men Are Mortal*), and the play *Les Bouches inutiles*, 1946 (*Useless Mouths*) are generally criticised for being *romans à thèse*, perhaps more philosophical than literary.

De Beauvoir was enormously influential in the post-war period, as a feminist and by setting an example in living her life freely and passionately. She devoted herself to the subject of women and her controversial work *Le Deuxième sexe*, 1949 (*The Second Sex*) shocked many of its readers. For many women, this study of women's oppression constituted an important first stage in their awareness of sexual inequality.

opposite L'Existentialisme 1946 Photograph by Willy Ronis © *Ronis/Rapho*

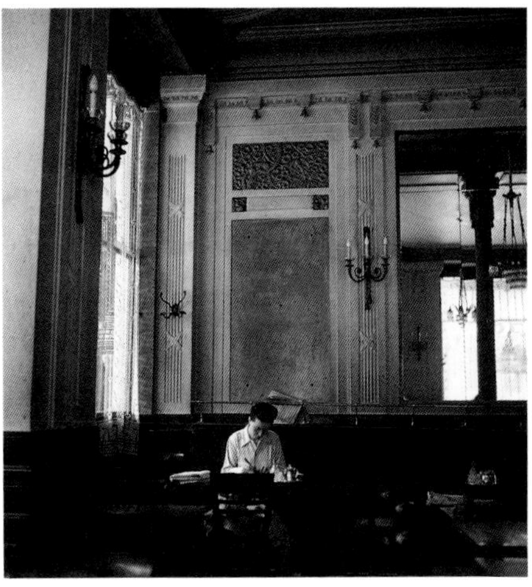

Simone de Beauvoir writing at the Café Les Deux Magots 1945 Photograph by Robert Doisneau © *Doisneau/Rapho*

Samuel Beckett (1906–1989)

Samuel Beckett was born in Dublin and first went to Paris, to teach English, in 1928. He settled there permanently in 1937. In Paris he was part of the literary circle around James Joyce; the importance of Joyce's influence on him is particularly evident in *Murphy*, Beckett's first novel, which was published in 1938.

The post-war decade was the most productive period in Beckett's life. His trilogy, *Molloy*, 1951, *Malone Meurt*, 1951 (*Malone Dies*), and *L'Innommable*, 1953 (*The Unnameable*), unveils the absurd character of life in an atmosphere of hopelessness, helplessness and despair. Aside from the influence of Joyce critics were quick to link Beckett's name with Kafka and Sartre. But apart from favourable notices in reviews such as *Les Temps Modernes*, *Fontaine* and *Transition*, Beckett remained little known until his plays were staged, to tremendous popular acclaim – due, perhaps, to the fact that the mood they convey coincided so well with that of post-war uncertainty. *En attendant Godot* (*Waiting for Godot*) was directed by Roger Blin in 1952, *Fin de partie* (*Endgame*) was premiered in 1957 and *Oh les beaux jours* (*Happy Days*) in 1963. Beckett's work explores notions of the void. His novels and plays are built round a language stripped bare, combined with a tragic humour. In his plays the terror of the void, of waiting, is incarnated in striking dramatic figures. Beckett's importance to the development of the 'new novel' is widely acknowledged.

Beckett also wrote criticism, both as a way of earning a living and as a means of working out his ideas. After the war his critical reviews and essays were exclusively concerned with painting. In 1945 he wrote about the Irish painter Jack B. Yeats, and from 1949 he wrote several pieces about two Dutch painters, Geer and Bram van Velde.

Although Beckett liked to dismiss his writings on the van Velde brothers as 'best forgotten', they have been very influential, and Beckett's opinion that Bram's paintings were 'inexpressive' is frequently quoted and often misunderstood. Much of Beckett's art criticism is really about language and its limitations. He admired art that resisted classification and that could not be reduced to verbal commentary. In this sense alone did he find Bram van Velde's paintings inexpressive. In *Le Monde et le pantalon*, 1945 (The world and the pair of trousers) Beckett argued that van Velde's painting involved the spectator in an exclusively pictorial, perceptual encounter: 'To write "purely visual perception" is to write a meaningless phrase. Obviously. Because every time we want to make words do a real job of transference, every time we want to make them express something other than words, they align themselves in such a way as to cancel each other out. This, no doubt, is what gives life so much charm. Because it is by no means a matter of awareness, but of vision, of simply seeing. Simply! And of the only field of vision that occasionally allows one merely to see, that doesn't always insist on being misunderstood, that sometimes allows its followers to ignore everything in it that is not appearance: the inner field.'

Beckett was a loyal and supportive friend to Bram van Velde. He also admired and respected Giacometti; they first met in the 1930s but only became close friends later, meeting frequently during the mid-1950s. Giacometti designed the set for the 1961 revival of *Waiting for Godot* at the Théâter de l'Odéan, Paris.

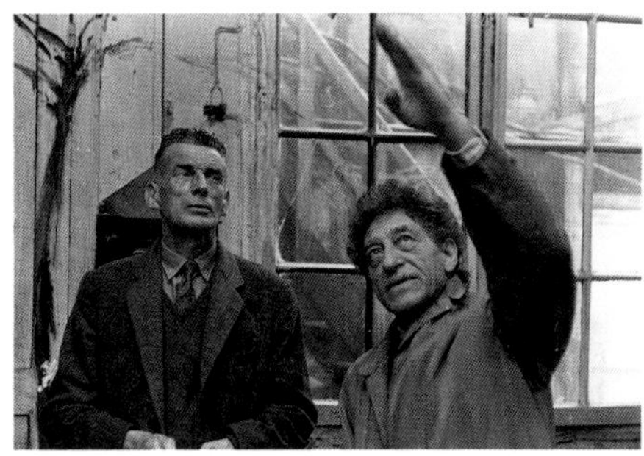

Giacometti in his Studio with Samuel Beckett, 22 April 1961 Photograph by Georges Pierre © *Georges Pierre*

Albert Camus (1913–1960)

Albert Camus is one of the most important literary figures of the post-war period. The ideas developed in his philosophical writings, fiction and plays were crucial to the intellectual and political debates of his time, and exercised a deep influence on the ethical beliefs of this generation.

Camus was born in Algeria and moved to France during the war. He became an important member of the Resistance in 1941 through his involvement in the Combat resistance network and as co-editor of the clandestine newspaper of the same name. His *Lettres à un ami allemand*, an analysis of the moral basis for political struggle against Nazism, was published during that period.

Camus became more widely known as a writer in 1942 when he published *L'Etranger* (*The Outsider*) and *Le Mythe de Sisyphe*. His novel *La Peste*, 1947 (*The Plague*), his role as editor of the Combat newspaper after the Liberation and his plays (*Le Malentendu*, 1944, *Caligula*, 1946, *L'Etat de siège*, 1948 and *Les Justes*, 1949) all contributed to his increasing fame. Camus had a passion for the theatre: as a writer, director, actor and producer he found ways to express the world's meaninglessness. Camus's work explores the feeling of absurdity that arises from the conflict between our desire for rationality and hope and the irrational, meaningless nature of the world. In 1944 he wrote in *Combat*: 'It is true that only one thing has ever been asked of our generation, and that is that it should be able to cope with despair'.

More of a moralist than a philosopher, Camus preached lucidity and rebellion as the only ways of overcoming the absurdity of our condition. 'If we are aware of nothingness and meaninglessness, if we find the outside world absurd and the human condition intolerable, that is not the end of everything. We can't leave things at that. Suicide apart, man's reaction is instinctive rebellion … Hence, our awareness of the absurd leads us to see something beyond it.' This is the message of *La Peste*, a fictional allegory of Resistance, occupied France and more general forms of rebellion against oppression. Camus emphasises the need for fraternity and collective struggle against evil. In *L'Homme révolté*, 1951 (*The Rebel*) however, Camus warns of the potential for disaster in such struggles and denounces state terrorism and dictatorships of either left or right. This was an implicit attack on the Soviet Union and its use of concentration camps. According to Camus no ends could justify unjust means. Camus's views were widely criticised by the revolutionary left wing and by Sartre, his former friend.

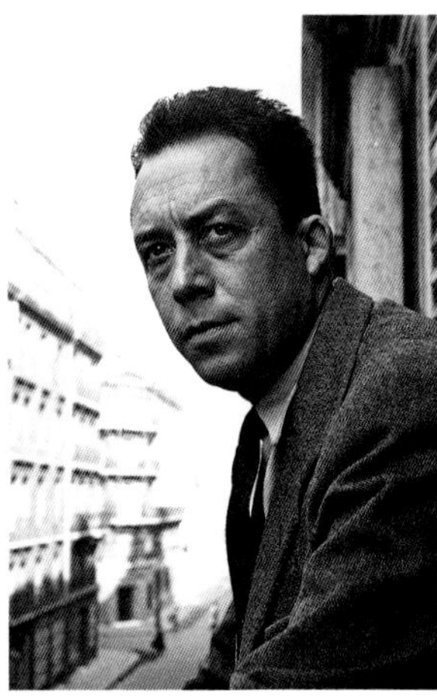

Albert Camus 1952 Photograph by Izis © *Izis/Rapho*

Jean Genet (1910–1986)

During the war Jean Cocteau read the manuscript of *Notre-Dame-des-Fleurs*, 1944 by a then unknown author, Jean Genet. He described Genet and his work as 'Terrible. Obscene. Unpublishable. Inevitable. You never know how to approach him. He is. He will be … For me, he is the great event of our times. He revolts me and enchants me … He is pure, with an intrinsic purity, a purity that is all of a piece. Pure in the sense in which Maritain said that the Devil is pure because he can only do evil. Jean Genet's eye embarrasses and disturbs us. He is right and the rest of the world is wrong, but what can we do?' This uncompromising first novel and those that followed, *Querelle de Brest*, 1947, and *Pompes funèbres*, 1948 (*Funeral Rites*), were nevertheless published, largely thanks to Cocteau.

Genet was abandoned by his mother and was brought up in institutions including the notorious state reformatory, Mettray. He went on to experience the life of a homosexual prostitute, thief, vagrant and finally prisoner. He moved to Paris in 1941 and became involved in the theatre where he continued to express his opposition and his anger. Genet's main theatrical theme, explored in works such as Les Bonnes, 1947 (*The Maids*), and *Haute surveillance* (1949), is that society imposes an image upon the individual which deprives him of his freedom. His theatre represents the act of breaking free.

Genet's work is both attractive and repulsive. His autobiographical novel *Journal du voleur*, 1949 (*The Diary of a Thief*), is a remorseless, violent and uncompromisingly frank confession: 'Betrayal, theft and homosexuality are the essential subjects of this book. There is a connection between them'. He writes in a unique style, blending sordid reality (erotic fantasy and blasphemy) with a coarse yet ceremonial and ornate language.

Genet was introduced to Sartre and de Beauvoir in 1944. In 1952, Sartre wrote a lengthy text about him: *Saint Genet, comédien et martyr* (*Saint Genet: Actor and Martyr*), which was originally intended merely as a preface to Genet's complete works. Sartre depicted Genet as a Sartrian hero whose extraordinary life had been shaped by his own conscious choices and actions. Ironically, the effect of seeing himself laid bare in this gigantic literary and psychological study had the effect of putting Genet off writing for several years.

A solitary man, who did not belong in the literary and artistic worlds, Genet nevertheless found a spiritual companion in Giacometti, whose work he discussed in *L'Atelier d'Alberto Giacometti*, 1958 (*Alberto Giacometti's Studio*): 'Beauty has no other origin than the particular wound that every man carries within himself; it is different for everyone, it may be hidden or visible, but we all hold it dear and retreat to it when we want to leave the world and take refuge in temporary but profound solitude. So this art has nothing to do with what is known as "miserabilism". Giacometti's art seems to me to be aiming at exposing this secret wound in every being and even in every thing, thus allowing it to enlighten them.'

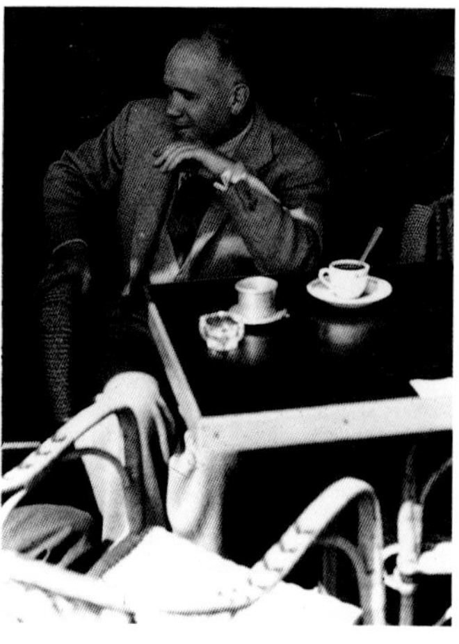

Portrait of Jean Genet Photograph by Georges Dudognon © *Georges Dudognon*

Michel Leiris (1901–1990)

Michel and Louise Leiris hosted the first reading of Picasso's *Le Désir attrapé par la queue* (*Desire Caught by the Tail*), which took place in front of an invited audience on 19 March 1944 and which had been rehearsed by Albert Camus. Leading parts were taken by Michel and Louise Leiris, Jean-Paul Sartre, Simone de Beauvoir, Dora Maar, Germaine Hugnet, Zamie and Jean Aubier, Raymond Queneau and Jacques-Laurent Bost.

Michel Leiris began as a Surrealist and cofounded the Collège de Sociologie with Georges Bataille and Roger Caillois. He was a well-known ethnologist establishing himself with *L'Afrique fantôme* (1934), later banned by the Vichy régime; he was also a writer, novelist, autobiographer and critic.

After the war he concentrated on ethnology and writing. As an ethnologist, working for the National Centre for Scientific Research, he visited Africa and the West Indies in 1945, 1948 and 1952, and in 1948 published *La Langue secrète des Dogons de Sanga*. As a committed writer, he was a member of the first management committee of *Les Temps Modernes* in 1945. In *Biffures*, 1948 (Erasures) and *Fourbis*, 1955 (Rubbish) he developed the original autobiographical approach of *L'Age d'homme*, 1939 (Manhood). These volumes are known collectively as *La Règle du jeu* and pursue an enquiry into the nature of existence, in which confession becomes a form of commitment or risk. Literature, like bullfighting, involves expression and courage. Michel Leiris reconstructed the past bit by bit, scrap by scrap, in order to extract 'the rules of the game' – of the game he was going to play from then on. In an important text of 1946 entitled 'De la Littérature considérée comme une tauromachie' (Literature considered as a bullfight), published in *Les Temps Modernes*, Leiris defined his commitment to and through literature, thus more or less aligning himself with the notions championed at the same period by Jean-Paul Sartre.

Leiris had close relationships with a number of

artists including Masson, Miró, Giacometti, Picasso and Francis Bacon. In discussing their work he developed an unusual style of writing on art: demonstrating his interest in these artists by introducing themes close to his heart – fetishism with Giacometti, the void with Miró –while never making use of them to talk about himself. 'When I write about Picasso, I talk about Picasso, not about myself.' His writings on art are rigorous, dense and precise. Neither the work of a historian nor of a critic, they are attempts at a kind of documentary transcription of visual perception, an exploration of the question of art starting from points in common, and a search for the self through the other.

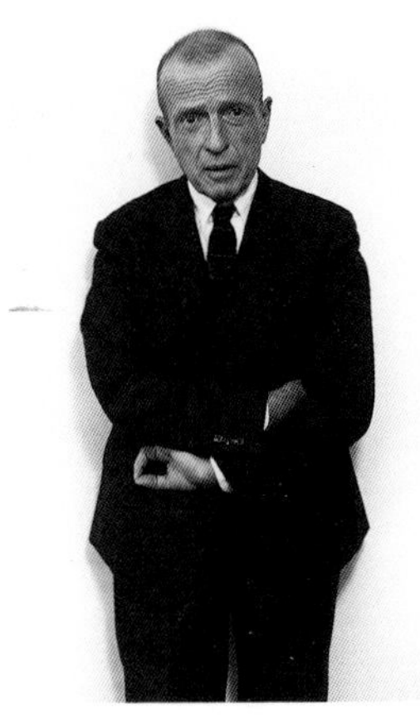

Michel Leiris 1966 Photograph by Daniel Faunières © *Daniel Faunières*

André Malraux (1901–1976)

According to Jean Cocteau, 'the great tragedy of France is that its politicians are unsuccessful writers and its writers are unsuccessful politicians'. Among the former he numbered de Gaulle and among the latter André Malraux, who served as de Gaulle's Minister of Culture from 1958–68. Aside from his controversial career as a politician Malraux had a spectacular and extraordinarily varied life as an archaeologist, adventurer, revolutionary, Resistance fighter, journalist, art critic, theorist and novelist.

During the 1920s Malraux's interest in archaeology took him to Indo-China, where he became involved in the smuggling of ancient statues. He then became embroiled in the nascent anti-Imperialist, revolutionary movement, participating as a journalist and propagandist. The following decade found him back in France fighting against the rise of Fascism – Malraux was one of the first to volunteer for the Republican cause in Spain. During the Second World War he fought as a private soldier. He was captured by the Germans but managed to escape and went on to distinguish himself in the Resistance. He met de Gaulle on the Alsatian front, and served as his Minister of Information from 1945–6.

Malraux established a reputation as a novelist with his third novel, *La Condition humaine*, 1933 (*Man's Fate*), in which he combined the style of a thriller with a cinematic technique. Its theme is anti-colonial: existential anxiety is appeased through revolutionary struggle. *L'Espoir*, 1937 (*Days of Hope*) was about his experiences in Spain. It was followed in 1943 by *Les Noyers de L'Altenburg* (*The Walnuts of Altenburg*), best known perhaps for its vivid recreation of the madness of Nietzsche. Malraux's novels are above all about human adventure, action, leadership and the exercise of will. Although they reveal his early left-wing leanings, Malraux's later swing to the right and his loyalty to de Gaulle are anticipated in the admiration they reveal for men of action.

In Paris, before the war, Malraux was a well-known society figure, involved in all aspects of French cultural life and, as artistic director of Gallimard's publishing house and a committee member of *La Nouvelle Revue Française*, an influential figure. He had been interested in contemporary visual art from a very early age, was a passionate admirer of Picasso and one of the first to appreciate the quality of Fautrier's work. To Malraux art, like other forms of action, was a way of questioning human destiny and responding to it. The message of his controversial *Les Voix du silence*, 1951 (of which *Le Musée imaginaire* was the first volume) was that art, unlike politics, is the only permanent expression of man's will over fate.

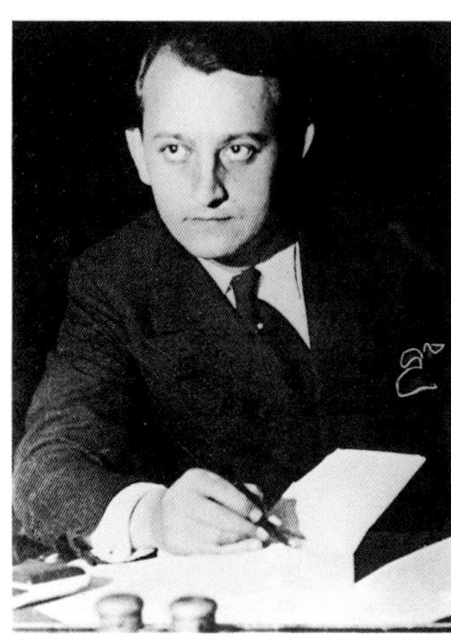

André Malraux 1945

Maurice Merleau-Ponty (1908–1961)

Certainly less well known than his friends and colleagues Jean-Paul Sartre and Simone de Beauvoir, Maurice Merleau-Ponty nevertheless played a vital role in the philosophical development of existentialism. He was a professor of philosophy at the Sorbonne and was given the prestigious chair of philosophy at the Collège de France in 1952. His retiring temperament prevented him from achieving wider acclaim.

In contrast to other French existentialists, Merleau-Ponty wrote no novels or plays and expressed himself largely through academic-philosophical works. His approach, like Sartre's, derived from German phenomenological sources, and Edmund Husserl was an enduring influence. Merleau-Ponty's major texts were *La Structure du comportement*, 1942 (*The Structure of Behaviour*) and *Phénoménologie de la perception*, 1945.

Merleau-Ponty's stated purpose was 'to understand the relations between consciousness and nature: organic, psychological or even social'. He found the key to these relationships in perception and his aim was to describe how perception works. Merleau-Ponty's view of human existence stressed the preconscious origin of man's conscious activity. He rejected a mind/matter dualism and argued that man's physical body is the basis of his perception, for 'things in the world are given to me with parts of my body, in a living connection, comparable or rather identical with that which exists between the various parts of my body'.

Art and artists figure prominently in Merleau-Ponty's writings. For him the human world was a world of contingence and ambiguity. He believed that it was above all in the arts – in literature, music and painting – that the meanings and truths bound up in physical reality and experienced only through the senses, could be unveiled. He was also interested in the process of painting. In *L'Oeil et l'esprit*, 1964 (*The Eye and the Mind*), published after his death, he wrote 'The painter ''apporte son corps'' (brings his body), as Paul Valéry said ... It is by lending his body to the world that the painter changes the world into painting. To understand these transubstantiations we have to discover the actual, effective body, the one that is not just a bit of space, a bundle of functions, but is an interweaving of vision and movement'. His writings were of enormous interest to artists experimenting with new materials and gestural techniques of expression.

As the political editor of *Les Temps Modernes*, Merleau-Ponty was also an influential political thinker and he played an important role, as Sartre himself confessed, in the latter's political education. In *Humanisme et terreur*, 1947

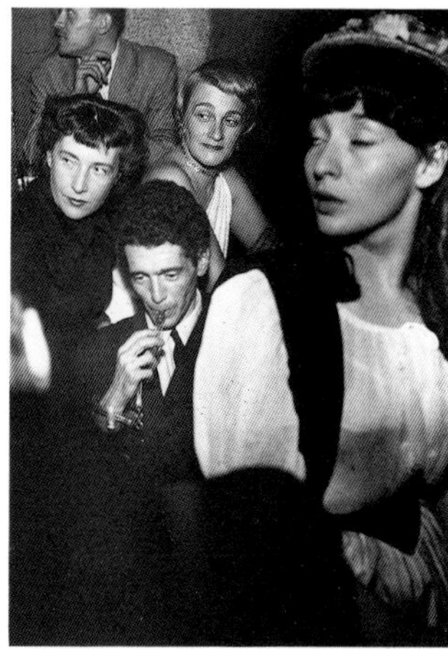

Portrait of Maurice Merleau-Ponty, with Nicole Védrès and Juliette Gréco Photograph by Georges Dudognon © *Georges Dudognon*

Merleau-Ponty affirmed his support for the Soviet Union but acknowledged the dilemmas faced by those on the left when confronted with the harsh realities of current Soviet practice. Merleau-Ponty gradually distanced himself from Communism and left *Les Temps Modernes* in 1952 as the review hardened its political views. In *Les Aventures de la Dialectique* 1955 he severely condemned the Soviet Union and denounced Sartre's 'ultra-bolshevism'.

Jean Paulhan (1884–1968)

By 1945 Jean Paulhan's reputation as editor and writer was already well established in Paris. He was the director of the prestigious literary review *La Nouvelle Revue Française*, published by Galli-mard, until 1940 when he was replaced by Pierre Drieu la Rochelle who proved willing to collabor-ate with the Nazi regime. Paulhan, unwilling to collaborate, moved onto the offensive and as part of his Resistance activities he helped launch and then manage the clandestine journal *Les Lettres Françaises*. After the Liberation Paulhan publically protested against the excesses of the *épuration*. He was especially critical of the cam-paign to purge collaborationist writers which was orchestrated by the National Writers' Committee. Paulhan's position in the publishing world made him a powerful behind-the-scenes figure and his patronage was often crucial to young writers. He was also a respected author in his own right and established a reputation with writings on linguis-tics and literature, notably *Les Fleurs de Tarbes*, 1941 and *Clef de la poésie*, 1944. *Sept causes célè-bres*, 1946 was a collection of shorter essays.

Paulhan was passionate about the visual arts and counted a number of artists among his closest friends. He collected art and used all his skills and contacts to promote the artists he most admired. Paulhan had first become interested in modern art during the 1920s and Paul Klee was an early influence. He discerned, in the art that moved him, a mysterious quality, which he often linked to the primitive, and which he found lack-ing in art which – like Surrealism – was created within a system. Georges Braque was the subject of his first essay on an artist, *Braque le Patron*, 1945. During the post-war decade he became a committed and articulate spokesman for less well known and often more controversial artists such as Antonin Artaud and Henri Michaux, both of whom he knew primarily as writers, and Ger-maine Richier and Wols. His great enthusiasms were for Jean Fautrier (*Fautrier L'enragé*, 1949) and Jean Dubuffet (*La Métromanie ou les dessous de la capitale*, 1949, Metromania or the underside of the capital).

He defended his original and often controver-sial aesthetic opinions in catalogue prefaces, cor-respondence and articles on art written for various reviews such as *Les Temps Modernes* (he sat on its original editorial board), the *Cahiers de la Pléiade* (a review he had created in 1946 and which was designed by Fautrier) and *La Nouvelle Nouvelle Revue Française* which he co-directed when it was relaunched in 1953.

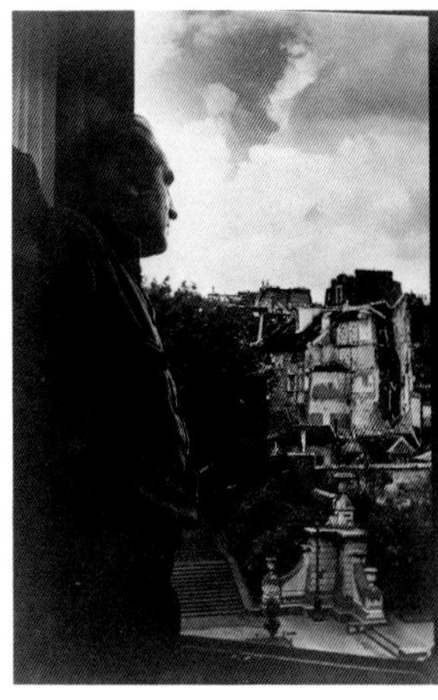

Portrait of Jean Paulhan at 5 rue des Arènes, Paris Photograph by Izis *Archives Paulhan* © *Izis*

Francis Ponge (1899–1988)

It was his collection of poetry, *Le Parti pris des choses*, 1942 (*The Voice of Things*) that brought Francis Ponge to the fore. Jean-Paul Sartre who reviewed it for *Les Temps Modernes* saw in Ponge's stance an example of the phenomenological dis-covery of the world. According to Sartre 'the things he speaks of are specially chosen. They inhabit him, they lie at the heart of his memory, they were present in him long before he had any problems with words: long before he decided to write about them, and his present undertaking is … to fish these seething, flowered monsters out of his inner depths and *express* them rather than to determine their qualities through scrupulous observation.'

Ponge's attitude to life, as explored in his poetry and related writings, shares the absurdist sensibility of Camus and Sartre. Ponge does not see absurdity as tragic but as the condition for self-realisation. After reading Camus's *Le Mythe de Sisyphe* in manuscript Ponge declared 'Expres-sion is my only resource. The cold fury of expres-sion. Another reason why I describe a million different possible or imaginable things is that I want to rub your nose in your own crap. *Why not a towel, a potato, anthracite? … In every possible tone of voice. In this world with which I have nothing in common, from which I have nothing to hope [for] (we're too wide of the mark), why shouldn't I begin, arbitrarily' (Francis Ponge, Pages bis*, 1941–3).

Devoting himself to 'things' – a wasp, a carna-tion, a branch of mimosa, a bar of soap, a shrimp – the poetry of Ponge describes his approach to and mental involvement with objects. His aim is to show the essence of the thing in itself. His is an infinitely realistic poetry, pure, free of all senti-ment or subjectivity.

After the war Ponge published several volumes of work including a group of short texts in *Proêmes*, 1949 (Preambles) and a collection of notes, recollections and essays in *La Rage de l'ex-pression*, 1952 (The passion for writing). Parallel

to his poems and essays and reflecting his friend-ships with a number of artists he also wrote art reviews including several important longer articles on art among them *Jean Dubuffet: Matière et Mémoire, ou les Lithographes à l'école*, 1945 (Matter and memory, or the study of litho-graphs); *Note sur Les Otages peintures de Fautrier*, 1946 (Jean Fautrier: Note on the Hostages group); *Georges Braque: Le Peintre à l'étude*, 1948 (Georges Braque: the painter at work). He also wrote about Jean Hélion, Germaine Richier and Alberto Giacometti. A feature of his art criticism is that he finds, in art, areas of interest analagous to his own. Furthermore his criticism, like his poetry, is not without humour.

Besides his 'poetic' writing Ponge was at differ-ent times a teacher, journalist and publisher. He was also, from before until shortly after the Second World War, a Communist. He was literary editor of the Communist weekly *Action*, from the Liberation until 1946. His work remained little known beyond a small coterie of French intellec-tuals until the 1960s.

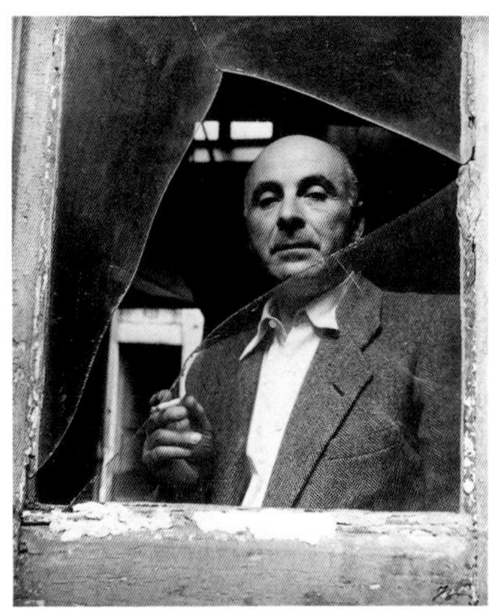

Portrait of Francis Ponge, 9 June 1948 Photograph by Izis *Ponge Collection, Paris* © *Izis*

Jacques Prévert (1900–1977)

Before the war Jacques Prévert had been assoc-iated with the Surrealists and had co-founded a radical theatre company, the Groupe Octobre, for which he wrote plays. He then turned to the cinema and wrote scripts and dialogues, most notably for Marcel Carné for whom he scripted *Le Jour se lève*, 1939 and *Les Enfants du paradis*, 1945.

Prévert wrote poetry throughout his life. His poems are vigorous, often amusing and fre-quently sentimental. He used the medium to attack pomposity and officialdom, and his poems are generally considered to be genuinely popular. One of his most characteristic works is the lengthy comic satire *Tentative de descriptions d'un dîner de têtes à Paris-France*, 1931 (Attempt at a description of a dinner of masked snobs) which was published in the magazine *Commerce*. As most of his other poems remained either unpublished or scattered among obscure reviews, Prévert's early reputation was largely due to word of mouth. It was greatly enhanced by the cabaret performance of his poems by such singers as Agnès Capri and Marianne Oswald; and after the war he collaborated with the composer Joseph Kosma, producing material for Juliette Gréco, Yves Montand, Mouloudji and the Frères Jacques.

In 1945 the writer René Bertelé brought a group of Prévert's poems together and the collection was published as *Paroles*, 1945 (*Words*). This brought him immediate popular acclaim. Other collections followed, including *Histoires*, 1946, *Spectacle*, 1951 and *La Pluie et le beau temps*, 1955 (*Rain and fine weather*).

Prévert's extraordinarily charismatic personality made him a prominent figure in left-bank society. He was a frequent visitor to the Café de Flore in Saint-Germain-des-Prés where his company of friends formed an alternative (sometimes overlapping) circle to that of Jean-Paul Sartre and Simone de Beauvoir. In 1946 Georges Bataille wrote 'his conversation is the most direct, and without exaggeration the most brilliant I have ever known'.

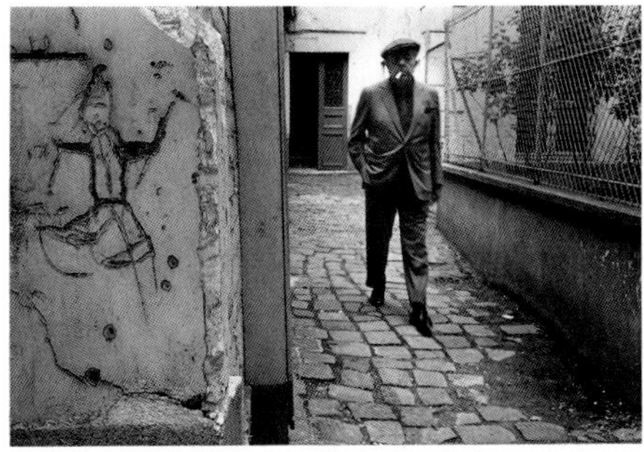

Portrait of Jacques Prévert Photograph by Robert Doisneau © *Doisneau/Rapho*

Jean-Paul Sartre (1905–1980)

As a writer, philosopher and political activist Jean-Paul Sartre was the great intellectual hero of the post-war period. Sartre's philosophical stance was explained in *L'Etre et le néant* (*Being and Nothingness*) published in occupied Paris in 1943. Sartre had worked on it during his time as a German prisoner of war from 1940–1 and then completed it back in Paris while involved in the Resistance. German existential phenomenology was a primary influence, especially the writings of Edmund Husserl and Martin Heidegger. Sartre adopted the phenomenological method which rejects abstract reasoning in favour of observation and description. He observed a fundamental distinction between consciousness (nothingness) and the phenomenal world of objects (being) which consciousness perceives. Beyond the dense and complex arguments the message that filtered through and that Sartre reiterated in countless texts – on art, philosophy and politics – was that in a godless universe man must both define himself and find his own reason for living.

Alienation, anguish and freedom are experienced when individuals confront the implications of this awesome truth.

Sartre's message is both hopeful and tragic. In an essay of 1944 he called on his contemporaries to assume responsibilty for themselves: 'Man must create his own essence; it is by throwing himself into the world, by suffering and fighting in it, that he gradually defines himself … Man cannot will anything until he has understood that he can count on no one but himself, that he is alone on earth, abandoned in the midst of infinite responsibilities, with neither help nor succour, with no other goal than the one he carves out for himself on this earth'. When he addressed a wider public in his 1945 lecture, 'L'Existentialisme est-il un humanisme?' (published in 1946), he explained the ethical dimension of his philosophy: in choosing for himself the individual commits the whole of humanity.

Sartre's plays, stories and novels anticipated and extended the scope of his philosophical writings. Together with the fictional writings of his companion Simone de Beauvoir they were the means by which existentialism was popularised. His first novel, *La Nausée*, 1938 (*Nausea*), describes the sensation of revulsion that its hero Roquentin experiences when he encounters the overwhelming physical existence of the material world around him. *Le Mur*, 1939 (*Intimacy*) is a collection of short stories in which the characters face an invisible wall preventing them from escaping their own existence. His most famous play is *Huis Clos*, 1944 (*In Camera*) in which three individuals, each of whom has been guilty of bad faith, meet in Hell. 'Hell is other people' is how one of the characters describes their torment. Issues of individualism versus collectivism were explored in the trilogy, *Les Chemins de la liberté*, 1945–9 (*The Roads to Freedom*).

Sartre's broad-ranging activities commanded critical attention from the press and respect and admiration among intellectuals at home and abroad. He was a local of Saint-Germain-des-Prés, home of the major French publishing houses, educational establishments, cheap accommodation and jazz-nightclubs. His presence there, and his public friendships with many of the younger set, including the singer Juliette Gréco and Boris Vian, helped draw the attention of the local and then the international press. During the post-war decade Sartre was both an intellectual and social celebrity, and 'existentialism' had both a serious intellectual constituency and a popular, fashionable following.

The need for a journal to reflect their own views encouraged Sartre and a group of likeminded individuals to found *Les Temps Modernes* in 1946. De Beauvoir, Raymond Aron, Merleau-Ponty, Paulhan and Leiris were also behind the review. *Les Temps Modernes* was the main outlet for Sartre's many articles on politics, philosophy and art during this period. His essays reflect his deepening involvement in French politics and although he never became a member of the Communist Party he was, until Soviet troops entered Budapest in 1956, a prominent admirer of the Soviet Union. Camus's opposing view, explained in *The Rebel*, prompted the quarrels that ended their close friendship. After 1956 Sartre evolved his own version of socialism in

which he tried to reconcile Marxism and existentialism. This is the subject of his *Critique de la raison dialectique*, 1960 (*The Problem of Method*).

Throughout his life Sartre was fascinated by creative individuals whose lives were dedicated to their art. He came to know and admire Giacometti, Genet, Ponge, Wols and André Masson. Sartre was interested in art that reflected his own philosophical interests, and also in the status of the work of art as an imaginary object. Although he never wrote a systematic study of aesthetics he devoted many articles to art and artists while his novels and plays are full of references to artists and works of art.

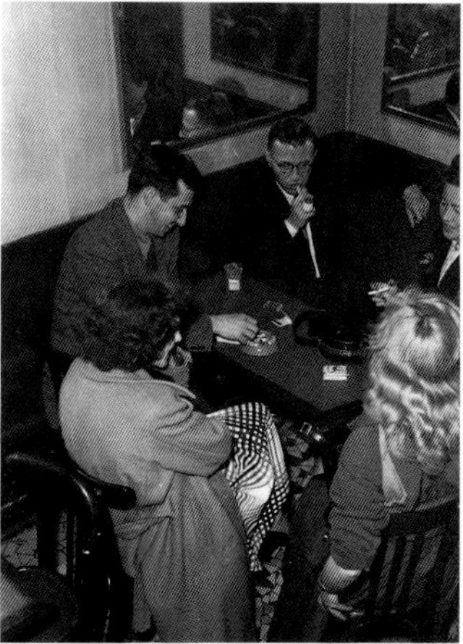

Corner Table with Jean-Paul Sartre, Simone de Beauvoir, Jacques Laurent and Olga Bost and Michelle Léglise, wife of Boris Vian Photograph by Georges Dudognon © *Georges Dudognon*

Michel Tapié (1909–1987)

It was after he had seen Fautrier's 'Otages' at the Galerie René Drouin in 1945 that Michel Tapié de Céléyran, a distant cousin of Toulouse-Lautrec, decided to devote his life to art. In the same year he met Jean Dubuffet, and then Henri Michaux, and was powerfully affected by their art. Shortly afterwards he began his career as a critic, essayist and adviser to many galleries. He was associated with the Galerie René Drouin, the Luxembourg, Galerie Colette Allendy and Galerie Facchetti.

Before the war Tapié had been an art student, jazz double-bass player and a member of Les Réverbères, a group influenced by Dada. He based his post-war activities on the Dadaist notion of a *tabula rasa* and declared that creative authenticity demanded extreme degrees of feeling and expression: 'Unless it is totally and passionately experienced, art is nothing.' Tapié became a fierce defender of the kind of abstraction then described as 'warm', as opposed to the 'cold' geometrical abstraction defended by such critics as Léon Degand.

Among the artists he supported, Tapié particularly admired the work of his friend Jean Dubuffet. In the catalogue to the exhibition

Mirobolus, Macadam et Cie: Hautes pâtes de Jean Dubuffet at the Galerie René Drouin in 1946 Tapié wrote: 'A page has definitely been turned. Only yesterday what was expected from a painting was a sense of permanence, of balance, if not of tranquility. But today the work of art we find most overwhelming is the one charged with the most dynamic, dionysiac power, a kind of living matter in a permanent state of magical ferment.' The following year Dubuffet invited Tapié to manage the *Foyer de l'art brut*, a space in the Galerie René Drouin specially dedicated to his collection of 'outsider art'. Later Tapié contributed to the creation of La Compagnie de l'Art Brut and included his own *art brut* objects in the 1948 exhibition *H.W.P.S.M.T.B* at the Galerie Colette Allendy.

Michel Tapié was the first to introduce the works of the young American artists, Jackson Pollock, Willem de Kooning and Sam Francis to Paris and to show them alongside French artists in the exhibition *Véhémences confrontées* (Opposing Forces) at the Galerie Nina Dausset in 1951. He gathered under his wing not only Fautrier, Dubuffet, Michaux and Wols, but also the younger generation which included Bryen, Hartung, Mathieu and Riopelle. The two exhibitions *Les Signifiants de l'informel* I and II held in 1951 and 1952 respectively and the international overview entitled *Un art autre* in 1952 (all at the Galerie Facchetti) gave Tapié the opportunity to present what he thought of as a radically new trend in art.

Tapié's book *Un art autre*, 1952 (A different art) expressed his views on this new trend in a style that was passionate and flamboyant. His message was for a radical reorientation of values. According to Tapié 'a different art' was urgently needed: 'Today, art cannot exist unless it stupefies. At a time when, for the best and the worst reasons, everything is brought into play to explain and popularise art, true creators know that the only possible way for them to express their unavoidable message is through the extraordinary – paroxysm, magic, total ecstasy.'

Yet Tapié was not aiming at founding a school, a movement. 'It is no longer movements that we consider interesting but – how much more rare! – authentic individuals.' In *Un art autre*, this critic-prophet speaks of ephemeral gatherings of individuals pursuing a common adventure which would transcend form, be full of future possibilities and go to the perilous limits of ambiguity. Its subject would be the human condition with all its fantastic marvels, and it would totally clarify the notions of Beauty, Eroticism, Mysticism and even the Aesthetic. 'And art, at that point, can only be a kind of extremely significant sorcery which leads us, with our eyes wide open, towards the magnificent vertigo of an incredibly violent test far beyond any consideration of "art criticism".'

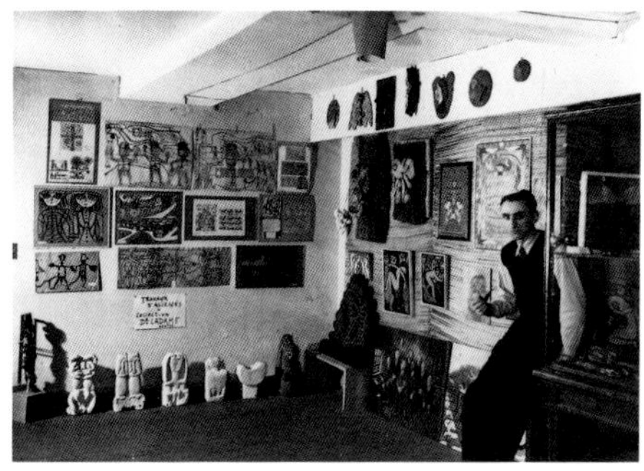

Michel Tapié with the Collection of *art brut* at the Galerie René Drouin c.1947–8 *V. Gille*

Boris Vian (1920–1959)

Boris Vian was intimately involved in Saint-Germain society after the war. His multi-faceted career, as a jazz musician, songwriter, playwright and novelist, brought him into contact with many of the most famous characters of the era. He portrayed his friends, among them Sartre and de Beauvoir, Juliette Gréco and Jacques Prévert, and other well-known personalities of the Left Bank, in his brilliant and irreverent *Manuel de Saint-Germain-des-Prés* published posthumously in 1974.

Boris Vian trained as an engineer but gave up the profession for music. He took up the trumpet and became well known in cellar bars such as Le Tabou. From 1946 he contributed a column to the review *Jazz Hot*. As a performer and music critic he was involved with many of the great black American jazz musicians who made their careers in post-war Paris. Although Vian rarely played the trumpet after 1947, during the 1950s he became an active enthusiast for the nascent rock-and-roll movement in France. He also wrote and performed his own songs, including the anti-militarist ballad, *Le Déserteur*, recorded at the height of the Algerian War.

Vian was first and foremost a writer and is still best known for his first novel, *L'Ecume des jours* (*Froth on the Daydream*), published in 1947, which was described by Raymond Queneau as 'the most heartbreaking contemporary love story'. The novel contains Vian's famous parody of Sartre's influence on French youth. His style is witty – often hilarious – and highly original in its use of word-play. Three further novels confirmed his talent. *L'Automne à Pékin*, 1947, and *L'Arrache-coeur*, 1953 (*Heartsnatcher*) combine humour and disillusion, maintaining a serious and sometimes tragic undercurrent beneath the light-hearted style. His theatrical works include the anarchistic vaudeville *L'Equarrissage pour tous* (*The Knacker's ABC*) – first performed in 1950, three years after its radio transmission – which mocks patriotism and other pretensions, and *Le Goûter des généraux*, 1951 (*The Generals' Tea Party*) an anti-militarist comedy.

Vian also published a number of American-style thrillers under the pseudonym Vernon Sullivan. One of these, *J'irai cracher sur vos tombes*, 1946 (*I shall spit on your graves*), is both violent and erotic and it was widely denounced as decadent. Vian was briefly jailed on a pornography charge and the book was withdrawn from the market.

Vian was only thirty-nine when he died in 1959. In *Jujube*, Juliette Gréco evoked his personality, at once romantic, amusing and grave: 'Boris Vian was handsome, his romantic beauty came from his pallor and dreamy look. All this also concealed a terrible anxiety. A grimace of pain, of disgust, was lurking beneath his fierce smile. He was tall, and he leaned his head over to one side to listen to you talking, or laughing, or crying. With the same gravity as that which darkened his face when he gazed at his little trumpet in the hollow of his too-white hand.'

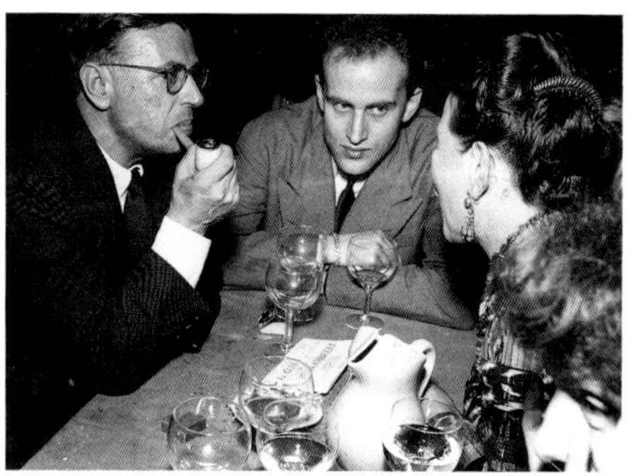

Boris Vian (centre) with Jean-Paul Sartre and Simone de Beauvoir Photograph by Georges Dudognon © *Georges Dudognon*

CHRONOLOGY

1944

THE ARTS

FEBRUARY
Première of Jean Anouilh's *Antigone* at the Théâtre de l'Atelier

MARCH
Death of Max Jacob in the Drancy camp

MAY
Première of Jean-Paul Sartre's *Huis clos* at the Théâtre du Vieux-Colombier

JUNE
Première of Albert Camus's *Malentendu* at the Théâtre des Mathurins

OCTOBER
Salon d'Automne (*Salon de la Libération*) – special Picasso show
Jean Dubuffet exhibition (Galerie René Drouin)

DECEMBER
Death of Wassily Kandinsky

FRANCE

JUNE
Massacre at Oradour-sur-Glane

JULY
Battle of the Vercors
First non-clandestine number of *Combat*

AUGUST
Liberation of Paris

SEPTEMBER
French Forces of the Interior (F.F.I.) incorporated into the army

OCTOBER
Statute on the right of women to vote

DECEMBER
First wave of nationalisations begins (coalmining)

THE WORLD

JUNE
Allied landings in Normandy

JULY
Bretton Woods Conference ends

OCTOBER
Warsaw uprising crushed with much bloodshed

LITERATURE Louis Aragon, *Aurélien*; Georges Bataille, *Le Coupable*; Albert Camus, *Caligula*; *Le Malentendu* (*Cross Purpose*); Paul Eluard, *Au rendez-vous allemand*; Jean Genet, *Notre-Dame-des-Fleurs*; Jean Paulhan, *Clef de la poésie*; Jean-Paul Sartre, *Huis clos* (*In Camera*)
Deaths of Jean Giraudoux, Max Jacob and Antoine de Saint-Exupéry

MUSIC Olivier Messiaen, *Vingt regards sur l'enfant Jésus*

CINEMA Jean Grémillon, *Le Ciel est à vous*
Prix Goncourt, Elsa Triolet, *Le Premier accroc coûte 200F* (*A Fine of Two Hundred Francs*)

1945

THE ARTS

FEBRUARY
Giacometti exhibition (Art of this Century Gallery, New York)

MARCH
First showing of Marcel Carné's and Jacques Prévert's film, *Les Enfants du paradis*
Hélion exhibition (Paul Rosenberg Gallery, New York)

APRIL
Dubuffet exhibition of lithographs, *Matière et mémoire* and *Les Murs* (Galerie André)

JUNE
Picasso libre exhibition (Galerie Louis Carré)

SEPTEMBER
Hommage à Matisse at the Salon d'Automne

OCTOBER
First issue of *Les Temps Modernes*
Exhibition of Fautrier's 'Otages' series (Galerie René Drouin)
Jean-Paul Sartre's lecture, 'L'Existentialisme est-il un humanisme?'

FRANCE

JANUARY
Brasillach condemned to death for collaboration. Charles Maurras sentenced to life imprisonment

APRIL
Marshal Pétain returns to Paris and gives himself up

JUNE
End of press censorship

AUGUST
Pétain's trial ends

OCTOBER
Reform of French social security

NOVEMBER
General de Gaulle becomes head of government

DECEMBER
Reintroduction of bread rationing
Second wave of nationalisations (banks)

THE WORLD

JANUARY
Auschwitz liberated by the Red Army

FEBRUARY
Yalta Conference

MARCH
Proclamation of Independence by Vietnam and Cambodia

APRIL
Death of Franklin D. Roosevelt; Harry S. Truman succeeds him
Mussolini executed
Hitler and Goebbels commit suicide

MAY
Nazi Germany surrenders

JUNE
Signing of the UN Charter

JULY
Potsdam Conference
Labour victory in England

1945 continued

THE ARTS	FRANCE	THE WORLD

THE ARTS

DECEMBER
Exhibition of drawings by Wols (Galerie René Drouin)
Exhibition of Picasso and Matisse (Victoria and Albert Museum, London)
Crimes Hitlériens exhibition (Grand Palais)

THE WORLD

AUGUST
Atom bomb dropped on Hiroshima
Atom bomb dropped on Nagasaki
Japan surrenders
Ho Chi Minh calls for a general uprising

LITERATURE   Louis Aragon, *La Diane française*; Antonin Artaud, *Au pays des Tarahumaras*; René Char, *Seuls demeurent*; Paul Claudel, *Poèmes et paroles durant la guerre de trente ans*; François Mauriac, *Les Mal Aimés*; Maurice Merleau-Ponty, *Phénoménologie de la perception*; Henri Michaux, *Epreuves, exorcismes*; Jacques Prévert, *Paroles*; Raymond Queneau, *Loin de Rueil* (*The Skin of Dreams*); Jean-Paul Sartre, *Les Chemins de la liberté* (*The Roads to Freedom*)
Deaths of Robert Desnos, Pierre Drieu la Rochelle and Paul Valéry

MUSIC   Richard Strauss, *Metamorphosen*; Beginning of Bebop (Charlie Parker, Dizzy Gillespie, Thelonious Monk)

CINEMA   Robert Bresson, *Les Dames du bois de Boulogne*; Marcel Carné and Jacques Prévert, *Les Enfants du paradis*; André Malraux, *L'Espoir* (*Days of Hope*); Roberto Rossellini, *Open City*

1946

THE ARTS

JANUARY
First *Lettriste* demonstration in Saint-Germain-des-Prés

FEBRUARY
Exhibition, *Art et Résistance* (Musée national d'art moderne)

MARCH
Bram van Velde exhibition (Galerie Mai)
Kandinsky exhibition (Galerie René Drouin)

APRIL
First number of *Cahiers de la Pléiade*
Exhibition of Georges Braque and Georges Rouault at the Tate Gallery

MAY
Michaux exhibition (Galerie Rive Gauche)
Dubuffet exhibition, *Mirobolus, Macadam et Cie* (Galerie René Drouin)

JUNE
Picasso exhibition (Galerie Louis Carré)
Picasso retrospective exhibition, *Fifty Years of his Art* (The Museum of Modern Art, New York)
Soirée in honour of Artaud at the Théâtre Sarah Bernhardt
Artaud benefit auction (Galerie Pierre)
Resumption of the Cannes Festival

OCTOBER
First number of *Cahiers de l'Art Brut*

DECEMBER
Exhibition, *Le Noir est une couleur* (Galerie Maeght)

FRANCE

JANUARY
Resignation of General de Gaulle

MAY
Referendum rejects draft constitution

JUNE
General de Gaulle's speech at Bayeux

OCTOBER
Referendum accepts constitution of the Fourth Republic

DECEMBER
Léon Blum becomes head of government

THE WORLD

MARCH
Churchill's 'Iron Curtain' speech at Fulton

JUNE
Proclamation of the Italian Republic

DECEMBER
Uprising in Hanoi. Beginning of the war in Indo-China

LITERATURE   Arthur Adamov, *L'Aveu*; Antonin Artaud, *Lettres de Rodez*; René Char, *Feuillets d'Hypnos* (*Leaves of Hypnos*); Jean Cocteau, *L'Aigle à deux têtes* (*The Two-Headed Eagle*); Jean Dubuffet, *Prospectus aux amateurs de tout genre*; Paul Eluard, *Poésie ininterrompue* (*Uninterrupted Poetry*); Jean Genet, *Les Bonnes* (*The Maids*); André Gide, *Thésée*; Marcel Jouhandeau, *Essai sur moi-même*; Saint-John Perse, *Vents*; André Pieyre de Mandiargues, *Le Musée noir*; Jean-Paul Sartre, *L'Existentialisme est un humanisme* (*Existentialism and Humanism*), *La P . . . respectueuse* (*The Respectful Prostitute*); Boris Vian, *J'irai cracher sur vos tombes*

MUSIC   Pierre Boulez, First Sonata; Benjamin Britten, *Peter Grimes*; John Cage, Sixteen Sonatas and Four Preludes for Prepared Piano

1946 continued

CINEMA   René Clément and Jean Cocteau, *La Belle et la bête*; René Clément, *La Bataille du rail*; Jean Delannoy, *Symphonie pastorale*; Billy Wilder, *The Lost Weekend*

1947

THE ARTS

JANUARY
Lecture, 'Tête-à-tête', by Artaud at the Théâtre du Vieux-Colombier
Death of Pierre Bonnard
Dubuffet exhibition (Pierre Matisse Gallery, New York)
Van Gogh exhibition (Orangerie)

APRIL
Lecture by Tristan Tzara at the Sorbonne, 'Le Surréalisme et l'après-guerre'
Opening of the club Le Tabou in Saint-Germain-des-Prés
Inauguration of the Musée de l'impressionisme at the Jeu de Paume

MAY
Exhibitions: Braque (Galerie Maeght), Wols (Galerie René Drouin), Hélion (Galerie Renou et Colle)

JUNE
Inauguration of the Musée national d'art moderne
Death of Albert Marquet
Exhibition, *Automatisme* (Galerie du Luxembourg)

JULY
International Surrealist Exhibition (Galerie Maeght)
Exhibition of Artaud's drawings (Galerie Pierre)

SEPTEMBER
Publication of *Jazz* by Matisse
Richier exhibition (Anglo-French Art Centre, London)

OCTOBER
Dubuffet exhibition, *Portraits* (Galerie René Drouin)

NOVEMBER
Opening of the *Foyer de l'art brut* (Galerie René Drouin)

DECEMBER
Première of Henri Pichette's *Epiphanies* at the Théâtre des Noctambules
L'Imaginaire exhibition (Arp, Atlan, Brauner, Hartung, Picasso, Riopelle, de Solier, Ubac, Vulliamy, Wols) (Galerie du Luxembourg)

FRANCE

JANUARY
Monnet plan for reconstruction
Vincent Auriol elected president of the Republic
Ramadier head of government

APRIL
Wave of strikes in France throughout the spring
Establishment of the R.P.F. Party (Rally of the French People) by General de Gaulle

MAY
Ramadier dismisses the Communist ministers from his government

DECEMBER
Split within the C.G.T. (General Confederation of Labour)
Establishment of the F.O. (Force ouvrière) union

THE WORLD

MARCH
Military repression in Madagascar

JUNE
Introduction of the Marshall Plan

AUGUST
Declaration of Independence by India and Pakistan

OCTOBER
Establishment of the Cominform

NOVEMBER
UN votes to partition Palestine
Arab countries reject the creation of a Jewish state

LITERATURE   Robert Antelme, *L'Espèce humaine*; Antonin Artaud, *Van Gogh, le suicidé de la société*; André Breton, *Arcanes 17*; Albert Camus, *La Peste (The Plague)*; André Malraux, *Le Musée imaginaire (Museum Without Walls)*; Henry de Montherlant, *Le Maître de Santiago (The Master of Santiago)*; Raymond Queneau, *Exercices de style (Exercises in Style)*; Boris Vian, *L'Ecume des jours (Froth on the Daydream)*
Deaths of Tristan Bernard and Léon-Paul Fargue
Nobel Prize: André Gide

MUSIC   Arthur Honegger, *Deliciae basilienses*; André Jolivet, *Concerto pour ondes martenot*; Benjamin Britten, *Albert Herring*; Arnold Schoenberg, *A Survivor from Warsaw*

CINEMA   Claude Autant-Lara. *Le Diable au corps*; Marcel Carné. *Les Portes de la nuit (Gates of Night)*; Henri-Georges Clouzot. *Quai des orfèvres*

1948

THE ARTS

JANUARY
Giacometti exhibition (Pierre Matisse Gallery, New York)

FEBRUARY
Paul Klee exhibition (Musée national d'art moderne)

MARCH
Death of Artaud

APRIL
Première of Sartre's *Les Mains sales* at the Théâtre Antoine
Première of *J'irai cracher sur vos tombes* by Boris Vian/Vernon Sullivan at the Théâtre Verlaine
Completion of the church of Assy
Exhibition *H.W.P.S.M.T.B.* (Hans Hartung, Wols, Francis Picabia, François Stahly, Georges Mathieu, Michel Tapié, Camille Bryen) (Galerie Colette Allendy)
Michaux exhibition (Galerie René Drouin)

JUNE
Fernand Léger exhibition (Galerie Louis Carré)
Foundation of the Compagnie de l'Art Brut by Dubuffet
Bram and Geer van Velde exhibition (Galerie Maeght)

JULY
Exhibition, *White and Black* (Arp, Atlan, Fautrier, Mathieu, Wols) at the Galerie des deux îles

SEPTEMBER
Opening of the Rose Rouge club in Saint-Germain-des-Prés
Georges Braque awarded the *Grand Prix* of the Venice Biennale

OCTOBER
Picasso exhibition (Galerie Louise Leiris)
Exhibition, *Solution surréaliste* (Galerie Nina Dausset)
Richier exhibition (Galerie Maeght)

NOVEMBER
Picasso exhibition (Maison de la pensée française)
Foundation of the Cobra group

DECEMBER
Death of Francis Gruber

FRANCE

JANUARY
Devaluation of the franc

JUNE
Bread rationing: 250 grammes per head

OCTOBER
Wave of strikes in France, particularly in the coal mines

NOVEMBER
The army intervenes in the coal strike
Coal strike ends

DECEMBER
'Zoé', France's first nuclear reactor, starts operating

THE WORLD

JANUARY
Mahatma Gandhi assassinated

FEBRUARY
Soviet influence in Czechoslovakia

MAY
Establishment of the State of Israel

JUNE
Beginning of the Berlin blockade
Beginning of the American air lift (lasts until May 1949)

NOVEMBER
President Truman re-elected

DECEMBER
Universal Declaration of the Rights of Man accepted by the UN

LITERATURE — Maurice Blanchot, *L'Arrêt de mort*; Jean Giono, *Un roi sans divertissement*; Julien Gracq, *Le Roi pêcheur*; Michel Leiris, *Biffures*; Francis Ponge; *Proêmes*; Antoine de Saint-Exupéry, *Citadelle* (*The Wisdom of the Sands*); Nathalie Sarraute, *Portrait d'un inconnu* (*Portrait of a Man Unknown*); Jean-Paul Sartre, *Les Mains sales* (*Dirty Hands*); Norman Mailer; *The Naked and the Dead*; Ezra Pound, *Pisan cantos*
Deaths of Artaud and Georges Bernanos

MUSIC — Pierre Boulez, Sonata No.2; Henri Dutilleux, Sonata for Piano; Olivier Messiaen, *Turangalîla Symphony*; Pierre Schaeffer, *Concert de bruit* (the first work of concrete music); Richard Strauss, *Four Last Songs*

CINEMA — Jean Cocteau, *Les Parents terribles*; Christian-Jacque, *La Chartreuse de Parme*; Vittorio de Sica, *Bicycle Thieves*; Luigi Visconti, *La Terra trema*

1949

THE ARTS

FEBRUARY
Première of Jean Genet's *Haute surveillance* at the Théâtre des Mathurins
Picasso paints 'The Dove of Peace'. Louis Aragon chooses it to feature on the poster advertising the April Paris Peace Congress

APRIL
Première of Raymond Queneau's *Exercices de style* at the Rose Rouge

JUNE
Matisse retrospective (Musée national d'art moderne)

OCTOBER
Exhibition, *Art brut préféré aux arts culturels* (Galerie René Drouin)

NOVEMBER
Publication of Jean Paulhan's *Fautrier l'enragé* (Galerie Billiet-Caputo)
Ferdnand Léger retrospective (Musée national d'art moderne)
Francis Bacon exhibition (Hanover Gallery, London)

FRANCE

JANUARY
Price freeze

JULY
Dissolution of the courts dealing with the purges

NOVEMBER
End of food rationing

THE WORLD

JANUARY
Mao Tse-Tung's troops seize Peking
Establishment of the Council of Europe
Establishment of Comecon

FEBRUARY
Armistice signed between Israel and Egypt. Peace rapidly spreads to the neighbouring countries

MARCH
First Peace Congress

APRIL
North Atlantic Treaty signed

MAY
End of Berlin blockade
Federal Republic of Germany (West Germany) established

JUNE
Bao Dai enters Saigon

JULY
First Soviet atom bomb tested

OCTOBER
Proclamation of the People's Republic of China
German Democratic Republic (East Germany) established

NOVEMBER
Integration of West Germany into the Western bloc

LITERATURE Louis Aragon, *Les Communistes*; Simone de Beauvoir, *Le Deuxième sexe* (*The Second Sex*); Georges Bernanos, *Le Dialogue des Carmelites* (*The Carmelites*); René Char, *Le Soleil des eaux*; Emile Cioran, *Précis de décomposition* (*Short History of Decay*); Jean Genet, *Journal du voleur* (*The Diary of a Thief*); Claude Lévi-Strauss, *Structures élémentaires de la parenté* (*The Elementary Structures of Kinship*); Jean Paulhan, *Fautrier l'enragé*; Henri Pichette, *Apoèmes*; Curzio Malaparte, *The Skin*; Yukio Mishima, *Confessions of a Mask*; George Orwell, *1984*

MUSIC Pierre Schaeffer and Pierre Henry, *Symphonie pour un homme seul*

CINEMA Yves Allégret, *Une si jolie petite plage*; Claude Autant-Lara, *Occupe-toi d'Amélie*; Jacques Becker, *Les Rendez-vous de juillet*; Jacques Tati, *Jour de fête*; Carol Reed, *The Third Man*

1950

THE ARTS

JANUARY
Braque exhibition (Galerie Maeght)

MARCH
Fautrier exhibition, *Aeply Replicas* (Gimpel Fils Gallery, London)

APRIL
Gruber exhibition (Musée national d'art moderne)

MAY
Première of Ionesco's *La Cantatrice chauve* at the Théâtre des Noctambules
The review *Arts d'Aujourd'hui* founded

AUGUST
Consecration of the church of Assy
Henri Matisse and Ossip Zadkine awarded the *Grand Prix* of the Venice Biennale

FRANCE

FEBRUARY
Establishment of the S.M.I.G. (guaranteed minimum wage)

MARCH
Death of Léon Blum
Dock strike in Marseilles

THE WORLD

MARCH
Stockholm appeals for the banning of the atom bomb

JUNE
North Korea invades South Korea

JULY
United States intervenes in Korea

SEPTEMBER
McCarthyism at its height: the U.S. Senate passes a law outlawing all Communist activities

OCTOBER
China invades Tibet

NOVEMBER
China intervenes in Korea

1950 continued

THE ARTS	FRANCE	THE WORLD

THE ARTS

OCTOBER
Exhibition, *Young Painters in US and France*
includes De Kooning, Pollock, Dubuffet and Wols
(Sidney Janis Gallery, New York)

NOVEMBER
Picasso exhibition (Maison de la pensée française)
Giacometti exhibition (Pierre Matisse Gallery,
New York)
Première of Arthur Adamov's *L'Invasion* at the
Studio des Champs Elysées

DECEMBER
First Salon du Jazz (Atlan, Doucet, Dmitrienko,
Dumitresco, Gauthier, Istrati)

LITERATURE Marcel Aymé, *Clérambard*; George Bataille, *L'Abbé C*; René Char, *Les Matinaux* (*The Dawn Breakers*); Marguerite Duras, *Un Barrage contre le Pacifique* (*The Sea Wall*); Julien Gracq, *La Littérature à l'estomac*; Pierre-Jean Jouve, *Ode*; Henri Michaux, *Mouvements*; Pablo Neruda, *Canto general*; Roger Nimier, *Le Hussard bleu* (*The Blue Hussar*)
Death of Joë Bousquet

MUSIC Georges Auric, *Phèdre*; Francis Poulenc, *Stabat Mater*; Arnold Schoenberg, Psalm 130, 'De Profundis'

CINEMA Yves Allégret, *Manèges* (*The Wanton*) René Clair, *La Beauté du diable*; Jean Cocteau, *Orphée*; Nicole Védrès, *La Vie commence demain*; John Huston, *Asphalt Jungle*; Akira Kurosawa, *Rashomon*; Billy Wilder, *Sunset Boulevard*

1951

THE ARTS	FRANCE	THE WORLD

THE ARTS

JANUARY
Première of Ionesco's *La Leçon* at the Théâtre de
Poche
Exhibition, *L'Ecole de Paris 1900–1950* includes
Giacometti, Gruber, Fautrier and Hélion (Royal
Academy of Arts, London)
Dubuffet exhibition, *Corps de Dames* (Pierre
Matisse Gallery, New York)

MARCH
Véhémences confrontées exhibition (Bryen,
Capogrossi, De Kooning, Hartung, Mathieu,
Pollock, Riopelle, Russell, Wols) (Galerie Nina
Dausset)

APRIL
Hélion exhibition (Hanover Gallery, London)
Cobra exhibition (Galerie Pierre)

MAY
Première of Jacques Prévert's *Dîner de têtes* at the
Fontaine des Quatre Saisons

JUNE
Consecration of Matisse's Chapel of the Rosary in
Vence
Giacometti exhibition (Galerie Maeght)

JULY
Inauguration of the Galerie Paul Facchetti

SEPTEMBER
Death of Wols

OCTOBER
Signifiants de l'Informel exhibition (Dubuffet,
Fautrier, Mathieu, Michaux, Riopelle, Serpan)
(Galerie Paul Facchetti)

FRANCE

JUNE
General election. Gains by the Gaullist and
Communist parties

JULY
Death of Marshal Pétain

THE WORLD

JANUARY
Vietminh offensive in Vietnam
UN forces halt the Sino-Korean offensive and
start to recapture South Korea

MARCH
Nationalisation of oil in Iran. Britain organises a
naval blockade of Iran

APRIL
Ethel and Julius Rosenberg sentenced to death in
the United States
Foundation of the European Coal and Steel
Community

OCTOBER
Britain: victory of the Conservatives, led by
Winston Churchill

NOVEMBER
Cease-fire agreements in Korea

1951 continued

THE ARTS	FRANCE	THE WORLD

DECEMBER
Bacon exhibition (Hanover Gallery, London)
Braque starts decorating the ceiling of the
Etruscan Room in the Louvre
Lecture by Dubuffet, 'Anticultural Positions', Arts
Club of Chicago

LITERATURE Jean Giono, *Le Hussard sur le toit* (*The Horseman on the Roof*); Julien Gracq, *Le Rivage des Syrtes*; André Malraux, *Les Voix du silence* (*The Voices of Silence*); Henry de Montherlant, *La Ville dont le prince est un enfant* (*The Town whose Prince is a Child*); Jean-Paul Sartre, *Le Diable et le bon Dieu* (*Lucifer and the Lord*); Jean Tardieu, *Monsieur Monsieur*; Marguerite Yourcenar, *Les Mémoires d'Hadrien* (*The Memoirs of Hadrian*); J.D. Salinger, *The Catcher in the Rye*
Deaths of André Gide and Alain

MUSIC Henri Dutilleux, First Symphony; Olivier Messiaen, *Livre d'orgue*; Karlheinz Stockhausen, *Kreuzspiel*
Death of Arnold Schoenberg

CINEMA Yves Allégret, *Les Miracles n'ont lieu qu'une fois*; Claude Autant-Lara, *L'Auberge rouge* (*The Red Inn*); Robert Bresson, *Le Journal d'un curé de campagne* (*The Diary of a Country Priest*); Alfred Hitchcock, *Strangers on a Train*

1952

THE ARTS	FRANCE	THE WORLD

THE ARTS

FEBRUARY
Bram van Velde exhibition (Galerie Maeght)

APRIL
Wols exhibition (Galerie Nina Dausset)

MAY
Première of Ionesco's *Les Chaises* at the Théâtre
du Nouveau Lancry
Jackson Pollock exhibition (Galerie Paul
Facchetti)

JUNE
Première of Adamov's *La Parodie* at the Théâtre
du Nouveau Lancry
Signifiants de l'Informel II exhibition (Galerie Paul
Facchetti)

JULY
La Chèvre de Picasso exhibition (Galerie de
Beaune)

AUGUST
Raoul Dufy awarded the *Grand Prix* of the Venice
Biennale
Exhibition *Recent Trends in Realistic Painting*
includes Gruber and Giacometti (Institute of
Contemporary Arts, London)

NOVEMBER
Inauguration of the Matisse Museum in Le
Cateau-Cambrésis

DECEMBER
Publication of Michel Tapié's *Un art autre*
Exhibition *Un art autre* (Appel, Brauner, Dubuffet,
Etienne-Martin, Fautrier, Francis, Hartung,
Marini, Mathieu, Matta, Michaux, Ossorio,
Pollock, Richier, Riopelle, Sironi, Soulages,
Sutherland, Tobey, Ubac, Wols) (Galerie Paul
Facchetti)

FRANCE

JANUARY
Fall of Pleven government. Edgar Faure forms a
government

FEBRUARY
Fall of Edgar Faure government. Antoine Pinay
forms a government

JULY
The Pinay government passes law on sliding
scale for salaries

DECEMBER
Resignation of the Pinay government

THE WORLD

JANUARY
Anti-French riots in Tunisia. Arrest of Bourguiba

FEBRUARY
Death of George VI. Elizabeth II succeeds

MAY
Signature of Bonn agreements ending the allied
occupation of West Germany
Signature of treaty for European Defence
Committee

JULY
Egypt: Nasser's *coup d'état* deposes King Farouk

AUGUST
Arrest of leaders of the non-violent campaign
against apartheid in South Africa

NOVEMBER
General Eisenhower elected President of the
United States. Richard Nixon Vice-president

DECEMBER
Riots in Casablanca

1952 continued

LITERATURE   Samuel Beckett, *En attendant Godot (Waiting for Godot)*; Marguerite Duras, *Le Marin de Gibraltar (The Sailor from Gibraltar)*; Jean-Paul Sartre, *Saint Genet, comédien et martyr*
Deaths of Paul Eluard and Charles Maurras
Nobel Prize: François Mauriac

MUSIC   George Auric, *Le Chemin de lumière*; Pierre Boulez, *Structures I* (for two pianos); John Cage, Concerto; Igor Stravinsky, Concertino

CINEMA   Jacques Becker, *Casque d'or (Golden Marie)*; André Cayatte, *Nous sommes tous des assassins (Are We all Murderers?)*; René Clair, *Les Belles de nuit*; René Clément, *Jeux interdits (Forbidden Games)*; Julien Duvivier, *Le Petit Monde de Don Camillo (The Little World of Don Camillo)*; Stanley Donen and Gene Kelly, *Singin' in the Rain*; Fred Zinnemann, *High Noon*

1953

THE ARTS

JANUARY
Première of Samuel Beckett's *En attendant Godot* at the Théâtre de Babylone
Exhibition, *Le Cubisme 1907–1914* (Musée national d'art moderne)

MARCH
International sculpture competition for *The Unknown Political Prisoner* (Tate Gallery)

MAY
Picasso exhibition (Galerie Louise Leiris)
Fautrier exhibition (Galerie de la Nouvelle Revue Française)

JUNE
Picasso retrospective (Musée de Lyon)
Publication of *Premier bilan de l'art actuel* (first survey of present-day art) by Les Editions du soleil noir

OCTOBER
Bacon exhibition (Durlacher Bros., New York, and Hanover Gallery, London)

NOVEMBER
Giacometti exhibition (Arts Club of Chicago)
Hélion exhibition (Galerie Chez Mayo)

FRANCE

JANUARY
René Mayer forms a government

MARCH
Introduction of a vast programme of publicly funded cheap housing (H.L.M.)

MAY
General de Gaulle quits the R.P.F. and allows Gaullist deputies their freedom
Fall of the Mayer government

JUNE
Joseph Laniel forms a government

JULY
The stationer-cum-bookseller Pierre Poujade starts his movement in defence of small shopkeepers

AUGUST
Widespread strikes in the public sector. The army is called to Paris

DECEMBER
René Coty elected President of the Republic

THE WORLD

MARCH
Death of Stalin. Malenkov succeeds him

APRIL
The Vietminh invade Laos

MAY
Edmund Hillary and Sherpa Tensing climb Mount Everest

JUNE
Coronation of Queen Elizabeth II
The Red Army puts down the East Berlin uprising
Proclamation of the Egyptian Republic
Execution of Ethel and Julius Rosenberg

AUGUST
First Soviet H-bomb exploded

SEPTEMBER
Krushchev becomes First Secretary of the Central Committee of the Communist Party

NOVEMBER
Several thousand French parachutists occupy Dien Bien Phu

LITERATURE   Jean Anouilh, *L'Alouette (The Lark)*; Roland Barthes, *Le Degré zéro de l'écriture (Writing Degree Zero)*; Pierre Klossowski, *Roberte ce soir*; Alain Robbe-Grillet, *Les Gommes (The Erasers)*; Nathalie Sarraute, *Martereau*; Boris Vian, *L'Arrache-coeur (Heartsnatcher)*

MUSIC   Henri Dutilleux, *Le Loup*; Oliver Messiaen, *Le Réveil des oiseaux*; Karlheinz Stockhausen, *Kontrapunkte*
Death of Prokofiev

CINEMA   Marcel Carné, *Thérèse Raquin*; Henri-Georges Clouzot, *Le Salaire de la Peur (The Wages of Fear)*; Jacques Tati, *Les Vacances de M. Hulot (Monsieur Hulot's Holiday)*

1954

THE ARTS

FEBRUARY
Death of Father Couturier, who had pioneered the restoration of sacred art

MARCH
Dubuffet retrospective (Cercle Volney)

MAY
Giacometti exhibition (Galerie Maeght)
Death of Henri Laurens

JUNE
Picasso exhibition (Maison de la pensée française)

SEPTEMBER
Death of André Derain
Max Ernst and Jean Arp awarded the *Grand Prix* of the Venice Biennale

NOVEMBER
Death of Henri Matisse

FRANCE

JANUARY
First nuclear-powered submarine

FEBRUARY
Cold spell in Paris. The Abbé Pierre appeals to Parisians to show solidarity with the homeless

JUNE
Fall of Laniel government. Pierre Mendès-France forms a government

JULY
Mendès-France grants Tunisia internal independence

AUGUST
The National Assembly refuses to agree the European Defence Committee negotiations

THE WORLD

MAY
Vietminh victory at Dien Bien Phu

JULY
Geneva agreement and end of the war in Indo-China. Vietnam partitioned on either side of the 17th parallel

NOVEMBER
Beginning of the Algerian insurrection

DECEMBER
American Senate passes a vote of censure against Joseph McCarthy, thus putting an end to his political career

LITERATURE Roland Barthes, *Michelet par lui-même*; Simone de Beauvoir, *Les Mandarins (The Mandarins)*; Albert Cohen, *Le Livre de ma mère*; Paul Léautaud, *Journal Littéraire (Journal of a Man of Letters)*; Clara Malraux, *Par de longs chemins*; François Mauriac, *L'Agneau (The Lamb)*; Françoise Sagan, *Bonjour tristesse*; William Golding, *Lord of the Flies*; Alberto Moravia, *Il Disprezzo (A Ghost at Noon)*
Death of Colette
Nobel Prize: Ernest Hemingway

MUSIC Jean-Louis Martinet, Trois mouvements symphoniques; Luigi Nono, *La Victoire de Guernica*; Edgar Varèse, *Déserts*; Iannis Xenakis, *Métastasis*
Bill Haley records 'Rock around the Clock'

CINEMA Claude Autant-Lara, *Le Rouge et le noir (Scarlet and Black)*; Jacques Becker, *Touchez pas au grisbi*; Marcel Carné, *L'Air de Paris*; René Clément, *M. Ripois (Knave of Hearts)*; Frederico Fellini, *La Strada*; Akira Kurosawa, *Seven Samurai*

1955

THE ARTS

JANUARY
Death of Yves Tanguy

MARCH
Death of Nicolas de Staël
Dubuffet exhibition (Institute of Contemporary Arts, London)

APRIL
Exhibition, *50 Years of Art in the United States* (Musée national d'art moderne)

MAY
Exhibition, *Les Objets de Fautrier* (Galerie Rive Droite)
Bram van Velde exhibition (Galerie Michel Warren)

JUNE
Giacometti exhibition (The Solomon R. Guggenheim Museum, New York)
Exhibition, *Bonnard, Vuillard et Les Nabis* (Musée national d'art moderne)
Picasso exhibition, *Peintures 1900–1955* (Musée des arts decoratifs)

JULY
Documenta I, Kassel

AUGUST
Death of Fernand Léger

FRANCE

JANUARY
Jacques Soustelle appointed Governor General of Algeria. French soldiers go into the attack in Les Aurès

FEBRUARY
Fall of the Mendès-France government. Edgar Faure forms a government

APRIL
The National Assembly decrees a State of Emergency in Algeria

AUGUST
Massacre of the French by anti-colonial forces in the Constantinois district of East Algeria
Reservists called up to serve in Algeria

DECEMBER
Edgar Faure dissolves the National Assembly

THE WORLD

APRIL
Winston Churchill resigns
Bandung conference: twenty-nine Third-World countries declare their non-alignment

MAY
West Germany joins NATO
Signature of the Warsaw Pact between the USSR and its satellite countries in Eastern Europe

SEPTEMBER
Prince Sihanouk proclaims the independence of Cambodia
First autonomous government in Tunisia
Coup d'état in Argentina overthrows the Perón régime

OCTOBER
Proclamation of the Republic of South Vietnam

NOVEMBER
End of the French protectorate in Morocco

DECEMBER
Ben Gurion becomes prime minister of Israel

1955 continued

THE ARTS	FRANCE	THE WORLD

SEPTEMBER
Hommage à Matisse (Salon d'Automne)
Hommage à Léger (Galerie Maeght)

LITERATURE — Arthur Adamov, *Ping pong*; Georges Bataille, *Lascaux ou la naissance de l'art*; Maurice Blanchot, *L'Espace littéraire* (*Space of Literature*); Claude Lévi-Strauss, *Tristes tropiques*; Alain Robbe-Grillet, *Le Voyeur*; Pierre Teilhard de Chardin, *Le Phénomène humain* (*The Phenomenon of Man*); Yasar Kemal, *Memed, My Hawk*; Herbert Marcuse, *Eros and Civilization*; Vladimir Nabokov, *Lolita*

MUSIC — Pierre Boulez, *Le Marteau sans maître*; Luigo Nono, *Inconti*
Death of Arthur Honegger

CINEMA — René Clair, *Les Grands Manoeuvres* (*Summer Manoeuvres*); Max Ophüls, *Lola Montès*; Jean Renoir, *French Cancan*; Charles Laughton, *The Night of the Hunter*; Nicholas Ray, *Rebel Without a Cause*; Satyajit Ray, *Pather Panchali* trilogy

THE ARTS	FRANCE	THE WORLD

LIST OF WORKS

Measurements are given in centimetres followed by inches in brackets, height before width

ANTONIN ARTAUD

1 **Couti the Anatomy** *c.* September 1945
Couti l'anatomi
Pencil and chalk on paper
65.4 × 50 ($25\frac{1}{4} \times 19\frac{5}{8}$)
Musée National d'Art Moderne, Centre
Georges Pompidou, Paris. Acquired 1985

ANTONIN ARTAUD

2 **The Machine of Being *or* Drawing to be**
Looked at Cockeyed *c.* January 1946
La Machine de l'être *ou* Dessin à regarder de traviole
Pencil and chalk on paper
64.5 × 49.6 ($25\frac{3}{8} \times 19\frac{1}{2}$)
Musée National d'Art Moderne, Centre
Georges Pompidou, Paris. Acquired 1988

ANTONIN ARTAUD

3 **The Illusions of the Soul** *c.* February 1946
Les Illusions de l'âme
Pencil and chalk on paper
62.5 × 47.8 ($24\frac{5}{8} \times 18\frac{7}{8}$)
Musée National d'Art Moderne, Centre
Georges Pompidou, Paris. Acquired 1987

ANTONIN ARTAUD

4 **Portrait of Jacques Prevel** 27 August 1946
Portrait de Jacques Prevel
Pencil on paper 28 × 22.5 ($11 \times 8\frac{7}{8}$)
Musée Cantini, Marseilles

ANTONIN ARTAUD

5 **Self-Portrait** 17 December 1946
Autoportrait
Pencil on paper 65 × 50 ($25\frac{5}{8} \times 19\frac{5}{8}$)
Florence Loeb

ANTONIN ARTAUD

6 **The Revolt of the Angels outside Limbo** 1946
La Révolte des anges sortis des Limbes
Charcoal and pencil on paper
65 × 49.5 ($25\frac{5}{8} \times 19\frac{1}{2}$)
Musée Cantini, Marseilles

ANTONIN ARTAUD

7 **Portrait of Jacques Prevel (in Profile)**
11 May 1947
Portrait de Jacques Prevel (de profil)
Pencil on paper 56.5 × 45 ($22\frac{1}{4} \times 17\frac{3}{4}$)
Musée Cantini, Marseilles

ANTONIN ARTAUD

8 **Portrait of Mania Oïfer** May 1947
Portrait de Mania Oïfer
Pencil on paper 64 × 50 ($25\frac{1}{4} \times 19\frac{5}{8}$)
Albert Loeb, Paris

ANTONIN ARTAUD

9 **Portrait of Minouche Pastier** 22 May 1947
Portrait de Minouche Pastier
Pencil and chalk on paper
63.5 × 47.8 ($25 \times 18\frac{7}{8}$)
Musée National d'Art Moderne, Centre
Georges Pompidou, Paris. Acquired 1984

ANTONIN ARTAUD

10 **Portrait of Arthur Adamov** *c.*17 June 1947
Portrait d'Arthur Adamov
Pencil and chalk on paper
65 × 50 ($25\frac{5}{8} \times 19\frac{5}{8}$)
Florence Loeb

ANTONIN ARTAUD

11 **Self-Portrait** 24 June 1947
Autoportrait
Pencil and chalk on paper
55 × 45 ($21\frac{5}{8} \times 17\frac{3}{4}$)
Private Collection, Brussels

ANTONIN ARTAUD

12 **Portrait of Henri Pichette *or* Gris-gris**
21 November 1947
Portrait d'Henri Pichette *ou* Gris-gris
Pencil on paper 64.7 × 49.8 ($25\frac{1}{2} \times 19\frac{5}{8}$)
Musée National d'Art Moderne, Centre
Georges Pompidou, Paris. Acquired 1986

ANTONIN ARTAUD

13 **Self-Portrait** *c.* December 1947
Autoportrait
Pencil on paper 37 × 27 ($14\frac{1}{2} \times 10\frac{5}{8}$)
Private Collection

ANTONIN ARTAUD

14 **Portraits** *c.* December 1947
Figures
Pencil on paper 63 × 50 ($24\frac{3}{4} \times 19\frac{5}{8}$)
Florence Loeb

JEAN DUBUFFET

15 **Smoker by a Wall** 1945
Fumeur au mur
Oil on canvas 116 × 89 ($45\frac{5}{8} \times 35$)
Mr and Mrs Julian J. Aberbach

JEAN DUBUFFET

16 **Monsieur Plume with Creases in his Trousers**
(Portrait of Henri Michaux) 1947
Monsieur Plume plis au pantalon (Portrait d'Henri Michaux)
Oil on canvas 130.2 × 96.5 ($51\frac{1}{4} \times 38$)
Tate Gallery. Purchased 1980

JEAN DUBUFFET

17 **Bertelé, Flowered Bouquet, Parade**
Portrait July–August 1947
Bertelé Bouquet Fleuri, Portrait de Parade
Oil on canvas 116 × 89 ($45\frac{5}{8} \times 35$)
Stephen Hahn

JEAN DUBUFFET

18 **The Geologist** 1950
Le Géologue
Oil on canvas 97 × 130 ($38\frac{1}{4} \times 51\frac{1}{8}$)
Private Collection

JEAN DUBUFFET

19 **The Uncertain Woman** 1950
L'Incertaine
Oil on canvas 116.5 × 89.5 ($45\frac{7}{8} \times 35\frac{1}{4}$)
Louisiana Museum of Modern Art, Humlebaek

JEAN DUBUFFET

20 **Gymnosophie** 1950
Oil on canvas 97 × 146 ($38\frac{1}{4} \times 57\frac{1}{2}$)
Musée National d'Art Moderne, Centre
Georges Pompidou, Paris. Acquired 1991

JEAN DUBUFFET

21 **The Busy Life** 1953
La Vie affairée
Oil on canvas 130.2 × 195.6 ($51\frac{1}{4} \times 77$)
Tate Gallery. Presented by the artist 1966

JEAN FAUTRIER

22 **Scored Head** 1940
Tête striée
Bronze (artist's proof)
18 × 10 × 15 ($7\frac{1}{8} \times 4 \times 5\frac{7}{8}$)
Private Collection

JEAN FAUTRIER

23 **The Eyes** 1940
Les Yeux
Bronze 14 × 15.5 ($5\frac{1}{2} \times 6\frac{1}{8}$)
Private Collection

JEAN FAUTRIER

24 **Large Tragic Head** 1942
Grande Tête tragique
Bronze 38.5 × 21 × 21.5 ($15\frac{1}{4} \times 8\frac{1}{4} \times 8\frac{1}{2}$)
Tate Gallery. Purchased 1991

JEAN FAUTRIER

25 **Hostage** 1943
Otage
Lead 48 ($18\frac{7}{8}$) high
Musée de l'Ile de France, Château de Sceaux,
Sceaux

JEAN FAUTRIER

26 **Sarah** 1942–3
Oil on paper pasted on canvas
116 × 89 ($45\frac{5}{8} \times 35$)
Private Collection, France. Courtesy Marc
Blondeau, Paris

JEAN FAUTRIER

27 **The Jewess** 1943
La Juive
Oil on paper pasted on canvas
73 × 115.5 ($28\frac{3}{4} \times 45\frac{1}{2}$)
Musée d'Art Moderne de la Ville de Paris.
Donation Jean Fautrier 1964

JEAN FAUTRIER
28 **Torso** 1943
Torse
Oil on paper pasted on canvas
46 × 38 (18⅛ × 15)
Private Collection

JEAN FAUTRIER
29 **Head of a Hostage** 1943
Tête d'otage
Oil on paper pasted on canvas
28 × 22 (11 × 8⅝)
Private Collection

JEAN FAUTRIER
30 **Head of a Hostage No.1** 1944
Tête d'otage no.1
Oil on paper pasted on canvas
35.6 × 26.7 (14 × 10½)
The Museum of Contemporary Art,
Los Angeles. The Panza Collection

JEAN FAUTRIER
31 **Head of a Hostage No.20** 1944
Tête d'otage no.20
Oil on paper pasted on canvas
33 × 24 (13 × 9½)
Private Collection

JEAN FAUTRIER
32 **Head of a Hostage No.22** 1944
Tête d'otage no.22
Oil on paper pasted on canvas
27 × 22 (10⅝ × 8⅝)
Gallery Limmer, Freiburg

JEAN FAUTRIER
33 **Head of a Hostage** 1945
Tête d'otage
Oil on paper pasted on canvas
35 × 27 (13¾ × 10⅝)
Private Collection

JEAN FAUTRIER
34 **Remains** 1945
Dépouille
Oil on paper pasted on canvas
114.3 × 144.8 (45 × 57)
The Museum of Contemporary Art,
Los Angeles. The Panza Collection

JEAN FAUTRIER
35 **Oradour-sur-Glane** 1945
Oil on paper pasted on canvas
145.1 × 113.7 (57⅛ × 44⅞)
The Menil Collection, Houston

JEAN FAUTRIER
36 **Head of a Hostage No.2** 1945
Tête d'otage no.2
Oil on paper pasted on canvas
35.5 × 26.5 (14 × 10⅜)
Galerie Di Meo, Paris

ALBERTO GIACOMETTI
37 **Head on a Rod** 1947
Tête sur tige
Bronze 62.2 × 14.6 × 15.2 (24½ × 5¾ × 6)
Acquavella Modern Art

ALBERTO GIACOMETTI
38 **Tall Figure** 1947
Grande Figure
Bronze 201.3 × 21.3 × 42.2 (79¼ × 8⅜ × 16⅝)
Hirshhorn Museum and Sculpture Garden,
Smithsonian Institution, Washington. Gift of
Joseph H. Hirshhorn 1966

ALBERTO GIACOMETTI
39 **Man Pointing** 1947
Homme signalant
Bronze 178 × 95 × 52 (70⅛ × 37⅜ × 20½)
Tate Gallery. Purchased 1949

ALBERTO GIACOMETTI
40 **Bust of a Man** 1950
Buste d'homme
Bronze 57 × 15.5 × 16.5 (22½ × 6⅛ × 6½)
Fondation Maeght, Saint-Paul

ALBERTO GIACOMETTI
41 **Four Figurines on a Base** 1950/1965, cast
c.1965–6
Quatre figurines sur base
Bronze
156.2 × 41.9 × 31.4 (61½ × 16½ × 12⅜)
Tate Gallery. Purchased with assistance from
the Friends of the Tate Gallery 1965

ALBERTO GIACOMETTI
42 **Place, Composition with Three Figures and a**
Head 1950
Place, Composition avec trois figures et une
tête
Painted bronze 58 × 57 × 42
(22⅞ × 22½ × 16½)
Städtische Kunsthalle Mannheim
[not exhibited]

ALBERTO GIACOMETTI
43 **Diego in a Sweater** 1953
Diego au chandail
Bronze 49 × 28 × 22.5 (19⅜ × 11 × 8⅞)
Alberto Giacometti-Stiftung, Kunsthaus Zurich

ALBERTO GIACOMETTI
44 **Bust of Diego** c.1954
Buste de Diego
Bronze 38.2 × 33.3 × 18.7 (15 × 13⅛ × 7¼)
Walker Art Center, Minneapolis. Gift of the
T.B. Walker Foundation 1957

ALBERTO GIACOMETTI
45 **Bust of Diego** 1955
Buste de Diego
Bronze 56.5 × 32 × 14.5 (22¼ × 12⅝ × 5¾)
Tate Gallery. Purchased with assistance from
the Friends of the Tate Gallery 1965

ALBERTO GIACOMETTI
46 **Venice Woman I** 1956
Femme de Venise I
Bronze 105 × 13 × 29.5 (41⅜ × 5⅛ × 11⅝)
Fondation Maeght, Saint-Paul

ALBERTO GIACOMETTI
47 **Venice Woman II** 1956
Femme de Venise II
Bronze 120.5 × 15.5 × 33 (47½ × 6⅛ × 13)
Fondation Maeght, Saint-Paul

ALBERTO GIACOMETTI
48 **Venice Woman III** 1956
Femme de Venise III
Bronze 119 × 17 × 33.5 (46⅞ × 6¼ × 13¼)
Fondation Maeght, Saint-Paul

ALBERTO GIACOMETTI
49 **Venice Woman IV** 1956
Femme de Venise IV
Bronze 117 × 16.5 × 34 (46 × 6½ × 13⅜)
Fondation Maeght, Saint-Paul

ALBERTO GIACOMETTI
50 **Venice Woman V** 1956
Femme de Venise V
Bronze 111 × 13.5 × 31 (43¾ × 5⅜ × 12¼)
Fondation Maeght, Saint-Paul

ALBERTO GIACOMETTI
51 **Venice Woman VI** 1956
Femme de Venise VI
Bronze 133.5 × 15.5 × 33 (52⅝ × 6⅛ × 13)
Fondation Maeght, Saint-Paul

ALBERTO GIACOMETTI
52 **Venice Woman VII** 1956
Femme de Venise VII
Bronze 117 × 16.5 × 36.5 (46⅛ × 6½ × 14⅜)
Charlotte and Irving W. Rabb, Cambridge,
Massachusetts

ALBERTO GIACOMETTI
53 **Venice Woman VIII** 1956
Femme de Venise VIII
Bronze 120.5 × 14.5 × 33 (47⅞ × 5¾ × 13)
Fondation Maeght, Saint-Paul

ALBERTO GIACOMETTI
54 **Venice Woman IX** 1956
Femme de Venise IX
Bronze 113 × 16.5 × 34.6 (44½ × 6½ × 13⅝)
Tate Gallery. Purchased 1959

ALBERTO GIACOMETTI
55 **Bust with Large Eyes** 1957
Buste aux grands yeux
Bronze 51.5 × 13.7 × 11 (20¼ × 5⅜ × 4⅜)
Private Collection, Paris

ALBERTO GIACOMETTI
56 **Bust of Diego** 1957
Buste de Diego
Bronze 60.6 × 24.8 × 16.2 (23⅞ × 9¾ × 6⅜)
Hirshhorn Museum and Sculpture Garden,
Smithsonian Institution, Washington. Gift of
Joseph H. Hirshhorn 1966

ALBERTO GIACOMETTI
57 **Portrait of Diego Seated, Head of a Woman,**
Heads
Portrait de Diego assis, Tête de femme, Têtes
Oil and pencil on wall of studio
153 × 185 (60¼ × 73)
Private Collection, Paris

ALBERTO GIACOMETTI
58 Walking Man, Standing Woman, Head of a Woman
L'Homme qui marche, Femme debout, Tête de femme
Oil and pencil on wall of studio
223×150 (88×59)
Private Collection, Paris

ALBERTO GIACOMETTI
59 Tall Woman, Annette, The Leg, Standing Woman
Grande Femme debout, Annette, La Jambe, Femme debout
Oil and engraving on wall of studio
189×141.5 ($74\frac{1}{4} \times 55\frac{3}{4}$)
Private Collection, Paris

ALBERTO GIACOMETTI
60 The Artist's Mother 1951
La Mère de l'artiste
Oil on canvas 91.8×72.7 ($36\frac{1}{8} \times 28\frac{5}{8}$)
Musée National d'Art Moderne, Centre Georges Pompidou, Paris. Dation 1982

ALBERTO GIACOMETTI
61 Jean Genet 1954–5
Oil on canvas 65.3×54.3 ($25\frac{3}{4} \times 21\frac{3}{8}$)
Tate Gallery. Accepted by the Commissioners of Inland Revenue in lieu of tax and allocated 1987

ALBERTO GIACOMETTI
62 Sketch 1957
Esquisse
Oil on canvas 73×60 ($28\frac{3}{4} \times 23\frac{5}{8}$)
Kunsthaus Zurich

ALBERTO GIACOMETTI
63 Annette Seated 1957
Annette assise
Oil on canvas 99.5×60.5 ($39\frac{1}{8} \times 23\frac{7}{8}$)
Kunstsammlung Nordrhein-Westfalen, Düsseldorf

ALBERTO GIACOMETTI
64 Standing Nude 1958
Nu Debout
Oil on canvas 155×69.5 ($61 \times 27\frac{3}{8}$)
Galerie Jan Krugier, Geneva

ALBERTO GIACOMETTI
65 Annette in the Studio 1961
Annette dans l'atelier
Oil on canvas 146×97 ($57\frac{1}{2} \times 38\frac{1}{4}$)
Kunsthalle, Hamburg

FRANCIS GRUBER
66 Woman Seated in Front of the Fireplace 1940
Femme assise devant la cheminée
Oil on canvas 91×72 ($35\frac{7}{8} \times 28\frac{3}{8}$)
Patrice Trigano, Paris

FRANCIS GRUBER
67 The Red Divan 1944
Le Divan rouge
Oil on canvas 89×116 ($35 \times 45\frac{5}{8}$)
Patrice Trigano, Paris

FRANCIS GRUBER
68 Job 1944
Oil on canvas 161.9×129.9 ($63\frac{3}{4} \times 51\frac{1}{8}$)
Tate Gallery. Purchased 1958

FRANCIS GRUBER
69 Nude in a Red Waistcoat 1944
Nu au gilet rouge
Oil on canvas 115×86 ($45\frac{1}{4} \times 33\frac{7}{8}$)
Musée d'Art Moderne de la Ville de Paris

JEAN HELION
70 Seated Nude, Nude Reclining 1949
Nu assis, nu couché
Oil on canvas 146×114 ($57\frac{1}{2} \times 44\frac{7}{8}$)
Private Collection

JEAN HELION
71 Four Seated Nudes 1949
Quatre nus assis
Oil on canvas 114×162 ($44\frac{7}{8} \times 63\frac{3}{4}$)
Private Collection. Courtesy Galerie Pierre Brullé, Paris

JEAN HELION
72 Star-Figure Nude with Smoker and Newspaper Reader 1949
Nu étoilé au fumeur et au journalier
Oil on canvas 150×200 ($59 \times 78\frac{3}{4}$)
Private Collection, Mulhouse

JEAN HELION
73 Men Reading Newspapers 1950
Grande Journalerie
Oil on canvas 129.5×195 ($51 \times 76\frac{3}{4}$)
Private Collection. Courtesy Robert Miller Gallery, New York

JEAN HELION
74 Large Mannequin Painting 1951
Grande Mannequinerie
Oil on canvas 129.5×161.5 ($51 \times 63\frac{5}{8}$)
Musée d'Art Moderne de la Ville de Paris

JEAN HELION
75 Nude with Loaves 1952
Dos aux pains
Oil on canvas 130.1×97 ($51\frac{1}{4} \times 38\frac{1}{4}$)
Tate Gallery. Purchased 1988

HENRI MICHAUX
76 Untitled 1946
Watercolour and ink on paper
31.7×23.7 ($12\frac{1}{2} \times 9\frac{3}{8}$)
Musée National d'Art Moderne, Centre Georges Pompidou, Paris. Donation Daniel Cordier 1976

HENRI MICHAUX
77 Untitled *c.*1946
Watercolour and ink on paper
47×30 ($18\frac{1}{2} \times 11\frac{3}{4}$)
Private Collection

HENRI MICHAUX
78 Untitled 1946–8
Gouache, ink and wash on paper
50.8×32.7 ($20 \times 12\frac{7}{8}$)
Musée National d'Art Moderne, Centre Georges Pompidou, Paris. Donation Daniel Cordier 1976

HENRI MICHAUX
79 Untitled 1946–8
Watercolour and ink on paper 50×32 ($19\frac{5}{8} \times 12\frac{5}{8}$)
Musée National d'Art Moderne, Centre Georges Pompidou, Paris. Donation Daniel Cordier 1976

HENRI MICHAUX
80 Untitled 1947–8
Watercolour and ink on paper
38×28 (15×11)
Private Collection

HENRI MICHAUX
81 Untitled 1947–8
Watercolour and ink on paper
46×30 ($18\frac{1}{4} \times 11\frac{3}{4}$)
Private Collection

HENRI MICHAUX
82 Untitled 1948
Ink and wash on paper 32×24 ($12\frac{5}{8} \times 9\frac{1}{2}$)
Private Collection. Courtesy Galerie Baudoin Lebon, Paris

HENRI MICHAUX
83 Untitled 1948
Watercolour and pencil on paper
39.1×29.2 ($15\frac{3}{8} \times 11\frac{1}{2}$)
Solomon R. Guggenheim Museum, New York

HENRI MICHAUX
84 Untitled *c.*1948
Watercolour on paper 49×32 ($19\frac{1}{4} \times 12\frac{5}{8}$)
Private Collection

HENRI MICHAUX
85 Untitled *c.*1948
Watercolour on paper 47.5×31 ($18\frac{3}{4} \times 12\frac{1}{4}$)
Private Collection

HENRI MICHAUX
86 Untitled *c.*1948
Watercolour on paper 49.5×32 ($19\frac{1}{2} \times 12\frac{5}{8}$)
Private Collection

HENRI MICHAUX
87 Untitled *c.*1948
Watercolour on paper 31.7×24.2 ($12\frac{1}{2} \times 9\frac{1}{2}$)
Private Collection

HENRI MICHAUX
88 Untitled 1948–9
Watercolour and ink on paper
31.5×23.5 ($12\frac{3}{8} \times 9\frac{1}{4}$)
Private Collection

HENRI MICHAUX
89 Untitled 1950
Ink on paper 23.5×21 ($9\frac{1}{4} \times 8\frac{1}{4}$)
Private Collection. Courtesy Galerie Baudoin Lebon, Paris

HENRI MICHAUX
90 Untitled *c.*1950
Watercolour on paper 39×27.5 ($15\frac{3}{8} \times 10\frac{7}{8}$)
Private Collection. Courtesy Galerie Baudoin Lebon, Paris

PABLO PICASSO
91 **Pitcher and Skeleton** 1945
Pichet et squelette
Oil on canvas 73 × 92.2 (28¾ × 36¼)
Musée Picasso, Paris

PABLO PICASSO
92 **Skull and Book** 1946
Tête de mort et livre
Oil on canvas 80 × 100 (31½ × 39⅜)
*Marina Picasso. Courtesy Galerie Jan Krugier,
Geneva*

PABLO PICASSO
93 **Still Life with Goat's Skull, Bottle and
Candle** 1952
Nature morte à la tête de chèvre, bouteille et
bougie
Oil on canvas 45 × 81 (17¾ × 31⅞)
*Marina Picasso. Courtesy Galerie Jan Krugier,
Geneva*

PABLO PICASSO
94 **Goat's Skull, Bottle and Candle** 1952
Crâne de chèvre, bouteille et bougie
Oil on canvas 89.2 × 116.2 (35⅛ × 45¾)
Tate Gallery. Purchased 1957

GERMAINE RICHIER
95 **Forest Man (Large Version)** 1945–6
L'Homme-forêt – Grand
Bronze 94.3 × 45 × 45 (37⅛ × 17¾ × 17¾)
Galerie Jan Krugier, Geneva

GERMAINE RICHIER
96 **Storm Man** 1947–8
L'Orage
Bronze 190.5 × 72 × 57.5 (75 × 28⅜ × 22⅝)
Louisiana Museum of Modern Art, Humlebaek

GERMAINE RICHIER
97 **Hurricane Woman** 1948–9
L'Ouragane
Bronze 179.5 × 71 × 47 (70⅝ × 28 × 18½)
Lousiana Museum of Modern Art, Humlebaek

GERMAINE RICHIER
98 **Ogre** 1949
L'Ogre
Bronze 80.5 × 45 × 41 (31¾ × 17¾ × 16⅛)
Private Collection

GERMAINE RICHIER
99 **Diabolo** 1950
Le Diabolo
Bronze 167.5 × 74 × 93 (66 × 29⅛ × 36⅝)
Galerie Jan Krugier, Geneva

GERMAINE RICHIER
100 **The Shepherd of Landes** 1951
Le Berger des Landes
Bronze 149.9 × 89 × 60 (59 × 35⅛ × 23⅝)
Lousiana Museum of Modern Art, Humlebaek

GERMAINE RICHIER
101 **Man with Claws** 1952
Le Griffu
Bronze 89 × 98 × 85 (35⅛ × 38⅝ × 33½)
Private Collection

GERMAINE RICHIER
102 **Pentacle** 1954
Le Pentacle
Bronze 82.9 × 36 × 22.5 (32⅝ × 14¼ × 8⅞)
Galerie Jan Krugier, Geneva

BRAM VAN VELDE
103 **Untitled, Montrouge** 1951
Oil on canvas 162 × 130 (63¾ × 51⅛)
Jacques Putman

BRAM VAN VELDE
104 **Untitled, Montrouge** 1951–2
Oil on canvas 130.5 × 162 (51⅛ × 63¾)
Franz Meyer, Zurich

BRAM VAN VELDE
105 **Untitled, Paris, Boulevard de la Gare** 1956
Oil on canvas 170 × 242.5 (66⅞ × 95½)
Musée d'Art Moderne de Saint-Etienne

BRAM VAN VELDE
106 **Untitled, Montrouge** 1945–8
Gouache 99 × 82 (39 × 32¼)
Private Collection

BRAM VAN VELDE
107 **Untitled, Montrouge** 1946–8
Gouache 116 × 73 (45⅝ × 28¾)
Catherine Béraud Putman

BRAM VAN VELDE
108 **Untitled, Montrouge** 1953
Gouache 146 × 108 (57½ × 42½)
Private Collection

BRAM VAN VELDE
109 **Untitled, Bourgogne** 1954
Gouache 150 × 202 (59 × 79½)
Private Collection

BRAM VAN VELDE
110 **Untitled, Fox-Amphoux** 1958
Gouache 124 × 94 (48⅞ × 37)
J. Benador, Geneva

WOLS (Alfred Otto Wolfgang Schulze)
111 **Painting** 1944–5
Oil on canvas 81 × 81.1 (31⅞ × 32)
*The Museum of Modern Art, New York. Gift of
D. and J. de Menil 1956*

WOLS (Alfred Otto Wolfgang Schulze)
112 **Composition IV** 1946
Oil on canvas 65 × 54 (25⅝ × 21⅛)
*Pinacoteca di Brera, Milan. Donazione Emilio e
Maria Jesi*

WOLS (Alfred Otto Wolfgang Schulze)
113 **Yes, Yes, Yes** 1946–7
Oui, Oui, Oui
Oil on canvas 80.6 × 64.2 (31⅜ × 25⅝)
The Menil Collection, Houston

WOLS (Alfred Otto Wolfgang Schulze)
114 **Untitled** 1946–7
Oil on canvas 81 × 81 (31⅞ × 31⅞)
The Menil Collection, Houston

WOLS (Alfred Otto Wolfgang Schulze)
115 **Manhattan** 1947
Oil on canvas 146 × 97.5 (57½ × 38⅜)
The Menil Collection, Houston

WOLS (Alfred Otto Wolfgang Schulze)
116 **Yellow Composition** 1947
Composition jaune
Oil on canvas 73 × 92 (28¾ × 36¼)
*Staatliche Museen zu Berlin, Nationalgalerie,
Berlin*

WOLS (Alfred Otto Wolfgang Schulze)
117 **Butterfly's Wing** 1947
Aile de papillon
Oil on canvas 55 × 46 (21⅝ × 18⅛)
*Musée National d'Art Moderne, Centre
Georges Pompidou, Paris. Don de M. René
de Montaigu 1979*

WOLS (Alfred Otto Wolfgang Schulze)
118 **The Pink Ship** 1949
Le Bateau rose
Oil on canvas 38 × 46 (15 × 18⅛)
Private Collection

WOLS (Alfred Otto Wolfgang Schulze)
119 **Bird** 1949
Oiseau
Oil on canvas 92.1 × 65.1 (36¼ × 25¾)
The Menil Collection, Houston

WOLS (Alfred Otto Wolfgang Schulze)
120 **Composition on Grey Ground** 1949
Composition sur fond gris
Oil on canvas 46 × 38 (18⅛ × 15)
Private Collection

WOLS (Alfred Otto Wolfgang Schulze)
121 **Composition Champigny** 1951
Oil on canvas 68 × 57 (26¾ × 22½)
Private Collection

WOLS (Alfred Otto Wolfgang Schulze)
122 **Untitled** 1940
Watercolour on paper 26.5 × 33 (10⅜ × 13)
Private Collection, London

WOLS (Alfred Otto Wolfgang Schulze)
123 **Untitled** 1942
Watercolour and ink on paper
18 × 26 (7⅛ × 10¼)
Private Collection

WOLS (Alfred Otto Wolfgang Schulze)
124 **Happy City** 1942–3
Ville heureuse
Watercolour, gouache and ink on paper
15.7 × 24 (6⅛ × 9½)
Philippe and Denyse Durand-Ruel, Paris

WOLS (Alfred Otto Wolfgang Schulze)
125 **Enchantment of a City** 1944
Féerie d'une ville
Watercolour, gouache and ink on paper
15.8 × 21 (6¼ × 8¼)
Philippe and Denyse Durand-Ruel, Paris

WOLS (Alfred Otto Wolfgang Schulze)
126 Vascello All'ancora 1944–5
Watercolour and ink on paper
13.5 × 13.5 ($5\frac{1}{4}$ × $5\frac{1}{4}$)
Private Collection

WOLS (Alfred Otto Wolfgang Schulze)
127 The City 1944–5
La Ville
Watercolour, gouache and ink on paper
9.8 × 16.2 ($3\frac{7}{8}$ × $6\frac{3}{8}$)
Philippe and Denyse Durand-Ruel, Paris

WOLS (Alfred Otto Wolfgang Schulze)
128 Branching Tree-Stumps in the Wind 1944–5
Trois souches dans le vent
Watercolour, gouache and ink on paper
15.7 × 10.5 ($6\frac{1}{8}$ × $4\frac{1}{8}$)
Private Collection, Paris

WOLS (Alfred Otto Wolfgang Schulze)
129 Nearby Star (Our Earth) 1944–5
Astre proche (notre terre)
Watercolour, gouache and ink on paper
16.7 × 12.3 ($6\frac{5}{8}$ × $4\frac{7}{8}$)
Private Collection, Paris

WOLS (Alfred Otto Wolfgang Schulze)
130 Untitled 1944–5
Watercolour, gouache and ink on paper
18.7 × 13.3 ($7\frac{3}{8}$ × $5\frac{1}{4}$)
Private Collection

WOLS (Alfred Otto Wolfgang Schulze)
131 Untitled c.1944–5
Watercolour and gouache on paper
9.2 × 13.5 ($3\frac{5}{8}$ × $5\frac{3}{8}$)
Tate Gallery. Purchased 1986

WOLS (Alfred Otto Wolfgang Schulze)
132 Ship on Green and Blue Ground 1945
Bateau sur fond vert et bleu
Watercolour and ink on paper
15.5 × 24 ($6\frac{1}{8}$ × $9\frac{1}{2}$)
Private Collection

WOLS (Alfred Otto Wolfgang Schulze)
133 Indonesia c.1945
Indonésie
Watercolour and ink on paper 20.5 × 12.5
($8\frac{1}{8}$ × $4\frac{7}{8}$)
Private Collection

WOLS (Alfred Otto Wolfgang Schulze)
134 The Mad Boar 1945
Le Sanglier fou
Watercolour, gouache and ink on paper
20.4 × 12.2 (8 × $4\frac{3}{4}$)
Private Collection

WOLS (Alfred Otto Wolfgang Schulze)
135 Untitled 1945–6
Watercolour, gouache and ink on paper
19.5 × 14 ($7\frac{5}{8}$ × $5\frac{1}{2}$)
Private Collection

WOLS (Alfred Otto Wolfgang Schulze)
136 The Red Leaf 1945–6
Le Feuille rouge
Watercolour, gouache and ink on paper
21 × 14.4 ($8\frac{1}{4}$ × $5\frac{5}{8}$)
Private Collection

WOLS (Alfred Otto Wolfgang Schulze)
137 The Pink City 1945–6
La Ville rose
Watercolour, gouache and ink on paper
18.5 × 25 ($7\frac{1}{4}$ × $9\frac{7}{8}$)
Private Collection

WOLS (Alfred Otto Wolfgang Schulze)
138 Untitled 1945–6
Watercolour, gouache and ink on paper
19 × 14.5 ($7\frac{1}{2}$ × $5\frac{3}{4}$)
Private Collection

WOLS (Alfred Otto Wolfgang Schulze)
139 Dark Sky 1946–7
Ciel sombre
Paint and casein on paper
16 × 12.2 ($6\frac{1}{4}$ × $4\frac{3}{4}$)
Private Collection

WOLS (Alfred Otto Wolfgang Schulze)
140 Untitled 1946–7
Watercolour, gouache, ink and casein on
paper 12 × 21.5 ($4\frac{3}{4}$ × $8\frac{1}{2}$)
Private Collection

WOLS (Alfred Otto Wolfgang Schulze)
141 Untitled 1949
Watercolour, gouache and ink on paper
25 × 16.2 ($9\frac{7}{8}$ × $6\frac{3}{8}$)
Private Collection

WOLS (Alfred Otto Wolfgang Schulze)
142 Untitled c.1949
Watercolour on paper 30 × 21.5 ($11\frac{3}{4}$ × $8\frac{1}{2}$)
Private Collection, London

WOLS (Alfred Otto Wolfgang Schulze)
143 Untitled 1950–1
Watercolour on paper 15.5 × 12 ($6\frac{1}{8}$ × $4\frac{3}{4}$)
Private Collection, London

DOCUMENTATION

144 Antonin Artaud, 'Gruber Louis XVI and Cagliostro his Valet' (left to right: Francis Tailleux, André Marchand and Francis Gruber) (Gruber Louis XVI et Cagliostro son valet) c.1937, ink on paper 28 × 50 (11 × $19\frac{5}{8}$)
Private Collection, London

145 Denise Colomb, 'Portrait of Antonin Artaud', photograph, 1947
© *Ministère de la Culture, France*

146 Denise Colomb, 'Antonin Artaud's Bedroom at the Clinic of Ivry-sur-Seine', photograph, 1947
© *Ministère de la Culture, France*

147 Antonin Artaud, *Au pays des tarahumaras*, Fontaine, Paris 1945
B. Gheerbrant

148 Antonin Artaud, letter to Jean Paulhan, 17 May 1946
Private Collection

149 *Hommage à Antonin Artaud*, publicity leaflet and exh. cat., Théâtre Sarah Bernhardt and Galerie Pierre, Paris 1946
Archives Paulhan

150 Antonin Artaud, *Van Gogh, le suicidé de la société*, K. Editeur, Paris 1947
B. Gheerbrant

151 *Portraits et dessins par Antonin Artaud*, exh. cat., Galerie Pierre, Paris 1947
Albert Loeb, Paris

152 Antonin Artaud, *Pour en finir avec le jugement de Dieu*, K. Editeur, Paris 1948
B. Gheerbrant

153 Antonin Artaud, 'Van Gogh, The Man Suicided By Society', *Tiger's Eye* (New York), vol.1, no.7, March 1949
Merlin James

154 Jean Dubuffet, 'Portrait of Jean Paulhan' (Portrait de Jean Paulhan) July 1945, gouache and ink on paper 37 × 29 ($14\frac{5}{8}$ × $11\frac{3}{8}$)
Private Collection

155 Jean Dubuffet, 'Wounded Figure by a Wall' (Mur et gisant) Jan. 1945, lithograph, image size 38 × 27 (15 × $10\frac{5}{8}$).
From Jean Dubuffet and Eugène Guillevic, *Les Murs*, Les Editions du Livre, Paris 1950
Fondation Jean Dubuffet, Périgny-sur-Yerres

156 Jean Dubuffet, 'Men Pissing against a Wall' (Pisseurs au mur) Jan. 1945, lithograph, image size 28.5 × 34.5 (11 × $13\frac{5}{8}$)

From Jean Dubuffet and Eugène Guillevic, *Les Murs*, Les Editions du Livre, Paris 1950
Fondation Jean Dubuffet, Périgny-sur-Yerres

157 Jean Dubuffet, 'Portrait of Francis Ponge' (Portrait de Francis Ponge) 1947, ink on paper 21 × 13.4 ($8\frac{1}{4} \times 5\frac{1}{2}$)
Armande Ponge, Paris

158 Robert Doisneau, 'Portrait of Jean Dubuffet in his Studio', photograph, 1951
© *Doisneau/Rapho*

159 *Exposition de tableaux et dessins de Jean Dubuffet*, exh. cat., Galerie René Drouin, Paris 1944
Tate Gallery Library

160 Jean Dubuffet and Francis Ponge, *Matière et Mémoire*, album of lithographs, Fernand Mourlot, Paris 1945
Private Collection, Paris

161 Jean Dubuffet, letter to Jean Paulhan [1945]
Archives Paulhan

162 Jean Dubuffet, *Prospectus aux amateurs de tout genre*, Gallimard, Paris 1946
Archives Gallimard

163 Jean Dubuffet, letter to Jean Paulhan [Summer 1946]
Archives Paulhan

164 *Mirobolus, Macadam et Cie, Hautes pâtes de Jean Dubuffet*, exh. cat., Galerie René Drouin, Paris 1946
Tate Gallery Library

165 *Portraits: Jean Dubuffet*, exh. cat., Galerie René Drouin, Paris 1947
Documentation du Musée National d'Art Moderne, Centre Georges Pompidou, Paris

166 *Lithographies: Jean Dubuffet*, exh. cat., Pierre Matisse Gallery, New York 1947
Tate Gallery Library

167 Jean Dubuffet and Jean Paulhan, *La Métromanie ou les dessous de la capitale*, Paris 1950
B. Gheerbrant

168 *Exhibition of Paintings by Jean Dubuffet*, exh. cat., Pierre Matisse Gallery, New York 1951
Documentation du Musée National d'Art Moderne, Centre Georges Pompidou, Paris

169 Jean Dubuffet, 'Anticultural Positions', MS 1951
Richard L. Feigen, New York

170 *Jean Dubuffet*, exh. cat., Galerie René Drouin, Paris 1954
Tate Gallery Library

171 Jean Fautrier, 'Reclining Woman IV' (Femme étendue IV) c.1942, pub. c.1960–4, etching on paper, image size 15.5 × 27.4 ($6\frac{1}{8} \times 10\frac{3}{4}$)
Tate Gallery. Purchased 1985

172 Jean Fautrier, 'The Executed' (Les Fusillés) 1943, pub. c.1960–4, etching on paper, image size 33.5 × 26.9 ($13\frac{1}{8} \times 10\frac{1}{2}$)
Tate Gallery. Purchased 1986

173 Jean Fautrier, 'Hostages on a Black Ground' (Otages fond noir) 1946, pub. c.1960–4, etching on paper, image size 24.2 × 32.7 ($9\frac{1}{2} \times 12\frac{7}{8}$)
Tate Gallery. Purchased 1985

174 Paul Facchetti, 'Portrait of Jean Fautrier', photograph, c.1952
© *Paul Facchetti*

175 *Les Otages peintures et sculptures de Fautrier*, exh. cat., Galerie René Drouin, Paris 1945
Documentation du Musée National d'Art Moderne, Centre Georges Pompidou, Paris

176 *Les Cahiers de la Pléiade* (Paris), no.1, May 1946. Cover by Fautrier
Archives Gallimard

177 Francis Ponge, *Note sur les Otages, peintures de Fautrier*, P. Seghers, Paris 1946
Bibliothèque Nationale, Département des Imprimés, Paris

178 Jean Fautrier and Georges Bataille, *L'Alleluiah*, A. Blaizot, Paris 1947
Musée de l'Ile de France, Château de Sceaux, Sceaux

179 Jean Paulhan, *Fautrier l'enragé*, A. Blaizot, Paris 1949
Musée de l'Ile de France, Château de Sceaux, Sceaux

180 Michel Tapié, 'Fautrier Paints a Picture', *Art News* (New York), Dec. 1955
Tate Gallery Library

181 Alberto Giacometti, 'Head of Simone de Beauvoir' (Tête de Simone de Beauvoir) 1946, bronze 13.4 × 4 × 4.1 ($5\frac{1}{4} \times 1\frac{5}{8} \times 1\frac{5}{8}$)
Private Collection, Paris

182 Alberto Giacometti, 'Portrait of Jean-Paul Sartre' (Portrait de Jean-Paul Sartre) 1946, pencil on paper 29 × 22 ($11\frac{3}{8} \times 8\frac{5}{8}$)
Private Collection, Paris

183 Alberto Giacometti, 'Portrait of Francis Gruber' (Portrait de Francis Gruber) 1946, pencil on paper 31 × 21 ($12\frac{1}{4} \times 8\frac{1}{4}$)
Private Collection, Paris

184 Alberto Giacometti, 'Portrait of Francis Gruber' (Portrait de Francis Gruber) 1946, pencil on paper 28 × 20 ($11 \times 7\frac{7}{8}$)
Private Collection, Paris

185 Sabine Weiss, 'Alberto Giacometti in his Studio', photograph, 1954
© *Weiss/Rapho*

186 Georges Bataille, *Histoire de rats*, Edition Minuit, Paris 1947
Bibliothèque Nationale, Réserve des Imprimés, Paris

187 Jean-Paul Sartre, 'La Recherche de l'absolu', *Les Temps Modernes* (Paris), no.28, Jan. 1948
French Institute Library, London

188 *Alberto Giacometti, Exhibition of Sculptures, Paintings, Drawings*, exh. cat., Pierre Matisse Gallery, New York 1948
Tate Gallery Library

189 *Alberto Giacometti*, exh. cat., Pierre Matisse Gallery, New York 1950
Documentation du Musée National d'Art Moderne, Centre Georges Pompidou, Paris

190 Francis Ponge, 'Réflexions sur les statuettes, figures et peintures d'Alberto Giacometti', *Cahiers d'Art* (Paris), 1951
Editions 'Cahiers d'Art'

191 *Derrière le Miroir* (Paris), nos.39–40, June–July 1951
Tate Gallery Library

192 Jean-Paul Sartre, 'Les Peintures de Giacometti', *Derrière le Miroir* (Paris) no.65, May 1954
Tate Gallery Library

193 Jean Genet, *Le Balcon*, L'Arbalète (Décines) 1956
Marc Barbezat, L'Arbalète, Décines

194 Jean Genet, 'L'Atelier d'Alberto Giacometti', *Derrière le Miroir* (Paris), no.98, June 1957
Tate Gallery Library

195 Marc Vaux, 'Portrait of Francis Gruber', photograph (n.d.)
Documentation du Musée National d'Art Moderne, Centre Georges Pompidou, Paris

196 Marc Vaux, 'Portrait of Francis Gruber in his Studio', photograph (n.d.)
Documentation du Musée National d'Art Moderne, Centre Georges Pompidou, Paris

197 Robert Wernik, 'Francis Gruber', *Labyrinth* (Geneva), 15 Dec. 1945
Private Collection, Paris

198 Madeleine Riffaud, 'Interviews et opinions: Francis Gruber', *Arts de France* (Paris), no.5, 1946
Merlin James

199 Jacques Lassaigne, 'Gruber, Prix national', *Panorama des Arts* (Paris), Dec. 1947
Merlin James

200 Tristan Tzara, 'Gruber', *Le Point* (Souillac), no.36, Dec. 1947
Tate Gallery Library

201 Louis Aragon, 'L'Enterrement à Thomery', *Les Lettres Françaises* (Paris), no.237, 4 Dec. 1948
Private Collection, Paris

202 *Francis Gruber*, exh. cat., Musée National
d'Art Moderne, Paris 1950
*Documentation du Musée National d'Art
Moderne, Centre Georges Pompidou, Paris*

203 *Francis Gruber*, exh.cat., Arts Council, Tate
Gallery, London 1959
Tate Gallery Library

204 Douglas Glass, 'Portrait of Jean Hélion in his
Studio', photograph, 1950
Mme Jacqueline Hélion

205 'Jean Hélion's Studio in Avenue de
l'Observatoire, Paris', photograph, 1953
Mme Jacqueline Hélion

206 *Eleven Europeans in America*, The Museum of
Modern Art Bulletin, New York, vol.12,
nos.4–5, 1946
Tate Gallery Library

207 Francis Ponge, 'Hélion', *Cahiers d'Art* (Paris),
1949
*Documentation du Musée National d'Art
Moderne, Centre Georges Pompidou, Paris*

208 Jean Hélion, 'Réponse à une enquête', *Esprit*
(Paris), no.168, June 1950
2 copies: (a) *French Institute Library, London;*
(b) *Merlin James*

209 Jean Hélion, *Notebook*, Jan. 1951
*Bibliothèque Nationale, Département des
Estampes, Paris*

210 *Hélion Paintings and Wotruba Sculpture*, exh.
cat., Hanover Gallery, London 1951
Tate Gallery Archives

211 Henri Michaux, 'Frottage' 1947, frottage
and graphite on paper 32×24 ($12\frac{5}{8} \times 9\frac{1}{2}$)
*Private Collection. Courtesy Galerie Baudoin
Lebon, Paris*

212 Paul Facchetti, 'Portrait of Henri Michaux',
photograph, 1953
© *Paul Facchetti*

213 André Gide, *Découvrons Henri Michaux*,
Gallimard, Paris 1941
B. Gheerbrant

214 *Henri Michaux peintures récentes*, invitation,
Galerie Rive Gauche, Paris 1944
*Documentation du Musée National d'Art
Moderne, Centre Georges Pompidou, Paris*

215 Henri Michaux, *Epreuves, exorcismes*,
Gallimard, Paris 1945
Archives Gallimard

216 Henri Michaux, *Peintures et dessins*, Le Point
du Jour, Paris 1946
Tate Gallery Library

217 *Michaux*, exh. cat., Galerie René Drouin,
Paris 1948
*Documentation du Musée National d'Art
Moderne, Centre Georges Pompidou, Paris*

218 Henri Michaux, *Meidosems*, Le Point du
Jour, Paris 1948
*Documentation du Musée National d'Art
Moderne, Centre Georges Pompidou, Paris*

219 Henri Michaux, *Mouvements*, Gallimard,
Paris 1951
Archives Gallimard

220 *Parcours Henri Michaux 1939 à 1956*, exh.
cat., Galerie René Drouin, Paris 1956
Tate Gallery Library

221 Pablo Picasso, 'Still Life with Skull' (Le
Pichet noir et la tête de mort) 1946,
lithograph on paper 31×24.5 ($12\frac{1}{4} \times 9\frac{5}{8}$)
Private Collection

222 Brassaï, 'Portrait of Picasso', photograph,
1948
*Bibliothèque Nationale, Département des
Estampes, Paris*
© *Gilberte Brassaï*

223 *Picasso libre*, exh. cat., Galerie Louis Carré,
Paris 1945
*Documentation du Musée National d'Art
Moderne, Centre Georges Pompidou, Paris*

224 Pablo Picasso, *Le Désir attrapé par la queue*,
Gallimard, Paris 1945
Archives Gallimard

225 Harriet and Sidney Janis, *Picasso, the Recent
Years 1939–1946*, Doubleday & Company
Inc., New York 1946
Tate Gallery Library

226 *Verve* (Paris), nos.19–20, 1948
Private Collection, Paris

227 Pablo Picasso, *Desire Caught by the Tail*,
Rider & Company, London 1950
Merlin James

228 Pablo Picasso, 'Portrait of Stalin', *Les Lettres
Françaises* (Paris), 12 March 1953
(photocopy)

229 *Picasso. Deux Periodes: 1900–1914 &
1950–1954*, exh. cat., Maison de la Pensée
Française, Paris 1954
*Documentation du Musée National d'Art
Moderne, Centre Georges Pompidou, Paris*

230 Germaine Richier, 'Forest Man' (L'Homme-
forêt [Petit]) 1945, maquette: wood and
clay 42.9 ($16\frac{7}{8}$) high
Private Collection

231 Germaine Richier, 'Untitled' 1948–51, pub.
1961, etching and aquatint on paper, image
size 38.6×29 ($15\frac{1}{4} \times 11\frac{1}{2}$)
*Tate Gallery. Presented by Mme Françoise
Guiter 1990*

232 Germaine Richier, 'Bat' (Chauve-souris)
1948–51, pub. 1955, etching and aquatint
on paper, image size 38.5×53.6
($15\frac{1}{8} \times 21\frac{1}{8}$)
*Tate Gallery. Presented by Mme Françoise
Guiter 1990*

233 Germaine Richier, 'Beetles' (Scarabées)
1948–51, pub. 1961, etching and aquatint
on paper, image size 24.8×19.8 ($9\frac{3}{4} \times 7\frac{3}{4}$)
*Tate Gallery. Presented by Mme Françoise
Guiter 1990*

234 Germaine Richier, Bust for 'The Shepherd of
Landes' (Le Berger des Landes -Buste) 1951,
brick and cement 16.9 ($6\frac{5}{8}$) high
Private Collection

235 Brassaï, ' "Diabolo" in Germaine Richier's
Studio', photograph (n.d.)
F. Guiter Collection

236 Brassaï, 'Portrait of Germaine Richier in her
Studio', photograph (n.d)
F. Guiter Collection

237 Brassaï, 'Germaine Richier in her Studio
with "Forest Man" ', photograph, 1948
F. Guiter Collection

238 *Sculptures of Germaine Richier; Engravings,
Studio of Roger Lacourière*, exh. cat., Anglo-
French Art Centre, London 1947
Tate Gallery Library

239 *Derrière le Miroir* (Paris), no.13, 1948
Tate Gallery Library

240 *Germaine Richier*, exh. cat., Hanover Gallery,
London 1955
Tate Gallery Library

241 *Germaine Richier*, exh. cat., Musée National
d'Art Moderne, Paris 1956
Tate Gallery Library

242 Maywald, 'Bram van Velde Reading the
Manuscript of Beckett's "Waiting for
Godot" ', photograph, c.1952
Archives Jacques Putman

243 Samuel Beckett, 'La Peinture des van Velde
ou le monde et le pantalon', *Cahiers d'Art*
(Paris), 1945–6
Editions 'Cahiers d'Art'

244 Samuel Beckett, 'Peintres de
l'empêchement', *Derrière le Miroir* (Paris),
nos.11–12, June 1948
Tate Gallery Library

245 Samuel Beckett, letter to Bram van Velde,
14 Jan. 1949
Archives Jacques Putman

246 Samuel Beckett, 'Some Sayings of Bram van
Velde', *Transition '49* (Paris), no.5, 1949
Tate Gallery Library

247 *Derrière le Miroir* (Paris), no.43, Feb. 1952
Tate Gallery Library

248 Samuel Beckett, letter to Jacques Putman,
25 March [1952]
Archives Jacques Putman

249 Samuel Beckett, text for Galerie Maeght
invitation, 1952
Archives Jacques Putman

250 Wols, [no title] *c.*1937–50, etching and
drypoint on paper, image size 13 × 8
(5 $\frac{1}{8}$ × 3 $\frac{1}{8}$)
Tate Gallery. Purchased 1983

251 Wols, [no title] *c.*1937–50, etching and
drypoint on paper, image size 6 × 9.8
(2 $\frac{3}{8}$ × 3 $\frac{7}{8}$)
Tate Gallery. Purchased 1983

252 Wols, [no title] *c.*1937–50, etching and
drypoint on paper, image size 10.2 × 12
(4 × 4 $\frac{3}{4}$)
Tate Gallery. Purchased 1983

253 Wols, [no title] *c.*1937–50, etching and
drypoint on paper, image size 11.8 × 9.5
(4 $\frac{5}{8}$ × 3 $\frac{3}{4}$)
Tate Gallery. Purchased 1983

254 'Wols's Bedroom at Champigny',
photograph, 1951
Private Collection

255 'Portrait of Wols', photograph, *c.*1946
Marc Johannès, Soissons

256 'Portrait of Wols at Champigny',
photograph, Aug. 1951
Private Collection

257 *Wols*, exh. cat., Galerie René Drouin, Paris
1945
*Documentation du Musée National d'Art
Moderne, Centre Georges Pompidou, Paris*

258 *Wols*, exh. cat., Galerie René Drouin, Paris
1947
*Documentation du Musée National d'Art
Moderne, Centre Georges Pompidou, Paris*

259 Jean-Paul Sartre, *Visages*, P. Seghers, Paris
1948. Illustrated by Wols
B. Gheerbrant

260 Jean-Paul Sartre, *Nourritures*, J. Damase,
Paris 1948. Illustrated by Wols
*Bibliothèque Nationale, Réserve des
Imprimés, Paris*

261 Wols, 'Les Paroles sont des caméléons', MS
*Documentation du Musée National d'Art
Moderne, Centre Georges Pompidou, Paris*

262 Jean-Paul Sartre, 'Doigts et non-doigts', MS
*Bibliothèque Nationale, Département des
Manuscrits, Paris*

263 Brassaï, 'Graffiti, Magic, Les Halles, Paris'
(Graffiti, La Magie, Les Halles, Paris) 1948,
gelatin-silver print 38.6 × 27.2 (15 $\frac{1}{4}$ × 10 $\frac{3}{4}$)
*Musée National d'Art Moderne, Centre
Georges Pompidou, Paris. Donation Daniel
Cordier 1989*
© *Gilberte Brassaï*

264 Brassaï, 'Graffiti' 1950, gelatin-silver print
84 × 54 (33 $\frac{1}{8}$ × 21 $\frac{1}{4}$)
*Musée National d'Art Moderne, Centre
Georges Pompidou, Paris. Donation Daniel
Cordier 1989*
© *Gilberte Brassaï*

265 Brassaï, 'Graffiti' 1950, gelatin-silver print
48 × 37.5 (18 $\frac{7}{8}$ × 14 $\frac{3}{4}$)
*Musée National d'Art Moderne, Centre
Georges Pompidou, Paris. Donation Daniel
Cordier 1989*
© *Gilberte Brassaï*

266 Brassaï, 'Graffiti' 1952, gelatin-silver print,
48.7 × 38.6 (19 $\frac{1}{8}$ × 15 $\frac{1}{4}$)
*Musée National d'Art Moderne, Centre
Georges Pompidou, Paris. Donation Daniel
Cordier 1989*
© *Gilberte Brassaï*

267 Brassaï, 'Graffiti "Birth of the Face,
Belleville, Paris" ' (Graffiti, 'Naissance du
visage, Belleville, Paris') 1952, gelatin-silver
print 47.7 × 38.7 (18 $\frac{3}{4}$ × 15 $\frac{1}{4}$)
*Musée National d'Art Moderne, Centre
Georges Pompidou, Paris. Donation Daniel
Cordier 1989*
© *Gilberte Brassaï*

268 Brassaï, 'Graffiti' 1952, Gelatin-silver print
38.2 × 28.5 (15 × 11 $\frac{1}{4}$)
*Musée National d'Art Moderne, Centre
Georges Pompidou, Paris. Donation Daniel
Cordier 1989*
© *Gilberte Brassaï*

269 Brassaï, 'Graffiti, Magic, "Demon", Belleville
Paris', (Graffiti, La Magie, "Démon",
Belleville, Paris) 1955, gelatin-silver print,
141 × 106.3 (55 $\frac{1}{2}$ × 41 $\frac{7}{8}$)
*Musée National d'Art Moderne, Centre
Georges Pompidou, Paris. Donation Daniel
Cordier 1989*
© *Gilberte Brassaï*

270 Brassaï, 'The Cast of *Desire Caught by the Tail*
in Picasso's Studio: Jacques Lacan, Cécile
Eluard, Pierre Reverdy, Louise Leiris, Zanie
de Campan, Picasso, Valentine Hugo,
Simone de Beauvoir, Jean-Paul Sartre,
Albert Camus, Michel Leiris, Jean Aubier',
photograph, 16 June 1944
© *Gilberte Brassaï*

271 Robert Doisneau, 'Simone de Beauvoir
Writing at the Café Les Deux Magots',
photograph, 1945
© *Doisneau/Rapho*

272 Robert Doisneau, 'Portrait of Jacques
Prévert', photograph, (n.d.)
© *Doisneau/Rapho*

273 Georges Dudognon, 'Corner Table with
Jean-Paul Sartre, Simone de Beauvoir,
Jacques Laurent and Olga Bost and Michelle
Léglise, wife of Boris Vian', photograph
(n.d.)
© *Georges Dudognon*

274 Georges Dudognon, 'Portrait of Jean Genet',
photograph (n.d.)
© *Georges Dudognon*

275 Izis, 'Portrait of Francis Ponge', photograph,
9 June 1948
Ponge Collection, Paris
© *Izis*

276 Izis, 'Portrait of Jean Paulhan at 5 rue des
Arènes, Paris', photograph (n.d.)
Archives Paulhan
© *Izis*

277 Georges Pierre, 'Giacometti in his Studio
with Samuel Beckett', photograph, 22 April
1961
© *Georges Pierre*

278 Willy Ronis, 'L'Existentialisme', photograph,
1946
© *Ronis/Rapho*

279 'Michel Tapié with the Collection of *Art Brut*
at the Galerie René Drouin, Paris',
photograph, *c.*1947–8
V. Gille

280 Simone de Beauvoir, *Le Deuxième sexe*,
Gallimard, Paris 1949
Archives Gallimard

281 Simone de Beauvoir, 'Les Mandarins', MS
*Bibliothèque Nationale, Département des
Manuscrits, Paris*

282 Simone de Beauvoir, *Les Mandarins*,
Gallimard, Paris 1954
Archives Gallimard

283 Simone de Beauvoir, *La Force des choses*,
Gallimard, Paris 1963 (1986)
Archives Gallimard

284 Samuel Beckett, *En attendant Godot*, theatre
programme, Théâtre de Babylone, Paris
1953
*Bibliothèque de la Société des Auteurs et
Compositeurs Dramatiques*

285 Albert Camus, *Caligula*, theatre programme,
Théâtre Herbertot, Paris 1945
*Bibliothèque de la Société des Auteurs et
Compositeurs Dramatiques*

286 Albert Camus, *La Peste*, Gallimard, Paris
1947
Archives Gallimard

287 Albert Camus, *L'Homme révolté*, Gallimard,
Paris 1951
Archives Gallimard

288 Albert Camus, *La Chute*, Gallimard, Paris 1956
Archives Gallimard

289 Jean Genet, *Journal du voleur*, Gallimard, Paris 1949 (1955)
Archives Gallimard

290 Jean Genet, *Haute surveillance*, theatre programme, Théâtre des Mathurins, Paris 1949
Bibliothèque de la Société des Auteurs et Compositeurs Dramatiques

291 Michel Leiris, *La Règle du jeu I: Biffures*, Gallimard, Paris 1948
Archives Gallimard

292 Michel Leiris, *La Règle du jeu II: Fourbis*, Gallimard, Paris 1955
Archives Gallimard

293 Michel Leiris, 'La Rose du désert', MS
Bibliothèque Nationale, Département des Manuscrits, Paris

294 Maurice Merleau-Ponty, *Phénoménologie de la perception*, Gallimard, Paris 1945 (1967)
Archives Gallimard

295 Maast [Jean Paulhan], *Sept causes célèbres*, Fontaine, Paris 1946
V. Gille

296 Francis Ponge, *Le Parti-pris des choses*, Gallimard, Paris 1942 (1945)
Archives Gallimard

297 Jacques Prévert, *Paroles*, Le Point du Jour, Paris 1947 (1959)
Archives Gallimard

298 Jean-Paul Sartre, *L'Etre et le néant*, Gallimard, Paris 1943 (1980)
Archives Gallimard

299 Jean-Paul Sartre, *Huis-clos*, theatre programme, Théâtre du Vieux Colombier, Paris 1944
Bibliothèque de la Société des Auteurs et Compositeurs Dramatiques

300 Jean-Paul Sartre, *Les Chemins de la liberté*, Gallimard, Paris 1945–9
Archives Gallimard

301 Jean-Paul Sartre, *L'Existentialisme est un humanisme*, Nagel, Paris 1946
Merlin James

302 Jean-Paul Sartre, 'Saint Genet, comédien et martyr', MS
Bibliothèque Nationale, Département des Manuscrits, Paris

303 Jean-Paul Sartre, *Saint Genet, comédien et martyr*, Gallimard, Paris 1951 (1952)
Archives Gallimard

304 Jacques Sennep, 'At the Pont Royal', ink on paper 22 × 29.5 ($8\frac{5}{8} \times 11\frac{5}{8}$)
Marie-Antoinette Pennès

305 Jacques Sennep, 'Pascal, from the café de Flore', ink on paper 17.2 × 11 ($6\frac{3}{4} \times 4\frac{3}{8}$)
Marie-Antoinette Pennès

306 Boris Vian, *L'Ecume des jours*, Gallimard, Paris 1947
La Fondation Boris Vian, Paris

307 Boris Vian, 'Manuel de Saint-Germain-des-Prés: Jean-Paul Sartre', MS, 1949–50
Fondation Boris Vian, Paris

308 Boris Vian, 'Manuel de Saint-Germain-des-Prés: Maurice Merleau-Ponty', MS, 1949–50
Fondation Boris Vian, Paris

309 *Les Temps Modernes* (Paris), no.8, May 1946
Archives Gallimard

310 *L'Imaginaire*, invitation card, Galerie du Luxembourg, Paris 1947
Documentation du Musée National d'Art Moderne, Centre Georges Pompidou, Paris

311 *H.W.P.S.M.T.B.*, exh. cat., Galerie Colette Allendy, Paris 1948
Documentation du Musée National d'Art Moderne, Centre Georges Pompidou, Paris

312 *L'Art brut préféré aux arts culturels*, exh. cat., Galerie René Drouin, Paris 1949
Documentation du Musée National d'Art Moderne, Centre Georges Pompidou, Paris

313 Michel Tapié, *Un art autre*, G. Giraud, Paris 1952
Documentation du Musée National d'Art Moderne, Centre Georges Pompidou, Paris

314 'Révolution à Saint-Germain-des-Prés', *Samedi Soir*, 2 July 1949
V. Gille

LENDERS

References are to catalogue numbers

Mr and Mrs Julian J. Aberbach 15
Acquavella Modern Art 37
Marc Barbezat 193
J. Benador 110
Catherine Béraud Putman 107
Staatliche Museen zu Berlin, Nationalgalerie 116
Bibliothèque Publique d'Information, Centres Georges Pompidou, Paris 228
Pinacoteca di Brera, Milan 112
Editions 'Cahiers d'Art' 190, 243
Musée Cantini, Marseilles 4, 6, 7
Galerie Di Meo, Paris 36
Fondation Jean Dubuffet 155, 156
Philippe and Denyse Durand-Ruel 124, 125, 127
Kunstsammlung Nordrhein-Westfalen, Düsseldorf 63
Richard L. Feigen 169
French Institute Library, London 187, 208
Archives Gallimard 162, 176, 215, 219, 224, 280, 282, 283, 286, 287, 288, 289, 291, 292, 294, 296, 297, 298, 300, 303, 309
B. Gheerbrant 147, 150, 152, 167, 213, 259
Alberto Giacometti-Stiftung, Kunsthaus Zurich 43
V. Gille 279, 295, 314
F. Guiter Collection 235, 236, 237
Solomon R. Guggenheim Museum, New York 83
Stephen Hahn 17
Kunsthalle, Hamburg 65
Jacqueline Hélion 204, 205
Hirshhorn Museum and Sculpture Garden, Smithsonian Institution, Washington 38, 56
Merlin James 153, 198, 199, 208, 227, 301,
Marc Johannès 255
Galerie Jan Krugier, Geneva 64, 95, 99, 102
Gallery Limmer, Freiburg 32
Albert Loeb 8, 151
Florence Loeb 5, 10, 14
The Museum of Contemporary Art, Los Angeles 30, 34
Louisiana Museum of Modern Art, Humlebaek 19, 96, 97, 100
Fondation Maeght, Saint-Paul 40, 46, 47, 48, 49, 50, 51, 53
Städtische Kunsthalle Mannheim 42
The Menil Collection, Houston 35, 113, 114, 115, 119
Franz Meyer 104
The Museum of Modern Art, New York 111
Bibliothèque Nationale, Paris 177, 186, 209, 222, 260, 262, 281, 293, 302

Musée d'Art Moderne de la Ville de Paris 27, 69, 74
Musée National d'Art Moderne, Centre Georges Pompidou, Paris 1, 2, 3, 9, 12, 20, 60, 76, 78, 79, 117
Documentation du Musée National d'Art Moderne, Centre Georges Pompidou, Paris 165, 168, 175, 189, 195, 196, 202, 207, 214, 217, 218, 223, 229, 257, 258, 261, 263, 264, 265, 266, 267, 268, 269, 310, 311, 312, 313
Archives Paulhan 149, 161, 163, 276
Marie Antoinette Pennès 304, 305
Marina Picasso 92, 93
Musée Picasso, Paris 91
Armande Ponge 157, 275
Private Collections 11, 13, 18, 22, 23, 26, 28, 29, 31, 33, 55, 57, 58, 59, 70, 71, 72, 73, 77, 80, 81, 82, 84, 85, 86, 87, 88, 89, 90, 98, 101, 106, 108, 109, 118, 120, 121, 122, 123, 126, 128, 129, 130, 132, 133, 134, 135, 136, 137, 138, 139, 140, 141, 142, 143, 144, 148, 154, 160, 181, 182, 183, 184, 197, 201, 211, 221, 226, 230, 234, 254, 256
Jacques Putman 103
Archives Jacques Putman 242, 245, 248, 249
Charlotte and Irving W. Rabb 52
Musée d'Art Moderne de Saint-Etienne 105
Musée de l'Ile de France, Sceaux 25, 178, 179
Bibliothèque de la Société des Auteurs et Compositeurs Dramatiques, Paris 284, 285, 290, 299
Tate Gallery 16, 21, 24, 39, 41, 45, 54, 61, 68, 75, 94, 131, 171, 172, 173, 231, 232, 233, 250, 251, 252, 253
Tate Gallery Archives 210
Tate Gallery Library 159, 164, 166, 170, 180, 188, 191, 192, 194, 200, 203, 206, 216, 220, 225, 238, 239, 240, 241, 244, 246, 247
Patrice Trigano 66, 67
Fondation Boris Vian 306, 307, 308
Walker Art Center, Minneapolis 44
Kunsthaus Zurich 62

The following works catalogued in the Documentation section are photographs: 145, 146, 158, 174, 185, 212, 270, 271, 272, 273, 274, 277, 278

WAYS OF GIVING TO THE TATE GALLERY

The Tate Gallery attracts funds from the private sector to support its programme of activities in London, Liverpool and St Ives. Support is raised from the business community, individuals, trusts and foundations, and includes sponsorships, donations, bequests and gifts of works of art. The Tate Gallery is recognised as a charity under Inland Revenue reference number X78055/1.

Trustees

Dennis Stevenson CBE (Chairman)

The Countess of Airlie CVO
The Hon. Mrs Janet de Botton
David Gordon
Christopher Le Brun
Sir Richard Carew Pole
Michael Craig-Martin
Richard Deacon
Sir Rex Richards
Paula Ridley
David Verey

Donations

There are a variety of ways through which you can make a donation to the Tate Gallery.

Donations All donations, however small, will be gratefully received and acknowledged by the Tate Gallery.

Covenants A Deed of Covenant, which must be taken out for a minimum of four years, will enable the Tate Gallery to claim back tax on your charitable donation. For example, a covenant for £100 per annum will allow the Gallery to claim a further £33 at present tax rates.

Gift-Aid For individuals and companies wishing to make donations of £250 and above, Gift-Aid allows the gallery to claim back tax on your charitable donation. In addition, if you are a higher rate taxpayer you will be able to claim tax relief on the donation. A Gift-Aid form and explanatory leaflet can be sent to you if you require further information.

Bequests You may wish to remember the Tate Gallery in your will or make a specific donation *In Memoriam*. A bequest may take the form of either a specific cash sum, a residual proportion of your estate or a specific item of property, such as a work of art. Certain tax advantages can be obtained by making a legacy in favour of the Tate Gallery. Please check with the Tate Gallery when you draw up your will that it is able to accept your bequest.

American Fund for the Tate Gallery The American Fund was formed in 1986 to facilitate gifts of works of art, donations and bequests to the Tate Gallery from the United States residents. It receives full tax exempt status from the IRS.

Individual Membership Programmes

FRIENDS OF THE TATE GALLERY

Since their formation in 1958, the Friends of the Tate Gallery have helped to buy major works of art for the Tate Gallery collection, from Stubbs to Hockney.

Members at £25 are entitled to immediate and unlimited free admission to Tate Gallery exhibitions with a guest, invitations to previews of Tate Gallery exhibitions, exclusive Friends Gallery Evenings, Friends newsletter, special events, *Friends Events* and *Tate Preview* magazines mailed three times a year, free admission to exhibitions at Tate Gallery Liverpool and Tate Gallery St Ives, and use of the Friends Room at the Tate Gallery.

Three categories of higher level memberships, Associate Fellow at £100, Deputy Fellow at £250, and Fellow at £500, entitle members to a range of extra benefits including guest cards and invitations to exclusive special events.

The Friends of the Tate Gallery are supported by Tate & Lyle PLC.

Further details on the Friends may be obtained from:

Friends of the Tate Gallery
Tate Gallery
Millbank
London SW1P 4RG

Tel: 071–821 1313

PATRONS OF THE TATE GALLERY

The Patrons of British Art support British painting and sculpture from the Elizabethan period through to the early twentieth century in the Tate Gallery's collection. They encourage knowledge and awareness of British art by providing an opportunity to study Britain's cultural heritage.

The Patrons of New Art support contemporary art in the Tate Gallery's collection. They promote a lively and informed interest in contemporary art and are associated with the Turner Prize, one of the most prestigious awards for the visual arts.

Annual membership of the Patrons ranges from £350 to £750, and funds the purchase of works of art for the Tate Gallery's collection.

Benefits for both groups include invitations to Tate Gallery receptions, an opportunity to sit on the Patrons' acquisitions committees, special events including visits to private and corporate collections and complimentary catalogues of Tate Gallery exhibitions.

Further details on the Patrons may be obtained from:

The Development Office
Tate Gallery
Millbank
London SW1P 4RG

Tel: 071–821 1313

Corporate Membership Programme

Membership of the Tate Gallery's Corporate Membership Programme offers companies outstanding value-for-money and provides opportunities for every employee to enjoy a closer knowledge of the Gallery, its collection and exhibitions.

Membership benefits are specifically geared to business needs and include private views for company employees, free and discount admission to exhibitions, discount in the Gallery shop, out-of-hours Gallery visits, behind-the-scenes tours, exclusive use of the Gallery for corporate entertainment, invitations to VIP events, copies of Gallery literature and acknowledgement in Gallery publications.

TATE GALLERY CORPORATE MEMBERS

Partners
ADT Group PLC
The British Petroleum Company plc
Glaxo Holdings p.l.c.
Manpower PLC
THORN EMI
Unilever

Associates
Bell Helicopter Textron
Brunswick Public Relations
Channel 4 Television
D.T.Z. Debenham Thorpe
Global Asset Management
KPMG Peat Marwick
Lazard Brothers & Co Ltd
Linklaters & Paines
Refco Overseas Ltd
Smith & Williamson
S.G. Warburg Group

Corporate sponsorship

The Tate Gallery works closely with sponsors to ensure that their business interests are well served, and has a reputation for developing imaginative fund-raising initiatives. Sponsorships can range from a few thousand pounds to considerable investment in long-term programmes; small businesses as well as multi-national corporations have benefited from the high profile and prestige of Tate Gallery sponsorship.

Opportunities available at Tate Gallery London, Liverpool and St Ives include exhibitions (some also tour the UK), education, conservation and research programmes, audience development, visitor access to the Collection and special events. Sponsorship benefits include national and regional publicity, targeted marketing to niche audiences, exclusive corporate entertainment, employee benefits and acknowledgment in Tate Gallery publications.

TATE GALLERY LONDON:
PRINCIPAL CORPORATE SPONSORS
(alphabetical order)

Barclays Bank PLC
  1991, *Constable*
The British Land Company PLC
  1990, *Joseph Wright of Derby**
The British Petroleum Company plc
  1990–4, *New Displays*
Channel 4 Television
  1991–3, The Turner Prize
Daimler-Benz AG
  1991, *Max Ernst*
Pearson plc
  1992–5 Elizabethan Curator Post
Reed International P.L.C.
  1990, *On Classic Ground: Picasso, Léger, de Chirico and the New Classicism, 1910–30*
Tate & Lyle PLC
  1991–3, Friends Relaunch Marketing Programme
Volkswagen
  1990–4, The Turner Scholarships

TATE GALLERY LONDON:
CORPORATE SPONSORS
(alphabetical order)

AFAA, Association Française d'Action Artistique, Ministère de Affaires Etrangères, The Cultural Service of the French Embassy, London
Agfa Graphic Systems Group
  1992, *Turner: The Fifth Decade**
Beck's
  1992, *Otto Dix*
Blackwall Green Ltd
  1991, International Conference on the Packing and Transportation of Paintings
Borghi Transporti Spedizioni SPA
  1991, International Conference on the Packing and Transportation of Paintings
James Bourlets & Sons
  1991, International Conference on the Packing and Transportation of Paintings
British Steel plc
  1990, *William Coldstream*
Carroll, Dempsey & Thirkell
  1990, *Anish Kapoor**

Clifton Nurseries
  1990–2, Christmas Tree (in kind)
D'Art Kunstspedition GmbH
  1991, International Conference on the Packing and Transportation of Paintings
Debenham Tewson & Chinnocks
  1990, *Turner, Painting and Poetry*
Digital Equipment Co Ltd
  1991–2, *From Turner's Studio*
Alfred Dunhill Limited
  1993, *Sir Edward Burne-Jones: Watercolours and Drawings*
Gander and White Shipping Ltd
  1991, International Conference on the Packing and Transportation of Paintings
Gerlach Art Packers & Shippers
  1991, International Conference on the Packing and Transportation of Paintings
Harsch Transports
  1991, International Conference on the Packing and Transportation of Paintings
Hasenkamp Internationle Transporte
  1991, International Conference on the Packing and Transportation of Paintings
The Independent
  1992, *Otto Dix* (in kind)
  1993, *Paris Post War: Art and Existentialism 1945–55*
KPMG Management Consulting
  1991, *Anthony Caro: Sculpture towards Architecture**
Kunsttrans Antiquitaten
  1991, International Conference on the Packing and Transportation of Paintings
Lloyd's of London
  1991, Friends Room
Martinspeed Ltd
  1991, International Conference on the Packing and Transportation of Paintings
Masterpiece International Ltd
  1991, International Conference on the Packing and Transportation of Paintings
Mat Securitas Express AG
  1991, International Conference on the Packing and Transportation of Paintings
Mobel Transport AG
  1991, International Conference on the Packing and Transportation of Paintings
Momart plc
  1991, International Conference on the Packing and Transportation of Paintings
Nuclear Electric plc
  1993, *Turner: The Final Years*
Propileo Transport
  1991, International Conference on the Packing and Transportation of Paintings
Rees Martin Art Service
  1991, International Conference on the Packing and Transportation of Paintings
SRU Limited
  1992, *Richard Hamilton**
Sun Life Assurance Society plc
  1993, *Robert Vernon's Gift*
THORN EMI
  1993 *Turner's Painting Techniques*
TSB Group plc
  1992, *Turner and Byron*
  1992–5, *William Blake* display series
Wingate & Johnston Ltd
  1991, International Conference on the Packing and Transportation of Paintings

*denotes a first-time sponsorship in the arts, recognised by an award under the Government's Business Sponsorship Incentive Scheme, administered by the Association for Business Sponsorship of the Arts.

TATE GALLERY LIVERPOOL:
CORPORATE SPONSORS
(alphabetical order)

AIB Bank
  1991, *Strongholds*
American Airlines
  1993, *David Hockney*
Barclays Bank PLC
  1990, *New Light on Sculpture*
BASF
  1990, *Lifelines*
Beck's
  1993, *Robert Gober*
British Alcan Aluminium plc
  1991, *Dynamism*
  1991, *Giacometti*
British Telecom plc
  1990, Outreach Programme
Concord Lighting
  1990, *New Light on Sculpture*
Cultural Relations Committee, Departments of Foreign Affairs, Ireland
  1991, *Strongholds*
English Estates
  1991, Mobile Art Programme
Granda Television plc
  1990, *New North*
Korean Air
  1992, *Working with Nature* (in kind)
The Littlewoods Organisation plc
  1992–5, *New Realities*
Merseyside Development Corporation
  1990, Outreach Programme
  1992, *Myth-Making*
  1992, *Stanley Spencer*
Mobil Oil Company Ltd
  1990, *New North*
Momart plc
  1990–2, The Momart Fellowship
NSK Bearings Europe Ltd
  1991, *A Cabinet of Signs: Contemporary Art from Post-Modern Japan*
Ryanair
  1991, *Strongholds* (in kind)
Samsung Electronics
  1992, *Working With Nature*
Volkswagen
  1991, Mobile Art Programme (in kind)

TATE GALLERY ST IVES:
CORPORATE SPONSOR

South Western Electricity plc (SWEB)
  1993–4, Education Programme

Tate Gallery Benefactors

London, Liverpool and St Ives

FOUNDING BENEFACTORS (date order)

Sir Henry Tate
Sir Joseph Duveen
Lord Duveen
The Clore Foundation

PRINCIPAL BENEFACTORS
(alphabetical order)

American Fund for the Tate Gallery
Calouste Gulbenkian Foundation
Friends of the Tate Gallery
The Henry Moore Foundation
National Heritage Memorial Fund
National Art Collections Fund
The Nomura Securities Co. Ltd
Patrons of New Art
Dr Mortimer and Theresa Sackler Foundation
St Ives Tate Action Group
The Wolfson Foundation and Family Charitable
    Trust

BENEFACTORS (alphabetical order)

The Baring Foundation
Gilbert and Janet de Botton
Mr Edwin C. Cohen
The John S. Cohen Foundation
The John Ellerman Foundation
Esmée Fairbairn Charitable Trust
Foundation for Sport and the Arts
The Getty Grant Program
Granada Group plc
John and Olivia Hughes
The Leverhulme Trust
John Lewis Partnership
Museums and Galleries Improvement Fund
Ocean Group plc (P.H. Holt Trust)
Patrons of British Art
Peter Moores Foundation
The Pilgrim Trust
GEC Plessey Telecommunications
The Eleanor Rathbone Charitable Trust
Mr John Ritblat
The Sainsbury Family Charitable Trusts
Save & Prosper Educational Trust
SRU Limited
Bernard Sunley Charitable Foundation
Weinberg Foundation

Tate Gallery Donors

LONDON (alphabetical order)

Professor Abbott
Hurry Armour Trust
Sir Richard Attenborough CBE
BAA plc
Friends of Nancy Balfour OBE
The Hon. Robin Baring
Mr Tom Bendhem
Michael and Marcia Blakenham
Miss Mary Boone
Botts & Company Limited
C.T. Bowring (Charitable Trust) Ltd
Caşenove & Co
Christie, Manson & Woods Ltd

Mr R.N. Collins
Mrs Dagny Corcoran
Mr and Mrs Kenneth Dayton
Anthony d'Offay Gallery
Miss W.A. Donner
Evelyn, Lady Downshire's Trust Fund
Mr Paul Dupee
Elephant Trust
European Arts Festival
Roberto Fainello Art Advisers Ltd
Gabo Trust for Sculpture Conservation
Miss Kate Ganz
The German Government
Mr and Mrs David Gilmour
Goethe Institut
The Worshipful Company of Goldsmiths
Sir Nicholas and Lady Goodison Charitable
    Settlement
Richard Green Fine Paintings
Gytha Trust
Mr Robert Horton
Idlewild Trust
The Italian Government
Sir Anthony and Lady Jacobs
Mrs Gabrielle Keiller
Knapping Fund
The Helena and Kenneth Levy Bequest
Mr and Mrs Lawrence Lowenthal
Midland Bank Artscard
Mr and Mrs Robert Mnuchin
Mr Peter Nahum
Old Possum's Practical Trust
Mr William Pegrum
Philips Fine Art Auctioneers
Reed International P.L.C.
Mrs Jill Ritblat
Mrs Jean Sainsbury
The Hon. Simon Sainsbury
Schroder Charity Trust
The Swan Trust
Tate Gallery Publications
Mr Barry and the Hon. Mrs Townsley
U.K. Charity Lotteries Ltd
Visiting Arts
Waley-Cohen Charitable Trust
The Andy Warhol Foundation for the Visual
    Arts, Inc.
Mr Mark Weiss
Willis Faber plc
Thomas and Odette Worrell
Mrs Jayne Wrightsman

and those donors who wish to remain
anonymous

LIVERPOOL (alphabetical order)

The Baring Foundation
David and Ruth Behrend Trust
Ivor Braka Ltd
The British Council
British Telecom plc
Calouste Gulbenkian Foundation
Mr and Mrs Henry Cotton
English Estates
European Arts Festival
Mrs Sue Hammerson OBE
Mr John Heyman
Liverpool Council for Voluntary Services
Merseyside Development Corporation
Momart plc
The Henry Moore Foundation

Ocean Group plc (P.H. Holt Trust)
Eleanor Rathbone Charitable Trust
Tate Gallery Liverpool Supporters
Bernard Sunley Charitable Foundation
Unilever
Visiting Arts

and those donors who wish to remain
anonymous

ST IVES (alphabetical order)

Donors to the Appeal coordinated by the Steering
    Group for the Tate Gallery St Ives and the
    St Ives Action Group.

Viscount Amory Charitable Trust
Barbinder Trust
Barclays Bank PLC
The Baring Foundation
BICC Group
Patricia, Lady Boyd and Viscount Boyd
British Telecom plc
Cable and Wireless plc
Carlton Communications
Mr Francis Carnwath
Christie, Manson & Woods Ltd
Mr Peter Cocks
John S. Cohen Foundation
Miss Jean Cooper
D'Oyly Carte Charitable Trust
David Museum Fine Paintings
Dewhurst House
Dixons Group plc
Mr Alan Driscoll
The John Ellerman Foundation
English China Clays Group
Esmée Fairbairn Charitable Trust
The Worshipful Company of Fishmongers
Foundation for Sport and the Arts
J. Paul Getty Jr Charitable Trust
Gimpel Fils
Grand Metropolitan Trust
Ms Judith Hodgson
Sir Geoffrey and Lady Holland
Mr Bernard Jacobson
Mr John Kilby
Lloyds Bank plc
Lord Leverhulme's Trust
The Manifold Trust
The Mayor Gallery
Marlborough Fine Art
The Worshipful Company of Mercers
Mercury Asset Management plc
Meyer International plc
The Henry Moore Foundation
National Westminster Bank plc
New Art Centre
Pall European Limited
The Pilgrim Trust
The Joseph Rank (1942) Charitable Trust
Mr Roy Ray
The Rayne Foundation
Royal Bank of Scotland
The Sainsbury Family Charitable Trusts
Mr Nicholas Serota
Mr Roger Slack
Trustee of the Carew Pote Family Trust
Trustees of H.E.W. Spurr Deceased
South West British Gas
South West Water plc
South Western Electricity plc
Sun Alliance Group

Television South West
The TSB Foundation for England and Wales
Unilever
Mrs Angela Verren Taunt
Weinberg Foundation
Wembley plc
Western Morning News, West Briton, Cornish
    Guardian and The Cornishman
Weslake & Co
Mr and Mrs Derek White
Mr and Mrs Graham Williams
Wingate Charitable Trust
Mrs Monica Wynter

and those donors who wish to remain
anonymous